Special Edition Using People Soft

Paul Greenberg,

Michael Fauscette,

Scott Fletcher, et al

que®

A Division of Macmillan USA
201 W. 103rd Street
Indianapolis, Indiana 46290

CONTENTS AT A GLANCE

SPECIAL EDITION USING PEOPLESOFT

Copyright © 2000 by Que Corporation

International Standard Book Number: 0-7897-1281-4

Library of Congress Catalog Card Number: 98-84641

Printed in the United States of America

First Printing: December 1999

01   00   99   4   3   2   1

TRADEMARKS

WARNING AND DISCLAIMER

Executive Editor
Randy Haubner

Acquisitions Editor
Holly Allender
Hugh Vandivier

Development Editor
Jeff Durham

Managing Editor
Lisa Wilson

Project Editor
Natalie Harris

Copy Editor
Margaret Berson

Indexer
Erika Millen

Proofreader
Benjamin Berg

Technical Edit Coordinator
Shae Donnelly

Technical Editors - Ernst & Young
Todd Beilis
Stephanie Blair
Susan Doherty
Mark Feinberg
Steven D Hazelrigg
Robert S Heffley
Andrew Jankowski
Tim Mateo
Syed M Mukhtar
Susan G Murray
Cheryl A Nelson
Adrian O Penka
Michelle J Roseman
Shelley Samoray
Christopher Spivey
Sharon Studley
David A Supinski
Christine J Volk
Becky A Weber

Team Coordinator
Cindy Teeters

Interior Design
Nathan Clement
Ruth C. Lewis

Cover Design
Dan Armstrong

CONTENTS

ABOUT THE AUTHORS

Paul Greenberg is executive vice-president of Live Wire, Inc., a PeopleSoft and e-commerce consulting firm headquartered in West Newton, MA. Paul has years of experience as an enterprise systems analyst, strategic planner, and business development specialist. He is married and lives very happily with his wife, Yvonne, and two cats in Manassas, VA.

Michael Fauscette was recently named vice president of client services engineering for Post Communications, Inc. an Internet Marketing start-up. With an extensive PeopleSoft background, he served most recently as the director of field support and Operations for the PeopleSoft, Inc. consulting organization.

In his career at PeopleSoft, Michael worked as a consultant, a project manager, a practice manager, and director of service operations. Prior to PeopleSoft, he worked in the high-tech industry as a consultant and project manager for two other software companies. His extensive experience as a complex project manager comes out of his 10-year career as a surface line officer in the U.S. Navy. Michael currently lives in Pleasanton, California with his wife Donna and two daughters, Jessica and Kendyl.

Scott Fletcher joined PeopleSoft in 1993. As director of european operations, he was instrumental in launching PeopleSoft's European business endeavors. Since his return to the United States, Scott has created and led PeopleSoft's Technology Consulting Division, where he was responsible for over 400 service professionals on worldwide assignments.

Currently, Scott is vice president of services at Annuncio Software, a leading provider of Internet Marketing Automation solutions, based in Mountain View, California. In this role, Scott is responsible for Application Hosting, Professional Services, Customer Education, and Customer Support on a worldwide basis.

ABOUT THE CONTRIBUTING AUTHORS

Lorraine Britto-Bernstein is a senior consultant in the consulting practice of KPMG, LLP. She has master's degrees in Industrial/Organizational Psychology from Radford University, Virginia and Bombay University, India. Lorraine also has a Certificate in Management Information Systems from Columbia University, New York.

Lorraine has held a variety of private and public sector positions in the United States and Asia. She has expertise in the areas of job analysis, development of methodologies for project implementation, design of training programs, analysis and design of business processes, programming, and documentation. Her interests include organizational behavior and client/server technology.

Dr. B. L. "Buddy" Bruner, vice president, Kaludis Consulting Group, has more than 30 years of higher education and industry experience in information systems, voice and data communications, and organizational and strategic planning. He currently manages higher education ERP implementations, leads business process and organizational change, designs approaches for the use of technology in learning, and champions the creative use of data analysis and modeling for performance evaluation and management decision support.

Prior to joining the Kaludis Group in 1986, he held teaching, research, and administrative positions at Yale University, The Mellon Institute, and the University of Kentucky. He also was manager of consulting for Telco Research Corporation and led two information technology start-up companies. He holds a BS degree from Purdue University and a PhD degree in Physical Chemistry from Iowa State University.

Bob Dunn is director of services at PeopleSoft eBusiness Solutions Division. Bob has 20 years of experience in information systems consulting. Prior to joining PeopleSoft, he was president of Synology, Inc, a consulting firm to Fortune 500 firms. He has an MBA and master's in Computer Engineering. He and his wife, Julie, live in Manhattan Beach, California.

Jennifer Ann Caria is a KPMG professional, holding marketing management positions in the firm's PeopleSoft and World-Class Human Resources e-business solutions. Her educational background includes a bachelor of arts degree from The George Washington University in Washington, DC, concentrated in journalism and economics; studies at l'Universita Italiana per i Stranieri in Perugia, Italy; and a master of business degree in International Business from St. Joseph's University in Philadelphia, Pennsylvania.

Jennifer lives in Pennsylvania's historic and scenic Valley Forge with her native Italian husband and the couple's bilingual cat.

Mark D. Gibson is a project manager with PeopleSoft USA, Inc. and has successfully implemented PeopleSoft in both the commercial and U.S. Government industry sectors. He has 14 years of progressive experience in project management, maintenance, implementation, and testing of major software automation initiatives.

Mark is experienced in all software development life cycle phases from requirement definition through implementation and software maintenance. Prior to joining PeopleSoft, he was employed by Information Technologies Consultants, Inc. and KPMG as a project management consultant and consulted on multiple business applications projects. He received his bachelor of science degree in mechanical engineering from Tulane University and master of engineering management degree from Old Dominion University.

Denise L. Hollo is a senior manager with KPMG LLP. She has more than 12 years of experience in financial systems consulting representing all phases of the life cycle, from requirements and package selection through implementation and support. She has worked with several mainframe and client/server financial packages and has been implementing PeopleSoft Financial Management applications for over three years, including implementations in the US and Europe.

Denise holds a degree in Systems Engineering/MIS from the University of Virginia. She currently resides in Manhattan.

Daniel W. Jamieson is a manager in the consulting practice of KPMG. He has over 25 years in consulting as well as in the practice of Controllership roles for American Standard, Inc. working with PeopleSoft software since 1992. His clients include NiSource and MicroWarehouse.

Upon graduation from St. Vincent College, in Latrobe, Pennsylvania, he was employed as an auditor with an international CPA firm. He is a CPA and member of the American Institute of CPAs as well as the Financial Executives Institute.

Daniel is married with two sons and resides in Edison, New Jersey.

James Jaworski is an Enterprise Packaged Solution consultant with KPMG LLP. He is a proud alumnus of the University of Iowa, where he received a master of arts degree in accounting. He resides in Chicago, Illinois.

Ari Katanick joined PeopleSoft's Professional Services Group (PSG) in 1994 and is currently the director of PSG's Enterprise Performance Management practice. He has consulted at over 70 PeopleSoft customers and specializes in enterprise reporting and decision support.

Lynn Ann Lew, CPP, is process specialist consultant with Peoplesoft, Inc. She has more than 25 years of experience in accounting, payroll, human resources, benefits, time and labor, and management and systems implementations. She has most recently been involved in a benefits and payroll implementation for Hewlett Packard.

Lynn currently is on the Board of Contributing Writers for the American Payroll Association. In 1994, Lynn was APA Payroll Woman of the Year.

Lynn has written numerous articles and is constantly striving towards sharing her knowledge. Lynn earned her Certified Payroll Professional (CPP) designation in 1986.

Nancy Marucci has over 10 years of experience in the human resources/payroll information systems field, and has been with PeopleSoft since 1994, currently as a senior HRMS project manager. During her numerous PeopleSoft implementation and upgrade projects (starting with version 3.11!), she provided systems analysis, design, and PeopleTools modifications, as well as conversion/interface support, upgrade planning and execution, and application/tools updates planning and execution. She has delivered over 30 presentations to regional and national HRIS user groups, as well as regional and national vendor conferences.

Matt McLelland is a process specialist with PeopleSoft's Professional Services Group. During his three years of consulting with PeopleSoft, Matt has been involved with a number of full system lifecycle implementations concentrated around PeopleSoft's Distribution and Financial Modules. Specifically, Matt's expertise lies within Order Management, Inventory, Purchasing, and Billing modules.

Prior to joining PeopleSoft, Matt was a consultant with Ernst & Young's Management Consulting group. In addition to working on PeopleSoft implementations, Matt was also heavily involved with a number of custom-developed client/server applications.

When unable to locate Matt at a customer implementation or in an airport en-route to his next consulting assignment, you can pretty much count on finding him strapped underneath one of his hang gliders flying high over his home near Lookout Mountain, Tennessee.

Raghu Natesan is an experienced ERP trainer, working at Atlantic Duncans International in Chantilly, Virginia. He has taught courses in PeopleSoft, SQR, Convoy, and Crystal Reports, often used as a trainer for customers by the vendor. Raghu lives happily in Northern Virginia with his wife and newly born daughter.

Patty Pasley is a communications specialist at PeopleSoft. For over seven years, she has written a variety of materials and publications for the company. She has also managed a number of communications-related disciplines, including employee communications, customer communications, User Conference communications, and most recently, executive communications.

Patty received a bachelor of science degree in technical communications from Michigan Tech University in 1987 and a master of arts degree in communications management from the University of Southern California in 1989.

Ramaswamy "Raj" Rajagopal is currently working with KPMG LLP as a senior manager in the PeopleSoft practice, and he heads up the Technology Assist Group. He has been managing and providing technical leadership for various PeopleSoft implementations for the last three years. He has also designed and implemented various Web solutions integrating with PeopleSoft for global deployment. Raj moved to the United States in 1990 and lives in the Detroit metro area. In his spare time he likes to play tennis, travel, and spend time with his wife and two lovely daughters.

Vlad Soran is an enterprise packaged applications manager with the Communication, Content, and Commerce practice of KPMG LLP. With more than 10 years of accounting, finance, and international systems implementation experience, Vlad is helping clients maximize the benefits of ERP implementations. A Georgia CPA, he is a graduate of University of South Carolina.

When Vlad is not implementing PeopleSoft or flying on planes, he shares a wonderful life with his wife and two lovely boys in Atlanta, Georgia.

Rob Townsend joined PeopleSoft's Professional Services Organization in 1997 and is currently a senior consultant from the Southeast region. He specializes in the Message Agent, Web Client, Three-Tier environment, as well as general infrastructure design and support.

Carl Upthegrove is director of the Office of Project Management for PeopleSoft Consulting. He possesses a BA in Accounting from California State University–Hayward and an MBA from California State University–Bakersfield. Carl spent over 20 years in the Consumer Package Goods industry designing, implementing, and managing business information systems both domestically and in Europe. He joined the application software industry where he has served as a consultant, project manager, and engagement manager for the past six years. Carl has taught in the Cal-State system and has spoken before several industry groups.

Tim Weaver is a consultant in the PeopleSoft Professional Services Group. With six years of ERP implementation experience, Tim has led many manufacturing and distribution companies through all phases of the implementation lifecycle. He has worked with the PeopleSoft Manufacturing suite for two years. Tim holds the CPIM and CIRM certificates from the American Production and Inventory Control Society (APICS).

In his spare time, Tim enjoys playing the trumpet, watching Miami Hurricanes football, and travelling internationally.

Jeff Wiesinger is Manager in the PeopleSoft practice of KPMG LLP. He lives in Indianapolis, Indiana, and has been with KPMG for eight years. Jeff has participated in several successful PeopleSoft Financials implementations. Prior to working with PeopleSoft, Jeff worked with one of KPMG's proprietary software packages focusing on software design and development, working closely with a state government.

Jeff is a Certified Public Accountant and holds a bachelor of science degree from Grace College in Winona Lake, Indiana.

Ronald K. Yeung, CPIM is a manager in the consulting practice of KPMG. He has over 18 years of business experience in manufacturing and distribution industry. Ronald has extensive hands-on consulting experience and solid technical background in the selection and implementation of integrated packaged software. He led and managed implementations of PeopleSoft Manufacturing and Distribution business applications for various industries that included electronic, industrial, consumer market, utility, and real estate. His experience includes business re-engineering, system requirement planning, information system strategies, package selection, system design, software development, project management, rapid implementation, application customization, data conversion, and training.

Prior to joining KPMG, Ronald held senior positions at three leading Enterprise Resource Planning software firms. At various times, he held the positions of director of reengineering/education, client services project manager, project leader, technical consultant, senior software developer, and senior system analyst.

Ronald received his BS degree in Accounting and Business Administration from Illinois State University. He is certified in American Production & Inventory Control Association (APICS). He is also a certified technical consultant of System Software Associates.

ACKNOWLEDGEMENTS

This has been a fascinating journey. Since the inception of this work, literally dozens of people have affected the production of this book in a positive way. The support varied in scope. Some of it was technical support. Some of it was moral support. Some of it was production support. Some of it was administrative support. The one thing that characterized all of it was…it was support. To that end, I'd like to thank those authors who stuck this book out from the beginning to the end and through all the incarnations and changes. I'd also like to thank those authors who jumped in at the last minute to perform the necessary heroics time and time again, save the book from what looked like apparent doom. I won't repeat the author's names: all those reading this book can see them on the previous pages. Suffice to say, I think that you are all champs for what you've done.

I'd like to thank my editors and collaborators, my "killer" Acquisitions editor, Holly Allender, and our coordinator/writer at KPMG, Jennifer Caria, who both persevered and persevered and persevered some more and made this book happen when it had to. I'd like to thank Bryan Gambrel and Angela Kozlowski for believing in this project through thick and thin.

I would particularly like to thank Hugh Vandivier, Jeff Durham and most of all, Randy Haubner, all of Que, who were unbelievable in driving this "thing" to completion. Additionally, I'd like to thank another PeopleSoft partner, Kaludis Consulting Group in Washington D.C., especially it's Vice President Buddy Bruner, one of our authors. He has been a class act and it is a classy company all the way. They responded quickly, professionally, and with grace, in a moment of need that shows their work quality and their work ethics, about the highest compliment I could pay a company or a person.

Often, you would think that a large company with over 100,000 employees would not be either nimble or even necessarily that friendly. Not so, when it comes to KPMG. Their responsiveness, leadership and quality of authorship made this long-awaited book worth it.

These were the internal forces that made things happen, but, believe me, I had an army of friends and family and business colleagues who supported me throughout the project. At ADI there were dozens of people who came to me and encouraged me that I could do this, even in my darkest, most pressure filled hours. The most encouraging were the President and CEO of ADI, Sanjay Puri, the COO of the company, Craig Thompson and a Revere Group Vice-President, Jeff Sacks and a terrific PeopleSoft trainer and friend who actually became an author of this book, Raghu Natesan. Thanks, guys.

Friends? Wow. There are myriads who spent time encouraging me. My closest friends in the world, Wayne and Dorothy Hintz, gave me moral support by simply being my friends. Sometimes the best way to write is to not think about writing and to simply be with those who love you and support you. That's my family. Mom and Dad, Abraham and Helen; my brother, Bob; my sister-in-law, Freyda; and my niece, Sara. My mother-in-law, Martha Reid, is always an inspiration to me, showing the strength and fortitude that I can draw on. What can I say? I may not have written the book in blood, but I was supported by my blood to a degree that was truly phenomenal. They were there at all times and any time over the past nearly one year of writing and information gathering. There's a reason I love them all.

They call the different segments of the book "elements." Well, I've left one "element" out of the configuration so far. As the line in the song by Vanessa Williams goes, I've "saved the best for last." My wife, Yvonne. She has been there for a lot more than my book, believe me. Anyone who would put up with me to the degree she did while I wrote this, not only should be acknowledged, but should be made an official saint.

Paul Greenberg

DEDICATIONS

Paul Greenberg

To my wife, Yvonne; my Mom, Helen; my Dad, Chet; my brother, Bob; my Sister-in-law Freyda; and my niece, Sara Rose: Greenbergs all. This is for you, and it always has been.

Michael Fauscette

To my wife, Donna, and daughters, Jessie and Kendyl, who keep me grounded and focused on what really matters.

Scott Fletcher

We all encounter people who influence the course of our lives for the better. I dedicate this book to Ype, who has helped me as both as a parent and a friend, on many occasions in my life. And to my wife, Lenny, and children; Ian, Emma, and Lydia; who never let me forget what a complete life that I led.

INTRODUCTION

Special Edition Using PeopleSoft fills a void. There are very few books on PeopleSoft on the market, and those that are there do not have the scope of this book. David Duffield, Chairman and President of PeopleSoft, says that "PeopleSoft was conceived on a beach in Maui." This book was conceived on a visit to Barnes and Noble. There was a noticeable dearth of books that explained exactly why PeopleSoft, this popular, exciting company with the peculiar name, had virtually no books out there on its behalf. Interestingly enough, Que Publishers had the same idea, and the result is this brainchild.

This is a reference work on PeopleSoft from roughly 5,000 feet up. It is for the decision makers who are deciding whether or not to implement PeopleSoft or the decision makers who are deciding what ERP packages to use. It is written for those decision makers who already have PeopleSoft at their institution and are looking at getting some sort of return on their investment via expansion or better use of their existing implementation. It is designed for the young consultant just beginning his career who is searching for what direction he should take or the older consultant who is changing his career. It is designed for the human resources or financial services professional who has been at it for 10 or 15 years and wants to get "radical" with a substantial shift in his or her life. It is designed for the end user at the company that already has PeopleSoft to aid in getting a better understanding of how the package works. Finally, it is designed for the computer-savvy person who is simply curious as to what the buzz is all about. In other words, it is written for a lot of people.

What This Book Is Not

There are a lot of things that this book isn't. It isn't a manual for every module of PeopleSoft. It isn't a comparison of all other Enterprise Resource Planning (ERP) packages with PeopleSoft. It isn't an implementation guide that will allow you to substitute the complexity of the implementation with the friendly nature of this tome. In other words, no matter how hard anyone tries, this book won't save you the money that it costs to do an implementation. But—it will save you time, effort, and needless expenditure if you use it properly.

However, there are some cautions. That 5,000-foot number mentioned earlier, although a breezy mention, is not a breezy concept. This book is *not* any kind of substitute for the manuals for the PeopleSoft modules. Using this book for an implementation would be a recipe for a disaster. The drilled-down details for the knowledge of the business processes and the technical specifics simply aren't here. *Special Edition Using PeopleSoft* is a guide to why you need PeopleSoft and what in PeopleSoft you need. There should be enough in here to aid and abet your decisions on the product, or we haven't done our job.

WHAT VERSION ARE WE TALKING ABOUT HERE?

This book is focused on the widely popular PeopleSoft version 7.5. This particular version is a dramatic change from all prior versions. At the time of the initial conception of this book, version 7.5 was just coming into use. Now it is the PeopleSoft standard. In writing this book, in some parts, we have had the benefits of the creators of a variety of the modules and the technical tools used to customize PeopleSoft. Otherwise, we are drawing on the vast experience of the authors, involved in combined dozens of PeopleSoft version 7.5 implementations.

HOW IS THIS BOOK ORGANIZED?

The book is organized for the convenience of the authors and the readers. PeopleSoft can be a tough subject. The book's organization makes it easier.

Part I—"Introducing PeopleSoft." This is the history and the *raison d'etre* of PeopleSoft. David Duffield, the founder, Chairman, and President of PeopleSoft, explains how and why he founded the company. The reasons that PeopleSoft and ERP exist are covered in this section.

Part II—"PeopleSoft Software." PeopleSoft is both functional and technical software. Although there are significant coding tools and toolkits designed for improving implementation times and efficiencies, what makes PeopleSoft and its class of software unique is the embedding of best business practices into the applications themselves. However, within PeopleSoft is the architectural ability to customize its look and feel and change those very same processes that govern the out-of-the-box version of the software so that they are specific to your needs. This section of the book covers the details from Mount Rainier with a look at the financial, manufacturing, human resources, student administration, and all other modules and the tools that are available to do the customization.

Part III—"Software for Re-engineering." To implement or not to implement PeopleSoft is a weighty issue. There are dozens of decisions that go into whether or not to do this. This part of the book covers those questions and answers and a few others also. For example, what do I have now at the company and what does it mean to be implementing this rather huge software? Ultimately, the value of this section to you should be to help you decide whether or not to implement PeopleSoft at your enterprise.

Part IV—"Getting the Implementation Ready." You've decided to do it; now what? Key to this process is not only purchasing the hardware and software, but winning the hearts and minds of the people at your company. All parts of the company have to buy into this process. There are a lot of considerations prior to implementation. Is this a plain-vanilla implementation at a very basic level, or does it involve a lot of customization? Should I use the vendor, a large integrator, or a small integrator? Is the company truly behind this yet?

Part V—"Starting the Implementation." Meat and potatoes time—how does the implementation process work? This section defines the basics of a PeopleSoft implementation. It covers the statement of work, the project management, the integration with legacy systems, the value of using interfaces, or converting entirely to the new system and much more.

Part VI—"As the System Rolls Out." Okay, now there is a pilot. It has been accepted. The next step is the rollout to the company as a whole and the preparations for that rollout, including the process of training and the post-implementation support.

Part VII—"Taking PeopleSoft to the Next Millennium." We've covered version 7.5 thoroughly in this book, but if there are three things that are inevitable they are death, taxes, and version 8.0. However, substantial initiatives are being thrust forward by PeopleSoft prior to the release of version 8.0. They range from supply chain management to e-commerce, to improvements in their existing applications, all as they move toward the millennium. What are they doing and where are they going with their future? This is Part VII of this opus.

Appendix A. This is the fun stuff. This appendix contains case studies, contact lists, Web sites, and a host of other useful and interesting information.

When you have finished this book, it will have served about half its purpose. It will have told you whether or not PeopleSoft is where you want to go in the future, either at your company internally, as a PeopleSoft partner, or as a PeopleSoft consultant. However, it serves its other half best if the book is not squirreled away on some shelf behind the Cajun cookbook that you stopped using in 1977. This should be a continuous reference for you when you need or want to know something about PeopleSoft. When version 8.0 comes out, there will be another book, but you have some time. Until then, read the book and then place it on the front shelf. If you have done both of these things, we are done with this and have done our jobs.

INTRODUCING PEOPLESOFT

DAVE'S STORY

by Dave Duffield

PeopleSoft was conceived on a beach in Maui. I'd been thinking of ways to leverage technologies that were relatively new at the time—Windows, relational databases, networking, application development tools—and I approached one of the most brilliant people I know, Ken Morris, with my thoughts. Interestingly, Ken had been mulling over the same opportunities. We were both working with mainframe technologies and applications at the time, and we felt strongly that a new computing paradigm was about to burst wide open. The industry called it "client/server." Ken called it "software for people." I called it "PeopleSoft." And so our story begins.

Our initial vision for PeopleSoft was to build a small-company alternative to ADP by offering flexible, easy-to-use software that gave organizations better control over their operations at reduced costs. At the outset, we defined four goals for our company. We were committed to delivering outstanding customer service; it was mandatory that every PeopleSoft employee have fun at work; we wanted to be profitable; and we would top out at 50 people (because we thought it would be impossible to have fun in a bigger company).

Had it not been for Ken's vision for PeopleTools, our development tool set, and the ongoing commitment to innovation at PeopleSoft, we would be that 50-person company today. PeopleTools enables rapid development with minimal programming, ease of use, ease of data access, and the flexibility to quickly customize applications. Although quite a remarkable concept then, PeopleTools has withstood the test of time and still offers PeopleSoft an innovative development environment and gives our customers the ability to easily maintain their PeopleSoft solutions.

With PeopleTools as our development backbone, we've turned loose our very smart application developers to create the best applications on the market—applications that world-class companies use to run their businesses. We take this responsibility very seriously; it's one of the primary reasons why we will always strive to set the pace in our industry. Our customers are relying on us to be enormously successful.

We've achieved the success we've enjoyed to date by being customer-driven, people-focused, and relentless. When PeopleSoft was founded, our industry had a reputation for mediocre service. We wanted to change that. We wanted to have the happiest, most successful customers in the world. Today, I'm very happy to say that our customer loyalty ratings are at an all-time high. We've blown way beyond the average rating for our industry, yet we know we can always improve.

Parallel to our customers, I think we also have the happiest employees in the world. (Think there's a correlation between employee satisfaction and customer satisfaction? I do.) Our culture is the heart of our business. We try very hard to maintain a working environment that promotes honesty, integrity, trust, and fun. We've also tried to keep our organization as flat as possible. Unnecessary bureaucracy and B.S. are not tolerated. We encourage people to work hard and play hard. And although we're a relatively large company, we try to "manage small" by organizing our people into highly focused, decentralized teams.

We've received a lot of recognition for our culture. Most notably, in 1997 we were rated by *Fortune Magazine* the twentieth best company to work for in America. This particular rating is perhaps the most important one for me, as our employees themselves provided the information that led *Fortune* to this conclusion.

Finally, one of my favorite quotes: "Most people think of pioneers as the people with the arrows in their backs. They also happen to be the people with all the land." (Anonymous)

Read on to find out more about the "land" that PeopleSoft owns today.

CHAPTER 2

PEOPLESOFT: WHERE IT CAME FROM AND HOW IT FITS

In this chapter   *by Paul Greenberg*

CHANGES IN THE WORLD AND IN HOW TO SURVIVE IN BUSINESS: THE FOUNDATION OF ERP

This world is frightening, especially for long-time business veterans, those just starting out, and, for that matter, everyone in between. Business survival and growth used to depend on producing a high-quality product or service for a customer. Customers would then stay with you for years because they had a high comfort level with your capabilities. Value-added services were something you did for old clients/friends because they asked, because you thought it would be good business, and because you liked them, too.

Unfortunately, that has gone the way of the good old days of the Studebaker, mom-and-pop candy stores, and 10-cent baseball cards. In the 1990s, the business climate has dramatically altered to show extremely rapid shifts in technology. Customer loyalties are based more on what their business demands are at the moment than on long-standing relationships to the vendors. There is rapid turnover in the workforce. The nature of goods and services demanded is in constant flux. Coupled with this are fears over technological problems such as Year 2000 (or, as it's euphemistically known, the *millennium bug*) and political/economic transitions, such as the European Monetary Union. In this new world, nightmares at 3 a.m. due to bad pizza become a welcome relief from the waking hours.

How do you deal with this? The bewildering matrix of change is perhaps the fundamental difference between now and the period from the 1950s through the 1980s. The production process has gone from quality-driven competition to customer-driven demand. It's imperative that you meet the needs of the end of the '90s, which means that your internal business processes have to be organized to handle these rapid shifts. On top of this, you also have to deal with the exigencies of crises such as the Year 2000 as a matter of survival of your long-standing business. What can you do?

ERP AND PEOPLESOFT: A FIRST LOOK

Oddly, in the midst of all these dramatic changes, *Enterprise Resource Planning (ERP)* and its stepchildren show up for the ride. ERP can be as confusing as the changes that created the need for it. The main reasons for your company using ERP are often very cloudy, although the supporting reasons for using it may not be. What are the benchmarks to determine how much return you can expect? Is it dollar value? Time savings? User friendliness? All these? None of these?

Just defining ERP is a chore. There are as many definitions of it as there are products supporting it. However, certain concepts that define ERP are pre-eminent. First, companies have highly complex business processes that govern the way they do things. "Things" could be from as seemingly straightforward as issuing an invoice to something as complex as administering a 401K plan. But is issuing an invoice as simple as it sounds? What are the invoice terms? Are the billings net 30 or net 15 or on demand? Do they include expenses always? Sometimes? Never? What format is the invoice in? How is it tracked once it is issued? Who is authorized to issue it? Who is authorized to follow it up if payment is late?

What is the procedure if there are errors or client complaints? *Ad infinitum.* The reality is that what seems simple and transparent has dozens of decisions, processes, and practices behind it. ERP consists of applications particularly focused in the financial, human resource, or manufacturing provinces that are designed to capture these processes and best practices or to change them for the better with generically embedded best practices.

However, things can get very confusing when you get past the stage of defining ERP. Then the question is posed: why PeopleSoft rather than SAP R/3, Baan, JD Edwards, or Oracle? Much of this chapter will be devoted to giving you a picture of how ERP came to be and how PeopleSoft, the company, and PeopleSoft, the applications, fit into the world of ERP— the beginning of the answer to the "whys" raised in this section.

The Venerable Ancestor of ERP: Materials Requirements Planning

In the traditional manufacturing world, resource planning has a long history. Old-timer *Material Requirements Planning (MRP)* and its younger sibling, MRP II, focus on how to use resources, capacity, and availability to balance all an enterprise's production elements. It's used to statically forecast supplier and customer need and to plan effectively for mid- and long-range efforts with these forecasts.

In the days of MRP, the focus was pretty strictly on materials and the ordering process for the supplier or the customer. The evolution to MRP II was more focused on a holistic view of the entire manufacturing environment. Both were revolutionary because they provided an organized way of identifying the processes that linked the production cycles of a manufacturing business and gave the business a means to plan what it would need for the future and where potential bottlenecks in the internal "supply chain" might be.

However, this wasn't sufficient for the 1990s. With the corporate thrust toward *Business Process Re-engineering (BPR)*, technology and business processes became increasingly integrated. A new model for planning had to be developed that involved the technologies used to facilitate these newly transformed business processes. This meant integrating such features as client/server architectures or integrated applications interfaces. Essentially, the automation of business processes through technology became the paradigm for the very large Fortune 1000-level corporations around the globe. In the early and even mid-1990s, it also began to mean accounting for supply-chain management through the Internet or EDI as suppliers and vendors became increasingly involved in the manufacturing processes and planning forecasts of the manufacturing enterprise. No longer were the materials focus of MRP or the island-like single enterprise core of MRP II sufficient. *Voilà*—Enterprise Resource Planning (ERP) was born.

ERP: A Brief Further Definition

ERP is technologically integrated, multi- or cross-enterprise, scalable, automated MRP II. With that mouthful said, let's look at it a bit more.

ERO VERSUS ERP

PeopleSoft's unique spin on ERP is called *Enterprise Resource Optimization (ERO)*. ERO seems to be the next step in the evolution of ERP and how business processes are looked at as technology changes at a sensational pace.

ERP is used in its literal meaning here to describe a particular, discrete set of processes—not the generic term for large-scale enterprise integration planning as it's used today. With all the obvious benefits of ERP, what's the problem? Fundamentally, it's an extended MRP II, which means pushing parts and materials through an assembly line process using computerized versions of manual production methods. Granted, the processes aren't necessarily a physical assembly line nor are they metal parts, but ERP is limited to tracking the process from its raw materials stage through its finished goods stage. In other words, it's materials-focused.

In contrast, PeopleSoft's Enterprise Resource Optimization (ERO) treats the parts, materials, and goods as a single piece of an integrated series of assets and constraints that make up the manufacturing process in its entirety. Capacity planning, the size of the workforce, the supply chain, and customer demand are all included in a planning engine that can build schedules and product plans and track changes in the total process. The underlying conceptual engine is customer-driven demand.

For example, one of the most successful models in the computer system production world is the "build-to-order" model of Dell Computers. This approach has made them a rip-roaring revenue success. All the major players in the industry, such as Gateway and Micron, are emulating their approach. The notion is that the customer is always right if he is ordering something. Although this might sound simple, the implications are staggering to a production process.

All of a sudden, if building to demand becomes the model, order management and fulfillment, real-time inventory management, manufacturing cycle time reduction, production planning, resource control, transaction methods, billing and scheduling—just to name a very few—go to warp speed levels. If significant changes are necessary due to a shift in the market, the build-to-order model has to allow for those changes or anticipate them so that they can occur without interrupting the production process or minimizing the production time loss.

MRP II or traditional ERP can't handle these changes. Table 2.1 shows the differences between MRP II, ERP, and PeopleSoft ERO.

TABLE 2.1   MRP II VERSUS ERP VERSUS ERO

Function	MRP II	ERP	ERO
Level of enterprise	Single plant	Cross-enterprise	Cross-enterprise

Function	MRP II	ERP	ERO
Conception	Parts/materials pushed through assembly line	Parts/materials pushed through assembly line in multiple enterprises; integrated technology/best practices	Parts/materials part of chain of assets/constraints including capacity, size of workforce, extranet suppliers/vendors, and so on; integrated planning engine
Time frame	Mid- to long-term	Mid- to long-term	Dynamic, near real-time
Orientation	Materials-oriented	Materials enterprise-oriented	Customer demand-oriented
Supply chain	Internally focused	Across the enterprise	Virtual manufacturing; extranet

Although there have been notable attempts to squeeze MRP II into the current customer-demand-driven business climate, they have been square-peg-into-round-hole efforts. MRP II can't answer real-time questions such as availability of inventory or the fundamental question, "Can I build it at all?" It can't take the supplier's resource availability into account when plans are being built. MRP II is far too set in planning for taking projected sales orders. It was never intended for handling near real-time changes in customer requirements or for anticipating shifts in the technology necessary to meet those demands. It is a dinosaur.

Also, MRP and MRP II software is basically inflexible. When an MRP II implementation is done, software "switches" are built into the applications. These switches allow the production facility to tailor the implementation. However, no other flexibility is built in and the switches are generic, so if there are contradictory needs across multiple facilities that are using a common database, this makes the MRP II switches—and thus, the software—dysfunctional.

ERP is also somewhat limited though much more customizable than MRP II. It does view the production process as a multiple enterprise venture but doesn't anticipate the real-time manufacturing changes necessary in a demand-based model. It's still a mid- and long-term process model that anticipates little re-engineering of business procedures over an extended period of time. PeopleSoft competitors such as SAP, Baan, and JD Edwards introduced a more flexible, modular, object-oriented approach in their recent releases. Baan purchased Berclain Software Ltd. and introduced what they call "Dynamic Enterprise Modeling," which works on a similar principle to ERO. SAP has introduced a much more modular approach with the version 4.0 Business Framework. But PeopleSoft was able to get a head start with its introduction of ERO in 1995.

WORKING WITH ERO IN PRACTICE

How does ERO address the problems of real-time business changes? Unlike ERP, which PeopleSoft calls a "push" technology, ERO is a "pull" technology, based on the rapidly changing customer demand. (In "push" technology, parts and materials are pushed through an assembly line because they're based on static anticipated sales orders in the mid- and long-term.) Actually, it's just another name for supply-based (push) versus demand-based (pull).

ERO treats the foundation of ERP and MRP II as part of a total complex global process that can span not only large numbers of internal enterprises but also across other companies and into the markets. So the production of the materials and parts is a piece of something that includes manufacturing capacity, the workforce, the suppliers, and their processes relative to inventory and customer demand. At this level, PeopleSoft uses an embedded planning engine based on the Red Pepper ResponseAgent.

PeopleSoft then uses workflow to link the planning and scheduling to more traditional MRP II and ERP modules that handle billing, routing, distribution, production, and cost management. Built into PeopleSoft Manufacturing is a Databridge that handles the links to traditional ERP/MRP/MRP II applications such as SAP R/3, Baan, and JD Edwards. With this workflow enablement, any change in a control or direction or process is immediately reflected throughout the whole system dynamically and in real time. Finally, a central data repository eliminates the data synchronization and duplication problems that exist when MRP II or its later ERP spawn deposit data from disparate sources.

Corporate Profile: Red Pepper

PeopleSoft practically applied ERO with the acquisition of Red Pepper, a United Kingdom-based software company for $225,000,000 in 1997. The supply chain management software developed by Red Pepper features an embedded planning engine, product configuration, workflow, and the use of PeopleTools, PeopleSoft's application development and customization toolset.

AN ERO IMPACT STATEMENT?

Businesses need to measure the impact of their expenditures on their business. There are certain processes that need to be identified and measurements created to calculate the effects of those processes. There are tools that are put into place that can do this. Some of the processes that PeopleSoft can identify and measure with ERO are as follows:

- **Inventory Reduction**

    Reduce finished goods inventory and works-in-progress

    Inventory turn

    Reduce obsolescence by quick changes in product mix

    Reduce safety stock by reacting faster to demand changes

- **Improved Throughput**

    Improve efficiency of plant resources

    Balance corporate-wide demand

    Increase facility output

    Delay capital investment

    Increase revenue

- **Increased Productivity**

    Increase labor productivity by 25%

    Increase planning productivity 100%

    Create proactive workforce that responds to change in real–time

    Move one step closer to paperless workplace

    Improve collaboration

- **Better-Managed Supplier Relationships**

    Share forecast and planning information with supply chain partners

    Source material optimally

- **Maximized Customer Demand**

    Achieve on-time delivery rates

    Real-time pricing

    Support make-to-order environment

    Better allocation of materials and capacity for new demand

This is good stuff, as Johnny Carson used to say. The material benefits of ERO aren't only in the processes but also in the results.

YEAR 2000: PANIC ISN'T NECESSARY—PEOPLESOFT TO THE RESCUE

Computers are very sensitive systems. One thing that's a given in all cases is that code written by human beings will by nature have bugs, especially when it's millions of lines.

For example, when the F16 fighter jet was first developed, a peculiar problem appeared in the simulator (which was a precise reproduction of the code used in the actual F16 production model). Every time it would cross the equator, it would fly upside down. It turned out to be a buggy piece of code that did nothing more than leave out the minus sign for latitudes south of the equator. Luckily, this was found and fixed in the simulator before the F16 actually flew.

The Y2K problem or "millennium bug" dwarfs anything like this. There are estimates now that potentially 90 percent of all accounting systems will fail when January 1, 2000 hits.

Because most of these systems accept *only* two-digit years and computers weren't all that popular in the year 1900, the 00 with the implied 19 has been essentially ignored throughout the century. If you try to enter a 00 into an accounting screen, errors, data exceptions, refusal to accept data as valid, or, even scarier, acceptance of the data as a valid year 1900 data set are very likely to occur. Transactions that mature in 2000 will suddenly be maturing in 1900, leaving a lot of incorrect dollar numbers in an accounting system or a complete system failure when the system can't understand the results. One implication of a dead or poorly transacting accounting system is the inability to cut or pay invoices or to accept or send money or even calculate payroll histories.

Many other kinds of problems present themselves. For example, the "date-in-key" problem occurs when a date is used as part of the key of an indexed file. This becomes a problem if the date has a two-digit year and the application depends on records in the file being in chronological order. Even if processing of the data doesn't depend on the records being in chronological order, it could result in records being listed in the wrong order in reports or onscreen displays. In 2000 and later, an application that's supposed to show the most recent items at the top, or on the first screen, would instead show 1999 items first, completely messing up the records access and slowing up the business process time. Multiply this by billions of potential transactions, and you have a serious slowdown.

Okay, these things are frightening. Look at some other Y2K facts to terrify you even more, and then we'll discuss the alternatives:

- According to the Gartner Group, more than 50% of all the companies in the world won't be Y2K-compliant by the end of 1999.

- By the end of 1997, 60 percent of IT managers surveyed had already experienced Year 2000 problems.

- The Year 2000 is a lawsuit magnet (think of banks that have your accounts messed up, causing you to lose interest and income—wouldn't you want to sue?), with an ABA estimate of over $1 trillion in lawsuits resulting from the Y2K problem.

- Although the Year 2000 issue is the most expensive IS predicament in history, the sole return on the investment in simply fixing the problem is the ability to stay in business.

- The estimated cost for fixing the problem through repair or replacement by business and government is expected to be between $300 billion and $600 billion.

THE ALTERNATIVES: FIX IT OR REPLACE IT?

Although most ERP vendors are Year 2000-compliant, PeopleSoft provides the most well-thought-out and elegant solution.

Since its founding in 1987, PeopleSoft has planned Year 2000 compliance. With version 7.0 of PeopleSoft and all subsequent versions, it is also Y2K-certified. Every single application has twenty-first-century dates systemically built in. This is focused on a Structured Query Language (SQL) relational database management system, which has a YYYY/MM/DD format for dates, and the PeopleTools development environment, which can support any SQL system. The SQL system date format varies among Oracle, Sybase, Informix, and DB/2, but the way that PeopleSoft handles those dates never varies from the YYYY/MM/DD format. PeopleTools handles the translation logic between the SQL database and PeopleSoft.

Regardless of the printed format (for example, May 30, 1998 or 05/30/98, and so on), PeopleSoft always handles the format as twenty-first-century-compliant. Using PeopleTools, you can create four-digit date fields easily so that there's no "conversion" to 2000; it's simply the day after December 31, 1999. PeopleSoft was smart enough to allow for habit by updating the default behavior for date entry to handle a two-digit entry. If the year entered is greater or equal to 40, the other two digits default to 19; if less than 50, the other two digits default to 50. Needless to say, after the year 2050, these date field defaults can be easily changed to contemporary behaviors.

PeopleSoft didn't ignore what seem to be the less spectacular problems of Y2K compliance, either, such as making sure that its PeopleSoft application toolsets are both commonly available Y2K-ready toolsets. For example, the toolsets to do the date manipulation are PeopleCode, which comes with PeopleSoft and PeopleTools; COBOL, which is coherent with the production of most of the Y2K code; and SQR, the 3GL programming language used by PeopleSoft to write internal reporting applications.

Also, PeopleTools developed Year 2000 solutions that use considerably less code than a similar solution in C++ or COBOL. This means more speed and efficiency in the execution of the applications.

PeopleSoft also supports centralized regular procedures for storage, input, retrieval, and manipulation of dates. For example, PeopleSoft has fully incorporated leap years through the twentieth and twenty-first centuries, which is crucial to future accurate date calculation.

Y2K as the Clock Runs Out: PeopleSoft's Template for Handling the Short Term

PeopleSoft has developed a rapid implementation approach for replacement designed to handle the Y2K problem before January 1, 2000. I am going to briefly summarize it here so that you can see that it's possible to still solve these problems as the Y2K clock ticks.

- Understand your business objectives. This is the most important step in the process. What do you hope to accomplish with your replacement system besides fixing the date fields? What business process changes do you want to implement?

- Assemble a dedicated project team with the appropriate skills. The project team needs to be skilled, experienced, and freed from all other tasks but the implementation. They have to be devoted body and soul to the project during its life.

- Recognize and capitalize on re-engineering opportunities. How can you leverage new functions and processes, not just redo the old ones? How can you trim your business processes or revamp them entirely?

- Leverage the experience of others. Work with your business partners, vendors, and your PeopleSoft account managers to carry the implementation forward. Use their experience—successes and failures—to make your implementation work more smoothly.

- Understand the system's capabilities. Do a study of the system's existing functionality and its hardware and software—an "as is" assessment so that you fully understand what you're working with.

- Explore new technology solutions. With the recognition that technological and functional change is continuous, choose the new technologies that you think will help you execute your business properly and better now and in the future. Just don't underestimate the amount of change that can ultimately affect what you've already transformed.

- Execute your implementation in phases. Deal with the basics first. Install your fundamental PeopleSoft functionality before you decide that everyone on the Australian staff needs Java-enabled Internet access.

- Customize by prototyping. Use PeopleTools to do rapid prototyping. When you need to build a feature, build it. When you need to improve the feature, add the improvements.

- Maintain a close relationship with your vendors. Teaming with a vendor such as PeopleSoft is invaluable. Aside from the knowledge that the staff could impart, you can participate in the forums provided by the vendor to improve the product, which can do you extensive good as PeopleSoft implements features that you need to drive your business.

- Follow a proven formula. Again, no need to fix what isn't broken. Follow the paths that other PeopleSoft implementation customers have used.

SPECIAL CASE: THE EURO AND PEOPLESOFT

Another transformation that has just occurred is at least as significant and could even have more impact on a global scale than Year 2000. That is the January 1, 1999, conversion to the euro, the currency unit replacing various European national currencies for multiple European countries.

THE EURO'S ORIGINS

In 1992, the 15 European Common Market nations signed the Maastricht Treaty establishing the European Monetary Union (EMU). The purpose of the EMU was to use currency consolidation and transformation to implement a merger of the capital markets of EMU member countries, establish a common European monetary policy, and to strengthen the trend toward a central European political and economic commonality that would allow the EMU members to compete on the level of the United States in world markets through a common currency and a single marketplace.

The implications of the single currency called the "euro" are staggering for international payment and settlement systems, specifically for banking and commerce. No longer are national currencies such as the pound, franc, or deutschmark as important in trading as they were. The holding of hard currency reserves in any country would be profoundly affected. The cost of goods and services would be dramatically altered because the common currency valuation would be determined by factors involving over 15 nations.

There's a lot more to add to the conversion confusion. Although January 1, 1999 is the date that the euro became the currency for 370 million Europeans, the national currencies of the EMU members will continue to coexist until 2002, when euro banknotes and coins become available. From January 1, 1999 until December 31, 2001, national banknotes—that is, pounds, lira, francs, and drachmas—will continue to exist, whereas checks, credit cards, bank transfers, and so on will be done in the euro. Pricing will be done in the euro for goods and services. Financial contracts will be priced in the euro. Financial institutions subject to government regulations, under the auspices of the European Central Bank (ECB) formed this year to deal with the euro conversion, will be required to report information in euros. Yet, even more confusing, membership in the EMU is voluntary and there is an "opt out" clause for any country that doesn't want to participate in the first round. Already, Denmark, Sweden, and Great Britain have exercised this clause, leaving 11 countries participating: Germany, France, Italy, Spain, the Netherlands, Belgium, Portugal, Finland, Ireland, Austria, and Luxembourg.

Also, until 2002, even the EMU countries don't have to use euros, but can if they want to. So Europe will have a number of countries transacting electronically in euros, spending their paper and coins in their own national currencies and dealing with countries that haven't supported the euro! Finally, several companies such as Siemens and Philips intend to switch their accounting systems to euros by 1999, which will create a very interesting situation for their vendors and suppliers. What confusion!

WHAT DOES THE EURO CONVERSION MEAN FOR INFORMATION TECHNOLOGY?

The countries that will be primarily affected will be all the nations of Europe and any country that does business in Europe—that is, just about every nation in the world. Even more cogent, according to a November 1997 report from the Hurwitz Group titled "The Coming Euro Mess: Conversion Means Opportunity for Packaged Software Vendors and Customers," any company doing over 20% of its business with Europe will be dramatically affected by this conversion.

The IT systems impact will be immense in several areas:

- Parallel currencies through 2002 will force the maintenance of multicurrency financial transaction systems.

- Until 2002, the workers in the European markets will be given the option to choose which currencies they will want to get paid in. This means multiple sets of books by the employers for payroll.

- Pricing will be normalized and thus restructured. All the implications for supply, fulfillment, international purchasing, and so on are there by extension.

- Partnerships are dramatically affected across Europe, as new models for business need to evolve to handle a true Common Market, affecting fundamental corporate business practices.

- Financial services, electronic transactions, credit, loans, contracts, budgets, and currency exchange are dramatically altered transactions forcing massive changes in the setup of systems.

- The euro conversion rate is entirely different than the current conversion rates between European currencies. For example, rather than convert from francs to marks, the conversion will have to be francs to euros and then euros to marks. This is called *triangulation*. It adds an extra step to financial systems transactions and the extra time can affect the national currency's exchange rate.

Legacy systems are facing huge amounts of custom coding or, as PeopleSoft proposes, replacements with "euro-ready" systems such as PeopleSoft. Dozens of companies, such as Lexmark, Eastman Chemical Corp., and Chase Manhattan Bank, have formed committees to examine the implications to their businesses and to make the recommendation on what to do. Financial systems, order entry, fulfillment, warehouse management, and other systems that have some tie to currencies will be affected and need to be changed—at a point that even the European Central Bank, the coordinating body for the euro, hasn't set the final set of rules and regulations.

PEOPLESOFT, THE EURO, AND THE PUBLIC

Many ERP vendors are coming forward with EMU solutions. PeopleSoft, SAP R/3, and JD Edwards are well under way with their planning with Oracle and Baan geared up. However, PeopleSoft has taken the EMU crisis a step further by bringing it to the public's attention, in an attempt to increase knowledge of this breathtaking change in business modality. Still, over 60% of the European population is unaware of the timetable for the changeover, so you can imagine the cognizance level of the U.S. population.

With this in mind, in February 1998, PeopleSoft and the distinguished publication, *The Economist*, cosponsored a successful conference titled *Economic and Monetary Union Executive Summit: Aimed at Raising Global Awareness of EMU.* The keynote speaker was former British Prime Minister John Major. It brought together a group of some of the important minds in the economic, financial services, political, and information technology worlds to discuss the EMU.

PeopleSoft has also involved itself in a number of public forums and appropriate organizations to make sure that its applications fit the specifications of this ever-evolving transition. For example, PeopleSoft sits on the EMU Committee of the Business and Accounting Developers Association of the United Kingdom. In fact, in late 1997, PeopleSoft publicly declared its support for the EMU in a press release.

PEOPLESOFT, THE EURO, AND IMPLEMENTING THE SOFTWARE

It's good to see PeopleSoft's public involvement. This seems to be the socially and politically conscious thing to do, but how does this affect the software?

PeopleSoft maintains consistency with its public posture in its applications and interfaces. If it publicly supports the EMU initiative, the applications will reflect the requirements for euro transactions, euro transitions, and euro transformations.

In version 7.0 and 7.5, PeopleSoft has implemented full support for the EMU. However, in version 6.0, introduced in 1996, PeopleSoft introduced the multibook architecture that laid the foundation for the later fuller support.

Multibook architecture is simple. It's a set of accounting capabilities embedded within PeopleSoft applications that allow users to create any number of ledgers within any single business unit or in multiple business units, each of which can be denominated in a different base currency. This differs from a multicurrency system that allows up to roughly three base currencies that can be converted during transactions and made available for transaction analysis. However, that limitation means that anything more complex than that is toast.

The embedded multibook architecture works to eliminate that constraint. When a currency becomes operational in the course of a transaction, a separate ledger in that currency becomes operational. This replaces enforced conversion with parallel running. Multiple currencies can be operational simultaneously. This means that if Country A is a member of the EMU and then decides to pull out, there is no effect on the transactions that have taken place or are taking place when that occurs. This allows the application of specific currency conversions, rounding, and calculation rules to the euro.

The Euro and PeopleSoft Version 7.5

In version 7.5, the introduction of new features completes the support of PeopleSoft for the euro. Among them are the following:

- Multibook functionality in the Accounts Payable and Accounts Receivable modules
- Currency "triangulation"–the conversion of currency to euro to another currency, a key compliance issue
- Multicurrency functionality in purchasing, order management, and billing, including invoice production in both the euro and the national currency of issuance
- Multicurrency functionality in budgets, for planning purposes
- Multicurrency employee time and expenses in the Expenses module
- PeopleSoft Treasury availability

SUMMARY

You've had a look at some of the reasons that there is a PeopleSoft today and some of the more mission-critical global reasons for its use throughout thousands of enterprises. Y2K certification, euro-readiness, and market responsiveness are only a few of the good reasons to take a look at the more in-depth treatment that you are being afforded with this book. Now, onward and upward to more on PeopleSoft!

PeopleSoft Software

PEOPLETOOLS

In this chapter

by Nancy Maruci

This section is intended as an overview to introduce you to the suite of building blocks provided by PeopleSoft to allow you to create, enhance, and maintain applications—PeopleTools. It is not intended to serve as a "how-to" training guide or to be used as a technical reference. PeopleSoft provides comprehensive and detailed technical reference information in its online PeopleBooks, as well as several excellent hands-on training courses that give specific usage detail for the various tools. It is highly recommended that anyone contemplating an implementation and development effort in PeopleTools should plan to make serious use of these resources.

If it is not practical to cover how-to detail in a chapter or two (the PeopleTools training documentation alone runs well over a thousand pages!), what can this chapter do to initiate you into the world of PeopleTools? First up is a basic definition of PeopleTools, followed by an exploration into the "motherlode" of PeopleTools, the Application Designer. The primary focus here is the Development Project Workspace; however, also included is a brief overview of the richly featured Upgrade Project Workspace.

Next is a section on "The Power of PeopleCode," the proprietary programming language used in the development of PeopleSoft applications.

Then we'll take a look at a sample application to understand how the logical steps of development fit into the integrated environment of the Application Designer.

The "Information, Please" section covers additional resources for learning about and troubleshooting your applications, from audit programs, to object reference reports, to PeopleSoft's online documentation, PeopleBooks.

The chapter finishes up with a "Quick Primer on Other PeopleTools," to give you at-a-glance definitions of other useful tools, many of which are covered in more detail in later chapters.

Along the way are several highlighted topics that give special attention to important concepts to consider when using PeopleTools.

Again, this chapter can serve only as a brief introduction to the wide variety of functionality and potential for using PeopleTools. Later chapters augment the basic information here with application specifics and creative usage of the technology. And, of course, updates, improvements, and new tools are continuously being developed and delivered by PeopleSoft.

As any long journey begins with a single step, we begin the PeopleTools journey in the next section with a definition of PeopleTools.

PEOPLETOOLS OVERVIEW

PeopleTools are a comprehensive toolkit used by PeopleSoft to build, maintain, customize, and upgrade PeopleSoft applications. Every PeopleSoft application is delivered with executable software programs that run when you work with the records, fields, panels, menus, and other objects that make up your application. These programs also allow the developer to maneuver the underlying SQL database from within the application's Windows environment on the client workstation. This toolkit is composed of and supported by several components, including software programs, SQR, SQL, proprietary utility scripts and reports, system messages, stored COBOL SQL statements, and database tables.

PeopleTools can be broken down into three categories:

- Development tools (for example, Application Designer, PeopleCode)
- Administration tools (Process Scheduler, Security Administrator)
- Reporting and Analysis tools (Query, Cube Manager)

The primary focus of this chapter is to provide detailed descriptions of several key PeopleTools, such as the Application Designer tools and PeopleCode. A comprehensive listing of additional PeopleTools, with definitions, is provided later in the chapter in the section "Quick Primer: Definitions and Uses of Other PeopleTools."

PART

II

CH

3

PEOPLETOOLS TABLES AND DATABASE TABLES

A PeopleSoft database is composed of three primary sets of tables: *Application Data Tables*, the *System Catalog Tables*, and the *PeopleTools Tables*.

Application Data Tables store data created by users, specific to the function of that application.

The System Catalog Tables (often referred to as the *database tables*) store indexes and physical characteristics of database tables, views, and columns.

When a PeopleSoft developer creates or modifies object definitions, using a variety of PeopleTools, these definitions are automatically updated in various corresponding PeopleTools tables. These tools tables store the PeopleSoft object definitions for records, views, fields, panels, menus, and more.

Caution

PeopleSoft maintains the structure and definition of all the tools tables. They can and do change with upgrades and new versions of the software. Customer developers should *never* change the tools tables structure or attempt to directly update the contents of these tables using native SQL—to do so would run the risk of database corruption. All changes should originate from within the Application Designer.

For efficiency and system integrity purposes, it is imperative that all these tables stay in sync. PeopleSoft provides auditing reports that help you monitor any inconsistencies within and between these tables. These audit reports are detailed later in the chapter in the section "PeopleSoft Delivered Auditing Reports."

Now that you have learned what PeopleTools are, it's time to further explore how they are used. In the next section, you'll take a look at the "motherlode" of development in PeopleTools, the Application Designer.

APPLICATION DESIGNER: THE MOTHERLODE

Whether designing a new business application, planning customizations, or learning record structures and requirements for conversion, you will be reviewing or manipulating a variety of object definitions. It would be helpful to have an easy-to-use, organized workspace for these activities.

The *Application Designer* is an integrated, visual development environment that enables the developer to create, maintain, customize, and upgrade PeopleSoft applications. Although several logical steps are necessary for each of these processes, most are accomplished using this single work-area, interactive tool. It provides the developer with the ability to work with several object definitions at the same time, enabling better understanding of object interrelationships.

WORKSPACES AND VIEWS

The workspace in Application Designer provides an integrated environment for both application development and upgrades. Two workspace views are provided, the *Development View* and the *Upgrade View*, which can be easily toggled using workbook tabs. Additional detail on the Upgrade View follows later in this section.

An interesting feature of Application Designer is the concept of a *Project*, and the *Project Workspace* (see Figure 3.1). Logically related object customizations can be grouped together into a named Project, which makes it much easier to track customizations, whether in development, for migrations during implementations, or for future upgrades. In the Project Workspace, you view and update projects and their associated object definitions. You can set up your Workspace to automatically or manually insert objects into Projects during development. Figure 3.1 shows the Project Workspace.

The Object Workspace is used to view, create, and modify object definitions, such as records, fields, and panels. Multiple objects can be opened at the same time and can be maximized, minimized, cascaded, or tiled within the workspace. The Object Workspace provides a comfortable flow of attention between the related objects in a development project.

A useful element of the workspace is the *Output Window*, a response window that displays informational or error messages and shows the results of SQL-builds or inquiries into where objects are referenced, and more. A convenient feature is the ability to double-click any of the related object definitions listed to open them.

Project Workspace   Object Workspace

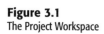
Figure 3.1
The Project Workspace

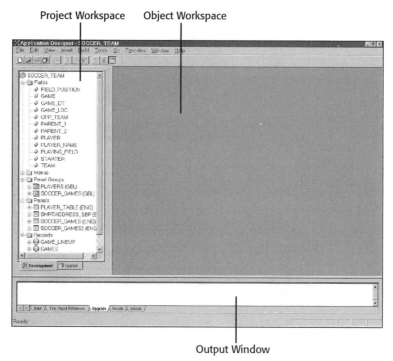

Output Window

PART

II

CH

3

And always, throughout the Application Designer, you can access context-sensitive pop-up menus with a right-click to add attributes, navigate to other objects, and perform actions such as copy and print.

DATA ADMINISTRATION FUNCTIONS

Data Administration functions are available within the Application Designer, to allow developers to directly manipulate the database with SQL from inside your PeopleSoft application. In fact, many of these functions must be performed within the Application Designer to build the underlying database components and keep them in sync with PeopleSoft object definitions (see the section on "PeopleSoft Delivered Audit Reports" in this chapter for further information about maintaining system integrity and synchronization).

Data Administration functions in the Application Designer include SQL Alter and Create for all types of database objects, index management, table space management, and DDL model management for tables, indexes, and table spaces. These functions are available on the Build and tools menus as shown in Figure 3.2.

Figure 3.2
The Build dialog box

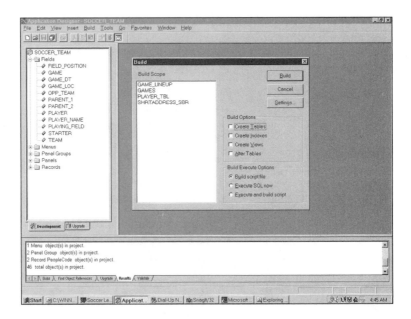

The *Build* function uses Data Definition Language (DDL) to construct a physical database component based on the record and field definitions you've created. It supports Create Table, Create View, and Create Index, as well as Alter Table actions, and can execute the SQL directly (depending on the database platform) or output to a script file for later use. You can choose to build a single record definition, a collection (for example, all views), or all the different record definitions contained within a project.

UPGRADE VIEW WORKSPACE

The Upgrade View is used to view, organize, and perform migration of objects from one PeopleSoft database to another. This tool is used for performing application release updates and upgrades, and for migrating selected new or customized PeopleSoft objects to a target database during an implementation.

Projects are used in the Upgrade View (see Figure 3.3), where folders indicate the various object definitions that are organized into an upgrade or migration project. For migrations during implementations, the developer decides which objects are contained in a project and selectively moves them to a test or production environment.

Figure 3.3
The Upgrade View
Workspace

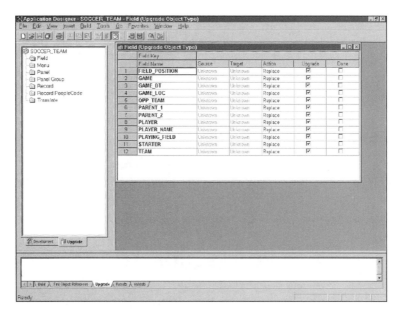

For application updates or upgrades post implementation, you should check whether any new updates would conflict with prior customizations to your system. PeopleSoft provides a mechanism in the Upgrade View workspace to compare your application object definitions with those supplied in a new release to find any conflicts (referred to as *compare programs*). These programs produce *compare reports* that identify conflicting object definitions between the original and new databases. Compare reports tell you whether and how the definition has changed in each database, to streamline decision-making about which versions to retain.

The same flow and ease of use of the Application Designer's graphic interface, seen in the Development View, also come into play in the Upgrade View. The visually integrated components make migrations and upgrades more manageable and straightforward.

APPLICATION DESIGNER: SOME PROJECT ADVICE

As you have seen, the Application Designer handles a variety of system functions, from application development to upgrades. Although its most obvious use is for developers to create and enhance applications, it can also be a useful tool for functional analysts and other nondeveloper members of a project team.

Technical project team members who are not necessarily slated to be PeopleTools developers should have a solid understanding of how to review and understand Application Designer tools. For example, conversion/interface teams responsible for data mapping and technical specifications for programs will need to understand record structures, field characteristics, and default values, as well as accommodate any PeopleCode-driven edits. All this can be easily researched with some basic Application Designer knowledge.

PART

II

CH

3

Functional analysts must be able to look up table, panel, and field use during fit analysis, data mapping, and base table data setup. Basic research-level knowledge of the Application Designer tools also helps with query design and development. This competency is important during functional system design, and analysts must have at least a rudimentary understanding of the tools, if only from knowledge transfer delivered by project developers who have been to formal training. Another alternative to informal in-house learning is a class that PeopleSoft developed especially for this need—the PeopleTools Overview class is designed for non-developers, managers, and analysts.

A few more good reasons for functional folks to learn how to navigate basic PeopleTools are increased self-sufficiency during the fit analysis/design phase, increased understanding of the impact of proposed customizations, and, it is hoped, more ability and willingness to find alternatives.

THE POWER OF PEOPLECODE

Sometimes standard delivered edits cannot accommodate the editing or processing requirement your design has placed on a field or a panel process. Or maybe you need specialized menu processing. In these cases, you may want to add PeopleCode to your application. *PeopleCode* is the proprietary structured programming language, built in to PeopleTools, used in the development of PeopleSoft applications (see Figure 3.4).

Figure 3.4
A sample of
PeopleCode

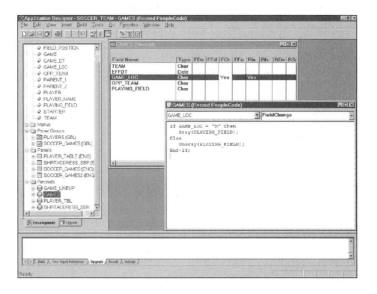

PeopleCode was originally developed to enforce business rules for data entry, such as conditional errors and warnings, field value edits, and controlling conditional field displays on panels. It has evolved and expanded over time to accommodate more complex application processing, such as validation of data on groups of panels, control data access in multiple-scroll panels, and creating command push buttons that trigger other panels or processes.

PeopleCode is attached to objects that you create and modify in Application Designer. Every PeopleCode program is associated with an object and an event and executes at specified events during application processing, such as panel initialization, a change in field value, or a row delete. The developer specifies which of several events will trigger the PeopleCode program associated with that object. Some events trigger when a field value is changed or added, such as `FieldChange` and `FieldEdit`. Others, such as `RowInsert` and `RowDelete`, affect actions on rows of data on a scrollbar. The `Save` PeopleCode events, such as `SaveEdit` and `SavePreChange`, will be invoked when a user attempts to save work on a panel record with this kind of PeopleCode associated with it.

Following is a list of PeopleCode events that are available to be associated with an object:

- `FieldDefault` event
- `RowSelect` event
- `SavePreChg` event
- `FieldEdit` event
- `RowInsert` event
- `Workflow` event
- `FieldChange` event
- `RowDelete` event
- `SavePostChg` event
- `FieldFormula` event
- `PrePopup` event
- `SearchInit` event
- `RowInit` event
- `SaveEdit` event
- `SearchSave` event

PART

II

CH

3

Note

In the example later in the chapter, additional field edits are provided by two PeopleCode events defined for the GAMES record. In the example, we want the field PLAYING_FIELD to gray or ungray for data entry, depending on the value in the field Game Location. This trigger needs to be invoked both when the field value is changed and when the panel itself initializes. Thus, we use FieldChange and RowInit PeopleCode events for the example.

PeopleCode uses built-in functions, system variables, meta-SQL, and language constructs. Anyone familiar with structured programming languages, relational database concepts, and SQL should be reasonably comfortable learning to interpret and write basic PeopleCode. Applications are delivered with several function libraries. Take a look at any of your application record definitions that are named FUNCLIBxx for examples. Developers can create, store, and call custom functions to facilitate modular programming and help make source maintenance easier.

Note

> You can always clone the delivered function definitions and modify them to fit your needs, but it is a good idea to house them as separately as possible from the delivered original code. It is recommended that you create your own Function Library record definition because it is practically guaranteed that PeopleSoft will change the functions in the delivered FUNCLIBxx records in new releases.

PeopleCode programs are primarily associated with a Record Field's attributes, that is to say, it is specific to a field's use on a particular record, not to the field itself. A PeopleCode program can also be attached to a menu item. You can input and edit PeopleCode from within a record or menu definition in Application Designer or while you are working with a panel definition in Panel Designer. The PeopleCode itself is not part of the record or menu definition; it is stored in its own tools table. An automatic association between the record/menu definition and related PeopleCode is created when the PeopleCode is saved. If you "clone" a record definition, you will be asked whether you also want to make a newly associated copy of the PeopleCode.

Automatic formatting and syntax checking are nice features of the PeopleCode Editor. It automatically converts field names to uppercase, indents statements, and highlights syntax errors. It also supports standard editing functions (Save, Cancel, Cut, Copy, Paste, Find, Replace, and Undo), as well as Windows Cut, Copy, and Paste keyboard shortcuts.

PeopleCode is powerful and, like all power tools, should be used or modified with caution by trained, knowledgeable developers. It is important to have a thorough understanding of how the Application Processor flows and interacts with PeopleCode, in order to avoid over-coding or time-consuming debugging. Some PeopleCode is very simple, easy to clone or modify, but other PeopleCode is very complex and involves several layers of drill-down before you understand what the code is doing and what you would be affecting downstream. For the most effective, efficient development effort, a PeopleCode class would be project time well spent!

In the next section, you will follow through a simple sample application built in the Application Designer using PeopleTools and PeopleCode.

ELEMENTS OF APPLICATION DESIGNER: A SOCCER LEAGUE APPLICATION

A working example makes explaining the elements of the Application Designer a little easier. We will walk through a custom application created to manage a soccer league's team, players, and game schedule/lineup. This simple application illustrates concepts such as field definitions, table creation, control tables, translate values, panel elements, subrecords, and much more. Remember, this is no substitute for a tools class! The intent here is to familiarize you with some basic elements and, I hope, encourage you toward further exploration and honing of your PeopleTools skills.

During the development process, it is important to understand the interrelationships of the objects you plan to create or modify, and the logical order of steps needed to implement customizations correctly. Table 3.1 is a good place to begin. In the upcoming Soccer League example, we will utilize the classic PeopleSoft "Nine Steps for Customization," made famous by PeopleBooks and tools instructors everywhere.

TABLE 3.1   THE CLASSIC PEOPLESOFT STEPS FOR CUSTOMIZATION

Development Step	PeopleTool
1—Design the application.	None
2—Create field definitions.	Application Designer
3—Create record definitions.	Application Designer
4—Build SQL objects.	Application Designer
5—Create panel definitions.	Application Designer
6—Create panel group definitions.	Application Designer
7—Create menu definitions.	Application Designer
8—Enable PeopleSoft security.	Security Administrator
9—Test the application.	Online System

STEP 1: DESIGNING THE APPLICATION

Imagine that you are the new League Commissioner for a junior boys and girls soccer league. Your coaches need an easy way to keep track of their players' personal and player information, as well as a way to line up the roster and schedule for each game. For this application, we will first design a panel for the Players Table to store information such as player name, address, position, and parents' names.

We then need a panel for coaches to track each game scheduled, with location and opposing team information, as well as the proposed lineup for that game. We'd also like to keep history data on all the games a team will play that season. This new panel will be the Soccer Games panel, supported by the Games and Game Lineup tables, seen in Figure 3.5 and Figure 3.6.

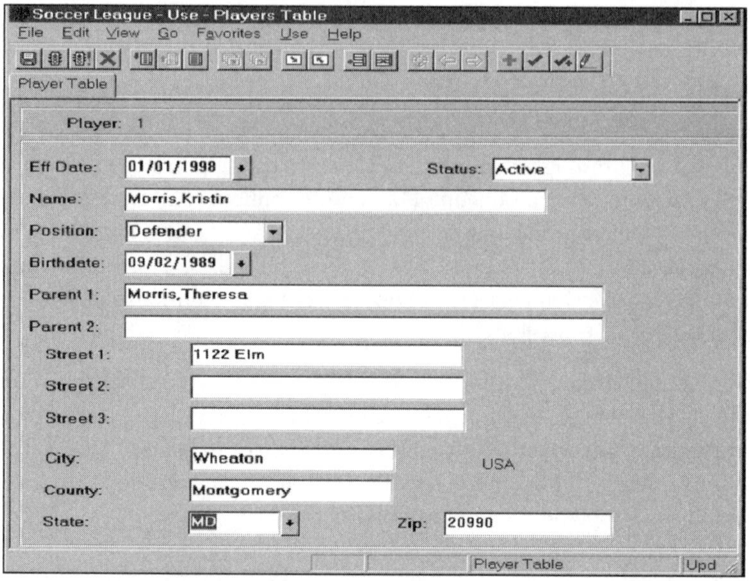

Figure 3.5
The Soccer Games panel

Figure 3.6
The Game Lineup tables

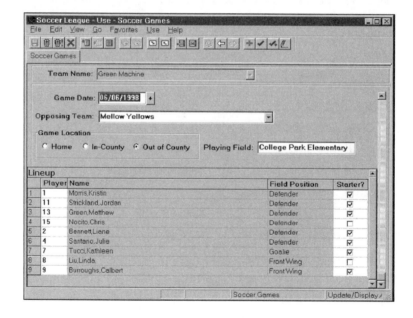

It's a good idea to map out visually what you need the panels to look like, in order to determine what fields your record definitions will require, what key structure will be most effective, and how you might best structure and edit the data in your tables. In this application, for example, there is a one-to-many relationship between the game and the roster of players, which would indicate that a parent-child table relationship is needed between the Games and Game Lineup tables. This relationship is indicated by the inner scrollbar on the panel. The outer scrollbar indicates the ability to track the history of a team's games over time.

Some field definitions may already exist in the delivered application; others, you will create. When planning the design of any new objects you yourself want to create, it is recommended that you reference the PeopleSoft Naming Standards and Conventions Guide, available in the online PeopleBooks documentation.

STEP 2: FIELD DEFINITIONS

Fields are initially defined independently of the record definitions that use them. Fields have *global* attributes, such as Length and Type, that remain the same anywhere the field is used. After a field is added to a Record definition, additional editing characteristics that are specific to use on that record can be added.

After you have opened the Application Designer in the Development View, you can create any new object by clicking File, New and selecting an object type. In this case, we created several new fields, for example, a field called PLAYER as the key identifier for each player's number. The Player field has been designated a Character field.

A variety of Field Types can be assigned. We also created another field, GAME_DT, with a field type of Date (see Figure 3.7).

PART

II

CH

3

Figure 3.7
Field Types available with the Application Designer

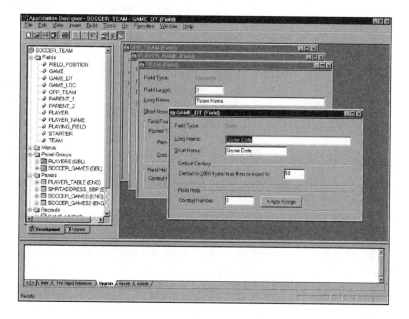

A field can be assigned an edit format. In this example, Parent Name uses the standard PeopleSoft Name format of LastName,FirstName[space] Middle Initial. Other examples of edit formats are Mixed case, Numbers Only, and Zip/Postal Code formats.

Data entered into a field can be set up to edit against the values stored in a table, for example, the State Code field would edit against a State Names table. In other situations, where there are only a few, static values to edit against, creating an entire edit table is overkill. An example to illustrate: The field Game Location will have only three choices—Home, In County, and Out of County. It doesn't make sense to create an entire database table to store three fairly static values to edit a field against. PeopleSoft applications provide one large edit table, the *Translate Table* (also known as the *Xlat Table*), for just such situations. It contains numerous delivered field translate definitions and can easily be customized to add your own.

We have defined a Field Object Property for *Translate Values* for the field Game Location, as shown in Figure 3.8.

Figure 3.8
Defining a Field Object Property for Translate Values

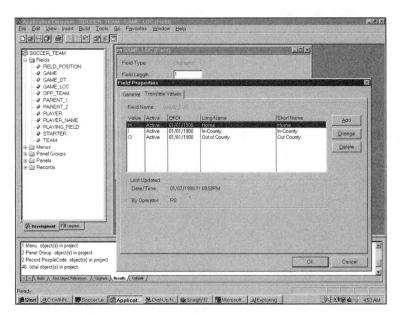

As the fields are created and saved, they can be added to the Project Workspace for inclusion into your Project (a *Project*, as discussed previously in this chapter, is a logically related group of objects that enables easier tracking and migration of customizations). You can do this manually or set a parameter to cause this to happen automatically.

The following section demonstrates how, after you have defined and saved all your new fields, you can use them along with existing field definitions to construct your new record definitions.

STEP 3: RECORD DEFINITIONS

Record definitions in PeopleSoft can define the database table structure and online characteristics of several types of objects: SQL tables, SQL Views, SubRecords, Derived/Work Records, Query Views, and Dynamic Views.

In the sample application, we created four new Record definitions for SQL tables.

- PLAYER_TBL—Tracks player information
- GAMES—Tracks game schedules
- GAME_LINEUP—Tracks player lineups by game
- SHRT_ADDRESS_SBR—Tracks player addresses

The SHRT_ADDRESS_SBR definition illustrates the concept of a SubRecord. A *SubRecord* is a record definition of a combined group of fields commonly used in other multiple record definitions. After you've defined it, you can add just the SubRecord object to other record definitions. This way, any changes to the group of fields can be made in one place, rather than on each record definition that the group of fields is used.

For example, Addresses are a pretty standard grouping of fields that are used in many record definitions across an application (see Figure 3.9. An Address SubRecord could be defined once and then used in as many record definitions as you want. Any future changes to the characteristics of the SubRecord would have to be made only in one place. SHRT_ADDRESS_SBR will become part of the PLAYER_TBL record definition.

PART

II

CH

3

Figure 3.9

Addresses as an example of grouping fields

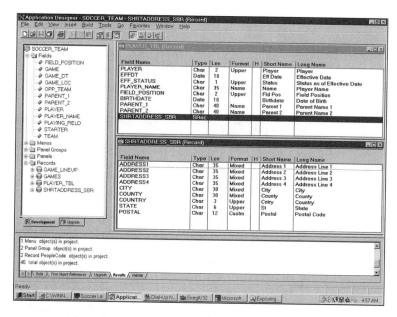

Fields can be added to a record definition in several ways. For example, they can be dragged and dropped from the fields in the Project Workspace, or they can be added from the menu via Insert, Field and selecting from a global field list.

When working with Record definitions, the Application Designer Object Workspace has four display views of attributes: Field Display, Use Display, Edits Display, and PeopleCode Display. Global field attributes (database-level attributes) that are part of the field's definition are displayed in the Field View of the Object Workspace (see the section preceding

Step 2, "Field Definitions," for more information on field attributes). When you're adding fields to define a record definition, additional record-specific characteristics for a field, such as Keys, Default values, Required, or Prompt Table edits, can be defined in the Use and Edits views of the Object Workspace. PeopleCode for a particular record field can be viewed and edited in the PeopleCode View (see Figure 3.10).

Figure 3.10
Using PeopleCode to edit or view a record field

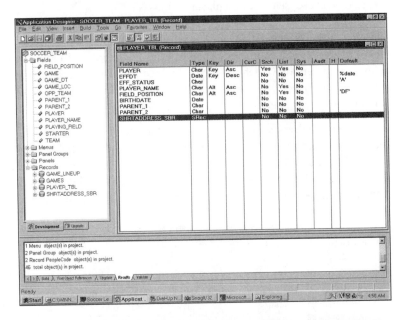

Figure 3.11
Providing additional field edits for PeopleCode events

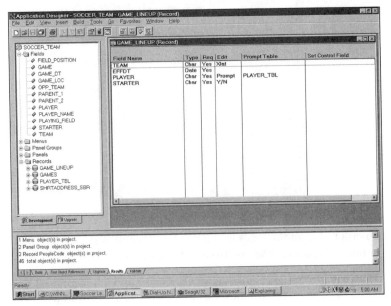

In this example, additional field edits are provided by two PeopleCode events defined for the GAMES record, as indicated by the Yes markers (see Figure 3.11). Clicking on the Yes will display the actual PeopleCode. In this example, you want the field PLAYING_FIELD to gray or ungray for data entry, depending on the value of the field GAME_LOC (see Figure 3.12).

Figure 3.12
Adding data to the
PLAYING FIELD field

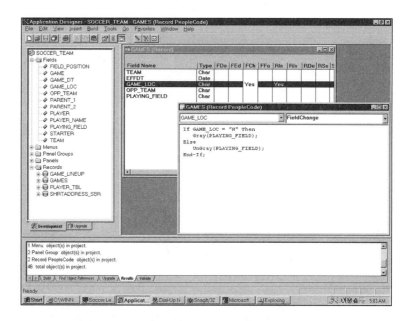

Note

Please refer to the section "The Power of PeopleCode" earlier in this chapter for more information about the definition and uses of PeopleCode.

Even though a Record definition is defined and saved in the Application Designer, the structural definition of the tables at the database level has not yet been created. This will be accomplished by Step 4, when we build the SQL objects.

STEP 4: BUILD SQL OBJECTS

The Build function in the Application Designer exists to easily enable the developer to execute the following SQL processes: Create Table, Create View, Create Indexes, and Alter Table. Using the Build function also serves to synchronize the database structure with what is defined in the Application Designer and stored in the PeopleTools record and index definitions. It allows a variety of settings to determine, for example, when a Create Table will be allowed, logging preferences, and where/when SQL script files will be generated and executed, plus much more.

PART

II

CH

3

In this example, the GAME_LINEUP, GAMES, and PLAYER_TBL tables need to be SQL-Created using the Build function. (Note that the SHRT_ADDRESS_SBR record definition will not be SQL-created at the database level because its record definition is actually a logical grouping of field definitions. The content of fields in a SubRecord is stored in the primary record structure where the SubRecord is referenced. See Figure 3.13.

Figure 3.13
The content of fields in a SubRecord is stored in the primary record structure.

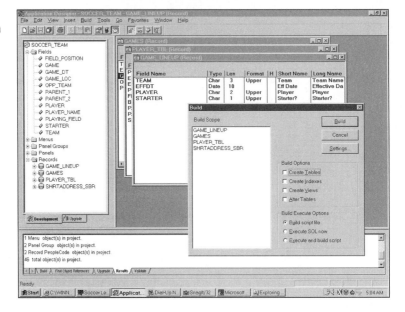

Now we are ready to begin constructing our panels. In the next section we discuss some basic elements of Step 5, Panel Definitions.

STEP 5: CREATE PANEL DEFINITIONS

This is the fun part! After you have a good design in place and have field and record definitions, you are ready to construct a panel. *Panel controls* are the elements of a panel definition, as shown in Figure 3.14.

Figure 3.14
Panel Controls

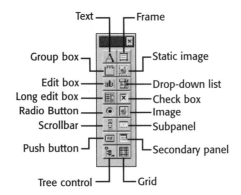

A variety of attributes can be assigned to each panel control. Our Players Table panel uses a wide range of Panel controls, as shown in Figure 3.15.

Figure 3.15
Using a wide array of panel controls

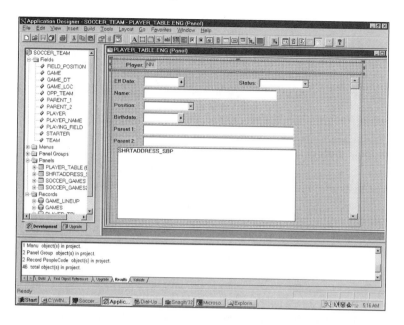

PART

II

CH

3

Note the SHRTADDRESS_SBP SubPanel area of the Players Table panel definition. We discussed the use and benefits of SubRecords in previous sections of this chapter; a *SubPanel* is a panel definition that corresponds to a SubRecord.

An important panel control to note is the scrollbar. *Scrollbars* are used to control rows of data being inserted into a single SQL table. Panels could have a single scrollbar, as in the Players Table panel, or two to three nested scrollbars. Sometimes it is more comfortable for the user, visually, for multiple occurrences of data in a scrollbar area to be displayed as a grid. The Soccer Games panel in Figure 3.16 illustrates grids and nested scrolls.

To use the panel we created, it must be first added to a Panel Group, and then the Panel Group added to a Menu Definition. Finally, panel security access must be granted. The next sections describe the PeopleTools elements that must be completed to get to the final all-important ninth step of customization, Testing.

STEP 6: PANEL GROUP DEFINITIONS

Panel groups are the link between panels and menus. The panels created for the Soccer application must be added to a panel group to access the via menus. Panel group definitions include

- Grouping of panels and labels
- Allowable user actions (Add, Update/Display, Update/Display All, Correction)
- Designated search records

Figure 3.16
Grids and nested
scrolls

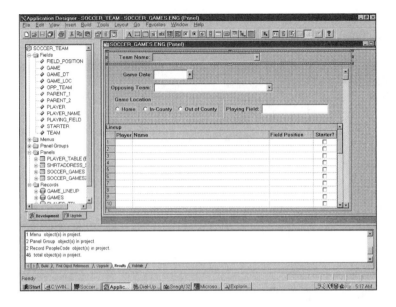

A *search record* is the record used to retrieve data into the panel. It also controls which search criteria fields appear in the search dialog box. A search record can be the same as the panel's primary controlling record, or another record that shares the same high-level keys. A view record definition can be used as the search record, to act as a filtering mechanism on data retrieved. Although search records can simply retrieve all the associated data for a panel, they often contain security processing components to filter data based on operator.

The Panel Groups for the Soccer application are Players and Soccer Games, as shown in Figure 3.17.

Figure 3.17
The Panel Groups for
the Soccer application
are Players and Soccer
Games

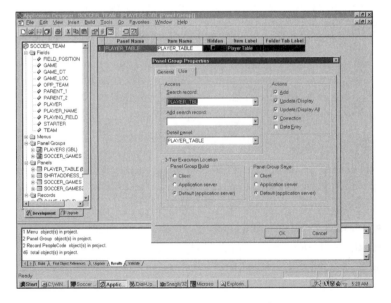

Next, you'll define the new menu and menu items.

STEP 7: MENU DEFINITIONS

After you've created your application's panel groups, you add them to menu definitions by associating them with menu items. You can also group several menu definitions together into menu groups.

The Soccer application has a defined standard menu, Soccer League, to allow access to the Soccer games and Players Table Panel Groups. Standard menus are displayed at the top of all PeopleSoft application windows and provide access primarily to an application's panel groups. (Pop-up menus are another kind of PeopleSoft menu, accessed by right-clicking panel fields, not covered here.) The standard menus in a PeopleSoft application are accessed via the Go menu bar. Menus, menu bars, and menu items are all parts of a standard menu definition.

The menu elements of the Soccer example are shown in Figure 3.18.

Figure 3.18
The menu elements of
the Soccer panel

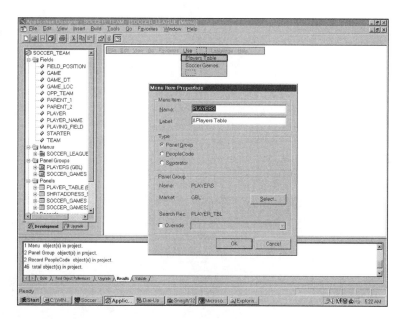

The next step is to grant security access to the new panels.

STEP 8: ENABLE PEOPLESOFT MENU/PANEL ACCESS SECURITY

After a panel group has been added to a new or existing menu definition, panel security access can be granted. The Security Administrator PeopleTool is used to grant menu and panel access, as well as determine allowable actions (Add, Update/Display, Update/Display All, Correction).

Menu/panel access is assigned to either an Operator profile or a Class of operators who have common profile attributes.

The Security Administrator enables control of many other profile attributes other than menu/panel access, such as sign-on times, passwords, Change Control access, operator Language Preference settings, and much more. For our development example here, we would only need Security Administrator for enabling menu and panel access for testing the application.

Figure 3.19
The Security
Administrator window

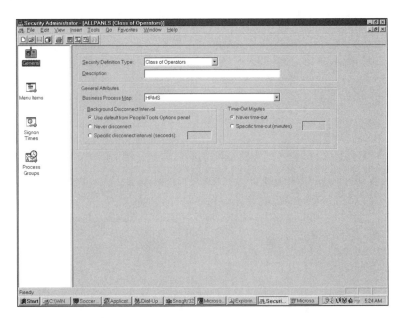

Figure 3.20
The Select Menu Items
window

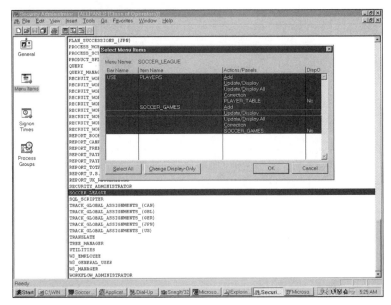

Now on to the last step, testing our new application.

STEP 9: TEST THE APPLICATION

The final step is to test the functionality of the new application. Some basic questions to test are: Does the panel show up on the menu? Will the panel retrieve? Do the field controls tab through in the proper order?

Other testing to consider: Perform all panel actions (Add, Insert, Delete, and Update rows). Confirm default values, and check fields that have prompt functions for correct list box display. Check PeopleCode edits and processes for expected results, and scroll down, if applicable, to view the effects of PeopleCode on any history rows.

If you have modified the delivered PeopleCode, it is assumed that adequate research has been done prior to customizing, to guard against unexpected downstream results. If customization was done to core PeopleCode modules, particularly on a record that spans several panels in a panel group, it is a good idea to test the business process through all the panels in the group, even at the unit testing stage.

To assist in your testing, you can print the record definitions for your panels, as well as a panel image and a panel definition in a formatted report.

PeopleSoft provides several excellent tools to help with tracing and debugging of applications, such as the Application Reviewer (for more information on these tools, refer to the PeopleSoft online documentation, PeopleBooks). In addition, cross-reference and audit reports help in managing and debugging your development efforts.

The next section, "Information, Please..." should get you started in the right direction.

INFORMATION, PLEASE: CROSS-REFERENCE REPORTS, AUDIT REPORTS, PEOPLEBOOKS

This section introduces several useful tools provided by PeopleSoft to assist you in your analysis, development, and debugging efforts: the PeopleTools Objects Cross-Reference Reports, Audit Reports, and those very useful online reference manuals, PeopleBooks.

PEOPLESOFT DELIVERED CROSS-REFERENCE REPORTS

We have previously discussed the PeopleTools tables that contain definitions and attributes of various application objects, such as Fields and Panels. When you're in the depths of implementation development, it would be handy to have a way to research these definitions without having to look them up, one by one, in the Application Designer.

You could, of course, construct your own SQR or Query reports, based on the record definitions of the tools tables. This assumes that you understand the structure of and values contained in those tables—not an easy task for the beginner. A faster, more handy way is to become familiar with the many PeopleSoft delivered Cross-Reference Reports. They are great to use "as is," or they can be cloned and modified for your particular need.

Cross-reference reports are easily identified. Look for the ones starting with XRF (standard delivered PeopleSoft reports follow a naming convention of a three-character prefix, such as PAY for Payroll reports, or GLX for General Ledger). Cross-reference reports can be run from either the Process Scheduler or the Query/Crystal reporting tool.

Caution

Some of these reports, if printed out, could kill several trees worth of paper!

Although sometimes there is no good substitute for seeing it on paper, an alternative is to Print to File and view the output report via a word processing tool such as MS Word. This enables faster word searches on a specific element you may be looking for. If you must print to paper, you may want to consider scheduling the print job for off hours.

Reports and descriptions are listed in Table 3.2.

TABLE 3.2   PEOPLESOFT OBJECTS CROSS-REFERENCE REPORTS

Report Name	Description
XRFFLPN—Fields and Panels	**Lists all fields in alphabetical order, with names of all record and panel definitions** in which the field occurs, and lists the field Long Name.
XRFRCFL—Fields and Records	**Lists all fields in alphabetical order** by associated record definition name. The report details the Long Name, Field Type, Field Length, and Formatting specified for the field.
XRFFLRC—Records and Fields	**Lists all fields in alphabetical order.** The report lists the Long Name, Field Type, Field Length, and Formatting specified for the field and includes the names of all record definitions that contain the field.
XRFAPFL—Applications and Fields	**Lists all menus, such as General Tables, in alphabetical order and the fields within each menu.** For each field, the report lists the Field Name, Field Type, Length, and Format and all the record and panel definitions that contain the field (within the window).
XRFIELDS—Field Listing	**Lists all fields in alphabetical order.** The report includes Field Type, Length, Format, Long Name, and Short Name.

continues

Report Name	Description
XRFFLPC—Fields Referenced by PeopleCode Programs	**Lists all PeopleCode programs in alphabetical order** by associated record definition and field. The report lists the type of field for all fields referenced in the PeopleCode program.
XRFMENU—Menu Listing	**Lists all menus in alphabetical order and all panel definitions within each menu.** It also includes the associated search record definition name and detail panel definition name.
XRFPANEL—Panel Listing	**Lists all panel definitions in alphabetical order.**
XRFPCFL—PeopleCode Programs and Field References	**Lists record definitions that contain fields with PeopleCode program attributes.** The report includes the Field Name, as well as the associated record definitions and fields referenced in the PeopleCode program.
XRFPNPC—Panels with PeopleCode	**Lists all panels that contain fields with PeopleCode attributes.** For each panel, the report includes the name of the record definition(s) that contain the field, as well as the Field Name and Type.
XRFRCPN—Records and Panels	**Lists all record definitions in alphabetical order.** The report includes the menu and panel definitions associated with each record definition.
XRFWIN—Window Listing	**Lists all application menu windows in alphabetical order.**

PART

II

CH

3

PeopleSoft Delivered Auditing Reports

The Application Designer allows a developer to create and modify object definitions, and these definitions are stored in various PeopleTools tables. Objects such as record and field definitions also have physical characteristic definitions at the database level, stored in the System Catalog tables (this occurs automatically during the Build process). For efficiency and system integrity purposes, it is imperative that these tables stay in sync. PeopleSoft provides auditing reports that help you monitor any inconsistencies.

DDDAUDIT

DDDAUDIT audits between the PeopleTools tables and the System Catalog tables, by using an SQR that compares data structures defined in the PeopleTools tables against the underlying database. Some examples of the type of inconsistencies that DDDAUDIT can uncover are when a record definition of a table is defined in the Application Designer, but not found in the database, or conversely, when a SQL table is defined in the database, but no corresponding record definition exists in the Application Designer. An example of how these situations can occur would be when a developer creates and saves a record definition using Application Designer and then forgets to do the Build step, creating a situation where he can see the record in PeopleSoft, but not in the database when he tries to access it via SQL.

SYSAUDIT

SYSAUDIT audits within the PeopleTools tables that define each object type, via an SQR that identifies "orphaned" PeopleSoft objects and other inconsistencies within your system. It will indicate, for example, whether field definitions are missing for fields used on a panel definition (someone deleted a field without checking where it is used first, or didn't do the necessary cleanup). Other examples of "orphaned" objects would be a module of PeopleCode that exists, but is not connected to any other objects in the system, or perhaps a panel definition that is not referenced on any menu definition.

When you run either the DDDAUDIT.SQR or the SYSAUDIT.SQR, the results are written to a corresponding .LIS file that can be reviewed and debugged against exception listings detailed in the PeopleTools PeopleBooks documentation. These audit reports are invaluable during an initial implementation development effort and especially during subsequent product upgrades. It's a good idea to become familiar with them and build them into your system administration processes from the beginning.

PEOPLEBOOKS AND OTHER PEOPLESOFT DOCUMENTATION SOURCES

PeopleSoft delivers documentation to its customers and business partners in several ways: PeopleBooks, hard copy, and selected information on a Continuous Documentation Web site.

PeopleBooks are downloadable CD-ROM–based "reference manuals" that come with the specific products a customer has purchased. (They are created using Folio VIEWS infobases .NFO files.)

PeopleBooks have proven to be a big hit with project teams and users alike—easy to learn, simple to search and find just the information you are looking for, and they can be printed out by the page, by selected sections, or as a whole. PeopleBooks quickly become an essential research and learning tool, especially during the fit analysis and design segments of an implementation.

Even with the ease of use of PeopleBooks, some people still prefer hard-copy manuals. Although you yourself can print out PeopleBooks, you can also order printed, bound volumes of the same PeopleSoft online documentation from PeopleSoft Press.

Another very useful and convenient source of the latest and greatest information is the World Wide Web site called *Continuous Documentation*, maintained by the PeopleSoft Communication Services group. This site does not contain the full documentation delivered in PeopleBooks; rather, it is an additional source of information for customers. The site delivers a variety of materials such as white papers, Product Deliverable Updates, Prerelease Notes, Release Notes, and selected updates to PeopleBooks.

QUICK PRIMER: DEFINITIONS AND USES OF OTHER PEOPLETOOLS

This Quick Primer is a basic introduction to some of the other PeopleTools, provided by PeopleSoft, that allow you to create, enhance, and maintain applications. This section is intended to give you at-a-glance definitions of other useful tools, many of which are covered in more detail in later chapters.

This primer of PeopleTools is divided into three basic categories: Development tools, Administration tools, and Reporting tools.

PART

II

CH

3

DEVELOPMENT TOOLS

The Development tools include Application Designer, PeopleCode, Application Reviewer, Message Agent, EDI Manager, Application Engine, and Business Process Designer, which are briefly described in the following sections.

APPLICATION DESIGNER

Application Designer is the integrated development environment, which allows customers to view, add, or modify application objects. It integrates several tools into one workspace, such as Data Designer, Panel Designer, Menu Designer, Business Process Designer, and the Application Upgrader.

PEOPLECODE

PeopleCode is the PeopleSoft proprietary structured programming language, which is used for custom field-level edits, calculations, defaults, and processes. (See the earlier section titled "The Power of PeopleCode" for further explanation.)

APPLICATION REVIEWER

Application Reviewer is a debugging tool to help developers and analysts identify and resolve modification/development issues during implementation.

MESSAGE AGENT

Message Agent is a tool to process messages sent by external systems (such as email, IVR systems, Internet/intranet), providing an API (Application Programming Interface) that enables communication and integration with PeopleSoft applications (the API can also be used to build connections between different PeopleSoft systems). It uses standard Microsoft Windows DLL routines, or dynamic data exchange, to communicate with the Message Agent.

EDI MANAGER

EDI Manager is used to define data mappings for electronic data interchange. This tool can also be used to build interfaces that leverage PeopleSoft's built-in error checking functionality. This eliminates the need for developers to build error checking into their interface programs and ensures that error checking is performed adequately and consistently throughout the application.

APPLICATION ENGINE

Application Engine is a tool designed to help develop, test, and run background SQL processing programs, bypassing the need to write COBOL or SQR programs. All resulting programs can be built, run, and debugged within PeopleTools, using PeopleSoft platform-independent meta-SQL.

BUSINESS PROCESS DESIGNER

Business Process Designer consists of tools used to design and build business processes, including workflow rules and routings (see more about this tool in Chapter 16, " PeopleSoft Web-Enabled Applications and Electronic Data Interchange").

ADMINISTRATION TOOLS

The Administration tools consist of Application Upgrader, Process Scheduler, Process Monitor, Import Manager, Data Mover, Security Administrator, Security Administration, Object Security, Mass Change, and Workflow Administrator.

APPLICATION UPGRADER

A part of the Application Designer, Application Upgrader is a tool used to facilitate object migration. New or modified objects such as fields, record and panel definitions, view definitions, and menu definitions, can easily be migrated between databases during implementation and ultimately moved up into production. This tool is also used to analyze and apply PeopleSoft-supplied updates.

PROCESS SCHEDULER

The Process Scheduler provides a way to process COBOL jobs and other executable programs involved in background processing. Process Scheduler enables users to initiate background processes from a client workstation, to run locally or on a server. Using Process

Definitions, processes can be scheduled to run immediately or at a specified date and time. A group of processes can be organized into a batch job and scheduled on a specific or next available server to run as a group.

PROCESS MONITOR

Used in conjunction with the Process Scheduler, Process Monitor is used to cancel or check the status on submitted background processes. The processes can be either server agent or user-initiated. Process Monitor indicates process status, for example, Queued, Initiated, Processing, Success, Cancelled, and Error.

IMPORT MANAGER

Import Manager is a tool to map data from source files and then load it into PeopleSoft application tables.

DATA MOVER

Data Mover allows the developer to write, edit, and execute scripts using a combination of SQL commands and proprietary Data Mover commands in order to move data between applications and across platforms. Data Mover is an essential tool during an application or tools upgrade.

SECURITY ADMINISTRATOR

Security Administrator is a tool to create profiles of access for users and classes of users. It provides the ability to define profile characteristics such as panel, menu, and data access, as well as logon restrictions.

OBJECT SECURITY

Object Security allows security control in the development environment, permitting read or modification access to definitions of individual objects or groups of objects, such as field, panel, or record definitions.

MASS CHANGE

Mass Change is a SQL generator tool that developers can use to set up a series of Insert, Update, or Delete SQL commands to allow system users to later execute a business process.

WORKFLOW ADMINISTRATOR

Workflow Administrator is a tool to access, monitor, analyze, and control workflow applications. (See more about this tool in Chapter 16, " PeopleSoft Web-Enabled Applications and Electronic Data Interchange.")

PART
II
CH
3

REPORTING AND ANALYSIS TOOLS

The Reporting and Analysis tools consist of PeopleSoft Query, PS/nVision, Tree Manager, and Cube Manager.

PEOPLESOFT QUERY

PeopleSoft Query is a SQL-generation tool with a friendly user interface, used to build SQL queries and extract data from an application database. It can generate output to the screen, link directly to an Microsoft Excel spreadsheet, or provide data to be used in Crystal Reports (a report designer and formatter from Crystal Services).

PS/NVISION

PS/nVision is a tool that integrates PS application data with Microsoft Excel to facilitate producing financial statements and other ad hoc financial reports and analyses.

TREE MANAGER

Tree Manager is a graphic tool that allows building hierarchical relationships between data elements in a given table. It is used to facilitate hierarchical reporting and also data access security.

CUBE MANAGER

Cube Manager is a tool to map data between PeopleSoft databases and hyperdimensional "cubes" using OLAP (online analytical processing).

SUMMARY

Creating or modifying applications can be a complicated activity. PeopleTools and the Application Designer can streamline implementation development projects. An integrated, visual workspace, combined with ease-of-use features like drag and drop and right-click pop-up menus, can make development almost fun. PeopleCode, other tools, utilities, reports, and a host of information resources round out the package.

Although this chapter is necessarily only a brief overview of the functionality of PeopleTools, it offers basic insight and should prompt a desire for further exploration of the depth and potential of the toolset.

PEOPLETOOLS REPORTING

In this chapter   *by Ari Katanick*

INTRODUCTION

PeopleSoft's applications contain a rich repository of business information. The ultimate goal of this information is to create reports that will aid you in making business decisions. To help facilitate this goal, PeopleSoft comes delivered with a wide range of integrated reporting tools and options. The following sections discuss these options in detail.

Enterprise reporting can be broken into three separate classifications: ad hoc, production, and analytical. PeopleSoft delivers integration with several reporting tools that fit within these classifications. Customers can pick and choose their standard tools according to their reporting needs. Although most customers have reporting requirements that fall into all three classifications, few customers use all PeopleSoft's delivered tools. Generally, a subset of the delivered reporting tools are used and standardized at each customer. To choose your tools, you need to first understand the different classifications.

PRODUCTION REPORTING

Production reporting is the most common classification. Production reporting is intended for the masses. Reports of this classification are standard, with minimal user interface, and require little or no interaction from the user. Production reports are more commonly distributed via push technology. They are generally scheduled to run at a set time and the users receive them via some distribution channel (email, hard copy, set file directory location, and so on).

Production reports can also be set up as an on-request job, but the report's layout is fixed. Interaction from the report requestor is restricted to only a few input parameters that allow for data filtering. The users who receive these reports don't need to understand the source PeopleSoft application that holds the data; they need to understand only the business information contained in the report. Production reporting tools are scalable and can be used for high and low volumes of data. Implementation issues for production reporting include output distribution and output management of the reports. Examples of production reporting are creating a report that generates a list of open orders or a report that lists the posted journals for the month.

AD HOC REPORTING

Ad hoc reporting is very interactive in nature. Users of these reporting tools need to have a strong understanding of PeopleSoft's applications and the information in the database tables behind these applications. Users also need to understand how to write efficient SQL, the importance of indexes, and how to form a "where clause." Ad hoc reporting can solve additional business questions that result from investigating information contained in production. Ad hoc reporting can also solve questions about uncommon occurrences generated from a transactional batch run. Individual ad hoc reports are generally run once or infrequently and are used to solve a specific and immediate business question.

Ad hoc reporting uses pull technology, and its capabilities are intended for a very small group of users. Because of the technical nature of these tools, only power users will use these tools to create reports. The power users might also, in turn, support other business users with information and data gathering.

Ad hoc reporting is intended for accessing a relatively low amount of data (at most, a few thousand rows) through a single select query. Examples of ad hoc reporting are generating a list of employees who have been with the company for over 10 years to determine a one-time bonus payout, or creating a report to follow up on a journal that didn't post during the previous night's batch run.

Implementation issues for ad hoc reporting include security issues for the users with ad hoc ability and performance issues for poorly written queries.

Security for ad hoc report writers is important to consider because of the flexibility of ad hoc tools. Views should be created on database tables to restrict users from sensitive data.

Ad hoc reporting can be very dangerous if in the wrong hands. A poorly written query can affect the performance of the entire system. Generally, only a handful of users, with a strong SQL background and a good understanding of PeopleSoft's conceptual data dictionary, should be allowed to use these tools.

Ad hoc reporting tools are the most flexible of the three classifications of reporting tools. They offer you the greatest amount of freedom in obtaining information from your PeopleSoft applications.

ANALYTICAL REPORTING

Analytical reporting enables you to view data at many different levels of aggregation in order to test conclusions or compare alternative strategies. Analytical reporting is highly interactive and highly strategic in nature. Users of these reporting tools need a great understanding of the business data contained in PeopleSoft's applications and of the key performance indicators that measure how their business is performing. These users do not need to know the details of their PeopleSoft applications, but they do need to understand the business fits and uses of the applications.

Analytical reporting is generally limited to business and financial analysts who use pull technology to analyze various business measurements. Analytical reporting is intended for analyzing aggregated information and not for reporting on the detail data. PeopleSoft delivers several processes to take your detail information and aggregate it according to a predefined hierarchy (or tree). The results of this aggregation are then used for analytical reporting.

Analytical reporting also offers the concept of *drilling down* or *slicing and dicing*. It gives users the ability to view their information at many different views and levels and to explore, interact with, and analyze this information.

PART

II

CH

4

Implementation issues for analytical reporting include training and distribution issues. Analytical reporting forces users to think of their business in multidimensional concepts, and teaching people to think in these terms takes time. Distributing analytic reports might also be difficult, because the nature of the report requires that the user have access to the source system. Examples of analytical reporting include generating a profit-and-loss statement or creating a head-count report broken down by department or division.

PEOPLESOFT'S REPORTING TOOLS AND OPTIONS

Peoplesoft delivers many different reporting tools and options.

PEOPLESOFT'S AD HOC REPORTING TOOLS

PeopleSoft delivers PS/Query for ad hoc reporting. PS/Query is a graphical tool that enables users to build data inquiries against PeopleSoft application data. PS/Query is developed by PeopleSoft and is fully integrated with PeopleSoft's meta-data and data dictionary. PS/Query leverages your predefined PeopleSoft security and PeopleSoft meta-data constructs, such as trees, effective dates, translate values, join relationships, and prompt tables. PS/Query's graphical interface enables you to use visual representations of your PeopleSoft database to create and run database queries without having to write SQL statements. The resulting queries can be used one time or can be saved if used more than once. PS/Query is limited to database select statements only and cannot be used for database updates, inserts, or deletions. Users who have access to PS/Query need to have some understanding of SQL and of writing optimized queries. Without it, they can create a query that will bring the performance of the entire system to its knees.

PeopleSoft delivers an Open Query Application Programming Interface (API) that enables third-party reporting tools to integrate with PS/Query and Tree Manager. This API shields developers from the underlying data structures of PeopleSoft tables and automatically handles user authorization, data security, runtime prompting, effective date selection, and set-ID mapping.

PeopleSoft publishes and supports this API so that other third-party reporting vendors can take advantage of it. The API is based on the ODBC API, which has become a standard for data access. This is delivered in the form of an ODBC driver. The driver can be installed as part of your standard workstation installation, and this registers it to any Microsoft Windows application that supports ODBC.

This API enables PS/Query to be used in combination with any third-party ODBC-based reporting tool. PeopleSoft delivers Open Query API integration with Crystal Reports Pro, Excel, PS/nVision, Actuate, and Cube Manager.

PeopleSoft Inquiry Screens can also be used for ad hoc reporting. An *Inquiry Screen* in PeopleSoft is a panel or group of panels that enables users to query against specific tables or information based on the user's filed-in parameters. PeopleSoft delivers many Inquiry Screens with its applications. Some Inquiry Screens enable direct access to transactional panels where the information can be updated. This type of investigative querying enables Inquiry Screens to be used as an analytical tool as well as an ad hoc tool.

Because Inquiry Screens are built with PeopleSoft's technical backbone, PeopleTools, it enjoys the ultimate flexibility of any PeopleTools' command. Popular uses of Inquiry Screens include online query access to and correction of the results of a previously run batch process. Also, because Inquiry Screens are a combination of PeopleTools and PeopleCode, they can also be Web-deployed via PeopleSoft's Web Client.

Table 4.1 diagrams the differences between PeopleSoft's ad hoc reporting tools.

TABLE 4.1   AD HOC REPORTING TOOLS AT A GLANCE

	PS/Query	**Inquiry Screens**
PeopleSoft meta-data integration	Yes	Panel integration only
Necessary skills for report development	PeopleSoft table/data knowledge, strong SQL knowledge	PeopleTools, PeopleCode, Application Designer, PeopleSoft table/data knowledge
Architecture and infrastructure	Any PeopleSoft-supported platform	Any PeopleSoft-supported platform
Report outputs and distribution	Open Query API, PS/Query navigator, screen display grid, Excel	PeopleSoft client or PeopleSoft Web client
Component security	Tables/groups of tables, row-level security	Based on the user's PeopleSoft security profile
SQL engine	It is its own SQL engine	Panel-generated SQL and native SQL through PeopleCode
Procedural/conditional logic	None	Both, through PeopleCode
SQL commands supported	Select only	All (DML only)

PEOPLESOFT'S PRODUCTION REPORTING TOOLS

PeopleSoft comes delivered with two production reporting tools: Sqribe's SQR and Seagate's Crystal Reports Pro. PeopleSoft also integrates with other third-party production reporting tools, such as Actuate.

Table 4.2 gives an overview and comparison of PeopleSoft's production reporting tools.

TABLE 4.2   PRODUCTION REPORTING TOOLS AT A GLANCE

	Crystal	SQR
PeopleSoft meta-data integration	Yes	No (native SQL integration only)
Necessary skills for report development	Understanding PS/Query, Microsoft Windows	Technical coding SQL, database tables/data
Architecture and infrastructure	Windows-based platforms only	Any PeopleSoft-supported platform
Report outputs	Crystal client (.RPT) output is automatic, other formats are supported but require manual intervention or a custom process	Text-based
Component security	Handled through PS/Query	Must be built manually
SQL engine	PS/Query	Native SQL
Report distribution	File Server, Crystal Info	File Server, Report Mart
Procedural/conditional logic	Conditional only	Both
SQL commands supported	Select only	All (DML and DDL)

SEAGATE SOFTWARE'S CRYSTAL REPORTS PRO

Crystal Reports Pro is a graphical report writer from Seagate Software. Crystal is linked to PeopleSoft via the Open Query API. Therefore, any query created via PS/Query can be accessed in a Crystal Report. Crystal has an excellent graphical user interface for creating report layouts. Users can paint and format fields and graphical components onscreen exactly as they would appear on the resulting report. Report development time is relatively short when using Crystal because of its easy graphical interface and its integration with PS/Query. Crystal is limited to only Windows-based operating systems.

SQRIBE'S SQR

SQR is a third-generation programming language that extracts data from any SQL-based relational database and prints or displays that information in a predefined output format. SQR does not have a direct tie to PeopleSoft meta-data; to access data, it uses SQL statements against your native database.

SQR is generally used for high-volume transactional reporting, complex reporting that requires more than one SQL statement, reporting that requires procedural logic, or any reporting that needs to be executed on a non–Windows-based server. SQR programs can be developed using any ASCII text editor. Because SQR can also be used to make global updates to your database and to load and unload tables, it is often also used for interface and conversion programs, data imports, and utilities.

SQR programming should be done only by experienced personnel who understand data constructs and have a strong SQL and programming background. Because SQR accesses the system via SQL against your native database, it has the capability of bypassing all the security in your PeopleSoft database. For this reason, programming should never be done against the production database, and if programming is to be done on tables with sensitive data, those tables should be filled with sample data only. SQR is another reporting tool that, if used improperly, will affect overall system performance. In order to avoid this, the programmer must have a strong understanding of SQL and of writing optimized queries.

ANALYTICAL REPORTING TOOLS

PeopleSoft delivers PS/nVision for relational analytical reporting and Cube Manager for defining multidimensional analysis models for analytical reporting. PeopleSoft partners with Hyperion's Essbase and Cognos' Powerplay for OLAP Reporting. PeopleSoft also delivers an enterprise warehouse for relational OLAP reporting.

Table 4.3 gives an overview and comparison of PeopleSoft's analytical reporting tools.

TABLE 4.3   ANALYTICAL REPORTING TOOLS AT A GLANCE

	nVision	OLAP
PeopleSoft meta-data integration	Yes through PS/Query, ledger tables, trees, timespans, and chart of accounts	Yes, through PS/Query and trees
Necessary skills for report development	PS/Query, Tree Manager, PeopleSoft's General Ledger, Excel	PS/Query, trees, multidimensional concepts, skills in the associated OLAP reporting tool

continues

TABLE 4.3   CONTINUED

	nVision	**OLAP**
Architecture and infrastructure	Windows-based platforms only	Depends on the vendor
Report outputs	Excel	Depends on the vendor
Component security	Tables/groups of tables, row-level security	Table and row-level access of the user who built the cube
SQL engine	PS/Query, ledger tables	PS/Query
Report distribution	Report books to run in batch, file server	Depends on the vendor
Procedural/ conditional logic	Both (through Excel and macros)	Conditional only
SQL commands supported	Select only	Select only

PS/NVISION

PS/nVision was originally developed to generate financial statements for PeopleSoft's General Ledger product. It has since become a general-purpose tool for generating matrix reports in an Excel spreadsheet. PS/nVision enables you to associate columns in Excel with PS/Queries, columns from your PeopleSoft Ledger table, or time-related variables. The rows of your PS/nVision report are associated with detail values or nodes on your PeopleSoft trees. PS/nVision is fully integrated with PeopleSoft's meta-data.

Simply put, PS/nVision is a data extractor from PeopleSoft that builds aggregated information according to your PeopleSoft trees and populates an Excel spreadsheet. After your data is in Excel, you can use any Excel functionality—such as macros, calculations, graphing and so on—on your data. PS/nVision enables you to view aggregated information and drill down to the underlining detail that made up those data values.

PS/nVision is both a real-time and a batch reporting tool. PS/nVision's Report Books feature enables reports to be grouped and run in batch. The generated reports are Excel files that can be mailed out to users or put on a file server for sharing and retrieving. This batch reporting and distribution functionality enables PS/nVision to be considered both an analytical and production reporting tool.

Because PS/nVision queries directly against your PeopleSoft transactional tables, it makes it a powerful tool for getting fresh data out of your PeopleSoft system. Any report that requires aggregation from real-time data would be a good candidate for PS/nVision. Examples of PS/nVision reports are trail balances and profit-and-loss statements required during the month-end close process.

CUBE MANAGER

PeopleSoft's Cube Manager enables you to define a multidimensional model in PeopleSoft by using PeopleSoft's current constructs and meta-data. Cube Manager's Cube Builder process then extracts detail data and dimensional definitions out of PeopleSoft and populates either a Hyperion Essbase or Cognos Powerplay multidimensional database. In future releases, Cube Manager will also be able to generate a Relational OLAP (ROLAP) star schema.

OLAP tools can access data stored at the desktop level, the server level, or in a relational star schema. Because the technologies used to implement OLAP vary by the amount of available data and the platform, it is important to choose tools appropriate for the needs of your users. There are three levels of OLAP tools that PeopleSoft supports:

- Desktop OLAP tools work best when users need to analyze a relatively small amount of data (up to 500MB). Desktop OLAP tools are a great choice for line managers and executives who need fast and easy access to information about their departments or groups.

  These tools usually do not require much training to use. They're also a good choice for users who travel or work remotely. Desktop OLAP tools typically require minimal support from the IS group.

  PeopleSoft partners with Cognos to bring you Desktop OLAP functionality.

- Server-level OLAP tools are appropriate for groups of people who need to analyze the same data in detail. The databases that these tools access are commonly called *data marts*. The users of the data mart typically comprise a department whose function includes significant analysis of ongoing operations (such as a finance or human resources department). The data in the data mart tends to be specific to one subject (such as finance or employee compensation). The IS group typically installs the hardware and software and sets up the data extraction processes, but trained users can administer the system, including restructuring dimensions and adding new calculated values. Data marts can typically grow to about 500GB. PeopleSoft partners with Hyperion's Essbase to bring you server-level OLAP functionality.

- Relational OLAP tools are appropriate for large, diverse groups of users who need access to a broad range of related data. Various groups across the enterprise must access the data, which comes from PeopleSoft's human resource, distribution, manufacturing, and financial systems. The challenges of managing large amounts of data (often more than 500GB) require significant IS support, from the initial design and development through implementation. PeopleSoft delivers its Enterprise Warehouse for relational OLAP functionality.

PART

II

CH

4

BUILDING A SOUND PEOPLESOFT REPORTING INFRASTRUCTURE

Reporting Infrastructure is the combination of people, processes, and procedures required in a reporting implementation prior to report development. In other words, it's everything that you need to think about before you start coding your first report.

Ensuring a successful PeopleSoft reporting project requires a sound infrastructure. Building a successful PeopleSoft reporting infrastructure involves ten steps:

1. Organizing your reporting project team according to roles and responsibilities
2. Identifying your end users
3. Defining the high-level reporting requirements
4. Determining the report distribution needs
5. Defining the global security needs
6. Configuring a reporting architecture
7. Selecting your reporting tools
8. Setting reporting standards
9. Dealing with performance considerations
10. Defining your report writing methodology

ORGANIZING YOUR REPORTING PROJECT TEAM

There are five types of roles in a reporting implementation. One or more team members fulfills each role on your project. Depending on the size of your implementation, you might also have one individual serve several roles. The following roles are required in your reporting implementation:

- Project manager
- Systems architect
- Data architect
- Power user/developer
- DBA

PROJECT MANAGER

A project manager in a reporting implementation must have a strong knowledge of the transactional application's business objectives. He or she needs to understand the business reasons for implementing PeopleSoft in order to prioritize, plan, and set direction for the application's reports. The project manager needs to have a high-level understanding of the standard reporting tools so that he or she can assign report requests to team members, choose the reporting tool, and estimate the work effort involved. The project manager needs to understand the implementation's project plan and user requirements in order to ensure the proper timing and rollout of the reports. This person is empowered to drive the development process, resolve issues, and coordinate resources (both project resources and end users). For the project to be successful and stay within budget, a good project manager ensures that issues are resolved quickly and that the other team members have the necessary skills and knowledge to get their job done.

The project manager has many responsibilities, including developing the reporting project plan managing scope, and tracking progress. Because the project manager keeps project sponsors updated with project status, it is important that he or she is well aware of the other team members' issues and status. The project manager is the final decision-maker on all report-related issues and plans training rollout for the controlled and end user community, as well as project team training. The project manager also markets the project to the end users to encourage use of new application reports. This ensures that when the project gets rolled out, users will be willing to use the system for their informational needs.

SYSTEMS ARCHITECT

The systems architect must have a strong knowledge of hardware and software configuration, report and data/informational distribution mechanisms, and network issues. The systems architect needs a good understanding of where the end users are located, their hardware/software configurations, distribution mechanisms, and their reporting needs.

The systems architect's responsibilities include standardizing and modeling the report distribution methods, building the reporting architecture, and resolving network issues. The system architect also plans and executes the software rollout to the end users and maintains system software and hardware upgrades.

DATA ARCHITECT

The data architect must have a strong knowledge of PeopleSoft's application and PeopleTools tables and the system's Conceptual Data Model. To support reporting, it is not necessary for the data architect to understand PeopleSoft's entire Entity Relationship Diagram (ERD). PeopleSoft comes delivered with thousands of tables, and only a small percentage of these are used for reporting. The tables required for reporting make up the Conceptual Data Model, and it is the data architect's responsibility to maintain this model. PeopleSoft's conceptual data model is housed in PS/Query and maintained via Query Trees in PeopleSoft's Tree Manager. By maintaining the model, the data architect will help the other team members choose the correct reporting tables for their reports. The data architect needs to understand the end users' data access allowances and the need for data retention.

The data architect must work closely with application team members to determine the system's data and security requirements. The data architect determines user security, creates new users, and grants them classes and levels of access into PeopleSoft. The data architect models the data archiving plan and determines when and how data will be taken out of the PeopleSoft system.

POWER USER/DEVELOPER

The developer must have a thorough knowledge of PeopleSoft's delivered reporting tools, the strengths and weaknesses of these tools, and the roles that they play within PeopleSoft. He or she must have a strong knowledge of the applications and the data contained within them. The developer must also have a good knowledge of the business need for the reports and the various informational uses that the users have for these reports. It is up to the developer to make recommendations on ways and methods of improving the reports and better utilizing the delivered PeopleSoft reporting tools. Developers are generally centralized resources that support the different types of centralized and decentralized end users.

Developer responsibilities include gathering reporting requirements from end users and using these requirements to determine and create reporting standards and reporting templates. The developer must ensure that reports are flexible and maintainable to meet organizational changes. By creating these reports, the developer validates the completeness and accuracy of the data source. This also creates a natural check against the work of the application team members. The developer must consider performance and maintenance issues in report design and work closely with the DBA to determine optimal query performance. The developer must also coordinate and roll out training for the end users he or she supports.

DATABASE ADMINISTRATOR (DBA)

The DBA must have a strong knowledge of the database design, ERD, and underlining PeopleSoft database tables. The DBA must also possess strong database tuning skills essential for a successful reporting implementation.

In a PeopleSoft implementation, the DBA has responsibilities to the transactional side of the implementation as well as for the reporting effort. The DBA's responsibilities for the reporting effort include maintaining table spaces, reporting indexes, and working with developers to determine optimal query performance. The DBA also monitors server performance, including query performance, RAM, and CPU utilization; database sizes; and disk capacity. The DBA is also responsible for the backup and restoration processes.

IDENTIFYING YOUR END USERS

After you establish your project team, you want to identify your end users. Although your project might consist of multiple phases, when you take an inventory of your end users, it is important to consider *all* your end users, including those who won't be influenced until future phases. It is important that you identify who your end users are, their hardware/software configurations, where they are located, and their type. Your end users will be divided into three types: power users/developers, controlled users, and auto-fed users.

Power users/developers create reports according to established standards. These users support the controlled users and some auto-fed users in their business area. The power users are generally located in a central location (same location as the implementation team); however, for large projects, they can be dispersed into various business locations. They will coordinate end user training for the controlled and auto-fed users. The power users are generally located in a central location and support the controlled users.

Controlled users are located in the business locations and support the business users of the reports. The controlled users will do some report creation based on templates and standards created by the power users. These users will need a strong knowledge of the business needs for the reports, a good knowledge of the PeopleSoft applications, and the data contained within the applications. They will be the first line of technical user support for the auto-fed users.

Auto-fed users make up the majority of report users. These users are spoon-fed their reports and information. Their reports are generally pushed to them. They might run reports, but only production, canned reports. These users do not need to have a working knowledge of the reporting tools or the PeopleSoft database tables and application processes behind the reports. They only need to understand the report, the data in the report, and how the information affects their business. Auto-fed users help the power and controlled users during the design phase by providing samples of their report requests or by generating informational requirements. They work with the controlled and power users to define current and future functionality and reporting requirements. During report creation, they validate reports for system data accuracy, informational requirement accuracy, and overall usability.

DEFINING REPORTING REQUIREMENTS

After you identify your end users, you need to understand their reporting requirements. At this stage, you don't want to dive into individual reports, but you do want to get a good understanding of the types of reports that your users are interested in having. Specifically, you want to know

- What data is required—Which tables are required for building the reports? This is the first step in maintaining the project's conceptual data model. From the user's requirements comes the list of tables to support those requirements.

- The timeliness required of the data—Generally speaking, the freshness of the data (if the data resides on a nontransactional table, the freshness is the time stamp from when the data was last refreshed) is directly relational to the report response performance (how long it takes the report to execute and generate). If your users want up-to-the-minute data from their transactional system, the report might take some time to generate. If your users can live with day-old data, you can build aggregate or denormalized tables to house this information, or recommend an OLAP or data warehouse solution.

- What level of summarization or aggregation is required in the reports?—A relational database stores raw data. It is designed to make the day-to-day processing of corporate data manageable. The raw data stored in relational databases does not lend itself well to summarized or aggregated reporting. The data is two-dimensional or *flat* and stored at the detail level. To view corporate data from multiple dimensions or perspectives, data needs to be gathered from several tables and aggregated. This process can take a lot of processing time. A relational database is created for data accuracy and isn't intended for multidimensional analysis.

An OLAP solution (either a multidimensional database or a relational star schema) is created to optimize reporting (ease of access and quickness of response time). It can create and store aggregations and combinations of your detail data. The performance of reporting from an OLAP solution is immediate and quick. The process to build the solution isn't an immediate job and is usually run as a batch job during off-hours. Therefore, the data in an OLAP solution is only as fresh as the last time it was built.

■ Is there a need for combining data from several tables, applications, subsystems, or even external sources?—A report that combines data from several tables might require joins that are complex. Creating views that combine these tables might ease the developers from recreating the wheel with every new report.

If there is a need for combining data from disparate systems, you might be a good candidate for PeopleSoft's EPM (Enterprise Performance Management) line of products. The EPM line includes an enterprise data warehouse to combine data from several systems, analytic applications to enrich the data, and workbenches to report from the data.

■ What are your data retention requirements?—How much history retention is needed on your transactional system for transactional purposes versus for reporting purposes? Do you need an archiving solution to pull data out of your transactional tables into historical reporting tables? In this step you define your archiving and data retention requirements.

DETERMINING REPORT DISTRIBUTION NEEDS

Depending on your users' needs, there are many different mechanisms for distributing reports. A user can request that a report be run on demand or view reports online that have already been run (both of these are types of *pull technology*). Users can also have reports distributed to them automatically on a scheduled basis or have alerts make them aware of exception conditions (both of these are types of *push technology*). Reports can be broadcast on the Web, distributed on a file server, or emailed to the intended users. Users can view their reports either online or via a hard-copy, paper-based report. Reports can be run in batch or on demand, and users can create their own ad hoc queries.

In this step of building your reporting infrastructure, you determine what technologies and distribution methods are required and will be made available to each user. PeopleSoft's different reporting options support different methods of distribution. Before you select your reporting tools, you must understand your users' distribution needs.

DEFINING GLOBAL SECURITY NEEDS

At this step of building your reporting infrastructure, your data architect should be looking at an overall security plan. PeopleSoft offers several different security options: menu and panel security, object security, and row-level security. By combining these security options, you create your overall security plan. An individual user or group of users might be restricted from a tool or panel (such as Tree Manager), an individual object from that tool or panel (such as a particular tree), and/or a group of values from an instance of that tool or panel (such as nodes from that tree). Row-level security enables you to secure information at the database table, column, or row level. Your data architect should make some early recommendations on tables that are candidates for row-level security, user groups that will share security traits, and menu security.

Your reporting security requirements might differ from the security scheme for your transactional system. Your reporting requirements reflect a "needs to know" basis, and your transactional requirements reflect a "needs to affect" basis.

CONFIGURING A REPORTING ARCHITECTURE

In this step of building your reporting infrastructure, your systems architect will lead the effort to model your hardware and software configuration. A solid reporting architecture can optimize report delivery performance by reducing network traffic and by configuring table structures for optimal data access.

There are three common techniques to configuring a PeopleSoft reporting architecture. These techniques can be combined to suit your needs. In choosing your architecture configuration, you need to consider your anticipated data volumes, global reporting requirements, and reporting batch window.

The first configuration technique is to report directly from your transactional tables. Indexes can be created on these tables to optimize report performance. This technique is the easiest and least costly to implement. It is also the least practical for high volume. PeopleSoft's transactional tables are tuned for transactional processing, and reporting from these tables can result in poor performance.

The second configuration technique is to write processes to build reporting tables from your transactional tables. This is a common practice, and PeopleSoft delivers several examples of this, such as the PS_EMPLOYEES table in human resources and summary ledgers in the financial applications. These tables generally get populated every night and are optimized for reporting purposes only. These tables speed up your report processing time, but because they are a nightly reflection of your transactional system, the data contained in the tables are only as fresh as the last time that you extracted the data from the source transactional tables. Generally speaking, if the timeliness of the data is important, you need to report from your transactional system. If report performance is important, this technique *might* be of some use.

The third configuration technique involves duplicating your transactional database or transferring several database tables to a separate server for reporting purposes. By moving your reporting to another server, you keep your transactional system from having to share resources with your reporting users. This is the best solution for large companies with global reporting requirements. PeopleSoft delivers the Enterprise Warehouse from its EPM line of products for this purpose. PeopleSoft's Enterprise Warehouse is discussed in more detail in Chapter 34, "The Enterprise Warehouse."

PART
II
CH
4

SELECTING YOUR REPORTING TOOLS

PeopleSoft comes delivered with several reporting options. Earlier sections of this chapter presented these tools in detail. During this step of building your reporting infrastructure, you define and standardize the reporting tools that you will use in your implementation. Very few PeopleSoft customers use all PeopleSoft's delivered reporting options. Most customers choose to standardize on a selected group of them. This decision needs to be made now so that the project team can obtain proper training. When choosing your reporting tools, you want to find the best balance of user needs, distribution requirements, and reporting architecture support.

SETTING REPORTING STANDARDS

As you embark on your reporting implementation, it is important to define and adhere to report creation standards. Reporting standards include establishing a particular look and feel for your reports. It also includes establishing templates and code reuse procedures. Report naming standards prevent reports from getting created more than once, and file and directory structure standards make it easy to find report layouts. Power users will be responsible for documenting and communicating these standards to the casual users, who might also be responsible for creating and maintaining reports.

To document report requests, a standard request form will help facilitate the assignment of reports to developers and document the conversations between the developer and the requester. A report inventory will help match requests from several different users that can be combined into one report layout. Establishing these inventory guidelines and creating an online subsystem that manages your report requests will save you a lot of time by

- Managing your report requests and allowing for a medium where both the users and developers can communicate ideas and the status of the reporting process
- Giving a feel for the amount of staff required to implement the reports
- Creating a system to prioritize the report deliverables
- Allowing for easier maintenance of the reports and report documentation
- Facilitating the reporting team's collaboration in creating reusable code and an easy search mechanism to identify reports that might be cloned

PeopleSoft does not deliver a report repository or suggested standards. Standards should focus on gathering requirements, report format, and object naming. Reporting standards should also follow your own established project standards. In general, reporting standards should cover

- File server directory structure
- File naming conventions
- PeopleTool object naming conventions
- Migration procedures

- Change control procedures
- Documentation standards within reports

DEALING WITH PERFORMANCE CONSIDERATIONS

Before coding your first reports, you should take a high-level look at system performance considerations. This will include an audit of your hardware and software configurations and ensuring that there are no system bottlenecks. You want to have your DBA document performance-tuning considerations and to separate these considerations by each reporting tool. The tuning document should also include references to proper SQL statement writing and understanding database table indexes. The tuning document should be shared with all power users/developers to ensure that they consider performance implications in their coding.

Understanding your data retention and data growth requirements is also required at this point. Although it is early in your implementation, you want to consider which tables will be good candidates for an archiving solution.

DEFINING YOUR REPORT WRITING METHODOLOGIES

Creating individual reports should follow a report writing methodology. This methodology would help ensure quality reporting from all your developers. The recommended methodology steps for creating reports are

1. Gathering report requirements
2. Designing/prototyping
3. Receiving user approval
4. Complete coding
5. Testing
6. User sign-off
7. Migration

GATHERING REPORT REQUIREMENTS

In this step, the developer should ask the business user to talk about the report requirements. The developer can facilitate the conversation by asking questions, such as

- What is the business need for the report?
- Which business processes or applications does the report belong to?
- What types of information will you gather from the report?
- Will this report replace an existing report? Are there additional requirements/needs not covered on the existing report (additional columns, totals, and so on)?
- What are the data requirements? Which tables and fields will be needed for the report?
- Is aggregation required? If so, which trees support the aggregation? Is drill-down

required, and if so, to what level?

- Are there any calculations or derived fields on the report?
- What are the selection criteria?
- Will there be a need for runtime prompts?
- Is there a preferred sort sequence?
- How often is this report run (daily, weekly, monthly)? At what time? Will this be a scheduled or on-demand job?
- Which output formats are required for this report (Web, hard copy, online, and so on)?
- Will the person requesting the report have access to the PeopleSoft system (that is, a valid PeopleSoft user ID and password)?
- What are the report timeliness and data freshness requirements?
- Which groups of users will be using this report? Are there language requirements? Are there data security or restriction requirements?
- What are the report or data retention requirements? Can this report or table data be archived?

DESIGNING/PROTOTYPING

In this phase, the developer will do the following:

1. Code the report according to user requirements.
2. Create enough test data to present the layout of the report.
3. Create a list of test conditions and test data for testing the report.

RECEIVING USER APPROVAL

In this phase, the end user and developer will

1. Review the layout and content of the report to ensure that all the report requirements will be met. Any modifications to the report will also be discussed at this time.
2. Review the list of test conditions and test data and discuss any other special test conditions that the user wants tested.

COMPLETE CODING

In this phase, the developer will

1. Complete the report layout according to report requirements.
2. If there are performance issues that the developer cannot identify, have the team DBA review the report SQL.
3. Create a "run control" panel (if needed for Crystal/Query, SQR, or OLAP cube building).

TESTING

In the testing phase, the developer will

1. Create enough test data to test all user report requirements.
2. Thoroughly test the report.

USER SIGN-OFF

In this phase, the following will be done:

1. The developer and user will review the layout and content of the report to ensure that all the report requirements were met.
2. The developer will show the user the results of the report testing.
3. The developer will show the user how to run or retrieve the report.
4. The user will review the report and sign-off.

MIGRATION

In the migration phase, the developer will

1. Move the report from the test environment to production.
2. Upgrade any "run control" records, panels, and menus from test to production.
3. Run one final test to ensure that the report works in the new environment.

PART

II

CH

4

DEFINING AN OLAP CUBE BUILDING METHODOLOGY

The process of building a PeopleSoft OLAP cube is iterative in nature. After the first round of data is loaded into the OLAP cube and users have had a chance to see what data is available to them, there will be changes and additions requested. So, before rolling out an OLAP solution to your entire company, a pilot project is recommended. A pilot project will enable your users to get their feet wet, gain experience, and see the value of their OLAP information. The pilot project might even serve as a proof-of-concept for higher management or for a steering committee. The pilot project is rarely a throwaway. From it, you will gain experience with the full life cycle of implementing a decision support system. You will also gain experience in Cube Manager and an understanding of how all the components fit together. Your pilot should be designed with an eye toward the future.

The methodology of building your PeopleSoft OLAP cube should be structured in the following order:

- Planning
- Gathering data requirements
- Data mapping using the PeopleSoft Cube Manager panels
- Data extraction and load using PeopleSoft's Cube Builder

- Data validation and testing
- Creating reports from the cube
- Automating the data extraction process
- Training
- Rollout

PLANNING

In the planning step, the following should be done:

- Define the scope of your project. Clarify the purpose and goal of the pilot project.
- Choose a PeopleSoft module for the pilot. A popular first cube is the PS_LEDGER table from PeopleSoft's General Ledger because it reveals revenue information and is well suited for multidimensional modeling.
- Determine your OLAP tool. Will you use Desktop OLAP, a server-based product, or a relational star schema? This tool determination should be done based on the number of users accessing the cube, the intended size of the cube, and the OLAP features and functionality required by the users.
- Determine the number of cubes to be built. Will you build one large cube with department security or will you create a separate cube per department?
- Estimate your cube size and begin capacity planning. How much data will be stored on a cube? How will you refresh or update the data in the cube?
- Determine report and cube distribution. Will you distribute cubes to the desktop via push or pull technology, or will you place them on a server? How will your reports be written and distributed? Who will write your reports?
- Determine your initial set of users.
- Define the project tasks and deliverables. Assign those tasks to your team members.
- Define the final project deliverables.

GATHERING DATA REQUIREMENTS

In the gathering data requirements step, you need to determine what informational needs the users have for iterative analysis. You need to understand how users currently conduct their business, what data they currently use, and what data they would like to have in the future. This will be an iterative process; as the users begin to use their OLAP tool, they will generate new data requirements.

You should interview people from many different groups. Ask them about their current reports and find out what they look for (find out what is highlighted). At what level do they currently perform most of their analysis versus what level of detail is stored in your PeopleSoft application? Are there multiple PeopleSoft trees that represent the hierarchies of the data?

Analyze their current reports. How do they currently process their totals, subtotals, grand totals? How do they want these things summarized on their new OLAP reports? Do they need the detail in their reports or are they just searching for the totals?

Make them come up with a reporting wish list. Tell them to think outside the current system boundaries when developing their wish list. What are the corporate objectives and how are these measured? What are the critical success factors for meeting these objectives? What opportunities exist to improve? What new types of business information will help your users do their jobs?

DATA MAPPING AND MODELING

In the data mapping step, the goal is to map your detail source data (a query from PS/Query) to PeopleSoft hierarchies that will summarize this data. Your end users should get comfortable using PeopleSoft's Tree Manager to define their hierarchies. The detail query and hierarchies will be used to map your OLAP cube's dimensions and measures through PeopleSoft's Cube Manager panels (Dimension Build and Analysis Model).

DATA EXTRACTION AND LOAD

Define any post-build OLAP scripts. For Hyperion's Essbase, a post-build script is an Esscmd file. If you are using Cognos's PowerPlay, the post-build script is an additional mdl file. Use the run control panel to kick off the PeopleSoft process to build the cubes. PeopleSoft's Cube Builder process extracts the detail data and the hierarchies out of PeopleSoft and populates either a Hyperion Essbase or Cognos cube. When the cube is loaded, Cube Builder kicks off the vendor's own cube building process (Transformer for Cognos and the default calculation for Essbase). After the cube is built, Cube Builder will run any post-build script and then complete.

DATA VALIDATION AND TESTING

Use an OLAP reporting tool to test to make sure your data has been migrated correctly. Was the detail data able to map to the trees? Check the Cube Builder log file for any system-generated messages at this time. The most common error at this step is data mapping and this is fixed by either adding members to a hierarchy or removing them from a query.

CREATING REPORTS FROM THE CUBE

When the data is deemed to be correct, you want to produce several reports to give your users some experience with the new type of reports. OLAP reporting tools generally support the following report types:

- Parameter-based reports (the user can change parameters such as department, products, time period, and so on)
- Web access to predefined reports or existing cubes
- Full analysis
- Hard-copy reports

This is a good time to try several different types of reporting formats to get feedback from your user community.

AUTOMATING THE DATA EXTRACTION PROCESS

Cube Manager enables incremental builds for both Hyperion Essbase and a relational star schema. Incremental cube building means that your OLAP target doesn't need to be fully refreshed with the entire detail source or the hierarchies every time it is built. Cube Manager gives you the option of sending it a file of changes to add onto what has already been built. In this step, you will build queries that will enable incremental builds and create processes and procedures for building and updating your cubes.

TRAINING

To gain real business value from your OLAP cube development efforts, users need to be trained in the scope of the data in the OLAP cube and in the front-end access tool and report writers. You must realize that your users might not embrace these new reports right away for several reasons. Some of them would rather access several different reports for their information, rather than learn a whole new sophisticated system. The status quo always seems easier to those people. Other users might find it difficult to get used to thinking in a multidimensional mind-set. That skill is learned and improved on as it is used. It is quite different than their current flat file mind-set. As a result, your training should include the following:

- An introduction to multidimensional concepts
- An introduction to the data contained in the cubes and how it relates to reports or systems that the user is already familiar with
- The mechanics of using the tool
- The types of analysis that can be performed
- Most importantly, your patience and encouragement

Also, be sure to teach the tool while going against your own data that the user knows and can identify with.

ROLLOUT

Help desk support should be in place to answer questions about the validity of the data, how to use the front-end tool, and basic troubleshooting. Get people excited about using the new product through positive reinforcement. Upper management should support the use of the new system and should recognize individuals who have embraced the new technology to improve their business processes.

Leveraging PeopleSoft's Reporting Options and Tools

At this point, you are ready to start leveraging some of the reporting tools that you've learned about. This section gives advice and hints on how to use these tools.

Using PS/Query in PeopleSoft

Before using PS/Query, you need to have a good understanding of PeopleSoft's conceptual data model. PS/Query comes delivered with a tree representation of PeopleSoft's reporting tables within each application. This tree is your first source to understanding PeopleSoft's data tables. If the PS/Query trees don't give you all the information that you need, other methods to learn PeopleSoft's conceptual data model include running SQL traces on panels as you enter information into them and running traces on the batch processes that affect the tables you are reporting from. Without a thorough knowledge of PeopleSoft's tables and their relationships, you run the risk of writing queries that pull from tables that don't contain the information you are looking for or of writing very inefficient queries that can affect system performance.

The steps in building a query with PS/Query are very similar to the steps in building a SQL statement. The first step is to determine the PeopleSoft table or group of tables that holds the data you want to access. If you are selecting an effective date table, PS/Query asks you what effective date range of values you'd like. This is the first introduction of meta-data integration in PS/Query. After the tables are selected, you pick the fields that you want to select and filter on. PS/Query helps you do this by giving you the descriptions of the columns, their format, and an indication of whether these fields have related records or translate values. When selecting fields, you can also indicate the order of the columns, any aggregation, and whether you want to join on a related record or the translate table.

PS/Query supports all the standard SQL filter statements. After you've selected your filters, you can view the generated SQL and test-run the query to a grid control. PS/Query can be used as an ad hoc tool, or if you feel comfortable with the query you've created and its results, you can save the query as either a public query (any user can access) or a private query (only you can access). Your query can now be accessed by any ODBC-compliant reporting tool.

PS/Query is fully integrated with PeopleSoft's meta-data, which means that instead of having to create all the SQL constructs yourself, PS/Query will create them for you. Instances of this are effective dates, trees, translate tables, parent-child joins, security, and related records. PeopleSoft's trees provide a great example of this. PeopleSoft delivers Tree Manager, which is a GUI tool that enables you to easily build representations of your organizational hierarchies. Behind the scenes of Tree Manager are six PeopleTools database tables. Writing queries against these tables could require joining all six tables. PS/Query saves you from having to do all that work. When you are using PS/Query to pull a list of valid departments that fall below a particular division in a PeopleSoft tree, you need to specify only that you want to select departments where they fall under this divisional tree node. There is no need to figure out the tables behind PeopleSoft's trees, because PS/Query takes care of that behind the scenes for you. The PS/Query meta-data integration is important because it enables you to concentrate on determining the information that you want and not on the technical tables that you need to pull it from.

After you write and save your queries in PS/Query, they can be used for many different uses:

- Report queries—Through Open Query API, PS/Query can be used with PS/nVision, Crystal, Excel, Actuate, Business Objects, Cube Manager, or any other ODBC-compliant reporting tool.

- View queries—You can use PS/Query to define SQL views in Application Designer. These views can be virtual views, which can be referenced in PeopleSoft panels and processes. They might also be used to define actual database table views.

- Search queries—Many of the search dialog boxes in PeopleSoft's applications enable you to select a predefined query or to create a new one to search for a particular record.

- Database agent and role queries—If you use PeopleSoft Workflow, you can write queries to detect conditions to trigger business events. These queries can also be scheduled on a regular basis. In Workflow, you can also write queries to determine who to send emails, forms, or worklist entries to.

USING INQUIRY SCREENS IN PEOPLESOFT

Inquiry Screens are a panel or group of panels in PeopleSoft whose sole purpose is to report information. PeopleSoft comes delivered with many Inquiry Screens, the most frequent use of which is to find specific transactions based on higher-level data or user-defined clues. Inquiry Screens enable the user to navigate back to the transactional screen for updating that transaction. Inquiry Screens are very powerful when there is a need to search a large table for specific data for which you don't have all the details.

To build an Inquiry Screen in PeopleSoft, select either the transactional panel where you'd like to conclude or pinpoint the detail source of the information that the user will want to find. This will serve as your result panel, and the rest of the panels in the group of Inquiry Screens will be built from there. Inquiry screens are built with a combination of PeopleTools and PeopleCode, and the developer of these is required to have a strong PeopleTools and programming background.

The easiest way to learn how to build a full-blown Inquiry Screen is to investigate and dissect one that is delivered. Most of the constructs that you'll want to use can be cloned, and there is no need to reinvent the wheel. The two most common constructs used on Inquiry Screens are search dialog boxes and panel transfer pushbuttons. Search dialog boxes enable end users to define the criteria they would like to query on. Panel transfer pushbuttons enable the user to either drill down into more information on the resulting list or to visit the panel that will enable the user to make data changes. PeopleSoft's Inquiry Screens make a powerful reporting tool because they offer the user the power of structured ad hoc querying combined with interactive analysis.

USING CRYSTAL REPORTS IN PEOPLESOFT

Seagate Software's Crystal Reports Pro is a report writer that helps you generate nicely formatted printed reports containing data from your PeopleSoft applications. Crystal is delivered with your PeopleSoft applications and integrated with PeopleSoft through the Open Query API in PS/Query.

To build a Crystal Report, you must start with PS/Query to generate your data source. From within PS/Query, after you've built a query, run the query and specify the output to Crystal. Crystal Reports will start automatically, and your query will be painted onscreen in Crystal's best guess of how you'd like your report to look. At this point, you can click and drag the columns in your report to their desired locations and change the font or look of the columns and headings.

Crystal Reports are broken up into five main sections: a report header, a page header, a detail section, a page footer, and a report footer. You can insert any combination of OLE objects, pictures, data columns, text fields, report variables, and so on into these sections. Crystal Reports also has grouping and sorting functionality that includes duplicate suppression, aggregate functions, calculations, and group and grand totals. You can use Crystal Reports to create cross-tab reports, graphs, labels, and mail-merge documents. Like PeopleSoft's other report offerings, Crystal is fully integrated with PeopleSoft's Process Scheduler and can be scheduled as a batch job that will run at night; or it can be set up as an on-demand job.

USING SQR REPORTS IN PEOPLESOFT

Sqribe's SQR reporting tool is delivered with your PeopleSoft applications. Although not integrated with PS/Query, SQR offers full support of the data manipulation capabilities of SQL, a high-level programming language, and portability across multiple platforms and relational database management systems. For those reasons, SQR is also used to build interface and conversion programs.

Strong programming and SQL skills are required to write an SQR report. It is recommended that the user clone an existing SQR report when writing a new report, rather than start from scratch. Cloning enables the user to strip out the meat of the program while keeping the necessary SQR structure intact.

SQR programs are built around SQL statements. SQR enables the user to write programming statements from within an SQL statement—and for reporting purposes, much of the user's programming logic will be located there. SQR automatically loops within a SQL select statement until all rows have been processed. This enables the user to focus on the business logic and formatting of the report rather than the looping and programming logic. Because SQR is a programming language that was created for reporting purposes, it has a lot of formatting features that enable nice output formatting. These features enable you to format a report directly from your SQL select statement or write to several different files at one time. SQR is also very portable and can run on any of PeopleSoft's supported platforms.

USING PS/nVISION IN PEOPLESOFT

PS/nVision enables you to import information directly from your PeopleSoft database into a Microsoft Excel spreadsheet. After the data is imported, you can use familiar Excel commands to format and analyze the data. PS/nVision works from within Excel, so that you can leverage Excel's formulas, formatting, and graphics. You access PS/nVision features from a special menu in Excel.

When you create a PS/nVision report, you define a report layout that specifies what data appears in the report and how it's formatted. A PS/nVision report layout is a template that enables you to specify what data the report includes and how that data will appear in your reports. Layouts are really spreadsheets themselves, but instead of specific data they contain formulas and data retrieval information. When you run a report, PS/nVision uses the layout to determine what data to retrieve and how to display it.

PS/nVision offers two kinds of report layouts. The major difference between them is how they specify what data to retrieve from the database:

- Matrix layouts have data selection criteria associated with columns and rows in the spreadsheet, creating a criteria matrix. The data retrieved for an individual cell is determined by a combination of the criteria for its column and its row.

- Tabular layouts use a standard query to retrieve data. The columns in the report correspond to the fields returned by the query; the rows in the report correspond to the rows in the query result set.

PS/nVision is delivered with a number of typical report layouts, such as Balance Sheet, Profit & Loss, and Operations Summary for the PeopleSoft Financials applications. These reports have been created based on data from the PeopleSoft demo database. You use these reports as examples to aid in learning and applying the PS/nVision tool. As with any spreadsheet, layouts can be cloned and modified, so it is not necessary to build one from scratch. After you select or create a layout, you choose a business unit to report on, and select or create a request for that business unit. Additional request specifications include the scope of the report, "as of" reporting dates, and file and directory names for the report results.

The layout and request are all you need to run your report. As the report is run, a copy of the layout, called an *instance*, is populated with data and is defined as a normal spreadsheet file. Depending on the scope of your report, you might produce several instances from one layout.

USING CUBE MANAGER IN PEOPLESOFT

Cube Manager was created by PeopleSoft to offer its customers an easy method of extracting data and hierarchies from their PeopleSoft applications for building multidimensional databases. Defining OLAP cubes in PeopleSoft is a three-step process:

1. In the Dimension Build panel, you define your dimensional hierarchies by using either Trees, Parent/Child definition queries or a combination of the two. This enables you a lot of flexibility in the way you define your hierarchies. In the Dimension Build panel, you might also build alternative hierarchy definitions and define dimensional attributes. You can also cut the size of the OLAP hierarchy by trimming a PeopleSoft tree—from the top by specifying a top node, or from the bottom by specifying a bottom level. You can also append a prefix or suffix to your dimension members to ensure dimensional uniqueness. PeopleSoft enables duplicate member names across its dimensions, but your OLAP tool might not. These options force PeopleSoft's trees to adhere to the OLAP vendor's hierarchical rules. The overall goal of the Dimension Build panel is to define your cube dimensions and the hierarchies that aggregate your dimension detail. All the options in this panel are there to ensure proper transferring of data from PeopleSoft to your OLAP cube.

2. After defining your dimensions, you use the Analysis Model panels to map your detail query to your dimensions. Here, you link your detail values to the hierarchies that will aggregate them. This panel also enables you to join several different sources of detail data to create one cube.

   Use the Build Cube Template panel to define any OLAP product-specific parameters, such as location of the cube, security, and so on. In this group of panels, you define the target platform of the cube (Cognos Powerplay or Hyperion Essbase). If it is a Cognos cube, you must specify the location of the mdc and mdl files. If it is a Hyperion cube, you need to identify the server, application, and database. This set of panels is very flexible because it enables you to define one cube template and build it on either platform.

After you've defined your cubes in PeopleSoft, the last step is to run the Cube Builder process. The Cube Builder process is a batch program that builds your cube for you. The Cube Builder process is accessed by the Build Cube panel or through an application-specific panel that includes prompting for binding variables. In release 7.5, the Cube Builder process can be run only on Windows-based machines. In future releases, it will include support for UNIX as well. After the Cube Builder process is complete, your cube has been built and you may report from it.

SUMMARY

PeopleSoft's applications offer the user many tools to facilitate business information. These tools are then used to create reports that can help users make better business decisions. To aid companies in achieving these goals, PeopleSoft delivers a wide range of integrated reporting tools and options. The bulk of this type of enterprise reporting is categorized into three components: ad hoc, production, and analytical reporting. PeopleSoft delivers integration with several reporting tools that fit within these classifications. From there, users can decide which components best fit their reporting needs.

CHAPTER 5

Start with HRMS

In this chapter

by Lorraine Britto-Bernstein

Because employees are vital to the success of an organization, maintaining accurate employee information is essential. PeopleSoft enterprisewide solutions have been developed to maintain accurate employee information can and therefore contribute to the effectiveness and success of a human resources department, as well as the organization overall. PeopleSoft Human Resources Enterprise Systems is one of the leading software packages used by human resources departments.

PeopleSoft Human Resources Management System (HRMS) consists of three major components, which are Human Resources, Benefits, and Payroll (see Figure 5.1). Each component consists of various modules. For example, the Benefits component contains the Base Benefits, Benefits Administration, and Flexible Spending Account modules. These modules are briefly described in this chapter.

Figure 5.1
The PeopleSoft HRMS.

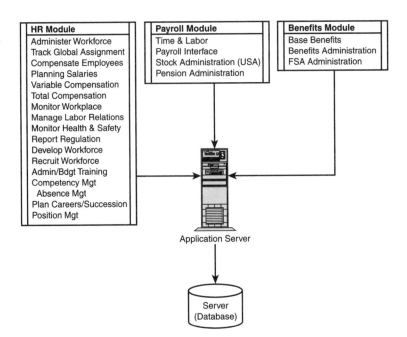

The PeopleSoft Human Resources software package is modular, global, and flexible. These features are described in the section, "PeopleSoft 7.5 Features." The package can be tailored to the unique requirements of various types of organizations. PeopleSoft processes enable executives to manage compensation and positions, as well as recruit, hire, terminate, and train employees. They can also track global assignments, promotion, retirements, and other status changes.

PeopleSoft's Security features enable users to control availability of employee information. This is a valuable feature, given the sensitivity of some human resource information. For example, an organization might not want to give managers responsible for promotion access to employees' birthdates.

Release 7.5 was launched in March 1998. It incorporates global functionality, adding multinational support for Belgium, the Netherlands, and Japan. It also expands the global and local functionality of PeopleSoft Human Resources modules for companies doing business in Canada, France, Germany, the United Kingdom, and the United States. The new functionality includes diversity tracking, preferred language tracking, and multilingual reporting capabilities. Stock and Pension administration functionality are also added for the United States.

PEOPLESOFT 7.5 FEATURES

In this section, various features of PeopleSoft 7.5 are presented.

CENTRALIZED AND INTEGRATED HUMAN RESOURCES SYSTEM

PeopleSoft 7.5 is a three-tier system. All employee data is stored in one centralized database, which facilitates accessibility, as well as running reports.

The PeopleSoft HRMS is fully integrated, allowing users to easily access and share information for the Benefits, Human Resources, and Payroll Processing modules.

The difference between a two-tier and three-tier connection lies in the server to which you connect. In a two-tier system, the client connects directly to the database server, whereas in a three-tier system, the client connects to an application server. Some of the advantages of connecting to an application server include faster access to data, increased scalability, improved capability to support Web clients, and the option of choosing between a two-tier or three-tier system.

FLEXIBILITY

PeopleSoft is a flexible package, which can be adapted to work in a variety of human resources environments. For example, it can be used effectively in both *centralized* (where all processing occurs in one area) and *decentralized* (where processing may occur in various areas while accessing a single database) human resources environments.

ACCESS BASED ON SECURITY

Access to employee information is based on one's operator class. Operator classes must be clearly defined in terms of department and type of data required. These operator classes will have access only to departments and information necessary to complete their tasks. PeopleSoft includes special global security that allows users to access the global panels, but limits any user's or group's access to data for their specific country.

USER FRIENDLY

The panels, reports, and menus of PeopleSoft are Windows-based and have a graphical user interface (GUI), which makes them easy to learn. Additionally, the user-friendly interface makes the Human Resources modules easy to navigate.

GLOBAL HUMAN RESOURCES PROCESSES

PeopleSoft can help organizations effectively manage their global workforce by allowing organizations to monitor international assignments, hire globally, and accommodate international regulations and labor agreements. Also, an organization can obtain local information from global core panels and give multinational users access to secure information.

CORE VERSUS LOCAL FUNCTIONALITY

Core functionality is the functionality that is common to all human resources business processes across countries, whereas *local functionality* is specific to a single country.

The Recruit Workforce (global) process and the country-specific Recruit Workforce process allow access to core and local functionalities for meeting domestic and international recruiting needs. For example, whereas general human resources data such as employee names would be maintained as a core functionality, country-specific information such as EEO (Equal Employment Opportunity) codes for the United States would be maintained as local functionality.

EASILY UPGRADABLE

Because the PeopleSoft HRMS is fully integrated, it is easy to upgrade and maintain provided there are only minimal customizations. If an organization develops or modifies records or panels, standard naming conventions (such as adding a prefix) should be followed. Organizations should employ and document standardized methods of naming customized objects. For example, XYZ corporations might have a prefix of XYZ.Fieldname. These prefixes allow the customized objects to be easily identified for upgrade.

MODULAR

PeopleSoft HRMS is composed of several Human Resources processes. These processes are organized into modules that may be used individually or in conjunction, depending on organizational requirements. For example, the core Human Resource module may be used independently or with other modules such as the Track Global Assignments module. The core Human Resource module is the base module that is necessary for the implementation of all other modules. This module contains employees' personal and job-related data.

SCALABILITY AND OPEN ENVIRONMENT

PeopleSoft HRMS is compatible with a variety of databases and operating systems. It is designed to run efficiently on multiple database platforms and various hardware environments. Also, the data and objects can be easily migrated to other platforms if standards or requirements change.

AD HOC REPORTING

Ad hoc query/reporting tools enable users to query data and create reports using various selection criteria, formats, formulas, and so on. PeopleSoft has integrated various ad hoc reporting tools into its applications. Some of the ad hoc reporting tools used by Human Resources Management System modules are as follows.

PeopleSoft Query offers the ability to create and run database queries without having to write SQL statements. Queries can range from very simple to complex, and they can be saved after being defined, so they can be run repeatedly.

Some of the features and functions offered by *Crystal Reporting Tool* are retrieving data by using specific selection criteria, sorting and grouping of data, and calculating grand total, subtotal sum, average, standard deviation, or variance of values in a group and percentage. Also, the user can create form letters and mailing labels. These reports can be saved and used later.

PEOPLETOOLS

PeopleSoft HRMS contains development tools that can be used for application customization, system administration, reporting and analysis, and customization or development of workflow. They can also be used for development and maintenance of applications.

WORKFLOW

PeopleSoft Workflow allows organizations to gain understanding of, streamline, and automate business processes. For example, when a new hire is entered in PeopleSoft HRMS, a process is initiated that encompasses all the activities related to hiring an employee and alerts staff to complete these tasks.

Also, PeopleSoft Human Resources packages deliver several workflow processes for standard business processes.

WEB-ENABLED APPLICATIONS

PeopleSoft Human Resources Management System 7.5 offers Web-enabled technology. For example, with the self-service module, employees can view their personal information, enroll for training, view job postings, and apply for positions online, as well as view and update benefits. PeopleSoft HRMS uses the standard Web browser functionality. Because it is Web enabled, these modules can be delivered to a wide range of external users.

STANDARD REPORTS

PeopleSoft HRMS modules contain several standard reports, which support a wide range of human resources business processes. Some of these reports include EEO and OSHA regulatory reports for United States–based organizations, company car reports for the UK, and WCB and EECRS reporting for organizations with Canadian employees. The company car reports calculate car and fuel benefit amounts for employees using company cars. These modules also have additional reports such as mailing labels, job postings, and new hire summaries.

The reporting tools also allow organizations to develop and customize reports according to their requirements. For example, the organization can create termination letters based on various predefined parameters such as As-of-Date and From-Thru dates. The data from the database will be accurately populated in these letters, eliminating the potential for human error.

This section reviews various features offered by PeopleSoft Human Resources modules. In the next section, the various Human Resources modules are described.

PEOPLESOFT HRMS

The PeopleSoft HRMS consists of three major modules. These modules are Human Resources, Payroll, and Benefits. The components of each module are described briefly in the following sections. Each module can help organizations perform necessary functions and activities (also known as *business processes*). Relevant business rules are identified and defined in specific PeopleSoft modules. For example, the Track Global Assignments module contains business rules that help organizations perform the task of tracking employees who have overseas assignments.

HUMAN RESOURCES MODULE

The Administer Workforce module is the core module that is necessary for the functioning of all other Human Resources modules. The Human Resources module is global and supports a wide variety of human resources needs. Multinational workforces in the United States, Canada, Germany, France, and the United Kingdom can be administered using the Administer Workforce(Global) windows. For a specific country, use the Administer Workforce windows for that country.

This module consists of foundation and employee-related data tables. The module assists employers in setting up codes for areas such as visas and permits, salary classifications, unions, labor relations, and even checklists. These codes are defined based on business rules and policies of the specific organization.

This module can validate the data entries for various fields against the predefined values and business rules. This ensures accuracy and consistency in record keeping across functions of your HRMS, from recruitment to benefits.

It should be noted that foundation tables contain codes that provide the basic structure for an organization's Human Resources system. These codes are set up in the foundation tables. For example, when you enter a job code in panels, the job title and other related information will appear. Employee-related tables are where employee data is stored.

This module maintains an employee's personal and employment data. It includes relevant employee information, from the time an employee is hired/rehired to termination. The Human Resources module maintains historical, current, and future-dated employee data. These core employee-related tables are essential for all Human Resources modules. There are three core tables in the Human Resources module:

Personal Data—This record includes employees' personal information, such as name, date of birth, address, and so on.

Employment—This record contains current employment data.

Job—This record contains historical, current, and future-dated employment data.

Figure 5.2 shows the Administer Workforce menu.

Although the Human Resources module is the core module, PeopleSoft contains additional modules that are briefly described in the following sections.

TRACK GLOBAL ASSIGNMENT

The Track Global Assignment module maintains data on expatriates and their dependents as they move from one country to another. This module also maintains home/host information on employees. It enables organizations to monitor assignment type and organize travel data such as passports and visas, pet information, and standard checklists. Also, this module stores information on dependent data such as schools and colleges, language classes, and so on, to ease employee transitions. The Track Global Assignment menu displays panels for maintaining expatriate data.

Figure 5.2
The Administer
Workforce menu.

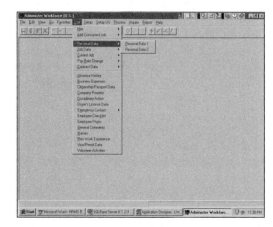

Figure 5.3
The Recruit Workforce
menu.

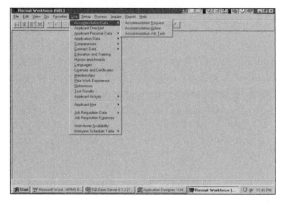

RECRUIT WORKFORCE

The Recruit Workforce module allows organizations to maintain data on employees and nonemployees who applied for positions. It can also monitor recruitment-related expenses, perform applicant job matches, and track recruitment activity. Additionally, the Recruit Workforce module can automatically generate offer, regret, and confirmation letters based on relevant data. Figure 5.3 shows the Recruit Workforce menu displaying panels pertaining to recruitment.

ADMINISTER AND BUDGET TRAINING

The Administer and Budget Training module aids organizations in maintaining data on employee and nonemployee training. This module can automatically generate enrollment and cancellation letters, use wait-listing options to track course demand, and maintain student-training history for all employees. It also contains a budgeting component that monitors administrative training costs and can compare them to pre-established budget guidelines. Figure 5.4 shows the Administer Training menu.

Figure 5.4
The Administer Training menu.

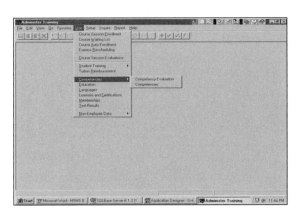

PLANNING CAREERS AND SUCCESSIONS

The Planning Career and Successions module maintains an inventory of employees' knowledge, skills, and abilities. Based on that information, this module allows an organization to define career paths and goals and develop career plans.

This module allows organizations to identify career paths for specific jobs. This enables employers to create an online network of jobs that employees can view. The Planning Career and Successions module also enables an organization to maintain performance-rating information; assign forced ranking and career potential ratings; and track career goals, strengths, and development plans. Figure 5.5 shows the Career Planning and Succession menu.

Figure 5.5
The Career Planning and Succession menu.

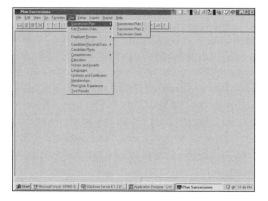

MANAGE COMPETENCIES

The Manage Competencies module utilizes data from Recruit Workforce, Plan Careers and Successions, and Administer Training functionality within HRMS. This component monitors two processes:

- Maintains data on expertise and proficiency required for each job or project team
- Matches employee qualifications with job or project team requirements

The Manage Competencies component allows organizations to allocate and maximize resources effectively while allowing optimal employee career growth. Figure 5.6 shows the Manage Competencies menu.

Figure 5.6
The Manage Competencies menu.

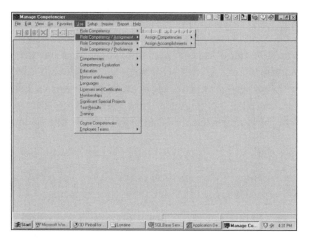

Manage Positions

The Manage Positions module enables organizations to arrange human resources data by position. This information is stored in position-specific tables. The user can identify information associated with specific positions, such as job title, phone number, and mail stop, whether an employee occupies the position or not. This component allows users to track all or only key positions in the organization. The PeopleSoft HRMS allows you to conduct searches based on position or employee. If an organization chooses Position, it will need to enable Position Management. Because employee-related (such as birthdate, hire date, and so on) and position-related (such as position number) data already exist, organizations can benefit in various ways. For example, because data for a specific position is already defined, it does not have to be re-entered for each new hire. Also, the potential for data entry errors is minimized.

Figure 5.7 shows the Manage Positions menu.

Figure 5.7
The Manage Positions menu.

Planning Salaries

The Planning Salaries module allows organizations to perform functions such as developing salary increase plans, budgeting salaries by department, developing salary plans for employees and/or departments, generating standard salary matrices, reviewing rating scales with salary grades, providing online salary modeling, and maintaining up-to-date salary plans by geographic location, currency, or organization. Figure 5.8 shows the Planning Salaries menu.

Variable Compensation

The Variable Compensation module enables organizations to identify and administer various types of incentive packages for individuals and project teams.

This module provides users with basic information regarding employee incentive plans, including their values and how employees may become vested. The Variable Compensation module also allows users to develop a comprehensive set of plan types, plan eligibility criteria and calculations, and determine payoff amounts. Users can also identify and administer group build rules, set goals, and determine employee eligibility for incentives. In this module, users can calculate award amounts, which can be fed to the HRMS Payroll module for employee payments.

Figure 5.8
The Planning Salaries menu.

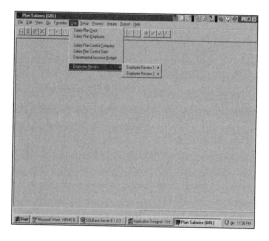

TOTAL COMPENSATION

The Total Compensation module analyzes and determines the value of all elements in an employment package. These elements may include salary, bonuses, long-term incentives, benefits, and other rewards of working.

MANAGE LABOR RELATIONS

The Manage Labor Relations module tracks grievances that employee applicants and unions might file in an organization. These grievances can be categorized as follows: employee disputes, group disputes, and disputes caused by unions representing their members. The system also monitors the type of disputes and the steps managers may take to resolve specific grievances.

This functionality is available for the U.S. (Manage Labor Relations). For all other countries, this information is monitored in the Manage Labor Relations (GBL) component.

MONITOR HEALTH AND SAFETY

The Monitor Health and Safety module allows organizations to maintain health and safety information issues in their workplace as subject to government regulations. This system enables users to organize incident data by criteria such as injuries and illnesses to individuals, damage sustained by vehicles and heavy equipment, and locations, as well as claims management data. Maintaining accurate and easily accessible incident-related information prepares employers to handle a variety of claims. Based on types of incidence, employers can develop need-based health and safety programs. Figure 5.9 shows the Monitor Health and Safety menu.

Figure 5.9
The Monitor Health and Safety menu.

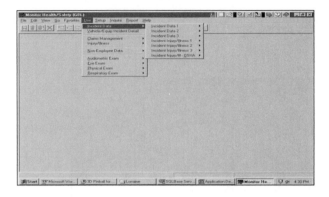

REPORT REGULATION

The Report Regulation module is specific to the U.S. and Canada. It aids employers in the U.S. in meeting federal regulations in the following areas: EEO/AA, OSHA, and accommodations made to comply with the Americans with Disabilities Act (ADA). The Report Regulation module is designed to meet federal requirements regarding workforce distribution in an organization by gender and ethnicity. It also reports the number of employees who have been hired, promoted, or terminated based on their ethnicity and gender. It enables Canadian organizations to meet government criteria for pay equity, employment equity, and official language requirements.

Because all relevant information such as age, gender, and ethnicity is available in the database, users can easily access and run EEO/AA reports by gender and ethnicity. Based on these reports, users can also develop affirmative action goals and timetables, as well as generate reports to comply with federal regulations on equal employment opportunities and affirmative action. Information on requests by disabled employees can also be maintained.

A specific country functionality for the United Kingdom enables users to accommodate company car reporting requirements. Also, specific country functionality for France allows users to monitor and evaluate professional elections for workers. Figure 5.10 shows the Report Regulation menu.

Figure 5.10
The Report Regulation menu.

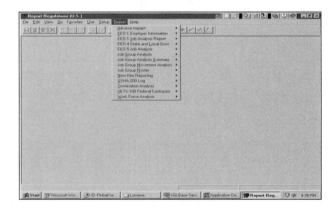

SUPPLEMENTAL FUNCTIONS

PeopleSoft also provides additional functions, which may be necessary for additional needs of human resources departments. These functions include tracking grievances and disciplinary actions. PeopleSoft Human Resources modules enable organizations to maintain grievance-related information filed by employees or applicants, unions, or other sources and to track the steps taken to resolve grievances. It also allows managers to identify various types of employee violations and related disciplinary actions.

Organizations can also use PeopleSoft modules to develop and track employment contracts, automatically generating letters (for example, termination or hire) according to predefined criteria.

PEOPLESOFT PAYROLL MODULE

The PeopleSoft Payroll module contains various standard business processes that can contribute to efficient payroll operation. These business processes include the following:

- Payroll calculations—The Payroll module can automatically calculate and pay employee wages based on business rules defined by an organization. This module can also calculate salaries based on predefined criteria such as salary pay rates, hours, additional earnings, tax methods, and accounting information.

- Tax computation—Maintains government tax requirements for specific countries. The PeopleSoft Payroll module provides regular updates to the tax rate tables based on government regulations. For example, in the United States, the PeopleSoft module can provide yearly updates to tax processes based on federal, state, and local regulations. The tax processes provided by the PeopleSoft Payroll module can enable an organization to calculate an employee's tax and wage rates.

- Automated check process—This system enables organizations to process check requests automatically for terminated employees and to define final check programs that identify the earnings, leave accruals, and deductions that apply to final checks. This module can also calculate gross to net pay and update balances for W2 reporting. Electronic file transfers (EFT) to banks are possible with additional customization. PeopleSoft does not currently provide this functionality (EFT) for the Payroll module.

- Global payroll system—The capacity to process payroll requirements of organizations in North America, Europe, Asia/Pacific, and other regions.

- Effective-dated data—Because the HRMS maintains historical, current, and future-date employee information, it enables organizations to perform a variety of tasks, such as automatically calculating pay based on hire or termination dates.

- Accurate and adjustable payroll calculations—The system can run and rerun calculations rapidly. Because this payroll calculation process is automatic, it is not susceptible to human error factors. If errors are found, human intervention may be necessary in order to correct data. After the data has been corrected, the system can rerun the payroll calculations until desired results as defined by the users are obtained.

■ Payroll reporting—The PeopleSoft Payroll module provides the following reports: deductions register, payroll register, cost centers, other earnings register, deductions in arrears, deductions not taken, employee earnings, payroll summary, and more. These reports can be customized according to organizational needs.

The PeopleSoft Payroll module interfaces with the Human Resources, Benefits, and General Ledger modules, enabling organizations to obtain information from these modules. This module can also perform automatic benefit deduction calculations. For example, the Payroll module can obtain employee deductions to calculate payroll. This reduces data entry time while providing accurate and reliable employee data necessary for payroll processing. Figure 5.11 shows the Payroll menu.

Figure 5.11
The Payroll menu.

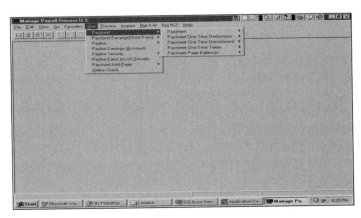

PEOPLESOFT TIME AND LABOR

The PeopleSoft Time and Labor module allows organizations to automatically monitor and control all aspects of time-keeping processes. These processes include time reporting, task reporting, and updating payroll. It also allows organizations to distribute labor expenses and make time-reporting adjustments for prior periods.

This module also enables employees to record the details of their daily work in a single place. The Time and Labor module is also capable of supporting specific time reporting needs of organizations, as well as managing payroll, financial/cost accounting, project management, and employee benefits processes.

With the PeopleSoft 7.5 Web-enabled feature, employees can view and report their own time regardless of their location, and supervisors can approve time over the Web.

This module also can be integrated with other PeopleSoft modules, such as Human Resources, Benefits, and Payroll.

PEOPLESOFT PAYROLL INTERFACE

The PeopleSoft Payroll Interface module enables organizations to use third-party payroll vendors to process payroll information. This module interfaces with the Human Resources and Benefits modules, which must be implemented beforehand. Benefits deduction calculations can be performed in the Benefits module, and employees' personal and job information is maintained in the Human Resources module. This eliminates some of the processes previously performed by the third-party vendor, thus reducing cost. The Payroll Interface module can export payroll-related data to the vendor based on the vendor's requirements. Also, this module can import payroll-related data from the third-party vendor into the PeopleSoft tables, making payroll information easily accessible to the organization.

The Payroll Interface module writes and reads sequential ASCII files containing data in formats compatible with various payroll systems. Figure 5.12 shows the Payroll Interface menu.

Figure 5.12
The Payroll Interface menu.

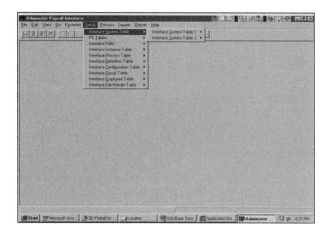

STOCK ADMINISTRATION (USA)

The Stock Administration module enables organizations to grant, monitor, and manage stock options and ESPP plans. This module is available only for the United States Stock Administration processes and is not present in releases prior to release 7.5. The users can define business rules and data validation for this module. This module can also interface with PeopleSoft payroll modules to determine whether an employee is eligible or has requested ESPP options.

PENSION ADMINISTRATION (USA)

The Pension Administration module maintains data on qualified and nonqualified employees, employee contributions, final pay, career averages, and cash balance plans. This module is based on regulations specified for U.S. benefits plans.

PeopleSoft Pension Administration modules provide organizations with the flexibility to define business and validation rules for pension plans according to their specific needs. The effective-dated functionality allows the organizations to maintain chronological data for each plan.

BENEFITS MODULE

The Benefits module consists of the Base Benefits, Benefits Administration, and Flexible Spending Account (FSA) components. Each component is described briefly in the following sections.

BASE BENEFITS

The PeopleSoft Base Benefits module enables an organization to manage a variety of benefits that are offered, such as health, life insurance, flexible spending accounts, and so on.

A *benefit plan* is a group of benefits, such as health, life insurance, or retirement plans specific to a job group.

In this module, the user defines and manages benefit plans offered by an organization. Users can also define the business rules associated with these benefit plans, which include plan types, plans, rates, and calculation rules. Employees and their dependents can be enrolled into these plans through various online panels. This module also enables organizations to identify highly compensated employees and then perform nondiscrimination testing.

Additionally, users can run various standard benefits and summary reports for employees.

This module also interfaces with the payroll module where employee benefit deductions are maintained, enabling it to calculate payroll deductions. The Web-enabled feature of this module enables employees to view their benefit information online. Figure 5.13 shows the Base Benefits menu.

Figure 5.13
The Base Benefits menu.

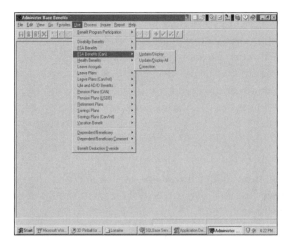

BENEFITS ADMINISTRATION MODULE

The PeopleSoft Benefits Administration module is an addition to the PeopleSoft Base Benefits module. To implement this module, organizations must first implement the Base Benefits module.

The Benefits Administration module enables organizations to automate their benefits enrollment process. This automation occurs in the following manner: The user first defines eligibility criteria required to enroll employees into benefit plans. Employee records are then validated against these criteria. Based on this validation process, employees are automatically enrolled into the appropriate plan. This module also determines and processes a variety of flexible credits, both general and plan-based. Figure 5.14 shows the Benefits Administration menu.

FLEXIBLE SPENDING ACCOUNTS ADMINISTRATION (FSA)

The Flexible Spending Accounts (FSA) module enables organizations to maintain employee contribution information for Health and Dependent Care Spending Accounts. These FSA plans must be defined in the benefit plan tables and are based on business rules defined by the users. This component may also be used to define contribution frequencies and employer contributions. This component also interfaces with the Payroll System, enabling FSA deductions to be processed by the payroll system. Figure 5.15 shows the Flexible Spending Account (FSA) menu.

Figure 5.14
The Benefits
Administration menu.

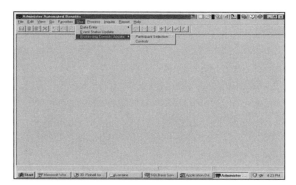

PART

II

CH

5

In this section, Human Resource modules were briefly described. In the next section, the advantages and disadvantages of customization are explored.

Figure 5.15
The Flexible Spending
Account (FSA) menu.

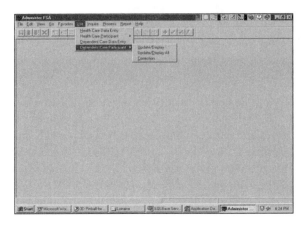

STANDARD VERSUS CUSTOMIZATION OF PEOPLESOFT HUMAN RESOURCES MODULES

The PeopleSoft HRMS modules can be used without alteration, or they can be customized according to the specific needs of an organization. Each format has advantages and limitations.

ADVANTAGES OF STANDARD PEOPLESOFT

- Limited testing—Because the organization is not making any modifications to the PeopleSoft module, minimal testing is required. This can save organizations time, resources, and money.

- Less need for additional development—Minimal additional development is required, which is cost effective.

- Less need for additional support—Using standard processes enables organizations to be less dependent on additional information or support services.

- Easier upgrades—Minimal modifications enable the entire system to be easily upgraded. This minimal effort required to upgrade will enable organizations to stay current and take advantage of new features.

- Ease of training—Pre-existing training documentation may be used because no modifications to the Human Resources modules have been made.

- Less need for additional documentation—PeopleSoft documentation will be adequate because no modifications have been made to the existing system.

- Easy interfacing—Because no modifications have been made, the PeopleSoft modules can easily interface with other modules without necessarily requiring modifications for those modules.

- Extensive product development—The standard version allows organizations to take advantages of the extensive product development that has been devoted to the standard PeopleSoft Human Resources modules.

- Quicker implementation—The standard version can be implemented with less time and effort than the customized version.

DISADVANTAGES OF STANDARD PEOPLESOFT HUMAN RESOURCES MODULES

- Unique organizational needs—Organizations may have specific needs that Standard PeopleSoft may be unable to address.

- Unique organizational culture—Organizations have unique cultures that Standard PeopleSoft may be unable to address.

- Interface modifications—These modules may require modifications to enable them to interface with other modules, such as third-party vendors.

- Standard/customizations—If an organization implements the standard version in the interest of convenience and efficiency, it may overlook factors that ultimately could have made the customized version more desirable.

ADVANTAGES OF CUSTOMIZATION

- Meeting unique organizational needs—Customizing PeopleSoft Human Resources modules may be necessary to address specific organizational needs that the standard version is unable to meet.

- Meeting unique organizational culture—Modifying PeopleSoft Human Resources modules may enable organizations to address their unique organizational cultures in ways that the standard version cannot.

- Meeting interface modifications—Customizations of the standard version may be necessary to enable it to interface with other modules used by an organization, such as third-party vendors.

- Facilitating documentation—The process of customization may facilitate more accurate and detailed documentation.

DISADVANTAGES OF CUSTOMIZATION

- Extensive testing—Modifications to the PeopleSoft Standard modules make extensive testing necessary. Organizations must allocate time, resources, and money to the testing process.

- Additional development—Modifying the standard version requires organizations to also allocate resources for additional development.

- Additional support—Additional information and support services are necessary because the standard processes have been modified.

- Difficulty upgrading—Because modifications have been made to the PeopleSoft Standard modules, considerable effort may be necessary to upgrade.

- Additional training—Modifications to the PeopleSoft modules will make standard documentation insufficient. Additional training materials will have to be developed.

- Additional documentation—Standard PeopleSoft documentation will be inadequate, and additional documentation will be necessary.

PART

II

CH

5

- Difficulty interfacing—The PeopleSoft modules may require further development to interface with other modules.
- Slower implementation—Because modifications are being made, implementation will require additional time and effort.

REQUIREMENTS FOR THE OPTIMAL IMPLEMENTATION OF THE HUMAN RESOURCES MODULES

Some important aspects for the implementation of the PeopleSoft Human Resources Modules are briefly described in this section.

REQUIREMENTS AND PLANNING

This aspect of PeopleSoft implementation for the Human Resources module consists of identifying business requirements for various human resources processes. Prior to determining its specific requirements, an organization should conduct a thorough needs assessment and evaluate the functions and processes of various human resources packages to determine whether the PeopleSoft Human Resources package is appropriate for their needs.

If it is determined that the PeopleSoft Human Resources modules are appropriate for an organization's needs, the organization can proceed to determine its specific requirements. Assessing requirements is important for organizations because it helps them determine which components of the PeopleSoft Human Resources package match their business processes, as well as ascertain the optimal order for implementation of these components.

When assessing requirements, organizations should conduct a needs analysis to identify processes and how the existing data fits into the existing PeopleSoft Human Resources modules. If an organization identifies processes that are not compatible with PeopleSoft Human Resources processes, they should evaluate the relative benefits of either re-engineering these processes or circumventing them by changing policies.

It should be noted that before converting to the PeopleSoft Human Resources modules, organizations should have clearly defined objectives and rationales for doing so.

CONVERSION/GAP ANALYSIS

After an organization has identified the Human Resources modules to be implemented, the organization should identify data to be converted from the legacy system to the PeopleSoft HRMS. Conversion processes and validation strategies should then be developed for converting this data. Organizations may find it beneficial to clean data before data is populated into the system tables. Testing conversion scripts and correcting errors are crucial during the conversion process.

PROTOTYPING AND DEVELOPMENT

Prototyping is an important aspect of the PeopleSoft developmental life cycle.

During the development phase the programmer develops or modifies interfaces, reports, and processes that users have identified. Interface and report designs, as well as programming specifications, should be documented in detail.

SYSTEM TESTING

Testing is crucial because it enables organizations to determine whether a system performs key business processes and meets policy requirements. Testing should be conducted against the requirements that have been identified during the analysis and design phase. Well-documented requirements will aid system testing. Contingency plans for all crucial processes should be developed.

A key aspect of system testing is developing accurate and detailed test scripts for the various business processes, as well as validation of business rules. It is important to develop clear test objectives, test schedules, and test acceptance criteria. Security, system configuration, and performance should also be tested. Test scripts can be modified for end-user training.

System testing for the Human Resources modules should include some of the following:

- Interface, reports, and business processes.
- Batch processes.
- System configuration.
- Validation and business rules identified.
- Import/export processes.
- Test foundation table values.
- Test data in employee-related tables—Test results are useful in determining priorities for enhancement requests.

PART

II

CH

5

END-USER TRAINING AND SUPPORT

The success of an implementation depends on the ability of the end users to operate and support a new application. For the users to use a new system and perform tasks effectively, training materials must be developed. Well-organized training allows information to be disseminated consistently and effectively. Customization of PeopleSoft Human Resources modules will require additional training documentation.

Identifying criteria for training is important and should include the following:

- Identifying the users and their needs—For example, are the users in one central place or are they geographically dispersed?
- Identifying the training objectives—An essential step for developing user training is to clearly define the training objectives. For example, an EEO coordinator who will be responsible for running EEO reports will require training in PeopleSoft functionality and associated business processes such as defining within an organization.

- Selecting appropriate training methods—Appropriate training methods may be selected based on criteria that include budget, geographical dispersion of users, users' background and level of training, infrastructure of organization, and so on. Some of the training methods including classroom training, computer-based training (CBT), training the trainer, or on-the-job training. Also, PeopleSoft provides a variety of training options, such as training classes in all modules and certification for trainers.

- Identifying the necessary resources for developing and conducting training.

- Developing training materials—For example, user documentation and software/hardware requirements for training.

- Allocating training budget.

TRAINING PROCEDURES

All employees who will be using PeopleSoft modules to perform their job duties will require training on PeopleSoft functions. Because PeopleSoft runs on a Windows NT platform, knowledge of Windows NT or Windows 95/98 is a prerequisite for employees. Users should be trained on modules that they are implementing and that are relevant to the needs of the organization. PeopleSoft training procedures should consist of functionality training, business process training, and help desk training, as described in the following sections.

FUNCTIONALITY TRAINING

Functionality training consists of training employees on the PeopleSoft functions required to perform their job. Computer Based Training (CBT) or instruction methods may be used effectively to train employees on PeopleSoft functionalities, because these functionalities remain essentially the same through various releases. Also, high staff turnover and geographically dispersed staffing should be considered when determining the specific training modality. Some PeopleSoft functions that users should learn include

- Entering data.

- Navigating between panels.

- Understanding the features of a panel, such as title, menu, and scrollbars.

- Understanding different types of data fields, such as date fields, text fields, and drop-down and list boxes.

- Understanding differences between *effective-dated* and *noneffective-dated* fields. A noneffective-dated field maintains only the current data; each time a user enters a new value, the old value is overwritten. An effective-dated field, however, maintains future, current, and historical data.

- Understanding action types, such as Update, Update/Display All, Add, and Correction. For example, if a user is adding new hire data to the system, he or she would use the Add action. If a user is adding additional benefits data that the employee has requested, the Update action would be used because the employee already exists in the system.

- Understanding steps for running a report, such as selecting a report from the menu bar, creating a run control ID, defining report parameters, entering a Process Scheduler request, running a report, viewing the Process Monitor, and printing a report.

- Performing searches with "key" fields, such as employee ID, last name, or full name.

- Understanding errors and warnings. A *warning* indicates that the value for a field may not be correct but will allow the user to do further processing. An *error message* requires the user to enter the correct value for that field in order to continue further processing.

BUSINESS PROCESS TRAINING

Business process training trains end users to use the PeopleSoft modules to perform their assigned task effectively. Business process training can be accomplished by the following means:

- Developing a training manual
- Classroom training
- Training the trainer
- Online help

HELP DESK TRAINING

Because help desk support staff provide assistance to end users, it is necessary to provide support staff with training on general information, application support, maintenance, and management.

SUMMARY

PeopleSoft HRMS is a fully integrated software package that enables human resources, benefits, and payroll departments to perform a wide variety of tasks. It is modular and customizable. Organization can select modules according to their specific needs. With the Web-enabled feature, users can view specific data online.

The PeopleSoft HRMS package is a well-designed tool that can fulfill practically every conceivable need of human resources departments. Constant enhancements by PeopleSoft, Inc., ensure continuing relevance to the rapidly changing organizational environment.

PART
II
CH
5

HRMS MODULES

In this chapter   *by Lynn Ann Lew*

PeopleSoft's Human Resources module, along with the other suite of Human Resource-related products—Base Benefits, Benefits Administration, Time & Labor, Payroll, Payroll Interface (if you choose not to use PeopleSoft's Payroll product), Flexible Spending Account (FSA) Administration, and Pension Administration—will provide you with the capabilities to track and process the complete set of information regarding an employee. In this chapter you will find out what business processes you need to define to best implement the Human Resources (HR) module and the other related business processes. Each business process provides the foundation for tracking your organization's employees from the day they are hired to the day they leave the company. Business processes can be best described as those processes that aid in the successful completion of your company's day-to-day processing activities.

SETTING UP THE HUMAN RESOURCES MODULE

Before you can actually begin to maintain all this employee data, the first step is to be able to capture the business processes and business rules of your organization. This is achieved by means of setting up the core tables of the PeopleSoft system. After you have set up these core tables, you will only need to enhance or maintain them. The Human Resources module contains many of the core tables that need to be defined and will also be used to interface with the other modules.

Note

PeopleSoft's Human Resources application includes functionality to plan salaries, careers, and successions; to manage positions, company cars, and competencies; to administer training and variable compensation programs; and to monitor absences, health, and safety. You can even track your employees' global assignments, and if you need to, process transactions related to recruiting your workforce.

THE BUSINESS UNIT AND TABLESET

In this age of technology and rapid information flow, it has become possible for you to view your organization on a more global level. It is very obvious that there are certain business processes that are common across the board (that is, for all entities of your organization), but there may also be a lot of differences. For example: Company A has locations in the United States and in Asia. Company A's departmental structure and job code structure are the same in both these locations, but the salary structure, the locations, and other characteristics are different. Version 7.5 introduced the concept of Business Unit and TableSet sharing. Because Business Unit is a new concept, this section will cover the concept in more detail. With the release of version 7.5, it has become possible for you to look at your organization, identify the similarities and differences, and decide whether you want to share data across different entities or keep the entities separate. You will now find it possible to share departmental and job code information between the two locations while at the same time keep the other discrete data separate, like the salary structure and locations. This concept will also be used to secure the data that you will deal with later.

The overall concept of Business Unit and TableSet Sharing is represented in Figure 6.1.

Figure 6.1
An overall perspective
of Business Unit and
TableSet Sharing.

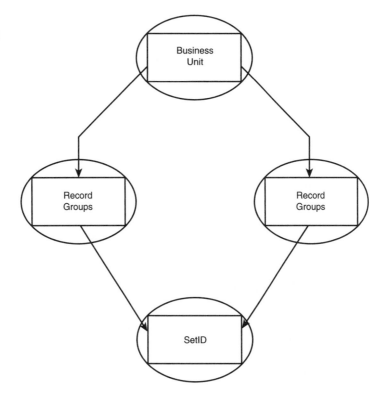

THE BUSINESS UNIT

The Business Unit sits at the top of the hierarchy, as shown in Figure 6.1. Think of a
Business Unit as a way of tracking and reporting specific business information for reporting
and other roll-up data collection. Business Units do not come with a predetermined definition, thereby giving you the flexibility to set them up the way your organization does business. This flexibility also comes with the possibility of leading to potential problems if
enough time is not spent on researching which structure will work best for your organization. It is required that you have at least one business unit to represent your organization.
In the middle between the Business Unit and Set ID are "Record Groups." PeopleSoft
Human Resources comes delivered with Record Groups. A Record Group is a set of logically and functionally related control tables and views provided by PeopleSoft. Record
Groups are further tied to Business Unit/SetID functionality. SetID is the label given to a
TableSet.

In Figure 6.2, you can see that the Business Unit USADM is tied to the default Record
Group SetID USA (which has been previously defined in another table). Again, the Business
Unit is tied to the TableSet Record Group Control.

Figure 6.2
An example of the Business Unit USADM with the SETID Record Group = to USA.

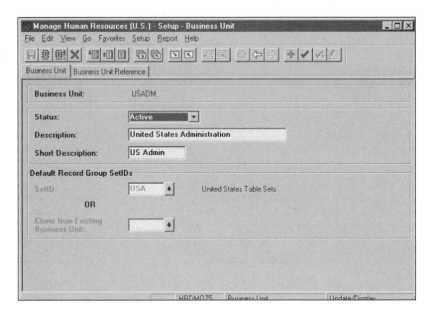

The panel shown in Figure 6.3 helps you to understand that the TableSet Record Group Control actually helps to tie multiple Record Groups together and that each of these Record Groups such as HR_01—Departments are tied to a SetID. Again, a Record Group consists of functionally and logically related records.

Figure 6.3
Example of Tableset Record Group Controls for USA, which is HR_01.

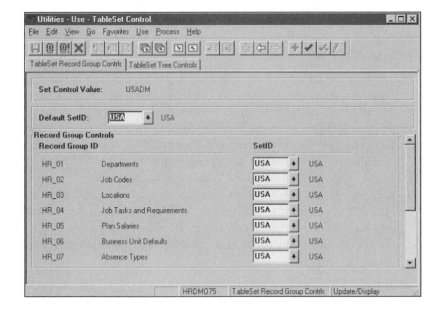

In Figure 6.4 it becomes clear that the Record Group HR_01—Departments actually groups Department-related records together.

Figure 6.4
Example of Record
Group HR_01—
Departments.

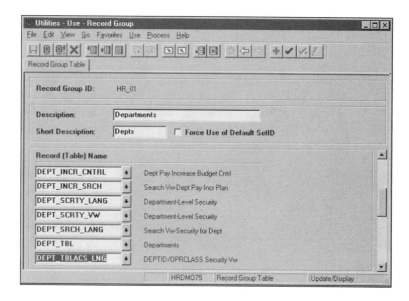

Let us now revisit the previous example, about the organization having locations in the United States and in Asia where the job codes and the Department structures are the same but other core data differs like the salary structure and locations. Assume that the United States Business Unit structure is USADMIN and that the record groups in this business unit are tied to the SetID USA. When you now define the structure for the Asia Business Unit, assume that the Business Unit is ASIADM. The Job Codes and Departments Record Group would be tied to the SetID USA for the ASIAADM, and the rest of the Record Groups would be tied to some other SetID, because they differ from the way business is done in the United States Business Unit. As you can see from this example, you have been successful in sharing redundant data and keeping the two Business Units separate for all other purposes.

TABLESET

A TableSet is a group of values in records that are keyed by the same SetID. SetID is just a label for a TableSet, and they are sometimes used interchangeably.

With this brief introduction to the Business Unit and TableSet Sharing concept, let's now move on and take a look at what other information needs to be set up that would be considered the core or the foundation of the HRMS system. These core tables shown in Table 6.1 need to be set up in a particular sequence to track the data of the organization.

THE CORE OF THE HRMS SYSTEM

The tables in the Human Resources Module as described in this section are the "foundation" tables for the entire system.

In this section you will be provided with an overview of the type of information you will be setting up. PeopleSoft's HRMS system is "table-driven." As your organization changes, you can always add information to the existing table with a new "effective date" as to when that information is effective. This allows you the flexibility to keep a history of what was originally input.

Example: When Company A originally installed the HRMS system on 1-1-95, they utilized only the HRMS modules and Payroll modules. Then on 1-1-99 they decided to also purchase PeopleSoft's Pension Administration module. Company A could indicate this by putting in a new effective dated record of 1-1-99 with Pension Administration added as a product they are now utilizing.

TABLE 6.1   HRMS CORE TABLES

Foundation Tables	Type of Data Stored
Company Table	Federal Employer Identification Number (FEIN)
Installation Table	Processing rules, products used
SetID	Identifies a set of rows in the control tables
Business Unit	Logical entity defining your company's structure
TableSet Control	Helps relate the SetIDs to Record Groups and in turn to Business Units
Operator Preferences	Defaults by Operator
Business Unit HR defaults	Defaults by Business Units
Establishment Table	Used for the purposes of EEO/AA reporting
Location Table	Physical locations of your organization as seen by the Human Resources requirements
Department Table	An organizational unit that is used for security
Salary Plan/Grade/Step	To track the salary plans or structures that are offered by your organizations
Job Code Table	Different job roles or attributes
Pay Group Table	Logical grouping of employees in your organization based on similarities such as how often they are paid

COMPANY TABLE

The company table helps in identifying the organizational information such as the address of the company, the date the company has become active, general ledger information such as the accounts for withholding of taxes, rules for the organization such as FICA taxes, and the Federal Employer Identification Number.

INSTALLATION TABLE

The Installation table identifies the products that you have implemented for the organization, certain IDs such as last employee ID assigned, and defaults such as standard hours and position management. The last IDs assigned are used for automatic generation of new employee IDs and also in keeping the uniqueness of employee IDs when the system goes into production. This table has a field called "calculation type," where you would indicate whether you are using PeopleSoft's Payroll product (= "Payroll") or interfacing to a third-party software like your legacy system (= "Deductions"). The calculation type lets the system know how the deductions, that are to be withheld from an employee's paycheck, are to be processed, either by PeopleSoft's payroll system or interfaced to the third-party software. You could also not be processing any payroll or deductions and just be using the HRMS system (= None).

BUSINESS UNIT

As discussed earlier, the concept of Business Unit and TableSet sharing is used to define and segregate business entities of the organization, and also in sharing information that is similar for the different business entities.

OPERATOR PREFERENCES

The various users of the system are considered operators. The defaults in the Operator Preferences table help in tailoring the system defaults to the Operator. When an operator who has the defaults associated signs on to the system, the defaults specified become the defaults at the employee level. The values that you associate with an operator will override the information that you set up in the Installation table.

BUSINESS UNIT HR DEFAULTS

In this table, you are given the ability to set up information such as default SetID, company, country, and standard hours. The defaults specified here will work similar to the defaults that are specified in the Installation table, except that the defaults in this table are based on SetID, which gives you the ability to share the defaults among multiple Business Units. So as discussed in the earlier example of Business Unit USAADM, you could choose to have the Locations for Business Unit USAADM be the ASIADM defaults for location instead of keeping them as USAADM locations.

ESTABLISHMENT TABLE

The Establishment table is used to specify information about each of the business establishments. The values that you specify for each of your business establishments are used for Equal Employment Opportunity (EE0)/Affirmative Action (AA) purposes. Establishments would be worksites where you have 100 or more employees in one location that require you to track EEO- and AA-related information.

LOCATION TABLE

The information in the Location table is used to identify the different physical locations such as headquarters of your organization, branch offices, and so on. Where your employees actually perform their work. If you use PeopleSoft Payroll, you must have one location for every taxing locality. For each state in which you have a location or locations, the state unemployment insurance tax for that location will default as the unemployment insurance jurisdiction. The employee's wages earned at that location are taxed for unemployment taxes. Otherwise, you can specify the locations using any grouping you want.

DEPARTMENT TABLE

The Department table contains information about the business entities. If you use PeopleSoft Payroll, the information in this table must be set up according to the Cost Centers where you charge your wages. If you do not use PeopleSoft's Payroll System, you may want to set up the departments based upon how you need the information to flow for reporting and general ledger purposes to the interfaces this information needs to be sent to.

The information in this table is also used as the basis for your departmental security tree. The Departmental Security tree helps you to secure employee data, that is, set up row-level security. You can set up the security to allow an employee to only be able to view how table information was set up but not be able to make changes to that information based on their security. You do not have to implement any of the other modules to have this departmental security tree functionality.

SALARY PLAN/GRADE AND STEP

Setting up a salary plan/grade and step within the plans helps you to create salary plans for the organization. You could create one salary plan that encompasses all the employees in the organization, or you could create multiple salary plans and grades and steps within them. The information here when tied to your location can help you build location-based salary plans.

JOB CODE TABLE

The Job Code table is used to classify the Job information for your organization. You could associate training programs, salary survey information, and job family information if you use this information for the organization. You could also associate a salary plan/grade and step to a job code. This helps in defaulting information to the employee level.

PAY GROUP TABLE

The Pay Group table is used to logically group employees based on certain criteria such as their pay frequency, work schedules, and so on. Grouping the employees together is very beneficial especially when you use PeopleSoft Payroll. It allows you to associate defaults with pay groups such as Benefit/Deduction programs and also helps you to streamline payroll processing. If you have set up the Salary Plan tables, you can also default the plan to the pay group.

Before you can actually hire employees or maintain employee information in the PeopleSoft Human Resources system, you must set up these tables. Each of these tables plays a role in capturing the business processes of your organization.

DEPARTMENTAL SECURITY TREE

Data security is very important due to the sensitive nature of the data maintained in the Human Resources database. By default, PeopleSoft uses the Departmental security tree that is built based on the information stored in the department table in conjunction with Operator Classes to administer security. The tree structure is built based on the organizational structure, but there is a major difference in these two trees, which is that inactive departments are maintained in the current security structure but not in the organizational structure. Security can also be applied based on other criteria such as Operator ID in conjunction with Departmental Security, or the tree can be built based on location. For security to be administered based on other criteria specific to your organization, you will have to modify what is delivered. As with any software, if you modify it, and something goes awry, PeopleSoft cannot support you if any customizations have been done to meet your company's specific needs. The departmental security tree is effective dated, which means that you have the ability to store the history of the changes that have forced a change in the security structure.

Figure 6.5 shows the hierarchical nature of the departmental security tree.

Figure 6.5
An example of the Department Security Tree.

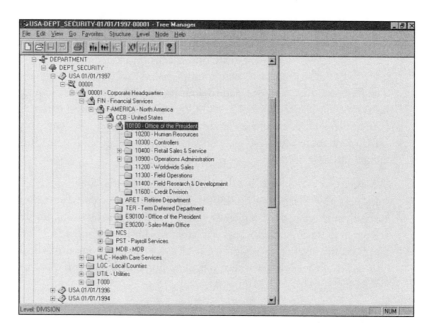

After the tree has been built and a process to update the system to look at the current tree has been run, you can view the changes you have made to the tree.

In the panel shown in Figure 6.6, you can see that the combination of SetID and Department ID in conjunction with Operator Class ALLPANLS is used to administer data security for any operator who belongs to the ALLPANLS class. The type of access can be set to Read/Write or No Access.

PART

II

CH

6

Figure 6.6
Example of an
Operator with
ALLPNLS class access.

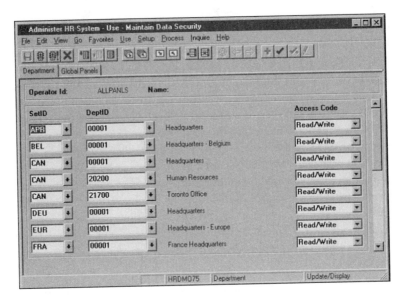

After security has been set up, it is possible for operators to be able to hire employees and maintain employee data in a secure environment.

ADMINISTERING YOUR WORKFORCE

The functions that you use in the Administer Workforce window are the foundation of your human resource management system. PeopleSoft Human Resources allows you the flexibility to implement based on how your business is organized—by company, agencies, subsidiaries, divisions, entities, departments, branch offices, and so on. It is up to you and your unique business needs.

Whether you are multinational (Global) or only United States-based, you will be able to track personnel salaries and reimbursements in multiple currencies, perhaps even multiple currency rate types, yet keep an eye on the bottom line by using one currency as a point of reference to track your expenses and costs worldwide. PeopleSoft Human Resources also gives you the flexibility to optimize your corporate and computing resources to meet the challenges of the global marketplace, including the changing requirements of the Economic and Monetary Union (EMU).

YOUR WORKFORCE AND THE ECONOMIC AND MONETARY UNION (EMU)

The delivered currency code table meets the International Standards Organization (ISO) standard of zero, two, and three decimal places. All currency-sensitive fields are 13 integers and two decimals (13.2). To meet your international business requirements, you can expand these amount fields to a maximum of 15 integers and three decimals (15.3).

With Version 7.50, PeopleSoft delivered regulatory or local country window functionality for Belgium, France, Germany, Japan, Netherlands, and the United Kingdom. In addition to tracking global information for employees such as their emergency contacts, volunteer activities, and banking information, you can also track country-specific information for workers in Belgium, Canada, France, and the Netherlands. Although none of these panels are required to be used, you will find them important for administering employees in these countries.

- Belgium—You will use additional panels delivered so you can record Belgian employment and end employment contract terms with employees, set up Claeys formula calculation data, and run the Claeys calculation to determine potential severance pay for an employee.
- Canada—You can record Ontario Employment Equity Commission (OEEC) workforce survey data for meeting regulatory reporting requirements for Ontario.
- France—You can track dependent data for French employees that impacts payroll processing, record military service information for your French employees to ensure that you can comply with required military service regulations, and record mandated data for works council participation by French employees in your organization.
- The Netherlands—If you maintain a Dutch workforce, you can use the Wet Bevordering Evenredige Arbeidsdeelname Allochtonen (WBEAA), or the "Law to promote equal labor participation for persons of a different ethnic origin." You will be able to track information on the national origin of an employee's birth parents for purposes of establishing the ethnic status of workers to comply with the WBEAA diversity law.

PeopleSoft's Human Resources application also comes delivered with some essential functionality to aid in retaining your most valuable resources—your employees.

PLANNING SALARIES

In PeopleSoft Human Resources, it is easy to set and maintain competitive salary structures. You will increase the timeliness and consistency of your data and gain flexibility in performing all your Plan Salaries tasks. And if you are creating plans in a multinational organization, you can set up salary structures for multiple currencies as well as multiple components of pay.

Depending on how you structure your compensation plans, you will use one or all three salary tables to set up your compensation business process. You can set up either salary grades only, or salary grades, salary steps, and salary step components. Many companies base their salary plans on salary surveys of organizations in their industry. Based on the increasingly competitive employment marketplace, you can change your salary plans easily by just inserting a new effective dated row with the new salary grades, rates, or steps functionality provided by planning salaries.

In the salary grade table found in Figure 6.7, you will enter minimum, maximum, and midpoint ranges.

PART
II
CH
6

Figure 6.7
Salary Grade table for Standard Pay Grade 1.

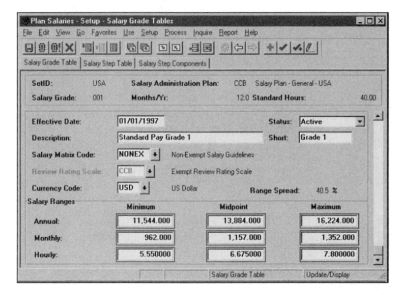

Salary Step tables are used to record hourly, monthly, and yearly rates for each step. For each salary step, you can also establish salary step components (see Figure 6.8).

Figure 6.8
Salary Step table for Standard Pay Grade 1.

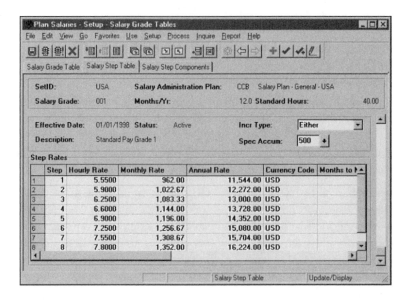

The salary components can be in the form of a specific amount, percent, or salary points. You can even tie a compensation package of several rate codes to a salary step (see Figure 6.9).

Figure 6.9
Salary Step components for Standard Pay Grade 1.

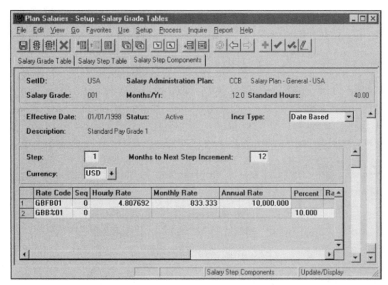

PLANNING CAREERS AND SUCCESSIONS

Retaining and motivating topnotch employees are important aspects of cost-effective human resources management. To ensure that your organization uses employee talents to their fullest, you will want to find out where employees have been in your organization and plan for where they are going.

PeopleSoft Human Resources helps you in managing your organizational growth and building employee skills. By working with your employees toward fulfilling their specific career objectives, you will retain top talent, thereby saving on recruitment costs. You will also end up keeping employees who are motivated because they will have a clear idea of where they are going in your organization. Planning careers also plays an important role in planning for successions in your organization. You never know when an employee who started out in your organization's mail room could end up through career planning on the track to becoming the company's next CEO.

You can use the career plans you set up for high-potential employees as the basis of preparation for moving into key positions in your organization.

Planning Careers enables you to plan and develop your employees' future career paths, and to record and track worker skills and knowledge, by providing a link with Managing Competencies. By linking career plans with competency evaluations, you can identify varying proficiencies and determine appropriate training courses for skill improvement. The system will use career path data to help you identify potential succession candidates quickly. You can also use other portions of career plans to create training and development plans for key employees, ensuring that they are adequately prepared to step into key positions.

PART

II

CH

6

You do not have to use career plans to create succession plans. But if you choose to use them, you will find that career plans are very useful for streamlining many of the tasks involved in managing effective successions in your organization.

MANAGING POSITIONS

The information you use to maintain and track positions in your organization can serve you in many areas of human resources, including organizational planning, budgeting, recruitment, and career planning. To help you maximize the usefulness of this data, PeopleSoft Human Resources offers several valuable features designed to help you retrieve and report on information for various functions, including career planning, budgeting, organizational planning, and recruitment.

You can maintain budgets by position or by job code, depending on the level of detail you want for a department. You can enter data on proposed, approved, or frozen positions. You can enter requested and approved budget amounts, and if you need to make changes after a budget has been approved, you can enter year-to-date adjustments. Managing position functionality provides you with a better way to keep track of the positions that have been filled, need to be filled, or are not to be filled at this time due to budget constraints.

If you use organization charts to assist you in organizational planning, you will want to see the reporting relationships among positions. You can get this information in two ways: by generating a report listing "reports-to" relationships among positions, or creating a position tree in the Tree Manager to view your organizational hierarchy in graphical form (see Figure 6.10). This information will be based on your organization's current structure—you do not have to use another type of media form like PowerPoint to illustrate your company's organizational structure. You will be providing the "true" hierarchical view of your company.

Figure 6.10
Maintaining position hierarchies in the Tree Manager.

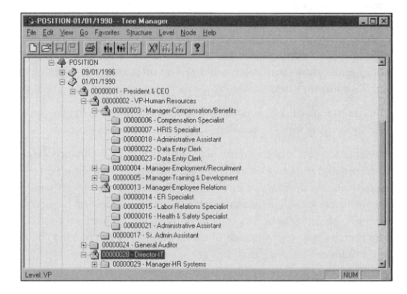

When you plan your organization's future, you will want to draw on position, incumbent, and budgeting data from the past and present. You can view this information via Summary panels of Position History.

Note

You can also manage positions at the employee level versus the position level. Position levels would not be employee-specific. Your company could have a total of five positions that you track as "Receptionist" versus tracking by each of the employees who has filled the receptionist position.

MANAGING COMPETENCIES

Manage Competencies features provided in PeopleSoft Human Resources exceed the traditional skill-tracking functionality you will find in most human resource management systems. Manage Competencies is a dynamic tool that empowers you to define your organization's jobs and positions in terms of key competencies, and perform real-time match and gap analyses between your workforce and your company's projects. With such a powerful tool, you will be able to plan your employee's careers with an eye to their current skills and their future growth based on the competency requirements that your company will need to grow and prosper in an increasingly competitive and ever-changing global marketplace. After you have defined your workforce competencies and accomplishments, you have the option of grouping these competencies into clusters that fit positions within your company. You can also opt to profile jobs, positions, or project teams using competencies alone. For example, the competencies you will use to track Human Resources personnel are different from the kinds of competencies you will find desirable for a software developer or accountant.

The system offers you the flexibility for grouping and organizing your competencies. You can categorize competencies by using categories and types on the Competency table (see Figure 6.11).

Figure 6.11
Competency table for "abstract thinking."

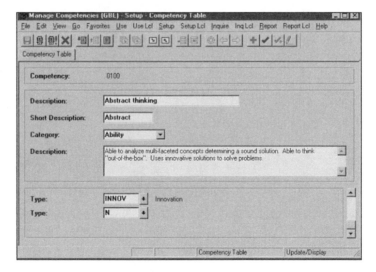

You can also cluster the kinds of skills that you require for each of your company's positions and assign them as a group to projects and positions all together (see Figure 6.12).

Figure 6.12
Competency Cluster table for technical professionals.

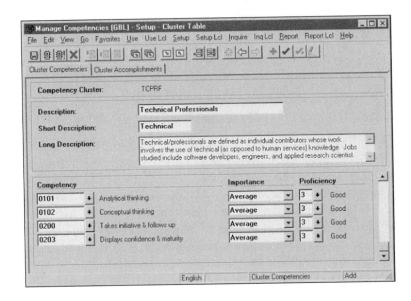

You can also group jobs together in Job Families and assign competency clusters to these families (see Figure 6.13).

Figure 6.13
Job Family table for Compensation Job Family.

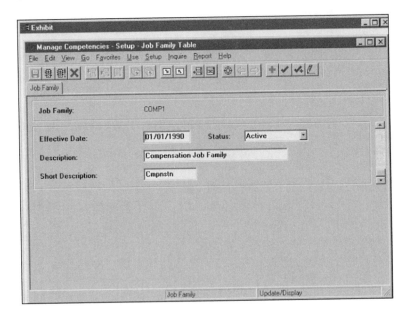

As you can see, the Human Resources module provides many delivered features that need to be defined and completed in order to successfully process your company's day-to-day HRMS-related business processes. Now that you have set these core foundation tables up, you can move on to setting up more company-specific information that will relate to your specific benefits plans, payroll, pension plans, and so on. Each of these products will utilize many of the defaults you have set up in the HRMS side.

INTRODUCTION TO BASE BENEFITS

PeopleSoft Base Benefits product makes it possible for your organization to effectively maintain and update any number of benefit plans. As the organization grows, there may be changes in the processing rules or in the rate structure, or it may be that the organization just wants to go to another provider that gives the employees better benefits. All of these changes will be very easy to maintain with PeopleSoft mainly because of the built-in flexibility. Instead of relying on hard-coded programs, the PeopleSoft system stores all the information in tables. This means that you have the flexibility to change the way you do business at any time without having to worry about which program needs to be changed or having to muddle through millions of lines of code to implement the change.

Just as in the case of implementation of Human Resources, there is a set of tables you need to set up before you can maintain employee benefit information. For example: Your company provides on-site day care while another company provides meal allowances and another provides commuting allowances. You can set up any type of benefit and track it for your employees. These tables store the information about the plans that you offer, the rate structure, how deductions affect the paycheck, and how the benefit-related deductions are to be calculated. Here's another example: You could set up your medical plans with the cost for the employee-only coverage being nothing to the employee, but the employee with one cost is $50/month, employee + 2 is $75/month, and so on. You are in control of what you need to set up. After these tables have been set up, you will set up a program called the Benefit Program. For example, you may offer a different type of benefit plan to the executives than to the part-time employees. By creating Benefit Programs, it is possible for you to segregate the plans for the executives and the part-time employees. The Benefit program mainly allows you to compile all the plans that belong to a benefit program and also helps you in creating the relationship between the different tables that you will set up for the Benefit Plans. The Benefit Program is then associated with the Pay Group table that you have already set up in Human Resources.

The advantage of tying the benefit program to the pay group is that when an employee becomes part of a pay group, this benefit program becomes the default at the employee level. So for the part-time employees, you may have benefit program PAR for them as the default, which only provides them with the ability to enroll in medical and dental coverage only. By contrast, the executive plan—EXE—allows the executives to enroll in a deferred compensation program, stock purchase, spouse insurance coverage, and so forth.

This default can also be overridden. After an employee is associated with a benefit program, he or she can only be enrolled in the plans within that program.

Implementation of Base Benefits can be broken down into the following steps:

- Setting up benefit plans and supporting tables
- Setting up the benefit program
- Enrolling the employees in the plans
- Calculating deductions

These steps will be illustrated in the following sections.

SETTING UP BENEFIT PLANS

All benefit plans have a common set of tables that need to set up, but for certain plans there are some specific tables that need to be set up. The following are the building blocks of a benefit plan.

PLAN TYPE

Plan type describes the generalities of the benefit plan that you are trying to set up, for example, Health, Life, or Disability type plans. Each of these categories is associated to a range of values so that the system can recognize the plan category. For example, Health Plans are in the range 10–19 or 1A–1Z. In this range, some of the values are already predetermined. Because PeopleSoft adds plan types starting from the beginning of the alphabet, if you needed to create a benefit plan that is not predetermined, PeopleSoft suggests you assign the plan type starting from 1Z and so on working backwards to A. The Plan Type value has to be a two-digit alphanumeric code.

BENEFIT PLAN

When you know the plan type, that is the category of the benefit that you are trying to set up, you can then get down to the details of the category. This is done in the Benefit Plan table. For example, you could be setting up an HMO plan. HMO plans would be in the Health Plans range 10-19, 1A to 1Z (see Figure 6.14).

You can see on the panel that Plan Type 10 represents the medical plan HMO1. You can also see that this medical plan is offered by Kaiser Permanente and the deduction code for this plan is MEDIC.

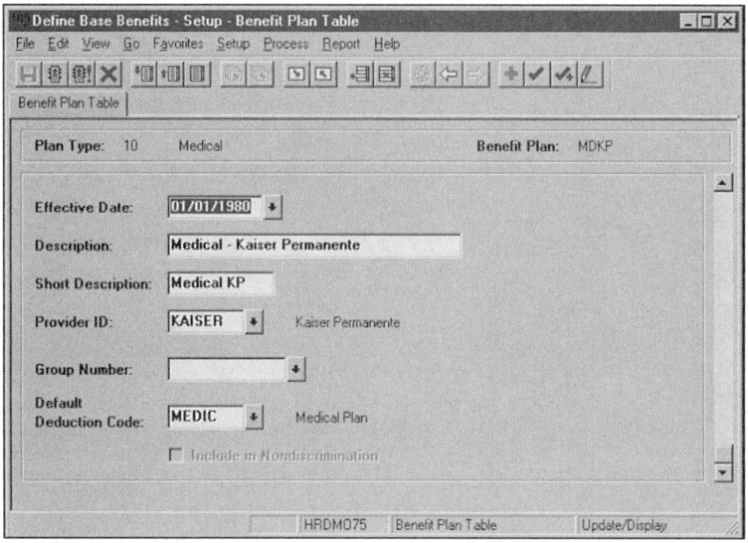

Figure 6.14
Example of HMO
Benefit Plan setup.

DEDUCTION CODE

A deduction code needs to be set up in order for deductions to be taken for the plan an employee participates in. While setting up deductions, you will specify how the deduction is to be processed, the priority of the deduction, tax implications, how to process arrears, frequency of deduction, limits if there are any limitations of deductions that can be taken in a year towards the plan. As can be seen following, the deduction table is a set of panels that allows you to specify the tax classification and other rules. Figures 6.15 and 6.16 provide you with an example of how you would fill out the deduction table for deduction code MEDIC, which is the deduction code for medical plan HMO1—Kaiser Permanente.

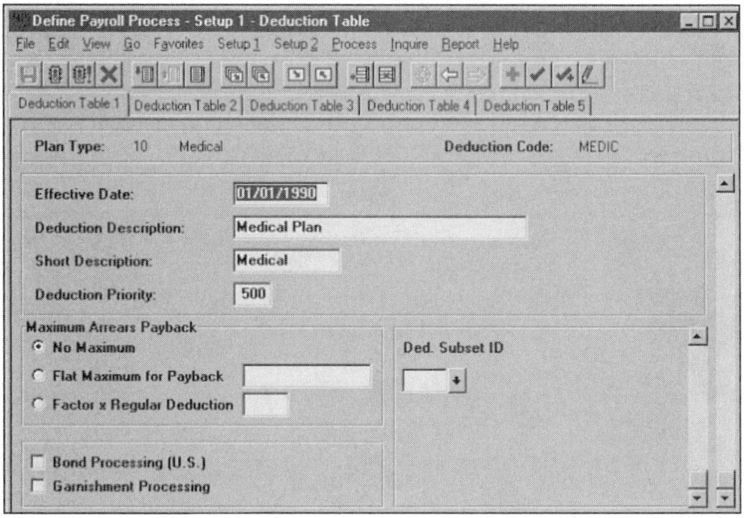

Figure 6.15
Deduction Table 1
Setup of MEDIC
Deduction Code.

PART

II

CH

6

Figure 6.16
Deduction Table 2
Setup of MEDIC
Deduction Code.

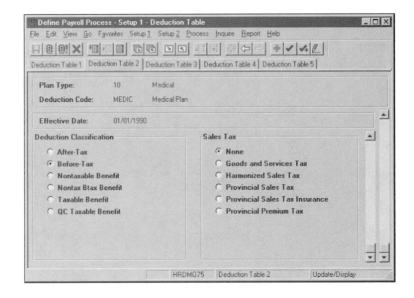

RATE TABLES

Rate tables need to be set up in order to specify the amount that needs to be deducted from the paycheck. Rate tables also allow you to define the employee/employer contributions, the premium frequency that determines how often the payment is made to the provider. There are mainly four different types of Rate tables: Flat Rate Table, Age-Graded Table, Service Rate Table, and Salary Percentage. The different types of tables that are provided give you the flexibility to set up the various plans that are offered by your organization (see Figure 6.17).

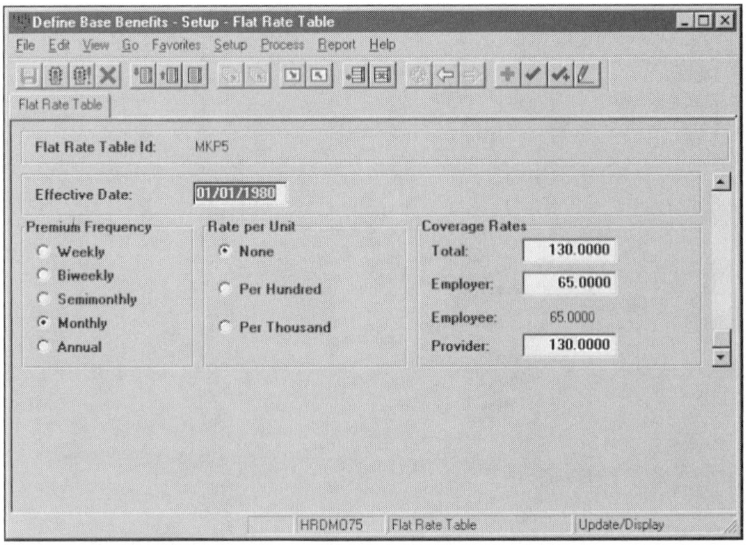

Figure 6.17
Example of Flat Rate
table setup.

CALCULATION RULES

The information in the Calculation Rules table controls how the deductions are calculated. These tables mainly control the mathematics behind the calculations. The information that can be stored in these tables consists of the rounding rules, the coverage maximums and minimums, the dates that need to be used to calculate age and service, and the base rate that is to be used to calculate coverage. The Calculation Rules table can be set up for any time of deduction. Figures 6.18 and 6.19 show you an example of how to define the calculation rules for a benefit that would be defined using CalcTbl ID 0001.

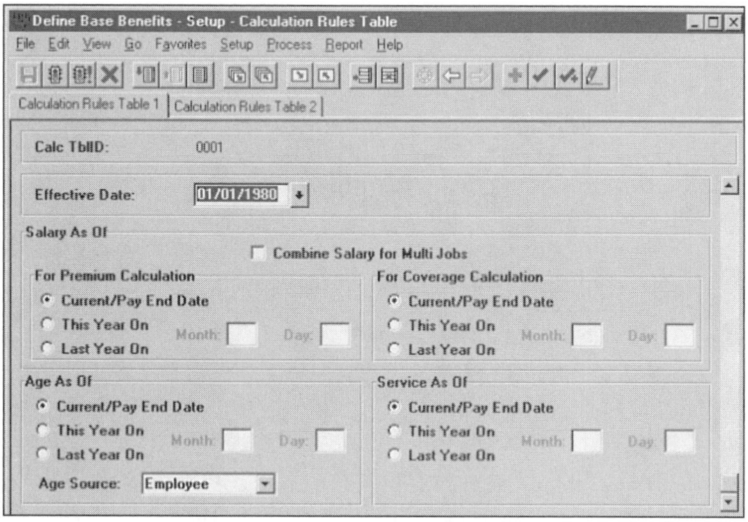

Figure 6.18
Example of setup of Calculation Rules Table 1 for CalcTbl ID 0001.

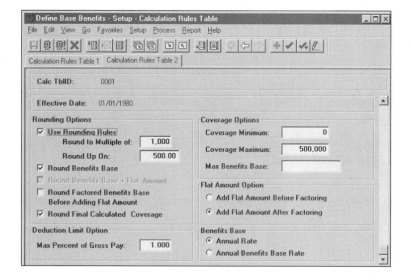

Figure 6.19
Example of setup of Calculation Rules Table 2 for CalcTbl ID 0001.

As mentioned earlier, almost all the benefit plans require you to set up a common set of tables, but some require other tables to be set up. The rule for these special plans is that for any plan with a plan type greater than or equal to 2x, it is necessary for you to set up the plan-specific table. Figure 6.20 shows the plan-specific table for a life plan (plan type 20).

Figure 6.20
Example of plan-specific table for Basic Life Plan—Plan Type 20.

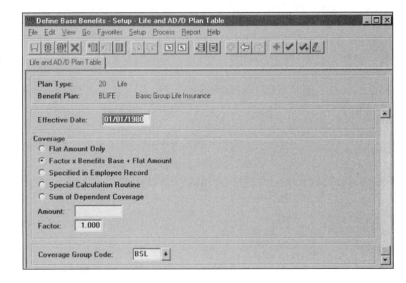

SETTING UP BENEFIT PROGRAMS

After all these tables that are the building blocks of a benefit plan have been set up, you will need to create the benefit program. In the Benefit Program table, you can tie together the different pieces that make up a benefit plan.

As you can see in Figure 6.21, medical plan MDKP has been tied to plan type 10, the plan offers multiple types of coverage, and the deduction code MEDIC has been associated with it. The cost associated with the plan and the different coverage options is associated on the Cost panel.

In Figure 6.22, the flat rate MDKP5 associated with the Benefit Plan MDKP and Coverage 1 is the cost structure that dictates the employee/employer contribution.

After the benefit program is created, it needs to be associated with the pay group table (Figure 6.23).

Figure 6.21
Example of a
Benefit/Deduction
Program table—BAS.

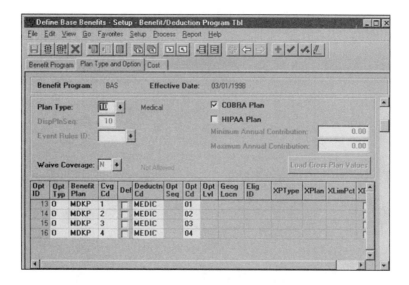

Figure 6.22
Example of the cost
associated with med-
ical plan MDKP.

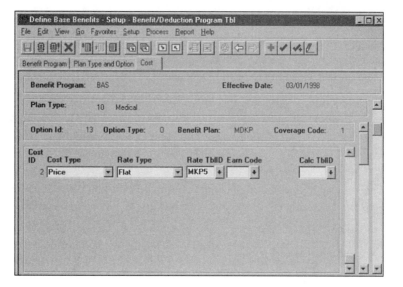

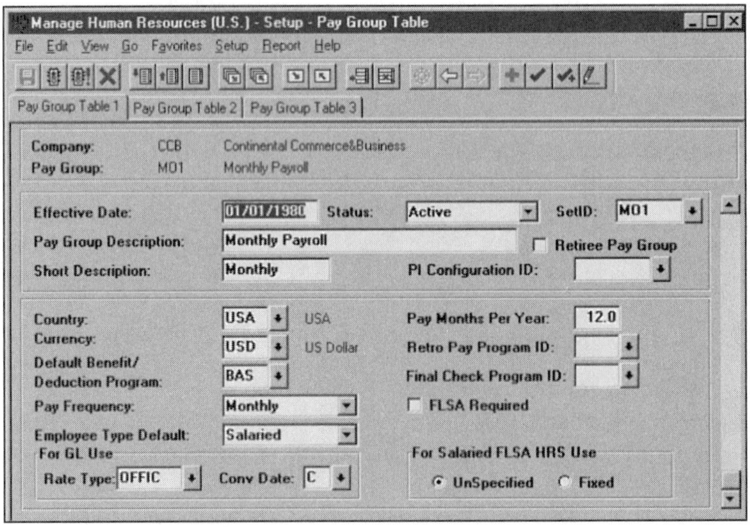

Figure 6.23
Example of a pay
group table.

ENROLLING EMPLOYEES IN A BENEFIT PROGRAM

The first step in enrollment is to associate the benefit program with the employee during the hiring process or while maintaining employee data. This is done on the Benefit Program Participation tab of Job Data panels.

As was mentioned earlier, at this time you would enroll a vice president who was just hired to the EXE benefit program, whereas you would enroll a part-time filing clerk to the PAR benefit program that offers only part-time medical and dental benefits.

CALCULATING DEDUCTIONS

The last step to maintaining benefits information is to process deductions. Before deductions can be calculated, it is necessary to set up the following information:

- Balance ID
- Pay Calendar
- Pay Run ID

The following sections will illustrate these setup processes.

BALANCE ID

Balance ID is set up in order to be able to maintain deduction balances, earnings balances, and so on. The Balance ID allows you to be able to maintain balances by calendar year or by fiscal year.

PAY CALENDAR

A pay calendar must be defined for every pay group. This is used to determine the benefit costs for an employee's pay frequency.

Pay Run IDs are defined before you are ready to run calculations and then tied to one or more pay calendars to process deductions for.

After these are set up, deduction calculations can be run.

With Base Benefits, it is possible to set up and maintain any number of benefit plans that the organization needs. It is also possible for you to be able to set up COBRA administration and Benefits Billing. As you can see, PeopleSoft's Base Benefits application is comprehensive in its ability to manage the needs of your organization.

In this section you learned about how to set up your benefit plan types, put them into a Benefit Program, and then associate them to a defaulted Paygroup. There was no discussion about eligibility rules. Many companies have rules about when an employee is eligible to participate in a benefit plan/program. The Benefits Administration product provides eligibility rules functionality in addition to event rules and open enrollment processing.

INTRODUCTION TO BENEFITS ADMINISTRATION

With PeopleSoft Base Benefits, it is possible to manage a number of benefit plans. It also allows you to manage and run COBRA processing and Benefits Billing if you set up these modules. However, with only Base Benefits functionality, there is no process provided that allows you to check whether an employee is eligible or ineligible for a particular benefit program. This is important functionality if your organization offers a number of different programs for your employees based on some criteria for enrolling the employees in the programs and plans. Eligibility enrollment depends entirely on the operator who does the enrolling of the employee to see if they are eligible for that particular program. If your organization has a number of employees and offers a number of benefit programs, this could become a very labor-intensive process. In addition, it is not just enrolling the employees in the plans that is required; you must also be able to keep track of all the changes that are requested by employees due to the occurrence of life events such as marriage or the birth of a child. Benefits Administration functionality provides you with the capabilities to automatically enroll the employees when eligible based on criteria that you will define. You will also be able to define event rules that trigger a change in benefits like marriage, birth of child, and so on. You will even be able to process your own Open Enrollment if you want.

PART

II

CH

6

OPEN ENROLLMENT AND EVENT MAINTENANCE PROCESSING

With Benefits Administration, it is possible for you to define the criteria for eligibility, and event rules that help alleviate the problems associated with manually administering benefits. It is also possible to define Open Enrollment processing to automate the administration of benefits enrollment of existing employees as well as new hires on an annual basis. The regular updates due to changes in benefits information of employees can be done by event maintenance. Both the event maintenance and open enrollment processes of Benefits Administration use the eligibility rules and event rules that you have defined. If there are any changes to the policies or criteria, all that needs to be done to implement these changes is to update these tables. It is important to note that Benefits Administration adds to the features of Base Benefits, so Base Benefits must be implemented first. Benefits Administration helps you to relate eligibility and event-processing rules to your benefit programs, which helps in automating the processing.

PAYROLL-RELATED TABLE AND FLEXIBLE CREDITS SETUP

When you work with benefits, you need to work with some payroll-related tables as well. With Benefits Administration, you may need to define flexible credit earnings for which an earnings code needs to be set up. After an earnings code is set up, it is then tied to an Earnings Program. The Earnings Program is a compilation of all the eligible earnings for a group of employees and is very similar in concept to the Benefit Program. The other payroll-related tables that you will come across are the Pay Group table, to which you tie the default Benefit Program and deductions, which help deduct amounts from the paycheck towards benefit-related or non-benefit-related payments. With Benefits Administration, it is possible to set up flexible credit deductions, which helps you define salary conversion (any benefit-related cost that the employee pays for in excess of the flexible credits earnings) and cash back (compensation in lieu of additional benefits based on the flexible credit earnings). Flexible credit earnings can be set up as general (credits that apply to a program) or plan-based credits (credits that apply to specific plan type). Earnings codes must be unique for a plan type within a program for Open Enrollment and Event Maintenance to work correctly. The calculation of Flexible Credit Earnings is based on the calculation rules and the rate tables that you set up using Base Benefits. When you create flexible credits, you associate a rate table with it.

Example: Your company provides each of its eligible employees with a flexible credit of $60/month. This $60/month can be used for any pretax benefit except 401(k). The employee enrolls in employee + spouse medical coverage with Kaiser, which costs $100/month. The $60/month flexible credit would be used up and the additional $40/month in cost ($100–$60 = $40) would be deducted from the employee's paycheck. You can also have a case where the employee waives medical coverage because he or she is covered under a spouse's medical coverage, so he or she does not get the full $60/month flexible credit but gets cash back as taxable income of $20/month.

ELIGIBILITY RULES

The Benefits Administration system depends on the eligibility rules, event classes, and event rules that are the core of the system. It is very vital to set up the eligibility tables properly in order for Benefits Administration to work. The eligibility rules come into the picture early on in the processing to determine which Benefit Program an employee is eligible for. This is done using the eligibility rules that are set up at the program level. Further, eligibility checks can be done at the plan level to determine the options that an employee has available. Creating well-defined eligibility rules is very important. This will help in restricting employees to be eligible for only one benefit program. Sometimes, despite all the care taken in defining the eligibility rules, you may find that employees are tied to the wrong benefit program or to an incorrect plan within the program. You can determine the problems and fix them using the Eligibility Debugging tool. This tool points out the problem areas and helps you to fix the problem(s).

DEFINING ELIGIBILITY RULES

In order to define eligibility rules, you need to set up the Eligibility Rules table and/or the Geographical Location Eligibility table. In the Eligibility Rules table, you can set up basic requirements for eligibility such as service required, age requirements, employee class, or FLSA status, Benefits Status (enables you to look at employee eligibility independent of employee status). This can be set up using the Action/Reason table. In effect, you can associate a benefit status to a particular action/reason. The benefit status is associated with the employee when action/reason is tied to the Employee, Company, Location, and many other parameters. You can also set up customized or organization-specific requirements using the Configurable Parameters panels or set up override parameters for specific employees.

The information for the Eligibility Rules table is defined using the Eligibility Rules panels. The following panels give you an idea of the type of information you can set up to define eligibility. On the first panel, you set up general information such as age requirements, service requirements, standard hour requirements, and what to base age and service calculations on. Figure 6.24 shows you further classifications such as the employee classes that are eligible, and the FLSA Status of an employee who is eligible. In Figure 6.25, note that the Benefits Status field shown in the panel tells you that only employees with the Benefit Status Active or Leave w/ben are considered eligible. But if you look at the FLSA status, the field is left blank. This implies that employees of any FLSA status are considered eligible.

Figure 6.24
Eligibility Rules–
Eligibility 1.

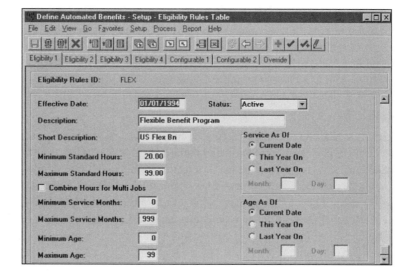

Figure 6.25
Eligibility Rules—
Eligibility 2.

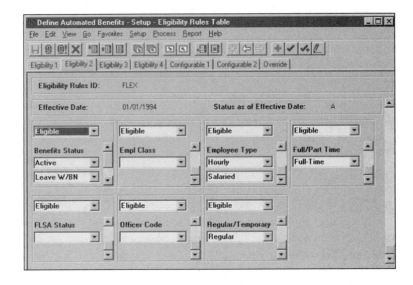

ELIGIBILITY CRITERIA

For an employee to be considered eligible for participating in the program or the plan that the eligibility rule is associated with, the employee has to pass all the criteria in the Eligibility Rules tables. It is also possible to set up exceptions to these rules by specifying the employees for whom the eligibility rules should be ignored. The system provides you with the capability to override the eligibility rules to allow an employee to participate in benefits that he or she would not normally be eligible for.

ELIGIBILITY BASED ON REGION

Sometimes, certain plans, such as an HMO plan, are available only within a particular geographical region. To accommodate such things, you can also set up geographical location eligibility rules. As illustrated by Figure 6.26, you can set up postal code ranges for employee home and work locations and tie these also to the plans.

DEFINING EVENT RULES

After the eligibility rules have been set up, you need to set up the event rules. Event rules govern the choice of options that an employee can make based on the event that has taken place and also when coverage under a plan is terminated for an employee who has become ineligible. It is very important to understand the boundaries between eligibility rules and event rules. The eligibility rules mainly evaluate the employee's eligibility for a program and the benefit plan options. Event rules are associated at the plan level. Event rules are usually defined for change in family status events like marriage, birth/adoption of child, death, divorce, and so on.

Figure 6.26
Benefits eligibility
based on region.

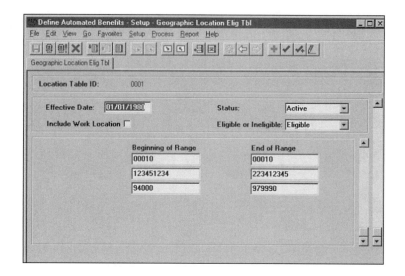

Event rules are very critical in the Benefits Administration process. To set up the event rules correctly, it is important to know the three main categories of events that can be triggered. They are as follows:

- Events triggered through employee data changes
- Events that are manually inserted
- Passive events that are predefined (such as the employee reaching retirement age)

Before you can set up event rules, you need to set up Event Classes. There are already some predefined classes delivered by PeopleSoft, example, New Hire = HIR. You can add more event classes to this list as required by your organization. Event rules are then set up to react to the occurrence of these events. This is done in the Event Rules tables.

DEFINING EVENT CLASSES

As can be seen, Figure 6.27 shows the event class Family Status Change (FSC). Figure 6.28 shows the event rules that are associated with the FSC event class, in this case FLEX. The Default Method and Select Allowed settings govern what changes can be made at the employee level. Just as you see the effect of FSC on this event rule, you need to set up the effect of other event classes.

ASSOCIATING PARAMETERS TO THE BENEFIT PROGRAM

After the Eligibility Rules, Event Rules, and the flexible credits have been defined, you are now ready to associate them to the Benefit program. Before you can set up an Automated Benefit Program, you must make sure that the Benefits Administration check box is turned on in the Installation table and also a start date is specified (see Figure 6.29). The significance of the start date is that it is used for Event Maintenance. The system looks at the employee events with a job effective date greater than or equal to the start date.

PART

II

CH

6

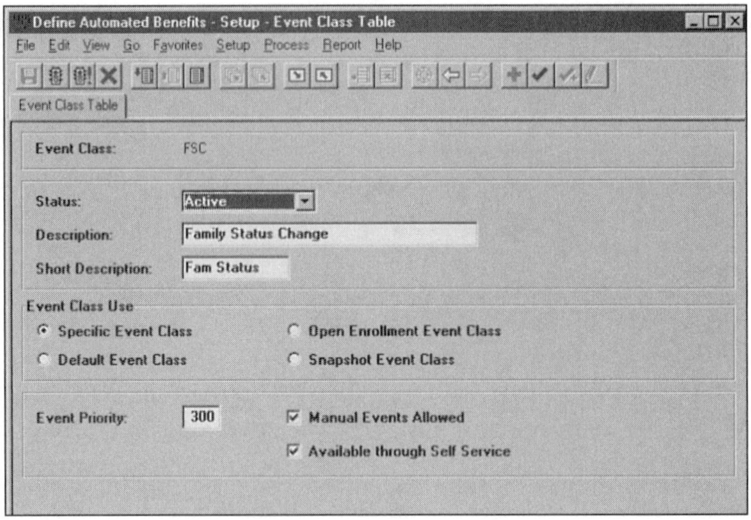

Figure 6.27
Event Class–Family
Status Change (FSC).

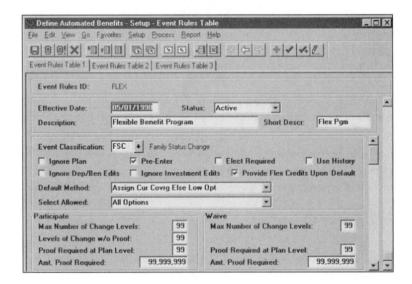

Figure 6.28
Event Rules Table
1–FLEX.

As you can see in Figure 6.29, the Benefits Administration Check box and the Benefits Admin Start Date are specified. You can now associate the eligibility rules, event rules, and flexible credit earnings with the Benefit program. When you set up the Automated Benefit Program, you need to set up a Program row (this is associated with the Plan Type 01). You can also set up a General credit as shown in Figures 6.30 and 6.31.

In Figure 6.30, the plan type and options panel, you will insert a row with Plan Type 01. Associated with the plan Type 01, at the bottom of the panel, is the eligibility rule FLEX for the option type P (program) and also a row with option type G, which defines a general credit. This is associated with a deduction code and also to a cost structure in the Cost panel as illustrated in Figure 6.31.

Figure 6.29
Installation table indicating Benefits Administration is being used and the Events Maintenance start date.

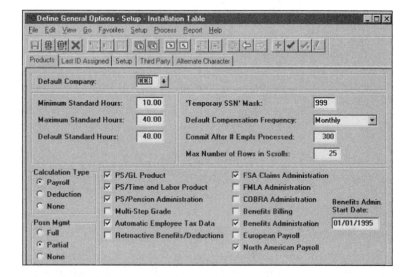

Figure 6.30
Plan Type and Option Setup for flexible credits.

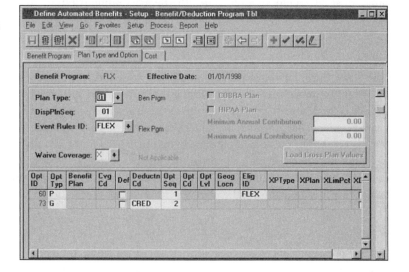

Figure 6.31
Cost of flexible credit.

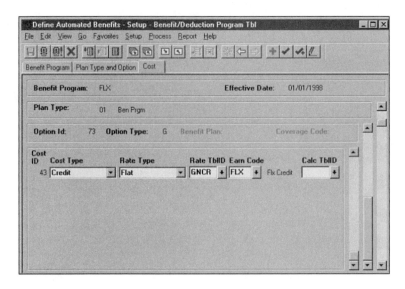

TYING THE BENEFIT PROGRAM TO THE PAY GROUP TABLE

After the benefit program has been set up, you can tie the benefit program to the Pay Group table. Now when an employee is hired, the benefit program becomes the default program at the employee level. When the Benefits Administration processes are run, such as Open Enrollment or event maintenance, the system identifies the program for which the employee is eligible and the options for which the person is eligible within the benefit program.

The Open Enrollment process is normally performed to re-enroll employees and new hires on an annual or semiannual basis. During this process, the system begins by determining the available choices for the participants. For each participant, the system identifies all the benefit options that are valid, including the associated prices and flexible credits. The system also identifies the default enrollments for new hires and those that do not have current elections, but are eligible for the program. The process ends when Open Enrollment is finalized. The Event Maintenance process is very similar to the Open Enrollment process except that it is done during the plan year to keep the information current and to keep track of the changes.

Now that you have finished defining the eligibility rules, and event rules, you are ready to do your open enrollment processing when the time comes. You are ready to start paying your employees. You will begin by setting up workgroup and taskgroup rules for your employees in Time and Labor.

INTRODUCTION TO TIME AND LABOR

PeopleSoft's Time and Labor application uses tables in Human Resources, Benefits, and Payroll to extract all the basic information about your company or companies. Tables used by Time and Labor in Human Resources include the Installation, Company, Location, Department, and Job Data tables. From the Benefits tables, Time and Labor uses the leave plan and accrual balances for determining leave accrual balances. In Payroll, Time and Labor uses the Earnings, Pay calendar, and Pay Group tables. One of the unique features of PeopleSoft's Time and Labor product is the capability to interface to Project Costing. Project costing is used by manufacturing, local, city, state, and federal government agencies. But it is also applicable to any organization who needs to track "project" costs.

TIME AND LABOR TABLES

Like all the other applications delivered by PeopleSoft, Time and Labor stores processing data in tables.

These tables can be adjusted as needed based on your company's changing business processes.

Time and Labor tables store processing data used during scheduling employees, creating time, and all areas of reporting time and updating to Payroll. You will use these tables to establish workgroups and taskgroups. The system uses the defaults specified on these tables to create time in advance of it being worked, creating employee schedules, creating time, and for labor distribution.

You will initially define your time periods for processing rules. Time periods can be days, weeks, or months. You may want to set up the time periods to match your general ledger if you interface to an application other than PeopleSoft.

Time and Labor offers you the option of scheduling your employees. If you choose to use this option, you will use the delivered Work Schedule templates. PeopleSoft recommends you use work schedule templates if your employees work on a complex or nonstandard work schedule (for example, three days on, two off), or if they work a fixed seven-day schedule but rotate through shifts (days, evenings, and nights). If you have employees that always work a repeating seven-day pattern and the same shift, the Workgroup tables will more than adequately handle this.

WORKGROUPS

Set up employees in workgroups who share identical compensation requirements. For example, members of a workgroup may include the following:

- All members are employees or non-employees. Time and Labor is designed so that you can easily report time for contract workers (non-employees). It does not send this information to Payroll but it will collect and maintain it.

PART

II

CH

6

- All members are "positive" reporting employees. This means they must submit their time in order to be paid. These are usually a company's hourly employees.

- All members are "exception" reporting employees. This means that even if an employee does not submit time, he or she will still be paid the standard hours. For example, a semimonthly employee is paid 86.67 hours a pay period. He will still be paid 86.67 hours even though he did not submit a time card for the pay period.

In addition to Workgroups, you can also keep track of information at the Time Reporting Code (TRC) level. This information is irrelevant to PeopleSoft Payroll but is useful, for example to keep track of tardiness information for the purpose of attendance monitoring. Time reporting codes can be defined as hours, dollars, or units. For example, Tardy Earnings Code (TAR) reduces regular hours in 15-minute increments. So, if I have reported Regular (REG) of 8 hours for Monday 4/12/99 and I was tardy 15 minutes, I would only be paid 7 hours and 45 minutes. (8.00 - .25 = 7.75) REG-TAR = Hours to be paid 4/12/99.

TASKGROUPS

All Time and Labor employees must belong to a taskgroup; otherwise, the system will not know how to distribute employee labor, which is one of the main functions of an automated Time and Labor application.

When you create a taskgroup, you are creating a means of grouping employees who share similar task-reporting requirements. You are also determining how you are going to administer the time they report.

For example, one group of employees may do project-level work such as developing software. When they report their time, you may want them to identify the time purposes for financial accounting, cost accounting, and project management. To do so, you may want to indicate the company they work for, the Department they are in, the Product they are working on, what the Project is, what the individual tasks are, and the Account Code. Time and Labor gives you the functionality to do this by using a Task Profile Template, as shown in Figure 6.32.

Employees will not automatically participate in Time and Labor just because they are hired into your PeopleSoft HRMS database. You must explicitly identify your Time and Labor employees and assign them to a Workgroup and Taskgroup.

Now that you have defined the workgroups and taskgroups, you are now ready to begin processing payroll.

Figure 6.32
Task Profile Template.

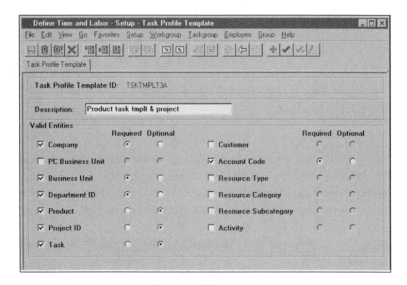

INTRODUCTION TO PAYROLL

Payroll is a comprehensive application. It is easy to use and powerful enough to meet the demanding, ever-changing payroll requirements of an organization. Like the other suite of applications, Payroll is also a table-driven application. A well-designed table-driven system puts you in control as opposed to the traditional designs, which tend to require extensive programming to make changes to something as simple as a state unemployment experience rate change. In Figure 6.33, Company State Tax Table 1 currently shows a rate of 3.50% effective back on 1/1/1993. If the rate increased effective 1/1/1999 to 3.70%, you would just need to insert a new row and input the new experience rate of 3.70(%).

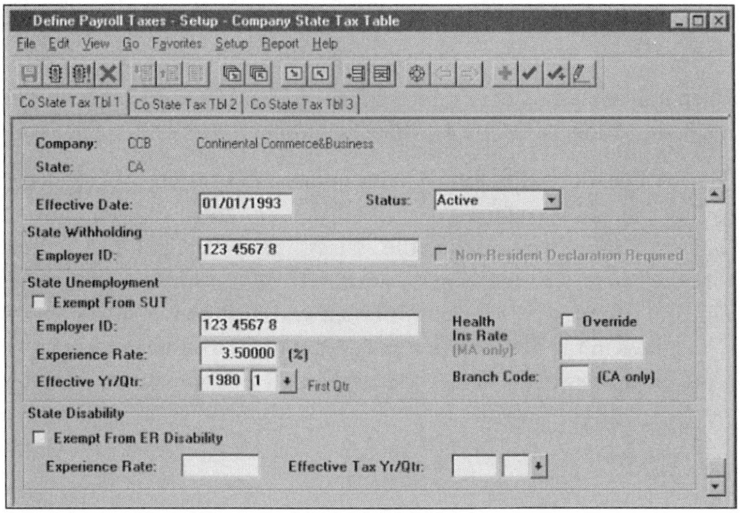

Figure 6.33
California Company
State Tax Table 1–
Unemployment Rate
example.

PeopleSoft provides and maintains the majority of tax tables in the Payroll system. PeopleSoft furnishes a complete set of tables with each release and updates as needed. Delivered are also extensive State Tax Reciprocity and Local Tax Reciprocity rules. You can also process and administer your own payroll tax filing and depositing and quarterly and year-end payroll tax reporting with the PeopleSoft Payroll application.

STORING PAYROLL INFORMATION

Let's take a look at how PeopleSoft Payroll stores information like locations for a company. Depending on how your organization is set up, you may have employees working in various locations throughout your company—some in corporate headquarters, others in remote offices or divisions scattered across the country, perhaps the world. In PeopleSoft you will store all these different locations in the Tax Location table (see Figure 6.34).

Figure 6.34
Tax Location Table 1.

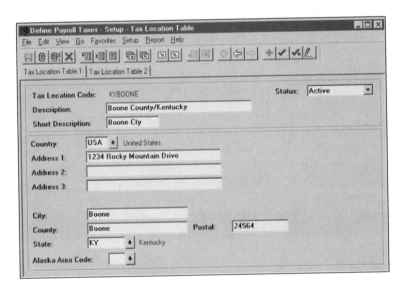

When you enter employee information, the Tax Location Table also defaults tax distribution information according to where an employee works (see Figure 6.35).

The Tax Location table also contains information specific to each location, such as the mailing address. If you need to mail information to all your employees who work in the Boone, KY office, you can find the address using the Tax Location table; you do not have to store the address of the Boone location with all the employee information. This way, if your company relocates the office from Boone to Lexington, you will only need to update the new address in the Tax Location table. And the next time you mail a packet of information to the employees in the Boone area, the new Lexington address will be used automatically.

Figure 6.35
Tax distribution
defaults.

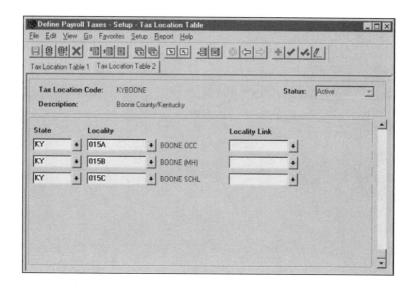

A more sophisticated example of the power of defining your processing rules via tables relates to the Benefits and Payroll application linkages. The PeopleSoft Life Insurance Table determines how the Payroll system calculates an employee's insurance based on the employee's coverage election, age, and sex. These tables typically support many different calculation options. As long as your benefit plans adhere to one of the available options, you can set up as many new plans as you need simply by adding new entries to the appropriate tables. In other words, you are no longer dependent on your in-house programmers to help you add new plans. If you are using the Benefits module, Payroll will automatically generate benefits-related deductions and employer contributions during payroll processing.

ITERATIVE PAYROLL CALCULATION FUNCTIONALITY

One of the most powerful features that PeopleSoft Payroll delivers is the iterative deduction and calculation processing functionality. Traditional payroll systems are often iterative in the sense that they allow you to enter data as many times as you need to. PeopleSoft Payroll takes this concept one step further in that it also allows for the calculation of deductions as an iterative process as well.

The system knows when it needs to calculate and when it does not need to. Typically payroll runs are large and time-consuming. Figure 6.36 illustrates that Payroll delivers functionality that allows you to "Only Calculate Where Needed." In other words, if you have made a change or an adjustment to an employee's data, the system will know that employee needs to have his/her paycheck calculated again, or when an employee's pay has not yet been calculated. In most cases, to minimize processing time, you should select "Only Calculate Where Needed".

You also have the option to "(Re)Calculate All Checks." You should use this option only when there has been a change to one of the non-employee-level tables affecting payroll

PART

II

CH

6

processing. An example of a table level change would be a change to the employee/employer deduction costs of the health benefit HMO1-Kaiser Permanente, deduction code MEDIC due to an insurance rate increase in premium.

Figure 6.36
The Pay Calculation Run control panel.

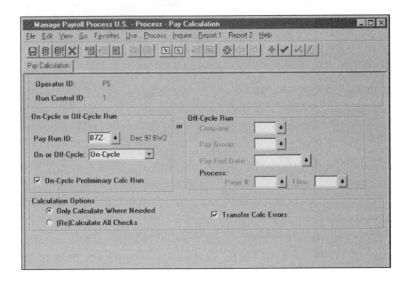

PeopleSoft Payroll uses an internal status flag on each pay earnings record to determine which employees to recalculate when the "Only Calculate Where Needed" option is turned on. When you select "(Re) Calculate All Checks," the system ignores the status flag and recalculates all pay earnings.

PeopleSoft Payroll also includes Retro Pay and extensive Garnishment processing functionality. Version 7.50 Payroll also delivered Final Check and Tip Allocation processing. Self-service web applications are also provided for employees to be able to review paychecks, change voluntary deductions, authorize direct deposit, change W-4 tax data, and request W-2 replacement.

Some employers provide retroactive pay increases to their employees. Retroactive pay processing functionality is delivered within PeopleSoft Payroll.

RETRO PAY PROGRAMS

To take advantage of the Retro Pay feature of PeopleSoft Payroll, you can set up Retro Pay programs to identify sets of Earnings Codes to be used for calculating and paying retroactive earnings. Retroactive earnings are usually for regular, shift, overtime, and double overtime payments. The Retro Pay programs you define can be assigned to specific pay groups to establish the Earnings Codes for which employees can be paid retroactively. Figures 6.37 and 6.38 illustrate the setup of a Retro Pay Program—RTP and Program Definition of the retroactive earnings that are eligible for retro pay.

Figure 6.37
Retro Pay Program
table–RTP.

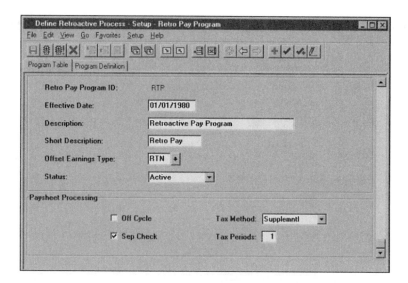

Figure 6.38
Retro Pay Program
Definition–earnings
eligible for retro pay.

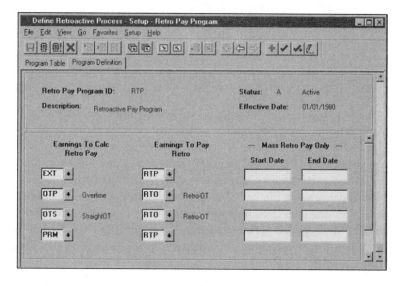

PART

II

CH

6

Within each Retro Pay Program you define, you can specify any number of Earnings Codes
as earnings for which Retro Pay can be calculated. For each of these Earnings Codes, you
can specify an Earnings Code to be used for paying the Retro pay earnings. You can review
and update the calculation results as well as rerun the calculation process as many times as
you need (see Figure 6.39).

Figure 6.39
Retro Pay review and update.

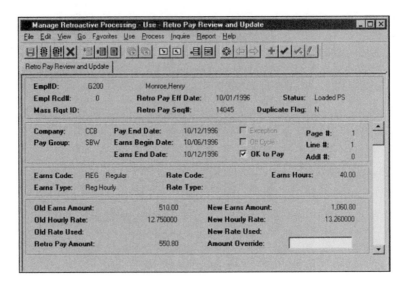

When you are satisfied with the calculation results, you can then load the Retro Pay data to the pay period for which you want to pay the retro pay.

GARNISHMENT PROCESSING

PeopleSoft Payroll provides you with unprecedented flexibility in garnishment processing. Not only can you set up ordinary automated garnishments within the Payroll system itself, the system will even process court orders that call for specific disposable earnings (DE). Disposable earnings are usually defined as Earnings less deductions required by law (statutory) like taxes = Disposable earnings. Sometimes allowable deductions can also include nonstatutory deductions like pretax medical benefits and other types of deductions that the court order specifies can be before disposable earnings. You can also set up individual deduction schedules to comply with court orders stipulating garnishments that vary in amount by pay period. There are a number of garnishment rules and disposable earnings definitions that are predefined and delivered from PeopleSoft: IRS Tax Levy, Chapter 13 Bankruptcy, and Child Support, to name a few.

The Garnishment process enables you to implement the following:

- Process multiple garnishments by priority or by proration rules. In the United States, certain states have rules regarding employees with more than one child support order or more than one writ of garnishment. When monies available for garnishment are not enough to cover all garnishments of the same type, you have the option of applying proration rules to determine how each garnishment should be handled. Figure 6.41 illustrates how you can set up a proration order.

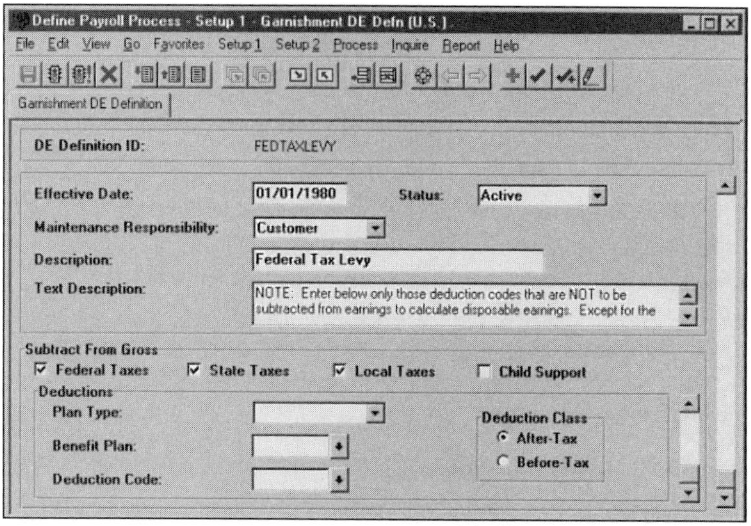

Figure 6.40
Garnishment
Disposable Earnings
Definition (U.S.).

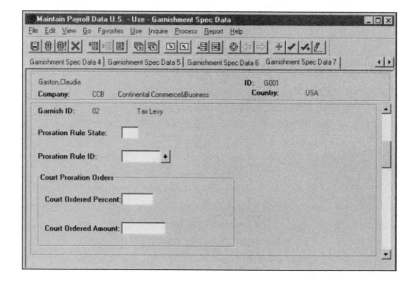

Figure 6.41
Specifying court
proration orders
(U.S. only).

- Refund garnishments. You can refund garnishment amounts withheld either partially or fully in error.

- Garnish manual checks. You can enter one-time garnishment data when entering a manual check, and the system will post the amounts and update the appropriate balances.

FINAL CHECK PROCESSING

When employment is terminated, regardless of the reason, employers are required by law to give employees their final wages. Some states require that the employee receive final wages before leaving the premises. PeopleSoft Payroll Final Check functionality eases the burden of creating final checks.

The Final Check process enables you to define a set of termination rules as a Final Check Program that identifies earnings, deductions, and leave plans to be processed when creating a final check. It then enables you to automate the application of these rules to provide a clean and speedy way of creating final checks. As long as the employee is set up in the payroll system, even if they were only temporarily employed (not from a temporary agency), the employee could be processed using the final check functionality. This functionality is not intended to be used for non-employees.

TIPS ALLOCATION PROCESSING

Most large food serving establishments are required to report additional information to the IRS concerning the establishments' receipts and the employees' tip income. A large establishment is any establishment that normally employs more than 10 people on a typical business day. If you are required to allocate tips, you will allocate according to establishments. Establishments are defined as individual restaurants, hotels, and so on. If you have 15 restaurants, you have to allocate tips separately for each of them. Figure 6.42 illustrates tip allocations by establishment, Tips Establishment ID 001.

Figure 6.42
Tip allocations by establishment data.

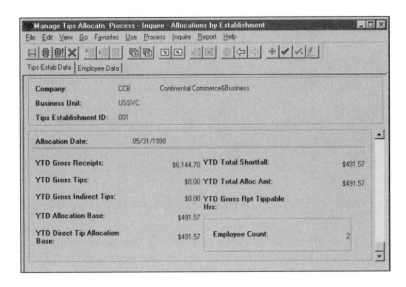

Allocated tips are not subject to tax withholding. However, the amount of allocated tips must be reported on the employee's Form W-2 in box 8. Therefore, you should store each allocated amount on the employee's earnings record and maintain Year-to-Date balances. Figure 6.43 provides the allocated tip detail for an individual employee.

Figure 6.43
Tip Allocations by
Employee Data.

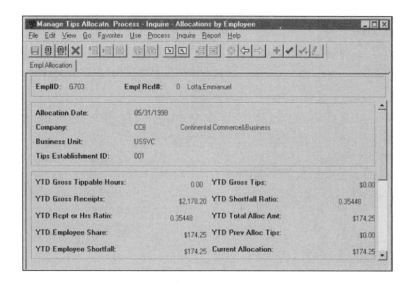

Up to now we have been defining and using the following products provided by PeopleSoft: HRMS, Base Benefits, Benefits Administration, Time and Labor, and Payroll. There will be situations where you might use all the products mentioned except Payroll. In these cases, you can use PeopleSoft's Payroll Interface product to exchange data between your own in-house payroll system or another third- party vendor.

INTRODUCTION TO PAYROLL INTERFACE

The purpose of PeopleSoft's Payroll Interface application is to exchange data between your PeopleSoft Human Resources system and your in-house legacy system or another third-party vendor application like SAP or Oracle's payroll product. (This also includes service bureaus that process payroll like Automatic Data Processsing [ADP]). Processing in PeopleSoft Payroll Interface will consist of calculating and confirming employee deductions and exporting and importing data between your payroll system and PeopleSoft.

When you implement PeopleSoft Payroll Interface, one of the major decisions you will make is which pay groups to set up. A *pay group* is a set of employees within a company for processing. The system processes one pay group at a time. The only earnings required for Payroll Interface are regular, overtime, and holiday. These are required fields in the Pay Group table (see Figure 6.44).

Payroll Interface does not calculate taxes, as that process is done either in your legacy system or by the third party. You can run the Deduction Calculation process as many times as you need to before you confirm them for export to your payroll system.

PART

II

CH

6

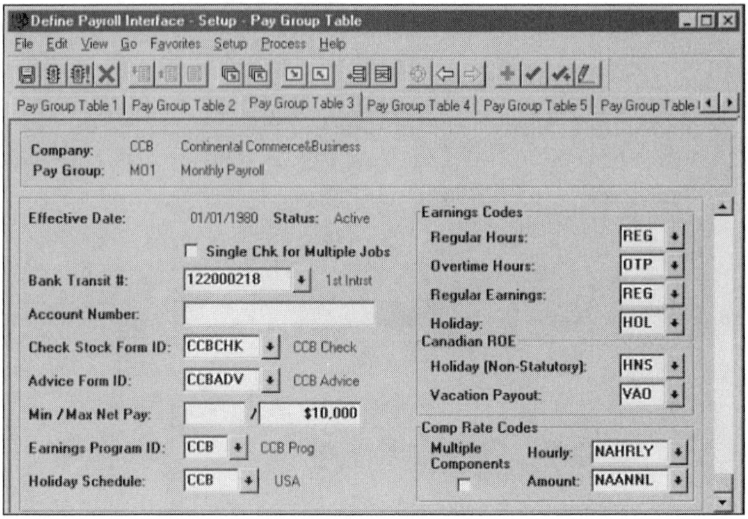

Figure 6.44
Pay Group table
showing required
Earnings Codes are
Regular, Overtime,
and Holiday.

RECORD TABLE AND RECORD FIELD TABLE

The PeopleSoft Record Table and PeopleSoft Record Field table determine the employee data to be extracted in the Payroll Interface process. PeopleSoft delivers all the definitions required to extract PeopleSoft records and fields. If you make changes to your PeopleSoft records and fields, you will need to update the PeopleSoft record and PeopleSoft Record Field tables on the PS Tables panel. No COBOL modifications are necessary.

INTERFACE FIELD TABLE

You will use the Interface Field Table to define your payroll system fields and the characteristics of those fields for Payroll Interface. A Field ID is required for each field you define. If your payroll system uses Field IDs, you may want to use those. If not, you can define your own Field ID for each field in your payroll system (see Figure 6.45).

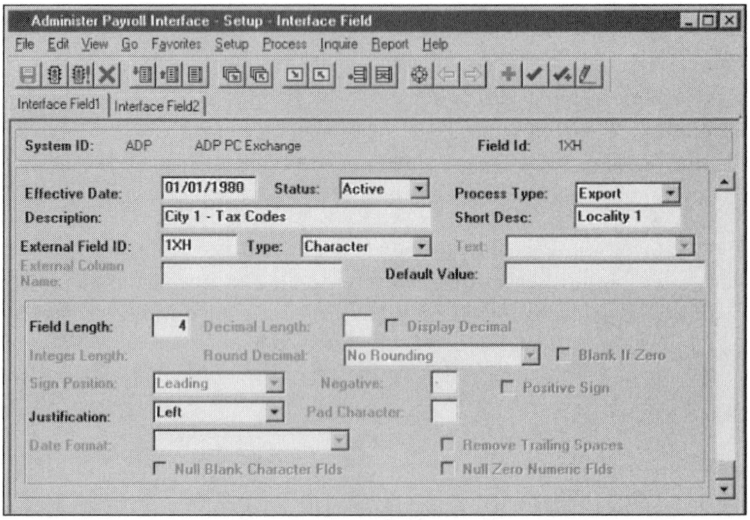

Figure 6.45
Interface Field ID
definition panel.

When you define a field of your payroll system to interface with your PeopleSoft system, you also need to define the rules for getting the data for that field from PeopleSoft. You will do this in the Interface Field 2 panel where you can specify which PeopleSoft fields the data comes from and any data translation rules for the data. Figure 6.46 illustrates the field name definition in PeopleSoft = PSField 1 and the corresponding value to that field in the payroll interface is defined in "PI Field."

Figure 6.46
Interface Field data
translation panel.

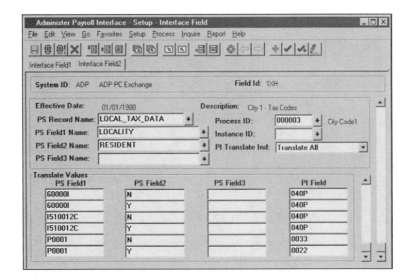

THE EXPORT PROCESS

The Export process is divided into two steps: compare and export. Compare involves extracting the employee data from PeopleSoft, translating and formatting this data as required, and then comparing the current values to those previously exported to your payroll system—identifying and recording the changed values.

After the compare step is completed, the export step creates the actual sequential output file. Thus the export file can be recreated when necessary, without the extensive processing required for the compare step.

The Import process imports checks and balance data from your payroll system into PeopleSoft tables so that you can view them online in your PeopleSoft database. Figure 6.47 is the output delivered back from ADP PC Exchange showing what was processed for employee "TATE, Ronnie" for the earnings and deductions.

As you can see, the Payroll Interface product is fairly straightforward to use. There are also some other products that PeopleSoft provides that your company may be interested in using if you do not outsource business processes, like Flexible Spending Account Administration and Pension Administration.

PART

II

CH

6

Figure 6.47
Interface Check
Summary detail.

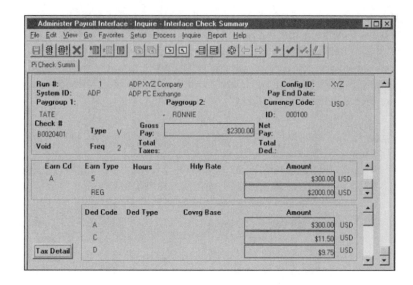

INTRODUCTION TO FLEXIBLE SPENDING ACCOUNT (FSA) ADMINISTRATION

FSA Administration is designed specifically to allow North American and Canadian organizations to manage their healthcare and dependent care flexible spending accounts. PeopleSoft FSA Administration is designed to be a supplement to PeopleSoft's Base Benefits application. You will not be able to run the processes and procedures until you have set up your Base Benefits system.

PeopleSoft FSA Administration does not support the multiple currency conversion required to perform premium calculations. For example, if you pay employees in Swiss francs and enroll them in a benefit program that uses U.S. dollars, PeopleSoft FSA Administration cannot perform a currency conversion to any base currency. If you do not use multiple currencies—for example, you pay employees in francs and enroll them in a benefit program that uses francs—you can easily process them using PeopleSoft FSA Administration.

SCHEDULING CLAIMS PROCESSING

With FSA Administration, you can schedule claims processing based on your operational needs. You can also choose a minimum check option. When you choose this option, the system automatically puts claims under the minimum into a pending file. When the total of the pending claim reaches the minimum, the system will print a check for the employee. You can also process pending claims. For example, if an employee submits a claim for more than the amount in the FSA account, you have the option to pay the claim and hold the excess in a pending account.

As mentioned earlier, in addition to being able to process FSA Claims, you can also process Pension Administration using PeopleSoft.

INTRODUCTION TO PENSION ADMINISTRATION

PeopleSoft Pension Administration enables you to automate and streamline your pension administration functions—from data storage and benefit calculations to retiree administration and payments. The system is integrated with PeopleSoft Human Resources, Payroll and Benefits, so your data collection and administrative chores can be done efficiently, with no duplication of effort or lengthy transfer of information between systems. The system assumes that a third-party trustee will determine tax withholding and calculate and print your final pension checks; a trustee extract provides the trustee with the necessary payment information.

PeopleSoft Pension Administration enables you to produce on-demand pension calculations for individuals or to schedule batch calculation runs. Estimates and "what if" calculations automatically incorporate the projection rules you have defined. Effective-dated plan rules enable you to produce historical calculations and allow for easy administration of grandfathering and "better of" benefits. You can use calculation results for employee counseling and benefit statements. The panels shown in Figures 6.48 and 6.49 provide easy access to the calculation results, and calculation worksheets offer detailed calculation breakdowns, showing each step used to produce a final amount in all its optional forms.

Figure 6.48
Benefits Calculation
Results panel.

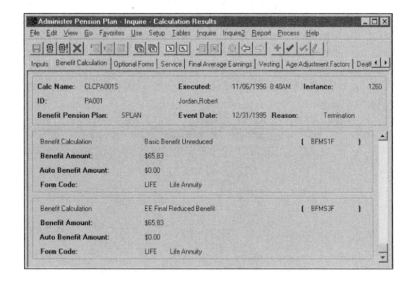

Figure 6.49
Optional Forms
Results panel.

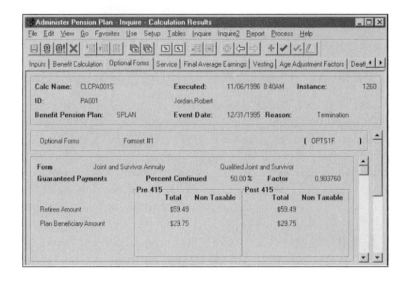

THE OPTIONAL FORMS PANEL

The Optional Forms panel will show each allowable payment formed offered by the plan. Single participants are ineligible for Joint & Survivor. Forms are described in terms of the Form, the number of years of Guaranteed Payments (for example 5 means five years, not five monthly payments), and the Percent Continued to the designated spouse beneficiary when the retiree dies. The Factor is the factor used to convert the benefit from its normal form to the optional form. Figures 6.50 and Figures 6.51 illustrate the calculation capabilities of the pension administration module. Figure 6.50 displays the "Final Average Earnings," based on Actual Earnings based on parameters you have defined. Figure 6.51 calculates the "Covered Compensation" for an employee averaging the actual Taxable Wage base for 35 years up to and including the year the employee meets Social Security retirement age.

Figure 6.50
Final Average
Earnings results
panel.

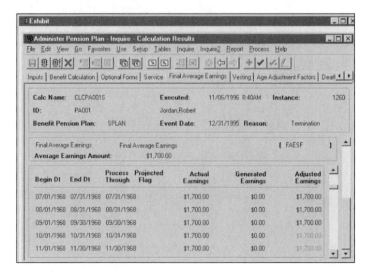

The Final Average Earnings function provides the amount calculated according to the plan's averaging rules that have been set up.

Figure 6.51
Covered Compensation results panel.

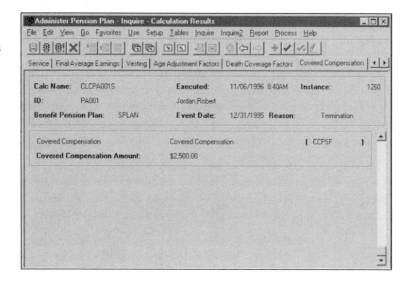

COVERED COMPENSATION FUNCTION

The Covered Compensation function calculates the Covered Compensation for the employee by averaging the Taxable Wage Base for the 35 years up to and including the year the employee reaches Social Security retirement age.

SOCIAL SECURITY FUNCTION

The Social Security function estimates an employee's Social Security Primary Insurance Amount (PIA) (see Figure 6.52).

Figure 6.52
Social Security results panel.

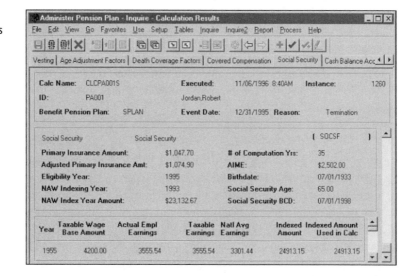

PART

II

CH

6

The Social Security results panel shows intermediate results as well as the final, adjusted PIA.

As you can see, PeopleSoft's Pension Administration system is comprehensive and complete. For you to be able to arrive at all the results that are displayed in Figure 6.52, you will need to enter all your calculation parameters. This will be the biggest implementation task you will undertake besides converting your employee data. PeopleSoft Pension Administration takes a modular approach to setting up the calculation rules. Because the modules are heavily interdependent, a key part of your analysis will be diagrams showing the relationships of the modules you need. Documenting and diagramming these relationships is extremely important, as it will be impossible for you to create any module until all of its prerequisite modules are in place. After you have completed your analysis, you will use your diagram as a road map for actually entering the data in the system.

This completes the discussion on the Human Resources products currently delivered by PeopleSoft. Next is a brief discussion about Global payroll functionality that is coming in Release 8 of PeopleSoft and a view of the "PeopleSoft Side of HRMS."

SPECIAL CASE: INTRODUCTION TO EUROPEAN PAYROLL

Version 7.50 delivered sound European functionality with the other PeopleSoft product lines, including support for the Economic and Monetary Union (EMU) that went into effect in Europe on 1/1/99.

Release 7.50 of Human Resources also added multinational support for Belgium and The Netherlands.

As of the time of this publication that are no details even at a high level of what will be included in the European Payroll product. Based only on speculation, the European Payroll product will be fully integrated with the Global Human Resources product. You will have to use the PeopleSoft Global Human Resources Product. Some of the issues to be addressed with the European Payroll product will be designed around changes due to social responsibilities for benefits, working hours, data protection, and labor law and regulations in Europe.

It will definitely be exciting when the product does become generally available because there currently is no other software application available to address the European marketplaces need.

THE PEOPLESIDE OF PEOPLESOFT HRMS

Since its launch in 1987, PeopleSoft has carefully cultivated the human touch. The Human Resources Management product has been the foundation software from which PeopleSoft has grown to now include financial, manufacturing, distribution, and student administration software. "PeoplePeople" all over the globe are committed to what is referred to as "positively outrageous customer service." There are even People Snaks and People News.

"People" is in everything PeopleSoft staff talk about. The customers are the most important people to PeopleSoft. PeopleSoft designates "PeopleDollars" for their customers to vote on what new functionality or enhancements they want to see in the product.

SUMMARY

PeopleSoft's culture is truly unique, even in a sector where almost all suppliers seem to emphasize human values. PeopleSoft is the undisputed leader in human resources software. PeopleSoft is comparatively easy to customize with the company's application tool set, PeopleTools. Due to the distributed nature of the PeopleSoft architecture, which is based on clearly defined components, re-engineering to accommodate future technology trends should also not prove too difficult. PeopleSoft Human Resources software can grow and change with your company's ever-changing needs and business requirements.

PART

II

CH

6

CHAPTER 7

GROWING WITH FINANCIAL MANAGEMENT

In this chapter

by Denise Hollo

In today's rapidly changing business environment, organizations require financial software that is more sophisticated and flexible than has been provided by traditional accounting packages.

For example, in the past, a reorganization of an organization's management reporting structure, let alone its legal structure, typically required an IT resource to make the required changes. With the rash of mergers, acquisitions, restructuring, and globalization that occurs now, today's financial management system must enable users to make frequent changes to its structure without the assistance of IT personnel.

As another example, in the traditional environment, the process of analyzing financial information was often very cumbersome. To see the detail that made up a number, a user would have to either wade through mountains of reports or make a call to the appropriate department (for example, Accounts Payable) to have it researched. Analysts often had to enter data from multiple reports into a spreadsheet to perform analysis. Clearly, information must be easily obtainable from the system, empowering users to perform analysis and manage profitability without redundant data entry or inefficient steps.

PeopleSoft's Financial Management product line delivers a new breed of financial software to cope with today's ever-evolving business horizon. It provides a streamlined, flexible, and scalable approach to the management of accounting and more.

This chapter explores the processes that are addressed by PeopleSoft Financial Management. It consists of a preview of the modules included in the Financial Management suite, followed by a section for each module. These sections discuss the business processes that PeopleSoft enables you to perform, touching on some of the functionality available to facilitate these processes. The next chapter, "Financial Modules," focuses more on the specific features delivered with each module and tips for implementation.

PEOPLESOFT FINANCIAL MANAGEMENT PROCESSES

PeopleSoft's Financial Management applications comprise the traditional accounting functions, plus some additional components to enable enhanced financial information management. These include the following:

- General Ledger
- Payables
- Receivables
- Asset Management
- Budgets
- Projects
- Treasury
- Expenses

Figure 7.1 shows these components and how they interact with each other and with other PeopleSoft modules.

Figure 7.1
The PeopleSoft Financial Management modules are tightly integrated to each other and to other PeopleSoft modules.

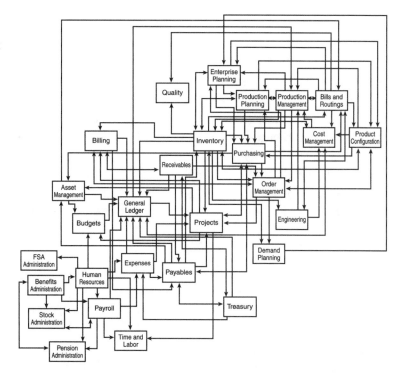

Each of these applications is designed to address the needs of a specific business function and to integrate seamlessly with other PeopleSoft modules. Although Chapter 8, "Financial Modules," provides a more detailed explanation of each of these components, it is important in this chapter to understand each application and the processes it performs.

GENERAL LEDGER

PeopleSoft General Ledger is a central component of the Financial Management product line. It encompasses the following processes:

- Structuring the Organization
- Defining Accounting Elements
- Entering, Importing, and Processing Journal Entries
- Processing Allocations
- Performing Consolidations
- Managing Year-End Processing
- Reviewing Financial Information

- Maintaining Budgets
- General Ledger Integration

These processes are explained in the following sections.

STRUCTURING THE ORGANIZATION

PeopleSoft General Ledger provides the ability to define your legal structure and maintain separate, balanced sets of books via business units.

A *business unit* is a representation of an entity within your organization, with its own set of processing rules. Although many organizations use business units to represent legal entities, you can define business units to represent operational or reporting entities as well. You can define as many business units as you need to capture the structure of your organization.

After your organizational structure is defined, you can begin to define the accounting elements that will enable you to capture accounting information the way you need to see it.

DEFINING ACCOUNTING ELEMENTS

The major accounting elements in PeopleSoft are ChartFields, Calendars, and Ledgers.

CHARTFIELDS   ChartFields define the information that you can capture with every financial transaction, including those that come from other PeopleSoft applications. ChartFields can be different for each business unit, or can be shared across business units.

PeopleSoft delivers predefined ChartFields that can help get you started quickly. These ChartFields include: Account, Department, Product, Project, Statistics Code, Currency Code, and Affiliate (to facilitate intercompany and consolidation).

Different industries might use the same ChartField to represent different kinds of information. For example, a consumer goods company might use the Product ChartField to represent types of goods that it manufactures or sells, whereas an investment firm might use the Product ChartField to differentiate the various funds it manages. If the delivered ChartFields do not support your company's structure, you can change their names or add new ChartFields.

The system edits each ChartField on every transaction, and can also edit them in combination according to rules you define (for example, a particular department can only use certain accounts).

You can summarize any ChartField by building a hierarchical tree over its values. Multiple trees can be defined for each ChartField, and the trees can be effective-dated.

CALENDARS   You use PeopleSoft Accounting Calendars to define the timespans you use to view and report on your data. Calendars are completely customizable, so you can define accounting periods to reflect your organization's fiscal and reporting periods. You define the number of periods and the beginning and ending dates for each period.

You can define multiple calendars, for example, separate calendars for actuals versus budgeting and forecasting. You can also share calendars across business units.

LEDGERS   You define PeopleSoft Ledgers, or sets of books that you can maintain within each business unit. You can define separate ledgers for financial, budget, and nonfinancial (statistical) transactions. You can share ledgers across multiple business units.

Ledgers also facilitate the Multibook feature, which enables you to capture transactions in multiple base currencies for a single business unit. Multibook functionality allows you to maintain a real-time balance in multiple currencies without having to run a monthly process to translate data.

ChartFields, calendars, and ledgers provide the basic infrastructure for your financial system. The next section explores the processes for making online journal entries, importing them into the General Ledger from another source, and processing journals.

ENTERING, IMPORTING, AND PROCESSING JOURNAL ENTRIES

The journal entry is the heart of the General Ledger. PeopleSoft provides the capability to enter journals online, including a number of features that make the process easy. When journals are in the system, they can be edited and posted. PeopleSoft also provides facilities to import journals from other sources.

ONLINE JOURNAL ENTRY   PeopleSoft General Ledger journals consist of two parts: the header and the entry lines. The header contains the identifying information for the journal. The entry lines contain the ChartField values and amounts for the journal.

PeopleSoft provides two features to maintain control over the online journal entry process:

- Control totals enable you to check the accuracy of your entry when you are entering numerous journal lines.

- Journal approval gives you the facility to control who can approve journal entries within a user-defined set of rules.

You can optionally set up the journals as adjusting or reversing entries, and you can specify currency information in the journal.

If you are entering a journal similar to one you have already entered, you can copy the original journal and change it. If the journal recurs on more than just a one-off basis, you can use either of the following two different types of Standard Journal Entries to facilitate entering journals of a repetitive nature:

- Use Recurring journals when you need to automate an entry that consistently charges the same amounts to the same accounting ChartFields. For example, you might set up monthly rent or amortization expense as a recurring journal.

- Use Template journals when an entry recurs with the same ChartFields but the amounts vary with each occurrence. For example, you might use template journals to set up utility and telecommunications charges or accrued interest.

You can automatically schedule either type of Standard Journal Entry.

After a journal entry is complete, you run the Journal Edit process to ensure that it adheres to the rules you have defined for your organization. The system checks to make sure that the journal is posting to an open period, is balanced if balancing is required, has valid ChartFields (alone and in combination), and matches control totals if applicable.

When a journal has been successfully edited with no errors, you run a simple process to post journals to the ledger. At this point, your journal entry cycle is complete.

SPECIAL JOURNAL ENTRY FEATURES   PeopleSoft supports several journal entry features that warrant mentioning:

- OpenItem Accounting enables you to monitor "subledger" detail for accounts that maintain a zero balance. For example, you might use OpenItem processing for employee advance accounts to ensure that the amount of the advance has been cleared and the items closed.

- InterUnit Accounting facilitates the automatic creation of offsetting Due To/Due From journal lines when you specify that the transaction is to be between two business units. This creation occurs during the Journal Edit process. For example, a central purchasing facility might buy computers on behalf of multiple business units. These computers can be "charged" to the appropriate business units, and the system will automatically create the offsetting InterUnit entries.

- Alternate Account is used to specify an alternative account code in addition to the original Account charged on a single transaction. This capability can be used to meet multinational statutory reporting requirements, or it can be used to facilitate statutory versus management reporting.

- VAT Transactions, to record the Value Added Tax required in certain countries, are supported in the General Ledger for non-receivable/non-payable items. VAT entries created in Receivables and Payables can also be posted using the VAT Posting feature. The VAT features require some additional analysis and setup.

- Average Balances, in conjunction with the nVision reporting tool, enable you to report prior day and current average balances. You can set up the system to calculate average balances on selected ChartFields, ChartField values and summarization rules, and time periods.

- Multiple Currency features enable you to adapt to today's globalization trends. PeopleSoft supports the European Monetary Union requirements for the euro, and provides a number of features to facilitate entry, processing, and reporting of multicurrency transactions.

IMPORTING JOURNALS   In addition to online journal entry, PeopleSoft provides two methods to import journals from other sources:

- Spreadsheet Journal Entry provides a front-end interface that enables you to create journals in a spreadsheet and import them into the ledger.

- Journal Generator is a PeopleSoft facility you run to find entries created in other PeopleSoft Financials modules and generate journals for the General Ledger that can be edited and posted. For example, entries produced from Payables from entry and payment of vouchers are imported into the General Ledger by using Journal Generator. Journal Generator also provides a generic definition and templates to facilitate importing entries from non-PeopleSoft systems.

This section covered journal entries and the features available to enter, import, edit, and post them. The next section looks at some of the processes that are performed on existing transactions.

PROCESSING ALLOCATIONS

As journal entries are accumulated in your general ledger, you will occasionally have the need to allocate balances across multiple areas in your organization. For example, you may have accrued expenses for telecommunications services in one department on behalf of many departments in your business unit.

PeopleSoft provides allocation functionality to enable you to perform allocations based on statistical quantities such as headcount or square footage. You can allocate across any ChartField, including product or project. PeopleSoft provides the capability to define multiple-step, or "stepdown" allocations.

Allocations create journal entries that can be edited and posted like any other journal entry.

After you have defined an allocation, you can save the specification to be rerun on an ad hoc basis, or you can schedule it to run automatically.

PERFORMING CONSOLIDATIONS

Organizations with more than one business unit will probably need to produce reports on a consolidated basis. Consolidation adds up all the assets and liabilities of the involved business units, and eliminates redundant entries such as intercompany and minority interest transactions, to produce a combined statement of the organization's financial position as if it were a single entity.

PeopleSoft consolidation is built upon trees that you define to represent your organization's hierarchical consolidation structure. You can perform consolidations on business units or, if required, other ChartFields. PeopleSoft provides an Equitization process that helps you to account for changes in consolidated results related to modification of a parent's investment in its subsidiaries. Reports are available to view the results of your consolidation.

MANAGING YEAR-END PROCESSING

PeopleSoft provides several features to help you transition smoothly from one fiscal year to the next:

- Managing accounting periods is easy with PeopleSoft. You control which periods are open for posting through a simple panel. To close a period, you simply modify the From or Through period and year.

- Automated Year-End Adjustments is a feature that enables you to isolate your closing adjustments into a period and year that you define. This frees you to choose whether to include adjusting entries in only those reports and inquiries where they will not cause a distortion of results.

- Defining Closing Rules is a very flexible process by which you decide precisely how you want to calculate retained earnings and carry forward your balances into the next year.

REVIEWING FINANCIAL INFORMATION

You've defined your business, entered your journals, performed your allocations and consolidations, and closed your books. Now how do you look at the data in a meaningful way?

PeopleSoft provides a variety of inquiries and reports that can help you locate, analyze, and summarize information to support research and decision-making needs. You can inquire on ledgers in summary and detail, journals, accounting lines, OpenItem accounts and status (open, closed, or both), and more. You can even drill down from a ledger transaction to the detail transactions in other PeopleSoft products such as Payables, Receivables, or Asset Management.

PeopleSoft's nVision reporting tool provides a robust reporting environment with which you can perform analysis and produce statutory and management reporting.

MAINTAINING BUDGETS

PeopleSoft General Ledger enables you to define and store budget information in a separate ledger, much like statistical or actual data. You can enter budget information in a variety of ways, including copying from spreadsheets, copying from other ledgers, entering summarized amounts and allocating, entering a lump sum and spreading across periods, or simply entering amounts directly.

If you have PeopleSoft Budgets, the budget preparation process is even more robust and easily managed, as you will see in the "Budgets" section later in this chapter.

GENERAL LEDGER INTEGRATION

PeopleSoft General Ledger is very closely integrated with all the other Financial Management modules, plus many of the Distribution and some Manufacturing modules. Figure 7.2 depicts all the modules that interface with the General Ledger.

Figure 7.2
PeopleSoft General Ledger is the central point of integration for the Financial Management modules.

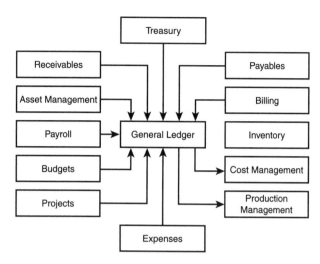

In summary, PeopleSoft General Ledger handles everything you need to assess and manage your financial status, from defining your legal and organizational structure to capturing and analyzing transactions and producing your legal and management reporting. Its tight integration with the other modules eliminates redundant data entry and facilitates quick and easy user access to information. The next sections discuss the Financial Management modules that feed and interact with the General Ledger.

PAYABLES

PeopleSoft Payables automates the processing of invoices and payments for vendors with whom your organization does business. It incorporates the following processes:

- Maintaining Vendor Information
- Managing Vouchers
- Processing Payments
- Taking Advantage of Global Features
- Integrating with Other Modules

These processes are explored in the following sections.

MAINTAINING VENDOR INFORMATION

Cost-containment initiatives require organizations to closely manage their vendor relationships to optimize cash flow. Capturing the right information and keeping it accessible enables you to research issues, manage conversations, and negotiate better payment terms.

PeopleSoft provides the means to enter a wealth of information for each vendor you establish, including:

- Basic vendor information such as name, employee versus supplier, status, and persistence, among others
- One or more physical addresses
- One or more vendor locations, for example, ordering, pricing, invoicing, remitting, and returning
- Vendor Internet information
- Procurement options to specify voucher processing rules such as approvals and error handling
- Tax options, including sales/use tax and VAT
- Payment options to specify how the vendor will be paid
- EFT payment options if the vendor is to be paid by EFT
- Vendor bank account information for routing of EFT payments
- Vendor contact information
- Informational items such as SIC codes and comments

You decide how much or how little of this information you need beyond the minimal required fields to effectively represent and manage your relationships.

On an ongoing basis, you can enter and catalog notes from conversations that you have with your vendors to keep track of the status of any outstanding issues or requests. A number of inquiries are provided so that vendor balances, voucher and payment information, vouchers on hold, overdue payments, or withholding information are at your fingertips for a specific vendor when you are on the phone with the vendor or an employee.

MANAGING VOUCHERS

In PeopleSoft Payables, a voucher can represent an invoice, request for payment, or adjustment. Vouchers can be entered online or interfaced into the system from an outside source using EDI Manager.

As depicted in Figure 7.3, the voucher processing life cycle comprises a number of steps, some required, others optional. You can enter vouchers on a standalone basis, or you can optionally enter them in control groups, or batches, that utilize control totals for accuracy and provide additional control features. When voucher entry is complete, the system edits the vouchers to ensure that they are complete and valid. You can optionally require vouchers to go through an approval process before they can be paid. Vouchers are posted within accounts payable to create accounting entries, which are then sent to the General Ledger as a journal entry whenever the Journal Generator process is run.

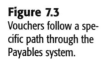
Figure 7.3
Vouchers follow a specific path through the Payables system.

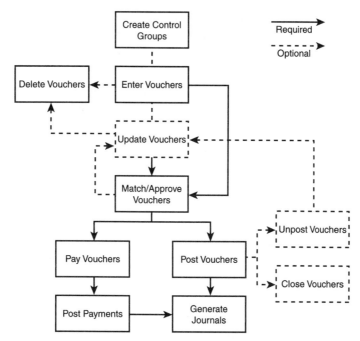

You can enter vouchers using a number of different entry formats, each with a specific use:

- Express vouchers enable you to enter simple vouchers quickly.

- Standard vouchers provide some additional flexibility.

- PO vouchers provide the facility to copy information from the purchase order or receiver, and enable you to control the matching process.

- Adjustment vouchers enable you to enter debit or credit memos related to a voucher that has already been entered, and to specify to the system the relationship between the adjustment and the original voucher.

- Journal vouchers provide you with the ability to reclassify accounting entries for a voucher that has already been posted without having to reverse and repost all the entries associated with the original voucher.

- Recurring voucher contracts enable you to establish and schedule repetitive vouchers that occur regularly, for example, rent or maintenance payments.

- You can save any voucher as a template voucher that you can call up to save time in entering similar future vouchers from the same vendor.

You can use control groups with any of these voucher types. Control groups give you a way of grouping vouchers, assigning them to various people for entry, and monitoring the status of open groups. You can specify defaults at the control group level to segregate vouchers that require different processing rules and save entry time. For example, you might have a different payment term for a group of vouchers that is consistent for the group but may override the payment terms specified for the vendors. You could specify the overriding payment term on the control group, and it will default to all the vouchers entered for that group.

Control groups also provide numerous balancing and control features that you can use to control the posting and payment of vouchers within a group.

Businesses can calculate, track, and report on tax information from entered vouchers, including sales/use tax and VAT. You can also enter discount information on the voucher, and the system will create the appropriate entries after the voucher is posted.

For vouchers that have been entered online, the voucher edit process runs automatically when you save the voucher in the system. Each voucher is checked to ensure that it is balanced, is not a duplicate invoice, and contains valid ChartField values and combinations. For vouchers that are loaded from an external source, you run the Voucher Edit process that performs the same functions in a batch mode for the interfaced vouchers.

You run a voucher posting process to create accounting entries from the vouchers that have been entered and passed the system edit. In addition to the ChartFields values and amounts entered on the voucher lines, system-generated entries such as discount, freight, and tax expense entries, use tax liability, and AP liability are created at the time the voucher is posted. When Journal Generator is run, these accounting entries are formatted into a journal entry and loaded into the General Ledger. When the Load Assets process is run, the system distributes accounting entries associated with an asset to the Asset Management module.

With the proper security, you can unpost, correct, and repost vouchers. If the accounting entries have already been sent to the General Ledger via Journal Generator or to Asset Management via the Load Assets process, the system creates reversing entries when you unpost.

You can require vouchers to be approved before they are made available for payment. If the voucher is PO-related, you can also require that the voucher be successfully matched with the invoice, receiver, and/or inspection notice prior to allowing payment. You are in control over when to run matching and how to process exceptions.

Let's take a look now at how PeopleSoft Payables processes payments from the vouchers that have been entered.

PROCESSING PAYMENTS

The Payables module is designed to help you keep your vendors satisfied, take advantage of early payment discounts, and better manage your organization's cash flow. When you set up vendor payment terms, bank information, and business calendar information, you are establishing the tools for the system to help you manage the payment process. In addition to these, you establish pay cycles to automate the selection and creation of payments according to your rules.

When a voucher is saved, the system automatically schedules it for payment by calculating the discount and net due dates based on the payment terms, and then calculating a scheduled due date based on the business calendar. You can override the scheduled due date at any time, or schedule multiple payments for a single voucher by using a panel in the voucher panel group.

A *pay cycle* is a collection of rules surrounding the selection and creation of payments. You specify

- Date Criteria including pay through and payment dates for this pay cycle and the next scheduled pay cycle (to establish discounts that may be lost), and accounting date for the payments.

- Preferences surrounding validation of business days available for payment, date change increment and whether or not to increment dates automatically, approval of the pay cycle, and other information.

- Source Criteria to specify whether you are paying Payables vouchers, Expense payments, or Treasury settlements.

- Business Unit Criteria to specify from which AP business unit(s) to look for scheduled payments.

- Bank/Payment Method Criteria to specify the bank(s), account(s), and payment method(s) for the payments to be generated. Available payment methods include system check, EFT, draft, and wire report.

- Pay Group Criteria to specify from which pay groups to select vouchers to pay. Pay groups allow you to group vendors that need to be paid under similar conditions, such as frequency, so that you can schedule them separately using this feature in the pay cycle.

- Bank Account Replacement to specify an alternative bank account from which to draw payments if the current bank account runs out of available funding.

With pay cycles, you can automate the selection of vouchers to pay. You also have the option to review the payments that have been selected prior to creating the actual payment records. The system will alert you to any potential lost discounts for vouchers not due for this pay cycle run but due before the next scheduled pay cycle, and gives you the option to include those payments in this run. Payables also alerts you to vendors with negative balances and foreign currency payments for which there is no current exchange rate.

After a pay cycle is approved, the payments can be generated. You specify the order in which checks are created and sorted. EFTs can be generated and sent to the bank in any of several predefined formats, and EFT data can be printed. Paper checks can be printed from the system, with a number of features. If you are using prenumbered stock, you can confirm the check numbers before you start printing and specify a number of alignment checks. Payables provides a restart feature that enables you to reprint a single check or a range of checks, with the option to reuse the check numbers or generate new ones. You can customize any payment format to fit your organization's needs.

In addition to regularly scheduled pay cycles, you can create an Express Check from the system on demand for any entered voucher that cannot wait for the next cycle to be paid. You can also manually enter payment information for a voucher that was paid outside the system.

After payments are generated, you run the payment posting process to create accounting entries. When Journal Generator is run, these accounting entries are formatted into a journal entry and loaded into the General Ledger.

You can cancel payments with the option to reopen the vouchers and reschedule for payment, reopen the vouchers and put them on hold, or close the vouchers altogether. The appropriate accounting entries are generated when you run payment post and, if you are closing the vouchers, voucher post.

Payables provides bank reconciliation functionality to help you manage your cash position. You can either interface the bank statement transactions electronically or enter them manually. You can run a process to automatically match and reconcile cleared payments, or you can perform this process manually.

PeopleSoft Payables also provides a cash clearing feature to maintain a greater degree of control over cash float. You specify an interim cash clearing account in addition to the cash account for each bank. When a payment is posted, the credit amount goes to the cash clearing account. After the payment has cleared the bank and been reconciled, you run a process to move the credit from the cash clearing account to the regular cash account.

TAKING ADVANTAGE OF GLOBAL FEATURES

PeopleSoft provides functionality in all the various applications to support organizations operating throughout the world. Global features provided in Payables 7.5 include the following:

- Document sequencing to adhere to regulations for European reporting and control.
- Multibook support to allow a single business unit to have multiple base currencies.
- The ability to be invoiced in one currency and pay in another.
- Global withholding features to process not only 1099 withholding for the U.S., but withholding that adheres to the standards of other countries as well.
- Support for Value Added Tax (VAT) setup, data capture, and reporting.
- Support for multilingual documents.
- Exchange rate triangulation in support of the European Monetary Union.

INTEGRATING WITH OTHER MODULES

Figure 7.4 depicts all the modules that interface with PeopleSoft Payables.

Figure 7.4
The PeopleSoft Payables module exchanges information with General Ledger, Asset Management, Expenses, Treasury, Receivables, Projects, Purchasing, Inventory, and Billing.

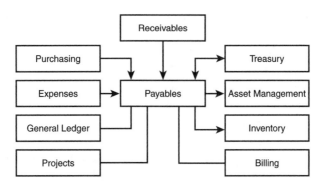

In summary, PeopleSoft Payables enables you to effectively manage your vendor relationships, efficiently process vouchers, produce payments, and manage your cash position. The next section discusses the PeopleSoft Receivables application.

RECEIVABLES

PeopleSoft Receivables automates the establishment of receivables and receipt of payments for your customers. The Receivables application comprises the following processes:

- Maintaining Customer Information
- Entering and Processing Receivables
- Receiving and Processing Payments
- Taking Advantage of Global and Other Special Features
- Integrating with Other Modules

These processes are explored in the following sections.

MAINTAINING CUSTOMER INFORMATION

Keeping track of customers and your relationship with them is a key part of the Receivables process. PeopleSoft Receivables subdivides customers into specific roles that they play. When you establish a customer to the system, you enter basic information, plus information specific to each role that is applicable to that customer. These are as follows:

- Basic customer information such as name, status, type, associated vendor, subcustomer hierarchies, address information, and which roles the customer will play in your organization.
- Corporate customer is the customer ID that this customer points to for rollup purposes, to enable you to view receivables and apply cash at a corporate customer level. You can also build trees to establish customer hierarchies.

PART

II

CH

7

- Sold To customers place orders with your organization. You can enter options for the customer's ordering preferences, define product catalogs specific to the Sold To customer, and enter the customer's aliases for these products. A Sold To customer can have multiple Bill To and Ship To customers.

- Bill To customers receive invoices from your organization. You can enter invoicing options for the Bill To customer such as payment method, payment terms, billing cycles, invoice formats, and PO/blanket PO information.

- Ship To customers receive shipments of goods from your organization. You can enter shipping options such as delivery routing, label formats, just-in-time parameters, freight terms and carriers, required customs documents, and days when shipment cannot be accepted.

- Remit From Information may be collected if the customer is a Bill To customer. You specify information about the paying entity within your customer's organization.

- Correspondence Information may be collected if the customer is a Bill To customer. You specify the addresses that need to appear on invoices, statements and letters to this customer, plus dunning, finance charge, and statement options.

- Consolidation customer is available for Bill To customers to enable the customer to receive multiple bills on one consolidated bill.

If a customer is also a vendor for your organization, you can link the customer to a Payables vendor ID. This will enable you to produce a report that nets receivables and payables for that organization.

You can maintain multiple contact names, addresses, phone numbers, and email information for your customers. You can also record the customer contact's credit card information.

Credit information is available for Bill To customers and Corporate customers only. You can establish a credit profile for your customer that includes credit check information.

You can group customers that share similar parameters and assign defaults at the group level to save time during data entry. Defaults that you can set include account distribution, price rule, pricing structure, reports, sales contracts, lead times, and tax information, including VAT.

You can attach messages to customer records that users within your organization can view. You can also define notes to your customer that print on documents sent to the customer according to rules you specify.

ENTERING AND MANAGING RECEIVABLES

Receivables are initially represented in the system as pending items. Pending items can be entered online or interfaced from either PeopleSoft Billing or an external billing system.

When you enter pending items online, you enter information such as:

- Group identifying information such as control totals, dates, currency, and assignment of the group.
- Specific information for each pending item, such as customer, amount, payment terms, discounts, dispute information, collection agency and dunning notification status, pay method, personnel responsibilities, and tax information, including VAT.
- Accounting entry information to be passed to the General Ledger.

You run the Receivables Update process to post pending items to Receivables, which updates the customer balance and creates accounting entries from the pending items. This process also performs edits on pending items that are interfaced from an external source. After a pending item has been posted, it becomes an open item.

Receivables provides functionality for maintaining open or closed items. You can change payment terms, payment method, credit status, and personnel responsibilities on a single item. You can also use a maintenance worksheet to match open debit and credit items, record writeoffs, create new items for open balances, record refunds, and perform other maintenance activities. Items can also be transferred between customers or within hierarchical levels of a customer.

You can run the Aging process to age the open items. This process designates items into aging categories based on how long the receivable has been outstanding. You can choose to age only customers who have had activity since the last aging run, customers who have not been aged since a particular aging run, or a combination.

You have the option to create formats for follow-up letters and dunning notices in the system that can be created from the system according to rules you specify. You can also produce statements and process finance charges.

RECEIVING AND PROCESSING PAYMENTS

PeopleSoft Receivables enables you to perform the following three processes related to cash payments:

- Entering Payments
- Applying Cash
- Creating Accounting Entries

These processes are described in the following sections.

ENTERING PAYMENTS   You can use any combination of the following methods to enter payments into PeopleSoft Receivables:

- Regular Deposit is the most basic method to enter your payments online. Cash application is accomplished via a separate process using Payment Predictor or a payment worksheet (discussed in the following section, "Applying Cash").

- Express Deposit provides a streamlined way to quickly enter payments online and perform cash application in the same process (also discussed in the following section, "Applying Cash").

- Lockbox is a method in which payments received in a bank lockbox are electronically sent in a file from the bank and interfaced to PeopleSoft Receivables.

- Electronic Data Interchange (EDI) is another electronic means of interfacing payments. Receivables supports both European and U.S. EDI formats. EDI can receive the cash and remittance records separately, and provides split-stream functionality to match the two components. PeopleSoft supports direct debit EFT payments and both vendor- and customer-initiated drafts.

- Bank Statements can also be interfaced electronically from the bank. This method requires that the statement be loaded into the PeopleSoft Treasury module. PeopleSoft supports European cash control functionality to debit cash when received payments have been reconciled to deposits on a bank statement.

After the payment is in the system, you must identify it to facilitate cash application. You can identify regular payments by customer ID or any other information supplied with the payment. On electronic payments, MICR ID can be used as well as customer ID or any other predefined reference.

APPLYING CASH   PeopleSoft provides three ways you can apply cash: Express Deposit (discussed in the previous section), Payment Predictor, or payment worksheets.

With Express Deposit, you enter the payment and apply it in the same process. You enter an item ID to identify the payment to one or more open items. If the payment can be fully identified in this process, the result is an applied payment; otherwise, you generate a payment worksheet to enable you to further apply the payment.

Payment Predictor is an automated cash application process that enables you to define rules in advance for matching payments with open items. You select payments to apply, and then run the process. Payments that can be fully applied are then ready to post without intervention. For payments that are not fully applied after running the Payment Predictor process, generate a payment worksheet.

Payment worksheets provide the means for you to manually match payments with open items. You can also make adjustments such as write-offs, deductions, or prepayments.

After payments are fully applied, they are ready to be posted.

CREATING ACCOUNTING ENTRIES   The Receivables Update process that is run to post receivables is also used to post payments. The process updates the customer balances and creates accounting entries. When you run Journal Generator, the system formats these entries into a journal to send to the General Ledger.

TAKING ADVANTAGE OF GLOBAL AND OTHER SPECIAL FEATURES

Global features provided in Receivables 7.5 include

- Document sequencing to adhere to regulations for European reporting and control.
- Multibook support to allow a single business unit to have multiple base currencies.
- The ability to invoice in one currency and receive payment in another.
- Support for Value Added Tax (VAT) setup, data capture, and reporting.
- Support for multilingual documents.
- Exchange rate triangulation in support of the European Monetary Union.

A final specialized feature of Receivables is self-service Web applications. Self-service Web applications give customers more information and reduce time spent answering customer inquiries by providing inquiry-only panels that the customers can access through the Internet to view their information. Two such panels are delivered with Receivables:

- An inquiry on the customer's account balance, credit limit, activity, and aging
- An inquiry on payments and their application to open receivable items

Security is placed on these Web applications such that customers can view only data for which they are authorized.

INTEGRATING WITH OTHER MODULES

Figure 7.5 depicts all the modules that interface with PeopleSoft Receivables.

In summary, PeopleSoft Receivables enables you to effectively manage your customer relationships by efficiently entering and tracking receivables, receiving payments, and applying cash.

The next section discusses the PeopleSoft Asset Management application.

Figure 7.5
The PeopleSoft Receivables module exchanges information with General Ledger, Billing, Order Management, Treasury, and Payables.

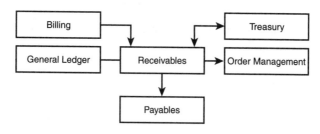

ASSET MANAGEMENT

PeopleSoft Asset Management facilitates the tracking, control, and reporting of your organization's assets. It encompasses the following processes:

- Planning Capital Acquisitions
- Adding and Maintaining Assets

- Depreciating Assets
- Tracking Physical Asset Inventory
- Taking Advantage of Global Features
- Integrating with Other Modules

These processes are described in the following sections.

PLANNING CAPITAL ACQUISITIONS

PeopleSoft Asset Management's capital acquisition planning functionality provides you with the capability to plan your appropriations and track expenses as they occur throughout a project.

You set up a plan by entering identification information, accounting information, an estimate of costs, and a cost limit and/or tolerance. You can plan for one or multiple assets in a single plan, and you can establish a master plan to roll up multiple plans. You can enter justification information and authorizations for each asset expenditure.

As you acquire and add assets to the system, you can link the asset to the plan by providing a capital acquisition plan number at the time of entry. A summary of all assets associated with a particular plan is available when viewing the plan. Additionally, you can view cost summary information for the plan by asset, by lease, and in total by status of the asset. This enables you to track your acquisition costs throughout the asset life cycle.

ADDING AND MAINTAINING ASSETS

To add assets, you specify both financial and physical information. Financial information includes cost, book, tax, and depreciation information, and physical information includes physical attributes, manufacturer, tag number, location, and custodial information. PeopleSoft Asset Management provides you with the flexibility to enter all information at once, or enter financial and physical information separately according to the information available at different points in your asset acquisition process.

The Basic Add method provides you with full asset addition functionality, including physical and financial information, in one set of panels. You can choose to enter only part of the information and finish at a later time if need be. This method is typically used when you initially have only physical information available, and is also used to enter additional information when it becomes available.

The Express Add feature provides you with the capability to quickly enter financial information for an asset without having to worry about paging through all the physical information. Depreciation can begin as soon as the financial information is added. You can then use the Basic Add panels to fill in the physical information when it becomes available.

Adding an asset is made easier with Asset Profiles. You can predefine book, depreciation method, proration convention, useful life, and tax credit information into an asset profile. When you link an asset to an asset profile, all the defaulted information from the profile is populated for you. An asset copy feature, enabling you to copy an entire asset and change only the information you need to, is also available to make data entry easier and more efficient.

Another way to save time adding assets is through the integration of PeopleSoft Payables and Purchasing. Payables sends financial and capitalization asset information from vouchers. Purchasing sends physical asset information, either capitalized or non-capitalized, from receipts. If Purchasing creates non-capitalized assets, voucher information from Payables can be used to capitalize the asset later.

Parent-child functionality gives you the flexibility to specify components of a larger asset. You can track cost, depreciation, and physical information for the composite, or parent, asset along with all its components, or children. Alternatively, you can specify the parent asset as a rollup only, so that information is tracked only for the children and rolled up into the parent. For example, if you add a desktop PC, you can either choose to track cost basis; depreciation; and physical information for the CPU, monitor, keyboard, and mouse only, using the PC as a rollup; or you can track this information for the composite PC along with all its components. You could also simply add the PC as a single asset and track it as one entity.

Throughout the life of your assets, you can make adjustments to cost, quantity, or other information. You can transfer assets within a business unit, or you can transfer them to other business units, and the system will automatically generate the appropriate intercompany entries. You can also recategorize assets, track repairs, and retire assets.

In addition to owned assets, PeopleSoft provides functionality to enter and maintain leased assets. You define the lease, terms, and cost information and calculate the lease payment schedule. You can define step leases when your payment timing or amounts vary over the lease term. You can transfer, retire, or reinstate leases, and a number of reports are provided to track the lease status.

All asset additions, adjustments, transfers, and retirements generate accounting entries. To create the accounting entries, you must first run a process to calculate depreciation on the asset transactions you have entered. Then you run the Accounting Entry Creation process to generate entries for all non-depreciation transactions. These entries will be sent to the General Ledger when you run Journal Generator.

DEPRECIATING ASSETS

PeopleSoft Asset Management provides you with a full range of depreciation options. It supports most standard depreciation methods and proration, and provides robust tax functionality. To help the system automatically calculate depreciation entries, you provide the following information about each asset:

- Depreciation Method
- Prorate Convention
- Depreciable Cost Basis
- Estimated Useful Life
- In-Service Date

You can specify these attributes as defaults when you define the books for your business units and in asset profiles, or you can specify it individually when you add the asset itself if the information differs from that defined in the profile. You can change these attributes at any time during the life of the asset; you just need to rerun the depreciation calculation.

If the depreciation methods that PeopleSoft provides do not cover your needs, you can define your own depreciation method by modifying the delivered tables and/or formulas. You can copy an existing method to use in defining a new one.

You run a process to calculate depreciation. You need to rerun this process to recalculate depreciation whenever you have a transaction that affects depreciation, for example, asset additions, adjustments, transfers, retirements, or changes to an asset's depreciation attributes. You run the Depreciation Close process at month-end to create depreciation accounting entries. These are sent to the General Ledger when you run Journal Generator.

TRACKING PHYSICAL ASSET INVENTORY

PeopleSoft supports interfacing with third-party physical inventory methods to capture asset inventory data.

If you use barcode scanning to perform your physical inventory, you can extract all potential PeopleSoft asset locations into a sequential file that you load into your scanning system. You can generate files for scanning, for label printing, or both. You also define a scan scope to specify which assets are expected to be in the physical locations you are inventorying. When you perform your physical inventory, the scanning system creates a sequential file of scanned information that you load back into PeopleSoft. Asset Management compares the assets you've scanned with those that are expected to be in each location, based on the scan scope. Differences create move, add, and retirement transactions.

PeopleSoft also supports performing inventory for technology equipment using a third-party asset discovery tool. A discovery tool is used to collect information about equipment over a network. This data is kept in a file that can be loaded into Asset Management similarly to the scan file. With this type of tool, you do not need to tag or barcode your technology assets.

TAKING ADVANTAGE OF GLOBAL FEATURES

PeopleSoft Asset Management supports the following global features:

- Multibook support to allow a single business unit to have multiple base currencies.
- Exchange rate triangulation in support of the European Monetary Union.
- Support for Australian tax requirements such as asset research and development categorization, tax credit allowance, and capital gains tax calculation.
- Capital cost allowance reporting to support Canadian depreciation calculation.
- Support for the German Staffel depreciation method to depreciate buildings.

INTEGRATING WITH OTHER MODULES

Figure 7.6 depicts all the modules that interface with PeopleSoft Receivables.

Figure 7.6
The PeopleSoft Asset Management module exchanges information with General Ledger, Purchasing, Payables, Projects, Budgets, and Bills and Routings.

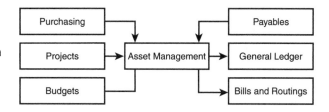

In summary, PeopleSoft Asset Management enables you to plan for and keep track of the cost, depreciation, tax, and physical information associated with your assets. The next section focuses on the Projects module.

PROJECTS

PeopleSoft Projects facilitates the tracking of costs by project. Any transaction within the Financial Management suite can be linked to a project and the costs captured for analysis purposes. Projects encompasses the following processes:

- Structuring Projects and Project Trees
- Maintaining Projects
- Integrating with Other Modules
- Analyzing Projects
- Taking Advantage of Global and Other Special Features

These processes are described in the following sections.

STRUCTURING PROJECTS AND PROJECT TREES

Projects contain a number of components that you define to establish your project environment. These include, at a high level

- Projects are the main component of the project environment. A project is a ChartField, and thus provides the link with all other modules. Projects can be grouped together using Project Types that you predefine.
- Activities are the tasks that are performed within a project. Activities can be grouped together using Activity Types that you predefine, enabling you to report on the same kinds of activities across projects.
- Resource Types identify the transactions that flow through the Projects system. For example, you might track Resource Types of Parts versus Labor in a manufacturing project. You can use Resource Categories and Subcategories to subdivide your Resource Types at a more granular level, and you can define Resource Groups to roll your Resource Types up to a higher level.

PART

II

CH

7

- Analysis Types are used to differentiate the kinds of transactions tracked by resource. For example, you may have Analysis Types to represent budgeted, committed, forecast, and actual amounts related to a project. You can define Analysis Groups to report on related analysis types.

- Accounting Entry Templates help you define how the system will generate accounting entries to send to the General Ledger based on user-defined Transaction Types, or events.

- You set up Integration Templates to define how transactions will be interfaced between Projects and the other modules. Asset Profiles enable you to capitalize and retire assets from the Projects module.

- Additional project components that you can define include parameters to describe project status, employee job codes, billing parameters, interest calculation, and quality.

The following section explains the process for maintaining projects in the system.

Maintaining Projects

When you set up a project, you enter basic information about the project, and then set the current project status, establish its location, and identify a project manager and team members.

Optionally, you can also identify project phases to track costs by phase, add a project justification, and link external documents to the project (for example, a workplan or a detailed description).

You can set up an approval chain for the project based on events that occur within the project life. You can require different approval criteria and different approvers at each event you define.

You can use the Funding feature to specify a cost limit, or budget, for the project by analysis type. You can then enter activity and resource transactions up to the funding limit for that analysis type.

To complete the project setup, you add Activities to it. Similar to the project itself, you create the activity, add a description, set status information, and establish a location.

Integrating with Other Modules

The integration of PeopleSoft Projects with other modules is the primary way transactions are accumulated for a project. Figure 7.7 shows the modules that integrate with PeopleSoft Projects.

Figure 7.7
The PeopleSoft Projects module exchanges information with Budgets, Purchasing, Inventory, Payables, Order Management, Time & Labor, Expenses, Billing, Asset Management, and General Ledger.

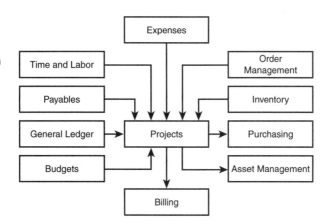

Because these integration points are intrinsic to the process of project information gathering, they are described briefly as follows.

- Budgets—You can create a budget at the project level in the PeopleSoft Budgets module and import the budget into Projects. You can also transfer Projects transactions (actual and budget) to the Budgets module to be used as the basis for future budget preparation.

- Purchasing—You can enter requisition lines into the Projects module to be sent to Purchasing where they can be used to create purchase orders. Or you can import requisitions and purchase orders that have been created within Purchasing into the Projects module to track commitments against a project. You can also process adjustments to purchase orders and requisitions.

- Inventory—You can use Projects to generate a demand that is sent to the Inventory module. If the demand can be fulfilled, costing information is sent back to Projects.

- Payables—You can import posted voucher transactions into the Projects module to track actual costs against a project.

- Order Management—You can import scheduled orders from the Order Management module into Projects to track orders against a project.

- Time & Labor—You can track your labor costs against a project by importing either estimated time and labor accruals during a payroll period, or actual time and labor costs after a payroll period is closed.

- Expenses—You can import approved expense transactions into the Projects Module to track employee expenses against a project.

- Billing—When you set up contracts within Projects, you can run a process that calculates a billing worksheet from all the billable transactions collected for labor, expenses, and so on. You can review the billing worksheet and make adjustments as needed. When you approve the billing worksheet and issue an invoice, the invoice transactions are sent to the Billing module to print.

- Asset Management—When you use Projects to track assets, you link resources to assets or to asset profiles. You can periodically run a process to summarize the transactions and send the capitalization information to Asset Management.

- General Ledger—Transactions accumulated in Projects can be sent to the General Ledger via the Journal Generator. For those transactions that originate outside the Projects module, you can either send transactions from the source system to both Projects and General Ledger simultaneously, or send transactions sequentially from the source system to Projects and from Projects to the General Ledger. For transactions that originate within Projects, you create accounting templates to automatically offset single-sided transactions that you enter and run a process to generate the entries. Then you run Journal Generator to send all applicable complete entries to the General Ledger. Additionally, allocations performed in the General Ledger to allocate costs between projects can be sent back to Projects.

The next section discusses the various features available to analyze projects.

ANALYZING PROJECTS

As you start to accumulate transactions related to your projects, you can perform analysis on them using the following features:

- Express Project Panels give you a condensed view of the most commonly used project information. Using this feature, you can create a project and add activities and resources all in one step, you can specify or view cost and revenue integration information, and you can drill down into source transactions from other modules that affect your projects. You can also generate project reports.

- Flexible Analysis Drilldown enables you to select an analysis group, and then specify your own analysis parameters to drill down to the project and/or resource level, to individual transactions, and all the way to source transactions from other modules.

- Project Drillup enables you to select a resource transaction and view the information for the project associated with it.

- Flexible Time Span Analysis enables you to see project information summarized by time spans that you specify.

- PeopleSoft Projects also provides a number of inquiry features that enable you to view project information in a variety of ways, including groupings by source data for transactions that originate from other PeopleSoft modules, such as by purchase order, voucher, employee, asset, and so on.

TAKING ADVANTAGE OF GLOBAL AND OTHER SPECIAL FEATURES

PeopleSoft Projects incorporates the following special features:

- Multicurrency capabilities for processing project information in multiple currencies.
- Exchange rate triangulation in support of the European Monetary Union.
- Interest calculation to enable interest to be accumulated in projects based on criteria you specify.
- Control features for incoming transactions from other modules to enable you to define, by project status, for which analysis types the system will allow transactions to be imported. You can also specify tolerances and enable threshold checking so that a transaction will be rejected if it causes an overrun of the tolerance.
- Investment incentives enable you to track project transactions associated with various government-issued investment incentives, such as grants, rebates, tax cuts, and so on.

In summary, the Projects module enables you to track costs and revenue associated with projects in your organization. You can integrate Projects with other PeopleSoft modules to budget for your project, track procurement commitments and actual costs, create demand for inventory, track employee labor and expenses, create billings for project customers, and send relevant accounting entries to the General Ledger. A number of specialized analysis features are available for you to keep track of your project.

The next section focuses on the Budgets module.

BUDGETS

PeopleSoft Budgets streamlines the budget preparation process within your organization. It builds upon the structures you created and maintained in the General Ledger, such as ChartField components, ledgers, and organizational rollup tree structures. Budgets encompasses the following processes:

- Creating the Budgets Cube
- Defining Budget Phases
- Preparing Your Budget
- Importing Your Budget to the General Ledger
- Integrating with Other Modules

CREATING THE BUDGETS CUBE

To prepare your budgets, you build a budgets cube, a multidimensional storage facility provided by Arbor Essbase technology. To build the cube, you need to establish the components that are used to define each dimension of the cube.

You establish the time dimension by defining the periods you want to use and building a tree to roll them up into quarters, years, and so on.

You establish the ledger type dimension by specifying the ledgers from which you want to extract data to help in the budget preparation process. For example, you might want to extract data from budget, actuals, and statistical ledgers.

The third dimension you specify is the ChartFields you want to use to create your budgets. One of these will become your central budgeting ChartField, or Budget Center. For example, you can budget primarily by department.

Optionally, you can define multicurrency options for your cube. You can also import depreciation data from Asset Management, and employee position information from Human Resources to use in your cube.

After you've defined your cube dimensions and logical structure, you establish a cube template to specify how the cube will be built. Then you run a process to extract the data and build the cube.

DEFINING BUDGET PHASES

You define the timing of the budgeting process with Budget Phases, and monitor them using the Phase Monitor. The system can send emails at the beginning and end of each phase to alert users to the tasks they need to perform. You establish which users have access to which data at which times.

PREPARING YOUR BUDGET

Budget preparers use the Budgets Explorer interface to access data in the cube based on security that you define, and manipulate the information to produce their budgets. For example, you might create a cube using a department ChartField rollup tree, last year's budget ledger, this year's actuals ledger, and some headcount statistics. A particular budget preparer might have access to only a single node on the Department rollup tree.

At the beginning of the phase, the budget preparer receives an email with instructions, and then accesses his or her part of the cube to prepare the budget. The preparer can "slice and dice" information in the cube and perform calculations based on statistics to facilitate the budget preparation.

A "checkout" feature enables the preparer to take his or her portion of the cube and work on it offline, and then check it back in when complete. Each preparer authorizes his or her own budget when finished, and then the next budget user in the hierarchy can review, change, and authorize it.

The coordinator can easily monitor the tasks being completed and the people working on them using the Phase Monitor.

IMPORTING YOUR BUDGET TO THE GENERAL LEDGER

At the end of the budget cycle, the coordinator runs a process to load the completed budget information into the budget ledger in the General Ledger. This process can be run at any time and rerun during the budget process. When data is back in the General Ledger, you can still manipulate the data using allocations and flexible formulas.

INTEGRATING WITH OTHER MODULES

Figure 7.8 depicts all the modules that interface with PeopleSoft Budgets.

Figure 7.8
The PeopleSoft
Budgets module
exchanges information
with General Ledger,
Asset Management,
Projects, and Human
Resources.

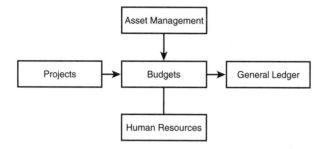

In summary, PeopleSoft Budgets enables you to structure and streamline your budget preparation process. The next section will explain the Treasury module.

TREASURY

PeopleSoft Treasury provides you with the means to automate your treasury function. The processes involved in the Treasury module include:

- Processing Bank Statements
- Transferring Funds Between Bank Accounts
- Executing Treasury Settlements
- Managing Positions and Deals
- Integrating with Other Modules

These processes are described in the following sections.

PROCESSING BANK STATEMENTS

PeopleSoft Treasury enables you to enter bank statements online, or interface them into the system using EDI. To enter the statement online, you establish identifying information such as external bank ID, bank account number, and a unique statement ID. You then enter the statement transactions, including the reference, the date, the amount, the kind of transaction, and its reconciliation status. You can use the same panels to view bank statements that were electronically loaded from a bank file.

The system also enables you to manually enter bank balances and look at balances across business units.

After the bank statement is in the system, PeopleSoft Treasury gives you several options to reconcile them:

- Manual Reconciliation is used to reconcile transactions when your bank doesn't send you an electronic bank statement, and you don't enter the bank statement online. The system displays the transactions, and you mark each one as you go through your bank statement.

- Semi-Manual Reconciliation is used when you've entered your bank statement online, or when you have exceptions from the Automatic Reconciliation. The system displays both bank and system transactions, and you select all transactions you want to reconcile. As long as the transactions balance and meet all criteria, they will all be marked when you click Reconcile.

- Automatic Reconciliation is a process that automatically reconciles system transactions with those loaded from an electronic bank file. It reconciles all items that match exactly. You can use the Semi-Manual Reconciliation panel to match the exceptions. You also have the option to force the reconciliation.

- Bank Balance Reconciliation is a process whereby you enter the bank balance and then run a process that sums system transactions that would not be on this bank statement, such as deposits in transit or fees that haven't been accounted for. These are added to a starting balance to obtain an ending balance, which is then compared to the bank's ending balance you entered.

- Credit Card Reconciliation is a process to compare system transactions with those loaded from a credit card clearinghouse file.

PeopleSoft provides a number of reconciliation reports to keep you on top of your bank statement activity. You run a process to generate accounting entries for the reconciliation activities you've performed. These entries are sent to the General Ledger when you run Journal Generator.

TRANSFERRING FUNDS BETWEEN BANK ACCOUNTS

PeopleSoft supports the need to transfer funds between bank accounts. You can perform either of the following two types of transfer:

- Internal transfers between two internal bank accounts
- External transfers between two external bank accounts

The system updates cash position and bank balances, and generates accounting entries when you run the accounting process. If you perform the same type of transfer on a regular basis, you can set up a template that can be reused.

EXECUTING TREASURY SETTLEMENTS

You can use PeopleSoft Treasury to manage and generate payments resulting from treasury transactions. This function enables you to select transactions for payment, net them to reduce the number of payments generated, and approve the payments to be sent to Payables where the payments will be generated.

MANAGING POSITIONS AND DEALS

You can use PeopleSoft trees to help manage your treasury positions. PeopleSoft provides the following position analyses:

- Cash Position worksheets help you to monitor your cash position with a variety of options.

- Exposure Position management enables you to manage the risk associated with your positions.

PeopleSoft Treasury provides additional functionality that enables you to revalue your positions using complex analytical tools, and to enter and administer deals and trades.

INTEGRATING WITH OTHER MODULES

Figure 7.9 depicts all the modules that interface with PeopleSoft Treasury.

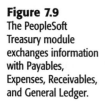

Figure 7.9
The PeopleSoft Treasury module exchanges information with Payables, Expenses, Receivables, and General Ledger.

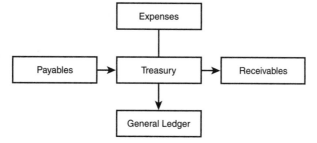

In summary, PeopleSoft Treasury enables you to manage and reconcile your bank statement activities, execute transfers and settlements, and perform extensive analysis. The next section explains the Expenses module.

EXPENSES

PeopleSoft Expenses helps you streamline the process of reimbursing your employees for work-related expenses. The processes involved in the Expenses module are

- Processing and Reconciling Cash Advances
- Processing Expense Sheets
- Making Expense Payments
- Integrating with Other Modules

These processes are described in the following sections.

PART

II

CH

7

PROCESSING AND RECONCILING CASH ADVANCES

PeopleSoft Expenses provides the facility for you to enter cash advances for employee travel. To enter an advance, you enter a description including the business purpose of the trip and advance lines by source of funding (for example, system-generated check, travelers checks). Based on your source definitions, each line may or may not generate payment from the system.

You can set up approval and audit rules separately. An employee cannot approve or audit his or her own cash advance, and the advance must be fully approved before it is audited. PeopleSoft provides many auditing options, including random auditing (for example, every tenth advance), audits based on criteria such as advances submitted from the Expense Traveler application, or audits for all advances.

You can set controls by employee such as cash advance maximums. When reviewing a cash advance, you can see whether or not the employee has any outstanding unreconciled advances.

After the advance has been fully approved and/or audited, the system will pay the employee the amount that is to be generated by the system (that is, net of outside sources such as travelers checks).

After completing the trip, the employee completes an expense sheet to submit travel expenses. As part of the expense sheet, the employee enters the Advance ID, which will then be used to offset the expense amount paid to the employee. You use an advance reconciliation panel to reconcile an advance against its offsets. You reconcile the advance amount against its affiliated expense sheet if one exists. You can also reconcile an advance against a check from the employee. When you are satisfied that the amounts are reconciled, you click a button to change the status of the advance. An employee cannot reconcile his or her own advance.

You run a posting process to create cash advance-related accounting entries. For cash advance lines that generate payment from the system, accounting entries to debit the employee advances account and credit the expense accrual account are both generated by the system using the ChartFields specified in the Accounting Entry Template. For cash advance lines that do not generate payment, the system debits the employee advances account from the Accounting Entry Template, and credits the account you specified when you set up the non–payment-generating funding source, such as Travelers Checks Payable. These entries are sent to the General Ledger when you run Journal Generator.

PROCESSING EXPENSE SHEETS

PeopleSoft Expenses provides robust features to streamline the entry, approval, audit, and tax reporting of expense transactions.

There are four origins for expense sheets:

- Online entry using panels
- Web self-service entry using Web client

- Corporate credit card transactions loaded from your credit card company using EDI Manager

- Expenses Traveler transactions loaded from PeopleSoft's mobile client application

These are described in the following sections.

ONLINE ENTRY   For online entry, you start with a description. You enter the business purpose, advance ID to link the expense to a paid cash advance, reference information, and a receipt ID to link the expense sheet to the receipts you send in as backup. Your default ChartField information is displayed, and you can allocate all the expense to this combination, or specify percentages to allocate the expenses to different business units, departments, and/or products.

You then enter expense line information to describe specific expense information such as date, method of expenditure, type of expense, description, location, merchant, amount of expense, currency information, and the like. Expenditure methods are elements that you set up to indicate how the expense was paid and whom to reimburse. Reimbursement can be designated to the employee, the vendor, or prepaid (no reimbursement).

Certain types of expense require additional information. For example, a hotel stay will prompt you for the number of nights, airfare requires a ticket number, and driving distance is required for mileage reimbursement. You can also indicate that an expense line has no receipt and enter a justification. Sort and copy features are available to streamline entry of expense lines.

You can optionally enter VAT information if you paid value added tax on any of your expenses. PeopleSoft provides reporting on VAT information to enable your company to be reimbursed for the appropriate amounts.

You can review and edit the accounting distribution for your expense lines. You can also specify project information to aid in the tracking and billing of expenses against projects.

A summary panel is available for you to review your expense sheet. It shows the total of all expense lines submitted and subtracts all nonreimbursable expense items such as personal expenses, prepaid expenses, items to be paid directly to a vendor, and related cash advances. The difference is either owed to the employee or owed to the company by the employee.

When you are finished reviewing your expense sheet, you submit the expense.

WEB SELF-SERVICE   PeopleSoft Expenses provides templates to enter expense data by using the Web client. This mode of entry can be quite useful for employees who are traveling, as it enables them to record their expense information, or approve requests from other employees, while they are away from the office.

Templates are provided for the following processes:

- Entering Expenses
- Requesting a Cash Advance

PART

II

CH

7

- Reviewing Expense Information
- Granting Entry Authority
- Approving Expenses
- Approving Cash Advances

These templates function in a similar way to the online panels described in the previous section.

CORPORATE CREDIT CARD   PeopleSoft Expenses provides you with the means to load expense transactions from your corporate credit card. You set up EDI Manager to import the credit card transactions to the staging tables. When this is complete, you run a process to load the transactions into the expenses tables.

PeopleSoft provides an online panel where you can review loaded credit card expense lines by employee ID, and verify them against receipts submitted by the employee. When you have verified all receipts, the system generates an expense sheet containing all verified lines, which you then submit as you would an online expense sheet.

EXPENSES TRAVELER   PeopleSoft's Expenses Traveler enables employees to enter expense sheets and request cash advances while on the road. You specify control data, such as business purposes or employee data, that the employee can download to his/her hard drive. The employee can refresh this data during any connection with the server.

The employee can prepare expense sheets and cash advance requests in a similar manner to the online panels. In addition, the traveling employees can define their own attendee and merchant lists to use in preparation of expense sheets. Additional tools provided to the traveling employee include a calculator, backup and restore facilities, and print preview. To submit an expense or advance request, the employee must connect to the network.

Regardless of origin, the posting process creates accounting entries for approved expenses to debit the ChartFields specified on the expense line accounting panel. The system generates the offsetting credit to an Expenses Accrual account, which you define in the Accounting Entry Template. These entries are sent to the General Ledger when you run Journal Generator.

MAKING EXPENSE PAYMENTS

To create payments for approved expense sheets and cash advances, you first run a staging process. This process selects all eligible transactions to pay and populates staging tables. You can review the staged payments, and you have the opportunity to change bank information and put payments on hold for an employee or vendor, prior to sending them to Payables to create the actual payments to employees and/or vendors using pay cycles.

You run the payment posting process to create accounting entries that debit the Expenses Accrual account and credit the cash account specified in the bank account definition. These entries are sent to the General Ledger when you run Journal Generator.

INTEGRATING WITH OTHER MODULES

Figure 7.10 depicts all the modules that interface with PeopleSoft Expenses.

Figure 7.10
The PeopleSoft Expenses module exchanges information with General Ledger, Payables, Treasury, Projects and Billing, Payroll, and Human Resources.

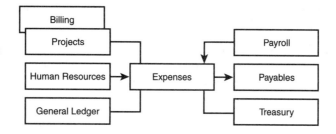

In summary, PeopleSoft Expenses enables you to reimburse your employees for expenditures incurred on behalf of your organization.

CONCLUSION

PeopleSoft Financial Management provides you with the tools you need to manage and retain a clear picture of your financial position at any time.

To recap the basic functionality of each module

- The General Ledger holds your organization structure and financial data. It also enables you to perform allocations, consolidations, and year-end processing, and it facilitates statutory and management reporting.

- Payables helps you manage your vendor relationships, invoice entry, and payment function.

- Receivables helps you maintain customer information, process receivables, and apply payments.

- Asset Management enables you to plan for your acquisitions, maintain and depreciate your assets, and track physical inventory.

- Projects facilitates the tracking and analysis of project budgets and related costs.

- Budgets help you in the process of preparing your annual budget and related forecasts.

- Treasury helps automate bank statement reconciliation, bank account transfers and settlement processing, and position and deal management.

- Expenses enables cash advance, expense, and payment processing.

These modules provide you with lots of functionality and options to give the maximum flexibility in your financial management. Inevitably, there will be processes or functions that your company performs that PeopleSoft Financial Management, or any packaged financial software, cannot accommodate as delivered. To handle these "gaps," you can either change the software or change the process.

PART

II

CH

7

PeopleSoft provides the tools to make customizations simple. You can use these tools to make panel modifications, add fields, change programs, and more. The drawback of modifying the delivered software is that you have to analyze each modification during every upgrade to ensure it is still required. This can add quite a bit of complexity and time to your upgrade process.

Many organizations opt instead to change their processes and use PeopleSoft as delivered. Although this option is sometimes very successful, it doesn't represent the best solution in every situation. Factors in each organization, such as resistance to change and complexity of processes, figure into the feasibility of this solution.

In each case, it is up to your organization to decide whether changing the system or changing your process, or a combination of the two, offers the best solution.

In summary, PeopleSoft Financial Management will help your organization to meet the increasing demands of today's rapidly evolving business landscape. In the next chapter, the modules will be discussed in more detail.

CHAPTER 8

FINANCIAL MODULES

by Dan Jamieson, James Jaworski,
Vlad Soran, and Jeffrey W. Wiesinger

In this chapter

GENERAL LEDGER

The General Ledger's main function is to serve as the repository for all financial transactions. The amounts captured in the General Ledger are used in producing financial statements and other financial reports. PeopleSoft's G/L was designed to enable organizational, processing, and reporting flexibility. The G/L Business Unit encapsulates all the accounting rules and related processes, foreign currency processing, reporting, and security. By using the Table Set Sharing feature, two or more G/L Business Units can have a different Chart of Accounts (COA), calendar (which will determine accounting periods and year ends), base currency, and reporting structure. An important item to note is that as long as the Ledger table structure is the same, G/L Business Units with different COAs can be consolidated automatically in the PeopleSoft General Ledger module. In PeopleSoft, there are two types of Ledgers: Detail and Summary. These two components will be discussed in the following sections.

DETAIL LEDGER

Detail Ledgers are grouped by a Ledger Group. In a ledger group, you can define multiple ledgers. You need to define more than one ledger if

- You have multiple base currency transactions (for example, a French subsidiary of an American company may need to keep the accounting books in both French francs and U.S. dollars).

- You need to keep track of budgeted amounts in a Budget Ledger.

- You need to capture statistical information to be used for various reporting purposes in a Statistics Ledger.

- You need to track average daily balances.

- You determine that you need one because of consolidation requirements. Each Ledger Group must have one Primary Ledger and can have up to nine Secondary Ledgers. PeopleSoft posts automatically to all the Ledgers, based on rules determined in the Ledger setup.

SUMMARY LEDGER

Summary Ledgers are used to enable faster reporting, by summarizing accounting ledger information. Using Summary Ledgers, information from detail ledgers is summarized at the Chartfield level (that is, Account) in a background process. The results are stored in the Summary Ledger tables. Having the data summarized and stored speeds the query process. Information can be summarized at any Chartfield level, either from the Detail Ledger fields or from the rollup trees. Rollup trees are trees that summarize individual Chartfields. An example would be that departments 100, 200, and 300 are all marketing departments. A rollup tree would include a node called Marketing on the Dept Rollup tree that would summarize the amounts for the three departments.

UNDERSTANDING CHARTFIELDS

In PeopleSoft, the individual elements of the COA structure are called Chartfields. The COA elements can be used to maximize the reporting and processing requirements of your organization. Table 8.1 details the PeopleSoft-delivered Chartfields.

TABLE 8.1   PEOPLESOFT-DELIVERED CHARTFIELDS

Chartfield Name	Field Length	Purpose
Account	6	Classic Account, the anchor of the COA
Department	10	Responsibility or cost center
Product	6	Additional field to enable easy product reporting
Project ID	15	Field user for project tracking
Statistics	3	Field used to track non-monetary amounts
Currency Code	3	Currencies
Affiliate	5	Enables automatic inter-company balancing and accounting using one inter-company account by Business Unit

Chartfields can be added, field lengths can be changed, and Chartfield names can be modified to suit your business needs. Depending on which database platform you use, you may have some database limitations as to how many Chartfields you can add. Careful consideration should be given to modifying and adding Chartfields. Such an evaluation should take into consideration what it will take to promulgate the change to the entire database (that is, the required tables, records, subrecords, panels, PeopleCode, SQRs, SQCs, various functions, and so on), as well as potentially having to repeat the process with each version upgrade. A very important distinction should be made in relation to the affiliate Chartfield. Unlike the other Chartfields (Account, Department, Product, and Project), the affiliate Chartfield has significant inter-company processing rules tied to it. Customizing or deleting the affiliate Chartfield directly impacts inter-company processing.

HOW PEOPLESOFT STORES INFORMATION IN THE LEDGER TABLE

Each ledger stores the net activity for the period at the Chartfield level. If needed, one can post total Debit and total Credit amounts for the period to the Ledger table. Year to-date-balances are calculated at the inquiry or reporting time. The period is determined by the calendar to which the respective G/L Business Unit is pointing. There are three periods that are reserved for PeopleSoft internal use: Period 0, Period 998, and Period 999. Period 0 is used to capture balance forward amounts, Period 998 stores the adjustments for a specific year, and Period 999 the year end closing amounts.

The data flow of accounting-related information is summarized in Figure 8.1.

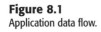

Figure 8.1
Application data flow.

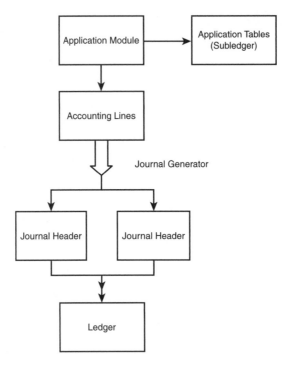

Thus, the various Application Modules (AM, A/P, A/R, Projects, Inventory, and so on) are creating Accounting lines. Accounting Lines are the detail Debit and Credit lines from which the Journal Generator will create the Journal Lines. These Accounting Lines are captured by the Journal Generator process. The Journal Generator creates the Journals, which are first edited and than posted to the Ledger. In the setup, one can decide to keep all the detail amounts in the Ledger from the application or to summarize the amounts in the Journals generated from the applications at various levels. Such summarization will increase performance by decreasing the lines in the Journal Line table. It will have a direct impact on the Edit and Post processes, as well as Reporting (more on Edit and Post later in the chapter). In addition to the Journals generated in the various other PeopleSoft applications, the General Ledger creates its own online Journals. These Journals pass the same edits and post processes to have their summarized amounts in the respective Ledgers.

TREES

The introduction to this chapter mentions the flexible design of the Ledger module. This section expands on one feature, which enhances such flexibility: the Tree Manager and, specifically, the PeopleSoft trees. Trees are a graphical representation of a certain hierarchical structure. Trees can be used for a variety of purposes. You can create a tree to reflect all the organization's Business Units' rollup and reporting structure. You can create one tree for internal and one for external reporting purposes. Another tree can be used for consolidation purposes. Yet another can reflect the Balance Sheet accounts and their respective classifications (Current Assets, Fixed Assets, Prepaids, and so on). One powerful feature of trees is effective dating. The effective date of the tree indicates when the structure represented by the tree is in effect. If your structure changes, you have the option of changing the original tree or making a new copy of the old structure, making the change to the structure, and having the effective date reflect the date that the change should become effective. By using trees, any changes to the tree will automatically be reflected in all the various processes using that tree. Such a direct link ensures up-to-date information, consistency in reporting, and flexibility to integrate changes.

How can trees be used? Trees can be used to indicate how various Chartfields should be summarized and how the rollup of various nodes needs to be done to perform the following functions:

- Summary Ledgers
- Consolidations
- Allocations
- Reporting (nVision)

An additional benefit is that being a graphical representation makes it a more intuitive representation of the hierarchical structure. In Figure 8.2, you can see the Account Rollup used in consolidation. The figure shows the summarized tree nodes for the Balance Sheet and the Income Statement. I have expanded the Cash and Salaries and Benefits nodes to show the detail ranges of accounts for the respective Balance Sheet and Income Statement nodes.

Figure 8.2
Account Rollup.

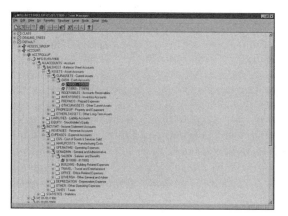

Having covered the main features of the G/L module, the following section presents other features that may be used as part of your application setup to maximize the enhancement and features of the PeopleSoft G/L.

OPEN ITEM ACCOUNTING

Open Item Accounting enables you to have, for the specified account selected, all the detail transactions until such time that all activity sums up to zero. For example, if you choose to keep track of employee advances using Open Item Accounting, you will send all the transactions to a respective employee until he or she has repaid the outstanding balance. If you choose to use Open Item accounting, you need to specify the Key field. In our example, let's say that the Key field is the employee ID. By using Open Item accounting, you do not have to use a separate Chartfield called Employee ID to track employee advances. Every time you enter a Journal Entry into the Employee Advance account, you need to specify the employee ID to keep track of the respective employee's advances. Depending on the volume of transactions, there are two modes for reconciling open item transactions: batch and online.

SPEED TYPES

Speed Types are predetermined Chartfield combination shortcuts used to speed data entry. For example, if you have to pay rent and charge the rent amount to specific Dept ID and Product, create a Rent Speed Type and PeopleSoft will automatically fill in the Dept ID and Product on the respective Journal Line.

ALTERNATE ACCOUNT

This feature enables organizations to maintain two COAs simultaneously on the same Business Unit. It was specifically created to provide for the statutory accounting and reporting requirements in Europe where, for statutory purposes, organizations have to have a standard COA. The feature is not fully functional. In order to obtain full functionality, you need to complete a set of modifications.

CHARTFIELD COMBINATION EDITING (COMBO EDIT)

The Combination Edit (Combo Edit) feature is designed to create Chartfield combinations that you, as a user, define as being valid. Only Journals having these valid Chartfield combinations will be posted to the Ledger. Thus, Combo Edit ensures the Chartfield Combinations' data validity in the Ledger. What is a Chartfield Combination? Recall from the previous discussion that Chartfields are the different elements of the PeopleSoft COA. You can define, for example, that Marketing Expense (Account 300001) can be charged only to certain departments (Dept. ID 222222) and certain products (Product ABC). If you set up a Combo Edit to include the three elements—Account, Department, and Product (that is, 300001, 222222, and ABC), any journal lines charged to Account 300001 have to be charged to Department 222222 and to Product ABC to be allowed to post to the Ledger. A good rule of thumb is to not set up Combo Edits on more than three Chartfields. Combo Edit rules can be set up on specific Chartfield values or rollup trees. You can create your own Combo Edit table or use the Combo Edit Explosion process, which populates a very large table with all the possible Chartfield Combinations. If you use the PeopleSoft process, indexes to optimize performance are also created. Indexes on the Combo Edit table speed the Combo Edit process by facilitating SQL statements to find and retrieve the data from the Combo Edit table. Depending on the data volumes, you may want to further tune the table to gain improvements in the Edit process. If you have used trees in creating your combination rules, any change in the tree values must be reflected in the Combo Edit table. The process is not automatic. After a manual change to the tree, you must run the Data Validation process to ensure that only valid rows are included in the Combo Edit table.

ALLOCATIONS

Allocation provides a systematic repeatable process to allocate costs based on certain criteria from one or many accounts/Chartfields to other accounts or Chartfield Values. An example of such a process is allocating Rent Expense to various departments based on their respective square footage. The results of the allocation process are Journal Entries to be posted to specified Ledgers. If the Ledgers involved are not the actual Ledgers, you may need to customize various work records to fit your particular needs. Complex allocations can have more that one step. You can first calculate a certain amount based on one set of criteria and then distribute the amounts to their final targets. Such multiple steps together create an Allocation Process Group. Allocations can span multiple G/L Business Units. The journals that are created can have user-defined dates and can also be automatically reversed if need-ed. PeopleSoft delivers an allocation log that records each step in the allocation process to provide the required audit trail.

JOURNAL ENTRIES

Online Journal Entries can be of two types: Regular J/E and Standard J/E. Regular Journals are online journals. The Standard J/E can be either Recurring or Template. Recurring Journals are identical journals that need to be processed based on a certain frequency. An example is a monthly lease payment. PeopleSoft enables you to set up the frequency, the start, and the end dates and automatically creates the Journal to be posted to the Ledger. First, you create a model J/E. Then you use the model J/E to create your standard J/E (Recurring or Template). Figure 8.3 shows the Standard Journal Entry panel.

Figure 8.3
The Standard Journal
Entry panel.

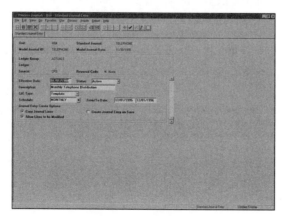

The Template Journals are journals that you may want to use either on request or based on a certain schedule. The difference between the Template and the Standard Journals is that in Template Journals you have Chartfield values being automatically pre-populated but not the amounts. Thus, if you need to have a standard account distribution for a telephone bill but the monthly amounts may differ, you can use a Template Journal to speed up data entry. The Standard entry, such as a Recurring entry, will have the same information each time it posts to the Ledger.

Each Journal has two components: Journal Header and Journal Lines. The Journal Header contains all the Key fields to specifically identify the Journal and to quickly enable the user to set it up as a Reversing or Adjusting entry. Recall that Adjusting entries are special entries recorded in Period 998 of the Adjustment Year, as specified in the G/L setup options. A Reversing entry automatically reverses the amounts at a day specified in the Journal Header Panel. Figure 8.4 shows a screen panel of the Journal Entry Header tab.

Figure 8.4
The Journal Entry Header tab.

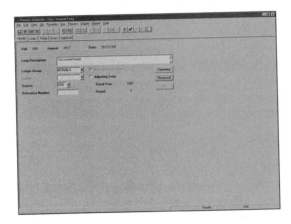

Some features present in the panel are the tabs for Header, Lines, Totals, Errors, and Approval. The Totals tab enables you to enter a control total for the Debits and Credits. It can be useful when entering a Journal with many lines. After the Journal has been edited, any errors are detailed on the Error tab panel. The Journal Approval process can be tailored to your organization. Using workflow, Journals can be routed for approval before being posted to the Ledger.

During the Ledger setup, in addition to the specific Ledgers for your G/L Business Unit, you have to decide and configure the error handling options. PeopleSoft enables the following error handling options for the Journal Entries: Default to Higher Value, Recycle, and Suspend. The first option defaults to the configuration set up in the Business Unit/Ledger for a Unit. Recycle stops the Journal containing errors from being posted to the Ledger. You need to make the correction, re-edit, and post. The Suspend option requires you to set up a Suspense account, which handles any errors in the journal processing. This Suspense account is a catchall account, which, if used, needs to be reconciled in order to ensure Ledger accuracy. Journals in error automatically create whatever Journal

Line is needed to balance the Journal; if a Chartfield Combination is in error, it posts these lines to the Suspense account. Before Journals are posted to the Ledger, they need to be marked to post. Depending on your specific business process regarding Journal review, PeopleSoft provides the option of posting Journals after they are edited (by marking to post in the Edit process), or going through the Mark and Post Journals process. The additional steps are designed to allow a supervisor to review the Journals prior to posting to the J/L. Journals can be unposted and deleted if necessary.

MULTI-CURRENCY PROCESSING

PeopleSoft provides flexibility in how you configure the system to answer your multi-currency processing and reporting needs. You can have multiple currency Journal lines in the same Ledger or, if required, you can set up multiple Ledgers for each currency. Using the multi-book approach, you can have separate Ledgers for each base currency needed. If the KLS (Keep Ledgers in Synch) option is selected, posting a Journal with foreign currency lines in one Ledger automatically creates all the required Journals for all the other Ledgers. PeopleSoft is also compliant with the currency exchange rates calculations required by the new EMU (European Monetary Unit) rules. All journals must balance by the respective Ledger's base currency. In PeopleSoft, you can maintain multiple rates for each currency type (Average, Current, Spot, and so on). PeopleSoft automatically performs currency conversions. Any transactions denominated in a currency other than the base currency of the G/L Business Unit is converted, and the amounts stored both in the base and foreign currency. This process can occur at the Accounting Line creation or the Journal Edit time. Other processes involved in processing foreign currency transactions are Re-measurement or Re-evaluation. The Re-evaluation process revalues the selected asset and liability accounts to reflect currency fluctuations from month to month. The differences are captured in revaluation gain/loss accounts. In cases where account balances need to be reported in a different currency than the G/L Business Unit base currency, the translation process produces account balances in the reporting currency. In the translation process, you can set up different rates for various types of accounts (Current rate for Balance Sheet accounts and Average rate for the Income Statement).

CONSOLIDATIONS

PeopleSoft provides the tools and processes to perform organizational consolidations, to account for minority interest, to automatically create Elimination Entries, and to account for the investment in subsidiaries based on the equity method. Elimination Entries are journals recorded in the Consolidation/Elimination Business Unit with the purpose of eliminating the impact of inter-company transactions. The PeopleSoft General Ledger enables you to define which parent maintains controlling influence over specific subsidiaries. In consolidating a subsidiary's books with those of the parent company, you want to credit the parent with only the portion of the subsidiary that it actually owns, leaving aside what is owned by minority investors. The General Ledger reports the value of minority interests in consolidations in terms of the aggregate net assets (equity), rather than in terms of a fractional equity in each of the specific assets and liabilities of the subsidiary.

To reflect minority interests in this manner, the General Ledger generates an adjustment entry that debits the parent's investment in the subsidiary account and credits a minority interest account. It calculates the amount of the adjustment by multiplying the percentage of minority interest in the subsidiary times the total equity of the subsidiary. Minority interest is the percentage of ownership in the net assets to be recorded against the investment in the subsidiary. You can consolidate at the Business Unit or any Chartfield combination level. PeopleSoft performs consolidations at the Business Unit level.

You can set up Consolidation trees to consolidate multiple divisions from the organization into the consolidated corporate entity. For each consolidation tree, you need to set up an Elimination Unit. Figure 8.5 shows a consolidation tree for a corporation consolidating the headquarters; the manufacturing division, including the Americas, Europe, and the Middle East, and Asia-Pacific; the health care; and the financial services divisions. Each division has an Elimination Unit (CE for corporate, ME1 for Americas, and ME3 for Eur-All).

Figure 8.5
The Consolidation tree.

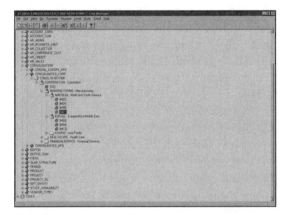

The Elimination Unit eliminates the inter-company transactions within the respective Elimination Set. The Elimination Set defines which sets of accounts will be eliminated in the consolidation process. Figure 8.6 shows one such Elimination Set using the Affiliate Method.

Figure 8.6
An Elimination Set using the Affiliate Method.

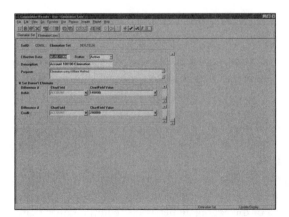

The advantage in using the Affiliate Method to account for inter-company transactions is that PeopleSoft automatically creates the inter-company balancing entries. If the Affiliate Method is not used, individual Elimination Sets need to be set up for each Business Unit/Inter-company Account combination. See Figure 8.7.

Figure 8.7
An Elimination Set without using the Affiliate Method.

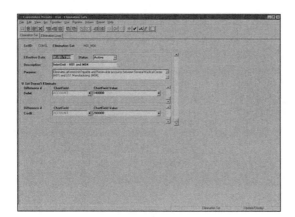

By using consolidation trees, it is relatively easy to consolidate various parts of your organization for internal purposes and still create the corporate consolidation for the entire corporate entity. Another advantage of the trees is that maintenance to accounts or organizational structure is easier to perform. In practical terms, some organizations have saved three to four days in their month-end closing by using the allocations and automatic consolidation process. The consolidation process provides a full audit trail to track the elimination and consolidating entries, minority interest calculations, and out-of-balance Elimination sets.

ONLINE LEDGER BALANCE INQUIRY

PeopleSoft provides a variety of tools to perform online account balance inquiries. This section illustrates the online G/L panels. Figure 8.8 shows the first panel in the Ledger Inquiry panel, the Ledger Criteria.

Figure 8.8
The Ledger Criteria tab of the Ledger Inquiry panel.

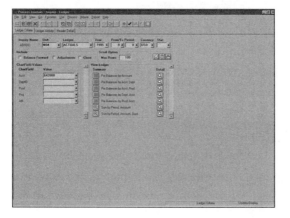

In this case, we are investigating the account 642000 for all postings in fiscal year 1995, Period 8. The Ledger Activity tab shows the detail Journals that posted amounts to the selected G/L account. On this panel, the user can review the Journal IDs and the total amounts for a specified account. See Figure 8.9.

Figure 8.9
The Ledger Activity tab of the Ledger Inquiry panel.

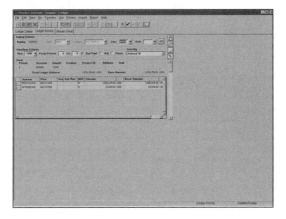

The Header Detail tab enables you to select the particular Journal for further investigation. See Figure 8.10.

Figure 8.10
The Header Activity tab of the Ledger Inquiry panel.

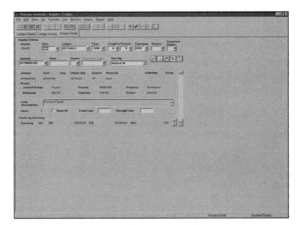

Thus, as illustrated, there is a full drill-down option, from Ledger balance to Journal Line by accounting period.

JOURNAL UPLOAD

There are five ways a user can get Journals into the PeopleSoft Journal tables. You have explored the online Journal entry method. In addition, there is a Journal Upload feature that enables users to enter journals in Excel and upload the Journals in PeopleSoft. This method requires that the user be logged in to the PeopleSoft database and have Excel and nVision running. A different variation of the Journal Upload is the Workbook Upload. The Excel Journals are saved to flat files that are uploaded using an SQR process into PeopleSoft. Excel Journals can be emailed from remote users to be uploaded to the PeopleSoft tables, using either nVision or the delivered Message Agent API. A higher-volume tool is the GLS 9002.SQR. The SQR uploads the data from a flat file into the PeopleSoft Journal Header and Journal Line.

REPORTING

As with other applications, PeopleSoft provides various tools to create both ad hoc and batch reports. nVision was designed to provide an easy and user-friendly interface to financial reporting by using a familiar platform—Excel spreadsheet. nVision Reports, such as Financial Statements, most likely will be created as part of the implementation effort. Report Books can create a number of individual reports deemed necessary are run together to create a Report Book. The user has the option of drilling down from a summary line in the nVision report to the detail Journal line. By using Time Spans, nVision can report account balances for any time period required. Time Spans are another feature of PeopleSoft by which users can define various time intervals. These predefined time intervals can then be used in both online panels and nVision layouts. Some examples of Time Spans are Current Period Last Year or Last Quarter. Any Time Span needs to be set up using the delivered Time Span Set Up panels. PeopleSoft delivers a Trial Balance and G/L account activity SQR report. Queries can be used to inquire as to Journal Status, account balances, and so forth.

This concludes the General Ledger overview. You may want to take a deep breath and have a good stretch before plunging into the depths of the Accounts Payable waters.

ACCOUNTS PAYABLE

Accounts Payable (AP) from PeopleSoft is very flexible and empowering. It has the capability of continuing processing company disbursements within your existing conventions or enabling changes that allow more control and efficiency.

For instance, suppose the organization needs to have distributed entry of vouchers at the local Business Unit. However, analysis indicates that centralized disbursement is required in order to maximize the efficiency of check distribution and electronic commerce. Separate AP Business Units can be created, and security will allow processing of approved vouchers for payment at the central processing location.

CONTROL HIERARCHY

It is important to understand the control hierarchy of this module. These components are as follows:

- Business Unit
- Origin

- Control Group
- Vendor
- Voucher

Default values are set at the top of the hierarchy (Business Unit), which ultimately facilitates voucher entry and processing. However, you can override the defaults, as necessary for special situations, at the lower levels.

Your organization may not need to use all levels. Levels of control such as these give you more flexibility. As you create processing options in levels other than Business Unit, the system frequently prompts you with the opportunity to USE DEFAULT. The following sections discuss these levels in more detail.

BUSINESS UNIT

With PeopleSoft, the organization must create at least one Business Unit for Accounts Payable. This Business Unit is unique from the General Ledger Business Unit. It is created to be an independent processing entry. Detail transactions and default settings are stored at this level.

Your Accounts Payables processing may currently be centralized, reporting to one or more General Ledgers, distributed throughout the organization with multiple General Ledgers, or some other variation. It is important to decide what form and processes the organization will follow for the Accounts Payables function. An AP Business Unit will be linked to only *one* General Ledger Business Unit. General Ledger Business Units, however, can have multiple AP Business Units reporting to them.

The following are the roles of Business Units in PeopleSoft accounts payable. Keep these in mind when designing your structure:

- Vouchers are entered by BU.
- Batch processing is requested by BU.
- You can request reports by BU.
- Chartfields may be different for each BU.
- InterUnit Accounting is based on BU.
- BU is specified for TableSet sharing.

ORIGIN

Origin identifies an entry point of PeopleSoft Accounts Payable. Examples are batch versus online, or types of expenditures, such as materials, contractors, and so on.

CONTROL GROUP

This level is generally used to identify voucher input control points. Vouchers can be assigned to personnel and the input verified by Control Group.

VENDORS

PeopleSoft Payables captures and tracks vendor information to ensure that you always have the right answer at your fingertips to satisfy your vendors. It is easy to create vendor profiles that will serve your business interests. All vendor information—for regular vendors, one-time vendors, and permanent vendors—is stored on the same set of vendor tables. You manage the vendor relationship, as shown in Figure 8.11.

Figure 8.11
Vendor relationship
flow chart.

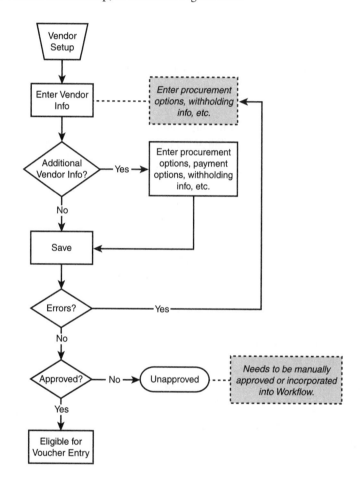

Duplicate invoice checking can be determined at the Vendor level in the hierarchy.

Additionally, if the vendor is also a customer, the appropriate number reference can be associated with the vendor. The system is capable of interfacing with the Accounts Receivable system to enable offset where necessary and/or appropriate.

Vendor location is available as multiple options. A large vendor may have multiple ship-from and pay-to locations, depending on where the Business Unit is located or on the type of product being purchased. In order to avoid having multiple vendor numbers, the use of location is used in the vendor profile.

VOUCHER PROCESSING

Processing vouchers is performed within a Business Unit. The information for voucher entry includes BU, Origin, Control unit, Vendor, and Voucher. As mentioned, Business Units sit on top of a default hierarchy that facilitates both voucher entry and payment processing. Default values entered at the Business Unit level default to the transaction level, unless you override the defaults with values stored at an intermediate level, such as voucher origin, control group, or vendor. The result is increased flexibility and control at the points where you need them to fit your business needs.

PeopleSoft allows for increased productivity for voucher entry through various methods. Some examples include Speedcharts, auto-allocations of taxes and freight, and auto-matching.

SpeedCharts can greatly increase voucher entry efficiency by reducing the number of keystrokes required to enter frequently used ChartField combinations. SpeedChart codes can be defined with multiple accounting distributions and used by entering the SpeedChart code rather than the individual ChartField combinations during data input. Remember that SpeedChart is a delivered tool that enables a quick code entry (from a pull-down tab) to represent complex and numerous accounting journal lines.

Approval for payment of vouchers can be initiated with internal matching (two-way or three-way), online approval procedures, or a combination using the PeopleSoft Workflow process.

On this panel, you can select the level of three-way matching you want to use. Three-way matching is a matching process that approves vouchers by comparing receiving information with purchase orders and voucher transaction records. You select the level of matching to receiving documents you want to use for the Business Unit: Use receipts on voucher only, Sum all receipts for PO, or Find receipts by quantity. You need to determine the option that is right for your business environment. If you want to use PPV (purchase price variance) or ERV (exchange rate variance), you need to turn on the PPV and ERV check boxes.

This screen is an example of how the system offers multiple options for approval of a voucher. Workflow is defined in the rule set.

Payment options, when approved, include ACH, AFT, and checks. Payments are available online (real-time) or in batch processing for regular payments.

OTHER FEATURES

Accounting entry Templates is an integral feature of Accounts Payable, just as in the Journal entries of General Ledger. While the voucher entry processing is concentrating on expense or inventory distribution for items purchased, offsets and taxes are recorded automatically via a Template.

VAT, Multiple currency options (MultiBook), Payment selection options, and Reporting are all included in the PeopleSoft Accounts Payable module.

We have attempted to provide you with major considerations for the installation of Accounts Payable. Your integration team will be able to configure the processes to best fit your business needs now and in the future. The next section introduces you to Accounts Receivable.

ACCOUNTS RECEIVABLE

Your PeopleSoft Accounts Receivable (AR) software is capable of adapting to existing processes, but is loaded with features that will probably give you reasons to re-engineer for the future.

Some of these features include direct entry of invoices from billing systems, application of payments using predefined algorithms to increase accuracy and reduce time, electronic interfaces to banks, multiple aging options, real-time viewing of customer balances, and intelligent calculation of finance charges (that is, "client-built" or system-delivered algorithms that will calculate added charges, such as late fees or interest).

As with any of the financial modules of PeopleSoft, it is critical to decide what form of processing and reporting for Accounts Receivable will be required after installation. Remember, at least *one* Account Receivable Business Unit must be defined.

Review the existing operations. The following are questions you should ask:

Are customer number conventions consistent? Different parts of the organization (product lines, for example) may use different customer numbering for the same customers.

How are payments being applied? Is the application timely and accurate? Have aging reports been delayed?

Are customers EDI-enabled for billing and payment? Technologies have changed dramatically over recent years. It is possible to configure the AR software to maximize these changes for the benefit of the enterprise. See the section "Cash Application," later in this chapter, for some examples.

CUSTOMER MAINTENANCE

As a prelude to setting up customers, ask yourself whether a particular customer will exist in more than one Business Unit under the same customer ID. Consider whether your Business Units will be sharing customer information, such as name and address, or whether each Business Unit will have its own customer information, even if it is repetitive.

Customer information stored under a SetID can be shared by any number of Business Units. With customer information keyed by SetID, the advantages are similar to control tables keyed by SetID: You enter the information only once and then point it to as many Business Units as you choose. Each of these Business Units will be able to process invoices, payments, and other receivables transactions for that customer.

PeopleSoft AR also enables you to group customers with similar attributes for upstream reporting. Location, D&B, Remit From, and Corporate are a few examples. Furthermore, the relationships can be defined using Tree Manager. The customer hierarchy must be named AR_CUSTOMER_CUST.

CASH APPLICATION

You can enter deposits in five ways: online as a regular deposit, online as an express deposit, automatically through a lockbox interface, through EDI, and through electronic bank statement processing.

PeopleSoft has full lockbox electronic functionality. In fact, the latest architecture enables interfacing the lockbox deposits, EDI 820, EDI CREEXT, and the automated bank statement.

The AR module gives you a full range of payment identification and search features, creating a powerful worksheet to do the complex applications. Algorithms for application are delivered and can be easily enhanced, depending on your needs.

Express deposit enables companies that have payments received with item ID to apply the payment directly without employing a worksheet.

Payment Predictor is PeopleSoft Receivables' automatic cash application feature—the genie of payment application. It's one of the alternatives in an array of cash application options that also includes express deposit and payment worksheets. The Payment Predictor program handles payments entered in regular and express deposits or through a lockbox, bank statement reconciliation, and EDI. It then matches payments with open items according to methods selected at either the Business Unit or customer level.

CREDIT MANAGEMENT

The collection features of AR include online aging, follow- up letters, dunning letters, online correspondence records, and significant historical review.

The Profile by Corporate tree enables the credit manager to view the entire exposure with a particular customer across the enterprise (including foreign currency).

An individual unit's history and current status is available in this next screen. Note that this customer is part of the corporate profile presented previously. This information is available online and can be updated as required to have real-time information.

Detailed information for credit management is a critical component of any accounts receivable system. After you've reviewed customer information at a high level, you may need to use PeopleSoft Receivables' multiple inquiry formats to research your business at a lower level of detail. When questions are raised about a customer's account, you use the item inquiry conversations panels to explore information about specific items, purchase orders, bills of lading, and the like.

AGING REPORTS

Aged Trial Balances are delivered in multiple formats depending on the business needs. They can be summarized or detailed, printed or online, and in various styles of aging buckets.

OTHER FEATURES

Monitoring activity can be done with the screen shown in Figure 8.12. Note that it enables you to identify multiple types of activity at a Business Unit level for a specific period.

Figure 8.12
The Monitor
Receivable Activity
panel.

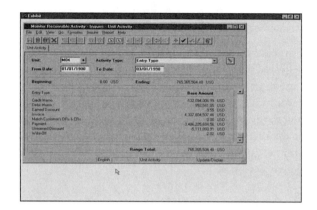

PeopleSoft has included the capability of calculating and accounting for multi-currency and VAT with your AR processing. If your customers are also vendors, this relationship can be defined so that reports are available for review.

PeopleSoft Accounts Receivable software has the versatility and features that should satisfy almost any organization's requirements, both in Treasury and Credit. The integration with Billing, General Ledger, and Accounts Payable, along with delivered reporting and monitoring tools, are added benefits of the PeopleSoft financial suite of products.

PEOPLESOFT EXPENSES

For years, companies have been trying to find an efficient and cost-effective method of reimbursing employees for business travel expenses incurred. They have encountered many obstacles along the way:

- The process involves too much manual work.
- The finance department has difficulty accounting for transactions.
- Payment was not received in a timely manner.
- Tracking activity is too difficult.

PeopleSoft Expenses provides a very simple and effective solution to this recurring problem. The flexibility of Expenses enables you to structure your reimbursement process to your company's requirements. PeopleSoft delivers a product that serves the essential needs of the reimbursement process: process expense sheet and cash advance requests, generate payment, and post journal entries. However, the complexity depends entirely on the tracking and reporting needs of the company. It also provides multilevel security, which presents a very manageable solution to a company's security issues. The strength of Expenses is how well it is integrated with the other PeopleSoft products, such as Human Resources, Projects, General Ledger, and Payables. By incorporating these functions into a single database, it reduces maintenance, reconciliation, and data integrity problems. PeopleSoft delivers simple mechanisms that link the different products, although it is the structure of these links that enables the separate applications to work effectively with non-PeopleSoft products as well.

The structure and processing rules that drive the Expenses module are stored in core tables. These tables are delivered with and shared among many PeopleSoft applications. For example, if you already use other PeopleSoft applications, such as PeopleSoft General Ledger, much of the framework will already be set up. Because the implementation of PeopleSoft Expenses is common to the implementation of all PeopleSoft applications, this section focuses only on the options and processes specific to the Expenses module. It looks more closely at the different configuration options, or setup, of Expenses and the major business processes that Expenses performs.

CONFIGURATION OF PEOPLESOFT EXPENSES

The core configuration of PeopleSoft Expenses consists of four groupings: Policy Definition, Security, Employee Data, and Classification of Expenses.

POLICY DEFINITION

You determine the policies that each Business Unit must follow in order to approve expense sheets and cash advances. The approval and audit rules will automatically be applied to the expense sheet or cash advance when submitted by employees. Based on the approval and audit rules that you define, expense sheet and cash advance requests can be paid immediately after submission or they can progress slowly through one or more review checkpoints.

You can specify that all expense sheets and/or all cash advance requests will require approval. Also, you can limit the approval requirements. Approval is required only when

- The expense item exceeded a certain amount.
- A receipt is not submitted for the expense item.
- The expense sheet included VAT items.

Audit rules can be applied to expense sheets and/or cash advances in lieu of or in addition to the approval policies. They are defined in a very similar fashion. In addition to the same three circumstances used by the approval rules, other options can be selected that require the audit of the expense sheet. You can require that the expense sheet be audited if the expense sheet originated from the Expenses Traveler. You can elect to audit expense sheets on a specific basis. You specify how often that you want to audit by entering the number. For example, you indicate that you want every third sheet audited. The audit of cash advances can be refined further than the expense sheets. You can designate that specific employees, Business Units, or departments will automatically require an audit of their cash advance request.

SECURITY

PeopleSoft applications use multilevel security in order to provide a very flexible and efficient solution to a company's security issues. Each staff member is assigned an operator ID that is authorized to access the panels and menus of his or her expense information. However, the company may have a separate staff, such as a travel and expense department, that is responsible for submitting the expense sheets on behalf of the employees. In this case, the operator IDs for these staff members are authorized to access the panels of the Expenses system.

Granting approval authority to a specific operator is very similar. For each operator ID, you grant Read/Write access specific to every Business Unit and department combination that you enter. The operator is explicitly denied access to any combination not entered on this panel.

EMPLOYEE DATA

The main customers of the reimbursement process are your employees. Therefore, the employee data is the foundation of the Expenses module. In order to ensure a central repository for personnel information, most of the employee profile used by the Expenses module can be loaded only from the Human Resources and Payroll system. PeopleSoft provides a process for you to export human resources data needed for use in the Expenses module. Certain employee information, such as the following, is stored specifically in the Expenses module:

- The method of payment used to reimburse expenses for the employee—The options are automated clearing house, electronic funds transfer (EFT), or system check. If the automated clearing house or EFT option is chosen, the bank account to which reimbursement will be deposited must be defined.
- The employee's maximum allowable cash advance limit.
- The credit card vendor and account number for the employee—This option applies only if the company elects to make direct payments on behalf of employees to credit card vendors.

CLASSIFICATION OF EXPENSES

The flexibility of the Expenses module enables you to classify and track expenses for reporting and analysis purposes very easily. Specific classifications are defined during setup that are required by the user during input. These classifications also enable you to specify dollar amount limitations for approval and audit policies. Such classifications include expense location group, expense location, expense type group, expense type, and business purpose. These components are discussed in the following sections.

EXPENSE LOCATION GROUP

Expense location group enables you to designate more than one city or travel destination to a common classification, such as Europe or Italy.

EXPENSE LOCATION

You define each city or travel destination in an expense location and assign each one to an expense location group. This gives you the means by which you can track and verify that reasonable spending policies are being practiced by employees during business travel. For example, you expect to pay more for a hotel in Japan than you would in Mexico.

EXPENSE TYPE GROUP

You classify typical employee expenses into an expense type group, such as airfare, hotel, meals, and so on, for tracking purposes. This also enables you to enter default accounting information, such as account number or department for each expense type group. For example, all transactions using the airfare expense type group post to the Airfare Travel Expense account number specified.

EXPENSE TYPE

Expense type enables you to further define the type of expense incurred by employees. It also assists in refining the amount of information required during input. By selecting certain options, you can require the employees to enter additional information, such as the airline ticket number, the names of individuals who attended the dinner, the number of nights in a hotel, the number of miles traveled by automobile, and so on.

BUSINESS PURPOSE

Business purpose enables you to justify the reason for a particular business expense, such as a meeting or trade show.

By using the classifications defined earlier, you can establish authorized spending limits for a particular expense type. The Expenses module then compares the input of the employee for a particular expense item to the amount established in the company policies and determines whether the expense should be denied, be approved, or require additional approval.

FUNCTIONS OF PEOPLESOFT EXPENSES

The main functions of PeopleSoft Expenses are to compile four distinct business processes: Process Cash Advance, Process Expense Sheet, Generate Payment, and Post Journal Entries. Two of these procedures take place solely within the Expenses module: process cash advance and expense sheet requests. However, the remaining two functions, generate payment and post journal entries, extract data from the Expenses module into the Payables and General Ledger modules, respectively. Let's take a look at these four processes more closely.

PROCESSING AND PREPARING THE CASH ADVANCE

Companies provide employees who travel on behalf of the company with cash to pay for items such as meals, ground transportation, or gratuities in order to minimize the impact of business travel on their personal finances. The Expenses module enables you to process these cash advances to specific employees.

The employee requesting the cash advance creates a new cash advance by providing the necessary information for the required fields. He or she must select the business purpose and source of payment from a predetermined list of choices that was created when you set up the Expenses module. He or she must also enter the amount of cash requested. When he or she is satisfied that all cash advance information is correct, the cash advance is submitted to the approval process. The system checks the approval and audit rules previously set up in order to determine where the cash advance should be sent. The panel indicates how many levels of authorization are required for this cash advance: None, Individual and Auditor, Individual Only, or Auditor Only.

APPROVING THE CASH ADVANCE

If the cash advance requires an approval, the designated individual must approve the cash advance before it is eligible for auditing or payment. The designated individual should be the only person who has access to the approval panel. Employees cannot approve their own cash advances. He or she then must decide whether to approve, hold, or deny the cash advance request. If the cash advance is denied, the individual must enter a description to indicate why it was not approved. He or she also has the option of returning the cash advance request to the employee for modifications.

AUDITING THE CASH ADVANCE

If required by the audit rules, the auditor must approve the cash advance before it is eligible for payment. The audit process is almost identical to the approval process. The designated auditor also must decide whether to allow, hold, or deny the cash advance request. If not approved, the auditor must enter a description as to why it was not approved, and he or she has the option of returning the cash advance to the employee for modifications.

PROCESSING AND PREPARING THE EXPENSE SHEET

Employees who travel on behalf of their company sometimes pay for items, such as airfare, hotel, or meals, out of their personal finances and are later reimbursed from the company. The Expenses module enables you to process these reimbursement requests to specific employees. The employee requesting the reimbursement will create a new expense sheet by providing the necessary information for the required fields. He or she must select the business purpose, expenditure payment method, expense type, and expense location from a predetermined list of choices that was created when you set up the Expenses module. He or she must also enter the amount of expense item and whether a receipt will be submitted with the expense. You may have activated an expense type edit that requires additional information, such as airline ticket number, the names of individuals who attended the dinner, and so on. The Business Unit, account number, and department fields should be populated based on the criteria previously entered during setup. However, these fields can be edited if necessary. When he or she is satisfied that all expense sheet information is correct, the expense sheet is submitted to the approval process. The system checks the approval and audit rules previously set up in order to determine where the expense sheet should be sent.

The panel will indicate how many levels of authorization are required for this expense sheet: None, Individual and Auditor, Individual Only, or Auditor Only.

APPROVING THE EXPENSE SHEET

If the expense sheet requires an approval, the designated individual must approve the cash advance before it is eligible for auditing or payment. The designated individual should be the only person who has access to the approval panel. Employees cannot approve their own expense sheets. He or she then must decide whether to approve or deny each individual expense line. If an expense line is denied approval, the line will be marked as a personal expense and is therefore non-reimbursable to the employee. Therefore, the entire expense sheet does not have to be approved in order for a partial payment process to continue. The individual must decide whether to approve, hold, or deny the entire expense sheet request. If the expense sheet is approved, only those individual lines previously marked approved will be available for auditing or payment. If the expense sheet is denied, the individual has the option of returning the expense sheet to the employee for modifications.

AUDIT EXPENSE SHEET

If required by the audit rules, the auditor must approve the expense sheet before it is eligible for payment. The audit process is almost identical to the approval process. The designated auditor must decide whether to approve or deny each individual expense line, as well as approve, hold, or deny the entire expense sheet request. If the entire request sheet is approved, only those individual lines previously marked approved will be ready for payment. If the expense sheet is denied, the auditor has the option of returning the expense sheet to the employee for modifications.

GENERATING PAYMENT

After both the cash advance and expense sheet requests have completed the approval and/or audit process, they are ready for payment. The Expenses module comes delivered with two defined source transactions, one for expense sheets (EXPN) and the other for cash advances (EXAD). They are also referred to as payment sources. These source transactions provide the link between the Expenses module and the Payables module. In order to generate payments in the Payables module, a Pay Cycle must be defined in the Payables module. The transaction source must be completed as part of the Pay Cycle definition. Entering EXPN and/or EXAD as the source transaction notifies the Payables module to generate payments based on the expense sheets and/or cash advances that have been approved for payment in the Expenses module.

POSTING JOURNAL ENTRIES

POST PAYMENT

Within PeopleSoft, payments do not automatically post to the General Ledger as a result of being generated. A separate process needs to be run for the results of the payments to be posted to the General Ledger. The journal entry resulting from the generation of payments follows:

- DR Expenses Accrual (defined during setup of Expenses)
- CR Cash (defined during setup of Payables)

The actual account numbers that represent the Expenses Accrual and Employee Advances line items are defined in the Accounting Entry Template panel of the PeopleSoft General Ledger.

POST LIABILITY

Similar to payments, the journal entries generated from the approval and/or audit process do not automatically post to the General Ledger. A separate process needs to be run in order for the expense transactions to post to the General Ledger. The journal entries created as a result of the expense transactions differ between expense sheets and cash advances.

For example, airfare and lodging costs are incurred and entered into the Expenses module by an employee. The following journal entry would be created:

Expense sheet transaction

DR Airfare Expense (defined by employee during input)

DR Lodging Expense (defined by employee during input)

CR Expenses Accrual (defined during setup of Expenses)

An employee submits a request to receive a cash advance for a future business trip. The check will be generated from the AP system. The following journal entry would be created:

Cash advance transaction that generates payment in Payables

DR Employee Advances (defined during setup of Expenses)

CR Expenses Accrual (defined during setup of Expenses)

An employee records a cash advance that he or she has received from the petty cash fund. Therefore, a check will not be generated from the AP system. The following journal entry would be created:

Cash advance transaction that does not generate payment in Payables

DR Employee Advances (defined during setup of Expenses)

CR Cash (defined during setup of Expenses)

EXPENSES TRAVELER

Up to now, you have looked at working online within PeopleSoft Expenses. However, there is an alternative to processing expense sheet and cash advance requests. It is called the Expenses Traveler. The Expenses Traveler is a third-party mobile client that your employees can use to enter expense sheet and cash advance requests while they are not connected to your company network. The Expenses Traveler has some of the same functionality as PeopleSoft Expenses, only to a lesser degree. Users have the ability to enter and submit for approval both expense sheet and cash advance requests. The panels on the Expenses Traveler look almost identical to the corresponding PeopleSoft Expenses' panels. The Expenses Traveler stores control data, expense sheet and cash advance data, and user-defined lists from PeopleSoft Expenses. It is recommended that you download the control data periodically from PeopleSoft Expenses to the Expenses Traveler so that the drop-down lists contain the most recent company information. PeopleSoft delivers a download mechanism that is quick and simple to use. After you have completed and saved an expense sheet and/ or cash advance request, you are ready to connect to your company's network and submit the request to PeopleSoft Expenses for further processing. The data is validated before the request is submitted to PeopleSoft Expenses. Also, during the submission process, the control data in the Expenses Traveler is refreshed with the most current data in PeopleSoft Expenses.

The flexibility of the Expenses module makes it a very efficient application for all users. Its integration with other PeopleSoft and non-PeopleSoft products provides companies with the opportunity to reimburse employees for travel expenses incurred in a routine manner. The next section discusses Asset Management.

THE ASSET MANAGEMENT MODULE

The PeopleSoft Asset Management (PS AM) module enables the control, recording, and reporting of all activities, costs, expenses, and relevant information related to asset transactions. PS AM enables tracking of capitalized and noncapitalized costs.

The AM module was created to enable full asset transaction life cycle control. Depending on which modules are used and the integration level between the PS modules, a fully integrated PeopleSoft system can track asset transactions through the following stages:

■ Purchase Requisition

■ Purchase Order

■ Asset Consolidation/Unitization

■ Vendor Invoice

■ Project Costing (if the cost is part of a Construction In Progress project)

■ Capital Plan tracking (Authorized amount versus budgeted versus capitalized)

■ Asset Capitalization (Additions)

■ Asset Changes (Adjustments, Recategorizations, Transfers)

■ Asset Disposals

In addition to the stages and activities mentioned, the AM module will also control and track

- Asset cost history
- Depreciation Expense
- Budgeted Depreciation and "what if" calculations
- Gain or Loss on Disposal
- Physical Inventory
- Asset Maintenance
- Research and Development (R&D)
- Capitalized Leases
- Replacement Values and asset reevaluations (for insurance purposes)
- Joint Venture Accounting for assets
- Group Asset (mostly used in the utilities industry)

AM INTEGRATION WITH OTHER MODULES

The Asset Management (AM) module integrates with the following PS modules: Purchasing, Accounts Payable, Project Costing, Budgets, General Ledger, and an external interface to various Property Tax Systems. Asset Management was designed to receive asset-relevant information from AP and the Purchasing Modules as well as Project Costing. When entering an AP voucher, the operator can indicate that the item is an asset. Later, a batch program will add the assets in the AM tables to start its depreciation. (See Figure 8.13.)

Figure 8.13
Entering voucher information.

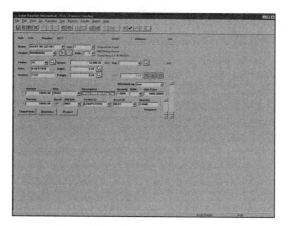

In the case of a Construction In Progress asset scenario, operators can accumulate a pool of project costs, grouping various cost lines as one or more assets. Two mass changes can capitalize the items as assets in the AM tables. The transfer from PC to AM is quite laborious because of multiple steps and detail information that needs to be captured at the resource-line level in the Project Costing to be able to automatically generate assets in the AM module. Careful planning and testing, either in the Conference Room Pilot or in the initial System Test Phase, should be performed to ensure optimal process and information flow.

NEW FEATURES IN PEOPLESOFT ASSET MANAGEMENT 7.5

The following are the new or radically revamped features introduced in version 7.5, which was the first version to include expanded international support. Some specific features include

- Inflation adjustments calculations for Chile, Argentina, and Mexico. These calculations enable country-specific statutory restatement of asset values.

- Tax reports for Australia and Canada.

- Depreciation methods for Germany.

- Interunit transfers with fixed markup or percentage of cost markup.

- Document sequencing—Document sequencing is a statutory requirement more prevalent in the Latin accounting model countries. The authorities issue prenumbered invoices, shipping documents, and so on, stamped by the respective regulatory entity. These documents can be audited later to verify completeness. PeopleSoft enables the assignment of unique numbers to each recorded transaction.

The following are new or expanded features in version 7.5:

- Web Self Service templates for Asset Listings by Location/Departments/Custodian— This feature enables users to get asset listings via the Web.

- Joint Venture Processing—This feature enables joint venture setup. You can establish a joint venture with multiple participants. Each joint venture participant may have a different percentage equity in the joint venture. Transactions at the Joint Venture Business Unit will affect the joint venture participants (cost, depreciation gain/loss) based on individual equity percentages in the Joint Venture Business Unit.

- Tax Reporting—Capital Gains, Tax Credits, and FAS 109.

- Physical Inventory—This is a new functionality with delivered integration to Tangram's Asset Insight. Asset Insight replaces barcoding for networked assets. It can query over the network and report on various PC components, such as memory, hard drive, and so on.

- Leases processing and reporting—This enables improved tracking of operating and capital leases.

- Research and development processing and reports.

ASSET MANAGEMENT KEY FEATURES

This section explores some of the key building blocks of the AM module. As with all other PS modules, AM was designed to provide a high level of flexibility in the system configuration and setup. The combination of asset profile, category, class, and cost type provides increased reporting and recording flexibility.

ASSET MANAGEMENT BUSINESS UNIT

The Application Management Business Unit (AM BU) has a many-to-one relationship to the G/L BU, which means that you can have multiple AM BUs posting transactions to one G/L BU. One word of caution: The more AM BUs you set up, the larger the control tables and the record control group tables will get. A significant increase in the number of rows in these tables will adversely impact performance for both online and batch transaction processing.

ASSET BOOKS

Asset Books are a very powerful feature in PS AM. Books enable grouping and tracking assets for different purposes. The systems enable the configuration of an unlimited number of Asset Books. Books enable the flexibility to track asset characteristics, such as cost, accumulated depreciation, life, depreciation methods (Straight Line, Double Declining Balance, and so on), and depreciation convention (Actual Month, Half Year, and so on) differently and independently in each book. Table 8.2 illustrates a potential example: US_GAAP is the Accounting Book, US_TAX is the Tax Book, and MEX_LOCAL is the Mexican Local Statutory Book.

TABLE 8.2   AN ASSET BOOK EXAMPLE

	US_GAAP	US_TAX	MEX_LOCAL
Cost	1,000.00	1,100.00	100.00
Accumulated Depreciation	800.00	600.00	60.00
Life (monthly periods)	60	120	84
Convention	AM (Actual Month)	MQ (Mid Quarter)	FM (Following Month)
AM Calendar	CY (Calendar Year)	FY (Fiscal Year)	CY
Depreciation Method	SL (Straight Line)	DDB150 (double declining balance 150%)	UD (User Defined)
Currency	USD	USD	MXP
Rate Type	Current	Current	Average

The following are a few considerations you should be aware of when deciding on setting up AM books:

- There is a one-to-one relationship between Book and Currency.
- There is a one-to-one relationship between Book and Ledger. Only one book can create accounting entries to a ledger (The US_GAAP book can create Accounting entries to the GAAP Ledger only. More on General Ledger Ledgers in the GL section).

- There is only one calendar per book.
- There is only one Capitalization Minimum amount per book.

Depending on reporting requirements, various books can be set up to accomplish property tax, ACE Depreciation, and various what if scenarios. In PS AM, there is an option, Keep All Books In Synch, to be set up at the AM BU level. If turned on, any asset transactions will be automatically reflected in all existing sets of books. Thus, if an asset is added, PS AM will automatically add the cost to all the books set up for that respective BU.

ASSET PROFILES

One of the building blocks of PS AM is the Asset Profile. Careful analysis and planning should be done before setting up Asset Profiles to ensure that PS AM will match corporate, statutory, and operational requirements. The purpose of the Asset Profile is to streamline data entry and to ensure consistency when performing asset transactions. The asset profile groups together asset characteristics such as

- Asset Books
- Asset Category
- Depreciation Status (depreciable or not)
- Salvage Value (either an absolute value or percentage of cost)
- R&D information
- Depreciation Limits (dictated by IRS based on tax years)
- Depreciation Attributes, such as Life, Depreciation Convention, Depreciation Method, and Retirement Convention
- Tax Attributes, such as Personal or Real Property, 1245 or 1250, Regulation, Guideline Class, Listed Property, Percentage Business use, and various Tax Credit information

When performing an asset Add, by defaulting the profile, all these asset attributes are automatically captured in the system. The result is faster, more accurate, and consistent data entry.

ASSET CATEGORIES/TRANSACTION TYPES

Asset Categories were created to drive the posting from AM to the General Ledger. For example, if in the GL you have Building and Accumulated Depreciation Buildings accounts, you will set up a Building AM category.

Transaction types in combination with asset categories will be applied to Accounting Templates to generate the accounting lines. The transaction types in AM are Additions, Adjustments, Retirements, Recategorizations, and Transfers. The AM accounting lines are the detail information for the Journal Entries generated from AM to the GL.

ASSET CLASSES/COST TYPES

These two attributes were created to provide increased granularity in both reporting and in the accounting posting to the G/L.

GROUP AND COMPOSITE ASSET

These two features relate to very specialized industry requirements. Group assets depreciate at the group-asset level while maintaining the cost at the individual group-member level. Composite assets do not maintain any information at the detail level. All cost and depreciation amounts are tracked at the Composite asset level.

PARENT/CHILD ASSET GROUPING

In PS AM, there are three options regarding tracking assets:

- Tracking items as individual assets.

- Creating a parent component—An example is a computer. One of the components (the PC unit) is the parent component, and the keyboard, monitor, and external scanner are its children.

- Parent only—The parent is created only for the purpose of grouping together the children. All children have individual costs and depreciate at the children level.

ASSET MANAGEMENT TRANSACTION FLOW

In understanding PS AM, it is very important to cover the transaction flows and the interactions between each stage during the monthly process. See Figure 8.14 for an illustration of the process flow.

Figure 8.14
PeopleSoft asset management transaction flow.

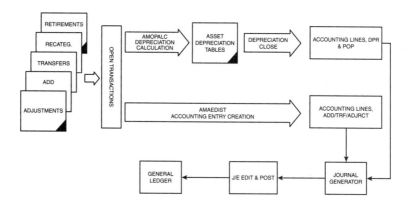

The first process we will look at is Asset Depreciation.

ASSET DEPRECIATION

When an asset is added to PeopleSoft, it creates an Open Transaction in the OPEN_TRANS table. The OPEN_TRANS table keeps track of two process statuses:

- Has the asset been depreciated?
- Has the transaction been captured in the form of Accounting Lines to be passed to the G/L?

PS AM uses the Depreciation Process to calculate Depreciation from the time the Asset was added to the end of its life. The information is stored by year in the Depreciation Table. Using inquiry panels, a user can inquire by Asset Book, by year, by period, by the Net Book Value, by Accumulated Depreciation, and by Depreciation Expense amounts for each asset. (See Figure 8.15.)

Figure 8.15
Inquiring about net book value of asset depreciation.

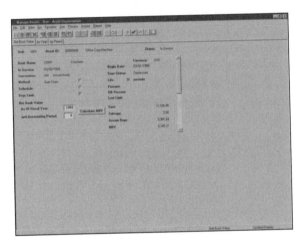

Every time a user changes one of the attributes that have an impact on Depreciation Calculation (Useful Life, Depreciation Convention, Cost, Retirements, and so on), Depreciation Calculation must be run. PS AM has two options regarding Depreciation. It can be run automatically every time a change in an asset created an Open Transaction, or it can be run as a batch program.

As mentioned earlier, PS AM calculates the Depreciation to the end of the asset's life. Thus, for budgeting purposes, if you need to know how much the depreciation expense will be for the whole asset base or for various categories of assets in the future (in one, two, or x years from now) the information is stored in the PS AM tables (DEPRECIATION and DEPR_EXP_PD3_VW). An additional feature related to Depreciation is the PS-delivered Net Book Value table. By running the Load Net Book Value program, PS loads the Cost, Accumulated Depreciation, Net Book Value, and As of Date in a table. Using Query or the delivered PS Crystal reports, users can get the Net Book Value for various ranges of assets. This information can be downloaded in a spreadsheet for further analysis.

ASSET ACCOUNTING ENTRY CREATION

As with all other PS modules, the accounting impact of AM transactions is captured via the AM Accounting lines. The key to creating accounting lines is the Accounting Template. An Accounting Template defines the General Ledger accounts for each type of transaction. In the Accounting Template, you can specify what kind of detail is needed in the G/L from the PS AM module. Accounting templates need to be set up for all the Transaction Type/Category/Class/Cost Type combinations. By using Cost Type and Asset Class, you can post transactions to very specific G/L accounts. Creating all these Accounting Templates can be quite laborious but must be done accurately to prevent Accounting Line Creation and the Journal Generator from failing. (See Figure 8.16.)

Figure 8.16
Creating accounting entry templates.

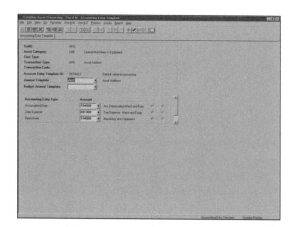

The types of transactions that create accounting lines are Asset Adds, Retirements, Recategorizations, Transfers, Cost Adjustments, and Depreciation. PS generates the AM Accounting Lines using two processes: Asset Accounting Lines Creation (AMAEDIST.SQR) and the Depreciation Close (AMDPCLOSE.SQR). For all the Depreciation transactions, the Depreciation Close creates the Depreciation Accounting Lines. For all other transactions (Adds, Transfers, Recategorizations, Retirements, and Adjustments), the Asset Accounting Line Creation will create the respective Accounting Lines.

DEPRECIATION CLOSE

The Depreciation Close process creates the Accounting Lines for all related Depreciation Transactions and Leases. If the AM BU has transactions denominated in a different currency than the G/L BU the AM BU is posting to, both the exchange rate type and the exchange rates need to be specified before running the Depreciation Close. In the accounting lines, both the AM amount and the G/L translated transaction amount will be captured, thus creating a detail audit trail. Usually, the Depreciation Close is run at month-end after the AM activities have been completed for the month. You can rerun the Depreciation Close process. In this case, all Depreciation-related accounting entries will be deleted and new accounting lines for Depreciation transactions will be created. The Depreciation Close process has an option to run the Budgeted Depreciation process. This process will create the Budgeted Depreciation and post the amounts to the Budget Ledger for review. An important word of caution: You cannot rerun Depreciation Close if the Journal Generator has created Journals from the Accounting Lines related to Depreciation transactions for the period. In other words, pay attention to the order of the processes between Depreciation Expense (AMDPCALC), Accounting Entry Creation (AMAEDIST), Depreciation Close (AMDPCLOSE), and Journal Generator (FSPGJGEN).

ASSET MANAGEMENT PERIOD CLOSE

The AM period can be closed the same way an accounting period is closed. When the process is run, no transactions can be processed with that accounting date. This process prevents overdepreciating assets for a specific period. When closed, an AM period cannot be reopened via PS panels the same way an accounting period can. Thus, be sure that you really want to close the AM period before you do it.

ASSET CONVERSION

In the case of Asset Management, many feel that the asset conversion is 80 percent of the headache. AM is not a high-volume online transaction processing application. When converted, most assets have a relatively low turnover. In PeopleSoft, AM assets are depreciated based on their depreciation lives. The difficulty in conversion stems from the fact that legacy business rules need to be translated and mapped to PeopleSoft profiles, categories, and cost types. You need to understand Life to Date versus Remaining Life PeopleSoft calculations, the accounting date and transaction date implications, and many other technical details related to asset conversions. PeopleBooks, the PeopleSoft online documentation, has some very good information in relation to converting assets to PeopleSoft. Careful and in-depth review of these sections is an absolute prerequisite to any successful conversion activity. In-depth coverage of the conversion is beyond the scope of this chapter. Instead, we will explore some highlights and some key issues.

The conversion process in PeopleSoft AM can take two routes depending on your Asset Management legacy system and/or your choice. If you convert from Best's FAS2000, PeopleSoft delivers conversion programs. In this case, you should review the Conversion Loader SQR's (AMCV1000 and AMCV2000). You may want to change some default fields and review precision (number of decimals) while testing conversion. The process is as follows:

1. Load the data from FAS2000 into the Conversion tables.
2. Load it to the three interface tables (INTFC_FIN, INTFC_PHY_A, and INTFC_PHY_B).
3. Run the Transaction Edit to ensure that valid data is being loaded in the PS AM system.
4. Load the transactions via the Transaction Loader (AMIF1000.SQR) into the PS AM tables.
5. Run the Depreciation process to complete the conversion.

If you do not convert from FAS2000, skip step 1. Instead, you need to create your own process to load the Interface tables with the Asset legacy data. The following is information that you should be aware of before starting the PS AM conversion:

- Read PeopleBooks regarding Accounting and Transaction Date options in the AMIF1000.sqr. Most of the time, in a conversion, the asset Cost and Depreciation amounts are captured in the G/L for the last accounting period (that is, if you convert on January 2, you already have the previous December's balances in the GL.) In your custom SQR, make TRANS_DATE and ACCOUNTING_DATE 12/31/XX. Make sure that in the AMIF1000, you set the following options:

```
! Do Insert-Open_Trans
! Do Insert-Open_Trans-Profile

do Process-Conversion-Open-Trans
```

    If you want the AMIF1000 to set the TRANS_DATE and ACCOUNTING_DATE to be the first date of the next accounting period, use the following options in AMIF1000:

```
Do Insert-Open_Trans
Do Insert-Open_Trans-Profile

! do Process-Conversion-Open-Trans
```

- Make friends with your DBA. Asset Management conversion can be a difficult issue depending on the number of assets converted. Allow plenty of rollback space and extents. AMDPCALC is notorious for requiring a lot of troubleshooting regarding performance. How much space is required for an AM conversion? You allocate the biggest space to the Depreciation Table. It stores one row per each asset per each book per each year of its useful life. Thus, if you have an asset with six years life and four books, you will end up with 24 rows in the depreciation table for that asset, assuming no PDP (Prior Depreciation Period) rows. Additional space reserves should be allocated to various temporary tables used by the Depreciation Process in calculating the depreciation amounts.

- Allow plenty of time to depreciate converted assets. Between running AMIF1000 (loading the assets) and AMDPCALC (depreciating the assets), it can be quite time-consuming. This should be a consideration if you have large data sets.

- Do not exceed more than 10,000 OPEN_TRANS IDs per RUN_CONTROL when running AMIF1000 and AMDPCALC.

- In the conversion, if you do not populate a valid profile ID, you should populate the field with a value. Otherwise, you will not be able to perform any transactions on the assets after they are converted.

- Review and understand the Life to Date and Remaining Life Depreciation methods. If you like the Depreciation amounts to date from your legacy system, use the following options:

    - Remaining Life for all converted assets except current fiscal year additions
    - Life to Date for current year additions

PeopleSoft AM is using Remaining Life to take the Net Book Value and prorate it over the remaining useful life of the asset. Under the Life to Date option, it recalculates the Accumulated Depreciation and records a PDP for any amount different than the Accumulated Depreciation amount loaded as of the conversion date.

- Coordinate with the G/L team which transactions generated from PS AM require posting to the G/L.
- Reconcile the Cost and Accumulated Depreciation amounts loaded in the conversion with the data from the Legacy system as of the conversion date.

To review briefly, the PeopleSoft Asset Management module enables the user to have an overall grasp of asset transactions.

Now that Asset Management has been covered, your next task is to gain an understanding of the Budgets module within PeopleSoft.

THE BUDGETS MODULE

The Budgets module is a unique part of the PeopleSoft software package. Your General Ledger will continue to have multiple budget ledgers; the data will flow from the Budgets module with unlimited iterations.

Budgets enables you to extract data from tables, manipulate it using intuitive and easy-to-use tools, and then move it back into the original tables (that is, General Ledger).

The Budgets process brings together components from PeopleSoft (ledger and nonledger) and Arbor Essbase to provide a robust budgeting environment. The following sections give a graphical description of the processes and interactions.

ESSBASE

Budget data is prepared and reviewed via an Essbase cube, a separate, *multidimensional* storage facility with an Excel-based user interface. It is the heart of PeopleSoft Budgets. PeopleSoft ledger and nonledger data can be loaded into the cube, or budgets can be directly entered into the cube. The Message Agent facilitates the movement of data.

Typically, historical General Ledger information is downloaded in the Cube. Additionally, other data, such as salary history, position information, economic data, and so on can be loaded.

Data can be manipulated, reviewed, and approved using Budgets Explorer, a budget-specific user interface facility for Essbase that is delivered with PeopleSoft Budgets 7.5.

COORDINATOR

The information for Budgets is controlled centrally. This can be for an individual or a department. The Coordinator is provided utilities, which include panels, processes, and PeopleTools objects. He or she must be involved from start to finish.

The Coordinator is responsible for creating a reporting structure using Tree Manager. This determines the relationships across the various OLAP dimensions, as well as responsibilities for preparation and review.

BUDGETS EXPLORER

The Budgets Explorer is the Budgets User's interface into the Budgets Cube—for ledger data—and to associate nonledger data stored in your PeopleSoft database. The Budgets Explorer enables the person responsible for preparing or reviewing budget data to view, manipulate, and edit data with functions specific to the budgeting process.

Budgets Explorer is installed separately. PeopleSoft is not required on every desktop. Budgets Explorer can be used in either online or offline mode.

OTHER FEATURES

Because the Budgets Explorer exists outside the PeopleSoft Financials Database, it uses Message Agent to facilitate the movement of data.

Another key feature is the use of Phase Monitor. This is the business process that monitors the budget cycles by updating phase statuses, sending email notifications, and granting access to budget data through Budgets Explorer. It works behind the scenes, based on the information provided by the Budget Controller through the phase panels.

Only when the Controller is satisfied that a particular budget cycle or phase is complete does he or she upload the budget data to the appropriate General Ledger for comparative reporting. There are no limits to the number of budgets, forecasts, or iterations of each.

PEOPLESOFT TREASURY

PeopleSoft 7.5 brought many functional improvements to its already robust suite of financial software. One of those advancements is the advent of PeopleSoft Treasury. This global, multi-currency module finally gives Treasury Manager one tool to monitor cash, debt, and investment transactions, and to integrate the related accounting events into the General Ledger. This section introduces the PeopleSoft Treasury module. This module is very new to the marketplace. Because its general release was in June 1998, only a few organizations have completed their implementation of PeopleSoft Treasury. However, over 100 companies have purchased the software and plan to implement it.

PeopleSoft Treasury puts cash, debt, and investment information in one place to better control the issues facing today's Treasury Manager. As the business environment changes and globalization continues, Treasury Manager face

- Greater expectations from executive management on cash utilization
- Cost management of bank charges and department overhead
- Increased complexity of financial instruments
- Continued mergers and acquisitions of sometimes smaller, less sophisticated companies without a full-time treasury function
- Managing multiple bank accounts
- Moving toward shared services without adding personnel

PeopleSoft Treasury is designed to be installed with PeopleSoft General Ledger 7.5, but it can be run as a standalone system. Unlike other treasury systems, PeopleSoft Treasury integrates with other PeopleSoft modules to provide a complete financial picture of your cash inflows and outflows. In addition, accounting events from the financial transactions created in PeopleSoft Treasury can be processed into journal entries in PeopleSoft General Ledger. This saves you time by not rekeying data between multiple systems.

UNDERSTANDING THE COMPONENTS OF PEOPLESOFT TREASURY

Treasury is comprised of three modules—Cash Management, Deal Management, and Risk Management:

- Cash Management is the foundation of the PeopleSoft Treasury and provides the ability to analyze current and future cash positions, perform bank reconciliation, initiate payments and bank transfers, maintain banking relationships, and even operate an in-house bank.
- Deal Management enables Treasury managers to capture deals, generate confirmations, perform settlements, integrate accounting entries, and monitor deal positions.
- Risk Management provides support for valuation and analysis of a treasury's portfolio of debt and investments.

These three tools can be configured in the following ways:

- Cash Management
- Cash Management and Deal Management
- Cash Management, Deal Management, and Risk Management

These components are discussed in more depth in the following sections.

CASH MANAGEMENT

Many treasury departments manage cash with spreadsheets. PeopleSoft Treasury provides the facilities to bring the spreadsheet information into one system. This provides greater control over cash funds, particularly in an organization with many bank accounts, and higher-quality reporting information. Cash Management pulls cash-related dates from Accounts Receivable, Accounts Payable, Expenses, and other PeopleSoft modules to provide current and future cash flow information. The biggest benefit to using PeopleSoft Treasury's Cash Management is the Cash Positions Worksheet.

The Worksheet provides a snapshot view of your cash position over varying time periods with the ability to drill down through the components of the cash balance. The Cash Positions Worksheet is also tree-driven. This provides a great deal of flexibility in defining a rollup structure that best fits your needs. You can even define more than one tree structure and view your cash position in many different ways. Figure 8.17 shows an example of a Cash Positions tree that comes in the PeopleSoft Single User Version 7.5.

Figure 8.17
The Cash Positions
tree.

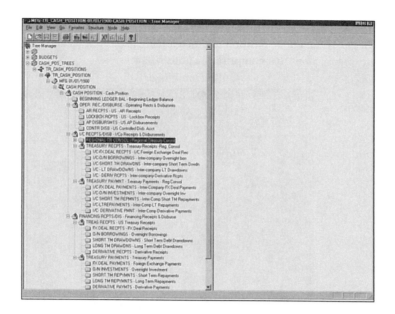

If you are familiar with PeopleSoft trees, you will notice there are no detail values in the Cash Positions tree. The Cash Positions Worksheet uses only Nodes on the tree, and there are special Node Definitions to further refine the transactions included in the Worksheet. Figure 8.18 illustrates the Selection Criteria panel of the Node Definition and the process to define the data included in the Cash Positions Worksheet.

Figure 8.18
The Selection Criteria
tab of the Cash
Positions tree.

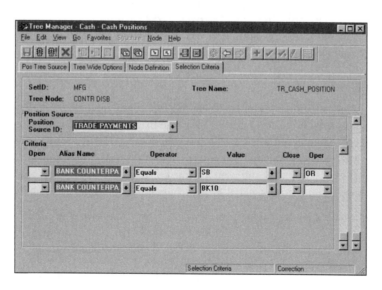

The backbone of the Cash Management module is the Cash Positions Worksheet. The drill-down capabilities provide a powerful tool to see the details of your cash flows in one place. Figure 8.19 shows the Cash Positions Worksheet, and you will notice the footstep buttons to enable you to drill down to the next node on the Cash Positions tree. When you reach the bottom node position, the magnifying glass appears and enables you to drill to the source transactions that comprise the node balance.

Figure 8.19
The Cash Positions Worksheet.

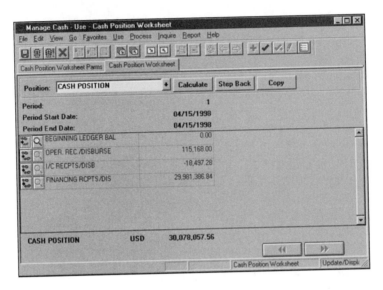

OTHER FEATURES OF PEOPLESOFT TREASURY

Much of the other operating functionality of PeopleSoft Treasury looks similar to that of Accounts Payable. In particular, Bank Reconciliation, and Paycycles are now contained in PeopleSoft Treasury—although you do not have to purchase this module to get these features if you own Accounts Payable.

BANK RECONCILIATION

Bank reconciliation, an important component of any internal control system, is made more manageable with the automated transaction matching functionality. Most banks can provide a data file of your account transactions, which can be loaded into PeopleSoft through the EDI Manager and matched to the transactions on your books. Exceptions to the matching process can be reported and used in your book-to-bank reconciliation. Figure 8.20 illustrates the AutoRecon Manager panel, which controls the automated reconciliation process.

If your bank cannot provide your account transactions electronically, PeopleSoft Treasury also provides a manual reconciliation process. You can take your paper bank statement and match the transactions to the items on the Manual Reconciliation panel (see Figure 8.21).

Figure 8.20
The AutoRecon
Manager panel.

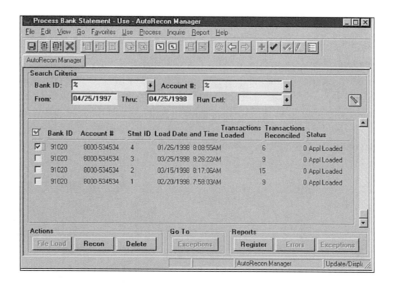

When the proper bank and book items have been matched, PeopleSoft Treasury provides
reports of outstanding items to be used in your book-to-bank reconciliation.

Figure 8.21
The Manual
Reconciliation panel.

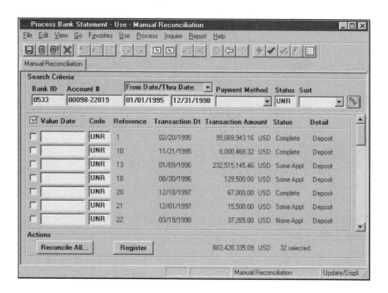

PAYCYCLES

Treasury settlement transactions are processed through the Paycycle to create EFT, Wire, or System Check transactions. The Paycycle functionality used in PeopleSoft Treasury is similar to previous versions of Accounts Payable, with one additional panel. To accommodate PeopleSoft Treasury and PeopleSoft Expenses, in addition to Vouchers from Accounts Payable, the Source Criteria panel enables you to tailor one or more Pay cycles for treasury transactions by specifying a source of Treasury Settlement Transactions. Figure 8.22 shows the new panel in Pay cycle definition.

Figure 8.22
Establishing the pay cycle.

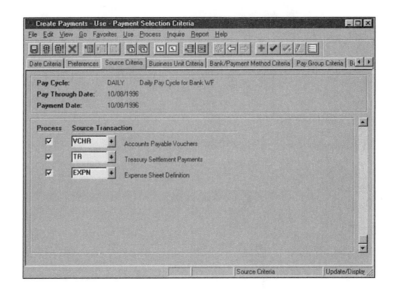

The Cash Management module enables you to consolidate all the spreadsheets into one tool and get a more complete view of the cash position of your entire organization.

DEAL MANAGEMENT

Deal Management (both debts and investments) in PeopleSoft Treasury has two basic components: Instrument definition and Deal capture. Defining Instruments creates the basis for the deals your company initiates. PeopleSoft refers to these Instrument definitions as *building blocks*. Instruments are combined to create deals, or *positions*. In PeopleSoft Treasury, a *deal* is a financial transaction, either an investment or a debt instrument, with another entity or financial institution.

PeopleSoft Treasury is delivered with five basic instrument types: Interest Rate Swap, Interest Rate Physical, Option, Option—Binary Payoff, and FX (Foreign Exchange) Deal Physical. Using these instrument types and other deal characteristics, the building blocks are shaped to be used individually to form simple deals or in tandem to form complicated deals.

Using the Instrument Definition panel group, the following instrument aspects can be defined:

- Instrument descriptions in detail
- Approval requirements
- User-defined attributes for the instrument
- Date-specific information for each core instrument type
- Combinations of a simple instrument into complex instruments
- Deal templates to be used later for similar

Figure 8.23 illustrates the building blocks concept for deal management.

Figure 8.23
The building blocks concept for deal management.

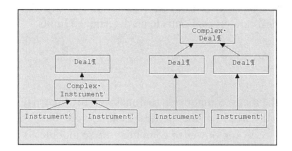

Managing risk is also a vital part of the treasury function. The PeopleSoft Treasury Deal Management module enables the user to manage the current status of positions, forecast future positions with current data, and review historical positions with current data. PeopleSoft Treasury provides the ability to manage currency risk, interest rate risk, counterparty risk, and country risk. Controls can also be placed on individual dealer's activities, instrument limits, and Business Unit limits.

RISK MANAGEMENT

PeopleSoft Treasury's Risk Management module enables you to the valuation and analysis of your debt and investment instruments. With new reporting requirements for GAAP and the SEC, the importance of an effective risk management tool is even more crucial.

One added advantage of the PeopleSoft Risk Management module is the ease with which market data can be imported into PeopleSoft. Any third-party pricing tools that operate in Microsoft Excel can be loaded into PeopleSoft to get the most up-to-date market pricing. This enables you to mark your portfolio to market rates.

The Risk Management module also provides the ability to calculate your value-at-risk and create a file compatible with JP Morgan's FourFifteen format. This system provides an internal risk management tool to analyze different investment strategies, restructure your exposures, and generate reports compliant with SEC requirements.

WORKFLOW

As you may have read in other chapters, the concept of workflow is an important part of making the PeopleSoft system work more efficiently for its users. PeopleSoft Treasury is no exception. Workflow in PeopleSoft Treasury provides the structure to effectively segregate the duties between data entry and transaction approval. The system can also notify supervisors of deals that require maintenance on dates for interest calculations. Cash Management and Deal Management both use workflow for electronic transaction approval processing:

- Approving Settlements—In Cash Management, settlement transactions can be approved by an authorized person before being eligible for payment.

- Approving Deals—In Deal Management, authorized people are notified of pending deal activity, new instrument types can be reviewed before being used, and management can be notified when deals are created outside predetermined limits.

SUMMARY

This chapter covered the many components that make up the financial backbone of PeopleSoft. Through a discussion of the General Ledger, trees, budget, and the PeopleSoft Treasury modules, the scope and power of combining these modules is apparent. Through a well-thought-out integration of these modules, the organization can possess a powerful and formidable financial reporting and analysis tool.

CHAPTER 9

MANUFACTURING MODULES

In this chapter

by Tim Weaver

This chapter discusses the key features of the PeopleSoft Manufacturing suite of business applications in detail. The applications discussed are Bills and Routings, Cost Management, Engineering, Production Management, Quality, and Production Planning. For each application, specific examples, tips, and figures illustrate how to use the PeopleSoft product most effectively.

INTRODUCTION TO BILLS AND ROUTINGS

PeopleSoft Bills and Routings is the foundation for the rest of PeopleSoft Manufacturing. To start our discussion of this module, let's first define some key concepts.

A recipe for chocolate cake involves both a bill of material and a routing. The *bill of material (BOM)* consists of chocolate, eggs, flour, and other ingredients. The *routing* is the direction to mix the ingredients together and bake it in an oven. This simple analysis is required to manufacture even the world's most complex industrial products, such as a jet airplane. The following discussion of PeopleSoft Bills and Routings will explain how to set up and use bills of material and routings in a manufacturing company.

A bill of material (BOM) is a listing showing the relationship of items to each other. Think of a bill of material as a detailed list of ingredients, but instead of making a chocolate cake, we're setting up all the ingredients needed to manufacture items. BOMs can be simple when the number of items involved is small (for example, when making coins) or very complex (for example, when making cars). They usually have multiple levels resulting in a tree branch-like structure. In PeopleSoft, you'll see the levels represented by a series of numbers where level zero is the absolute highest level assembly, like a car. Level one items, commonly referred to as "children" of the level zero "parent," might be purchased items or subassemblies, which would have level two children, and so on. For example, the pistons of a car engine are at level two of the BOM for a car because the engine is at level one, but they would be at level one of the BOM for the engine.

A *routing* is the series of steps needed to methodically produce an item. To prepare a cake, you might have three steps:

1. Mix the ingredients.
2. Bake the cake.
3. Cut it into pieces.

Routings can also be complex, and usually there are subassemblies that are intermediate items used in the production of yet another item. An example of a subassembly could be the radiator of a car, which ultimately becomes part of the car.

ROUTING OPERATIONS AND TASKS

Specific operations are what comprise a routing. Each operation represents a step in the production process. For example, "welding the frame" might be an operation. For ease and consistency, tasks are also available for common operations. A task called "welding the frame" could be defined and applied to all routings that need an operation called "welding the frame." Tasks make development and maintenance of routings very streamlined.

CREWS, MACHINES, AND TOOLS

Crews,machines, and tools are the components that implement production work. These resources are assigned to the individual operations of a routing. For example, a welding operation might consist of the following two resources:

- One welding crew of three people
- One arc welding machine

WORKCENTER

Each operation of a routing is performed in a workcenter. The "welding the frame" operation might take place in the workcenter "arc welding." Many operations can take place in a single workcenter. Figure 9.1 shows a sample routing summary panel and its operation, task, and workcenter fields.

Figure 9.1
Basic routing information is on the Routing Summary tab.

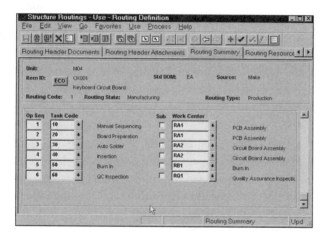

SETUP, RUN, AND POST-PRODUCTION

For each operation, specific times for different production activities are defined. Let's elaborate on our welding example. Say it requires some programming setup time, actual run time, and teardown time. You can establish setup, run, and post-production times, so that the standard cost of the operation can be calculated and so that you can see how long it'll take for proper scheduling. Each operation should also have codes that represent either the labor or machine rates for the work performed. For "welding the frame," the run rate for the code might be $45 per hour, but the setup and post-production rates might be $65 per hour.

MAINTAINING BOMs

PeopleSoft BOMs have plenty of features. These features make the construction of the BOM more powerful, more complete, and easier to maintain.

PHANTOMS

One way to modularize the construction of your BOMs is to utilize phantom BOMs. Some subassemblies may be very common but are seldom stocked or considered saleable items. For example, the dashboard of a car might be constructed as a phantom level in the BOM structure. To facilitate BOM maintenance, it's a good idea to create phantoms to make it easier to change the one phantom instead of every assembly in which the common sub-assembly is used. The same dashboard might be used on multiple car models. Sometimes, it's referred to as a blowthrough assembly because component requirements are calculated through the phantom in the PeopleSoft planning engine.

INCREMENTAL CONSUMPTION

If your assembly has long manufacturing lead time, it can help your planning and scheduling to define operation sequences where the components are used. By doing so, you plan the components to be available when they are needed in the production process rather than right at the beginning. The exterior paint for a car, for instance, is one of the last components needed to make a car. If paint is associated with the "apply paint" operation on the BOM, the planning engine would plan the delivery of paint to be available when the "apply paint" operation starts instead of when the first operation starts.

NON-OWNED STATUS

If desired, items can be marked as non-owned in PeopleSoft Inventory. If so, they are non-owned anywhere they are used. A non-owned status indicates that the item carries no value on your organization's financial statements. As a consequence of this, you cannot create a standard cost for non-owned items. PeopleSoft Bills and Routings allows you to define an owned item as non-owned on BOMs on an exception basis. You can treat a component as having value on one assembly for costing purposes, whereas on another assembly's BOM, it is non-owned and doesn't contribute to the cost. An automotive subcontractor might take a computer chip owned by Honda and place it in a protective casing containing many computer controls. To the subcontractor, the computer chip is non-owned because it was given to them for inclusion in the casing. It carries no value but it's important to track it so that the casing is properly made.

BOM QUANTITY

Using BOM quantity, you can express the set of quantity per's on each component in terms of an end quantity of assemblies. If you have a component where 1 kilogram can make 1000 units of the end item, you could set the BOM quantity to 1000 and quantity per of the component to 1. For example, a gold-plated electronic device contains very small amounts of the element gold. A BOM Quantity would be very useful in establishing the BOM relationship between gold and the device. Otherwise, you'd express the quantity per in terms of what would be required to make 1 unit of the end item.

COMPONENT YIELD

When there is an expected percentage of component scrap, you can set a yield on the component. Doing so will inflate the component requirement by the yield percentage for both planning and costing purposes.

COMPONENT AND ASSEMBLY TEXT

Attach a text note to the assembly or to any component for special instructions. This prints on the production documents. Maybe the component needs to be cleaned in a solution before assembly. By placing a note on the BOM, you can provide instruction to personnel, especially if they are not accustomed to that item.

COMPONENT AND ASSEMBLY DOCUMENTS

Documents stored in an external document vault such as Documentum can be linked to either the assembly item or to any of the components on the BOM. Examples of documents in the vault might be AutoCAD drawings of the transmission of a car or engineering specifications for acceptable tolerances of an engine's properties. The documents can be queried, checked out from the vault, and used to provide instruction or reference for the build. The document can refer to the assembly or any of the components on the BOM. This feature is available only if PeopleSoft Engineering is installed.

COMPONENT AND ASSEMBLY FILE ATTACHMENTS

Files containing text, diagrams, or other information can be launched directly from a PeopleSoft BOM panel. These files can refer to the assembly or any of the components on the BOM. This is a good option to use if you don't need a more robust solution like Documentum.

DIMENSION INFORMATION

Some industries will require the storage of dimensions on the BOM. PeopleSoft Bills and Routings has a tab to store this type of information for components. Examples include length, width, weight, volume, and size.

REFERENCE DESIGNATORS

If you require reference designators, you can define one or more designators for each component. A reference designator is electronic industry-specific functionality. The placement of electronic components such as resistors, capacitors, and so on is aided by having a coding scheme in place for designating where to place each component. These codes are placed on the BOM for such components and are reference designators.

EFFECTIVITY DATING

Components on BOMs are effective date-controlled. This means that each component has both an effective date and an obsolete date. A component is effective between these dates, which means it is a valid item on the BOM. Often, effective dates are controlled using revision control on the assembly or, if PeopleSoft Engineering is installed, ECO control. For example, the circuit board that controls a car's digital controls may be revision-controlled. Over time, some components are replaced or eliminated for better performance or other reasons. By tracking these changes, buyers ultimately know not to buy more of a component when it becomes obsolete according to the BOM.

Within PeopleSoft Bills and Routings, you can copy, delete, and verify manufacturing BOMs.

COPYING A MANUFACTURING BOM

Why would you want to copy a manufacturing BOM? Well, you might have five new assemblies whose product structure is identical except for the color of the paint used. By creating the BOM for one item and then copying it to other items, you can save considerable time. With the copy BOM function, you can select some or all properties for copying, such as component or assembly text, documents, and attachments. In addition, you can control which properties are copied, limiting by specifying a range of items. Finally, you can copy manufacturing BOMs across business units, which would be valuable if you were going to produce the same item in more than one plant.

DELETING A MANUFACTURING BOM

Deleting a manufacturing BOM is necessary for cleanup and performance of your production database. It's good practice to periodically delete obsolete BOMs. You can delete manufacturing BOMs by specifying one or a range of items. If the item is no longer manufactured, there is little reason to keep an active BOM out there. For example, the Pontiac Fiero, out of production for years, would be a good candidate to delete.

BOM VERIFICATION

Finally, PeopleSoft Bills and Routings provides a process whereby you can verify that the BOMs are structurally valid. With complex product structures, it's always a good idea to check the logic of your structures. Defining that an engine is made out of an engine will not get you very far. Checking for these loops can be done online or through a background process.

Note

Complex, deep BOM structures can hinder performance of BOM maintenance. It's better to check for loops using the background process if you have complex structures and never verify BOMs online.

REVISION CONTROL

Revision control refers to the method of tracking changes in the way an item is manufactured. Specifically, replacing a component like a printed circuit board with a better-performing one might necessitate a new revision number for items in which the change occurs. Revisions are a way of keeping tighter control over introducing or "obsoleting" components on BOMs. Within PeopleSoft, items are either controlled by revision or more generically by effective date.

When a revision-controlled item is specified in production, the system selects components by determining which revision is in effect at the start of production and which components are in effect for that revision. You can optionally build non-current revisions by selecting a previous or planned revision for the item. When an alternate revision is specified, the system builds a BOM using only those components associated with the specified revision. This is pretty important in the electronics industry where there might be a need to build many different revisions of the item for replacement or on a spot basis.

At this point, our discussion of BOM concepts has focused on traditional manufacturing BOMs and their features within PeopleSoft. Later in this chapter, the engineering BOM (and routing) will be fully discussed. To conclude our introduction to BOMs, it is worth discussing a special type of BOM, called a *Planning BOM*.

PLANNING BOMs

Planning BOMs are artificial groupings of items. They can be used to forecast items through PeopleSoft Production and Enterprise Planning. For example, you could establish a planning BOM for Chevrolet car models. Based on sales projections, create a planning BOM for "Chevrolet cars" and the components are "Chevette," "Camaro," "Cavalier," and so on. Each component's quantity per should be in proportion to the sales projections. Then you can forecast total sales and use the planning BOM to plan component requirements. There's really no one way to use planning BOMs, however.

For planning bills, the parent item of the BOM is always a non-stockable item that represents a group or family of parts like Chevrolet cars. It also represents a planning part that, although forecasted, can't be ordered. Because planning parts can be components of other planning parts, you can create multiple levels of planning bills.

BOM INQUIRIES

PeopleSoft Bills and Routings have a robust set of inquiries for viewing BOMs. From within PeopleSoft, you can navigate through menus or icons to reach these panels. They are:

- BOM Inquiry—View all information about the BOM, including text, documents, files, reference designators, and dimensions.
- Summarized BOM Inquiry—Shows the exploded BOM with just the essentials, such as quantity per and level. It can be viewed unindented or indented. Indented BOMs can be easier to view because they more clearly demarcate the levels of the BOM. See Figure 9.2 for a summarized BOM Inquiry example.

Figure 9.2
The indented
BOM inquiry is a
convenient way
of reviewing your
product structures.

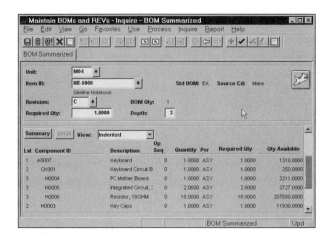

- Costed BOM Inquiry—Shows the rolled-up cost of each item, based on the quantity per and BOM quantity of the item.

- BOM Verification Status—Shows the results of the BOM Verification process by displaying those BOMs that have loops in them and must be corrected.

- Component Where Used Inquiry—Shows all assemblies where the component specified is used. If you need to know what effect a component change might have, this feature shows you immediately the degree to which a component is used. This inquiry is run for manufacturing BOMs only within PeopleSoft Bills and Routings. You can view revision or effective date information. Also, you can limit the output to show only the top-level assemblies, which is helpful if you want to get an idea of what saleable items the component belongs to. For an example of a Component Where Used Inquiry, see Figure 9.3.

Figure 9.3
Finding out where an
item is used quickly
helps many functional
areas in a manufac-
turing plant.

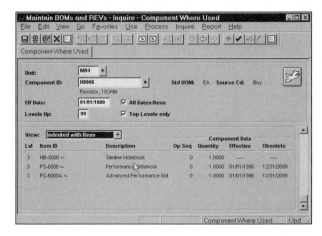

To complete the sweep through the BOM functionality, some considerations about developing BOMs are necessary; namely, the source codes of items must be consistent with their placement on BOMs; and finally, the decimal precision of numerical relationship between BOM levels should be ascertained.

SOURCE CODES FOR ITEMS

When constructing BOMs, you should be concerned with the source code of the item. The source code identifies the nature of the item. PeopleSoft has three source codes:

- Make—To get an item with a make source code, you need to produce it.

- Buy—To get an item with a buy source code, you need to procure it from a supplier.

- Floor Stock—To get an item with a floor stock source code, you should look on the factory floor. Examples are nuts, bolts, and rubber gloves.

Generally, a BOM should never have a make item at its lowest level. If that were the case, how would you get that item when you have to make it and it has no BOM? All BOMs should have items with a source code of either buy or floor stock at the lowest levels.

Floor stock items, even though they can appear on BOMs, are not included in picking plans, material consumption, or in any planning or costing functions. They are there merely for reference as a required part in the production of the item. To manage the inventory levels of floor stock items, you should use inventory replenishment, a kind of reorder point technique that is workflow-enabled. When issued to the production floor, they are expensed using the miscellaneous issues/returns transaction.

DECIMAL PRECISION

A good reason to have accurate BOMs is to give planning a chance to get the right parts to the right place at the right time. Missing components on the BOM most assuredly would cause planning personnel considerable grief—not to mention the shop floor when they have part shortages everywhere! A subtler problem occurs sometimes with the decimal precision of a component's quantity per assembly. In semiconductor manufacturing, for instance, small amounts of metal content require a quantity per on a BOM to be expressed to a high degree of precision. PeopleSoft offers up to 10 decimal places to the right of the decimal for you to define any such relationship. When combined with large volumes, the BOM should still generate accurate information. Preventing decimal precision rounding errors allows planning and costing functions to fulfill their organizational responsibilities.

MAINTAINING ROUTINGS

As with BOMs, PeopleSoft provides a breadth of functions to execute production. Features like operation overlap help you more closely model production cycle time. Moreover, subcontracting functionality ties seamlessly with PeopleSoft Purchasing to provide an excellent solution for outside processing activities. These and other features are discussed next.

PeopleSoft Routings have plenty of features, as described in the following sections.

PART
II
CH
9

HEADER AND OPERATION TEXT, DOCUMENTS, AND ATTACHMENTS

Each routing and each operation of a routing can be supplemented with descriptive text, documents from a data warehouse, or file attachments. This information can provide additional details concerning how to succeed in producing the item.

OPERATION OVERLAP   Operation overlap enables you to indicate numerically that an operation can begin prior to the completion of the previous operation. You have three choices for operation overlap. You can define no operation overlap, an overlap by a percentage of elapsed run time completed, or an overlap by a specific quantity completed at the operation. This feature is helpful in more accurately depicting shop floor realities. Production order lead times are more accurate, resulting in better planning and scheduling. Whenever production can continue to the next operation before the entire order quantity passes through the current operation, operation overlap is a useful feature.

SUBCONTRACTED OPERATIONS

For work that is performed for you by a vendor, you must indicate which operation(s) represent the outside work. These operations receive special treatment.

ROUTING TIMES

Each operation has piece rates. That is, how long does it take to perform the operation? PeopleSoft offers an extensive array of choices for defining routing times. You define the times used for costing purposes as separate from planning times. This may be the best piece of functionality in Bills and Routings because it gives you the flexibility to plan in a completely different manner from the way you derive manufacturing costs. You could, for example, assign a fixed time of one hour for planning purposes; whereas for costing, you might define a rate of five units per machine hour. See Table 9.1 for a list of the available routing time types and Figure 9.4 for the Routing Times tab of the Routing Definition where you actually define the times.

TABLE 9.1   MAINTAINING ROUTINGS

Costing and Planning	Description Labor and Machine
Setup Time	The amount of time required to prepare an item, machine, or work center for production.
Run Time	The amount of time necessary to process one unit-rate, expressed in minutes, hours, or days, or the number of units that can be processed in one time period. The rate is expressed in units per minute, units per hour, or units per day.
Fixed Run Time	The amount of time necessary to complete the task, regardless of the number of units processed.
Post Production Time	The amount of time required to clean up, flush, or break down a machine, work center, or area once production has been completed.

Costing and Planning	Description Labor and Machine
Special Times	Used only without Production Planning.
Queue Time	The amount of time that units must wait in an operation before setup (if there is setup) or processing can begin.
Intransit Time	The amount of time required to transport units from one operation to the next.

Figure 9.4
The Routing Times tab is where you define how long an operation takes.

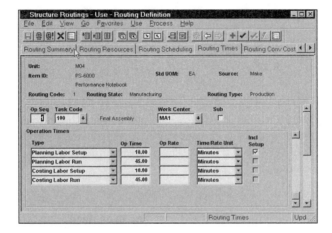

You can use task, workcenter, or "resource where used" inquiries if you're interested in where you've defined these entities in your routings.

COPY ROUTING, DELETE ROUTING, AND MASTER (REFERENCE) ROUTINGS

Bills and Routings both copy and delete routing functionality to assist in maintaining the set of manufacturing routings.

With the copy routing function, you can select some or all properties for copying, such as times, resources, and documents associated with the operations. In addition, you can control which properties are copied to which operation sequences. This is pretty powerful stuff. Finally, you can copy engineering routings across business units, which would be valuable if you were going to produce the same item in more than one plant. For instance, suppose a new Chevy truck model has finished design and development and is now ready to go into production. The problem is that five plants across North America must produce the same truck. If you copy the original routing from one plant to the other four, there is guaranteed consistency in how the product is made (at least from a systems perspective).

Delete routing functionality could be used to delete those item routings for which all production is complete and closed to accounting and for which there is no expectation of future production. Delete routings only if you're sure they won't be used again! For a sample delete routing request, see Figure 9.5.

Figure 9.5
Deleting a routing that is no longer used helps to maintain good system house-keeping.

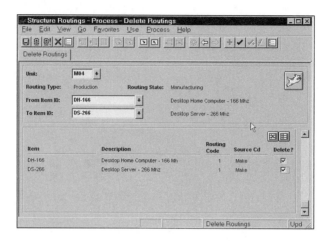

In some industries, many items have the same routing. To reduce the setup and mainte-nance of routings in this case, use master routings. By referring to another item's routing, many items can share the same routing. The master routing is then used for all planning, scheduling, and costing activities.

There are three ways to reference master routings:

- By item—Directly link the item to the routing of another item.

- By item group—Item is assigned to an item group, which is in turn assigned an item whose route is the master for the whole group.

- By item family—item is assigned to an item family, which is assigned an item whose routing is the master for the whole group.

After all the links are made, it is much easier to maintain routings overall.

Bills and Routings are the building blocks for all manufacturing systems. The ability to plan and execute production depends largely on the accuracy of the BOM and Routings, as well as on the ongoing accuracy of inventory levels throughout the enterprise. The upcoming dis-cussions on Cost Management, Engineering, and Production Planning are all fundamentally grounded in BOM and routing concepts.

INTRODUCTION TO COST MANAGEMENT

Manufacturing organizations utilize cost tracking and analysis to improve their bottom line by identifying and eliminating cost in their production operations. With Cost Management, companies can track the performance of resources and analyze the data to improve opera-tions and account for costs. The two primary activities within Cost Management are prod-uct costing and inventory accounting. *Product costing* consists of establishing standard costs for manufacturing, whereas *inventory accounting* involves keeping track of the money involved when material is moved around the organization.

PRODUCT COSTING

PeopleSoft Manufacturing is a *standard cost system*, which means that all items associated with production must have a preset cost, called the standard cost. The standard is periodically changed to adjust for market change, but costs do not change on a transaction-by-transaction basis, as is the case with other valuation methods like actual or average costing. When an item is purchased at a cost other than the standard, a variance is recorded. Likewise, when the cost of manufacture is more or less than the standard, a variance is calculated.

So the first step in implementing a standard cost system is to create the standard costs. Table 9.2 shows the setup required to establish standard costs for your items.

TABLE 9.2   STEPS NECESSARY TO ESTABLISH STANDARD COSTS FOR AN ITEM

Task	Purpose
Create Cost Type	Specifies whether to use current or forecasted costs for purchased items.
Define Conversion Codes	Attached to routing, to cost direct machinery or labor.
Define Conversion Overhead Codes	Attached to routing to cost production overhead.
Create Cost Version	Adds version and defines the set of rates, for the conversion codes and conversion overhead codes (i.e. code X is $20/hr).
Define Purchase Costs	Specifies current purchase costs or forecasted costs for your "buy" items depending on how you have defined cost type.
Create BOMs and Routings	Be sure to assign conversion and conversion overhead codes to routing and establish routing times.
Cost Rollup	Specifies Cost Type and Version defined above for this process. It gives potential standard costs for you to review. Change and rerun rollup as appropriate.
Update Production Costs	Specifies Cost Type and Version defined above for this process. Establishes the standard cost.

Tip

You need to establish a manufacturing business unit if you want to establish standard costs for manufactured items. In addition, a manufacturing business unit is required for other activities such as material planning and production. There is always a one-to-one correspondence between a manufacturing business unit and an inventory business unit.

Standard costs for manufactured items like a car are usually built from the bottom up. For example, electrical wire has a cost in and of itself. So when it is used in the steering column of a steering wheel, the steering wheel's cost is partially comprised of the wire's cost. Applying this principle to all the other components of a car, such as the doors, engine, and transmission, will help to give an overall standard cost for a car. Now, we'll see how to construct the environment in PeopleSoft to cost products.

COST TYPES AND VERSIONS

Cost Management has an architecture that lets you develop virtually unlimited product costing scenarios. By utilizing different combinations of Cost Types and Cost Versions, you can perform "what-if" cost simulations. You accomplish this by selecting these different combinations when submitting the cost rollup process. For instance, you might do three different cost rollups representing best case, worst case, and best estimate labor costs. In this example (see Table 9.3), the cost type remains "S99" because the same material costs are used for each scenario but the cost version is different.

TABLE 9.3   YOU CAN HAVE MULTIPLE COST VERSIONS TO REPRESENT DIFFERENT SETS OF COSTS

Business Unit	Cost Type	Cost Version
PL1	S99	99BEST
PL1	S99	99WORST
PL1	S99	99EST

A Cost Type defines what type of material cost to use for the cost rollup: current or forecasted. You define the Cost Types on the Cost Types panel in the Define Cost Foundation panel group (see Figure 9.6) You choose a cost type when you perform a cost rollup. It tells the process to "Go get me the purchase costs from..." The current purchase cost of an item is maintained on the Item Attributes by Unit panel (see Figure 9.7). The current purchase cost is per standard unit of measure and is used by the rollup process if the Cost Type specifies current for purchase cost used. Forecasted costs are entered on the Forecasted Costs by Item panel (see Figure 9.8) and are used by the rollup process if the Cost Type specifies the purchase cost used.

If the cost type is chocolate, let's say that the cost version is the peanut butter. They ultimately go together, but are made from different ingredients. Cost types are made of material cost, whereas cost versions are made of labor, machine, and overhead costs.

A cost version represents a set of value added costs: labor, machine, overhead, and so on. The cost version really retains all cost except material (see Figure 9.9). The first thing to do is to establish at least one cost version. Notice that it is here where you establish the linkages between the cost type and the cost version. If you want, you can link one cost version to many cost types or vice versa. Just keep inserting those rows.

Tip

Put the year into the name of your cost types and versions. It'll be easier to identify them as the years go by.

Figure 9.6
Here is where you define the Cost Type.

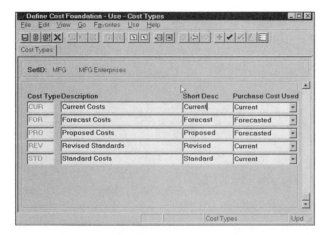

Figure 9.7
The current purchase cost here may become the standard cost for a purchased item.

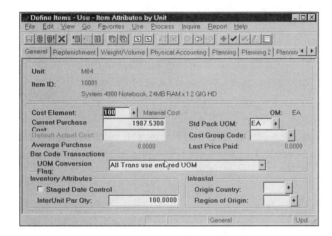

Figure 9.8
Forecasted costs may become the standard costs and are defined here.

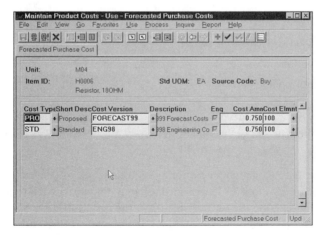

Figure 9.9
Define all cost versions for a manufacturing business unit here.

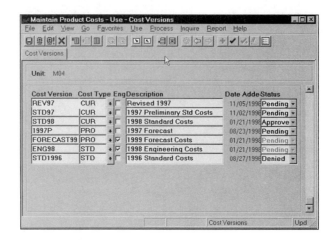

The cost type and version represent an overall method for establishing standard costs. Each element of cost, such as the cost of paint, the cost of assembling a transmission, or the supervision of a production work area contribute to the total cost of manufacture. These are all examples of cost elements, the next topic of discussion.

COST ELEMENTS

Cost elements are the building blocks of PeopleSoft Cost Management. A *cost element* is a user-defined kind of cost. Common examples include the following:

- Raw material
- Labor
- Labor overhead
- Machine
- Machine overhead
- Outside processing (subcontracting)
- Inbound inspection
- Outbound shipping

Typically, the cost of a manufactured item consists of many different elements, each contributing a portion of the overall cost. Figure 9.10 shows the Cost Element definition panel.

By using elements to model your accounting requirements, you have complete control of how your costs are sent to the General Ledger. In other words, each transaction, item, or cost element combination is a separate record in the database, so that you could send part of an item's cost for a particular transaction to one account, other cost elements to another account, and so on.

Figure 9.10
Cost elements are the building blocks of all product costs.

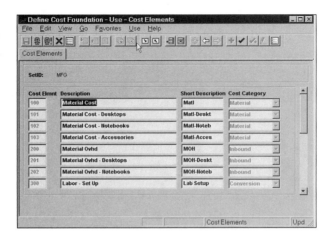

> **Tip**
>
> Be careful not to define excessive cost elements. You could probably get by with basic cost elements such as material, labor, machine, and overhead and then add new ones when there are specific reasons for more detail. Each cost element generates its own accounting lines and, as a result, the inventory accounting can yield data at a tremendous level of detail and volume.

CONVERSION AND CONVERSION OVERHEAD CODES

Let's get into the guts of the setup for tracking value added costs. Here's a workflow diagram to describe how things go together. Each step in the setup moves you closer to defining conversion costs on a production routing:

Cost Version -> Conversion Rates -> Conversion Codes -> Production Workcenters/Tasks -> Production Operations

You attach codes to production workcenters or tasks (see Figure 9.11). Then, for a particular cost version, you define what the rate is for each code. There is a panel for attaching rates to conversion codes and a panel for attaching rates to conversion overhead codes (see Figure 9.12). This allows you to model different sets of rates for same code(s). Cost Version 99BEST might have a rate of $20 per hour for code X, but Cost Version 99WORST might put the rate at $30 per hour. What's the impact? Run a Compare Cost Versions report to find out. To run the report, request it by specifying the cost versions to compare. In this case, you would say 99BEST and 99WORST. An example request panel for the Compare Cost Versions report is found in Figure 9.13.

Figure 9.11
Attaching codes to the individual operation is required to the cost operation step.

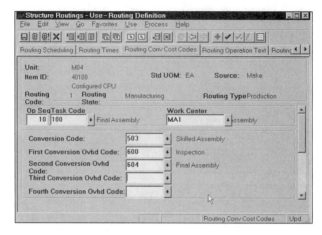

Figure 9.12
Defining rates for each type of conversion defined on the routing is required.

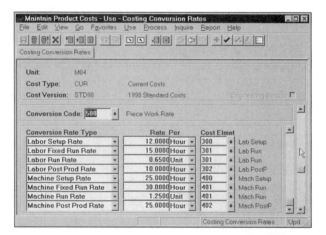

Figure 9.13
Comparing different cost versions is useful for analysis.

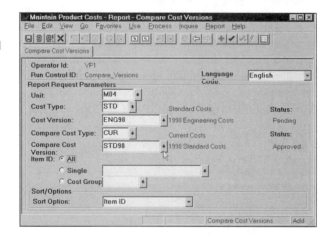

There are two different codes. These will be discussed in the following sections.

CONVERSION CODES

To convert material into a more valuable commodity, you convert the raw material into the finished product. For example, you take some metal and turn it into the frame of a car. This conversion involves the use of machinery and people operating the machines. *Conversion codes* represent the direct labor or machine costs incurred in such a conversion. Labor or machine setup, run, fixed run, or post-production costs are the conversion code types available to model your production. One excellent feature of PeopleSoft is that it separates costing and planning times. Planning Labor Run and Costing Labor Run are defined separately and can be completely different. The result is that the material planners can change the planning labor run rates for better scheduling flexibility without affecting how an item is costed. These conversion codes are attached to tasks and workcenters. Then, any use of these tasks and workcenters when setting up routings will automatically copy this cost information to the routing itself. The routing is where the information must be for use in costing the item through the cost rollup process. For example, let's say bending a metal sheet is one of the operations necessary to make a car frame. An operation is a step in the manufacturing process (routing). Bending involves setting up a press for the appropriate model, running some frames through, and then tearing down the press. You might define Costing Machine Setup, Costing Machine Run, and Post-Production for this operation. All machine time would be costed based on the conversion code tied to operation 20.

CONVERSION OVERHEAD CODES

Conversion overhead codes are used to allocate manufacturing overhead to production. For example, the production control systems and management are part of the overall cost of car frame manufacturing, so each individual frame will absorb a piece of that total cost. A good approach would be to base overhead on a percentage of direct machine cost, because costing machine run is defined. This is one of the five different methods available for applying overhead costs:

- per unit of production
- as a percentage of direct labor cost
- as a percentage of direct machine cost
- as an amount per labor hour
- as an amount per machine hour

If necessary, you can establish up to four conversion overhead codes per workcenter or task.

Tip

Be sure to define conversion codes and conversion overhead codes on your workcenters or tasks *before* you create routings using either a workcenter or task. That way the codes default to the individual operations. It is very easy to create a workcenter and immediately create routings using that workcenter before setting up the costing for the workcenter. This causes a lot of extra work later because you have to add the costs to each routing created.

You can use the same conversion or conversion overhead code for one or many workcenters. The code could even be the same across the enterprise if the business units share the same SetID.

After the material and conversion costs are established, it is time to develop the standard costs. In some cases, the standard cost is just the purchase cost of the material, as with raw steel. In the majority of cases, however, the standard cost is developed from a variety of materials, manufacturing processes, and supporting personnel. The cost rollup process will gather the costs based on the bills of material, routings, and raw material costs.

COST ROLLUPS

Utilizing the cost versions established, you can perform a cost rollup to get total costs for each item. If an item has a deep bill of material, all those lower-level component costs are included. This is where the idea of a "rollup" comes from, because you are including all costs whether it's at the next level in the bill of material or a purchased item at the very bottom of the product structure. The result of a cost rollup is a set of costs stored for review and for possible later use as an input into establishing frozen standard costs through the update production costs process. For any particular item, the product's cost is broken into its individual cost elements. In addition, the costs are classified as occurring at "this level," meaning the top level of the BOM or at "lower level," all other levels. See Figure 9.14 for an example of a manufactured item where the labor cost is at "this level," whereas the material costs of its components are all at lower level. In this example, a 300MHz desktop computer has an item cost made up of many cost elements, including labor and materials. The material costs come from the purchase costs of the components, such as resistors, power supplies, cables, and a cooling fan. All these components are linked to the desktop computer through bills of material.

Figure 9.14
The rolled up cost of a make item usually contains many cost elements.

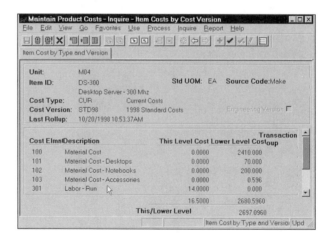

UPDATE PRODUCTION COSTS

The last step to establish the standard costs is to run the Update Production Costs process. It takes the results of a cost rollup for a cost type or version and creates the frozen standard costs. This process is very serious because you are revaluing the inventory in your business unit. The request panel (see Figure 9.15) gives three options for running the process at the bottom left corner. If you're not sure about the impact of an update, you can run the process in a report-only mode. Nothing happens to your standards already in place—but you can see what would happen on a real update. In other words, you can see the reevaluations that would occur. The cost of a car might increase from $5,200 to $5,500. Factors in the increase might include increasing cost for metal, a new union contract resulting in higher labor costs plantwide, or a huge jump in the price of platinum. The last two options in Figure 9.15 will actually update standards and subsequently create transactions called "inventory reevaluations" to account for the differences in inventory value. These differences in value are variances that can be posted directly to the ledger.

Figure 9.15
The most important process in all of Cost Management: Update Production Costs.

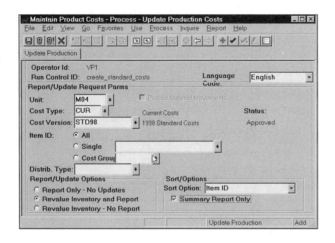

> **Tip**
>
> You cannot perform any inventory movement for an owned, standard costed item until you've given it a standard cost. The system gives an error if you attempt to place units in inventory. This is a quite common problem during implementations with separate finance and manufacturing teams because usually the finance group knows what the costs are, but manufacturing people are the ones trying to get inventory into the system for testing. Keep in mind that non-owned items do not have cost by definition, so you can put away these types of items immediately after defining them and their inventory locations.

INVENTORY ACCOUNTING

Just how does PeopleSoft Manufacturing send information to PeopleSoft Financials? Refer to Figure 9.16 to understand the basic flow of the inventory accounting functionality. The input of standard cost is required to run the transaction costing process, and a set of account distributions is required to perform accounting line creation. Note that transactions like shipping and receiving occur principally within the inventory business unit. Therefore, you can think of this flow occurring for each inventory business unit defined. Also, some important accounting lines have their origins in the manufacturing business unit. For example, shop floor variances generate within the manufacturing business unit and are picked up at accounting line creation. Purchase price variances are another example here. Many of the calculated transaction groups, such as variances, have already been costed at time of receipt or at production order close time and, therefore, do not actually show in the inventory accounting flow until the accounting line creation process.

Figure 9.16
The flow of data for inventory accounting involves three key background processes.

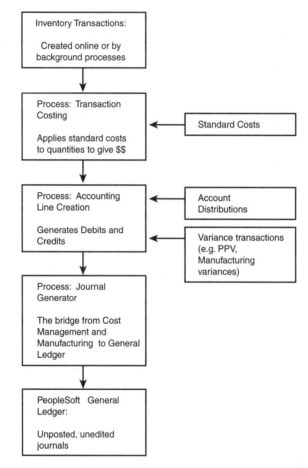

TRANSACTION COSTING

The transaction costing process runs in the background and takes care of assigning a cost to a transaction. The user is concerned with units of inventory movement, but this process takes the number of units in a particular transaction and multiplies it by the standard cost per unit to give a monetary value to the transaction. This is a preparatory step to the accounting line creation process.

ACCOUNTING DISTRIBUTIONS AND ACCOUNTING LINE CREATION

The accounting line creation process takes each costed transaction and assigns a debit and credit account to it. If necessary, other chartfields such as department, product, and project can also be utilized. The input to the process is the account distributions. An account distribution is definited by the transaction group, which chartfield to debit or credit when a transaction is processed by accounting line creation. For example, an issue normally debits a "cost of goods sold" account and credits an inventory account. Considerable flexibility is available when setting up these distributions, and you need to make wise decisions about setup. The volume of distributions can get out of hand pretty quickly. You need a complete set of distributions for each inventory business unit.

PART

II

CH

9

Transaction Group, Item Group, and Item Levels for Account Distributions

Account distributions can be created using transaction groups, item groups, or item IDs. The level of detail needed in the General Ledger is the key consideration for deciding the proper level of detail within inventory accounting.

A *transaction group* is system-defined and represents a certain type of inventory or manufacturing transaction, including variances. For example, a cycle count adjustment is one example of a transaction group. Each PeopleSoft Manufacturing/Inventory transaction falls into one of the following Transaction Groups:

- Receipt to Inspection
- Return to Vendor From Stores
- Return to Vendor From Inspection
- Stocking
- WIP Receipt
- IBU Receipts
- Customer Returns
- Issue
- Interbusiness Unit Shipments
- Non-Stock Shipments
- Shipments on Behalf of Other Business Unit
- Physical Accounting
- Cycle Count Adjustments
- IBU Transfer Adjustments
- Adjustments
- Inventory Scrap
- Shipping Adjustment
- Miscellaneous Issue/Return
- Bin-to-Bin Transfer
- Inventory Re-evaluation
- Inventory Re-evaluation: Inspection
- Average Cost Adjustment

- WIP Re-evaluation
- Component Kit
- Route to Production Kit
- Component Consumption
- Earned Labor
- Assembly Scrap
- Material Variances
- Conversion Variances
- Rework Expense
- Outside Processing PPV
- Gain/Loss on Transfer Price
- PPV (Purchase Price Variance)
- PPV Update to Weighted Average Cost
- ERV (Exchange Rate Variance)
- ERV for Weighted Average Cost
- Write Off From Average Cost PPV and Average Cost ERV
- Miscellaneous Charges
- Freight Charges

An *item group* is an extremely important method of classifying the totality of your items. The primary use of the item group field is for inventory accounting. You can assign items to an item group and ultimately treat them similarly from an accounting standpoint by establishing account distributions by item group.

The item ID identifies the item and is also available for use in account distribution setup. If you decide to use item ID level account distributions, use them with caution. They can really complicate your setup. For instance, one transaction group like "issue" defined at this level for 20,000 items will create 40,000 rows of data, given a debit and a credit row. Item IDs constitute the lowest possible level of detail allowed when defining account distributions.

PARAMETERS FOR ASSIGNING ACCOUNT DISTRIBUTIONS

What rules are followed to assign account distributions during the accounting line creation process? The purpose of the accounting line process is to create accounting lines representing the debit and credit entries for each costed transaction. For every transaction, it identifies the level at which to pick up a distribution. From low to high, it searches in the following order until it finds a record:

1. An item ID level distribution search is launched.

2. An item group level distribution search is initiated.

3. Finally, a transaction group level distribution for the transaction is begun.

The account line creation program picks up the first distribution found according to the order shown in the preceding numbered list. You should always have a default for each transaction group so as to properly capture all possible activity.

When the program knows the level at which to work, there are several other important checks before the debits and credits are assigned.

DISTRIBUTION TYPES

A *distribution type* is a field found on most online transaction panels in PeopleSoft Inventory. Set up and choose a distribution type on the online panel if you want special handling of that transaction. The distribution type field is passed to the accounting line creation program where it's matched to an account distribution with that distribution type.

COST ELEMENTS

A *cost element* is a certain part of product cost such as material, labor, and overhead. If necessary, you can distribute cost elements to different chartfields. This functionality is excellent, but it can also be overwhelming especially with large numbers of cost elements. In many cases, it's sufficient to send the full value of the product to the same General Ledger account. To isolate and financially track a specific portion of cost, however, use cost-element-specific account distributions.

DRILL DOWN ON ACCOUNTING LINES

To look at the results of the accounting line creation process online, you can go to any transaction and drill down to the accounting lines it creates as well as the journal in the General Ledger that was created. This capability also works the other way. This gives you considerable online flexibility in researching the source of a journal entry from manufacturing. The example in Figure 9.17 shows journal ID 5282, line 1 and lists all the accounting lines involved. Note that by right-clicking on a line, you can drill up or down to important transactional or General Ledger information.

As an alternative to online analysis, you can print both the transaction register and the accounting register, which give a complete history of transactions entered or accounting lines created over a period of time.

Note

The choice of whether to use location accounting is an important one. Location accounting allows you to associate a General Ledger account with each storage area and production area defined in the system. Doing so gives considerably more control over your inventory accounting. The system automatically debits and credits the associated accounts when value flows in and out of the storage and production areas. Setting up account distributions is simplified with location accounting, but you then have the additional setup of attaching an account to each of your storage areas. Thus, setup is about the same. The decision to use location accounting is done at the SetID level in PeopleSoft, which means it must be a decision made early in the implementation and not changed.

Figure 9.17
Online drill up and drill down makes analyzing accounting information easy within Cost Management.

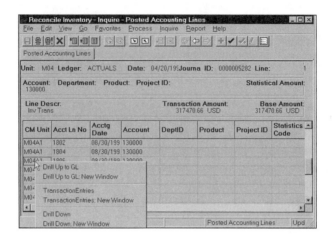

This concludes the discussion of PeopleSoft Cost Management. Along with effective cost management, product and process design are important support activities in which a manufacturing enterprise engages. When introducing new products or revisions of existing products into production, there must be an effective information system to store and track designs, bills of material, routings, and other information. PeopleSoft Engineering provides this capability.

INTRODUCTION TO ENGINEERING

PeopleSoft Engineering provides tools for developing new products and processes in a manufacturing environment. As a design engineer, you can use PeopleSoft Engineering to construct preliminary BOMs and routings in order to estimate product cost, organize the development effort, and identify new material requirements. The PeopleSoft Engineering product manages changes in production processes through Engineering Change Requests and Engineering Change Orders.

THE ENGINEERING CHANGE FLOW

Engineering changes are managed through a sequence of requests, approvals, and updates. Like many business processes within the PeopleSoft ERO solution, PeopleSoft Engineering utilizes workflow to accomplish tasks. Specifically, the engineering change process can be managed using PeopleSoft Workflow. You can use Workflow to send Engineering Change Requests (ECRs) and Engineering Change Orders (ECOs) for approval to the designated person(s).

ENGINEERING CHANGE REQUESTS (ECRs)

ECRs are requests usually made by purchasing, production, or engineering personnel that describe a change needed to the existing bill of material and/or routing. For example, Paul, a quality control inspector, notes that the Slimline series of laptop computers is overheating and warping the casing. He could submit an ECR describing the problem and identifying the affected items in the Slimline series. See Figure 9.18 for this ECR example. Another example might be engineering personnel requesting component changes to improve product performance. In either case, ECRs enable an organization to track problems and begin a systematic process of change control.

Figure 9.18
Paul's Engineering Change Request involves a warped casing on the item NB-5000.

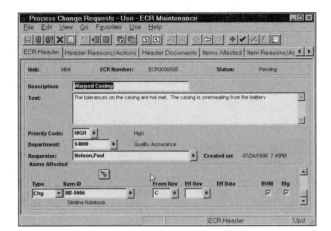

ENGINEERING CHANGE ORDERS (ECOs)

An ECO is created to bring about changes to product configurations in a systematic and timely manner. Typically, the introduction of new component specifications or production methods is felt across a series of items, thereby necessitating a formal method of change control. ECOs provide this capability in PeopleSoft Engineering. Generally, someone in design or manufacturing engineering will either enter and/or approve ECOs. See Figure 9.19 for an example transfer controlled by ECO. In the previous example, Paul had submitted an ECR because of overheating causing the warping of the Slimline series of products. A review by engineering now results in adding a fan to the Slimline design. This BOM change of adding a fan is introduced across all Slimline models using an ECO.

Revision control is a structured way to facilitate the introduction of new models and configurations of items currently in production. Revision control of items is defined by items, and each revision is given an effective date. If an item is not revision controlled, the timing of introducing ECOs is handled directly with effectivity dates.

ENGINEERING BOMs VERSUS MANUFACTURING BOMs AND ROUTINGS

PeopleSoft Engineering is integrated with PeopleSoft Cost Management, Production Management, and Bills and Routings, but it is also an island to itself. All work done in the Engineering workbench, from developing engineering BOMs and routings to creating ECOs, does not affect current planning or production. But when it's time to move BOM and routing data between, say, the engineering department and production management, copy and transfer tools are there to accomplish this task. All the features of manufacturing

BOMs and routings (as discussed previously in the Bills and Routings section) are included in the functionality of engineering BOMs and routings. Because of this you do not have to recreate anything when the BOM is copied for use in Manufacturing.

Figure 9.19
Transferring through ECO is a good way of controlling the introduction of new product and process designs.

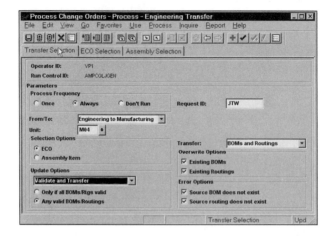

ENGINEERING BOMs

Engineering BOMs are used to construct product structures for new or revised products for later use by manufacturing. Unlike manufacturing BOMs, engineering BOMs allow you to use items that are not yet approved as assemblies or components, and you can even use "placeholders" for components that haven't been identified. These placeholders are great while developing new BOMs, allowing you to continue work before purchasing and inventory personnel define the actual items. As you might expect, however, you cannot cost placeholders. Any final cost analysis would have to have all items in place.

COPYING, DELETING, COMPARING, AND VERIFYING ENGINEERING BOMs

Within PeopleSoft Engineering, you can copy, delete, and compare engineering BOMs.

The copy feature, importantly, also lets you copy engineering BOMs to manufacturing BOMs and vice versa. To move BOMs between manufacturing and engineering using ECOs, you must use the transfer method. Why would you want to copy an engineering BOM? Well, you might have five new assemblies whose product structure is identical except for the color of the paint used. Using the workbench, create an engineering BOM with all the relevant details for the first item. Then copy the BOM to the other four items. By changing the paint color on the four new ones, you've now efficiently created five brand new BOMs and saved a ton of time. With the copy BOM function, you can select some or all properties for copying such as component or assembly text, documents, and attachments. In addition, you can control which properties are copied, limiting by specifying a range of items. Finally, you can copy engineering BOMs across business units, which would be valuable if you were going to produce the same item in more than one plant.

Deleting an engineering BOM is necessary for cleanup of the engineering workbench. You can delete engineering BOMs by specifying one or a range of items.

When you're developing new product lines, one handy way to ensure that BOMs are consistent or to find problems with BOMs is to be able to compare them. PeopleSoft Engineering provides an inquiry for thoroughly comparing an engineering BOM with either another engineering BOM or a manufacturing BOM. Every tab of the BOM definition panel group is compared. You can look at results onscreen. Figure 9.20 shows a comparison between item NB-5000's engineering BOM and manufacturing BOM.

Figure 9.20
A comparison reveals some differences between the manufacturing and engineering BOMs.

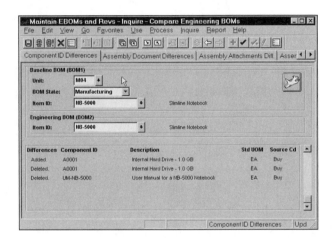

VERIFYING ENGINEERING BOMs

Finally, PeopleSoft Engineering provides a process whereby you can verify that BOMs are structurally valid. With complex product structures, it's a good idea to check the logic of your structures! In particular, mistakes are quite common when first developing BOMs, which is a principal activity within PeopleSoft Engineering.

SEARCHING FOR A COMPONENT

Within the PeopleSoft Engineering solution, there is a "component where used" inquiry. This inquiry shows all assemblies where the component entered is used. If you need to know what effect a component change might have, this feature shows you immediately the degree to which a component is used. The inquiry is run over either manufacturing BOMs or engineering BOMs from PeopleSoft Engineering.

BOM MASS MAINTENANCE FOR EITHER ENGINEERING OR MANUFACTURING BOMs

Mass Maintenance refers to the general ability to make the same change once and have it affect many similar structures. It's like having 100 TVs all operating off the same remote control. If you punch a new channel, all 100 TVs switch to that new channel. BOM Mass Maintenance is a powerful function of PeopleSoft Engineering. With it you can add or change components and their characteristics for a large number of BOMs at one time. The BOMs can be either Engineering BOMs or Manufacturing BOMs.

To set up this maintenance, the first step is to define a Mass Maintenance code. By selecting what to search for on the BOMs and designating the changes to make and/or the components to add, you establish a Mass Maintenance code. The selection criteria can be just about anything on the BOM, including the component ID, the quantity per assembly, reference designators, yield, and specific dimensions. For example, you might want to search for where resistor 46O has a yield of 90% on BOMs. Resistor 4 might be on 100 different printed circuit board BOMs, but maybe only 40 have a yield of 90% defined for resistor 4 as determined when you hit the count button on the panel. Figure 9.21 shows the panel where you define mass maintenance codes.

Figure 9.21
Mass maintenance is a powerful feature with a high degree of flexibility.

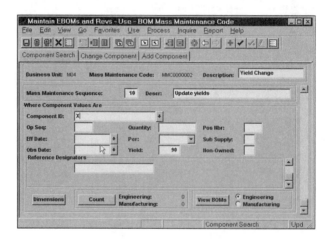

This search criterion would bring back a count of just those 40 items. What can you do with these 40 items? You can change any of the component's attributes on all 40 items. Or perhaps you'd like to add an inductor 34Y everywhere there is a resistor 4 with a yield 90%. The possibilities are extensive. To specify an "or" condition, use two or more mass maintenance sequences. For example, if resistor 4 or inductor 3 is on a BOM, add capacitor 1. Here, the search criteria sequence 10 is for resistor 4 and sequence 20 is for inductor 3. If either or both exist, capacitor 1 is added to all BOM structures.

To execute BOM mass maintenance, you have two options:

- Apply by mass maintenance code
- Apply by ECO

The option chosen depends on whether you want the mass maintenance connected to your engineering change process. If so, there's the extra step of attaching the mass maintenance codes to the relevant ECOs before applying the ECOs. This gives tighter control over the changes made to BOM structures.

In either option, you choose whether to apply the mass maintenance code to implement the following:

- Engineering or manufacturing BOMs
- A range or a list of assembly items which you specify
- Validate the BOMs only or to validate and update the BOMs

ENGINEERING ROUTINGS

Engineering routings are used to develop build instructions and steps for new products or products made from redesigned manufacturing processes. Unlike manufacturing routing, however, you can develop an engineering routing for a pending item. By relaxing this requirement, you are able to create the routing for an item before it's approved by other functional groups within your organization. All other definitions are identical between the manufacturing and engineering routing. This enables complete integration between these two types of routings. Some of the utilities for maintaining routings like copy and delete routings are also available in PeopleSoft Engineering. For an example of copying an engineering routing, see Figure 9.22. These were discussed previously in the "Understanding Bills and Routings" section. Comparing routings, however, is a unique tool used within Engineering.

PART

II

CH

9

Figure 9.22
Example of copying an existing manufacturing routing to become an engineering routing.

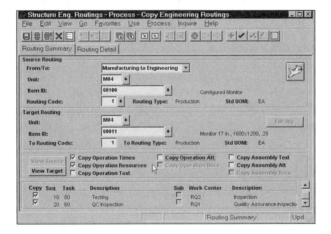

COMPARING ROUTINGS

When you're developing new product lines, one handy way to ensure that routings are consistent or to find problems with routings is to be able to compare routings. PeopleSoft Engineering provides an inquiry for thoroughly comparing engineering routings. Every tab of the routing definition panel group is compared. You can look at results onscreen. You can compare two different items or, if alternate routings are defined, you can compare two different routings for the same item. The routing code keeps track of multiple routings for an item. Finally, you can compare either two engineering routings or an engineering routing to a manufacturing routing. It's pretty flexible.

COST ROLLUPS USING COST VERSIONS

PeopleSoft Engineering and Cost Management work together when evaluating the product costs of items. You can establish a unique set of material costs and labor, machine, and overhead rates to cost out your items. Special engineering cost versions can be used to develop simulated product costs but can never be used to create frozen standard costs. It's a security measure to keep engineers from affecting live production, but allow them to analyze costs as part of the development process.

COPY AND TRANSFER INTEGRATION

The transfer method of integration between PeopleSoft Engineering and PeopleSoft Bills and Routings is different from the Copy BOM and Routing functions previously discussed. See Table 9.4 for some subtle differences. There is considerably more control with the transfer method. You can validate the transfer in a kind of simulation and review the problems. If you want to create a bunch of manufacturing BOMs from work done on the engineering side, the transfer method is the way to go.

TABLE 9.4   THE COPY FUNCTION AND THE TRANSFER FUNCTION HAVE SOME IMPORTANT DIFFERENCES

Feature	Copy	Transfer
ECO Control	N	Y
Move several BOMs or routings at once	N	Y
Copy within Engineering	Y	N
Copy across Business Units	Y	N

PEOPLESOFT DOCUMENTUM INTERFACE

PeopleSoft Engineering has embedded support for the Documentum Enterprise Document Management System (EDMS), which provides a complete document management solution. Currently, there are 13 panels or panel groups that are linked up. Among these are the Indented Engineering and Manufacturing BOM Inquiries, the Engineering and Manufacturing Routing Inquiries, and the Component and Operation Lists. The idea behind the interface is to give real-time visibility to documents and drawings necessary to produce an item by launching them directly from PeopleSoft. In addition, the Documentum EDMS securely vaults all different types of documents, such as drawings from AutoCAD, for use in engineering and production activities. PeopleSoft only controls the references to the documents while Documentum owns them.

Up to this point, the discussion of Bills and Routings, Cost Management, and Engineering, has been largely about creating an environment in which production can take place. From developing accurate BOMs and routings to establishing standard costs, the preparation involved in gearing up for production is important and requires work. At this point, it's time to begin our discussion of PeopleSoft Production Management, which will manage the people, machines, and materials involved in production activity.

INTRODUCTION TO PRODUCTION MANAGEMENT

PeopleSoft Production Management is the central module of PeopleSoft Manufacturing. With this module, manufacturers manage the flow of material throughout the manufacturing process by tracking production orders from their initial creation all the way through to the order's closure. It relies heavily on the data from other PeopleSoft modules such as the following:

PART

II

CH

9

- Inventory—Provides for the creation of items and stock locations for use by Production Management

- Bills and Routings—Provides the infrastructure in the form of BOMs and Routings, which are the build instructions for execution of production orders in Production Management

- Cost Management—Provides the standard costs of the items involved in manufacturing

- Production Planning—Provides a plan to satisfy demand and sends build messages to Production Management

- Purchasing—Sends back purchase receipt information as part of the subcontracting process

MANUFACTURING CALENDARS

Before production can begin, you must establish a calendar to represent which days your manufacturing business unit is operational. The calendar is a vital input when calculating the lead time for a production operation, because it considers only the available time specified on the calendar in scheduling the orders.

The production scheduling and planning functions use a hierarchy of calendars to determine when a workcenter is available. The workcenter is where work is performed, so it makes sense that this is the controlling entity when it comes to defining operational hours. If there is a work center calendar, it takes first priority. Otherwise, the system looks for the production calendar, which indicates for the entire manufacturing business unit which shifts are working on which days, and so forth. If no production calendar exists, the system assumes a five-day workweek.

SOME TIPS ON CALENDARS

It is, of course, highly recommended that you set up a production calendar. Work center calendars are necessary only if you have a lot of variability when machines operate over a period of time. In other words, use work center calendars when there are exceptions to the overall production calendar.

You have to run a process to give planning the ability to see the new calendars. Oftentimes, this is overlooked because it seems as if you've created them online by specifying all the information, and so on.

PRODUCTION AREA SETUP

The production area is the foundation of Production Management. It is used to structure the manufacturing operation within one manufacturing business unit. For each item you want to manufacture, you must tie it to one or more production areas. Production areas can represent product lines, product classes, a manufacturing process, or any high-level grouping of work. The area is a logical grouping of one or more physical workcenters or buildings. For example, to make a Chevy truck, multiple production areas such as "Engine Manufacturing," "Transmission Shop," and "Final Assembly" would probably be involved. The engine would be made in the "Engine Manufacturing" production area, and the truck would be completed in the "Final Assembly" area.

Refer to Figure 9.23 for a screenshot of setting up a production area. To establish a production area, you must specify WIP locations and General Ledger chartfields, as described in the next two sections.

Figure 9.23
Production Area setup is a fundamental aspect of Production Management.

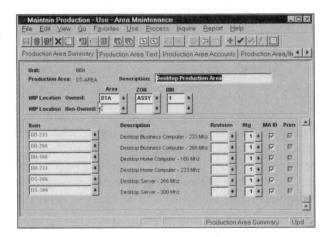

SPECIFY WIP LOCATIONS

A *WIP location* is an inventory storage location that is physically located on the factory floor. When material is sent to the factory floor for use in manufacturing, it is automatically routed and stored in the WIP location until it is used in production. One place where WIP locations are specified is on a production area.

SPECIFY GENERAL LEDGER CHARTFIELDS

This part is required only if location accounting is on. The account chartfield is required, whereas the other chartfields are optional but can give more detailed WIP tracking. Speaking of detail, if you want to retain different cost elements in different WIP accounts, you can do so by defining each cost element and their associated chartfields. Finally, if you want to classify work in process that is being reworked separately from regular production, you can also specify different chartfields for rework orders.

For each item, you specify a good deal of information on how to go about manufacturing it in that production area. Refer to Figure 9.24 for a look at production area/item details. First, there's the Maintain Production IDs check box. This flag tells the system whether to create discrete orders called Production Ids, or simply create production schedules based on production rates and shifts to satisfy demand. Second, the way in which components are issued to either the production ID or schedule is controlled by the component issue method selected. There are four different methods that are discussed later under the section "Component Issue Methods." They are Issue, Kit, Replenish, and Use Component's Method. Finally, you specify the routing code that represents which routing to use for the item. Usually this will be the primary routing (code = 1).

Figure 9.24
Any item to be produced in an area should be defined under that area.

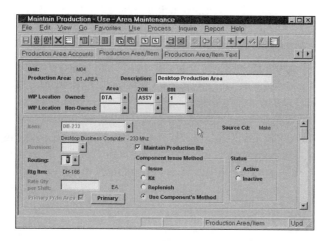

TIPS ON PRODUCTION AREAS

It is easy to forget to associate items with production areas. It is also easy to overlook the assignment of a routing code to each item in the production area. Missing either of these steps will prohibit you from creating production IDs or schedules.

There is a place in PeopleSoft Inventory Item Attributes by Unit to specify the production area of the item. This field enables the production area/item inquiry panel, but there doesn't seem to be any other use for it. The key association is linking items to production areas in Production Management, not Inventory.

Each production area can have its own WIP inventory account when using location accounting. Location accounting ties General Ledger accounts directly to storage areas and production areas. When you consume material in a production process, for example, the account tied to that production area is automatically debited for the material's value and the account tied to the storage area from which it came is credited. Refer back to "Introduction to Cost Management" for more information on location accounting.

CREATING PIDs AND SCHEDULES

The two ways to track manufacturing in PeopleSoft are production IDs and production schedules. A *Production ID (PID)* is a work order for a specific quantity due on a specific day. For example, a lamp manufacturer can create a production ID to make 15 Luxury Collection brown table lamps due the fifteenth of next month.

A *production schedule*, on the other hand, is a flow- or process-oriented way of representing production. A schedule will list out the volume or amount to produce daily, weekly, or monthly. For instance, a soap manufacturer can create a production schedule to make 5 million bars of soap per month for the entire year. As the production is completed, they would continually report against the outstanding production schedule all throughout the year.

There are four ways to create production IDs (PIDs) and production schedules.

- If you have Production Planning installed, accepting planning-generated messages that suggest the creation of PIDs or production schedules will create those orders

- If you want to create a PID or production schedule manually, you can enter them in Production Management one at a time

- If you are using the PS/nVision utility, you can change production quantities using a PS/nVision spreadsheet. The spreadsheet is actually a Microsoft Excel document, which can be uploaded using PS/nVision. Then, when these changes are exported back into Production Management, they will create PIDs and/or production schedules

- If you have Product Configurator installed, PIDs can be created by using the configurator. You could also create a manual PID for a configured item. Production Configurator is a rule-based generator of PIDs useful in configure-to-order manufacturing environments

PRODUCTION STATUSES

As progress is made on PIDs and schedules, the production status changes. PeopleSoft Production Management tracks production orders using eight distinct statuses. Refer to Table 9.5 for a brief description of these statuses.

TABLE 9.5   PRODUCTION ORDERS MAY HAVE THESE STATUSES DURING THEIR LIFETIMES

Production Status	Description
Firm	The order is seen as a source of supply, and you can change anything on the order but no component or operation list exists yet.
Released	For regular production, the Bills of Material and Routing are copied to create the component and operation lists, respectively. While changes can be made to the order, it may now result in the recreation of the component and operation lists. For rework production, the component list contains the item as a component of itself for rework. No operation list is created.

Production Status	Description
In Process	Status after you've either recorded actual hours or completions and/or scrap for the order.
Pending Complete	Status specifying that production is complete on the order itself.
Complete	No material completions or component consumption allowed in this order status. Run close production process to get here.
Closed for Labor	No actual hours or material completions allowed in this order status. Run close production process to get here.
Closed for Accounting	Production variances transactions are created when the close production process moves the order to this status. No changes can be made to the order unless it's reopened.
Cancelled	You may cancel orders that are in firm or released status only. Once you start work on them, it is necessary to close by making adjustments to production quantity, and so on.

RELEASING PRODUCTION

When you're developing a plan to produce, one method of getting ready is to create PIDs or production schedules in advance and specify a firm order status. The firm status means that you have every intention of making the item but have not yet released the order to the factory floor. Releasing PIDs or schedules from firm status is accomplished in one of two ways:

- Release one order at a time using an online panel
- Submit a process to release selected PIDs or schedules

The production release process is particularly noteworthy because it creates the component list and operation list.

The *component list* is a copy of the current production bill of material for the item that is tied directly and uniquely to the one released PID or schedule for that item. Changes to the component list do not change the production bill of material. Therefore, changes such as adding a component or deleting a component from the component list have no effect on future orders. They result in variances only for the one order.

The *operation list*, similarly, is a copy of the current production routing for the item. If a change is required to the production steps, you change the operation list and nothing on the production routing is affected. Future orders use the production routing and do not see the changes made on any operation list.

Tip

Here is a quick tip on releasing production: Run the process to release a whole bunch of orders at a time.

Releasing production is not a time-consuming process because usually it's done once a day at the most. The method depends largely on the type of business environment. If you are a configure-to-order manufacturer, PIDs can come directly to Production Management through the configurator rules. Or, more likely, PeopleSoft Planning has generated the optimal plan and has released orders on that basis. After a PID or schedule is released through one of the methods discussed, it's time to start making sure the material needed for manufacture is in the right place at the right time.

COMPONENT ISSUE METHODS: ISSUE, REPLENISH, AND KITTING

Issuing components to production orders is accomplished in one of three ways.

The *issue method* requires the items needed for production to be picked using a picking plan, and the picked components are then released to a WIP location. When the picked components are at the WIP location, PIDs or schedules consume these components when an operator records either completed or scrapped assemblies. A case of metal brackets whose method is "issue," for example, would be released and effectively transferred to the WIP location. But it might be a few days before the finished order was actually manufactured. During this stretch of time, the brackets reside in a material storage location and are not directly allocated to the original order that caused their release to the factory floor.

The *kit method* requires that the components are picked using a picking process, but in this case the components are released directly to the PID or schedule. The components never enter or leave the WIP location. Clearly, the kit method provides tighter control of inventory. In an aircraft manufacturing facility, the kit method could be used to dedicate cockpit control parts for use on assembling a portion of the pilot's visual displays. They are earmarked for a singular purpose and would have to be returned to the warehouse before being kitted to any other PID.

The *replenish method* does not require that the items be picked. Rather, replenishment logic kicks off a workflow notification when the stock level falls below the replenishment point at the WIP location. When the worklist is accessed, the item and location default into the Production Replenishment Transfer panel for ease of use. Whenever a raw material is used ubiquitously and frequently, it is a good candidate for replenishment. The coil used to make coins is an example of where it's not necessary to have issuing or kitting because literally every PID or schedule needs the raw material. It's much easier to control the flow using reorder point logic and workflow.

When you tie a make item to a production area, you specify how you want to issue components for that item when you're ready to produce it. Refer back to Figure 9.24 to see where to assign the component issue method. You can select issue, replenish, or kit, or you can opt to use the individual components' issue methods. In the last case, there could very likely be a mixed bag of methods. For example, you might have five components whose issue is through the kitting method, two components that are replenished, and three components that use the issue method. In any event, by the time you record completions and scrap, all the components should be a part of work-in-process inventory.

The picking plan is generated to pick components using either the issue or kit methods. Refer to Figure 9.25 for a screenshot of the Picking Plan Request panel. There are many options for selecting which components to pick, such as lead days and date ranges based on the operation start times, and also for sorting the output, such as by component or production area. You also have the option whether the system will decide the location from which to pick the components (the PUSH method) or will list out the locations where the component can be found so that the picker can provide feedback.

Figure 9.25
Production picking lists are very flexible.

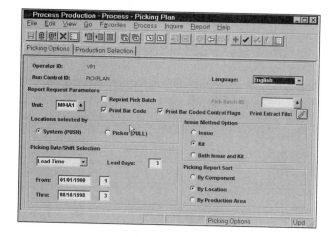

CONFIRMATION AND MATERIAL RELEASE PROCESS

Two other required steps after running a pick plan are the confirmation process and the material release process. The confirmation step is done online and must be followed by running a background process to complete the confirmation. Confirmation is the feedback loop to the system that says, "Yes, I picked this component from this location in this quantity."

The last step is the material release process. For components using the issue method, the components are released to the WIP location determined through the component and operation lists. Specifically, if the component has a non-zero operation sequence on the component list, the WIP location is taken as that operation sequence's workcenter. Otherwise, the WIP location is taken from the definition of the production area at which the item is being produced. For kit method components, the material release process sends the components directly into the PID or schedule, eliminating the need to backflush components.

Tip

Here are some component issue tips: You are allowed to drive inventory negative in PeopleSoft Production Management when picking or consuming components. There is a flag at the business unit level that allows it and another flag that will give you a warning every time it happens. So, for example, you could record a completion and consume some components even if no components were currently at the WIP location. In a lot of cases, this can be handy because of the timing of transactions.

If you utilize one of the component issue methods with due diligence, the component materials should not only be available physically, but for the system to utilize. Now when production commences, the PeopleSoft system can accurately record material consumption. It is now time to look at the process of entering into PeopleSoft information about the work completed on the production floor.

RECORDING PRODUCTION COMPLETIONS AND ASSEMBLY SCRAP

Tracking the progress of the production process is accomplished by entering information about material completions and scrap. PeopleSoft Production Management supports automated data collection in this area and others. You can also record completions of good units or scrap of bad units online. For a look at this panel, see Figure 9.26.

Figure 9.26
You record the progress of production by specifying units completed and/or scrapped by operation sequence.

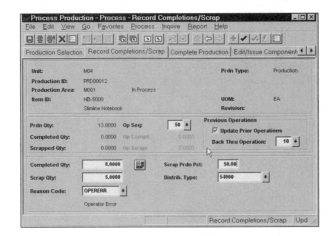

You can enter completions and scrap by operation for a PID. If desirable, you can also enter the information for any operation, say the last, and have the system automatically record the same numbers of completions and/or scrap back through a range of previous operations. In many cases, particularly if production times are short, it is easiest to record just at the last operation and back through all operations, recording just one time for the entire PID.

You enter completions and scrap for production schedules without specifying operations, even if the operation list has many steps.

The recording of completions and scrap will backflush all issue or replenishment component issue method items from the WIP locations. *Backflushing* is the recognition that components were used at the time the finished item is recorded complete. As such, the inventory for the components is reduced at the same time a completion occurs in the amount that went into making the product. Remember that kit components are already a part of the WIP inventory value, having been issued directly to the PID or schedule. It is at this point also that Production Management will generate earned labor transactions for the standard costs of conversion: labor, machine, and overhead costs defined through the item's routing.

When production is complete, you have the option of sending the product directly to an inventory storage location straight from the PID or schedule, or you can stage the item, sending the inventory to a table for batch processing, warehouse confirmation, or interface purposes.

> **Tip**
>
> You can close a PID or schedule short. In other words, you can make 900 units only, even if the PID or schedule quantity is for 1000 units. There is a check box on the close production process that needs to be on in order to do this.
>
> The reason code is required only if you scrap assemblies. The distribution type is optional for scrap and can be used to direct the scrap expense on a one-time basis to a special set of General Ledger chartfields. Additional account distributions are required for this to work.

RECORDING ACTUAL HOURS

As shop floor personnel perform work, you can have them enter it into PeopleSoft using the Actual Hours functionality. The idea here is to capture actual time spent so as to monitor performance. By comparing the actual time spent on an operation and comparing the standard costs, you get an indication of performance as well as insight into how aggressively you've set your standards. None of these efficiency or utilization variances can actually post to PeopleSoft General Ledger. They are available only within PeopleSoft Manufacturing.

CLOSING PRODUCTION ORDERS

PeopleSoft Production Management has a number of different production statuses that you might consider to be a closed status. When an order has a status of in-process, you can close it to any status that is further downstream. Refer to Figure 9.27 to see how you can close orders in one status to another status. The close production process must be used if you want to make an order have the status of complete, closed for labor, or closed for accounting. The last step, closed for accounting, is when production variances like configuration variance and routing process variance are posted. You can run the process in report mode only. Doing so enables you to see the production variances that will generate if you close orders for accounting in a simulation environment. If you don't like what you see, there's time to make some calls and take corrective action before the close. As a last resort, you can always run the reopen production process. This process reverses all variances posted if the order was previously closed for accounting. You can make the necessary changes and close again. This closing and reopening should be minimized.

It might be a business practice to close orders to labor those orders that are a week past their due date and to close for accounting those orders that are a month past their due date. All you need to do is set up run control IDs for the close production process and run the process through the process scheduler.

Figure 9.27
Completed orders
must be closed for
accounting purposes.

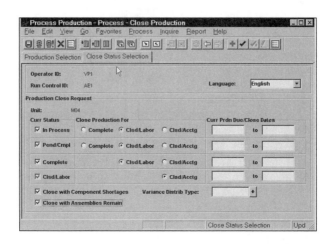

PRODUCTION VARIANCES SENT TO COST MANAGEMENT

All manufacturing variances accumulate in Work in Process (WIP) as production proceeds.
When the production ID or schedule is closed for accounting, variance transactions can be
generated. If the close production process is run in report mode only, the table is populated
temporarily for reporting but is then rolled back at the end of the process. Refer to
Table 9.6 to see which transactions might occur.

TABLE 9.6   VARIANCES INCURRED BY THE MANUFACTURING PROCESS ARE POSTED TO THE
PEOPLESOFT GENERAL LEDGER UNDER THESE TRANSACTION GROUPS

Transaction Group	Description	Manufacturing Variances Involved
261	Material Variance	Configuration, Usage, Component Yield, Material Lot Size
262	Conversion Variance	Routing Process, Conversion Lot Size
263	Outside Processing Purchase Price Variance	Outside Processing PPV
264	Rework Expense	Material Rework Expense, Conversion Rework Expense

To explain how these particular variances can occur, it is necessary to open up a rather
extensive example for discussion. Each type of variance is the result of a decision made
regarding a PID or schedule. It primarily involves changes to the component and operation
lists necessitated by one-time factors. For this analysis, I'll start with a standard costed
printed circuit board, a PCB. Its BOM and routing are shown in Figure 9.28.

Figure 9.28
This simple Bill of
Material explains the
different manufactur-
ing variances.

PART

II

CH

9

The standard cost of the PCB is composed of the material cost of a transistor and a green board, as well as the cost of the insertion and welding operations, including manufacturing overhead. It's a very simple, non-functional PCB but will be useful for discussion purposes. All variances are deviations from this standard cost. The standard is composed of "this level" and "lower-level" costs by cost element. All variances discussed are broken out by cost elements for reporting and accounting purposes. To fully understand what each reported variance represents, review the following hypothetical situations for each type of manufacturing variance.

CONFIGURATION VARIANCE

Configuration variance is the difference between the BOM used as the benchmark for establishing standard costs and the BOM used at some later date to create the order's component list.

With standard cost established, Susan, the manufacturing supervisor, decides that the BOM needs a little tweaking. She includes a resistor in the BOM. Remember that the standard cost includes the transistor and green board only in the material cost, but now we've got the transistor, green board, and resistor thanks to Susan.

The resistor is not part of the standard cost, but it certainly costs money. A standard cost system requires that inventory be valued at its standard cost. Therefore, when the PCB is sent to stores, it goes in at the standard that includes only the material cost of the transistor and green board. The system accounts for what was issued to production of resistors as configuration variance. This type of variance is also known as Methods BOM Variance.

Susan might have also changed the component list instead. When a production ID is released, a copy of the BOM is taken to create the component list. If Susan just changes the component list, only this one order would have a configuration variance. On the other hand, changing the BOM itself would affect all orders released after the change until the standard cost was updated to include the resistor.

Another way to get configuration variance would be to delete the transistor or green board from the BOM or component list. A change in the quantity per (for example, instead of one transistor to make one PCB, change the relationship to four transistors to make one PCB) would also cause configuration variance.

Configuration variance is a fancy name for the production BOM not being the same as it was when costs were established. If standards change more often than manufacturing processes, it is very likely to encounter this variance.

USAGE VARIANCE

Usage variance results when too much or too little of a component is backflushed into WIP according to the current component list for the order.

Bob, the shop foreman, uses more transistors and resistors than scheduled on the BOM for a particular item. Maybe one of his team bent the transistor on insertion and just broke the leads off some resistors.

The transistor, green board, and resistor are all on the BOM (remember, Susan added the resistor). Any difference between what the component list says is the scheduled quantity needed and what Bob actually used becomes usage variance.

The scheduled quantity is adjusted for any expected yield if the component has a yield factor. Sometimes you build in a yield factor if you know there is going to be some component loss in the manufacturing process. Thus, if your yield factor bumps up the scheduled quantity by five, the five units are taken out for any usage variance calculation.

Usage variance is probably the most common variance because any slight deviation from what the BOM says will create this variance. It is especially common in industries where raw materials are measured in mass or volume due to inherent inexactness.

COMPONENT YIELD VARIANCE

Component yield variance is the difference between the expected yield loss for a particular component and the actual yield loss during manufacturing.

Joe, the trusted process engineer, has previously added a yield factor of 90% to the transistor of the PCB. Let's assume it was always a part of the standard cost of the PCB. Thus, he expects that to make 100 PCBs, he'll need 111.11 transistors, not 100. Later, in recording the issuing of components to the production order, Bob's team reports that only 3.0 extra transistors were needed.

This would result in a so-called "favorable" variance because the production went better than Joe's estimate. (With a favorable situation, the debits and credits of accounting will be reversed downstream.) The process used 103 total, giving a favorable variance of 8.11 times the cost of the transistor.

The Edit/Issue Component panel clearly separates the issue quantity and yield loss quantity. The sum of these quantities is what is truly consumed by the manufacturing process. The former is tied directly to usage variance, and the latter is linked to component yield variance.

The value of 111.11 really makes sense only for weight, volume, or length units of measure. It would be hard to realistically schedule 111.11 transistors! Yield factors enjoy wide use in process manufacturing.

Component yield variance and usage variance are similar. Just as with usage variance, component yield variance is measuring the actual versus the standard. Here, though, it is the standard yield expected versus the actual yield observed.

LOT SIZE VARIANCES

Lot size variance occurs when costs that occur per order are figured into a standard cost per unit based on the normal production run size, but the production run size differs from the normal.

Vanessa is a cost engineer and has set an average order quantity (AOQ) for the PCB because some costs are defined on a per order basis. The standard cost uses the AOQ as a basis to determine per unit costs. When the production quantity completed of the PCB differs from its established AOQ, there is the possibility of lot size variances; either material, conversion, or both.

Lot size variance has nothing to do with the concept of lot control. Lot size variance refers only to the size of the production order.

MATERIAL LOT SIZE VARIANCES

To get material lot size variances, the way in which the component is defined on the BOM is important. A component can have a quantity per relationship of either (1) per assembly or (2) per order. That is, the production process may require one transistor for every PCB (the assembly) produced or one transistor each time some PCBs are made, regardless of the quantity of PCBs produced. In this case, the transistor would clearly be on a per assembly basis. Material lot sizes, however, result if a component is per order and the production quantity is different than the AOQ.

This makes sense because if the component was per assembly, the fact that the production quantity differs from the average order quantity would be irrelevant. It is when you have to spread the cost of the transistor over some quantity of PCBs that discrepancies would arise. The standard is based on the AOQ. A larger production quantity will yield lower costs per unit of PCB than the standard.

CONVERSION LOT SIZE VARIANCES

Conversion lot size variances come from setup, fixed run, and post-production times. If these times are defined per order rather than per unit and the production quantity differs from the AOQ, you get conversion lot size variances.

Here again, the standard cost of the PCB would be based on the AOQ. With any cost defined per order, the system must have an AOQ in order to calculate standard cost, which is always on a per unit basis. Each operation, insertion and welding, might have setup, fixed run, and post-production elements of conversion. So these variances might come from neither, one, or both of these routing steps.

Both material and conversion lot size variances are infrequently encountered. Many companies do not use the average order quantity concept to cost their products.

ROUTING PROCESS VARIANCES

Routing process variance occurs when the routing or operation list of an item changes. Adding, deleting, or changing some portion of an operation step can result in variance from the original standard.

The production team leader Carmen decides that an additional routing step called inspection is needed for a run of PCBs. She adds the inspection task as operation 030 to the operation list because she thinks there could be a quality issue.

The change increases the cost of conversion. Still, the standard cost of the PCB has not changed. An unfavorable routing process variance results. Any addition, deletion, or change of operations in either the routing or the operation list could give a routing process variance. Invoking alternate routings or flat-out skipping operations are other examples where you'll get routing process variance. This variance is also known as methods routing variance.

Changes in the costing labor run, costing setup, and so forth or a change of conversion code per rate will also create routing process variance. For example, the welding operation might normally have a labor rate of $20 per hour, which is the established standard. But if Carmen changes the conversion code and the labor rate goes to $25 per hour, routing process variance is the result. Assigning the welding operation to a different workcenter could have the same effect.

Routing process variance will result whenever the routing or operation list changes from the standard routing. Any change will precipitate this variance, so it is very common to see this variance.

REWORK EXPENSE

Rework expense is basically the cost of extra work involved in fixing orders that physically have problems.

Mike is the quality manager for the circuit board division and he needs to rework the PCB. He creates a rework production ID. The component list has only the PCB on it. You issue the item to itself in a rework situation, which makes sense. Mike goes on to add a capacitor and an inductor to the component list and adds an operation called Rework to the operation list. He completes the rework PID.

All cost except for the PCB itself becomes rework expense. The cost of capacitor and inductor components, as well as the cost of fixing the PCB at the Rework operation is treated as rework expense. All rework expense is unfavorable because anything that's done is in addition to the standard production costs.

If the standard cost of the PCB is $100 and Mike's reworking one PCB, $100 goes into WIP when the PCB is issued to itself. Then, when the PCB is put back into inventory, that $100 goes right back into inventory at standard. The rest of it, including all other components needed for rework and all labor and overhead, is treated as rework expense. On the production variance report, rework expense is separated out by material and conversion rework expense. Ultimately, however, it all becomes a part of the rework expense transaction.

Rework expense is a variance resulting exclusively for the extra material, labor, and overhead expended to correct manufacturing problems through rework.

Outside Processing PPV

Janet, manager of vendor relations, has created a routing in which Wally's Welding, a great shop just down the street, does the welding. This is outside processing. Wally wants more money for his welding because he knows he's good. So Janet pays him a little extra because he's worth it. The problem is that Janet established the standard cost of the welding operation when Wally was charging less. So now she'll get outside processing purchase price variances.

The purchase order price compared to the welding operation cost is the variance. The operation cost defaults into the PO schedule line price but in this case, Janet overrode the value with the new PO price. This variance could also be favorable. Then again, who ever heard of a service getting cheaper?

Operations are marked as subcontracted by checking a box on the routing. Both rework and regular production IDs can have a subcontracted operation and PPV.

Subcontracting can result in outside processing PPV when the purchase order price differs from the standard cost associated with that type of subcontracting activity.

Summary of Manufacturing Variances

The financial outcome of manufacturing activity in PeopleSoft is in part a set of variances that post to the PeopleSoft General Ledger. These variances are the result of any allowable change in production. Consistent variance is an indication of an item that might need to be revalued.

It is possible to have every one of the variances generate for one production order. Each would fall under a transaction group as defined earlier. The accounting line creation process and the journal generator must run to see these variances as journal entries in the General Ledger.

Two variances that do not post to the General Ledger are efficiency variance and utilization variance. Both require the recording of actual labor and/or machine hours. To view them, you must run the PeopleSoft Efficiency and Utilization Report within Production Management. Efficiency is defined as the Standard hours versus Actual hours, while Utilization is Actual hours versus Available hours.

Production Management Reports and Inquiries

Production Management has a number of "out of the box" reports. They are available on the panels of Production Management and are requested like other reports through run control IDs. Here they are with a brief description:

- Picking Plan—Shows the components and the locations at which they are located for use by the warehouse in retrieving materials.
- Dispatch List—Also available online, this report gives supervisors and operators a look at what is scheduled by workcenter by day or hour.

- Production Documents—Also known as the shop paperwork or shop traveler, it lists the components and operations required for a PID or schedule.

- Efficiency and Utilization—With the recording of actual hours, it displays these measures of productivity. These variances are not posted to the General Ledger. *Efficiency* is the standard hours vs. the actual hours by operation, and *utilization* is the actual hours vs. available hours as defined on the workcenter.

- WIP Inventory Value—Shows the current work in process at standard cost. Includes material, labor, overhead, and other types of costs.

- Potential Production Variance—For PIDs and schedules that are not yet closed for accounting, it shows the current variance picture based on the transactions recorded to date.

- Close Production—As part of the close process, this report generates. It is very similar to the potential production variances report.

- Production Variance—Shows only variances that have posted as a result of closing for accounting or reopening PIDs and schedules.

- Shortage—Lists different levels of component shortages based on system-defined rules. Helps to get materials to the right place.

- Production—A listing of the key information about PIDs and schedules. Many different options for selecting including order status, start dates, items, and production areas. You can also sort it many different ways.

Production Management also has a number of useful inquiries accessible through the delivered panels. Here they are with a brief description:

- Production Schedules by Production Area—Shows all the production schedules over a week in one area.

- Component and Operation Lists—Shows the components of a specific PID and all the details associated with it. Likewise, shows the operations required in order to make a PID.

- Production for an Item—Shows all orders for specific items.

- Production—Shows the details on a specific PID or schedule.

- Production Areas for an Item—Shows production areas at which an item can be manufactured.

- Dispatch List—Shows which PIDs and schedules are scheduled at a workcenter for a given day or week.

- Scrap, Earned Cost, and Actual Hours—Shows a detailed breakdown of what materials have been scrapped for a particular PID, the completions in terms of dollars produced, and the real time spent on an order as reported by the shop floor personnel.

INTRODUCTION TO PEOPLESOFT QUALITY 7.5

Quality control is a key function within any manufacturing organization. By ensuring that the products are meeting predefined quality specifications, organizations can monitor processes and ultimately make improvements in their operations based on the collected information. A baseball bat manufacturer, for example, would weigh each bat to make sure it is the number of ounces intended. Selling a bat that is not the weight promised is not a good business practice. As part of an overall quality initiative, there is a need for software to store, monitor, and analyze quantitative measurements taken for the purpose of statistical process control. Part of the PeopleSoft manufacturing solution is PeopleSoft Quality.

PART

II

CH

9

PeopleSoft Quality is based on the Salerno quality system, purchased outright by PeopleSoft and reprogrammed using PeopleTools. The Salerno quality system was a market-leading product of Salerno Manufacturing Systems, so its purchase represents a significant addition to the PeopleSoft enterprise solution. PeopleSoft Quality combines online statistical process control (SPC) data collection with the power of a relational database for top-flight quality analysis. With Quality you can configure your process environment, use industry-standard quality controls or create your own, monitor process performance, and perform online quality data analysis using the interactive tools it provides.

INPUTS NEEDED FROM PEOPLESOFT MANUFACTURING

PeopleSoft Quality enables you to track and manage quality data in your manufacturing operation. It relies heavily on the rest of PeopleSoft Manufacturing for the items, machines, and workcenters against which the measurements are made. To start the setup of PeopleSoft Quality, you must have quality business units, items, workcenter, and machines, as described in the following sections.

QUALITY BUSINESS UNITS

There must be a one-to-one correspondence between the manufacturing business unit and the quality business unit. The quality business unit is where you will store the data collected from observations as well as define the structure of the quality tests performed. Note that every other module discussed within PeopleSoft Manufacturing is based on the manufacturing business unit, but Quality is its own animal that has its own business unit structure. If you have a plant in Omaha, Nebraska, both the manufacturing and quality business units can be the same name, but the two separate definitions are still required. Along similar lines, it is worth noting that PeopleSoft also has business unit definitions specific to modules like Order Management, Inventory, and the General Ledger, just to name a few.

ITEMS

To measure the quality of a product or process, it's clear that you'll need approved items defined within PeopleSoft Inventory. An electrical device manufactured by an electronics company, for example, usually requires a quality check. By hooking an ammeter to the device, you can measure the electrical current. Such measurements are the basis for the statistical analysis performed in PeopleSoft Quality. Quality control (QC) steps such as "test electric current on device" are linked to these items, providing a mechanism to set up the process controls, enter samples, and analyze the reported values using tools like Pareto charts and histograms.

WORKCENTERS

Workcenters are established in PeopleSoft Bills and Routings. The implication of needing workcenters is that there must be a place where some measurable manufacturing activity is taking place. A *workcenter* is a group of resources (machines and/or people) operating at the same cost.

MACHINES

Machines are also set up in Bills and Routings. A machine such as a drill press operates according to its settings, which are usually programmed by the machine operator. Monitoring the manufacturing process is done using quality control (QC) stations. A drill press quality control station is linked directly to the definition of the drill press machine itself. Physically, there might be a quality inspector assigned to the drill press who is to take measurements and record them in PeopleSoft Quality.

Refer to Figure 9.29 for a graphical depiction of these interrelationships.

Figure 9.29
PeopleSoft
Manufacturing supports electronic data collection for most types of transactions.

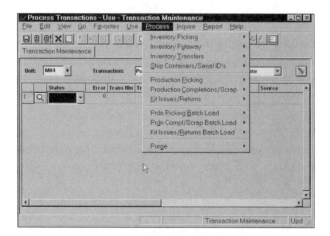

ESTABLISHING QC STEPS: CHARACTERISTICS, TRACE SETS, AND DISTRIBUTIONS LISTS

The Quality Control (QC) step is the key concept of PeopleSoft Quality. For each step, you can define one or more quality characteristics. For example, the length of a piece of cut wire might be a measurable quality characteristic. Each characteristic is recorded, tracked, and analyzed using control procedures, tests, and charts. Importantly, each characteristic must have a data type. A variable data type is used for measuring characteristics such as length, mass, or time. In addition, any characteristic derived through a user-defined formula would have a variable data type. A defect data type represents the number of defects observed per unit. Examples might be a dent, smudge, or a missing component. A defective data type is for pass/fail characteristics, a count of how many units are defective. Refer to Figure 9.30 for a breakdown of the types of control charts available and the valid subgroup size for each type.

Figure 9.30
Serial control shown here as well as lot control give tighter control of shop floor activities.

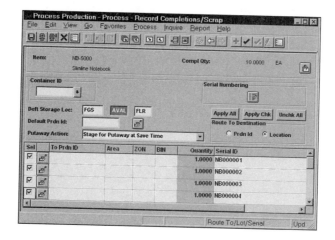

For each QC step, you define the level of traceability. By assigning a user-defined trace set, every time an operator records sample results, he/she will have to enter the trace field(s) as well. Trace fields might include the operator ID, the lot ID, the serial ID, the production ID, or other production information associated with the sample. You can define trace fields to pop up online for each individual sample or just for the subgroup. If you capture specific information about the production process such as lot numbers at the time of sampling, taking corrective action is much easier because you already know which lots to rework.

For each QC step, you can also define a distribution list. If a violation of one of the control tests occurs, the distribution list will send out an "alarm" to notify the appropriate people. This notification will be an email or, if PeopleSoft Workflow is utilized, a message on the PeopleSoft worklist.

ATTRIBUTE CATEGORIES

Attribute categories are predefined lists of defects, causes, and actions. Based on historical knowledge, a paint factory knows that quality problems are usually chipping, peeling, and bubbling of the paint. By listing these defects upfront in the setup, the operator taking the reading does not have to continually enter these values. Similarly, likely causes can be listed beforehand. Some causes might be high humidity, excessive handling, or paint chemistry. Finally, what actions are taken in the event a quality problem is detected? All the possible actions can be set up in advance. With the cause, defect, and action attribute setup, most of the data entry is streamlined. It is as easy as pulling down the selection criteria list at each sampling.

DEFINE QUALITY CONTROLS: CONTROL CHARTS, TESTS, AND PROCEDURES

How do you evaluate the data for each QC characteristic? Without a meaningful method of testing, the data will not provide useful information. The idea is to identify quality problems to prevent nonconformities from continuing throughout the production process. With this in mind, you must establish control charts, tests, and procedures consistent with your company's quality policies and programs. PeopleSoft Quality allows you to customize these important controls. If you want, you can create your own control charts, tests, and procedures. Many industry standards, however, come delivered with the software.

The seven standard control charts ready to use in PeopleSoft Quality are

- X and Moving Range
- Xbar and Sigma
- Xbar and Range
- c chart
- u chart
- p chart
- np chart

Many control tests come ready to use with PeopleSoft Quality. These tests are grouped together into control procedures. A control procedure is then attached to the QC characteristic. Data on the QC characteristic is analyzed using the control procedure specified.

Control tests commonly used in industry include upper and lower control limit violations, shift, trend, systematic variables, and stratification. Each type of variation here can be captured by one or more of the delivered control tests.

The delivered control procedures I–IV include some combination of the delivered control tests. Control procedure I contains only a few control tests, and control procedure IV is the most stringent, providing the most rigorous procedure. Again, control procedures can be customized to fit your particular needs.

COLLECTING THE QUALITY DATA ON THE MANUFACTURING FLOOR

After all the controls are established including control charts, tests, procedures, QC steps, and QC characteristics, it is time to begin the data collection. Operators on the manufacturing floor can enter their data directly into a PeopleSoft panel for a sampling session (see Figure 9.31 for an example). Plans are currently under way to support a wide range of automatic data collection through an advanced Application Program Interface (API). In the meantime, users have to enter everything manually. The panel enables an operator to view the control chart associated with the characteristic by just clicking a button. Furthermore, other buttons enable the calculation of derived characteristics and provide areas to enter the defects and actions to take. Each of the sampling sessions is tracked individually. At any time, someone can return to a session to edit it or review its findings.

Figure 9.31
PeopleSoft Quality uses inputs from other Manufacturing modules.

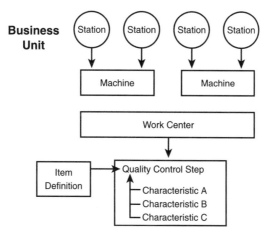

DISTRIBUTE ALARMS FOR FAILED TESTS

Whenever a violation of control test occurs, an alarm is issued. The form of the alarm is a message sent to those employees who need to know about the violation. Using the distribution lists, you can organize the issuance of these alarms to the appropriate people. All alarms appear in the operator's alarm queue, which looks like your email list at work. Reviewing them is easy—you just pick one and look at the detail.

EXTRACTING DATA THROUGH QUERIES

Queries offload the data entered through the sampling sessions. For safety, all data is extracted to an isolated storage area that is external to the production database and cannot be used to update production. Such queries or extractions are user-defined, SQL-driven, and reusable. After the data is extracted, it is manipulated by user-defined graphical preferences. One important example is specifying one of five types of available transformations including the following:

- Inverse
- Square
- Square root
- Log
- Natural log

PeopleSoft Quality can fit data to a normal distribution (normality assumed), assess non-normal distributions, and utilize the Pearson best-fit method of least squares. When using tests for normality, the delivered methodology measures the skewness and kurtosis of the distribution at a 95% confidence interval. If the test for normality indicates a non-normal distribution, the Pearson best-fit criteria is used.

Many of the standard statistics are available for analysis, including

- Mean
- Variance
- Covariance
- Range
- Minimum
- Maximum
- Skewness
- Kurtosis
- Z scores
- Sum
- Upper and lower 3 sigma
- Quartiles
- Median
- Capability indices
- Defect statistics including sum, per unit, per hundred, per thousand, and per million

QUALITY ANALYSIS TOOLS

PeopleSoft Quality contains six quality analysis tools ready to use. All the tools are run on the Quality Server, which is really just a utility within PeopleSoft Quality that stores and displays the data extracted. Each tool is interactive, colorful, and easy to use and customize. The delivered analysis tools are as follows:

- Control Chart
- Histogram
- Pareto Chart
- Bar Graph
- Box Plot
- Line Graph

The features of each tool include the capability to mask any point such as an outlier and recalculate the statistics without the data point. You can change control procedures, and the system will automatically apply the new procedures and generate the relevant violations. Also, you can export the data and graphics to a number of file formats including Microsoft Excel and HTML. For examples of the analysis tools, refer to Table 9.7 and Figure 9.32.

TABLE 9.7   EACH OF THE THREE DATA TYPES HAS ITS OWN CONTROL CHARTS

PS Characteristic Data Type	Also Known As	Control Charts Available	Valid Subgroup Size
Variable	Variable	X and Moving Range, Xbar and Range, Xbar and Sigma	1-50
Defects	Nonconformities	c, u	0-50
Defectives	Nonconforming	p, np	0-500,000

Figure 9.32
You enter the QC readings on the Maintain Sampling panel.

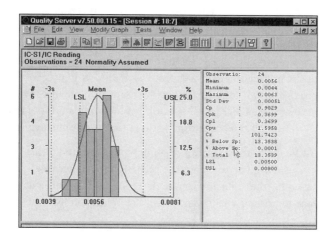

With PeopleSoft Quality, the collection and analysis of quality data is made easy. Working as part of the overall manufacturing solution, the continuous quality improvement activities are fully supported through this flexible software.

INTRODUCTION TO PRODUCTION PLANNING

The ability to effectively manage a manufacturing organization depends heavily on having the right people, machines, and materials in the right place at the right time. Maximizing the way scarce resources such as your valued employees are put to work has a tremendous effect on the efficiency and effectiveness of a manufacturing operation. PeopleSoft Planning is a resource optimizer. That is, it maximizes the use of people, materials, and machines.

THE PEOPLESOFT PLANNING APPROACH

PeopleSoft's Production Planning is an Enterprise Resource Optimization (ERO) product. As a planning tool, it can be thought of as the next generation of requirements planning.

It is one of the first manufacturing applications to embed advanced planning and scheduling capabilities for optimizing the supply chain and all assets in the plant. The purpose of this section is to focus on plant-specific optimization. Based on Goldratt's Theory of Constraints and fully integrated with the rest of PeopleSoft Manufacturing, Production Planning is a great tool to improve the effectiveness of your manufacturing and distribution operations. While maintaining the capability to perform similarly to MRP or MRPII systems, Production Planning allows you to optimize your production plan, taking into consideration potentially many constraints at one time or, more common in practice, iteratively solving the business plan by applying one set of constraints followed by another set. Constraints measure the feasibility and quality of a schedule. You set the relative importance of a constraint by specifying weights and penalty functions.

In the simplest PeopleSoft terms, MRP can be run by optimizing on PeopleSoft's buildable inventory and raw material shortage constraints. That is, MRP evaluates the time-phased availability of material by considering lead times for both production (buildable inventory) and purchasing (raw materials). MRPII considers all resources including people and machines so that the production plan is more reasonable. In PeopleSoft, the aggregate capacity constraint, along with the first two constraints of buildable inventory and raw material shortages serve to model an MRPII type of production plan. Note that one optimization run can consider all MRPII type constraints at one time without solving for each separately.

The advantage of PeopleSoft Production Planning over the traditional approaches like MRP or MRPII is that it enables you to weigh the relative importance of each constraint so that the optimal solution for the company can be determined. If promise dates to your customers are the single most important business criteria, turn on that constraint 100% and weight the others less.

PRODUCTION PLANNING VERSUS ENTERPRISE PLANNING

PeopleSoft Production Planning and Enterprise Planning are powered by an embedded optimization engine that was originally developed by the company called Red Pepper, acquired by PeopleSoft in 1996. Through this optimization engine, planning data is analyzed for use by production and procurement (PP) and for the entire distribution supply chain (EP). For a full discussion of the Enterprise Planning module, refer to Chapter 11, "Distribution Modules." For a discussion of Supply Chain Management, refer to Chapter 19, "Should I Do It?" Production Planning focuses optimizations on plant-level problems like getting the right part at the right time and scheduling the right amount of work for a production area. Enterprise Planning is more concerned with overall issues like overall order fulfillment and aggregate capacity concerns for your whole enterprise that might include hundreds of plants, distribution warehouses, and satellite locations.

REQUIRED INPUTS

To have any kind of useful production plan, there is plenty of required setup within PeopleSoft Manufacturing. What good is an optimization without accurate Bills of Material and Routings? It is of very little use. Such a setup effort is not trivial when you're getting started with an implementation. It is wise to give a great deal of thought to your production planning goals and objectives and seek professional training and assistance early in the process. Some of the major setup needed to run any meaningful optimization includes the following:

- **Machines**—What are your machines? How many available hours per shift? How many like machines do you have? What is the labor involved with them?

- **Workcenters**—How is your shop floor structured? Do you want the optimizer to see a group of machines as one workcenter or many?

- **Routings**—How are your products made? What sequence of steps is involved and how long does each take? What resources like people, tools, and machines go into the production effort?

- **Item Attributes**—What are the characteristics of your items? Do you need safety stock of the item? What are your minimum purchase or production lots of this item?

- **BOMs**—What purchase items and/or subassemblies compose your production items? Do you want to represent product lines through planning BOMs?

- **Forecasts**—What is the expected demand of your items? Do you have any firm orders? If not, what does your knowledge of the business, history, and demand planning modeling tell you about upcoming demand?

THE PLANNING DATALINK

The integration of PeopleSoft Manufacturing with PeopleSoft Production Planning is performed entirely through the Planning Datalink. The optimization engine runs on its own server, so data is transported over to the planning server, and when you have an acceptable plan, you transfer information back to PeopleSoft Manufacturing. The Datalink can be run at any time, as many times as necessary, and a variety of user-defined settings control what information to send. Refer to Figure 9.33. Note that the tabs at the top of the figure represent other panels where setup is required. Included are such things as demand and supply options. In other words, you must specify whether you want existing supply in the form of purchase orders, production orders, and transfer orders to be included in the data sent to the optimization engine. Similarly, demand such as forecasts, sales orders, sales order quotes, and transfers can be included or excluded from the model individually.

Other options set in the Planning Datalink include any number of fences. A *fence* is an arbitrary point in time that you define to limit the visibility to information either before or after the fence date. Looking at demand over one year out, for example, might not be worthwhile, so you could set a planning time fence of one year. Many other fences including start, end, purchase, early, late, and demand time are used to construct the environment to your liking. Fences are a fairly advanced topic and because there are so many different ones, the whole subject can become very confusing. If you don't know what a fence is supposed to do, it is often best just to leave it at zero and hope for the best!

Figure 9.33
A histogram plotted with 24 observations and normality assumed.

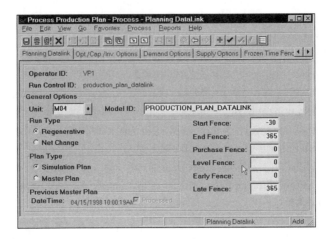

The Planning Datalink is the control station for all data flow into the optimization engine. When you run the datalink, you create a command file that will contain all the data to be used by the optimizer.

RED PEPPER OPTIMIZER

The planning server is where the optimization, that is, the planning, actually occurs. To begin, the data from the datalink run is loaded into memory on the server by opening the command file. When the data is in the server memory, you are free to view the input data using the data browser feature, and prepare to optimize by defining the control panel.

CONTROL PANEL

The control panel is where you establish the weights of each constraint. For a look at the control panel, see Table 9.8. In other words, here is where your business objectives like promise dates to customers are defined quantitatively by expressing a percentage from 0 to 100% for each constraint. There are both a primary and an optional control panel where you can define constraint weightings. After you have established the control panel to your liking, you are ready to begin an optimization.

TABLE 9.8   PRODUCTION PLANNING CAN CONSIDER ANY COMBINATIONS OF THESE CONSTRAINTS WHEN OPTIMIZING

Constraint	Description	Type of Constraint
Request Date	Ship product to the customer when he requests it	Business
Promise Date	Ship product to the customer when you promise it	Business
Safety Stock	Maintain a level of safety stock to ensure product availability	Business

Constraint	Description	Type of Constraint
Excess Stock	Minimize the cost of carrying inventory	Business
Buildable Inventory	Availability of finished goods and/or subassemblies	Resource
Raw Material	Availability of raw material/ purchased inventory	Resource
Aggregate Capacity	Availability of people, machines, or other resources over a period of time	Resource
Capacity	Availability of people, machines, or other resources at any point in time	Additional
Capacity by Period	Over a period time, set up preferred utilization ranges for resources	Additional
Reduce Routing Slack	Checks for the time between scheduled tasks where no job is scheduled for a workcenter	Additional
Changeover	Minimize workcenter changeover cost based on cost structure	Additional
Purchase Contract	Checks for a violation of the maximum purchase quantity for a vendor oritem combination over a period of time	Additional
Build Contract	Checks for a violation of the maximum production quantity for an inventory item over a period of time	Additional

The optimization takes the data from the datalink and the control panel settings as its principal inputs. Using advanced planning and scheduling logic, the optimizer iteratively searches for the best solution. You can see it working as it displays a graphic showing a history of its workings. The best-optimized score is zero, which indicates that with the given inputs, all constraints are met without any violations.

A *violation* is one instance where a constraint is not optimally met. For example, the capacity of a workcenter in a week is, say, 40 hours and the aggregate capacity constraint was turned on at 100%. If the planned workload (as calculated by the optimization engine in a given week) is 41 hours, a violation would occur and would show up under the aggregate capacity constraint in the scorecard.

Note that other constraints in this case probably prohibited the optimizer from shifting work to another workcenter or to another week. The optimizer is considering all chosen weighted constraints simultaneously and attempts to come up with the best solution given the inputs. There is no guarantee that a perfect solution will result; only the best solution under the constraints imposed. Note also that the end of an optimization can be controlled by the number of iterations run, the elapsed time, or by manually ending the run.

At the end of an optimization, you can view the results through a variety of means. The current data is viewed using the data browser. Figure 9.34 shows the data browser interface.

Figure 9.34
The Planning Datalink sends data to the optimization engine running on a different server.

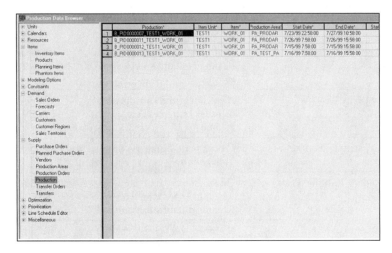

Note that it's very similar to Microsoft Windows Explorer where you click down through the hierarchy to get to the type of data in which you're interested. For example, demand followed by sales orders will show a list of all sales orders currently in memory. At any time, you can save the current plan to a file for reference later. Such a picture is called a *snapshot*.

The violations are best viewed through the scorecard. The scorecard shows the outcome of the optimization from the perspective of each constraint. Each constraint is given a rating, and if the constraint is colored red, it indicates that many violations occurred. A primary activity of the planner is to recognize, analyze, and attempt to adjust the schedule to eliminate these violations.

Analysis tools like inventory histograms and line charts are available to assist the planner. For any item or workcenter, for example, detailed graphical capabilities enable the planner to see exactly where the trouble begins. The specific task or order is easy to identify and move within the graph.

FEEDBACK FROM THE OPTIMIZATION ENGINE: TRANSFER, PURCHASE, MANUFACTURING MESSAGES, AND HORIZONTAL PLANNING REPORT

When the planner is ready to accept the plan generated through optimizations and potentially manual changes, he or she is ready to send the data back to PeopleSoft Manufacturing. The link back to PeopleSoft is called "Receive Planning Data" instead of a fancy name like the Datalink. Two types of data are sent back, as shown in the following list:

1. The messages related to production, purchase, and transfer order including actions to take and exceptions

2. The data necessary to print a horizontal planning report

It is only necessary to bring over the messages if you are not utilizing the horizontal planning report. Action messages from the optimization are concerned with changes that are recommended to align business activity with the optimized production plan. You might be required to open new production orders, cancel orders, or move orders in or out in time. There are three separate places to make all the changes. First, production ID and schedule changes are reviewed, approved, and applied through the Maintain Production menu. The optimization can recommend the creation of a number of new production IDs, ostensibly to satisfy some demand out there. The planner approves these new orders and then runs a quick process in the background to apply the changes. Similarly, material planners have a panel for approving transfer order messages and another panel for approving purchase order messages. They worked similarly to the production order message panel.

The horizontal planning report is a powerful and flexible reporting option. If you bring the report data over from the optimization engine, you have the capability of printing an excellent report to give you an instant supply versus demand analysis. The selection criteria of the report are extensive and include the capability to print data by item family, buyer, item category, item, vendor, and planner code. In addition, each type of supply and demand can be included or excluded from the output. There are more than 20 different types of supply and demand. This report can be customized quickly for any individual interested in viewing planning data.

SUMMARY

PeopleSoft Production Planning has a very powerful optimization engine that is fully integrated with PeopleSoft Purchasing, Inventory, and Production Management. Through the use of advanced in-memory optimization techniques, the system is capable of producing a plan that is optimal in terms of the weighted criteria planners provide. Simple criteria such as buildable inventory and raw material shortages when taken alone are similar to traditional MRP approaches. With the additional capability to model capacity, production changeovers, safety stock, and other constraints simultaneously, the planning module provides real-time, valuable information to any manufacturer or distributor.

CHAPTER 10

UTILIZING DISTRIBUTION

In this chapter

by Matt McLelland

UNDERSTANDING THE COMPONENTS OF DISTRIBUTION

The Distribution product line is a key aspect of PeopleSoft's Enterprise Resource Optimization (ERO) solution. Consisting of eight modules, Distribution collectively brings a fresh approach to the disciplines of materials and supply chain management. From materials procurement through complex outbound logistics, PeopleSoft Distribution capitalizes on the integration of these eight modules to help customers manage their supply chain and streamline business processes. Distribution works in concert with PeopleSoft's Financial, Manufacturing, and Human Resource solutions to help customers manage all aspects of their enterprise. The eight modules of Distribution are as follows:

Purchasing

Inventory

Order Management

Billing

Enterprise Planning

Product Configurator

Demand Planning

Order Promising

At this point you might be asking, "Just what does Distribution mean anyway? How does it differ from Manufacturing? How does it integrate with the rest of PeopleSoft's Enterprise Solution?" Before we answer these questions and explore the business processes associated with PeopleSoft Distribution, an understanding of the components making up the Distribution product line is required. Although a more detailed explanation of these products is provided in the next chapter, we need to take a moment and define these components before moving forward.

The Distribution product line at this time consists of individual applications that focus on business processes. Each application in Distribution is composed of application objects designed to address global business requirements, perform specific application processes and functions, and link seamlessly to other application objects within a single product or product line. Although the full potential of this product line is best illustrated when all modules are working together, it is possible to use individual modules if functionality provided in others is not needed. Table 10.1 shows where Distribution fits into PeopleSoft's enterprise business solution.

TABLE 10.1   MODULES IN PEOPLESOFT'S ENTERPRISE BUSINESS SOLUTION

Financials	Distribution	Manufacturing	HRMS
General Ledger	Purchasing	Bills and Routings	Human Resources
Payables	Inventory	Production Management	Benefits Administration

Financials	Distribution	Manufacturing	HRMS
Receivables	Order Management	Production Planning	FSA Administration
Asset Management	Billing	Cost Management	Payroll
Projects	Enterprise Planning	Engineering	Payroll Interface
Budgets	Product Configurator		Pension Administration
Expenses	Demand Planning		Time and Labor
Treasury	Order Promising		

Table 10.1 provides a complete listing of the Distribution product components. More information about how these products interact with other products in the Distribution, Manufacturing, and Financial Product lines is covered in the next chapter. But for now, a 30,000-foot overview of these components is required.

INVENTORY

Inventory's primary function is to assist in managing items and storage locations, shipping items to customers, and keeping inventory at optimum levels. It provides detailed costing information and up-to-date views of all inventory levels. Additionally, as each Inventory process is completed, information is immediately made available to other PeopleSoft Distribution, Financial, and Manufacturing products using a seamless interface. Synchronized planning and execution models enable automatic replenishment orders throughout the enterprise. Use of advanced technologies provides features like EDI, workflow, and RF data collection. Whether the focus is on maintaining item information, tracking stock fulfillment requests, maintaining appropriate on-hand balances, or analyzing inventory value, users will find a wide range of tools to accomplish critical tasks.

ORDER MANAGEMENT

Integrated tightly with Inventory, Order Management manages the entire sales order process by passing demand through the supply chain. Created in Order Management and filled via Inventory, sales orders can be filled by a local or regional warehouse, a distribution center, production facility, or even drop-shipped to a supplier. It allows for multiple order entry methods, contracts, order quotes, drop ships, alternate product lists, flexible pricing, and commissions. In addition, complete functionality is provided for when the customer returns materials (RMAs), as well as for applying hold codes, creating multiple schedules, and managing complex accounting distributions.

BILLING

PeopleSoft Billing addresses both informational and operational business needs, streamlining the billing process and providing for easy customization of billing requirements. Designed to create bills generated from PeopleSoft Order Management, Projects, or online entry panels, Billing can also accept billing data from external systems as well. Invoices are easily customized to fit the customer's specific needs. After bills have been finalized and printed, Billing passes information to PeopleSoft Receivables and General Ledger. With functions such as Bill Adjustments, you can adjust an entire bill, credit a bill, or adjust a single line.

PURCHASING

Efficient, cost-effective procurement of raw materials, goods, and services is a key to the success of any enterprise. PeopleSoft Purchasing helps a company align itself with these goals by allowing users to manage requisitions, vendor contracts, purchase orders, and purchase order receipts. It also supports EDI transactions, automatic faxing of purchase orders, sourcing of items from electronic catalogs, streamlined requisitioning, purchase order contracts, requests for quotes, change orders, and sophisticated data procurement analysis. Finally, it integrates tightly with Accounts Payables for Matching, Order Management for drop ships, Assets for Asset ID identification, and Inventory for auto-putaway.

ENTERPRISE PLANNING

Enterprise Planning utilizes the Red Pepper response agent to provide an advanced planning and scheduling system that enables simultaneous, real-time optimization of enterprise-wide procurement, production, and distribution resources. It provides multisite planning and scheduling by looking at all demands and constraints throughout the supply chain. When these demands and constraints are known, Enterprise Planning simultaneously considers all parameters to produce a timely, accurate, and cost-effective production plan.

DEMAND PLANNING

Demand Planning represents a new approach to demand forecasting. Rather than projecting future demand based on historical data, Demand Planning relies on current information from across the enterprise. Product lifecycle data, promotion plans, sales data, competitor promotion plans, custom buying plans, supply chain capacity, and—to some extent—human intuition from across the sales, marketing, manufacturing, finance, and distribution departments are all used to generate a reliable forecast. A demand plan created with enterprise-wide information results in lower inventories, reduced transportation costs, and improved customer satisfaction.

PRODUCT CONFIGURATOR

The Product Configurator uses patented technology to address the unique requirements of make, assemble, and configure-to-order manufacturers. This module essentially captures the knowledge of the marketing, engineering, distribution, and manufacturing departments to the laptops of company sales representatives—either at their desks or at customer sites. Armed with this knowledge, sales reps can create and price custom configured products to customers. Because of its tight integration with the Manufacturing product line, the Product Configurator automatically determines pricing based on the selected configuration at order entry time, generates production orders with corresponding Bills of Material, calculates standard costs for configurations, costs inventory, and source configurations on hand. Finally, Product Configurator helps to ensure quick distribution of new product information, engineering, or pricing changes for configured orders to both sales representatives and customers.

ORDER PROMISING

Order promising in today's manufacturing and distribution enterprises frequently falls short of meeting customer needs. The goal of Order Promising is simply this: Obtain a sound delivery date with an internally workable result, and analyze that impact before committing to the customer. PeopleSoft Order Promising enables real-time determination of a valid delivery date. It looks at available inventory across the enterprise and evaluates the capacity and material availability of the entire supply chain while the customer stays on the phone. With Order Promising, order takers can now confidently commit both date and quantity of product to a customer.

FLEXIBLE AND ADAPTABLE APPLICATIONS

In the hectic environment of today's global marketplace, many of the business operating principles and distribution processes put in place 20 years, five years, even a year ago no longer apply. Today's business strategies focus on flexibility, not size; teamwork and empowerment instead of command and control; and technology and outsourcing as opposed to layers of middle management. Success, if not survival, hinges on how quickly a company can re-evaluate, restructure, reorganize, or re-engineer the organization to cultivate a corporate culture that is lean, innovative, efficient, responsive, profitable, and customer-focused.

Distribution responds to these demands in a number of ways. First, its tight, seamless integration with other modules in PeopleSoft's ERO solution allows all aspects of the supply chain to be made aware of changes across the enterprise. Whether the enterprise is large or small, the immediate recognition of these changes greatly reduces any lag time between decision and action. This flexibility is perhaps the most important of all PeopleSoft's features.

Second, Distribution's adaptation of advanced technologies into its product line can greatly reduce distribution costs and increase responsiveness to customers. Through its overall use of three-tier architecture, OLAP, and Internet/intranet Web applets, PeopleSoft uses new technology to deliver key information to users in a more timely, efficient manner. Through its use of integrated EDI, Internet Web applets, radio frequency (RF) data collection, and electronic catalogs, Distribution offers both the flexibility to move quickly and the freedom to optimize corporate and computing resources.

Finally, the effective use of tools allows Distribution to change quickly as new business processes are defined. No business is static—especially in today's market. Change, along with death and taxes, is a fact no business can escape. Users want new reports, data requirements change, new company roles are established, and new business opportunities are undertaken. For an organization to embrace these changes, its supporting software must make concessions. PeopleSoft Distribution encourages these changes through use of the following tools.

AUTOMATIC DATE SENSITIVITY TO PREPARE FOR CHANGES

All the critical tables within PeopleSoft Distribution are keyed to an effective date—the date the information goes into effect. So you can store a history of what data in each table used to look like, and enter future information that allows you to project analyses, or create a what-if picture.

For example, if you know that new items are being introduced to the corporate product line at the beginning of the fiscal year, you can enter that data into PeopleSoft Inventory now. You can set up the items and establish the related information for each item today, and effective-date it for fiscal year 1999. When that date arrives, the system automatically makes the item available to PeopleSoft Distribution for cost calculations and other processes, integrating the item information with all existing transactions.

Effective-date design means you're better prepared to respond to change, because you can anticipate and institute changes well in advance of the date they will take effect.

INTEGRATED WORKFLOW

Running a business involves literally thousands of business processes, ranging from simple tasks like entering a telephone order to complex procedures like managing inventory, creating quarterly reports, and analyzing business trends. Coordinating these processes and keeping them running smoothly are at the heart of running a business.

The goal of workflow technology is to automate and streamline business processes throughout the enterprise. It automates the flow of information from one person to another. It can make processes run more efficiently, reduce the human labor involved in certain tasks, and guarantee that they are performed consistently by different people at different times.

To ensure that you get the right information to the right people at the right time, PeopleSoft Distribution makes workflow an integral part of its applications. PeopleSoft Workflow facilitates the flow of information throughout the enterprise solutions and among external systems that support business processes.

Workflow Example: Approving a New Customer Order

In Figure 10.1, you see Workflow implemented in approving a new customer order:

1. An order from a new customer is received.

2. Because the new customer is not yet established in the system, the customer's full address, contact, and billing information is requested.

3. A credit application is automatically faxed or emailed to the customer, and the order is saved pending additional customer information.

4. New customer information is received and forwarded through Workflow to the credit department.

5. The credit department checks a worklist, sees that a new customer must be set up, checks credit, and establishes an account for the customer.

6. The credit department automatically approves the sales order and takes the new customer off credit hold.

With the customer now in the system, the order flows through the system for fulfillment. Of course, workflow-enabled order management allows existing good credit customer orders to flow uninterrupted.

Figure 10.1
The Purchase Request workflow for a new customer order.

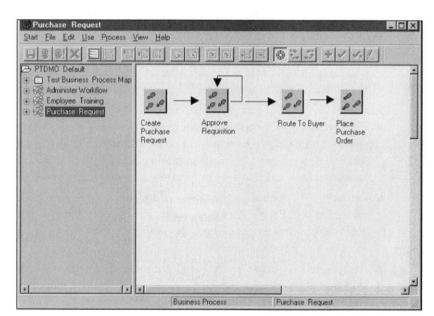

COHESIVE BUSINESS PROCESS DESIGN TOOLS

PeopleSoft Distribution menus organize panels and panel groups based on their related functions. For example, the menus in the Fulfill Stock window (in PeopleSoft Inventory) collect together all the panels related to maintaining orders and shipments. This organization makes sense, but it isn't always the most appropriate organization for day-to-day users. The Business Process Designer enables you to organize panels in cohesive business processes. You create graphical maps that show the activities and steps in the processes and enable users to start the panels associated with each step.

The Business Process Designer works with the PeopleSoft Navigator, a graphical "browser" that displays the maps you create in the Business Process Designer. For many users, the Navigator is a simpler and more straightforward means of moving around the system than the menus are. Maps and the Navigator supplement menus; they don't replace them. You can use either method of navigating, depending on which method is most appropriate for the panel you want to find.

INTEGRATED ELECTRONIC COMMERCE

PeopleSoft Distribution has a broad definition of electronic commerce. It is not limited to financial transactions, but encompasses all types of electronic information exchange. For PeopleSoft, electronic commerce is a new business operating environment, created by the convergence of computers and communications, that supports a new set of business processes. Electronic commerce is not simply technology, but a new method of doing business.

PeopleSoft Distribution views electronic commerce (EC) as a critical tool to help customers compete in today's business environment. Electronic commerce enables leadership, empowerment, flexibility, and responsiveness:

- Leadership—The combination of PeopleSoft's leading edge toolset and new EC technologies puts customers at the forefront of information technology. Because applications are designed around processes, PeopleSoft helps streamline an organization, thus improving efficiency, access to information, and ability to manage costs and production.

- Empowerment—Distribution applications already automate routine processing, enabling employees to focus on tasks that add more value to the enterprise. With the addition of electronic commerce technologies, employees, suppliers, and customers can more effectively work together to manage the virtual enterprise.

- Flexibility—PeopleSoft applications are designed to change as business changes. The combination of PeopleSoft's applications, its supporting toolset, and advanced technologies from its partners gives companies more choices and flexibility to design a complete solution that meets their needs.

- Responsiveness—Superior access to information facilitates better decision-making, keeping companies ahead of the competition. PeopleSoft applications, combined with electronic commerce technology, mean access to information anywhere, anytime. Armed with the latest data, companies can remain nimble, reacting to change in minutes instead of weeks.

INFORMATION ACCESS

By using PeopleSoft Distribution applications, customers can build an invaluable repository of business data. Query and analysis tools are designed to complement business applications so that customers can easily extract, analyze, and present vital information. You may have heard PeopleSoft contend that "EIS should not just be executive information systems, but *everybody's information systems:* easy-to-use, yet secure tools that make information readily available to everyone who needs it." By providing a suite of powerful reporting tools,

PeopleSoft makes information available to users of all skill levels. For instance, you can do any of the following:

- Build SQL queries without having to see SQL commands, much less know the language. And you'll be able to apply queries you create in many ways, not just for standard reporting.

- Use a natural language interface that enables you to query your database for information in your own words.

- Harness a wealth of formatting and report design tools to quickly and easily create reports, mailing labels, or forms—and present them using a variety of fonts, borders, and other special effects for emphasis and easy reference.

- Utilize a robust set of matrix reporting, drill-down, and tabular data retrieval features with the familiar face of a spreadsheet, so you can quickly develop reports for analysis without having to re-enter data.

- Facilitate ad hoc queries.

- Schedule programs and background processes to run once or regularly each day, week, or month.

QUICK RESPONSE TO CHANGE

PeopleSoft Distribution is built with PeopleTools. This robust, versatile application environment enables customers to develop, deploy, and evolve powerful business solutions. Unlike other client/server programming tools, which typically focus only on one phase of development and are oriented toward programmers, PeopleTools provides

- Easy-to-use tools that system analysts, business analysts, system administrators, and users can use throughout the lifecycle of your applications.

- Inherent business rules and functionality to streamline and simplify development.

- Dynamic system architecture that promotes open, scalable, portable, high-performance systems that conform to your complex hardware configurations and database preferences.

- A complement to existing programming and CASE tools, so customers can take advantage of PeopleTools' prototyping power without having to retrain your entire MIS staff.

- Inherent date sensitivity to maintain a complete history of all data in your application, so you can enter information to take effect automatically, on schedule. With this type of effective dating, you can easily track, control, and project past, present, and future data.

- Graphical tools to visually organize information stored in database tables. By using *trees* (a graphical hierarchical structure for expanding, collapsing, drilling down, or rolling up data), users gain a new way to view, analyze, and change information such as organization charts and department, accounting, and security structures.

- Multinational capabilities to support multiple language, currency, and country requirements as well as country-specific business processes.

■ Sophisticated database design techniques for easily sharing and separating data and data structures among multiple departments and operating entities throughout your organization. By sharing common values or sets of values among business units, you reduce data redundancy, simplify maintenance, and improve accuracy.

TRANSCENDING BOUNDARIES WITH GLOBAL SOLUTIONS

With the release of version 7.5, PeopleSoft begins the official globalization of PeopleSoft Distribution and Manufacturing. PeopleSoft has addressed complex language, currency, legal, and business process requirements of multinational corporations. Architecturally, they've managed to efficiently store and manage the flow of business information throughout an organization's worldwide network, regardless of where you work. Strategically, PeopleSoft provides the flexibility to implement localized and global solutions, yet still share information and reduce redundant data and effort.

The most recent release of PeopleSoft Distribution features significant enhancements in three major development areas—globalization, cross-product distribution solutions, and materials management and supply chain optimization. The following summary details new functionality that allows Distribution, as well as all other Enterprise product lines, to be a real global player in the Enterprise Software arena.

■ VAT/GST Processing—With this release, value-added and goods and services taxes can be calculated, accounted, and reported for distribution transactions.

■ Multilanguage—PeopleSoft supports multilanguage customer and supplier documents, invoices, and standard reports across the product line.

■ Multicurrency—PeopleSoft provides a flexible tool for you to capture and manage multicurrency information as your unique global requirements dictate.

■ Enhanced Currency Precision—With this release, PeopleSoft provides the option to expand currency fields to meet your multinational requirements.

■ Support for European Monetary Union—PeopleSoft Distribution supports the EMU and the introduction of the euro. PeopleSoft Distribution products also support multiple transaction currencies, allowing you to invoice in one currency and receive payment in another.

■ Intrastate Support—PeopleSoft Distribution provides the ability to track movement between EC member states.

SUMMARY

The Distribution product line is a major component of PeopleSoft's ERO solution. Distribution works to formulate a new approach to the disciplines of materials and supply chain management. From materials procurement through complex outbound logistics, PeopleSoft Distribution utilizes eight modules to help customers manage their supply chain and streamline business processes. Distribution works in sync with PeopleSoft's Financial,

Manufacturing, and Human Resource solutions to help customers manage all aspects of their enterprisewide configuration.

PART

II

CH

10

CHAPTER 11

DISTRIBUTION MODULES

In this chapter

by Ron Yeung

INTRODUCTION TO DISTRIBUTION MODULES

The PeopleSoft distribution suite includes the following modules: Order Management, Billing, Inventory, Enterprise Planning, Purchasing, and Product Configurator.

ORDER MANAGEMENT

PeopleSoft Order Management supports rapid order entry, as well as complex customer orders. Activities such as product management, customer administration, quote, pricing, credit checking, sales contract, order creation, commission, shipment, returned material management, and billing are the backbone of the PeopleSoft Order Management system.

PeopleSoft Order Management ensures order accuracy as it captures, maintains, and shares product and distribution information across your enterprise.

PeopleSoft Order Management provides an integrated system for the distribution of your product and service across multiple business units domestically and globally.

To support this comprehensive functionality, PeopleSoft Order Management integrates with PeopleSoft Inventory, Purchasing, Remote Order Entry, Product Configurator, Order Promising, Billing, and Receivables.

We will now examine in more detail some of the activities within PeopleSoft Order Management, such as product management, customer administration, flexible pricing, quote, sales contract, order creation, commission, order fulfillment and tracking, shipment, returned material management, billing integration, remote order entry, electronic data interchange, and Web enabling.

PRODUCT MANAGEMENT

Product Management is particularly crucial for companies that market and sell tangible commodities, such as computer hardware or consumer products. PeopleSoft Order Management, in conjunction with PeopleSoft Inventory, allows you to maintain and share product information effectively. You can place and track orders with your product numbers or use the corresponding customer part number.

PeopleSoft Order Management supports product catalogs, substitution, and kits. Product catalogs enable you to customize your product offerings for your customers. Catalogs can be created and attached to a customer in the database, thus expediting product selection and achieving rapid order entry. Product substitution helps you manage shipment during stock shortages. Product kit components can be stock items, drop ship items, services, or any combination. For example, kits are generally included to assemble a bicycle, or the manufacturer might offer assembly service at the dealer for a nominal fee. Kits can also be configured if PeopleSoft Product Configurator is installed.

CUSTOMER ADMINISTRATION

Customer Administration supports four types of customer roles. The *Sold To* defines the customer who places orders, the *Ship To* defines the customer who accepts the delivery of product or/and services, the *Bill To* defines the customer who receives invoice billing, and the *Corporate* defines the customer who groups the Sold To or Ship To customers for the same organization. For example, WalMart Corporation could be the *Corporate* customer. WalMart Central Purchasing could be the *Sold To* customer. Individual WalMart stores could be the *Ship To* customers.

FLEXIBLE PRICING

Effective pricing and best services are the key to a successful business. Pricing structure has always been complicated and complex in today's evolving and competitive markets. PeopleSoft Order Management supports standard list price, discounts, surcharges, promotional pricing, and giveaways based on a combination of products, customers, regions, and order quantity. Examples are Sold to Customer, Payment Type, Payment Terms ID, Product ID, Carrier ID, Export Carrier ID, Freight Terms, Export Terms, Ship To Customer, Ship Via Code, Export Shipping Method, Item ID, Commodity Code, Customer Grp, Product Group, and Region Code.

Price lists can be grouped by products or constructed by customer or customer group. PeopleSoft Order Management pricing can be maintained in multiple currencies and by effective dates. You can manage price maintenance and currency conversion selectively or globally by products or price lists. The process is flexible and quick.

PART

II

CH

11

QUOTE

Quotations in PeopleSoft Order Management are generated using the same functionality as creating a sales order. Most of the rules that apply to quotes also apply to orders. Examples are Pricing, Product/Customer Holds, Credit Check, and so on. You can manage the quotations by entering your best educated guess as to whether the quotation will result in a sales order. If the success percentage is more than the parameter defined in PeopleSoft Enterprise Planning, the quotations are considered as demand.

You can also limit your exposure by inputting an expiration date to indicate when the prices and terms of your quote are no longer valid. If your customer accepts a quote, you can convert the quote into a sales order by copying.

SALES CONTRACT

PeopleSoft Order Management allows you to structure sales contracts for customers or a group of customers such as WalMart stores. Sales contracts are constructed similarly to sales orders in the form of order header and detail. Your customers can include products in a sales contract, and sales orders can be generated automatically from contract releases. If shipment schedule is not known at the time of contract, sales orders can be created from contracts online when your customer calls.

To track and measure your sales contract performance, you can define rebates and penalties for each contract line. Rebates will be calculated within your defined time period. Likewise, penalties will be calculated if terms of the contract are not met.

ORDER CREATION

PeopleSoft Order Management gives you the option to quickly enter a sales order or take control of PeopleSoft's extensive Order Management functionality to create complex orders. For example, you can categorize orders in Order Groups. The groups apply default information to the orders, thus reducing data entry. Or you can create composite orders that require drop ship, export shipment, product substitution, configuration, or promotional pricing.

You must run the Order Completion Processes to complete the order information. The background processes take the order information, create the shipment schedules, calculate pricing by going through all the pricing table entries, check credit, and finish the addition of new sales order lines and schedules.

The Order Completion processes also complete orders received by Electronic Data Interchange, orders created from sales contracts, or replacement orders created as a result of Returned Material Authorization. The processes include Order Completion 1, 2, 3; Automatic Hold Check; Automatic Credit Check; and Populate Demand.

When sales orders are created, PeopleSoft Order Management generates demand for the PeopleSoft Inventory and buy orders for PeopleSoft Purchasing. It also generates shipping schedules to be used by the PeopleSoft Inventory and then sends shipped sales orders information to PeopleSoft Billing for invoice generation.

COMMISSION

PeopleSoft Order Management calculates commissions based on the percentage you defined for an order. Commission schedules and distribution can be customized by individual orders. PeopleSoft Order Management supports three methods for calculating commission. Two calculation methods are based on the team members involved in the sale. The third method is based on the product sold. You set up commission percentages for your sales people by team members, and product commission percents when you define your products.

PeopleSoft Order Management gives you the option of whether commission percentages can be applied to the entire order or to individual shipments.

ORDER FULFILLMENT AND TRACKING

PeopleSoft Order Management enables you to track an order throughout its fulfillment cycle. You can also drill down to additional detail on the order status in PeopleSoft Order Management, Inventory, Purchasing, Billing, and Receivables.

SHIPMENT

PeopleSoft Order Management enables you to view shipment information at three levels. Shipment by Header is a high-level view of order shipments. Shipment by Line breaks down shipment information for each product on an order. Shipment by Schedule displays detailed shipping information about an order at the schedule level.

RETURNED MATERIAL MANAGEMENT

Returned Material Management is an important service to customers as they are in order entry. PeopleSoft Order Management provides an efficient way to process and track returned material. When the returned goods are received, replacement sales orders or credit can be generated automatically. Restocking fees can be charged to your customers based on a percentage of the value of the returned goods or as a flat amount. Returned Material Authorization (RMA) can be created based on customers' shipment history. Serial IDs and Lot IDs can also be added to label the returned material.

Returned material can be received into the PeopleSoft Inventory business unit after the RMA process is completed. After the material receipt, you can use the inventory put-away processes to move the returned material to an inventory location.

BILLING INTEGRATION

PeopleSoft Order Management integrates PeopleSoft Billing to bill customers based on shipments or orders and to trigger a credit memo for returned material. Sales activity can be grouped and invoiced by contract number, sales order number, shipment ID, or purchase order number.

PART

II

CH

11

REMOTE ORDER ENTRY

PeopleSoft Remote Order Entry is a subset of the overall capabilities of PeopleSoft Order Management and PeopleSoft Product Configurator. Using Remote Order Entry, you can take regular and configured quotes and orders at customer sites. Remote Order Entry shares customer information, pricing, and orders from PeopleSoft Order Management.

PeopleSoft Remote Order Entry allows you to dial in to the main system and download and upload data. This feature is different from the Web-enabling e-business currently being developed by PeopleSoft.

ELECTRONIC DATA INTERCHANGE

PeopleSoft Order Management enables you to process inbound transactions such as Purchase Order and Request for Quote or outbound transactions such as Order Acknowledgement and Response to RFQ. PeopleSoft Order Management uses PeopleSoft Electronic Data Interface Manager and PeopleSoft Electronic Data Interface Agent to process inbound and outbound electronic transactions.

WEB ENABLING

PeopleSoft Order Management provides self-service applications on the Web where your customers can review and update customer address and contact information, check product availability, and monitor sales order status.

Giving your customer access to information on the Web reduces the workload for your customer service staff. This feature will be expanded in PeopleSoft E-Business Strategy.

This concludes the discussion of the backbone of the PeopleSoft Order Management. We will now examine PeopleSoft Billing, which is tightly coupled with PeopleSoft Order Management.

PEOPLESOFT BILLING

PeopleSoft Billing provides a direct invoice process that generates the invoices for the customer immediately after shipping of sales orders. PeopleSoft Billing allows you to store multiple levels of customer information and shares across business units. Customer information such as name and address has to be entered only once, and then it's available to PeopleSoft Order Management and PeopleSoft Receivables.

PeopleSoft Billing allows you easy access to customer account information. It also enables you to send information to PeopleSoft Receivables or PeopleSoft General Ledger whenever you choose. PeopleSoft Billing streamlines the billing process and provides easy customization of billing requirements. With extensive invoicing and reporting functionality, you can accurately and easily prepare, calculate, and submit invoices.

PeopleSoft Billing interfaces with other PeopleSoft applications, as well as non-PeopleSoft applications. PeopleSoft application interfaces include PeopleSoft Order Management, Payables, Receivables, Projects, and General Ledger.

CUSTOMER MANAGEMENT

PeopleSoft Billing allows you to enter customer information only once, and then it's available to PeopleSoft Order Management and PeopleSoft Receivables. PeopleSoft Billing enables you to

- Maintain customer data at the level of detail appropriate for your business requirement.
- Accommodate multiple customer addresses and contacts.
- Assign roles and designate relationships for your customers.
- Share customer information across business units.
- Define group billings based on a predefined invoice schedule.

SIMPLIFIED BILLING ENTRY

PeopleSoft Billing simplifies billing entry in two ways. The first is the manual method of entering billing data through online bill entry. During online entry, PeopleSoft Billing gives you the advantage of extensive defaults and overrides. The second includes the billing interface and recurring bills. By using the billing interface, you can import your billing information from outside billing sources such as legacy systems through the use of flat files. Recurring billing enables you to reproduce bills using templates.

BILLING INTERFACE

PeopleSoft Billing enables you to import a large number of bill lines into PeopleSoft Billing through the Billing Interface. PeopleSoft's Billing Interface verifies and validates the data integrity in the staging tables. It also defaults data from customer, bill source, and business unit. Billing Interface is also intelligent enough to decide whether the imported bill lines should be added to a new bill or to an existing bill.

RECURRING BILLING

PeopleSoft Billing enables you to reproduce bills, or portions of bills, and create invoices using templates. By defining the schedules and billing cycles, the bill is created automatically during each defined recurring period. In PeopleSoft Billing, schedules are used to automate and control the frequency of generating the recurring bills. The billing cycle links a schedule to a recurring bill template and defines the number of days before the invoice date a recurring bill can be generated.

PeopleSoft Billing also gives you the facility to copy bills easily. You can copy a single bill online or run the process to copy a group of bills, regardless of the status of those bills.

FLEXIBLE BILLING CYCLE

PeopleSoft Billing provides the ability to customize your billing cycle to meet your business requirements. You can define daily, biweekly, monthly, yearly, or custom invoice cycles. You also have the option of creating General Ledger entries and/or Accounts Receivable pending items separately or automatically combined with the billing cycle that you defined.

CUSTOM INVOICES

PeopleSoft Billing enables you to impress your customers by sending them as much invoicing information as they require. As a result, you receive your payment more quickly. For example, you may include your customer product numbers for their reference. PeopleSoft Billing gives you the facilities and programs to customize your invoices for your customers. When you define invoicing formats, you can choose from multiple layouts to best fit the style of your invoice.

BILL ADJUSTMENT

Bill adjustment is an activity that cannot be completely avoided during the billing cycle. PeopleSoft Billing Bill Adjustment allows you to adjust an entire bill, credit a bill, or adjust a single line or combination of lines. All bill adjustments completed in PeopleSoft Billing are logged. PeopleSoft Billing enables you to drill down and view the adjustment history of any specified invoice by using the Adjustment History panel.

GLOBAL SUPPORT

PeopleSoft Billing prints invoices in your customer's preferred language and billing reports in the language of your user. PeopleSoft Billing bills your customers in their preferred currency, which can be different from your base currency. PeopleSoft Billing supports Value Added tax on all process transactions, invoice bills, and printed documents. The printed invoices show totals in both bill and Euro currencies. Sequencing numbers are assigned to documents to meet European reporting and control requirements.

BILLING INTEGRATION

PeopleSoft Billing is integrated into the PeopleSoft's Sales and Logistics solution. By implementing other PeopleSoft applications, such as PeopleSoft Order Management, Projects, and Product Configurator, you can fully take advantage of PeopleSoft Billing functionality and efficiency. For example, PeopleSoft Order Management and Projects can furnish customer charges to PeopleSoft Billing. As a result, the billing process can be streamlined through direct invoicing. As you improve the rate of invoicing, you can expect quicker payment from your customers. In addition, PeopleSoft Order Management can directly transfer returned material authorization and credit card transactions to PeopleSoft Billing. The automation improves speedy and quality service to your customers.

PeopleSoft Order Management and Product Configurator enables you to configure and create customer orders. Through the integration, PeopleSoft Billing can print the invoice that reflects the configuration detail on any invoice line that was composed by PeopleSoft Product Configurator.

This concludes the discussion on PeopleSoft Billing. Now we will examine a critical module in both distribution and manufacturing environment, PeopleSoft Inventory.

PEOPLESOFT INVENTORY

Inventory Management is an integral component for an effective manufacturing and distribution environment. PeopleSoft Inventory enables you to perform stock management, automatic replenishment, material put-away, demand fulfillment, cart inventory, container management, lot and serial control, interunit transfer, returned stock management, physical inventory, product costing and valuation, and electronic data collection throughout the enterprise.

PeopleSoft Inventory directly integrates with PeopleSoft Purchasing, Order Management, Billing, Product Configurator, Enterprise Planning, Production Planning, Production Management, Cost Management, Projects, General Ledger, and third-party electronic data collection hardware and software.

Now we will examine some of PeopleSoft Inventory functions and features mentioned earlier.

STOCK MANAGEMENT

Using templates and defaults, PeopleSoft Inventory enables you to define your item master quickly without duplicating effort. You can copy item attributes within and across business units. You can also copy items within share tables. You can choose to approve new items before they are allowed for transactions. For example, a new product introduction normally requires notification and approval from multiple departments in a company.

In addition, PeopleSoft Inventory enables you to maintain historical, current, and future inventory information by using effective dates. For example, item attribute revisions can be kept in history, whereas new attributes can become effective at a future date.

PeopleSoft Inventory gives you the option to use lot and serial control over your inventory. Lot tracking covers the entire life cycle of a lot. Serial tracking starts from the time you receive or ship an item. However, you can expect additional data entries to support this feature.

STORAGE LOCATION

PeopleSoft Inventory supports single or multiple inventory business units. For example, you must define at least one or more inventory business unit(s) to support a manufacturing business unit. A stock warehouse can be defined as an inventory business unit. Inventory business units are designed to store all inventory-related transactions in PeopleSoft Inventory.

An inventory business unit is made up of storage areas. PeopleSoft Inventory enables multi-level storage structures in which each storage area supports four storage locations. For instance, you can define separate storage areas in your inventory business unit, such as finished goods, work in process, and raw materials. Storage location can be defined as aisle, row, section, and bin. In addition, you can assign attributes to the storage location. Any items transferred to the location will inherit the same attributes. For example, items become disabled when they are transferred to a suspended location.

NEGATIVE INVENTORY

Should inventory quantity ever go negative? PeopleSoft Inventory allows you to define the option of negative inventory for each inventory business unit. In that case, PeopleSoft Inventory enables transactions to drive inventory balances to negative. However, you can choose to display warning messages before accepting a transaction that will cause the inventory balance to be negative. As a result, you can continue to keep your production going and your customer shipment on track and resolve inventory discrepancies at a less critical time. For example, you need five pieces to fill a customer order. However, the system indicates that the quantity on hand is three. You found five pieces at the storage location when you picked the inventory. You reported to the system that the order is filled, and the quantity on hand was reduced to minus two as a result.

You can also enable PeopleSoft Workflow to help you manage your negative quantities and reconcile discrepancies.

ORDER FULFILLMENT

PeopleSoft Order Management and PeopleSoft Inventory are closely integrated. PeopleSoft Inventory is used to ship the products listed on an order.

PeopleSoft Inventory enables you to process stock fulfillment in three methods.

The first method is known as *Auto-Pick & Auto-Ship*. Auto-Pick & Auto-Ship does not provide picking and shipping feedback, but it streamlines your operation, maximizing efficiency and minimizing labor costs.

The second method is a multiple step fulfillment. PeopleSoft Inventory employs a six-step process to manage the order fulfillment in this method and enables you to control the individual steps more closely than the first method. The process includes material reservation, pick plan review, picking feedback, picking confirmation, and shipping and depletion of stocked materials.

The third fulfillment method is Express Issue. This method allows you to request, pick, and issue inventory from a single step. Express Issue is ideal for internal orders and walk-up customers.

PeopleSoft Inventory requires that an order must be approved for processing before you can reserve inventory to fulfill the order.

INVENTORY RESERVATION

PeopleSoft Inventory provides the option of reserving quantity for order fulfillment at the business unit level. However, PeopleSoft Inventory reserves quantity only for orders that have a schedule ship date between the current date and the date defined by the reservation lead days. If you cancel an order that has been reserved, PeopleSoft Inventory reverses the reserved quantity and releases the quantity for other orders. You can also reallocate reserved stock from one order to a higher priority order.

STOCK PICKING

PeopleSoft Inventory allows you to define picking rules for the business unit. For an item to appear on a picking plan, its storage location must have a status of open for picking. PeopleSoft Inventory supports two types of picking—push and pull. With a *push* picking plan, an allocation reserves the quantity. The allocated quantity then becomes unavailable for other demands. With a *pull* picking plan, pick locations are suggested, but no allocation is made.

ORDER SHIPMENT

PeopleSoft Inventory provides advanced shipment notification to customers through electronic data interchange. You can also build shipping containers to optimize material movement in the supply chain. PeopleSoft provides the option to assign serial numbers as well.

PeopleSoft Order Management uses PeopleSoft Inventory for its order shipment.

INVENTORY PUT-AWAY

PeopleSoft Inventory supports three inventory put-away methods in administering your materials processing.

Multistep put-away gives you the tightest control over your stocking process. Multistep put-away steps include staged item load and correction, put-away plan review, stockroom feedback, and put-away process. Auto put-away automates much of the stocking process. Auto put-away steps include staged item load and put-away process. Express put-away enables you to process miscellaneous receipts in one quick step.

MATERIAL REPLENISHMENT

PeopleSoft Inventory enables you to maintain and replenish on-hand inventory stock levels to meet your customer demand. The principle is to maintain your optimum stocking level to service your customers and yet keep the inventory and overhead cost as low as possible. PeopleSoft Inventory calculates the stock replenishment options based on historic demand analysis or values that you supplied.

PART

II

CH

11

PeopleSoft Inventory supports three material replenishment methods. With ad hoc replenishment, PeopleSoft Inventory enables you to specify and create ad hoc replenishment requests when you do not have enough on-hand quantity to fulfill a stock demand. With reorder point replenishment, you specify stocking levels for each item in your business unit. PeopleSoft Inventory uses replenishment attributes such as economic order quantity, reorder point, and safety stock in the calculation and generates a replenishment order when the available on-hand quantity drops below the stocking levels. With fixed-bin replenishment, PeopleSoft Inventory generates a restocking request when the on-hand quantities in the fixed storage location fall below the optimal quantity that you defined.

The difference between reorder point and fixed-bin replenishment is that reorder point considers other attributes to calculate variable, optimal replenishment quantity. Fixed-bin replenishment generates a request for the difference between the actual quantity on hand and the optional quantity defined at the location.

PeopleSoft Inventory supports material replenishment within an inventory business unit. PeopleSoft Enterprise Planning considers and supports inventory replenishment and transfer across business units.

BAR CODE

PeopleSoft Inventory supports bar code in data collection, labeling, and reporting. Bar-coded transactions can be accepted from bar code devices, third-party feeds, and manual data entry. All transactions will be validated before your inventory is updated. PeopleSoft Inventory supports various bar code transactions such as put-away, picking, shipping container and serial IDs, storage location transfers, physical inventory, and cycle counting. In addition, PeopleSoft Inventory supports six bar-coded labels—storage location, item storage, storage container, shipping carton, shipping container, and shipping serial. PeopleSoft Inventory produces two embedded bar-coded inventory reports that include a put-away plan and picking plan.

This concludes the discussion on some of the functionalities and features of PeopleSoft Inventory. We will move on to another PeopleSoft module that influences inventory management beyond an inventory business unit.

PEOPLESOFT ENTERPRISE PLANNING

PeopleSoft Enterprise Planning provides a real-time, net change planning solution that plans for multiple competing demands throughout your supply chain. It simultaneously considers constraints such as material availability and capacity across your enterprise to produce a timely plan that you can execute. By planning your distribution requirements in real time, you can respond rapidly to changes in customer demand.

PeopleSoft Enterprise Planning enables real-time planning and scheduling by embedding the Red Pepper Enterprise Response Agent technology. With real-time planning and decision support, PeopleSoft Enterprise Planning provides an advanced planning and scheduling system that enables simultaneous optimization of enterprisewide procurement, production, and distribution resources. Because the planning is continuously executed in memory, it dramatically reduces planning cycle time and allows you to respond to continuous change.

This section initiates an introduction to the PeopleSoft Enterprise Planning. A more in-depth discussion of Supply Chain and Enterprise Planning can be found in Chapter 19, "Should I Do It?"

NET CHANGE PLANNING

The optimizer will work to improve the schedule based on the settings on the Control Panel until there are no more constraints violated. The iterative repair approach allows you to process net change optimization. During net change planning, the plan is adjusted minimally to account for new requirements without complete plan regeneration.

MULTIPLE COMPETING DEMANDS

Demand is driven by sales order, sales forecast, internal demand, and safety stock and target stock levels. Sales order includes actual customer demand, whereas sales forecast is projected or expected customer demand. Internal demand may include interunit transfers or production orders. Safety stock and target stock levels are inventory balances that you maintain to provide a target level of customer services.

Enterprise Planning synchronizes your supply plans with your demand and inventory targets. Constraints are used and weighted to reflect your business environment and objectives. After the demands and constraints are known, Enterprise Planning simultaneously considers all the enterprise supply chain parameters and produces a timely, accurate, and cost-effective plan.

CONSTRAINTS

Constraints are, by their nature, often in conflict with one another. For example, minimizing capacity issues may violate promise date constraint. Or minimizing promise date exceptions may cause problems with material availability constraints. The key to feasible and optimized planning is the ability to simultaneously balance multiple business constraints.

Enterprise Planning optimizes constraints such as promise dates, request dates, inventory shortages, aggregate capacity, safety stocks, excess stocks, and raw material shortages. The goal is to produce a plan that best meets all the business objectives. If all constraints cannot be resolved simultaneously, Enterprise Planning will violate the less important constraints first.

Enterprise Planning resolves violations in iterations by rescheduling existing orders, creating new planned orders, and selecting an alternative sourcing option.

ESTABLISHING AN ENTERPRISE MODEL

To establish an enterprise-planning model, you need to define the structure of your enterprise. The enterprise model may start with the following structures:

- Business Unit Group
- Items
- Resources
- Routings
- Bills of Material
- Promise and Request Date Penalties
- Planning Attributes

BUSINESS UNIT GROUP

Business Unit Group defines and reflects the boundary of your enterprise model. The enterprise model should consist of at least a single or multiple inventory, manufacturing, order management, and purchasing business units. This will then allow your model to receive demand and plan for the supply.

ENTERPRISE PLANNING DATA

PeopleSoft Enterprise Planning data may include enterprise items, resources, routings, and bills of materials.

Only critical items that you defined in your model will be planned using Enterprise Planning. This allows you to send only critical end items or components that have to be planned. You will also define whether purchase orders or transfer orders are created from Production Planning or Enterprise Planning.

The purpose of enterprise resources is to create a plan that will analyze capacity loads for a resource in daily, weekly, or monthly buckets.

Enterprise resources may include production lines, work centers, tools, or machines that are critical to the enterprise's operation and need to be planned. However, Enterprise resources can be defined only if you are using PeopleSoft Manufacturing.

Enterprise Routings define the sequence of processing steps that are required to build the enterprise items. Enterprise Routings are less detailed than the production routings and do not affect production routings.

Enterprise Planning uses the enterprise Bill of Materials to model the product structure of manufactured items in the enterprise model. Every item on an enterprise Bill of Materials must be identified as an enterprise item. PeopleSoft Enterprise Planning gives you a verification process to identify and validate the enterprise items.

ENTERPRISE PLANNING ATTRIBUTES AND PENALTIES

Enterprise Planning attributes define how planning tracks inventory consumption and completion rates. It also manages forecast consumption.

PeopleSoft Enterprise Planning uses the penalty factor to assign penalty weights to violations on customer shipments. The Enterprise Planning uses these weights to calculate the score for the promise date and request date constraints that display on the scorecard.

A more in-depth discussion of PeopleSoft Enterprise Planning can be found in Chapter 19. We will now examine the last distribution module in this chapter—PeopleSoft Purchasing.

PEOPLESOFT PURCHASING

The Purchasing function and its associated business processes hold the key to achieving significant performance improvement. The focus in purchasing is driven not only by the potential for reduced spending but also by the rapid time frame in which the costs can be reduced.

Saving from purchasing directly affects the companies' bottom line. For example, a 5–10% savings on expenditures of one billion dollars represents a 50–100-million-dollar potential increase in net income.

PeopleSoft Purchasing enables you to manage item maintenance, vendor management, requisitions, request for quote, vendor contracts, pricing control, purchase orders, change order processing, accounts payable matching, and shipment receipts interactively. PeopleSoft Purchasing supports a centralized or decentralized purchasing model, an inbound or outbound electronic data interface, automatic faxing of purchase orders, and electronic catalogs. With PeopleSoft Purchasing, you can achieve a cost-effective and efficient procurement of raw materials, goods, and services.

PeopleSoft Purchasing is part of PeopleSoft Material Management solution. PeopleSoft Purchasing gives you the tools to automate your Purchasing business model and integrate it into your entire enterprise. PeopleSoft Purchasing fully integrates with PeopleSoft Inventory, Order Management, Payables, Asset Management, Projects, General Ledger, Production Management, and Production Planning.

We will discuss some of the PeopleSoft Purchasing processes ranging from the data setup through the creation and receipt of a purchase order.

ITEM MAINTENANCE

Item maintenance can be a tedious and time-consuming task when you consider all the possible attributes. PeopleSoft Purchasing enables you to effectively manage item information by assigning category default values that apply to each item in the category. You can also define a group of items as a purchasing kit similar to a bill of materials. PeopleSoft Purchasing also enables you to define an unlimited number of vendors and their priorities for each item. PeopleSoft Purchasing enables you to track the prices, quality, and service that you receive from your vendors by item, thus helping you make better purchasing decisions. When entering contracts, requests for quotes, requisitions, and purchase orders, you can access the item master or catalog quickly.

PeopleSoft Purchasing shares item attributes with PeopleSoft Inventory, Order Management, and Asset Management. PeopleSoft Purchasing enables you to define item attributes in one place. If PeopleSoft Inventory is also installed, purchasing and item attributes both must be entered. PeopleSoft Purchasing automatically copies item attributes to the transaction line level when you specify a defined item or assign a defined category to any item.

Item category streamlines requisition and purchase order entry by providing default item values at the transaction line level. Item catalogs can be tailored for individuals, departments, or groups of users.

PeopleSoft Purchasing allows you to identify a set of items as a purchasing kit with a single kit ID. When you enter a kit ID into a requisition or purchase order, it explodes into its component lines. Ordering by kits saves you time and effort while improving the accuracy and efficiency of your procurement operations.

VENDOR MANAGEMENT

Vendor management is an integral part of your purchasing system. The success of your business is often tied to your vendor relationships. PeopleSoft Purchasing enables you to effectively manage vendors by maintaining unlimited numbers of detailed, effective-dated vendor location and contact information. You can track conversation with your vendors and recall the notes easily by using search keywords. You can also certify vendors to control their use and payment terms. PeopleSoft Purchasing enables you to maintain effective-dated vendor item price schedules in any currency. You have the option of grouping vendors for payment and posting as well.

PeopleSoft Purchasing shares vendor tables with PeopleSoft Accounts Payable to avoid duplicate vendor data and provide consistent information among purchase orders, vouchers, and payments.

You can define a set of vendors for each business unit or share vendors across two or more business units. For every vendor you identify in the system, you can define default procurement options such as freight terms, shipping defaults, or payment terms.

PeopleSoft Purchasing enables you to establish and update prioritized item/supplier combinations, including vendor price and unit of measure. By maintaining your item/vendor relationships, you can also take advantage of Vendor Contract functionality.

PeopleSoft Purchasing allows you to set up a vendor contract even when you have minimum controlling information. PeopleSoft Purchasing allows you to maintain open, fixed-item, or service contracts of any complexity.

REQUISITION

PeopleSoft Purchasing enables you to generate requisitions online or through background processing from purchase requests entered by other departments. PeopleSoft Purchasing enables you to reduce requisition data entry through extensive use of operator and item defaults. You can also copy any previously entered requisition and then override the information that does not apply to the current requisition. You are allowed to choose items from online catalogs. PeopleSoft Purchasing enables you to specify multiple shipping schedules and accounting distributions for each line item at the line level. In addition, you have the option to order supplies for multiple departments by entering a single line on a requisition.

PeopleSoft Purchasing allows you to enter a single requisition that involves multiple vendors. PeopleSoft Purchasing provides automatic sourcing that consolidates and converts requisitions into purchase orders or inventory demand transactions.

PeopleSoft Requisition Loader is a process that considers all the possible sources of raw material demand and generates the appropriate requisitions. PeopleSoft Requisition Loader creates background requisitions from requests such as inventory stocking requests, third-party or external systems, costing resource planning, or order management drop ship requests.

PeopleSoft Purchasing supports self-service Web applications that empower your employees to enter, review, and approve requisitions through a user-friendly Web environment. This feature was developed before the E-Business Strategy and is not as comprehensive.

PURCHASE ORDER

PeopleSoft Purchasing enables you to prepare purchase orders interactively online, copy from existing purchase orders, or convert the information from contracts or requisitions. Using PeopleSoft Purchasing, you are able to consolidate multiple requisitions on a single purchase order either by vendor or both buyer and vendor. You can also specify multiple shipping instructions per purchase order, multiple internal delivery locations, and accounting distribution per shipment. You have the option of attaching comments to purchase orders for internal use or for communication with your vendors.

To help you better manage the change order, PeopleSoft Purchasing enables you to apply your own rule for determining what changes will generate a change order. For example, you can define whether any change in price or order quantity should generate a change order. A change order will then be created if you alter the quantity. You have the option to reprint the purchase order and notify your vendor of the changes.

PeopleSoft Purchasing allows you to dispatch purchase orders to vendors by print, fax, or electronic data interchange.

RECEIVE SHIPMENT

PeopleSoft Purchasing allows you to process the receipt and inspection of all shipments with or without an associated purchase order number. PeopleSoft Purchasing allows you to process multiple purchase orders on a single online receipt or receive partial shipments of a single purchase order on many receipts. PeopleSoft Purchasing enables you to automate the routing process from receiving to inspection if you choose to do so. You can also record receipt of assets and inventory put-away in PeopleSoft Purchasing.

VENDOR CONTRACT

PeopleSoft Purchasing enables you to establish contracts with your vendors even if you have very little information available at the time. Vendor contracts are agreements between your company and vendors about unit prices, items, minimum and maximum quantities, discounts, units of measure, and delivery schedules.

PeopleSoft Purchasing enables you to create both open- and fixed-item contracts. With an open-item contract, you can set up the header information, such as effective date, expiration date, total discount, and maximum amount. The open-item contract is a good way to set up blanket purchase orders. With a fixed-item contract, you can specify items, unit prices, shipping, and scheduling information. Defining a contract with fixed items does not preclude you from ordering open items.

PeopleSoft Purchasing supports both product and service contracts and enables you to share contracts across business units if you want.

PROCUREMENT CARD

A procurement card is a credit card, such as Visa or MasterCard, that you set up with your choice of bank. The bank will summarize your charged activities and send you the statement for payment.

The procurement card is quite popular because it empowers individuals to make credit card purchases on behalf of the organization. This feature reduces the number of small dollar purchases that often flow through the purchasing department.

PeopleSoft Purchasing enables you to set up data to control authorization, security, the general ledger account number, and spending limits.

In conjunction with PeopleSoft Electronic Data Interchange Manager, PeopleSoft Purchasing provides the ability to load the bank statement files and generate a procurement card statement. The cardholder, supervisor, or account payable personnel can review the statement online as it becomes available. PeopleSoft Purchasing enables you to review and reconcile transactions, override default accounts, add additional account distributions or purchasing item information, and track disputes.

CHAPTER 12

INDUSTRY-SPECIFIC SOLUTIONS

At the time of this writing, PeopleSoft continues to evolve its strategy and will do so for the next several years. Although its reputation in the early '90s was established in the "horizontal" world of specific cross-industry application modules such as Human Resources, PeopleSoft is recognizing that, to remain competitive, specialized industrywide solutions are a significant factor in the company's future. How does PeopleSoft account for the differences in each vertical industry and incorporate those differences into its applications without developing entirely new applications? Or should it develop entirely new applications? In 1999, its strategy seems to be to mix and match the existing modules with one another and integrate in a few highly specialized third-party solutions so that it can provide the most effective answer to specific industries. In this chapter, we will take a high-level look at some of the vertical solutions for such areas as Communications, Utilities and Transportation, Health-care, Financial, Retail, and High Tech services. The other PeopleSoft-designated vertical industries, such as Public Sector and Higher Education, are addressed elsewhere in the book.

THE GENERAL CHARACTERISTICS OF PEOPLESOFT VERTICAL INDUSTRY SOLUTIONS

PeopleSoft's vertical industry lines of business have several common features. This section describes how those common elements are embedded in all of PeopleSoft's vertical solutions regardless of the particular aspects of any industry.

SHARED SERVICES

Shared services are a natural fit for vertical industries. Although organizations in every industry vary, there are common management principles and practices that can be consolidated and "shared" in any given organization. Even if a corporation has segmented core administrative responsibilities down to the business unit level, certain processes are more successful operating as enterprisewide processes, and certain processes are better run at the local level. To illustrate the differences, imagine that you are an employee in the Accounting Department. Your best friend works in Personnel. In Accounting, a number of processes that are specific to accounts payable have no bearing on your friend's work (for example, the process for getting check signatures). However, Payroll affects both you in Accounting and your friend in Personnel. That is the difference between local and enterprisewide processes. Other examples of enterprisewide processes include the following:

- Payroll Processing and Production
- Billing and Collections (Receivables)
- Human Resource Administration
- General Corporate Accounting Functions (General Ledger, Accounts Payable)
- Corporate Purchasing and Contract Management with Suppliers/Vendors
- Event Management (setting up corporate meetings and seminars, trade show exhibitions, luncheons, and even internal conference room reservations)
- Employee Travel and Expense Management

Examples of local processes include the following:

- Sales Automation and Management
- Departmental Requisitioning and Receiving
- Project Management
- Training and Resource Management

Information Systems departments can be either local or enterprisewide, depending on the functions. For example, LAN maintenance is an enterprisewidefunction, but the use of PeopleSoft Financials could be restricted to a particular department such as Accounting or Financial Services.

Several approaches to the use of shared services for corporate business processes are possible:

- A vertical industry shared services standalone unit that consolidates enterprisewide functions in a business unit at either a single location or multiple locations
- Consolidation of all enterprisewide processes in a single location
- Business unit–level business process independence
- Successful shared services units such as those at the *New York Times*, which consolidated financial services, benefits, human resources, and communications into a single organization. Thus, at the *Times*, financial and human resources data reside in a single repository. Their foundation is the PeopleSoft Human Resources, Financials, Payroll, and Benefits systems.

PERFORMANCE MANAGEMENT: THE BENCHMARKS AND METRICS

When PeopleSoft developed its manufacturing modules using Enterprise Resource Optimization (ERO), it was a revolutionary way of approaching customer-driven enterprise activity and responsiveness. Within a year of ERO's introduction, PeopleSoft developed its Enterprise Performance Management (EPM) system in conjunction with Harvard University's Dr. Robert Kaplan, the creator of Stage IV Financial Management Systems and, more recently the "Balanced Scorecard" concept. Together, they defined a means of assessing the return on investment of corporate initiatives using tools that look at the normal parameters of financial measurement, customer profitability and expectations, the sizing and functioning of the workforce, shareholder value, and the effect of technology breakthroughs on the bottom line. These new assessment and measurement criteria are recognition of an instrumental breakthrough in the marketplace and customer activity.

By the end of 1997, PeopleSoft had solidified its key Enterprise Performance Measurement indicators. Activity Based Costing (ABC) was then introduced by PeopleSoft to assist financial analysts in making strategic cost decisions across the enterprise. Questions like "What was the difference in cost of issuing a utility bill to a Commonwealth Edison customer in New York City versus a Commonwealth Edison customer in East Meadow, Long Island, and New York? How would that cost affect the small margin of profit that Commonwealth Edison earned?" could now be answered.

Additionally, the calculation of profitability across various units in multiple dimensions, all determined from a single data repository, became possible. Planning, simulations, and the use of Online Analytical Processing (OLAP) tools all were fully integrated with the PeopleSoft financial modules such as General Ledger, Accounts Payable, Accounts Receivable, Asset Management, and so forth.

However, before a complete vertical solution was anointed, several steps were taken and functionality was increased to create what became known as the Enterprise Performance Management Analytical Applications, as of the 1998 PeopleSoft Users Conference in San Francisco, California.

THE ANALYTICAL APPLICATIONS

So, as the wise sage said, "Vat's the difference?" Tools, tools, more tools and a far more sophisticated data repository. The purpose of the analytical applications is simple: to provide a means to measure tangible and intangible assets in light of the defined operating strategy and vision of the organization.

Some examples of the analytic applications' functionality are

- The Balanced Scorecard—A series of key performance indicators developed by Dr. Robert Kaplan that incorporate both financial and non-financial measurements to derive a determination of "value."

- Workbench—Role-based user interfaces. One example would be a financial analyst who sees only that information gathered from multiple sources that is appropriate to his job. PeopleSoft prepackages these interfaces.

- Activity-Based Management (ABM)—A cost management application developed by Dr. Kaplan, PeopleSoft, and KPMG that utilizes cost parameters and augments them with non–cost based transactions. For example, a cost is assigned not only to the price of taking clients to lunch, but to all the activities associated with that transaction. To reduce costs, it follows that a reduction in the number of those cost-intensive transactions should occur. But does that reduction in cost-associated transactions create a gain or a loss of "value?" That won't be answered here.

- Total Compensation Management—As the market for employee additions and retention continues to remain fierce, understanding how changes in compensation impact an entire organization becomes a vital piece of knowledge. Total Compensation Management is designed to work with Human Resource managers to determine how those compensation decisions affect the overall enterprise.

- Enterprise Warehouse—This is a central PeopleSoft data repository that uses the PeopleSoft-designed Extract, Transform, and Load (ETL) technology to combine third-party external data with PeopleSoft applications data.

THE SPECIFIC: VERTICAL INDUSTRY BREAKDOWN

TRANSPORTATION, COMMUNICATIONS, AND UTILITIES

A common theme runs throughout the three verticals: Transportation, Communications, and Utilities. All are defined by their service to the public. Most of the major entities associated with the three are *quasigovernmental*, which means that they are subjected to both federal and state regulations but yet are deregulated. Their focus is consumer-oriented, even more than a commercial venture. They are distinguished by their integral role as a central part of any urban, suburban, or rural service grid. A failure can have life-and-death consequences. Their inability to satisfy need could have terrifying repercussions for the economy.

All three of these industries are project focused, capital intensive, and consumer responsive by mandate. Their procurement, billing, service offerings, reporting, and overall customer management processes are highly complex and diverse, yet need to be thoroughly integrated so that feedback is nearly instantaneous.

The Utilities industry has several additional specific requirements that are discussed in the following section.

- Transportation, Communications, Utilities Modules
- Human Resources Management
- Accounting and Control
- Treasury Management
- Project Management (integrates with Microsoft Project and Primavera)
- Performance Measurement
- Materials Management (Supply Chain)
- Supply Chain Planning (Supply Chain)
- Focused Modules
- Sales and Logistics (Supply Chain)
- Communication, Transportation
- Vertically Specific Modules
- CIS for Utilities

PART

II

CH

12

UTILITIES: SPECIAL NEEDS

The Utilities industry is the most diverse of the three when it comes to service offerings because of the variety of public services defined as utilities: for example, gas, water, and electricity. Real-time pricing is an essential part of any application for this vertical. Outage management is part of the daily work in this industry, especially during the weather extremes of the summer and winter. Even something as ordinarily accepted as meter reading must be a built-in part of any IT solution.

PeopleSoft is working with SPL WorldGroup to offer CIS Plus, designed for managing special requirements for the utilities industry. Two of the most outstanding features of this industry-specific PeopleSoft application are its real-time price delivery with real-time meter reading. It also handles the natural gas sector in the wake of its recent deregulation. Consumer service contracts can be customized to the entity regardless of geographic location, demographic data points, or financial status. It automates complex business processes such as evaluations of test marketing service offerings, definition of usage periods, payment processing, credit and collections, and price setting.

RETAIL

In 1998, PeopleSoft purchased Intrepid Systems, Inc., for an undisclosed sum. This has been an important decision for PeopleSoft's delivery of services to the retail industry because it introduced PeopleSoft Merchandise Management (which was Intrepid Systems' Evolution 4.0). Coupled with data warehousing and several traditional modules, PeopleSoft has been able to provide the retail industry with perhaps its most complete industry-specific solution.

INDUSTRY-SPECIFIC NEEDS

PeopleSoft segments the retail industry into two areas: retail merchandise management and restaurant/grocery retail. However, the supply chain is essentially the same for both. This vertical market is an excellent expression of PeopleSoft's ERO (see Chapter 2, "PeopleSoft: Where It Came From and How It Fits") with customer satisfaction and demand the lifeblood of the industry. The retail PeopleSoft solution set has the strongest ERO features of any vertical built in to its core processes.

WHAT IS THE RETAILER'S WORKFLOW AND SUPPLY CHAIN?

The workflow and supply chain for the retail industry is highly integrated. Their fundamental operations involve all the standard processes, including inventory management, procurement, sales, distribution, human resources, logistics, billing, routing, purchase orders, and so on. With the specific requirements of the retail industry in mind, PeopleSoft added Retail Merchandise Management to its application suite.

- Retail Merchandise Management
- Traditional Modules
- Human Resources Management
- Accounting and Control
- Treasury Management
- Performance Management
- Project Management
- Sales and Logistics (Supply Chain)
- Supply Chain Planning (Supply Chain)
- Procurement (Supply Chain)
- Industry-Specific Modules
- Merchandise Management

MERCHANDISE MANAGEMENT

One of the core processes of retailing is the management of inventory from the point of production to the time it is in the hands of the customer. Merchandise Management handles this task with the development of SKU Master. This tool manages inventory, maintains SKUs at the warehouse and in the stores, and handles the special deals that are crucial to customer satisfaction. Additionally, this tool supports the following:

- Vendor maintenance
- Price change management
- Cost change management
- Product specification
- Quote management
- Allocation of merchandise
- Demand forecasting
- Automatic replenishment
- Merchandise analysis
- Ordering
- Returns
- Receipt
- Departmental merchandise transfers
- Inventory and adjustments

DECISION SUPPORT REPOSITORY

Decision Support Repository is what may be the first retail industry-specific data warehouse. Here, information regarding merchandising, sales, inventory, and deal information can be sliced, diced, drilled down, or cut so that analysis and reports can be accessed for key, near-real-time decisions. It is compliant with Oracle, Microsoft SQL Server, DB2, Informix, Sybase, and other relational databases.

SUPPLY CHAIN MANAGEMENT

Logistics Management, Demand Planning, and Analytic Tools provide the foundation for PeopleSoft Supply Chain Management for retail. They are the primary combination of modules and applications that make up the vertical suite for the retail industry's supply chain.

THE SERVICES INDUSTRY

PeopleSoft has developed explicit vertical applications for a substantial part of the commercial and professional services industry. The needs of the service industry tend to be different from those of the more commodity-oriented retail industry or the quasipublic utilities industry. The following section covers those commercial service segments.

PART

II

CH

12

Financial Services

Risk management, services maintenance, globalization in its broadest sense, and financial analysis are the center of the PeopleSoft Financial Services vertical solution. With the increasingly wide variety of services offered by financial institutions, the explosive growth of online banking and other services, and the coming of the Euro, financial services institutions have a pressing need to manage a wide variety of processes. This includes service delivery, reporting requirements for governments, customers and investors, marketing, sophisticated online transaction activities, and management of the development of multiple layers of regulatory oversight. Assessment of the impact their offerings and processes have is paramount as the competition becomes increasingly fierce, and as increasingly similar services dominate what were previously clearly demarcated financial institutions. What a bank offered, a brokerage house couldn't. Now that both offer several service offerings that are identical, making competition for the customer that much fiercer. All this was exacerbated by the introduction of the Euro in January 1999 (see Chapter 2).

These changes, in conjunction with an increasingly antiquated General Ledger that is not structured to handle the real-time need for information, have brought PeopleSoft into the center of the millennial maelstrom in the financial services sector with a series of offerings designed to manage an industry undergoing fundamental, dramatic changes in a short time period.

Additionally, one financial services domain with highly specialized needs is the insurance industry. Their offerings have become increasingly complex and investment oriented with a wider and wider variety of plans. To handle policies, PeopleSoft teamed with Trimark Corp., the creator of the insurance industry–focused Transcend, a client/server application that handles product development, distribution, sales and marketing, regulatory compliance, knowledge management, customer service, cash control, and policy administration.

- General
- Financial Services Modules
- Human Resources Management
- Accounting and Control
- Treasury Management
- Project Management
- Service Revenue Management (Supply Chain)
- Procurement (Supply Chain)
- Industry-Specific Solutions
- Profitability Management
- Insurance Industry
- Insurance Services Modules
- Trimark Corporations "Transcend" for Policy Administration

FINANCIAL SERVICES: THE ANALYTIC APPLICATIONS

PeopleSoft attacked the need for performance management and profitability analysis in the financial services industry in 1997. With the development of several financial services–specific analytic applications by the end of 1998, PeopleSoft had tools in place to provide increased functionality to this vertical industry. They are as follows:

- Funds Transfer Pricing—This application determines the profitability of financial services across an enterprise.

- Risk Weighted Capital—By allocating risk to capital, this allows financial services institutions to understand the actual return on investment on multiple levels.

- Asset Liability Management—External factors such as market impact are used by ALM to do risk assessment on the holdings and investments of a financial services firm.

HEALTHCARE

Healthcare is a growing part of the PeopleSoft vertical solutions group. The centerpiece of PeopleSoft's approach to healthcare is cost containment and business flow analysis, specifically centered on the supply chain and Enterprise Performance Management (EPM). Using the front-end supply chain applications of PeopleSoft, including Demand Planning, the OLAP-based Cube Manager, Supply Chain Collaborator, and Order Promising, healthcare institutions can minimize their inventory costs, reduce the costs of purchase and delivery, and through the use of intranets, streamline communications and business processes. This is especially important in healthcare because of the complex network of primary care providers, specialists, pharmacies, pharmaceutical suppliers, employers, community service agencies, insurance companies, and so on, that rely on vital information from the healthcare organizations.

The second major focus in healthcare is in the implementation of a true EPM model. The distinction of this PeopleSoft tool within healthcare is the capability to merge standard PeopleSoft financial module data (for example, GL, AM, PC, AP) with "clinical" patient results to know the "true" costs of patient care.

- Traditional Modules
- Human Resources Management
- Accounting and Control
- Treasury Management
- Performance Management
- Project Management
- Service Revenue Management (Supply Chain)
- Supply Chain Planning (Supply Chain)
- Materials Management (Supply Chain)

PART

II

CH

12

HIGH TECH SERVICES

Although PeopleSoft includes the high tech services among the general Service Industry offerings, there are several distinguishing features that PeopleSoft thinks merit attention. They are as follows:

- Customer-centric order processing. Immediate turnaround of customized sales orders, perhaps best represented by the Dell Computer Corporation's build-to-order sales model that revolutionized the computer hardware industry in the late 1990s. This model allowed a customer to virtually build the computer from scratch with a large selection of prebuilt parts and then have that computer shipped nearly immediately (read: within a few days).

- Seriously reduced product life cycle and production cycle. This has forced high technology software and hardware companies to come to market more rapidly, with highly innovative, competitive, lower-cost products in order to attract potential customers.

- The globalization and simultaneous decentralization of the enterprise, coupled with the breakdown of national boundaries through online ordering and processing. This multinational and multientry approach is becoming increasingly prevalent as the Internet continues to revolutionize business.

PeopleSoft has designed another of its mix-and-match solutions that fits the high-tech industry like a glove. Using a number of its standard modules, submodules, and methodologies, PeopleSoft integrates Financials, Human Resources, Demand Planning, Workflow, and Enterprise Performance Management to define how the high tech business can run its operations. For example, Dell can use Demand Planning, based on current information, to identify which parts and how many of them will be needed over the next time period, given existing production cycles. Then, using PeopleSoft's workflow, this multidimensional forecast is routed to the appropriate personnel and departments for review, changes, and annotations. The changes are then reassembled into a single collaborative forecast for the coming time period.

The next step would be to enter the forecast/order into the production and distribution cycle. At the Dell manufacturing facility, PeopleSoft's Product Configurator would be used to create a temporary product (say a computer with 256MB RAM instead of 128MB RAM or a 21-inch monitor instead of the normal 17-inch monitor) that would be run through the Product Configurator rules. These rules could say, for example, that 256MB of RAM is fine, but a request for 341MB RAM cannot be met. Then the PeopleSoft Order Promising system is used to see what inventory exists to meet this temporary product and where that inventory exists. The product is procured, inventory moved and delivered, purchase orders issued, and the machine is then built.

THE OTHER SERVICES

PeopleSoft for Service Industries is an all-encompassing category covering multiple industries. Everything from Consulting and Systems Integration to Architecture, Engineering and Construction, Trade Associations, Staffing, Prepackaged Software, Hospitality and Gaming, and so on, are covered in the Business Services domain.

However, there are common applications/modules that we can identify for the Service offering:

- Services Modules
- Human Resources Management
- Accounting and Control
- Treasury Management
- Performance Management
- Project Management
- Service Revenue Management (Supply Chain)
- Procurement (Supply Chain)

CHAPTER 13

STUDENT ADMINISTRATION

by Buddy L. Bruner

In this chapter

THE SPECIAL ENTERPRISE REQUIREMENTS OF HIGHER EDUCATION

The higher education institution is a daunting venue in which to introduce an enterprise resource systems solution. First, the general processes used to deal with the delivery of coursework, the oversight of scholarly research, and the awarding of degrees are unlike those of any other service or product delivery business. Not only do the administrative needs differ from those of most other government agencies and businesses, but historic classification, affiliation, and size and culture differences among institutions of higher education have created a systems marketplace with myriad unique academic practices and, consequently, different business needs. The resulting administrative applications (and particularly those supporting student administration) are, as a result, some of the most demanding and complex ever deployed.

Until recently, virtually all accredited institutions of higher education operated as not-for-profits. The common profit motivators and measures are largely absent. In addition, the customer-first model is largely rejected and there is little concurrence even as to the identity of "the customer." Performance measures that are appropriate for business and industry are therefore rejected as irrelevant by most higher education institutions. In spite of these differences, PeopleSoft has been able to extend a meaningful message to institutional management and make the first major penetration into the higher education administrative systems marketplace in a quarter century. With their new systems, PeopleSoft has started a redefinition of the scope and nature of higher education enterprise software support.

PeopleSoft's success has not simply been due to technology or to a unique functionality. Although these factors are recognized as positive aspects of the PeopleSoft offerings, it is the potential for enabling and coping with change that has attracted most institutional adoptions of the software. Education lags most sectors of business and industry in experiencing the effects of mergers, just-in-time positioning, and demanding stockholders.

Still, virtually every campus executive has felt enough budgetary and board pressures to know that higher education must be more proactive and effective in the near future. Like their industrial counterparts, higher education executives see enterprise systems as a major and necessary element in coping with the nature and pace of change. Although many first considered PeopleSoft software to address deficiencies in legacy applications, overwhelmingly they are also seeking to use their PeopleSoft implementations to reorient and reposition their administrative units and business strategies. The major missing factor in these efforts is the absence in Student Administration of formal provisions to track outcome measures adequately. Without outcomes information, institutions lack the ability to determine their effectiveness in enabling the student to meet new challenges and opportunities. They also lack the ammunition to convince potential employers, donors, and other stakeholders to continue or expand their support.

Software, in itself, rarely makes a business dramatically more successful nor does it often produce or require a different management process. However, only very functional and flexible software can support major new management and enterprise initiatives such as we now see around us every day. In this chapter, we provide an overview of the functional scope of the present PeopleSoft 7.5 Student Administration release and the characteristics that make it a versatile and functional platform for higher education institutions that are actively moving to meet the demands of change and leverage tomorrow's new opportunities.

THE PEOPLESOFT HIGHER EDUCATION OFFERINGS

Historically, higher education institutions have separately created or purchased packaged software systems to support the their finance, human resource, and student administrative transactions.

FUNCTIONAL AND BUSINESS ORGANIZATION

In the last five years, a consensus has emerged on the advantages of having all major higher education administrative systems tightly coupled and supported by a common, nonredundant database. Increasingly, institutions are also seeking an enterprise environment in which end users initiate their own system transactions, the use of paper is reduced, information flows are electronic, and the associated manual transaction checking is replaced by automation. And most recently, institutions are requiring that most or all user interaction with such systems be supported through a Web browser such as Netscape Communicator or Microsoft Internet Explorer.

Today, PeopleSoft is one of the few vendors offering software to address these needs and to provide the functionality sought in all three systems. The PeopleSoft Higher Education offerings are shown in Table 13.1. The financials and human resources requirements for higher education institutions operating as not-for-profits are very similar to those for government and general not-for-profit entities. The same finance and human resource products are delivered to all these clients and can be configured during setup to accommodate the minor differences. There are, however, no products in either the for-profit or not-for-profit government arenas that meet the special needs for student administration.

PEOPLESOFT HIGHER EDUCATION ERP ARCHITECTURE

Architecturally, PeopleSoft utilizes the same database to support its higher education 7.5 HRMS and 7.5 Student Administration modules. Finance, at this time, is a release behind at 7.0 and utilizes a separate database. Although the modules were designed to operate independently to allow "best-of-breed" implementations with other products, they can be tightly integrated and set up to exchange information automatically when implemented as a total enterprise solution.

PART

II

CH

13

TABLE 13.1   PEOPLESOFT HIGHER EDUCATION ER PRODUCT

Finance	HRMS	Student Administration
General Ledger	Human Resources	Campus Community
Payables	Benefits Administration	Admissions
Receivables	FSA Administration	Student Records
Asset Management	Payroll	Financial Aid
Inventory	Payroll Interface	Academic Advising
Billing	Time and Labor	Student Finance
Budgets	Pension Administration	Advancement

Transactions within these modules can be processed in the traditional batch mode with accompanying edits to identify and treat errors or in near real time relying more heavily on entry edits. Information flow and provisions for control and review can be accommodated in a robust workflow capability that provides active user alerts when action needs to be taken or important information has been made available. A flexible suite of query and reporting tools is provided to augment the standard reports. Users can readily minimize the number of paper reports that will routinely be produced if that is one of their objectives.

Most of the standard panel groups can be viewed either in the PeopleSoft interface using Windows or using a Web client. These panel groups are necessarily complex, however, making them a poor choice for end-user input. PeopleSoft has recognized this and is moving to create a full suite of end-user oriented panels, specifically designed for end-user input over the Web. About 20 are currently available in the Student module. By release 8.0, all important panel functions should be similarly Web-enabled in HRMS, Finance, and Student.

Given the breadth of ERP functionality potential provided in the full higher education suite and the flexibility provided in its setup configurations, many institutions have found PeopleSoft software to be a powerful vehicle for business process change, thereby markedly increasing the potential return on their investment.

BUSINESS PROCESSES AND CHANGE

If an institution or organization is going to remake itself today, the most accepted means is to address its business activities not as discrete departmentally contained functions (the silo model), but as the components of all the fundamental activities that address a need (and make up a process that typically crosses several departments) from start to finish. PeopleSoft, as a vendor, does not sell process change support. The company has, however, departed from the philosophy of most software vendors by stressing the importance of the customer, addressing business processes, and refining both software and customer practice to optimally meet today's demanding and changing needs.

PeopleSoft has also pioneered the use of alliances with other companies to support their customers' implementations. They have partnered with software companies to provide integrated and extended functionality in specialized areas, with certified hardware vendors who provide equipment sized and tested to meet realistic industry demands, and with experienced implementation consultants who understand how to drive change in congress with software configuration and implementation. These alliances have been a major factor in the PeopleSoft successes and in the successes of the PeopleSoft customers.

To ensure that the individual PeopleSoft modules can be aligned with customer processes, PeopleSoft has made a major effort to compile an industry-wide perspective of the processes underlying the conduct of each business. For higher education, this has meant working with a panel of higher education institutions, associations, and consulting practices. The resulting group (almost an atlas) of student administration process models captures the common central elements of activity across large and small, undergraduate and graduate, public and private institutions and is documented in the Student PeopleBooks. These processes promise to be an increasingly important base for understanding how PeopleSoft will address future product releases like that anticipated for Performance Measurement in higher education.

USING PROCESS MODELS

At their overview level, the PeopleSoft business process models represent generic higher education processes. At their detail level, they illustrate how the software supports the business process and its associated steam of activities. The model, in its simplest form, is a series of boxes interconnected by arrows and branch points. The boxes represent either the use of a PeopleSoft application panel or the execution of a PeopleSoft background process. The associated text describes the business activity (for example, enroll a student, enter grades).

The models are meant to be a starting point for describing and guiding institutions' understanding of their new applications and how they will be used. Each customer will want to use the provided models as reference during Fit-Gap considerations and as a jumping-off point for exploring process redesign as part of its campus implementation. During their initial implementation of PeopleSoft, most institutions endeavor to refine and optimize those campus processes that provide an opportunity for significantly improved service or reduced costs. The resulting processes often depart from the generic atlas model at least in some detail. Even without process optimization, some institutional processes will be seen as "better" than the PeopleSoft generic model. Fortunately, PeopleSoft's flexibility of configuration and setup can accommodate a wide variation in institutional practice without major software customization.

STUDENT ADMINISTRATION BUSINESS PROCESSES

The process modeling input gathered by PeopleSoft led to ten mid-level processes: Plan the Mission; Manage Campus Community; Admit Student; Provide Financial Aid; Enroll Student; Teach, Learn, and Evaluate; Transition Student; Provide Financial Services; Advance the Organizational Goals; and Analyze Performance. Detail level models such as the one seen in Figure 13.1 underlie the overall Student Administration provided in Figure 13.2.

Figure 13.1
Calculate optional fees.

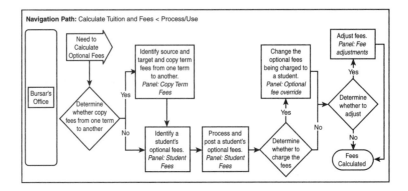

Figure 13.2
Student administration.

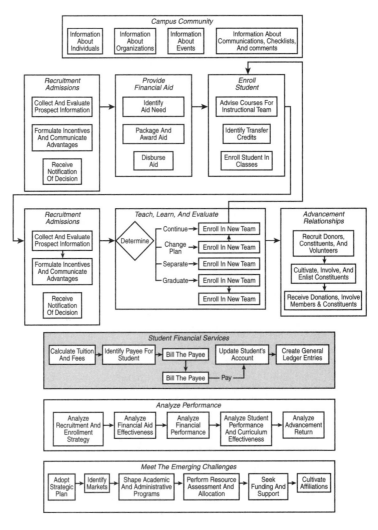

TABLE 13.2   STUDENT ADMINISTRATION PROCESSES AND ACTIVITIES

Plan the Mission	Strategic Planning (Academic and Administrative)
Manage Campus Community	Collect and track information about campus individuals, organizations, and events
Admit Student	Market, recruit, and admit
Provide Financial Aid	Analyze need, package aid and incentives
Enroll Student	Establish offerings, manage dependencies, register students
Teach, Learn, and Evaluate	Track enrollment, progress, grades, activities
Transition Student	Advise, advance, separate, graduate students
Provide Financial Services	Bill, collect, and refund tuition, fees, and other expenses
Advance the Organizational Goals	Manage constituents, volunteers, events, dues, donations, and pledges
Analyze Performance	Evaluate effectiveness of enrollment, student performance, curricular effectiveness, financial achievement, and advancement strategies

As the nature and scope of the models imply, an overall process focus and a process change commitment require goals, progress and performance measures, and a feedback methodology to sustain ongoing excellence. The PeopleSoft upgrade process, with its roughly annual timing and its mini-implementation nature, provides an excellent opportunity for not-for-profit institutions to refine their activities and their use and configuration of the PeopleSoft modules regularly. PeopleSoft's update-driven renewal is one of the key factors in sustaining a truly successful enterprise system deployment.

With the overall perspective of the processes in mind, we will describe the general characteristics of the current six Student modules and the new, closely related Advancement (Alumni/Development) module.

THE STUDENT ADMINISTRATION MODULES

The PeopleSoft Student Administration modules in their common order of implementation are Campus Community, Admissions, Student Records, Financial Aid, Student Financials, and Academic Advisement. Although Advancement is not strictly a student module, it uses the same HRMS database and is tightly integrated with Student. We include it in this discussion because of its treatment of the alumni postgraduate relationship with former students. The Student Administration modules are a young effort, drawing heavily on the needs and experiences of a seven-school *beta* program effort. The result is a fresh and innovative package, but one that some institutions may feel still does not address all common practices. The following sections discuss these modules in more detail.

CAMPUS COMMUNITY

The HRMS and Student Administration modules (here including Advancement) share a common database as well as common demographic data in the Campus Community module. PeopleSoft chose to combine personal and organizational information into a single hub of definitions and maintenance so that data commonly duplicated across systems will have only a single system instance. It is through this module that the institution will manage information about individuals (their demographic data and other general characteristics), events, committees, communications, checklists, and other associated organizational information. Gathered here is the commonly used student biographical and demographical data (and if HRMS is used, faculty and staff data as well).

Closely associated with the Campus Community information is detailing Academic Structure, Academic Programs, and the Academic Calendar. This information forms the foundation on which every other Student Administration module builds and operates. This core information is a critical prerequisite to serving the student properly and efficiently. It provides a rich repository for almost any sort of general student information, now or in the future. Grades, programs, and academic curricula are tabulated and related here. Although not strictly a transaction processing module, proper setup and maintenance in Campus Community is essential to the smooth integration of Student with HR and Finance.

ADMISSIONS

PeopleSoft's Admissions module brings together the marketing, recruiting, actual prospect application evaluation, and the resultant admissions processing. Prospect contacts, recruiter assignments, and applications handling progression can be readily tracked against the ongoing record of presentations, fairs, mailings, and conversations. Market segmentation and comparisons provide a sound basis for effective planning and targeted campaigns. The ability to handle (and electronically load) some twenty-odd standard test scores formats (SAT, and so on) provides a wide variety of prospect sources and value schemes.

Academic credentials, recommendations, and career goals can be related to incentive offers and institutional and program enrollment targets. Document imaging, Web applications, email responses, and a robust traditional correspondence program can be combined with electronic document interchange to support almost any desired approach to communication and follow up. Internal units can readily review prospect files without the need to physically copy or transfer records. After matriculation, the prospect is automatically moved to student status. No other maintenance is required.

Although a seamless integration with student aid and incentive modeling would be desirable, Admissions is one of the most polished and sophisticated modules in PeopleSoft's Student Administration. Few will want more, following the release of PeopleSoft's Campus Connection Web Portal and an associated set of user-friendly Web interfaces for inquiries, applications, fee payment, financial aid modeling, and acceptance. Schools with college or departmental admissions activity will appreciate the ability to leverage electronic workflow in place of circulating forms and credentials. The capability to support an aggressive program of "self-service" is well within the module's capabilities.

STUDENT RECORDS

PeopleSoft's Records module supports the maintenance of the student's institutional academic progress from the point of enrollment and matriculation (objectives, majors, coursework, activities, portfolios, honors, status, and so on). The objective of this module is to present a common interface to support tracking, evaluation, and monitoring of every element of a student's progress toward his or her academic goal. From the student's perspective, this record links all the elements in Figure 13.3.

Figure 13.3
Student records perspective.

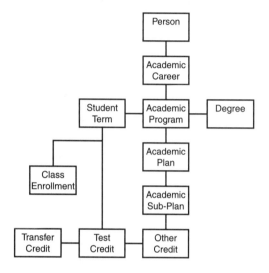

From the institution's perspective, student records link Academic Career, Group, Program, Plan, Sub-Plan, and Degree with Subject Area, Course, Class, Session, and Term. The Student Records module must therefore incorporate the definition and maintenance of these elements plus grading schemes, transfer equivalency rules, repeat rules, schedules, and catalogs (with class notes, course attributes, exam codes, instructors, advisors, level/load rules, CIP and HEGIS codes, facilities, room characteristics, time periods, and so on).

Students can be enrolled and de-enrolled. Their class attendance and extracurricular activities can be tracked, their academic progress evaluated, their honors and awards managed, and their eligibility for registration and other services tracked. The registration process can be easily integrated with third-party IVR products for telephone registration. In a number of cases, simple-to-use, Web applications are provided for use by the student (to research the course catalog, search for classes, investigate holds on their records and eligibility, register for classes, review their grades, and request transcript copies). The faculty can also use a simple Web format to enter and confirm their course grades. More such interfaces are expected in the next releases.

To complete the records picture, PeopleSoft provides both standardized statistics and reporting formats for the most common requirements. In addition, Cognos' Power Play desktop data warehouse capabilities are delivered with Student. PeopleSoft provides the

PART

II

CH

13

basic data cube parameters and loading capabilities to support initial use of this OLAP repository and the tools to refine the model to meet individual campus needs.

FINANCIAL AID

The Student Financial Aid module is one of the most critical elements for recruiting and retaining students. Ideally, such a package should integrate well with recruiting, admissions, student financials, and ongoing student evaluation through the point of graduation. The complexity of the needed functionality and continual regulatory changes make this a very demanding module to perfect.

PeopleSoft has designed a powerful module for this purpose. The module accepts and applies both Federal and institutional aid. Automated need and packaging calculations are provided to match budgets against resources and determine awards. A very flexible capability is provided to process and disburse the proceeds. Web inquiry capability is provided for student inspection of their aid summary. A variety of checks and oversight provisions are provided to minimize the possibility of errors and oversights (including oversubscription of need, the use of inapplicable funding sources, and missing eligible sources). Compatibility is provided for DOE Central Processing System and CommonLine loan services.

ADVISEMENT

The Advisement module is PeopleSoft's strong effort to address student advising and degree requirements auditing. Competing vendor efforts in this area have largely been undistinguished in both their capabilities and flexibility. The PeopleSoft module provides a basis for codifying curricular and degree requirements and policies, tying them to the specifications that govern when the student first entered his current academic career. As a student progresses toward potential graduation, the Advisement module provides an analysis of the unmet requirements—courses, seminars, internships, and so forth.

The most exciting capability is the potential for this module to be used in what-if modeling for the students, allowing them to compare alternative degree or curricular course requirement consequences. It lacks only a linkage to Student Financials/Financial Aid to clarify the accompanying cost and aid impacts as part of the process. For the faculty, the Advisement module provides a rigorous mechanism to certify eligibility for graduation and a program planning basis that does not preclude the normal complement of special requirements or considerations on a student-by-student basis.

STUDENT FINANCIALS

PeopleSoft's Student Financials module provides the capabilities to calculate all tuition and fees for each student and to support the resulting student and/or third-party customer billing accounts. The module provides the means to design and create bills, establish and maintain five different types of payment plans, age accounts, and manage collections (including the associated correspondence) and to post all net transactions directly to the general ledger.

Student Financials' cashiering module can be used to perform a wide variety of transactions quickly and accurately, including cashier and register support, credit card processing, and check cashing. A Campus Connection Web account inquiry capability is provided for direct student access. A variety of tracking and reporting capabilities are provided to support the base financial functions as well as student counseling. Student Financials can also transact in and convert to or from any currency the institution chooses.

ADVANCEMENT

PeopleSoft's newest student-related module provides a comprehensive solution to the need to manage complex campaign efforts, multifaceted events, volunteer efforts, and membership drives. The module provides a robust gift-processing capability that can handle pledges, matching gifts, tribute and memorial gifts, acknowledgments, and giving club membership maintenance. Direct posting to the general ledger is provided with the capability to track not only gifts, but endowment earnings, beneficiaries, and so on even if the original funds have been pooled.

The module incorporates a broad spectrum of information on members, prospects, and contributors, both individuals and organizations. Specialized functionality is provided to plan and manage initiatives and to sustain memberships and membership drives. Special attention has been given to organizing and supporting the activities of volunteers and the full cross-section of events, be they fund-raising or relationship-building. The financial support allows for flexible definition of appropriate handling of all proceeds and expenses with posting to the institutional general ledger or that for a separate entity as desired.

STUDENT ADMINISTRATION LIMITATIONS

We noted that PeopleSoft encourages relationships with other software vendors. These alliances have served to enrich the potential of the higher education PeopleSoft environment beyond the scope of the applications provided by PeopleSoft. Most of the PeopleSoft panels are Web-enabled. However, Web-enabling them has not made them truly user-friendly, and a more comprehensive end user Web presence still lies in the future.

Although PeopleSoft has a rich family of student applications, from the global perspective of higher education a number of important applications are not available in the 7.5 release. These include

- A library system
- A campus housing module
- A student affairs system
- A grants and contracts management system
- A placement module
- An outcomes tracking module
- A co-op/intern management module

PART

II

CH

13

- A class scheduling module
- A facilities work order system
- A registration and billing capability that is truly compatible with continuing and professional education needs
- A classroom space management module
- An integrated institutional analysis, modeling, and planning module

PeopleSoft also does not offer integrated ancillary technologies such as CTI, IVR, and imaging. However, its Alliance Partners do. As this volume is going to press, PeopleSoft is committed to providing a one-to-one Web interface, the Campus Connection. This Web framework will combine a Web portal linking applications, intranet, and extranet capabilities. The commitment includes a significant number of Web applications designed from the ground up to fully leverage the Web environment and to be user-oriented and friendly.

By release 8.0 in 2000, PeopleSoft does expect to offer a Housing module (addressing one major Student Affairs activity). This release should also include PeopleSoft's Grants and Contract Management software. Although PeopleSoft continues to evaluate the potential return and market share that it might get from additional functionality, it is likely that it will continue to draw heavily on the competencies that can be provided by software Alliance Partners.

SUMMARY

PeopleSoft's Student Administration has had two years of limited release and is now in its first full release to colleges and universities both in the United States and other countries. It is Year 2000 compliant, supports a variety of foreign languages, and can simultaneously handle a number of different currency systems. Its modules treat all the basic transactional academic tasks (and already additional modules have been announced or are under consideration). Though originally announced as a two-tier, client-server application, PeopleSoft Student is rapidly being transformed into a true Web-based client environment with integrated e-business capabilities.

The flexibility of the delivered modules and the inherent richness of the tools provided (for operations, communication, integration, import, program development, database manipulation, reporting, query, analysis, and so on) have stimulated an unprecedented rate of adoption by both large and small institutions. They have also served to sponsor some of the most serious review and innovative refinement of internal business processes since change became a management buzzword.

Implementing PeopleSoft Student Administration remains one of its biggest obstacles. The typical implementation still exceeds one year. New and added functionality will only increase the effort needed in the future. With new and significant software update releases scheduled annually, the unsophisticated client must weigh the clear advantages of PeopleSoft's capability and the significant gains for the business changes this software allows against the traditional IT model for administrative support.

CHAPTER 14

Federal Human Resources

In this chapter   *by Kara Kasprazak*

DEFINING EXISTING PRACTICES AND PROCEDURES FOR FEDERAL HUMAN RESOURCES

This chapter will look at PeopleSoft and the business processes defined specifically in the federal arena and where PeopleSoft applications might be appropriate (or inappropriate).

PeopleSoft established an HRMS beachhead on the banks of the Potomac River in 1995 and has driven the enemy to retreat to the safety and security of their only remaining fortress (the Pentagon). However, the walls of the Pentagon are crumbling, and there are very few safe places left to hide.

PeopleSoft Federal started and is winning a new Revolutionary War—a war on internal management issues. PeopleSoft partners are helping the U.S. federal government gear up for Year 2000, enhance customer service through Web-enabled applications, and gain control over their business through tailored software solutions and services.

PeopleSoft realized that to work successfully with industry professionals, you need to employ individuals with relevant backgrounds. By understanding this need to relate to federal customers and their issues and business rules, the Federal Business Unit has enabled its clients to meet the mandatory rules and regulations placed on their organizations by using the Federal HRMS product suite. PeopleSoft has been successful in meeting the needs of the client base by employing industry-knowledgeable individuals and providing a "federalized" HRMS suite of products along with financial, manufacturing, and distribution applications for a total enterprise-wide solution.

This decade has seen more changes in the U.S. federal government than the last several decades. Government is melding technical advances and reinvention initiatives to become more efficient and results-oriented.

Recent fundamental shifts in the way government conducts business affect human resources and line managers significantly. Each person and organization will be affected by these changes: the visionaries steering the path for the personnel systems, those developing the systems, those using the new technology, or those managing the workforce.

PeopleSoft understands the far-reaching implications of the changes taking place, and is committed to delivering innovative client/server applications that help its customers address those changes.

The Department of Veterans Affairs (with more than 260,000 employees) signed on September 1995 as PeopleSoft's first customer for the "federalized" HRMS product. Now PeopleSoft is the recognized leader for HRMS vendors in the federal market by a wide margin and has announced its entrance into the Federal Financials market. PeopleSoft is also marketing its Supply Chain products to a select group of federal customers and is evaluating more full-scale efforts in that arena.

Other customers:

- Library of Congress
- Navy Exchange Service Command
- Central Intelligence Agency
- Dept. of Justice
- Dept. of Energy
- Dept. of the Treasury (IRS, Customs, Bureau of Prisons, Drug Enforcement Agency)
- Social Security Administration
- U.S. Census Bureau
- U.S. Department of Agriculture (NRCS, FSA, RD)
- Environmental Protection Agency
- State Department
- Dept. of Labor
- U.S. Navy

PeopleSoft first released the Federal Human Resources product in version 5 of the software. Even in the early stages, PeopleSoft realized the need for a Year 2000-compliant application. This was a perfect fit for federal government clients who need to comply with federal regulations to have their systems implemented and Year 2000-compliant. Many government agencies were supposed to be in production with Year 2000-compliant systems by October 1998.

> **Note**
>
> The development and product management teams for PeopleSoft HRMS for U.S. Federal Government are located in Pleasanton, CA, and are part of the commercial HRMS development organization. PeopleSoft's emphasis is on analyzing and enhancing core commercial applications to meet the needs of federal agencies.

UNDERSTANDING THE COMPONENTS OF FEDERAL HRMS

PeopleSoft has tailored each federal product to help prepare agencies for the future. These industry-specific products enable an organization to fulfill its objectives and provide enhanced levels of service, such as

- Solutions tailored to the U.S. federal government
- Technology that supports best practices in human resources
- Year 2000-compliant solutions
- Flexible, adaptable applications
- Improved information access
- Intelligent process management

PART

II

CH

14

Now, PeopleSoft has "federalized" the following HRMS applications:

- Human Resources
- Benefits Administration
- Time and Labor
- Payroll
- Payroll Interface

HUMAN RESOURCES

With PeopleSoft Human Resources, customers can build a fully integrated base of human resource management information to share with other PeopleSoft applications (such as Benefits Administration, Payroll, Payroll Interface, Time and Labor, Financials, and Supply Chain) or interface with their current set of business applications. Object-based, content-sensitive, operator-class security preserves the confidentiality of all client data.

Recruiting is a never-ending process in any organization, federal or commercial. PeopleSoft Human Resources Recruiting processes include job requisitions, applicant rating and ranking, and applicant selection and hiring. With PeopleSoft Human Resources, customers perform both internal and external functions and complete personnel recruiting actions. After customers identify possible candidates, they can narrow down their selection and hire the best individual for the position.

Resumes of individuals who met the selection criteria but were not hired are held in a repository. PeopleSoft partners Restrac and Resumix offer mature software packages that can scan resumes and have queries run against them to find individuals who meet the selection criteria. These systems can interface with PeopleSoft Human Resources. The power of storing this information and searching on it time and time again is a significant cost reducer in today's expensive recruiting costs.

One major priority for a federal human resource employee is to process a change in personnel data. This change is termed a *personnel action request (PAR)*. A PAR must be initiated and moved through a number of approvals before the human resources representative can process and complete it. PeopleSoft offers the flexibility of using workflow to automatically push this process through, so you don't have to carry around that infamous piece of paper called a PAR paper. By using this work-in-progress routing system, including cancellation and correction functionality, retroactive action and detailing assignment processing, and Central Personnel Data File (CPDF) editing, an employee can easily process and track personnel actions.

Other features within the PeopleSoft Federal Human Resource application are Competency Management, Individual Development Plans (IDPs), and Training Administration. These three modules heavily share information on employees to help them enhance their career potential. By keeping all this data in a central repository, individuals can work with their managers to enhance their personal career goals by accessing the same information, making changes, and agreeing on a particular progression.

Compensation administration and planning have always been a tedious process for federal employees. To reduce the tedium, PeopleSoft offers integrated Performance Management and Salary Planning. Mass organizational changes and mass pay adjustments can be handled smoothly by using a multiple-step process for making changes. After changes are made, it is easy to generate detailed organizational charts in minutes. Automatic Within-Grade Increases (WGIs) are issued for employees who meet the requirements. Performance standards and performance reviews are coordinated. Performance Improvement Plans (PIPs) can be prepared and tracked along with salary grades and steps.

BENEFITS ADMINISTRATION

Managing employee benefits in the federal workplace is becoming more complex as each individual employee has to think about caring for themselves and their families. The baby boomer generation makes up a majority of the workforce. Baby boomers are more concerned about the benefits available to them through their employers. Offerings by organizations are changing and being prioritized differently.

PeopleSoft 7's Benefits for U.S. Federal Government application offers a robust set of federal specific benefits already included in the application. A benefits administrator has the ability to

- Define benefit plans, providers, and rates.
- Provide different types of rates for benefit/price calculations, including age-graded and service-step.
- Establish calculation and rounding rules for the determination of coverage amounts.
- Set up deferral percentages, flat dollar amounts, rollover options, and investment choices for savings plans, including the Thrift Savings Plan (TSP).
- Maintain information about dependents and beneficiaries.
- Dynamically calculate Federal Employee Group Life Insurance (FEGLI) basic coverage and premium amounts for wage grade employees. (This feature works with PeopleSoft's Federal Payroll product.)
- Arrange, track, and validate FEGLI living benefit elections for terminally ill employees.
- Manage retroactive benefits and deductions for individuals and groups.

PeopleSoft customers can track past, present, and future benefits for all employees. The Open Season benefit enrollment and event maintenance will provide a time savings to employees. PeopleSoft Benefits Administration for U.S. Federal Government for release 7 provides multiple, concurrent open seasons for FEHB, FEGLI, and TSP enrollments.

TIME AND LABOR

When tracking hourly, salaried, or any other type of employee, an organization needs complete control over time and labor tracking. Time and Labor Tracking is used to report time, interface with a payroll system, and provide information for analysis and reporting.

PeopleSoft has defined time reporting as the recording of any information required by an agency that can be attributed to an individual employee and expressed in hours.

PeopleSoft 7 Time and Labor for U.S. Federal Government gives the customer just that. The customer gets a system that provides a single, consistent, auditable repository of all time-related information. This Time and Labor system is fully integrated with PeopleSoft Human Resources, Benefits Administration, and Payroll for the U.S. Federal Government. Some of the major features of this application are the capabilities to

- Track employee compensatory time earned and taken, without manually sorting through paper files.

- Define how employees' time will be reported and summarized, how payroll will be updated, and how the system is presented to your time collectors and administrators.

- Schedule employees' time before they perform the work and future-post known exceptions.

- Distribute payroll expense back to the Employee Time Detail records.

PAYROLL

Whatever the size and diversity of your workforce, PeopleSoft Payroll provides all the tools you need to run an efficient payroll operation: calculate earnings and deductions, maintain balances, and report payroll data to external systems such as Department of Treasury, Office of Personnel Management (OPM), and Thrift Savings Board.

PeopleSoft's Payroll product is based on *paysheets*, PeopleSoft's online timesheet. Paysheets are used by both the Payroll and Time and Labor applications. With paysheets, you can view, enter, and change payroll information. The information in paysheets can be entered directly into the Time and Labor system or loaded into payroll from an external system.

PeopleSoft Payroll can calculate federal overtime and compensatory time (including locality adjustments) and Fair Labor Standards Act (FLSA). The system can apply them to employees paid for a specific number of hours—as well as to employees paid both an hourly rate and a piece rate—for weekly and biweekly frequencies.

Other features are

- Administration of mass changes, along with calculations on retroactive pay. Balances can be maintained by calendar, fiscal, or benefits year, or by another method.

- Scheduling of payments (SF1166), which authorizes the Treasury to disburse payments, can be generated.

- Calculation of Federal Employee Health Benefits (FEHB) premiums for part-time and temporary employees.

- Tracking and dating of U.S. Savings Bond purchases.

- Generation of monthly reports on workforce utilization SF-113A and SF113G.

- Multiagency processing, including a common paymaster.

These are only a few of the federal specifications that PeopleSoft has included in its version 7 Payroll for the U.S. Federal Government. If an agency wants to process its payroll from a service bureau and not in-house, PeopleSoft has developed the PeopleSoft 7 Payroll Interface for U.S. Federal Government.

PAYROLL INTERFACE

PeopleSoft 7 Payroll Interface for U.S. Federal Government was designed as an interface that could transfer data from PeopleSoft human resources application to a service bureau, so that federal employees can receive their paychecks. This interface was designed to be used as a generic template so that agencies can create their own customized interface to the system they choose. This way, each agency will not have to reinvent the wheel and start from scratch.

Interfaces can be extremely complicated and can take many hours of development time to create. PeopleSoft has taken that tedious process and created this template to help customers advance by leaps and bounds. This interface allows users to

- Create an external interface file formatted to the specifications of the specific payroll provider
- Export earnings and deduction information from the PeopleSoft HRMS database to their third-party payroll system or service bureau
- Import individual paycheck detail and balance data from any third-party payroll system to the PeopleSoft database

FUTURE PLANS

PeopleSoft's goal is to continue to make sure new functionality developed for its commercial customers is also made available in the federal marketplace. In addition, PeopleSoft will be developing new features specifically for federal agencies.

PeopleSoft works closely with its federal customer base to enhance its software packages. Customers participate in organized focus groups. These groups always have a facilitator and a scribe to capture all the information. These focus groups discuss the direction that the products will take. The outcome is taken to PeopleSoft's product strategy and development organizations to be evaluated and used in future development of the product. Customer feedback is used continually in the enhancement and development of PeopleSoft applications.

CUSTOMER SERVICES

- Account Management services is available for all federal customers. Account Managers are located in the PeopleSoft Bethesda, Dallas, and California offices.
- Professional Consulting Services are available for all federal customers.
- Education Services: Scheduled education courses are currently available in Bethesda. These include the following:

PART

II

CH

14

- Introduction to Federal Human Resources—Release 7
- PeopleTools I—Release 7.5
- PeopleTools 2—Release 7.5
- PeopleTools Overview—Release 7.5
- Introduction to Federal Benefits
- Federal Benefits Administration
- Overview of Federal Human Resources
- Federal Recruitment
- Federal Payroll

These courses are also offered onsite at the customers request.

■ Global Support Center

PeopleSoft Federal now has global support hubs in Pleasanton and Teaneck, NJ, with global support personnel staffing hotlines in both these locations.

Global support works closely with the PeopleSoft federal account management team, who act as the customers' voice. They work together to monitor critical cases and incidents, and act on resolving them for customers. Communication is a key factor in assisting customers in having a successful implementation of the PeopleSoft products they have chosen.

SUMMARY

PeopleSoft is always looking toward the future. The future holds many more releases of the applications and tools that drive the product. Some enhancements PeopleSoft is looking toward are vast and interesting. Perhaps this tour through PeopleSoft in a Federal Human Resource capacity has illustrated the vast potential of PeopleSoft.

CHAPTER 15

PEOPLESOFT FOR THE PUBLIC SECTOR

In this chapter *by Randy Tucker*

MANAGEMENT BUSINESS PROCESS WORKFLOW

At the heart of workflow lies the desire to create a more efficient and competitive operation. Workflow tools are designed to reduce operational costs and business process cycle—or even manufacturing cycle—times through automation of transaction handling and responsibilities associated with steps in a business process. Although a Workflow Engine is by definition a technology tool to facilitate business process automation, workflow itself is a marriage of technology tools and business process design—one influencing, but not driving, the other.

Successful implementation of business process workflow is the result of three principal areas of focus: business process analysis, the understanding and utilization of technology tools, and the ability to measure and monitor the resulting business process performance. PeopleSoft provides tools and services for the entire process of workflow implementation. The Business Process Designer tool is used to model your business process and provides graduated layers of granularity that support a methodical approach to business process design. The Workflow Engine facilitates the automation aspects and runtime results of system events. The Workflow Administrator tool enables you to define and manage business process rules as well as monitor process performance.

UNDERSTANDING YOUR OBJECTIVE

First, it is crucial to understand your objective. Are you launching a global re-engineering effort or implementing less radical isolated business process improvements? Considering this enables you to prepare your organization for the process and effects of this type of effort. At any level, re-engineering will, to some degree, be best accomplished by anticipating, sponsoring, and ultimately embracing change in the way your organization operates today. Although it is possible to automate existing business processes with workflow tools and achieve process performance improvement, larger performance improvements can be realized by taking a hard look at the rules that govern your business tasks and establishing a willingness to change them.

PROTOTYPING A BUSINESS PROCESS MODEL

PeopleSoft provides a tool called Business Process Designer, which enables you to design and illustrate a schematic diagram of a business process from start to finish. With PeopleSoft applications, this diagram serves three purposes. It provides a prototyping and design tool, provides definition for the runtime behavior of the Workflow Engine, and provides end users with an intuitive navigation alternative to the standard pull-down menus. The following are definitions that will help you understand the discussion on business process design:

> Business process—A procurement process, for example, is a collection of activities that define the process of requesting, approving, purchasing, and reconciling receipt.

Activity map—In the example of the procurement business process, you explored a number of activities. Requisition and the rules you have established for approval are an activity. An activity map is a diagram that illustrates the basic process flow within an activity.

Step map—A step map is a diagram that establishes the relationship between an event and an associated routing or routings. Additionally, a step map provides an alternative to pull-down menus and provides a graphical navigator for the end user.

Event—An event is a condition that is detected on the system. Detection can take place through a number of conventions that you will learn about later. But for now, understand that events can be an online event, such as the creation or change action by an end user, or a batch or background event, such as aging invoices.

Rule—Rules are used to define the path that a transaction or task will take when it is detected as an event. For example, a rule specifies that all requisitions are subject to approval by various levels (or roles) of authority in your organization. Rules also are used to define the level of authority associated with each role.

Routing—When an event takes place on the system, workflow uses a routing to tell somebody that something needs to be done. Routings come in three forms that will be presented in more detail later. But for now, consider that routings can be as simple as an email notification or as complex as an electronic transmission to another system.

As a process design tool, the Business Process Designer provides four levels of detail. The operator of the tool is presented with a palette of symbols and shapes that are dragged into a business diagram. Shapes can represent business processes on the whole or they can represent every activity and step through the process.

The highest level of detail is the business process map and is used to represent how the various individual business processes fit together in your enterprise. The next level of detail is an activity map. The activity map shows a more detailed look at each business process defined and illustrates, at a summary level, the various activities that make up a business process. The next level is the step map. Step maps provide a detailed illustration of the individual tasks within an activity. In addition, a step map provides a graphic illustration of the results of various types of events that take place within an activity. In other words, a step defines an event within an activity and directs the Workflow Engine to route information as a result of the event. At the most detailed level, the Business Process Designer provides the ability to apply properties to steps, events, and routings within a step map. It is here, at the step properties level that you specify the characteristics of the Workflow Engine.

BUSINESS PROCESS NAVIGATOR

The conventional method for accessing functions involves locating the appropriate menu and selecting it from the toolbar, and then locating the proper panel group within the menu and selecting it as well. This process has worked fine for years for users that have been trained on the navigation and location of functions within PeopleSoft.

When you define a step map, PeopleSoft automatically builds an intuitive alternative to the conventional method for navigating to the various steps that make up a business process. This alternative is called the *Navigator*. The navigator provides a graphical representation of a business process and provides a shortcut link to each step in the process. It enables you to see the "big picture." You can see the next step along the way, and a single click of a button takes you directly to the next required function. It is the same concept as a Web browser, where you rely on graphics to provide an intuitive means to get users to the most appropriate function.

Don't worry—even though the Business Process Designer automatically builds a navigation view, you still have the ability to select which processes will be available via the online navigator. In addition, the navigator takes advantage of your existing security setup. For example, when users are accessing functions by using the links on the business process diagram, they are subject to the same security and authorization schema as any other PeopleSoft operator. So users see the entire business process, including steps outside their span of permissions. If they try to link to a function that they do not have access to in the PeopleSoft operator security profiles, they will not be allowed to access the function.

Using the navigator is easy. It is invoked by using a toolbar icon that appears on the user desktop. The same icon is used to toggle between the navigator view and the menu view. When the navigator view has been launched, users click on the visual icons that represent specific events, or use a Next Step or Prev Step icon to move through the process.

UNDERSTANDING THE WORKFLOW ENGINE

The PeopleSoft Workflow Engine is the tools' ability to invoke runtime routings based on business events. Recall from the earlier discussion on Business Process Designer that an event is a condition that the system has detected. A routing is the transmission of information or responsibility to another person or system. In other words, the Workflow Engine facilitates a routing as a result of a business event. In order to understand how this is accomplished, you need to look at the components that make up the Workflow Engine.

WORKFLOW EVENTS

Events can be generated from a number of different sources. An event may be defined as a transaction entered or changed by a user, or an automatic event can be generated by the system. PeopleSoft provides the ability to place conditional logic around every event, regardless of its origin. An event is defined using PeopleCode. The advantage to using PeopleCode is that each event can be defined with conditional logic based on related field values or environmental conditions. Let's use an easy example. You would like to send an email routing to the human resources department as notification that an employee has made a change to his personal data profile. Using Peoplecode, you are able to distinguish between an "add" action and a "change" action. The logic in your PeopleCode would read like this:

```
If User action is "Change"
Then     Trigger a workflow routing to notify HR
End if
```

WORKFLOW ONLINE AGENTS

Workflow PeopleCode gets executed any time a record is saved using a PeopleSoft panel. Its easy to understand, then, how a user could trigger a workflow routing based on an event resulting from his or her use of a PeopleSoft panel. PeopleSoft refers to this type of online trigger as an *online agent*. Online agents are people using the Online panel interface to the PeopleSoft application.

Earlier, we explained that it is possible to create routings based on events from other types of system events as well—namely, database conditions or system interface transactions. To accomplish this, PeopleSoft has defined two additional types of agents and provides an architecture for providing workflow capability to them. A distinct advantage to PeopleSoft's approach is that all the agents rely on the same objects used to define your applications and business processes. The result is a consolidated set of application definitions and business process definitions, which means less to maintain when your business changes and less to upgrade.

WORKFLOW DATABASE AGENTS

Database agents are used when you need the system to evaluate the condition of transaction in your database and trigger a routing as a result. For example, a database agent can be used to scan your database every day looking for employees that are soon due for a performance or salary evaluation. This fantastic tool enables you to prevent data or transactions from becoming lost in the business process and keeps activities from falling through the cracks by automatically scanning the database at user-definable intervals. Because the database agent can be defined to run at intervals of everything—seconds, hours, days, weeks, or on-demand—they are suitable for tasks such as monitoring inventory levels in a manufacturing setting and proactive management of your work force.

QUERY, MAP DEFINITION, AND EVENT DEFINITION

There are three basic components to a database agent: a query, a map definition, and an event definition. This section explains how it works.

Using the Query tool, rows are selected from the database that match any criteria. The query can be a simple or complex query. This enables you to evaluate the database for just about any wild-eyed criteria you can imagine. The basic rule is: If you can return a row (or rows) using the Query tool, you can use the query in a database agent definition. Queries are then scheduled to run at intervals defined using the PeopleSoft Process Scheduler. PeopleSoft has provided a way to specify whether a query is a database agent query or a normal one. The reason for this distinction is that rows returned by a database agent query are handled differently than other types of queries.

Rows returned by a database agent query are processed one-by-one, through a map definition that takes each of the fields returned by the query and maps them into fields on an existing PeopleSoft panel. The database agent actually simulates a user in this fashion. Behind the scenes, it processes a panel in user simulation mode, using the returned fields from the query as keys for locating a specific row within the database. When the database agent saves the panel, the workflow PeopleCode that was used to define an event is executed. Events are triggered just as an online agent. In fact, it can be the same event definition used by online agents. This is an example of how PeopleSoft helps consolidate your application definition and business processing rules by sharing definition objects.

WORKFLOW MESSAGE AGENTS

Message agents are used when there is a need to exchange transactions with tools, applications, or a database that is considered a third party to PeopleSoft. The reality is that your information infrastructure is made up of many systems, databases, and applications that must communicate with one another. It is not sufficient to simply effect an interface from one system to another because a single business process may weave in and out of several existing systems during the life cycle of a business process. Moreover, PeopleSoft is dedicated to "working in your world," which means that it has provided a way to extend the functionality and value of the PeopleSoft applications to users who don't normally interact directly with the PeopleSoft applications. As an example, let's say that acquisitions for real estate need to be approved by an assigned member on your board of directors. In this case, the transaction starts in PeopleSoft, needs to be approved, and then flows to the another part of your organization for execution. Can you really expect that your board members understand how to go into PeopleSoft and perform an approval? Message agents enable you to take a transaction out of PeopleSoft and place it into a form that is best suited to the person or system responsible for the next action in the business process. In our example of the board member approval, it might be appropriate to convert a requisition approval to an electronic form that is distributed using your email system. This person would simply execute his or her approval (or denial) of the requisition using the electronic form, which would then flow right back into PeopleSoft for further processing.

A message agent can be best described as an interface channel to or from PeopleSoft that is tied to workflow events defined using PeopleCode. Are you surprised? PeopleSoft has provided a library of call programming routines that enable custom APIs to engage the message agent and process transactions through it. The advantage to using the message agent channel over a direct update to the database is that the message agent will take the transaction and process it as an online user would. It works much the same way as the database agent. Fields are mapped from the inbound transaction to PeopleSoft fields that are processed in user simulation mode. As transactions are saved using the message agent, PeopleCode is executed and any defined workflow event is triggered as a result. For transactions traveling from the PeopleSoft application to external applications, each field is mapped from the PeopleSoft application to the corresponding fields defined in the outbound API.

To summarize, there are three types of agents that are designed to accommodate the real world of business process flow. The agents handle online interaction, database conditions, and inbound or outbound interface requirements. All the agents leverage the existing application definition by processing PeopleCode in order to trigger routings as a result of defined workflow events. Because PeopleCode is used, conditional logic can be placed around the definition of each event.

ROUTINGS

Now that you have learned about events and the various ways to trigger them, it is an opportune time to talk about what you do with an event when it occurs. An event can generate a workflow routing. There can be any number of routings attached to a single business event. Routings can take on a number of different forms depending on how you conduct business. "Working in your world" means that several different types of routings need to be available so that you can provide the most suitable notification for the ergonomics of your organization. As each routing is described, keep in mind that there is some overlap in what each routing accomplishes. Choosing which routing is most appropriate should be driven primarily by its success in motivating information through your business processes.

EMAIL ROUTINGS

Email routings are the simplest to understand. They serve as a simple notification that an event has occurred on the system. PeopleSoft provides the ability to compose an email message using a combination of free text, transaction field values, and database field values. The Workflow Engine assembles the content of the message and dynamically establishes the recipient based on route control criteria. You'll learn more about route control criteria later. Using an email routing, it is easy to notify people that an event has taken place on the system. Using the earlier example of an employee performance evaluation, managers can be notified, using an email, that a performance appraisal will be due on a given date for a specific employee. Using a more esoteric example, an email could provide notification of system events, such as the successful completion of time-critical background processes and interfaces. If the email system supports paging, an administrator could be paged when system events occur. At the time of this writing, PeopleSoft has provided an API as part of the product that supports email messages to MAPI-compliant email systems. Invocation of the API is built into the product as delivered.

FORM ROUTINGS

Form routings enable people who do not have access or the desire to interact directly with PeopleSoft to actively participate in the business process. Like an email routing, a form routing enables you to define the contextual aspects of the form by mixing text, transaction, and database field data on the form. The difference is that a form routing provides a structure to accept an action executed by the recipient and process it back into the PeopleSoft application. In the case of an approval being executed by a member of the board of directors, a form is routed to the appropriate board member via route controls. The form provides background and context that is pertinent to the approval and provides a convention for approval or denial of the requisition. Certainly a form could enable the recipient to change data and add content as well. By selecting a form button that implies approval, the transaction is sent back to PeopleSoft and the business process continues.

WORKLIST ROUTINGS

Worklist routings can be viewed as an electronic To Do list. The worklist is presented to users by evaluating items placed into worklist tables as business events occur. When an event takes place on the system, an entry is placed into a database table that essentially serves three purposes. At the simplest level, this row serves as a list of actions that a user is responsible for performing to enable the business process to continue and contains fields that describe each task. The worklist also provides instant access to the PeopleSoft functions required for execution of a given task. So, in addition to containing fields that describe the action to the user, the worklist tables also contain information that enables a user to access a specific function by selecting the task on a worklist interface panel. The aspect of the worklist supports workflow administration. Conventions have been provided to ensure that tasks are selected or worked in user-defined orders of priority. It also provides for keeping track of the status of each worklist entry. Lastly, the Workflow Engine places a time stamp on each entry as it enters a worklist table or as it is worked. This time stamp provides useful information later, when you perform analysis on the efficiency of your business processes.

The underlying motive for workflow is efficiency. PeopleSoft recognized that asking the system to assign tasks to individual users based on predetermined criteria is not always best suited to streamlining your business. Often, a workforce is more fluid, with departments sharing the responsibility for a pool of tasks rather than assigning each task to a single user. For this reason, there are two types of worklist supported by the PeopleSoft product: *pooled* and *nonpooled*.

Email, forms, and both types of worklists are routed to the appropriate user, or users dynamically using route controls. The difference between a pooled and a nonpooled worklist is that a nonpooled worklist is dynamically assigned to a specific person within your organization. A nonpooled worklist is assigned to a role within your organization, which may be occupied by an entire group of people assigned to that role. This enables an entire department to work off a pooled set of tasks.

INTRANET/WEB ROUTINGS

PeopleSoft provides a native architecture that supports extending PeopleSoft worklists, panels, and queries to Web users. Chapter 18, "PeopleSoft and Supply Chain," discusses the PeopleSoft Web strategy in more detail, but it is important to view the Web technology as part of an overall workflow solution. Panel interfaces can be used to replace electronic forms for entry functions. Worklists are dynamic on the Web and show a real-time list of activities that must be performed by a pool or by an individual user. Again, the technique you choose should be based on its capability of successfully streamlining your business process. One of the big advantages to leveraging the Web for workflow solutions is the ability to include other enterprise partners in your business process solution. So far, we have explored using your own employee population as the main participants in a business process. The Web enables you to expand this perspective to include vendors, customers, and other value-added network partners into the business process. Even if it is simply to check the status of a transaction or order, the Web minimizes the manual aspects of providing this information and perhaps makes you a more appealing—and therefore competitive—business partner.

ROLES AND ROLE USERS

The Workflow Engine uses roles and route controls to determine which person or group of people is identified as the target recipient of workflow routings. It is a profoundly powerful tool that is the heart of the dynamic aspects of PeopleSoft workflow. A thorough understanding of these conventions enables you to implement workflow solutions that will embrace your changing business process and a fluid workforce with a minimal amount of hands-on maintenance. The PeopleSoft approach provides the ability to form complex metrics for determining how a transaction is routed. The three principles of this concept are roles, rules, and route controls. First, let's examine role definitions.

ROLE DEFINITIONS

A role in your organization can be described as a capacity within your organization. A role user is a person who is assigned to a role. An example of a role is a manager, vice president, or senior vice president. Of course, your organization may have several, if not many, individuals who serve within each capacity. Because your organization is evolving, a person in one role today might not be in the same role a week from now. For this reason, PeopleSoft has enabled you to define two types of roles.

A static role is a hard-coded relationship between a role and a role user. When a static role is defined, a single individual role user is defined as the role. As a result, when an event is triggered that generates a routing to a static role, the routing will always be sent to the individual identified as the static role role user.

A dynamic role is different because there is no role user assigned directly to the role. Instead, the Workflow Engine first determines which role a transaction should be routed to and then determines the target role user by a more sophisticated metrics of queries and route control definition.

BUSINESS RULE DEFINITION

Although it is possible to use PeopleCode to trigger events based upon certain conditions, business rules can be defined using the PeopleSoft tool. This tool enables you to minimize the amount of customization made to PeopleCode modules and places business rule information into tables that are more gracefully upgraded and maintained. This tool enables you to specify rules that govern what the operating thresholds of each role are within a given business process. When a business event calls the Virtual Approver, the Workflow Engine evaluates the rules and thresholds defined in order to determine what to do with the transaction. Each rule provides the ability to direct the Workflow Engine to a specific routing as a result of transaction field values and action taken by the user.

A requisition may be subject to approval based on its dollar amount, for example. Your controller and your internal audit department have determined that a requisition that totals $1,000 must be approved by a manager, a requisition that totals $1,000 to $10,000 must be approved by a vice president, and anything over that amount must be approved by a senior vice president. Because requisitions are created by employees, the role user in the appropriate role is notified that he or she is responsible for a requisition approval. Should the role user approve or deny the requisition, notification routings can be sent out accordingly.

The Virtual Approver enables you to specify the approval path for transactions, along with any business event processes that should be triggered as a result of role user actions. Remember that transactions can be approved, denied, or demoted in an approval chain. Each action constitutes events and may have various types of routings attached to it. The Virtual Approver supports multiple and parallel paths through an approval process. Although our example focused exclusively on total dollar amount, the Virtual Approver can base approval limits on field values or combinations of field values, including dollar amounts.

ROUTE CONTROLS

Let's pick up the example of the employee evaluation that is almost due. The scenario is that you have built a database agent that locates employees in your database who have a performance evaluation due next month. You know that that a manager is the appropriate role to notify that the appraisal is almost due. The question is, which of the many managers in your organization is the correct one?

Route controls establish the relationship between dynamic roles such as manager and the appropriate role user assigned to a role. Using route controls, you are able to create profiles that associate ranges of field values to a role user. In our example, a manager may have several departments that he or she is responsible for. A route control profile can be constructed to represent the range of departments that should be grouped for this specific purpose. One view of a collection of departments might be appropriate for employee evaluations, and another collection of departments might be appropriate for requisition approvals. As each route control profile is defined, it can be assigned to a specific role user within the system. At this point, you are pretty close to having the whole picture. You know you have an employee with an evaluation due next month, and you have managers who are assigned to a range of departments that are defined exclusively for the purpose of workforce administration. The only remaining activity is to ascertain which department the employee belongs to and compare it with the route control profiles you have built.

The process for doing this brings us back to a convention introduced when we explored the various routing types. For each of the routing types, you define the contents of each routing with text, transaction field values, or database field values. The convention is referred to as mapping fields. One of the fields that is present on all of the routing types is the target of the routing. In other words, for each routing you need to use information from the transaction to determine how to map the appropriate recipient name into the routing field that specifies the routing target. Although it is possible to map a hard-coded name into the target recipient field, this convention is rarely useful. The best way to establish the recipient of a routing is to use a query to identify the role user associated to the transaction by comparing data on the transaction to route control profiles you have established and the role users assigned to the route control profile. While doing this, it is possible to mix route control profile definitions with other application tables to determine the appropriate target for any given routing.

WORKFLOW ADMINISTRATION

Now that you have had an overview of how to automate your business processes with workflow, you should have a look at how best to maintain it once it is up and alive. PeopleSoft provides tools to perform everyday workflow administration for business rule definitions, role maintenance, role user maintenance, and routing maintenance.

BUSINESS RULE DEFINITION

Business rules are defined and maintained by a function that organizes business process rules by business process name. The procurement business process, for example, is organized into a series of rule steps. Each step contains information that specifies what the upper limit is for approval and what the appropriate routing event is based on particular user actions. This function enables your workflow administrator to add, change, or simplify existing business processing rules without fussing with the application code. As with other PeopleSoft functions, this function can be secured by providing access to your workflow administrator only via PeopleSofts Security Administration.

ROLE MAINTENANCE

Role maintenance enables your workflow administrator to add or change roles defined on your system. This simple function enables you to define both static and dynamic role definitions.

ROLE USER MANAGEMENT

There are several functions that are provided to maintain role users within the system. Each role user record has data associated with it that enables workflow to know the email address, employee ID, and other user-specific field values. So the first function provides the ability to locate a specific role user by role user name. This function will present the individual profile for each role user. Role user maintenance is also where you will define the relationship between role user and assigned roles. PeopleSoft has provided a function that enables you to locate role users by the role they are assigned and quickly place them into another role or remove them from an existing role. This function is especially useful when working with groups of role users rather than specific users.

Using these functions, your workflow administrator is able to make temporary changes in role user assignments to accommodate promotions, terminations, short or long leaves of absence, or temporary assignments.

ROUTING MAINTENANCE

The workflow administration functionality provides the ability to monitor the status of worklist routings. For example, your workflow administrator has the ability to view bottlenecks in a business process and redirect routings. There are a number of tools available to the workflow administrator in this regard. Worklist entries may be individually reassigned to other workflow users at the administrator's discretion. But for those processes that are prone to bottleneck as a result of fluid work force, poor individual performance, and spikes in workload, PeopleSoft has provided a timeout routing facility.

A worklist timeout routing enables the workflow administrator to automatically take a worklist entry from one role user worklist and generate another routing as a result. Timeout thresholds are completely user-definable and can be adjusted for a tolerance of minutes, hours, days, and so on. Using this convention, bottlenecks can be detected automatically and redistributed appropriately.

PROCESS PERFORMANCE MEASUREMENT

Remember that the whole reason for doing this in the first place was to make your business operate more efficiently. Process performance measurement provides the ability to evaluate improvements your workflow implementation effort has yielded. PeopleSoft workflow creates routings as a result of a business event, and we have established that any given event can have any number of routings attached to it. Workflow administrators are attaching worklists to events in a business process that create a virtual worklist. In this way, an event creates a time-stamped worklist entry that is routed to a fictitious role user in the organization. This routing does not hold up the business process, but it creates an entry that represents a point in time that the event occurred.

The virtual worklist becomes a probe. By placing a series of probes at strategic points along a business process path, workflow administrators are able to use queries and graphs to represent process performance and analysis trends. This is accomplished by relating entries and their corresponding time stamps with each other.

Using this convention, you will be able to prove statistically and graphically, that the procurement process that used to average 2 1/2 weeks, end-to-end, now averages four days. You will be able to better anticipate trends in workload to proactively reallocate your work force. You will be able to measure your work force's ability to handle volume, and increase or decrease accordingly. The capacity for workflow to support statistical analysis is enormous, with almost limitless possibilities. Best of all, PeopleSoft provides all the tools needed to perform this type of analysis. The PeopleSoft query tool has access to the PeopleSoft workflow tables and has the capability of exporting data into report format or Excel spreadhsheets.

SUMMARY

By now you have an understanding of the moving parts that make up the Workflow Engine. Events are embodied in business process definitions and can create routings of various types. Events can be triggered from a number of different sources and as a result produce a routing. Routings enable us to communicate a responsibility or transaction to a person or system by evaluating business rules and route control definitions. Route control definitions enable you to create complex decision metrics to determine the proper recipient of a particular routing. It's as simple as that.

There are many ways to achieve business process automation using PeopleSoft workflow tools. There are several workable solutions for any given business process scenario. When prototyping solutions, it is critical to keep a foot in each camp by considering the ergonomics and tendencies of your work force and the impact and benefit technology solutions will provide. It is an art that demands a special instinct for blending both these perspectives.

CHAPTER 16

PEOPLESOFT WEB-ENABLED APPLICATIONS AND ELECTRONIC DATA INTERCHANGE

In this chapter   *by Ramaswany Rajagopal*

The business processing environment has undergone a revolution in the current decade with the advent of globalization. The changes to business processing were complicated by the need to adjust to rapid changes in technology. Also, this decade saw the need for most businesses to remedy problems created by applications that are unable to handle the century change, commonly known as the *Y2K bug*. These factors allowed application software providers to develop products based on the industry's best practices and capture the imagination of the industry.

A major change to the business process involves opening the application to the source of data. The source of data can be internal or external to the organization, which can be another user or application. Prior to this paradigm shift, the applications were accessible to only a chosen few within the organization, which led to a large amount of information redundancy. The opening of applications has been speeded up with rapid innovations in technology, which include client/server applications and the Internet. This has been made possible by the advent of networking, both Local Area Networks (LAN) and Wide Area Networks (WAN). These ensure speed and, most importantly, security between the connections. PeopleSoft was the first Enterprise Resource Planning (ERP) solution that pioneered and delivered its product using client/server architecture from its very first release.

However, ERP solutions are not always sufficient to meet all business needs. The trend that all the ERP solution providers, including PeopleSoft, are following is to provide access points to their applications.

PeopleSoft's strategy is to extend the product by providing tools to accomplish various user requirements, as illustrated in Figure 16.1. The tools enable communication between PeopleSoft and external applications, or in some cases, enable the application to be viewed using methods other than PeopleSoft panels.

Figure 16.1
PeopleSoft's Internet communication process.

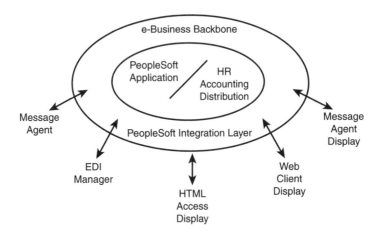

This chapter discusses the tools offered by PeopleSoft to facilitate the following:

- Access to PeopleSoft panels and associated business logic using message agents
- Web clients to facilitate intranet and Internet access to PeopleSoft panels
- Electronic Data Interchange (EDI) to transfer data between internal and external applications

MESSAGE AGENT

PeopleSoft panels, the online processing points to the PeopleSoft application, are a combination of user entry, validation rules, and business logic. The panels are stored in PeopleTools tables in the database. The panels and associated PeopleCode are extracted and executed by the PeopleSoft client in a two-tier configuration and a combination of PeopleSoft application server and client in a three-tier configuration. Access to PeopleSoft panels is accomplished through the use of the Message Agent API in conjunction with the message definition. This approach allows the panels and the associated business logic to be reused and integrated into applications other than PeopleSoft. The Message Agent architecture was first introduced in version 5 of PeopleSoft and has been converted to run as part of the three-tier architecture in PeopleSoft version 7.5.

The messages can be sent through an object linking and embedding (OLE) interface, a C function, or Dynamic Data Exchange (DDE). Any programming tool or language that supports these methods can be used to develop the message agent client application. Examples of such programming tools include Microsoft's Visual Basic and Visual C++.

MESSAGE AGENT ARCHITECTURE

The Message Agent architecture is shown in Figure 16.2.

Figure 16.2
The Message Agent
architecture.

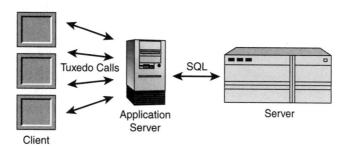

Tuxedo Calls   SQL

Client   Application Server   Server

The Message Agent runs on the PeopleSoft application server as another server (PSAPIS-RV) and processes the requests from external clients. The key components of the PeopleSoft Message Agent are as follows:

- Clients—PeopleSoft Message Agent client programs that have been developed using OLE, DDE, or C function calls.
- PeopleSoft Message Agent server (PSAPISRV)—A UNIX or Windows NT machine containing BEA's Tuxedo middleware product and running PeopleSoft server and PeopleSoft message agent server processes.
- PeopleSoft Database Server—Running any of the supported RDBMS/platform combinations.

MESSAGE AGENT FUNCTIONALITY

The Message Agent allows access to a PeopleSoft panel group by an external application using a message agent API. For the message agent to be functional, the following four steps must be completed:

1. A panel group must be designed or identified.
2. A message definition for the application that the Message Agent is to use must have been created or defined. A *message definition* allows the client programs to access PeopleSoft panel groups. The message definition is created using the Application Designer and allows the fields in the PeopleSoft panels to be populated from the client programs. The Application Designer is one of the development tools used to develop the PeopleSoft application and is the primary tool for defining PeopleSoft records, fields, views, and panels.
3. Develop Message Agent client programs using the Message Agent APIs. The Message Agent API allows the program to connect to the Message Agent server, set input field values, invoke the predefined message definition, retrieve the data returned, process any errors encountered, and close the connection. A large number of calls make up the Message Agent APIs, and a number of complex issues are associated with programming some parts of an external program.
4. Establish a connection between the Message Agent client and the application server running the Message Agent server process.

PeopleSoft includes a set of Message Agent definitions with each of its modules, which can be used out of the box.

BENEFITS OF USING MESSAGE AGENT

The Message Agent uses the panels and their associated business logic. In using the Message Agent to create access to external programs, the business logic is reused. This approach facilitates easier upgrades.

The Message Agent facilitates an open application framework, allowing external applications to reuse the PeopleSoft application without circumventing the edit, validation, and data integrity of the product.

The Message Agent server is stateless, meaning that the server does not maintain the status of the processed requests after it is serviced. Each request to the Message Agent server is totally self-contained. The servers can support many request processes, but only one external message agent request is processed at a time. This results in increased reliability and a robust performance of Message Agent clients. The failure of one Message Agent application server as the result of an operation has no effect on other Message Agent client programs.

The Message Agent is automatically linked to the application server, and the application server handles all the administrative functionality. There is no need to manually bring up the Message Agent application or make Message Agent connecting decisions. The PeopleSoft application server even administratively processes automatic restarts when necessary.

Because the PeopleSoft application server administrative process can run multiple copies of the Message Agent at the same time, the result is increased scalability.

LIMITATIONS OF MESSAGE AGENT

The access to the Message Agent server is through the Message Agent clients. This limits the platform on which the client application programs can be developed to Windows 95/98 and Windows NT.

The fact that the Message Agent is accessed using panel groups limits the capability of using it for volume or batch processing, because it will not meet the performance needs.

Upward compatibility is limited. The Message Agent architecture and API have undergone significant re-engineering since they were first released. As a result of the changes, the applications that were developed in earlier versions have to be modified as the PeopleSoft version is upgraded.

Many PeopleSoft application panels include one or more scrollbars, which enable them to display data from more than one row of data at a time. The application panels display more than one row when they are opened in an Update/Display All or Correction mode in PeopleSoft. For example, when you want to update more than one customer, you use the Maintain Customers panel with a selection criteria that brings up multiple rows. When you access such a panel using the Message Agent, you have access to multiple rows of data. The Message Agent can add or update only one row of data at a time. So, to add or update multiple rows inside a scroll, you will need to make repeated calls to process the message.

PeopleSoft 7.5 must be configured in a three-tier mode in order to use message agents.

TOOLS INTEGRATING MESSAGE AGENTS

NetDynamics and One Wave provide Web solutions to PeopleSoft customers who want to build Web applications or extend PeopleSoft applications using a single enterprise wide intranet tool. They access PeopleSoft applications through the PeopleSoft Message Agent, which contains the business rules that manage the integrity of the databases. You can get more information on NetDynamics at `www.netdynamics.com` and OneWave at `www.primix.com`.

REVIEW

Message Agent is the tool to integrate external applications to PeopleSoft. PeopleSoft has expanded the capabilities and performance of this tool since it was first introduced in version 5.0 and will continue to expand its capabilities. The pressure is on the ERP vendors to provide an open system that easily integrates with other applications. Other software vendors such as Siebel and Vantive integrate their CRM package to PeopleSoft using this technology. In this section, you saw a utility that extends PeopleSoft's capabilities by integrating to other applications. The next section addresses extending PeopleSoft applications to the source of the data, both within the organization (employees) and outside the organization (customers, suppliers).

PEOPLESOFT WEB CLIENT

The significant changes to technology have widened the reach of applications by extending access to the source of data. One of the key technologies that enables such a change is the Internet/intranet. This is possible because of the rapid improvement in the communication medium, in terms of both speed and security. As the technology improves, more organizations will be comfortable in performing real-time transactions online. For example, car manufacturers send purchase orders to their suppliers by programming the inventory monitoring application to generate a purchase order automatically when stock of the part depletes to certain configured levels. PeopleSoft delivers the extension to the product through Web-enabling the application and delivering a subset of the application on a Web client. The list of transactions that are available through the Web client is published in PeopleBooks. The Web client supports Universal Applications and extends workflow to the Web. It is also designed for seamless integration into existing corporate intranets. A Web client connection requires that a supported browser is installed on the workstation, and it requires access to a Web server containing PeopleSoft HTML and Java applets.

PeopleSoft n-tier architecture is based on the application server(s) used to process client requests. The application server connects to the database server to access the application data and the business logic associated with it, processes the client request, and transmits the result back to the client. The application server and the client use the middleware product from BEA called *Tuxedo*. Tuxedo is an Enterprise Transaction Processing System that provides the environment and features required for Online Transaction Processing (OLTP) applications that deliver enterprisewide, mission-critical services. Normally, the application server and the Windows 95/98 client communicate using Tuxedo Messages that are processed by the application server. The Web client uses the application server to process the request; this is achieved using BEA's Jolt product, which supports Web client connections. Jolt acts as the communications layer between the Java environment and Tuxedo. The PeopleSoft Web client architecture is shown in Figure 16.3.

Figure 16.3
The Web client architecture.

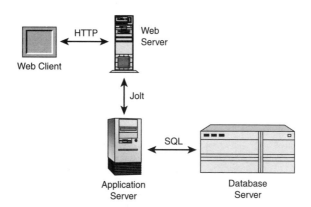

Web clients do not connect directly to the application server, but rather to a specified Jolt port. Jolt acts as the communication layer between the Java and C++ environments. After Jolt passes a Web client request to the application server (Tuxedo), the request is equivalent to a Windows client request. Jolt Internet Relay (JRLY) and Jolt Relay Adapter (JRAD) are companion products that provide a secure way to process Web client transactions over an Internet or intranet connection in cases where the Web server and the application server are on separate machines.

Web Client Connection

Table 16.1 presents an overview of the sequence events that occur within a Web client connection to an application server and the component responsible for each event. The Web client connection is very similar to the Windows client connection except that the client connects to the Java Station Listener (JSL) instead of the WSL. The Web client knows to connect to port 9000, for example, because the port number is hard-coded into the HTML downloaded from the Web site.

TABLE 16.1   EVENTS DURING WEB CLIENT CONNECTION

Event #	Component	Description
1	Client/Browser	Client workstation running a supported browser specifies the URL where the Web page containing the PeopleSoft HTML applet tag resides.

continues

TABLE 16.1   EVENTS DURING WEB CLIENT CONNECTION

Event #	Component	Description
2	Web Server	The Tuxedo Web Listener receives the incoming requests and allows the client to view the desired Web page. The Web page contains the PeopleSoft applet tag that specifies—among other parameters—the Jolt port (server_port) and the self-service application to be executed (CODE=).
3	Client/Browser	The browser downloads the information from the applet tag (server_port and CODE=), which specifies the Jolt port and the self-service application to be executed.
4	Java Station Listener (JSL)	The JSL is the single point of contact for Web clients. It "listens" for client requests, receives them, and distributes connections to the Java Station Handlers.
5	Java Station Handler (JSH)	Receives the transaction request from the JSL and sends the message to the JREPSVR.
6	Jolt Repository (JREPSVR)	The JREPSVR retrieves Jolt service definitions from the Jolt Repository and returns the service definitions to the JSH. The JREPSVR is a BEA process that reformats the Java message for Tuxedo.
7	Tuxedo Bulletin Board Liaison (BBL)	The Tuxedo BBL receives a client request and queues it for a particular PeopleSoft server process.
8	PeopleSoft Service	A PeopleSoft Service processes the queued requests from the BBL and runs SQL against the RDBMS.
9	RDBMS	Processes the SQL request and returns the result to the PeopleSoft Service, which sent the request.

DEPLOYING A WEB CLIENT

The Web client uses the same panels that are developed for a Windows client, which do not have certain features of PeopleTools that are not supported for Web clients. The following six steps must be completed in order to deploy a Web client:

1. Build or modify PeopleSoft panels using the Application Designer.

2. Create a panel group definition and insert the panel into the panel group. This step includes creating a search record.

3. Validate that your panel group or definition does not contain PeopleTools features not supported in a Web client. PeopleSoft has provided a tool as part of the Application Designer to validate the PeopleCode in Web client applications and to check the panel group for valid PeopleCode.

4. Attach the panel group to a menu. (A *panel group* is a set of panels linked together for business process requirements.) Although the menu will not be displayed on the screen, a panel group must exist on a menu and be referenced in the applet tag.

5. Grant security to the panel group. A single menu for all your panel groups will allow for easier deployment and security management. Remember that the Java applets use the same security as your Windows applications.

6. Create an applet tag with parameters it requires in HTML code within the Web page. Copy the applet and HTML to directories that are accessible by the Web server.

BENEFITS OF PEOPLESOFT WEB CLIENT

The Web client uses the same panels and PeopleCode associated with it as the Windows client. This eases the deployment of PeopleSoft applications over the Web.

LIMITATIONS OF PEOPLESOFT WEB CLIENT

PeopleSoft 7.5 must be configured in a three-tier mode in order to use message agents.

All the panels that are available may not be able to be deployed over the Web because some of the PeopleTools functionality is not supported for Web clients.

The JAR file that needs to be transmitted to the Web client in order for the applet to be instantiated is large and performs poorly over low bandwidth networks.

The Web client uses the same security access as the Windows client. Some of the self-service applications require access by a large number of users, and this may require significant effort from the user administrator. However, using the server-side user exits can reduce this effort. The exits expose interfaces that are utilized at the authentication sequence between the Web client and the Tuxedo application server. The first exit (pre-signon dialog) provides the user's signon information while bypassing the PeopleSoft Signon dialog. The second callout (post-signon dialog) applies supplemental authentication information to the PeopleSoft signon information. And the third callout validates the user's signon and authentication information at the application server.

REVIEW

The Web client provides access to occasional users of the PeopleSoft application without having to deploy the complete suite of PeopleSoft Windows client on their desktops. The PeopleTools technology has been designed to deploy most of the application panels to the Web client without the need to redevelop, thus reducing the need for dual development and maintenance. However, the Web client uses the Java applet that requires it to be downloaded to the Web client before execution, which can be stressful to the network. The following section discusses tools that are useful when network bandwidth becomes an issue.

HTML ACCESS

The Web client, as previously identified, requires the applets to be downloaded to the client, which will require reasonable network bandwidth. The low bandwidth is an issue when users try accessing the application from a Wide Area Network, especially in the case of dial-up access. For example, a traveling salesman would like to access the order management system at the customer location to check availability or to place a new order for a product. In most cases, such access is through a dial-up connection resulting in 28K or 56K modem access to the application.

To address the needs of low bandwidth requirements, PeopleSoft has provided a tool called HTML Access. This integration is achieved through a combination of Message Agent and Java Message Agent Client (JMAC). This architecture is shown in Figure 16.4.

Figure 16.4
The JMAC architecture.

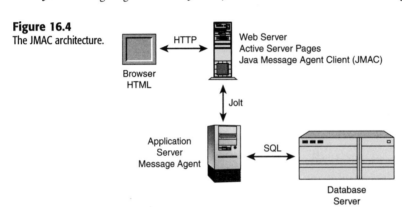

The core part of the architecture is the message agent that runs on the application server. The API provided by the message agent is accessed using the Java Message Agent client that runs on the Web server provided by PeopleSoft.

There are two usages to HTML access:

1. API access—In this usage, the JMAC calls are invoked from HTML pages. The JMAC calls, in turn, connect with the message agent on the application server invoking the appropriate message agent API. The HTML page and all the JMAC API calls have to be developed.

2. Framework Access—In this usage, the active server pages are created and stored in the Web server. These active pages are accessed using HTML pages.

The HTML access provides the user with the flexibility of integrating the data not only from PeopleSoft but also from other application sources. The user interface is developed and customized to user requirements.

Web Clients Versus HTML Access

Web clients and HTML access are the two methods to Web-enable PeopleSoft applications. Table 16.2 explains the key distinctions between the two tools.

Table 16.2   Web Client Versus HTML Access

Web Client	HTML Access
One of the PeopleSoft clients that allows panels to be presented in the Web browser	A tool that allows integrating Message Agent to the Web using Java Message Agent Client
Requires a specific browser as defined in PeopleSoft's product support	Any HTML 3.2 browser
Web clients are panel based	HTML access is forms based
Supported by PeopleSoft upgrade	No upgrade support
PeopleSoft's User Interface	No defined UI
Higher network bandwidth	Low network bandwidth
Available in version 7.0 and higher	Available in version 7.55 and higher

Part

II

Ch

16

Review

HTML access is the tool of choice for deploying PeopleSoft applications over the Web where network bandwidth is an issue. PeopleSoft has delivered the campus community with the Students Administration product using this technology, and it extends direct access to students to perform most of their administrative responsibilities. Prior to the major changes to technology due to the Internet and intranet, electronic communication between organizations was achieved through the technology called *Electronic Data Interchange* (EDI). Many application systems have already incorporated EDI into their processing, and hence ERP vendors such as PeopleSoft continue to provide mechanisms to integrate EDI technology to their application. The following section describes PeopleSoft's EDI integration.

Electronic Data Interchange (EDI)

The previous sections describes methods to integrate PeopleSoft applications with external applications and to provide access to PeopleSoft from a Web browser. One of the major changes that the business has undergone in recent years is that you can manage your commerce with your trading partners electronically. For example, you can submit your purchase orders to your vendor and manage the entire process, including paying for the order, electronically—without any paper changing hands or even contacting your vendor offline. The power of this interchange becomes even more valuable when the entire process can be automated by configurable applications. For example, you can configure your inventory management application to automatically send out purchase orders to your vendors when a part has reached a critical level. This electronic communication opens up a wide possibility for integrating your business to your trading partners.

EDI in a very simplistic sense is a message format that is agreed upon between the trading partners. The message formats are used to define the transaction type, for example, purchase order sent to the vendor, and transaction detail, which has direct relation to the transaction type. As you can see from this simple definition, endless possibilities of transactions can be communicated electronically between the trading partners. However, it is cumbersome for the businesses to agree to a format with each of its vendors. Another implication that has to be considered is that the meaning of the messages changes based on the direction, depending on whether you are transmitting a request (outbound) or receiving a request (inbound). For example, the same message will be a purchase transaction on outbound but will be an order management transaction on inbound. Various organizations have defined standards for EDI. Some of the common formats are as follows:

- ANSI X.12
- EDIFACT
- NACHA (National Automated Clearing House Association)
- BAI (Bankers Administration Institute)

Each of these standards defines the various transaction types, also known as *transaction sets*, that it supports and associated codes to facilitate the transaction details. Each message has significance based on whether it is an inbound or outbound message. Because the transactions that are communicated between trading partners are so different, the standards offer flexibility so that you can customize according to the requirements of the business. Consequentially, the systems developed to use EDI for communication will require adapting to the requirements of each of the trading partners.

PeopleSoft's approach to EDI is to provide a tool to define the transactions with associated translations and an automated agent to process inbound and outbound transactions.

PEOPLESOFT'S EDI ARCHITECTURE

PeopleSoft's EDI architecture is shown in Figure 16.5. The boxes above the dotted line represent services provided by third-party software, including services typically provided by the Value Added Network, which assists in the exchange of EDI transactions. The Value Added Network also provides secure network services for exchanging data between trading partners.

The transactions from the standard EDI formats X.12 or EDIFACT are converted into PeopleSoft Business Document format using the EDI translation software. The PeopleSoft Business Document is a flat file that is recognized by the standard input/output processing utilities provided by PeopleSoft. A PeopleSoft-supplied EDI agent reads the PeopleSoft Business Document files and places their data in staging tables in the PeopleSoft database. An EDI Application Load SQR transfers data from the staging tables to the appropriate application tables. After the data is loaded into the application table, it is similar to any other transaction and processed as such.

Figure 16.5
The EDI architecture.

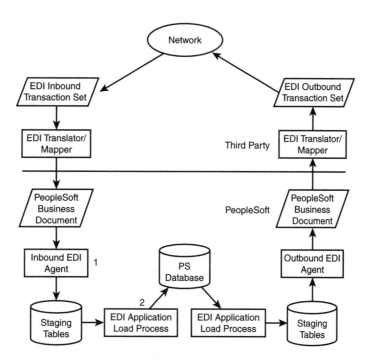

The process for outgoing transactions is similar. A PeopleSoft-supplied SQR is periodically run that extracts the appropriate data from the application tables and copies it to a set of staging tables. An EDI agent creates PeopleSoft Business Documents from this data. The PeopleSoft Business Document is then processed by the EDI translation/mapping program to be converted into standard formats such as X.12 or EDIFACT. The outbound transaction set is not ready to be transmitted to the trading partner.

The PeopleSoft portion of EDI processing has two stages:

1. Copying data from a PeopleSoft Business Document into staging tables in case of inbound transactions or from the staging tables into PeopleSoft Business Document in case of outbound transactions. This is achieved by the EDI agent using the data mappings in the EDI Manager.

2. Transferring the data from the staging tables into the transaction tables, performing the necessary data validations. This is performed by SQRs.

EDI MANAGER

The EDI Manager is the PeopleSoft application used to define the mappings that EDI agents require to convert PeopleSoft Business Documents into data for the staging tables, and vice versa. The EDI Manager is also used to maintain information about your vendors and other trading partners. The staging tables are a temporary storage area for EDI transaction data. When the EDI agent processes a PeopleSoft Business Document, it copies the data into your PeopleSoft database by adding it to the staging tables. Later, a transaction-specific "application load" process transfers the data from the staging tables into the application tables.

Much of the data that is transmitted using EDI is in the form of code and identification numbers. For example, each of your transaction types is assigned a Transaction ID. The application data is also stored in the form of codes by PeopleSoft. Some of these codes and IDs represent the same data as the codes and IDs in the EDI transaction, even though the codes themselves might be different. When the EDI agent processes a transaction, it copies the transaction data into the PeopleSoft database. As it does so, it can convert the external EDI codes into the internal PeopleSoft codes. Similarly, as it writes out the file for an outgoing EDI transaction, it can convert the PeopleSoft codes into codes that your trading partner will recognize. You specify how the EDI agent converts the codes using the EDI Manager.

EDI Manager allows definition of two types of conversion:

- Conversion of EDI event codes to PeopleSoft action codes, and vice versa. The EDI event codes are used to specify the action to be performed by the transaction. There are two types of event codes. *Primary event codes* specify the status of the transaction request (new, duplicate, status request, cancellation, and so on), and *secondary event codes* specify the type of transaction in detail. PeopleSoft has one action code to determine the action to be performed on a transaction. The EDI Manager allows the mapping of the EDI event codes to PeopleSoft action code by assigning a PeopleSoft action code to a combination of primary and secondary event codes.

- The data values that are used by the trading partner in many cases might not match the values in PeopleSoft. To accomplish this task, the EDI Manager provides a utility to define a conversion data profile. A conversion data profile takes the values from a particular PeopleSoft database table (such as the table holding bank transaction codes) and specifies how that value appears in PeopleSoft Business Documents. Multiple conversion data profiles can be created for the same table because you might need to create different conversions for different trading partners. For example, different banks might use different transaction codes.

PEOPLESOFT'S EDI AGENT

EDI agents copy EDI transaction data between PeopleSoft Business Documents and the PeopleSoft database, using the maps described in the preceding chapter. There are two types of EDI agents:

- Inbound EDI agents, which process incoming transactions by copying data from PeopleSoft Business Documents into the database

- Outbound EDI agents, which create PeopleSoft Business Documents from transaction data in the EDI staging tables

Creating EDI maps doesn't start an EDI agent running. You have to submit a Process Scheduler request that tells the system when, where, and how often to run each EDI agent. Apart from copying transaction data, EDI agents can also be set up to perform the following:

- Basic calculations like Averages, Sum, Min, and Max
- Assigning default values to certain fields like current date/time
- Inline data conversion/translation

The EDI agent can be integrated into the workflow to process errors that are detected by the EDI agents and assign them to the appropriate worklist. This is a powerful tool to facilitate timely correction of transaction errors.

The first task for implementing EDI with PeopleSoft is to define mapping for the EDI transactions. Mapping is necessary to extract data from PeopleSoft to create the PeopleSoft business document for outbound transactions and to map the PeopleSoft business document to EDI staging tables for inbound transactions. The following section describes how to map the EDI transactions.

MAPPING EDI TRANSACTIONS

PeopleSoft applications store their transaction data in tables in the PeopleSoft database. For an application to process an EDI transaction, it needs the transaction data in its tables. So, the first step in processing an EDI transaction is to transfer the data from an incoming EDI Transaction Set file into the application tables. Similarly, the first step in generating an EDI transaction for delivery to a trading partner is getting the transaction data out of the application tables into an EDI Transaction Set file.

You specify how the EDI agent transfers data between EDI Transaction Set files and application tables by creating electronic commerce maps. There are two kinds of electronic commerce maps:

- Inbound maps, which transfer incoming transaction data into your PeopleSoft database
- Outbound maps, which create outgoing EDI documents from transaction data in the database

PeopleSoft's EDI agent uses the transactions that are mapped as described, either to extract data from PeopleSoft to create a file called a *PeopleSoft Business Document* or to use the PeopleSoft Business Document to enter data into EDI staging tables. The following section provides a definition of a PeopleSoft Business Document.

PEOPLESOFT BUSINESS DOCUMENT

A PeopleSoft Business Document is an ASCII file containing one or more EDI transactions that can be processed by the EDI agent. The file consists of two types of records: control and transaction. The control record specifies the type of transaction contained in the following lines and the trading partners involved. Based on the control record, the EDI agent retrieves the mapping definition for the specified transaction and the data conversion options relevant to the trading partner. The EDI agent reads the records in the document one at a time. For each record following the control record, the EDI agent reads the value in the Record ID field and uses it to determine which PeopleSoft record definition to use to parse the rest of the record. The PeopleSoft record definition specifies the location, size, and data type of the remaining fields in the record. The EDI agent copies the data from the document into staging tables in the database, following the rules in the mapping definition.

When the EDI agent encounters a new control record—identified by the Record ID 999 or 998—it retrieves the mapping definition for the new transaction type and repeats the process.

Most transactions include a variety of record types: a header, detail lines, schedules, summary lines, and so on. The layout of the records within a PeopleSoft Business Document follows a logical pattern. All detail lines linked to a particular parent or header line must follow the parent record.

The EDI agent processes each transaction as a unit of work that can be rolled back in case of errors, and it is important for each transaction to be a unit of work.

PEOPLESOFT-SUPPLIED EDI TRANSACTIONS

PeopleSoft delivers standard EDI transaction sets for many of its applications, including Purchasing, Order Management, Inventory, Treasury, Billing, Accounts Payable, Accounts Receivable, HRMS, and Students Administration. To use them, you need to do the following:

1. Identify the transaction sets and associated EC maps.
2. Define trading partner profiles.
3. Define data mapping profiles.
4. Define your trading partner and associate them with the trading partner profile and data mapping profile.

In many cases, you may need to define a new set of transactions. This can be achieved using PeopleTools and following these steps:

1. Use PeopleTools to develop the application that processes the transaction. Create the database tables and the panels users need to process the transaction.
2. Define a PeopleSoft Business Document format based on the EDI format for the transaction. At this step, think about how the data from the EDI document needs to map to the application tables.
3. Write a translation program that converts EDI documents into PeopleSoft Document format. Usually, you'll have an EDI Translator program to handle this step.
4. Create staging tables to serve as a temporary holding area between the PeopleSoft Document and the application tables.

5. Create a mapping that copies data between the PeopleSoft Business Documents and the staging tables.

6. Write an application load procedure that transfers data from the staging tables to the application tables.

BENEFITS OF PEOPLESOFT'S EDI SOLUTION

There is more than one industry standard for exchanging data between applications using EDI, which makes the job of application software vendors difficult. The previous sections describe the PeopleSoft EDI solution. They illustrate an approach of extracting data from PeopleSoft and posting data into PeopleSoft using a two-stage approach with staging tables and PeopleSoft business documents. This solution has significant benefits.

The PeopleSoft solution provides a flexible approach to setting up and processing EDI transactions. The EDI transactions consist of codes and vary in format between the trading partners. The EDI Manager utility allows for defining any transformations that are required in order to process transaction requests. It is generic to the extent that with the combination of the EDI agent, it can be used for any data extraction that may be required.

The current version of PeopleSoft supports the files in a comma-delimited format for both inbound and outbound transactions.

The EDI agent can be set up to communicate errors through workflow worklists, allowing a control process to be set up to correct errors.

SUMMARY

This chapter covers the PeopleSoft solution to electronic commerce. In summary, the PeopleSoft solution is to provide integration tools to open the application. These tools enable the external applications to access the PeopleSoft panels and associated business logic. This is accomplished by a combination of message agent server and client programs with message agent API calls. The Message Agent is the backbone that is used to enable workflow. The tools allow the application to be Web enabled. PeopleSoft provides Web clients and HTML access to enable the applications to be deployed over the Web. The tools also enable communication to trading partners using EDI transactions. This is provided by the EDI Manager utility.

This strategy is being further enhanced by the PeopleSoft Business Network (PSBN) and e-business backbone that are being released in the next version of the product and are discussed in Chapter 17, "PeopleSoft Business Network (PSBN) and E-Business."

PeopleSoft Business Network (PSBN) and E-Business

In this chapter

by Bob Dunn

This chapter introduces PeopleSoft's unparalleled e-business vision and the robust architecture that supports this vision. PeopleSoft Business Network (PSBN) is not just a single product. PSBN is an integrated suite of products, partners, and technology under an umbrella strategy to enable an organization's competitive advantage. This chapter will begin with a discussion of the evolution of computing paradigms followed by the PSBN e-business strategy, vision, and architecture.

EVOLUTION OF TECHNOLOGY AND BUSINESS PARADIGMS

Technology paradigms have evolved over time to support new business structures and practices. These paradigm transformations did not occur at discrete points in time. The important distinction is the business purpose addressed by each. Host-centralized computing supported tall functional hierarchies and corporate forms, whereas centralized information services departments controlled corporate information. Host technology was focused on providing automation and centralized access and control to these corporate repositories (see Figure 17.1). This centralized access became increasingly unproductive and untimely as organizations shifted to decentralized operations. Mergers and acquisitions required many heterogeneous systems to be integrated. People also needed immediate access to information adapted for their needs. Desktop computing intervened in the 1980s and supported productivity by allowing individual control over personal task information. Client/server systems evolved and were adopted as an architecture in the late 80s and early 90s to meet the increasing needs for integrated, distributed, decentralized, and timely information.

Figure 17.1
The integration of business and technology evolutions.

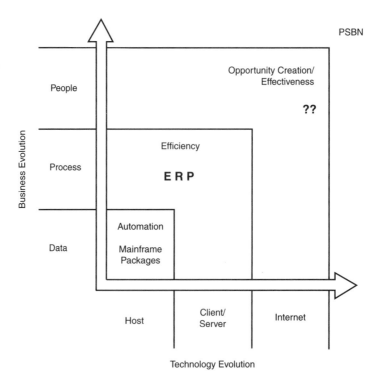

In the last few years, the Internet has been responsible for a more personalized approach to information distribution and access on a grand scale. A recent IDC research study by Ian Campbell, "The Pervasive Intranet," predicted that in 1998, 77% of all US companies would have an intranet (an internal Internet within a single company), and by the year 2001, there would be 133 million intranet users around the world. Morgan Stanley's 1997 report, "The Internet Retailing Report," predicts that the number of Internet users is also expected to accelerate, reaching 150 million by 2000. According to Michael Sullivan-Trainor in the IDC report "Global Infrastructure," 100% of the Fortune 1000 companies already have deployed intranets.

Client/server computing has enabled far-reaching technical advances driven by the demanding business environment in which most companies operate. The trend in the U.S. in the 1990s has been for companies to regain competitive advantage in the global marketplace by reinventing themselves. Decentralization, rightsizing, employee empowerment, business process re-engineering, continuous improvement, and rapid change have all directly led to client/server computing. Client/server computing has been exploited to reduce costs, reduce cycle time, increase productivity, and increase efficiency. The business case for migrating to client/server, however, is less dependent on financial considerations, such as the relative costs of new hardware and software versus the maintenance of the prior systems. Rather, the justification is the financial impact of increased productivity and better use and reuse of resources. ERP applications address this process-based efficiency market.

Client/server and ERP applications are integral to the business processes of an organization. They have an essential place in an organization's information backbone. ERP applications are predominantly targeted at selected people and processes in the organization versus having a pervasive, outward focus. Demands for a pervasive, relevant, integrated, distributed convergence of content to construct effective organizations are needed. All this suggests a fresh architecture that is open, scaleable, and prepared for the emerging global marketplace and marketspace. PeopleSoft understands that e-business is both revolutionary and evolutionary and must make use of the investment organizations have made in their operational and informational infrastructure. E-business is inevitable, and PSBN is the solution.

PEOPLESOFT'S E-BUSINESS VISION

PeopleSoft's e-business vision is a people-centric focus that will transform an organization's competitive landscape (see Figure 17.2). It is empowering, unique, and compelling. What is the PeopleSoft e-business vision for PSBN?

Figure 17.2
Using PeopleSoft
Enterprise Solutions
for organization
transformation.

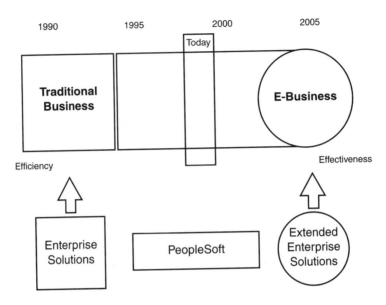

PeopleSoft believes e-business extends well beyond electronic commerce. Electronic commerce is the exchange of goods, services, and information electronically. Until recently, electronic data interchange (EDI) was the primary means of electronic commerce. EDI supports organizational efficiency. Electronic information exchange decreases the costs of doing business. However, transaction-based e-commerce doesn't really add any value in and of itself. It doesn't help people to make decisions better, wiser, and faster, and it doesn't create new opportunities. The Internet has seen electronic commerce expand exponentially to include businesses and consumers. It is still, however, primarily transaction-based. Forrester, in a 1998 "Sizing Commerce Software" study, predicts that business buying over the Internet is expected to grow from $20 billion in 1998 to over $350 billion in 2002. A Giga 1998 report states that the Organization for Economic Cooperation and Development (OECD) predicts that global electronic commerce will reach $1 trillion worldwide by 2003, with 80% consisting of business-to-business commerce.

Effective e-business exploits opportunities along the physical and virtual value chain. What is the value chain? The *value chain* is a collection of activities that are performed to deliver a firm's products and services. This includes internal logistics, production, marketing, and sales. It extends to a firm's customers and suppliers in the supply chain. As discussed, supply-chain collaboration traditionally was transaction-based EDI through private networks. The physical value chain adds value at each link in the chain. Industries involving physical goods operate through a familiar physical value chain (raw materials, production, distribution, marketing, and sales) in a physical market place. The virtual value chain is created through information gathering, organization, selection, synthesis, and distribution. This virtual value chain, conceived by John Sviokla of the Harvard Business School, is the information that can be used to create effectiveness. Information-based opportunities exist in a market space, through a virtual value chain. Value is created through synthesis, integration, and relevancy and the distribution of this content to the right people. This personal virtual value chain is based upon a person's role in the organization.

E-business then is about collaboration, building competitive advantage, and creating new opportunities. It provides timely, relevant, and integrated information to optimize decision making. It allows people to collaborate based on the role they play in their business value chain as well their own personal virtual value chain. PSBN is people- and role-focused to exploit such opportunities. As discussed in Porter and Millar's 1985 article, "How Information Gives You Competitive Advantage," in the Harvard Business Review, it is widely accepted and proven that competitive advantage can be gained by a firm that exploits technology to perform an activity better than its competitor. PSBN is that competitive advantage, and that is what e-business is all about.

For this e-business vision to be fully exploited, distributed computing technologies, messaging, and analytic applications must be deployed. Given PeopleSoft's vision for e-business, the architectural components that fulfill this vision will now be discussed.

OVERVIEW OF PSBN

There are four complementary architectural suites that support PSBN. The PSBN eBusiness Backbone provides the core ERP applications business processes that are the foundation of the business activity of the enterprise; ePerformance Management provides a relevance engine through analytics; the Enterprise Portal provides a single gateway to the sources of information for decision making; and eBusiness Communities provide relevancy and content convergence (see Figure 17.3). These architectural suites will now be examined.

eBUSINESS BACKBONE

The eBusiness Backbone consists of the organization's core ERP applications plus integration points to other content and applications. The eBusiness Backbone consists of the operational business processes represented by ERP applications, electronic commerce and marketplace, and value chain solutions. PeopleSoft provides suites of industry-specific business management applications in the eBusiness Backbone, such as:

- Human resource management
- Financial management
- Treasury management
- Procurement and materials management
- Sales and logistics
- Project management
- Production planning

Figure 17.3
The four complementary architectural suites that support PSBN.

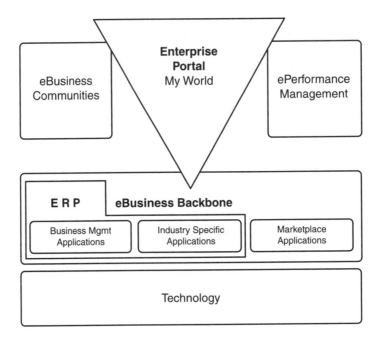

ePERFORMANCE MANAGEMENT

The infrastructure and tools that create information value through data transformation and aggregation based upon relevant rules is ePerformance Management (ePM). This supports forward-looking thought processes and trend analysis. The Web-enabled Workbench provides a framework that can be used to build different activity dashboards and different perspectives. A balanced scorecard engine evaluates goals against performance to provide a snapshot of organizational performance tailored to the metrics important to a person's role. The ePerformance Management architecture is integrated with the backbone and the Enterprise Data Warehouse (see Figure 17.4).

ENTERPRISE PORTAL

The Enterprise Portal provides the gateway to all relevant content based upon a person's role in the enterprise. People may have many roles within an organization, and distilled content is presented for a chosen role (see Figure 17.5). The Enterprise Portal provides comprehensive, role-based access to relevant business content and web-based applications. The portal provides for

- Role-based access
- Point of security
- External and internal content integration
- Taxonomy and categorization

- Searching
- Personalization and profile management
- Open and integrated workflow

Figure 17.4
A diagram of the infrastructure that generates information value through data transformation.

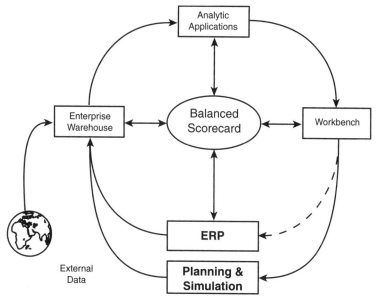

Figure 17.5
Relevant content present in the enterprise.

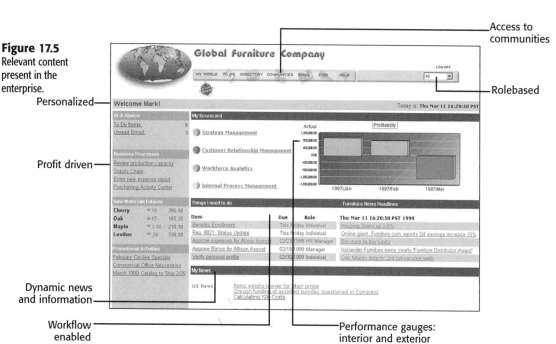

eBUSINESS COMMUNITIES

The eBusiness Communities are the workplaces where employees with differing roles perform their duties, evaluate and analyze their options, and conduct business. This section will define eBusiness Communities.

RELEVANCY, CONVERGENCE, AND INTEGRATION

The eBusiness Communities are the focal point for relevant content integration and convergence (see Figure 17.6). Content from merchants, the eBusiness Backbone, and ePM is brought together based upon a person's role in his or her community. People have many roles within an organization. PSBN is focused on enabling employees to be efficient in each of these roles, and the eBusiness Communities provide this congruence.

Figure 17.6
A graphic depiction of relevancy, convergence, and integration.

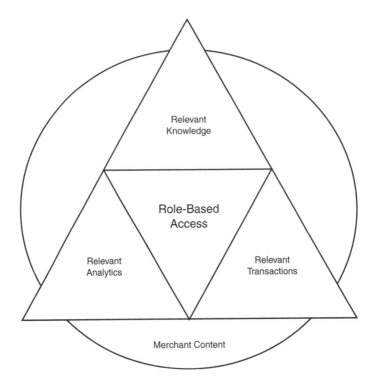

WHAT ARE eBUSINESS COMMUNITIES?

An e-business environment can be thought of as a set of communities where access to information is based upon role. The variety and number of communities are extensive. The organization as a whole has numerous processes and activities. Transactions, relevant analytics, collaboration with partners and people, and knowledge are formulated into related eBusiness Communities (see Figure 17.7). Communities are defined by discrete business activities such as benefits administration, travel and expense, and procurement. Virtually any business activity is a candidate for an eBusiness Community.

Unlike applications, eBusiness Communities converge rich content from several sources (see Figure 17.8). The primary sources of content are the ERP backbone, other contributing content partners, analytics, knowledge capital, policies and procedures, and groupware applications. They provide unified access to all relevant information and transactions about a business activity.

Figure 17.7
A graphic depiction of related eBusiness communities.

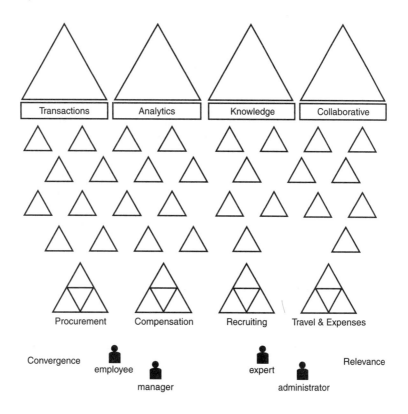

Figure 17.8
Bringing together content from several sources.

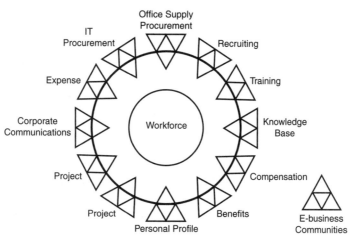

Based on the roles people play in the business world, they may access eBusiness Communities from multiple perspectives. For example, roles in the e-business community may include various levels of managers, employees, executives, and functional experts.

The following examples describe some possible e-business communities, roles, and actions:

- Procurement Community—A requisitioner (employee role) has access to information about approved products with policies and procedures for ordering them. A manager of employees accesses the community (manager role) where he views the list of purchase requisitions requiring approval for his department.

- Recruiting Community—Employees see a list of current job openings, interviewers see current interview schedules and complete interview evaluations, and managers evaluate the candidate. In this community, external people might log in to the community to see the job openings or get directions for getting to the interview.

- Benefits Community—Employees select benefits and conduct research on the various options available. Managers access the community to determine if employees have finished the benefits enrollment process for health, insurance, and 401K.

It is important to understand that the same individual in one case might sign into a community in a variety of roles. In each of the preceding examples, the manager may access the community as a manager or as an employee.

PSBN eBUSINESS COMMUNITIES ARCHITECTURE

The scalable and open architecture to support the eBusiness Communities is discussed in this section in terms of the conceptual and logical architecture. The conceptual architecture defines the system components in terms of function and capabilities independent of technology. The logical architecture maps this conceptual architecture to a high-level technology blueprint.

ARCHITECTURAL GOALS

The distinguishing attributes of any powerful architecture are characterized by the following:

- Maintainability—The ease of maintaining the architecture. The PeopleSoft toolsets and those of PeopleSoft's partners provide extensive and flexible control over an organization's information assets. An optimal architecture, such as PSBN, leverages the organization's current infrastructure and investment in personnel.

- Modularity—The ability to add, modify, and remove pieces of the architecture. There are two elements of modularity. The first is simplicity and ease of removing and replacing physical components covered under maintainability. The second is ease of development, collaboration, and reuse. The architecture is built with collaboration and reuse in mind. Objects are designed as autonomous agents to support high-level business concepts with abstraction layers that service the business components. The eBusiness Communities and Framework business object-based architecture are modular and loosely coupled. Object models are at different levels of abstraction that incorporate encapsulation and separation of implementation from behavior and leverage polymorphism.

- Openness and interoperability—The compliance of the architecture with open standards enables many of the other attributes and the ability to work in collaboration between multiple heterogeneous processing platforms. PSBN eBusiness Communities distributed architecture includes transaction and data independence through object and transaction request brokering. The architecture is also based upon common protocols such as XML, TCP/IP, and HTTP, which enables interoperability.

- Scalability—The ability to scale the architecture by the dimensions of transaction volume, data storage volume, and concurrent user base. The n-tiered architecture supports scalability. The architecture can be scaled horizontally and vertically.

- Availability—The system must be available to be of benefit. Through many local failover strategies, the architecture is resilient to multiple or single points of failure.

CONCEPTUAL ARCHITECTURE

The PSBN eBusiness Communities content is accessed in an n-tiered architecture through the Enterprise Portal. An Open Framework layer provides consistent presentation and broker APIs for building communities. Major features of the Open Framework include security, workflow, directory server integration, merchant and content integration and registration, mail and news integration, and backbone integration and transparency (see Figure 17.9).

Figure 17.9
Open framework features.

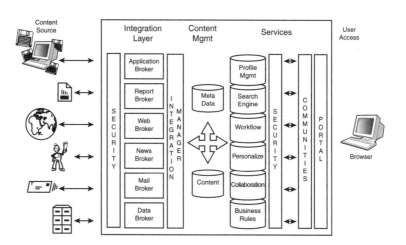

LOGICAL ARCHITECTURE

The PSBN eBusiness Communities architecture supports the seamless integration of PSBN eBusiness Communities technology with merchants, the ERP backbone, and ePM to produce an enriching, content-driven, fulfilling user experience. This seamless, scalable, distributed architecture collaborates through an Object and Transaction Request

Broker. The system architecture prescribes an n-tier model, which separates user interface, business components, and data access layers. This n-tiered architecture is server-centric, because it enables business components to run on servers instead of on clients as in two-tiered applications. The architecture supports several levels of abstraction to create a truly interoperable and service-oriented architecture. The PSBN eBusiness Communities architecture deploys presentation logic on desktop client browsers via the Web server, business components, data access components, and brokering/proxy components on middle-tier servers, data on dedicated database servers, and directory/security information in an LDAP-compliant directory server (see Figure 17.10).

Figure 17.10
The PSBN eBusiness Communities architecture.

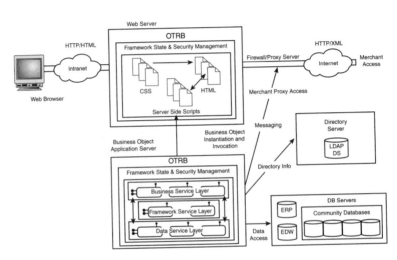

PSBN eBusiness Communities application components and data access layers are abstracted away to create immutable interfaces to public methods of business components. Encapsulation and abstraction of implementation is held private to each component. Components can be accessed in the same process, across processes, or across nodes in a network through the Object Transaction Request Broker (OTRB).

OBJECT TRANSACTION REQUEST BROKER (OTRB)

The distributed architecture of PSBN allows eBusiness Communities' components and third-party components to communicate, cooperate, and collaborate with each other in a well-defined manner. This distributed architecture enables applications and data to reside on different platforms and to seamlessly support various business services from the Web. The attributes of this architecture employ object and transaction brokering, which provide for the following:

- Location independence—Components do not need to exist in the same process space, on the same node, nor do they need to reside on the same network.

- Platform independence—Business components need not reside on the same host on the same operating system. Business components in the distributed architecture are ubiquitous.

- Programming language independence—Components can communicate with one another while utilizing best of breed tool sets or tool sets targeted at a certain need.

- Data independence—Objects can cooperate and collaborate to complete transactions across platforms and are data-independent.

The architecture provides for shared memory management between components for collaboration. It also allows for transparent remoting (cross-process or cross-network calling). There are multiple network transports, including HTTP, TCP, UDP, and IPX/SPX.

The OTRB provides a server-centric environment for developing and deploying n-tiered applications (see Figure 17.11). The primary functions performed by the OTRB include transaction management across objects, object management, security support, database connection pooling, and an object instantiation and invocation. eBusiness Community business components run on servers and are invoked by presentation-centric components running on clients. Business components' data service objects access datastores, messaging services, and other services. The objects are deployed as server and library instances, which provide a way to easily secure, manage, and deploy components as a group.

Figure 17.11
The Object Transaction
Request Broker
(OTRB).

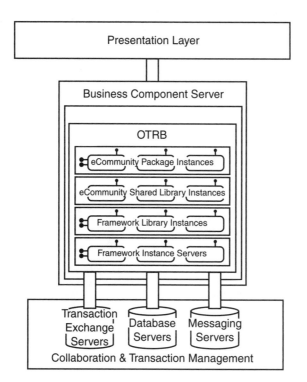

WEB BROWSER AND SERVER

Commonly available third-party Web browsers are the vehicle for rendering the user's portal to access all relevant content. Content is rendered as appropriate to the user's desires and roles. A mixture of content push and pull is provided by eBusiness Communities as appropriate for the necessary function. Content push to the user occurs in instances such as rendering analytics and organizational news. Content pull occurs in instances where the user requests information, such as benefits enrollment. The Web server provides the capability to deliver PSBN eBusiness Community pages to users via HTTP. In addition, an application mechanism will provide the ability to instantiate and invoke business components and services from the Web server.

SUMMARY

PSBN enables people to more effectively and efficiently accomplish business goals over the Internet. This includes not only e-commerce, commonly defined as buying and selling over the Internet, but also employee and management self-service, and the physical and virtual value chain. The PeopleSoft solution is people-centric and integrates both transactions and information to facilitate better decision making. Although many other companies facilitate e-commerce, PeopleSoft's focus is on e-business.

CHAPTER 18

PEOPLESOFT AND THE SUPPLY CHAIN

In this chapter   *by Ron Yeung*

RED PEPPER

Red Pepper is a collaborative planning engine across the enterprise. Red Pepper software's ResponseAgent enables manufacturers and distributors to respond to the needs of their customers in real time while minimizing total supply chain costs.

Red Pepper was purchased by PeopleSoft in 1996 and integrated into PeopleSoft Enterprise Resource Planning applications as its supply chain solution.

Supply Chain Management considers factors inside and outside the enterprise. It assesses and optimizes the resources of the enterprise to establish a feasible plan. To make the right decisions, planners need visibility to balance available capacity, material arrivals, inventory constraints, and customer requests within the plant and across the entire supply chain.

Red Pepper's ResponseAgent provides the visibility and optimized supply chains to

- Reduce inventory
- Minimize cycle time
- Improve on-time delivery
- Maximize capacity utilization

Traditionally, the production and distribution planning process is performed by individual groups who attempt to manage, to the best of their ability, within their domains but with little visibility of the effect of their actions on the rest of the company. The planning groups might include

- Financial forecast
- Marketing forecast
- Supply planning
- Order promising
- Manufacturing planning
- Material planning
- Distribution planning
- Shipment planning

Red Pepper's ResponseAgent revolutionizes the planning process with a collaborative planning across the entire enterprise. This provides each group with up-to-the-minute visibility of the effect of their actions on the rest of the organization.

THE PLANNING SUITE

The Red Pepper planning suite offers three products to help manage the supply chain:

- Enterprise Planning optimizes the plans and schedules across the supply chain. Enterprise ResponseAgent is the embedded technology for Enterprise Planning.

- Production Planning optimizes the plans and schedules of a single production facility. Production ResponseAgent is the embedded technology for Production Planning.

- Order Promising provides real-time sales order promising of supply chain resources. Sales ResponseAgent is the embedded technology for Order Promising.

ENTERPRISE RESPONSEAGENT

Enterprise ResponseAgent optimizes your entire supply chain, from key suppliers and available materials through production and distribution capacity.

Enterprise ResponseAgent considers key production resources and materials requirements simultaneously, first to produce a feasible plan and then to optimize it against the constraints and objectives of the enterprise. Enterprise ResponseAgent attempts to balance the constraints among material availability, plant capability, customer requests, and warehouse capacity and yet meet the company objectives in areas such as customer service, profit, and inventory level.

Enterprise ResponseAgent also enables you to build a complete representation of your enterprise supply chain, from suppliers to customers. Enterprise ResponseAgent generates an optimized multiplant Master Production Schedule (MPS), as well as an optimized Distribution Resource Plan (DRP). In addition, Enterprise ResponseAgent provides spreadsheets such as Horizontal MRP, Material Movement, and Capacity Overview.

Enterprise ResponseAgent produces an optimized schedule for your enterprise, based on the constraints you set on the Control Panel. The constraints include request dates, promise dates, buildable inventory shortage (finished goods, subassemblies), aggregate capacity, safety stock, excess stock, and raw material shortage.

The Control Panel regulates Enterprise ResponseAgent in how to make trade-offs. It enables you to control the relative weight that Enterprise ResponseAgent assigns to each constraint when optimizing the schedule. This is particularly helpful in an overconstrained environment, where it may not be possible to solve every constraint violation.

Enterprise ResponseAgent often helps you address many day-to-day operational questions. For example, you can determine which scheduled production is most important and discover whether these work orders were produced to forecast or to actual demand. If there is a material shortage in one plant, you can easily check availability in other plants and initiate an interplant transfer to solve the problem. If the local plant is overbooked, Enterprise ResponseAgent can help you evaluate whether it is better to make product earlier or to make it at another factory and incur the additional shipping costs.

Benefits of Enterprise ResponseAgent include simultaneous optimization of enterprisewide procurement, production, and distribution; integration with the Enterprise Resource Planning system; and collaborative decision making.

PRODUCTION RESPONSEAGENT

Production ResponseAgent supports single plant planning and scheduling. Production ResponseAgent optimizes among material, capacity, inventory targets, and customer orders to create the production schedule that best meets your company objectives.

PART

II

CH

18

Production ResponseAgent optimizes the plant-level production sequence to minimize the effect of work center changeover between orders. Production ResponseAgent uses the same set of overall objectives and constraints as Enterprise ResponseAgent and provides a feedback loop to Enterprise Planning to refine enterprise material requirements and interplant demand.

Production ResponseAgent produces an optimized schedule for each resource in the model based on the constraints you set on the Control Panel. The constraints include request dates, promise dates, inventory shortage, detailed capacity, aggregate capacity, changeover, safety stock, excess stock, and raw material shortage.

Use the Control Panel slider to set the relative value of constraint by dragging the slider to the left or right. A constraint with a value of 100 is top priority and not flexible. A constraint with a value that is turned off is of zero importance and will not be considered by Production ResponseAgent.

Production ResponseAgent provides spreadsheets such as Horizontal MRP, Build Schedules by Resources, Capacity Usage, and Purchase Order Requirements.

Production ResponseAgent helps you address many factory-specific planning situations as well as detailed scheduling situations. For example, when a line suddenly goes down for a day, you can determine where production can be rescheduled and whether promise dates will still be met. If the sales order exceeds projected forecasts, Production ResponseAgent can display whether the material and capacity are available to meet this additional demand, allowing for material lead time. Material often arrives late. Production ResponseAgent can help you determine how this alters the entire schedule and minimize its effect.

Benefits of Production ResponseAgent include simultaneous optimization of production schedules based on material, capacity, and customer demand constraints; improved customer satisfaction and return on assets; and reduced dependency on forecast accuracy.

SALES RESPONSEAGENT

Sales ResponseAgent considers the latest inventory and production status across your company's supply chain and enables real-time order promising. The process is known as *Capable to Promise*. Sales ResponseAgent provides the Capable to Promise feature by evaluating all available inventory, capacity, and raw materials across the enterprise. Sales ResponseAgent adjusts the enterprise build plan to accommodate the new demand. This gives customers the best possible promise date while maximizing supply chain output. It also serves to integrate customers directly into the planning process.

Sales ResponseAgent is designed to complement the order management system. The order management system sends the message to Sales ResponseAgent when a potential order is captured. Sales ResponseAgent responds with all potential shipping opportunities, enabling you to choose and commit to the best solution. After an order is committed, the inventory and capacity are reserved in Sales ResponseAgent.

Sales ResponseAgent provides real-time order promising across the entire supply chain. During initial customer inquiries, Sales ResponseAgent can help you answer many customer questions. For example, if the finished goods are unavailable, you can inform your customer of the promised delivery date based on the availability of productive resources across your company supply chain. If no raw materials are available to satisfy the customer order anywhere in your supply chain, you can inform your customer when the material will be available and which plan can ultimately produce the product at the lowest cost, including transportation cost.

The benefits of Sales ResponseAgent include reliable and fast delivery performance, increased customer satisfaction and sales channel productivity, and improved customer loyalty.

THE TECHNOLOGY

Red Pepper planning is an objected-oriented system. This means benefits such as high quality, easy maintenance, fast development, scalability, and adaptability. It also means that Red Pepper is more flexible and easier to customize.

Red Pepper planning uses a client/server architecture that allows many people to access the same planning data (server) while using their computers (client).

Red Pepper needs data to process and create an effective and optimized plan. Loading data is done through command files. Data Bridge creates command files. Data Bridge is used to import data into Red Pepper and export data out of Red Pepper. Data Bridge can accept input from database tables, flat files, and bulk load files. It is portable across many platforms, including UNIX, Solaris, AIX, and Windows NT. It can also communicate with any ODBC-compliant database such as Oracle, Sybase, and Informix.

The Red Pepper planning system can be used with or without PeopleSoft Manufacturing or Distribution. Companies that do not have a PeopleSoft application system can use Data Bridge for integration.

PART

II

CH

18

THE SUPPLY CHAIN SPECIALTY

In today's business world, challenges are often multidimensional. Competition is global. Pricing is competitive; cost must be low and efficient. Customers demand on-time deliveries, superior service, and the highest quality products. Manufacturers must continue to increase employee productivity, reduce lead time, and improve asset utilization to stay competitive.

Supply Chain Management attempts to synchronize the activities within the enterprise related to the delivery of goods and services to the customer. The enterprise often includes the suppliers as well. Supply Chain Management must be able to capture the business data quickly and accurately to provide purchase, production, and distribution plans. The plans should reflect the changes in supply and demand across the enterprise in a timely manner. Ultimately, the supply chain system should provide sophisticated decision support to minimize your operational costs, while maximizing the customer service level and product quality. More importantly, the system should give you maximum control of your supply chain so that you can be responsive to the constantly changing demands of the marketplace.

The PeopleSoft supply chain planning system powered by Red Pepper technology addresses planning, optimization, collaboration, and execution. PeopleSoft Supply Chain Management solution includes PeopleSoft Demand Planning, Enterprise Planning, Production Planning, Order Promising, Order Management, Product Configurator, Inventory Management, and Purchasing.

The Enterprise Planning, Production Planning, and Order Promising applications are designed around the concepts of constraint-based optimization. The planning systems are integrated with PeopleSoft's supply chain execution systems. This enables you to forecast demand; plan purchasing, production, and distribution activities; and give realistic promise dates to customers, all within a processing environment.

With PeopleSoft Supply Chain Management, the typical sequential Material Resource Planning (MRP II) processes—such as Master Production Schedule (MPS), Rough-Cut Capacity Planning (RCCP), Material Requirement Planning (MRP), Finite Forward Scheduling (FFS), Detailed Capacity Planning (DCP), and Distribution Requirement Planning (DRP)—are streamlined into a single planning process that considers material and capacity availability simultaneously.

ADVANCED PLANNING AND SCHEDULING

Managing complex supply chains requires constant analysis and monitoring to drive efficiency. Supply chain decision-support tools are required to resolve rapidly the demand and supply problems created by global competition, increasing product portfolios, and emerging sales and distribution channels. One of the leading supply chain decision-support tools is *Advanced Planning and Scheduling*. Advanced Planning and Scheduling is designed to integrate and drive the enterprise execution system, such as the PeopleSoft Manufacturing and Distribution application system. Advanced Planning and Scheduling provides competitive advantages of time and information to respond to market dynamics and reduce operating expenses by synchronizing the resources in minutes and hours instead of days.

Advanced Planning and Scheduling is an iterated process of balancing material and plant resources to best meet customer demand while achieving business goals. A good reason for implementing Advanced Planning and Scheduling is to improve the responsiveness and accuracy of customer due-date promising. Advanced Planning and Scheduling considers the capabilities of the entire supply chain to deliver product when it is requested.

Some of the leading Advanced Planning and Scheduling providers are Red Pepper, Berclain, Manugistics, i2 Technology, ProMIRA, Thru-Put Technology, and Optimax. Red Pepper was purchased by PeopleSoft in 1996 and integrated into PeopleSoft's Supply Chain Management. Berclain was purchased by Baan and integrated into Baan's Enterprise Resource Planning system. Computer Associates developed Quick Response Engine. SAP also developed its own Advanced Planning and Scheduling technology to drive the core planning of its R/3 system.

Advanced Planning and Scheduling considers the constraints and business objectives to derive the optimum plan. Typically, Advanced Planning and Scheduling establishes a feasible baseline schedule during the first pass through the data. Then Advanced Planning and Scheduling continues to optimize the plan on subsequent passes.

Most Advanced Planning and Scheduling products reside completely in memory to eliminate disk access time. They can require as much as 4GB (gigabytes) of computer memory or more.

Modeling is a required process of customizing the Advanced Planning and Scheduling product to a specific manufacturing environment. This process can take as few as 3 months for products with predefined models or as many as 18 months to model multiplant supply chains.

GLOBAL VISIBILITY

Manufacturers must have the ability to collaborate on a global basis to ensure that the available resources of the enterprise best satisfy customer demand. It is possible to have planners in Asia or Europe dial in to a worldwide planning session over the phone line on a portable workstation. When someone in the United States adjusts the schedule on the screen, all other participants can immediately see the changes. These planners can work together on the plan, creating multiple scenarios of how they want the enterprise to operate by comparing and contrasting different supply plans to meet target inventory and customer service levels. This provides real decision support for solving tough multisite enterprise problems. When all the planners are satisfied with the new plan, it can then be saved as the official plan. The result is a collaborative planning process that weighs the trade-offs associated with various options.

THE BALANCED SCORECARD

Planners need visibility to quickly pinpoint problem areas and devise quick resolutions. PeopleSoft's Balanced Scorecard displays the number of times each constraint is being violated, as well as the importance of the violations with a weighted value. The scores are color coded to indicate urgency—for example, red for critical, yellow for caution, and green for no issues.

The scorecard helps you quickly identify any problems with your supply plan. You can weigh and define the relative importance of constraints against one another and regenerate the plan interactively. PeopleSoft's planning engine enables you to use a slide-bar Control Panel to prioritize constraints. The scorecard reflects the quality of your current plan when the optimization was executed. PeopleSoft enables you to name and save any Control Panel setting and recall it any time you have to use the settings again.

When you need more information on a problem, you can drill down to detailed information and graphically display more information on the issue. The drill-down screens allow you to access the situation, consider the implications, and correct the problem without having to switch among multiple applications.

CONSTRAINTS MANAGEMENT

Constraints are a set of limitations and rules that influence the potential for meeting company objectives. Limitations can be material availability, labor skill, and machine capacity. Rules can include the machine maintenance schedule or customer demand over forecast.

Constraint Management assigns a weight indicating the relative importance of the constraints. Advanced Planning and Scheduling takes multiple passes to evaluate constraints. The first pass determines a feasible plan. In the subsequent passes, Advanced Planning and Scheduling uses all the constraints and attempts to optimize the plan.

The key to feasible and optimized planning is the ability to balance multiple business constraints.

CUSTOMER DUE-DATE PROMISING

One of the benefits of supply chain synchronization using Advanced Planning and Scheduling is the ability to offer Capable to promise. Customers always want to know when their orders will be ready so that they can plan their own schedules. Capable to promise uses the Advanced Planning and Scheduling engine to instantly access the feasibility of adding a new customer order to the existing production schedule and derive an estimated promise date.

Capable to promise helps you evaluate all available inventories, factory capacities, distribution constraints, and transportation alternatives across the entire supply chain. Rather than plan customer deliveries according to locally available inventory and capacity, you can accommodate new customer orders by reviewing sourcing alternatives across the enterprise and selecting the most cost-effective method to deliver on time to your customer. You can give your customer realistic delivery dates and cost-effective options for partial deliveries, and you can be assured that both material and production capacity have been reserved to meet the delivery promise. All this can be accomplished while the customer is on the phone, eliminating the chance of losing your customer to a competitor.

THE SUPPLY CHAIN COLLABORATOR

PeopleSoft Supply Chain Collaborator helps manage the sharing of planning data among entities in your supply chain. In real-time, you collaborate with suppliers and customers to offer competitive prices and quick response. With PeopleSoft Supply Chain Collaborator in place at both supplier and customer sites, you can communicate forecast and plan information. This enables multiple supply chain entities to function as one large enterprise. PeopleSoft Supply Chain Collaborator is free and can be downloaded from the Internet. Install and operate it right away.

SUPPLY CHAIN MODULES

ENTERPRISE PLANNING

A good enterprise planning system provides timely customer response, reduces planning cycle time, and enables the enterprise to respond to continuous change. PeopleSoft Enterprise Planning is one of the keys to effective supply chain planning.

PeopleSoft Enterprise Planning offers Advanced Planning and Scheduling capabilities that enable real-time, enterprisewide optimization of procurement, production, and distribution resources.

PeopleSoft Enterprise Planning enables you to weigh the business constraints, such as lead time, capacity, and inventory, that can affect your ability to respond to your customer.

ENTERPRISEWIDE OPTIMIZATION

Enterprise Planning accumulates all customer orders and forecasts and calculates planned replenishment orders to support customer needs. Enterprise Planning recommends purchase orders for raw materials and interunit transfer of material across the enterprise. Through this integrated approach to order fulfillment, customer orders are satisfied quickly at the lowest cost possible. As a result, you strengthen your customer relationships and your competitive position in the market.

PART

II

CH

18

DECISION MAKING

PeopleSoft Enterprise Planning processes distribution requirements planning, multisite production planning, and critical materials planning. It enables you to make sound decisions and immediately replan to meet new customer orders, handle changes in material delivery dates, optimize production capacity, and control inventory levels.

ENTERPRISE PLANNING VERSUS MRP

Typically, the MRP II model has been limited to a single plant. Each plant runs its own MPS and MRP. The flow of material among plants is seldom synchronized to the point where production can be planned based on multiple site requirements.

Distribution Requirement Planning (DRP) creates transfer orders between warehouses and creates requirements for inventory replenishment with MRP. However, MRP is unable to distinguish the demands between market and warehouse replenishment.

Traditionally, the cyclical process of developing a DRP, Master Production Schedule (MPS), Rough-Cut Capacity Plan (RCCP), and Material Requirement Plan (MRP) can take days to perform. After that, any problems uncovered in the MPS and MRP require changes to the DRP.

Disadvantages of the MRP process include

- Time-consuming sequential process
- Input/Output intensive
- Bucketed logic

- Data instead of information
- Single-level constraint process

PeopleSoft Enterprise Planning provides a real-time planning solution that simultaneously considers constraints such as material availability and capacity across your enterprise and produces timely plans so that you can respond rapidly to changes in customer demand. PeopleSoft Enterprise Planning creates material transfer and replenishment orders that maintain inventory levels. If material transfers are not sufficient, the system will look at alternative sourcing options. This ensures inventory availability to meet unexpected demand at all distribution facilities.

Enterprise Planning allows you to determine product availability, generate planned purchase orders, develop optimal inventory allocation to meet customer demands, maintain desired inventory levels by developing material transfer and replenishment plans, and specify inventory rules.

In comparison to MRP, Enterprise Planning has the following advantages:

- Intelligent decision support
- Adaptability to changing business needs
- Interactive process
- Consideration of all dependencies
- Real-time capability
- Graphical workbench
- Unlimited simulation

THE ENTERPRISE PLANNING DATA LINK

Before an optimized supply plan can be generated, Enterprise Planning gathers data from PeopleSoft applications through the Enterprise Planning Data Link. Data Link extracts required data from PeopleSoft Purchasing, Inventory, Order Management, Production Management, and Bills and Routing. The Data Link converts the data into object-oriented form in memory.

When the data is placed in Enterprise Planning, you can determine optimization settings on the Control Panel and create a new supply plan. Updating data in Enterprise Planning and executing optimization can be performed both in real-time or in a batch process, at the end of either each shift or each day.

When the plan completes the optimization process, Enterprise Planning generates spreadsheets and charts for you to view. Spreadsheets include new planned orders from existing orders, projected available inventory, supply and demand, and an aggregate capacity utilization profile. Charts include purchase, a production and transfer tasks timeline, inventory level, and resource load.

You have the ability to review the plans, run simulations to test alternative solutions, and improve the plan using your knowledge to minimize any problems.

When you are satisfied with the supply plan in Enterprise Planning, you can transfer the plan to PeopleSoft applications. The plan is loaded back into the PeopleSoft transaction database and stored in temporary tables for validation and review. You can review, manipulate, and approve the data before updating the production tables in PeopleSoft Production Management, Bills and Routing, and Inventory and Purchasing.

PRODUCTION PLANNING

PeopleSoft Production Planning is a detailed scheduling and planning tool. It handles the MPS, MRP, CRP, and sequencing requirements at a single factory location.

Unlike PeopleSoft Enterprise Planning, PeopleSoft Production Planning looks at detailed scheduling but can also handle aggregate planning for the longer term. Production Planning considers all items in the bill of material, second-by-second scheduling of all resources, sequence-dependent changeovers, and alternative routings.

The level of details that Production Planning processes is quite different from that of Enterprise Planning. The following lists these details:

Enterprise Planning

Key items

Aggregate capacity

Average changeover

Build/buy/transfer orders

Rough-cut planning

Production Planning

All items

Detailed and aggregate capacity

Detailed changeover

Build/buy orders

Detailed planning

Production Planning helps you address many operational issues. For example, Production Planning provides you with an optimized detailed schedule for your plant. You can review orders and decide which orders to dispatch. Production Planning allows you to respond to or modify a recommended schedule and lets you see the effect. You can also replan in the near term to react to local capacity or material changes.

PART

II

CH

18

MPS, MRP, AND CRP REPLACEMENT

Under Material Resource Planning (MRP II), the planning scope is usually limited to one plant at a time. Lead times are often static instead of dynamically calculated. No consideration is given to the interdependency of material availability and capacity. There is no feedback of actual results of efforts to improve the process and data. In addition, it lacks the capability to optimize the production schedule to improve throughput.

Master Production Schedule (MPS) is a high-level production plan that expresses sales forecasts of aggregated product families for the coming year. It lacks accuracy and does not react to business change quickly.

Material Requirement Planning (MRP) can calculate what materials are required, but it cannot determine when those materials are required. As a result, MRP cannot generate an accurate production schedule to response to customer needs and just-in-time deliveries.

Capacity Requirement Planning (CRP) assumes infinite capacity planning. CRP identifies overloaded work centers, but resolution must be made manually by leveling the master schedule or adding more capacity.

The cyclical process of developing an MPS, RCCP, MRP, and CRP can take days to perform. Furthermore, detailed problems uncovered in the MRP and CRP process might necessitate changes to the MPS.

PeopleSoft Production Planning provides real-time decision support tools that reduce the planning cycle time and give integrated optimization of procurement and production. PeopleSoft Production Planning creates a detailed production schedule that considers the specific sequence in which orders or operations should be processed to maximize plant throughput while still meeting customer due dates.

MODELING AND SEQUENCING

Modeling is one of the most important aspects of Advanced Planning and Scheduling. Modeling gives the planning and scheduling engine a multi-dimensional picture of the manufacturing and supply chain environment. The more powerful and complete the modeling capabilities are, the better the product responds and reflects the detailed requirements of a specific environment. You can define a model to capture the resource constraints, business goals, distribution limitations, customer preferences, and other factors that influence planning and scheduling decisions. PeopleSoft Production Planning offers graphical tools that reduce your effort in modeling your manufacturing and supply chain environment.

Sequencing is a special form of setup analysis commonly found in process/batch industries and some discrete manufacturing operations such as painting and plastic molding. Preferred or required production sequences are used to constrain the plan or schedule. For example, in a painting operation, a black part can follow a white part with minimal spray gun clean-out; a large setup penalty is incurred going from black to white. PeopleSoft Production Planning allows sequence attributes such as color to be specified for each part. A separate table is used to maintain the setup penalty between attributes. This makes it easier to add another color or flavor, because only the attribute relationship table has to be changed.

PLANNING ANALYSIS

PeopleSoft Production Planning produces a wide variety of spreadsheets to help you analyze and edit the production plan by shift, day, week, or month. Spreadsheets include Master Production Plan, Material Requirement Planning, Capacity Planning, Resource Load Overview, and Schedule Cost. You can use the Master Production Plan spreadsheet to balance supply and demand, including forecasts, actual dependent and independent demand, and projected availability of inventory items. The Horizontal Material Requirement Planning spreadsheet gives you the ability to view supply, demand, and on-hand inventory. The Capacity Planning spreadsheet can be used to view capacity utilization profiles of select resources. If you want to view and edit resource load, you use the Resource Load Overview spreadsheet. The Schedule Cost spreadsheet allows you to view all production costs, revenues, and profiles per period.

THE DATA INTERFACE

To create plans and schedules in Production Planning, the model requires data such as bills of material, routings, rates, on-hand inventory, planned orders, and demand from your application database. PeopleSoft Production Planning uses PeopleSoft-supplied software known as *Data Bridge* to import and export data in and out of the Production Planning server.

PeopleSoft Production Planning executes in virtual memory. After you've optimized a workable and satisfactory plan, you can bring that plan back into the PeopleSoft application database through the Data Bridge. After the plan is imported into the database, you can review, approve, or deny any suggestion that the planning engine makes.

PLANNING TO PRODUCTION

PeopleSoft Production Planning interfaces directly with PeopleSoft Production Management and Purchasing. You can review the planning messages and indicate which recommendations are approved for processing. When you convert approved planned production messages, PeopleSoft Production Management creates planned orders in the released status. Operation lists are created using the operation schedule and resource information provided by PeopleSoft Production Planning. Component lists are created based on the bills of material and go into effect as of the production's start date. The actual start date and time and actual due date and time are defined based on the dates and times recommended by Production Planning.

When PeopleSoft Production Planning suggests new purchase orders or makes adjustments to existing purchase orders, the messages are loaded into PeopleSoft Purchasing. You can review and approve the messages just as you do the production messages. Approved planning messages are stored in a temporary table ready for staging. PeopleSoft Purchasing gives you the option to convert the requisitions on the staging tables and build the purchase orders.

ORDER PROMISING

Order entry clerks often receive inquiries similar to this: "I will give you an order if you have the product. If you do not have the merchandise now, can you tell me when you could deliver it? If you can't, I will have to go elsewhere." More and more often, you must be prepared to determine a committed ship date while the customer is on the phone. You must quickly present fulfillment dates or suggest options if the customer's requested delivery date cannot be met. Otherwise, you lose a sale.

PeopleSoft Order Promising enables you to analyze in real-time to determine the result of accepting the delivery date before committing to the customers. PeopleSoft Order Promising gives you a valid delivery date or suggests shipping options based on the availability of production resources across the entire supply chain. At the same time, you can see which plants can produce the product at the lowest overall cost, including the cost of distribution. This is done while the customer is on the phone.

CAPABLE VERSUS AVAILABLE

Capable to promise is the process of determining a more accurate customer due-date promise based on either the allocation of products in the production schedule or the assignment of resources to produce the unscheduled items. Capable to promise is the next step after Available-to-Promise. Conventional Available-to-Promise searches for available inventory only in a local factory or warehouse. PeopleSoft Order Promising assesses the entire supply chain to determine the best location for fulfilling the customer order, considering customer request dates, product cost, and distribution costs. As a result, you can make commitments to customers based on real supply chain resource availability and capacity, rather than on static Master Production Schedules.

The Available-to-Promise approach generally allocates new demand against a previously approved Master Production Schedule that derives from a forecast. Disadvantages of Available-to-Promise include

- The focus on a single plant
- The dependancy on forecast
- The use of estimated lead time
- The Forced blind commitments
- The "Let me get back to you" approach

Order Promising evaluates the actual capacity and material availability of the entire supply chain for a solution that will satisfy the customer, based on the customer's requested delivery date and cost objectives. Order Promising provides a set of possible shipment dates, along with the cost of each shipment date. This process enables you to consider alternatives and derive a customer-satisfactory solution, given the constraints of time, money, and resources.

In comparison to the Available-to-Promise approach, PeopleSoft Order Promising offers the following advantages:

- Considers the entire supply chain
- Evaluates options
- Optimizes multiple constraints
- Processes the model in memory
- Presents the best date and cost
- Responds in real-time

PeopleSoft Order Promising does not work well in make-to-order, configure-to-order, and make-to-stock environments because of the nature of the manufacturing process. It is difficult to derive an accurate ship date at order entry time when the order is highly customized.

By the same token, if an item is not currently in stock or already scheduled for production, many factors such as raw material and labor availability and production capacity must be considered. The combination of resources used can significantly affect the cost of producing the item and the date the finished goods can be delivered.

CUSTOMER SATISFACTION AND LOYALTY

By leveraging the information from PeopleSoft Order Management, Enterprise Planning, and Production Planning, PeopleSoft Order Promising evaluates all possible shipping solutions and sorts the results on best cost or best date in order to give your customer a set of options for when and where the finished product can be produced and delivered, respectively. PeopleSoft Order Promising helps you improve customer satisfaction and delivery performance and reduce your dependency on forecasts.

PeopleSoft Order Promising enables your customer service to quote delivery dates even when there is no on-hand or planned finished goods inventory. Promises are made based on actual material and capacity available, eliminating the guesswork based on conventional estimated lead time or using a static Master Production Schedule in Available-to-Promise.

PeopleSoft Order Promising satisfies your customers with accurate delivery dates at order entry time, enabling you to set customer expectation up front. Thus, you present your customers with a cost and time trade-off.

ORDER INTEGRATION

PeopleSoft Order Promising integrates with PeopleSoft Order Management to maximize product delivery to your customers. You can decide whether you want to use Order Promising to determine availability while you are entering order. By accessing a popup menu on the sales order line, you can invoke PeopleSoft Order Promising. PeopleSoft Order Promising searches the entire supply chain, based on your parameters, to determine the best ship date for a customer order. Order Promising not only considers existing stock, planned purchases, transfers, and production but also checks open capacity and raw materials in case new production is required. When the search is completed, you can select from a list of possibilities that best suit your customer's requirements.

PeopleSoft Order Promising also integrates with PeopleSoft Product Configurator to determine availability for key components of configured products and to fix a delivery date based on the earliest date of all the available key components.

THE PLANNING INTERFACE

It is necessary to refresh the PeopleSoft Order Promising server with a new copy of optimized Enterprise Planning or Production Planning data. This makes it possible to evaluate the current available material and capacity across the enterprise.

PeopleSoft Order Promising uses a snapshot plan for evaluation. The planning server contains the most up-to-date information on changes in supply and nonsale order demand. The planning server can supply PeopleSoft Order Promising with the optimized plan from PeopleSoft Enterprise Planing and Production Planning.

On the other hand, as new demand (in the form of sales orders) is committed in the Order Promising server, the Order Promising snapshot of the plan is updated. All this information is included when all the subsequent orders are processed.

SUMMARY

Supply Chain Management utilizes various factors that exist both internally and externally in regard to the organization. It takes into consideration the various resources of the enterprise and from there creates a workable design for managing the supply chain. To have a successful supply chain management, planners must consider the following factors: available capacity, inventory constraints, material arrivals, and customer requests, both internally and across the entire supply chain.

PART III

SOFTWARE FOR RE-ENGINEERING

CHAPTER 19

SHOULD I DO IT?

In this chapter *by Perry Keating*

TODAY'S ORGANIZATIONAL STRUCTURES, PROCESSES, AND ADMINISTRATIVE SYSTEMS

Today, networks of computers interact worldwide in seconds. The complete works of William Shakespeare can be transmitted around the world over fiber optic cable in a hundredth of a second. In the manufacturing industry, design engineers can work simultaneously on the same design as though they were sitting next to other, and manufacturers can have an integrated, worldwide network of suppliers that meet the needs of their customers in real time. Traders in Europe and the Far East can be online with the Chicago Mercantile Exchange, and some of the authors of this book have never met in person—but here's the book! Retailers with thousands of shops all over the world can be linked to a central computer system so that wealth-generating processes can be monitored and adjusted as they happen. This is today's reality.

In contrast, most companies today have decades-old organizational structures, processes, and paper-based administrative systems. They employ hierarchical management structures that divide work into functional areas designed before information technology. Traditional enterprises have an executive heading each functional area with a title like Vice President of Marketing or Vice President of Finance. Often the functional areas are largely autonomous and there is little communication between functions. A manufacturing employee normally does not pick up the phone and make a joint decision with an employee in marketing. This is referred to as being organized into functional *silos*, which act to maximize their own structures, processes, and administrative systems but do little to increase market share, lower operating costs, or satisfy customers.

In most corporations, employees are trapped or locked in this organization structure. Within that structure, they think about what is visible to them—namely, their own department and what it does. If they are at a higher level, they might think about how their department interacts with other departments within their division. The problem with this is that most of the reinvention needs a broader viewpoint. The string of processes that satisfies customers, lowers operating costs, or increases market share that desperately needs reinventing often spans multiple departments, multiple divisions, and sometimes multiple corporations. The necessary reinvention often is not the responsibility of the department head and sometimes not even that of a division's vice president. Most people in an obsolete organization structure cannot change the organization. They build systems to aid or protect their own department or their division, and they tend to cast in concrete obsolete procedures that ought to be re-engineered.

The computer applications within each function or department have often been built independently by separate non-communicating teams. These are often referred to as *stovepipe systems*. Such systems often use incompatible data, which prevents or makes difficult communication between systems, even if they have "open" systems.

Today's computer systems have processes that cross multiple functions within an enterprise. Multiple handoffs occur as work progresses from one functional area to another. This causes delays and errors. It is difficult to trace things that have fallen through the cracks. Exceptions are time-consuming. There is no manager in charge of the whole process. In non-physical flows, such as approving a loan, the total work done adds up to an hour or two, but the customer has to wait weeks because the work sits waiting at the different handoff points.

For centuries, efficiency experts have tried to make work processes efficient by division of labor. These efficiency techniques reached their peak in the late nineteenth and early twentieth centuries through the work of Frederick Taylor. "Industrial efficiency" experts timed repetitive tasks and tried to minimize their duration. Division of labor was applied to both manufacturing and administrative work. Different people did the repetitive tasks of data entry, billing, processing invoices, and handling customer queries. Work in the office became similar to work done in the factory. The result was an ever-lengthening "factory line" for administrative processes, which may have helped a particular functional silo justify its existence, but did little for the overall company. At this stage of the twentieth century, that is no longer valid. Reinvention is needed by most companies and needed immediately.

The resulting administrative systems are a strung-together series of paper-based handoff forms, multiple data entry sites, and a maze of complex reports and consolidations needed to keep these silos in existence. These stovepipe computer systems are designed for a single department or, if they are for more than a single department, often entirely repetitive. Function and costs so outweigh benefits that many executives question their value.

OFFICE AUTOMATION: THE EARLY YEARS

In the 1980s, many corporations installed large mainframe systems to address their office automation needs. Although these systems did address many of the old issues, they often ate money in computer staff, analysts, programmers, and software and in some cases gave a negative net return on investment. Personal computers spread to everybody's desk. It is estimated that the total cost of operation (TCO) per desktop computer was well over $10,000 when supported costs were calculated. By the end of the '80s, this had become a river of concern, but the flood had yet to begin.

By the 1990s, the reasons for the problem became known: Corporations needed to drastically redesign their business processes to take advantage of information technology. Unfortunately, identifying a problem didn't mean solving it. Using today's technology to automate 20-year-old processes is like Marconi inventing radio and thinking that the only use for it is a point-to-point wireless telegraph. He did not initially recognize its potential for broadcasting. About the only regular use that was publicly espoused for broadcasting was the transmission of Sunday sermons, because that was the only apparent occasion when one man regularly addressed a mass public. This meant that the generic thinking of the era was that the mass public was the gathering place of many, instead of defining the power of radio to create a mass public audience through reaching individuals. This is truly "thinking in the box."

Most people fail to understand the potential of technology because they think of it in terms of solving only today's problems. For example, Tibetans invented the turbine mechanism but used it only for the rotation of prayer wheels. Most people ask, "How can we automate what already exists?" The great potential of technology is to replace what exists with something different and fundamentally better.

Today's enterprises are anxious to avoid disruption of their established organization. The introduction of office communications and new business processes was seen as costly not only due to the disruption, but also due to re-education of the workforce. That is why the "paperless office" promised by the technological revolution has quadrupled paper output over the last 10 years. Paper is comfortable; digitized bits are not.

IMPLEMENT FIRST, RE-ENGINEER SECOND?

Unfortunately, enterprise executives don't seem to realize that they need to change until after they've wasted millions of dollars automating their legacy systems. Despite the advice "Think before you automate," many executives automate first and then rethink the process—spend, then think, and then redo. This process is expensive and slow.

If you have to "spend, think, and then redo," be sure that the first steps are easily reversible. From 1975 to 1982, there was a massive drive to automate accounting in the U.S., but during this period the number of accountants increased by 40 percent. Many companies known for their superb financial management had top executives drowning in data they could not use. Some companies produced daily reports for top management containing product-by-product sales details on hundreds of thousands of items. There were reports that were literally over 12 feet high.

TOO MUCH EMPHASIS ON THE TECHNOLOGY, NOT ENOUGH ON THE PROCESS

Computer professionals acquire sophisticated knowledge about how to make their machinery work and how to create programs. The computer industry captivates its own professionals with mind-gripping fascination. However, few technical professionals think about how the business processes should be changed. They may think about how to automate a procedure that already exists, but this negates the value of technology. Its true value lies in its application to the changes in the business processes and its ability to enhance this capability, not in simple automation. The big challenge is reinventing the business, not applying the software and hardware. This is where PeopleSoft shines.

But, before the entry of PeopleSoft, there has to be a corporate refocusing, because often computer professionals are building the wrong applications and are not as connected to the business users as is necessary to craft solutions to meet the business needs. They are applying their advanced technical knowledge to outmoded processes.

The financial implications of this are staggering. Computing is now the world's largest profession. In most corporations, the IT budget is the largest capital expenditure. Also, hundreds of other costs are hidden beyond the budget. Poorly designed processes and systems, no matter how high-tech, are a losing proposition. The IT community must be tied more closely to the business needs. Software solutions must first address process issues, and then look to technology.

THE NEW ECONOMIC RESOURCE: KNOWLEDGE

A new approach to organizations is evolving that will change management structures, jobs (processes), and the supporting administrative systems everywhere. The results benefit employees. More "happy productivity" means a more profitable corporation. This late 1990s paradigm is the recognition that the true value of a corporation is its employees and the new basic economic resource is knowledge. How is value created? By applying knowledge to work. A corporation needs a technical infrastructure to maximize this use of knowledge. The successful uses of this technology will be those that maximize knowledge through the use of contemporary technologies. By maximizing knowledge in every way possible and putting that knowledge to best use, corporations will increase market share, lower operating costs, and satisfy customers. Knowledge, constantly renewed and enhanced, will become the primary source of competitive advantage.

Knowledge as a key economic resource represents a new paradigm in economic and business history. Contrast this to the post-World War II economic boom when the key resources were capital, raw materials, land, and labor. Knowledge, unlike traditional economical resources, can be endlessly replicated. It can be in the hardware, it can be part of PeopleSoft release 7.5 embedded in the software, it can be the cumulative work experience of a PeopleSoft implementation team. It can be transmitted worldwide in a fraction of a second. Worldwide networks are transmitting $4 trillion per day just between banks.

Contemporary businesses must constantly update their knowledge base to succeed. Only a tiny fraction of knowledge can be protected with copyright or patent laws, leaving openings for myriad cloned uses of knowledge. Organizations must rapidly learn from the success of their competitors. These all spill into the implementation area, and thank goodness for that! Almost no process improvements can be protected with intellectual property laws, which means that when PeopleSoft implementations are being done, they have a history of established practices and methodology, both built-in and in the work experience of the team. They have a library of mistakes not to make the second time around. One PeopleSoft client can learn from another, either directly or inadvertently. Thus, to stay ahead is to update your knowledge base faster and better than your competitors.

What does this mean for the enterprise model when the "era of intellectual capital" is mature? Who knows? We do know that they will be nothing like the enterprises of today. The most advanced corporations are already in transition, experimenting with new forms (organizations, processes, and administrative systems). They are living on the edge.

PART

III

CH

19

What is fascinating is that much of this organizational knowledge increasingly resides in software. The knowledge architecture of an enterprise and the related jobs are being reinvented so that all employees are challenged to improve the corporate know-how. New teams with new technology are designed to delight customers. The enterprise at all levels learns rapidly and efficiently and accumulates its learning procedures and its inventory of software. To survive, it must constantly improve its pool of know-how.

GLOBALIZATION

The new global markets seem of an infinite magnitude. Prosperity in one area can have wide-reaching effects; and conversely, as we have seen in the recent Asian economic crisis, regional economic difficulties can have disastrous effects on the global economy. Due to the enormous global coming-of-age of Generation X, a new consumer tsunami is hitting global economic shores. There is even more to come. By 2001, 2 billion teenagers will have a global reach and similar experiences. They will watch global networks like MTV and CNN, shop in worldwide chain stores or online, listen to the same pop music, go to the same movies. Most of them will want to better their economic situation. Fewer than 5% of them will be in America and Europe.

Germany and Japan became economic powerhouses after WWII because their old industries were destroyed and replaced with new high-tech factories that, along with a strong labor force, created the economic marvels they became.

The millennial leaders will be corporations designed for an era of intense, global, knowledge-driven competition, with worldwide electronic media, massive computer power, and management styles that challenge all employees to add value to a much greater extent than today. The corporation of the future will be designed to learn constantly at all levels, accumulate its learning, and put it to good use by empowering the workforce that it employs. All this is happening while customer demand is constantly shifting, yet driving the business processes and strategies of those same corporations. The post-war boom was based on high technology and sturdy backs, but the new boom is based on high technology and sturdy, flexible minds.

SURVIVING IN A NEW WORLD

As of late 1999, this kind of knowledge management is now in vogue. Although it may seem to be a trendy concept, in fact it is an essential part of survival for any corporation as it faces the millennium. A smooth workflow that takes advantage of the global knowledge of any enterprise (and, in some cases, its partners) can mean savings of millions of dollars to a company in a given time period. The use of this knowledge, when organized around effective business processes implemented through PeopleSoft, can mean the difference between failure and success in the management of changing customer demand, changing world conditions, changing internal procedures, and the implementation of best practices throughout an enterprise.

Implementation, re-engineering—both are somewhat daunting terms. Any software implementation is challenging. Tie in a process re-engineering project, and you certainly increase that challenge. But what is the cost of not moving forward? Can you afford to stay or compete in today's economic environment with your current systems and processes? You must ask yourself hard questions before you decide, but the pressure will only increase.

So, in a nutshell, should you do it? Yes. If you need to be able to respond well to the changes in your business with seamless integration of those changes, PeopleSoft is the software implementation to choose.

SUMMARY

This chapter has taken the time to discuss whether or not a PeopleSoft plan is for you or your organization. The chapter discussed such wide-ranging topics as office automation, re-engineering and restructuring, as well as globalization.

PART

III

CH

19

CHAPTER 20

ESTABLISHING THE BASELINE OR THE AS-IS STATE

In this chapter   *by Mark Gibson*

This chapter focuses on the current state of your organization, the baseline or "as-is state." The baseline establishes a starting point for all project activity and provides a means of comparing where your organization was to where you are going. As one of the first activities by the project team, creating the baseline is the first chance for team members to build a working relationship. Project managers will leverage this relationship, team synergy for the life of the project. The discussions of this chapter include:

1. Defining current business processes
2. Measuring those processes (getting internal measurements)
3. Identifying key performance indicators
4. Identifying critical success factors
5. Benchmarking those processes (getting external measurements)
6. Defining initial requirements
7. Defining industry best practices

DEFINING CURRENT BUSINESS PROCESSES

The most critical time in any project is the beginning. In the beginning, the strategic course of the project is established and a plan constructed to get there. How can the organization get anywhere if the organization doesn't know where it is? Imagine being blindfolded and taken to some unknown place, or being placed in the middle of the desert with no visible landmarks. The organization knows that it needs to change but is unsure how to change or how to affect that change. That is how it will feel for a team with no plan. In order to lead the team somewhere, you must be prepared to answer the questions: "Which direction do I head? How far is it? For that matter, do I pay in dollars, yen, francs, or the Euro?" The beginning of any project is to establish a starting point, the current business processes. As depicted in Figure 20.1, if the organization does not have a solid understanding of its current business processes, the path to change is unknown and appears to be an insurmountable task.

Figure 20.1
Understand the organization's business processes before proceeding with the project.

How do I Know which way to go, if I don't know where I am?

Before you can answer these questions, a project team must know where it is before it can begin working towards the end goal. This is the essence of the baseline or As-is model.

By defining the organization's current business processes, the project can establish a starting point. This starting point will act as an anchor to solidify the project plan and give it a basis of comparison. The project plan will outline how the organizations will "travel" from this starting point to the desired state, called the To Be model.

The desire for change is born from a level of discomfort in the process. The project manager should understand this discomfort from each element of the organization and how the project team feels about these areas of discomfort. By understanding these areas and each member of the organization's feelings about these areas, the project manager can better understand the course of events to follow and the motivations of the end-user community.

One of the most difficult aspects of project management is understanding why end users are so much more passionate about some requirements than others. Individuals are motivated by the areas in which they feel the most discomfort. These individuals tend to be more passionate about these areas and more vocal about the requirements that will make their jobs easier. During the course of developing an As-is model, the project manager should observe the proceedings with a keen ear and eye for those subprocesses that spawn the most passion from the end users.

The second observation point for project managers during the development of the As-is model is subprocesses that spawn extensive discussion/debate. These will represent areas of potential requirements risk. Especially in organizations that do not routinely work together but perform similar tasks, the details of these processes may be substantially different. Large differences in the business processes of organizations may be handled with the business unit structure of PeopleSoft, but can cause dissatisfaction with the end product. The prudent project manager pays special attention to these volatile areas and works diligently early in the project to ensure the satisfaction of all parties in the eventual product.

The organization can always remember the ways of the past and gain motivation and energy from the knowledge that the project will make conditions better than before. During the As-is model, the organization will highlight those business processes and subprocesses that require change. The knowledge that the project team will make the organization more efficient and desirable is an enormous rallying point for the project manager.

As with all projects, the motivation level of the team will fluctuate with the trials and tribulations of implementing software. Project team members may have to give up functionality or go back on promises they made to coworkers. These times can demotivate members, and the project manager can highlight to the members in dramatic terms the large contribution they have made. This contribution is well-documented in the As-is model.

Now, before a discussion of the benefits and uses of the baseline model, let's talk briefly about the modeling process.

Business process modeling is a well-established discipline. The concept achieved greater prominence with Edward Deming and his concepts of process improvement. Many different techniques and tools exist to document an organization's business process. Any tool or technique is satisfactory—the key point is for the organization to undergo the process of understanding how they currently do business, where they want to improve, and what are their new performance standards. As discussed earlier, the organization learns a great deal about itself during this enlightening period.

The members of the organization will understand better how they individually conduct business, how they fit into the organization as a whole, how others within the organization conduct similar business, and where their current methodologies have room for improvement. This process is especially enlightening for those individuals or organizations who do not routinely keep detailed process models or who do not routinely study their current business processes. Key points to remember are as follows:

- Document all business processes.
- Functional and technical managers should document this model.
- Functional and technical project team members should fully understand the As-is model.

DOCUMENT ALL BUSINESS PROCESSES

The first step is to document *all* business processes.

When performing software implementations or upgrades, many organizations limit their process modeling or engineering efforts to a few processes. All the processes of the business should be modeled even if they have existing automated tools and will not change. All the organization's processes should integrate seamlessly to achieve optimum results.

Thus, the combination of the implementation's in-scope business processes and those of existing systems or manual processes should pave the way for identifying the required integration points. The lack of defined integration points can create significant issues during and after an implementation if the upstream and downstream impacts are not considered and tested thoroughly. For example, if you are replacing the General Ledger, not considering where your data is coming from or going to could have huge business implications.

When performing software implementations or upgrades, many organizations limit their process modeling or engineering efforts to a few processes. These omissions tend to fall into two areas:

1. Business processes deemed outside the project's scope because the processes are supported by existing legacy systems
2. Processes that won't change

Figure 20.2 depicts an organization that has identified an interface to a legacy General Ledger system. By virtue of its inclusion, an interface to this legacy system is defined. Without the inclusion in this model, it could have been overlooked. Also associated with this system is the coordination with the system owners on project elements such as human and computing resources, and the compatibility of the operating systems and database engines. A high-level technical design including the data transfer mechanisms and media can be negotiated based on this As-is model. Functional tasks such as the conceptual data mapping and technical tasks such as the logical data mapping are achievable based on this model. Project managers are able to scope the resource requirements for this interface and negotiate the timing of resource expenditure with this information. Training requirements for each organization's technical and functional staff can begin after the technical and functional tasks described earlier are complete.

Figure 20.2
Organizations should include all connected legacy systems in the model.

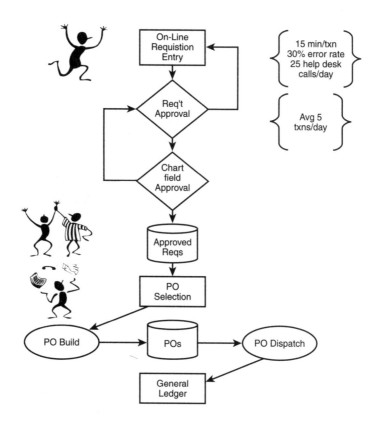

Figure 20.3 depicts an organization under one of two scenarios. The purchasing module is either a PeopleSoft module not destined for customization or a legacy system. In either case, the inclusion of this module highlights the need for interfaces, functional and technical training, as referred to in Figure 20.3. It also facilitates the functional and technical design of the interfaces and scoping.

All the processes of the business should be modeled even if they have existing automated tools and will not change. All the organization's processes should seamlessly integrate to achieve optimum results. Without identifying the modules and integration points, organizations will risk omission of elements. One of the major risks associated with all projects is the creeping of requirements. Process modeling enables project managers to think through the entire system at a required level of detail. The more thorough the requirements scope efforts, the lower the risk of omission or creeping of requirements.

Figure 20.3
Organizations should include all interconnected systems in the model.

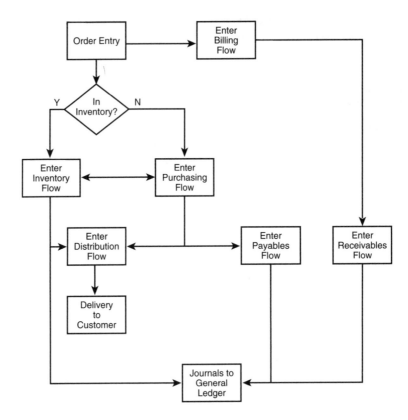

The interface points between the existing systems are identified, paving the way to identifying the interface points in the new system. Given a thorough model of an organization's existing system, this knowledge can be enlightening to some organizations. This new view of the organization's system architecture may facilitate identifying a more efficient To Be system architecture. Figure 20.4 highlights this concept.

In Figure 20.4, the organization's system architecture has evolved over time without management review. The organization began without a good purchasing system, so individual suborganizations built their own systems to meet their individual needs. Later, the organization implemented a credit card program and its associated purchasing system. This system was implemented in addition to the organization's existing purchasing systems. To keep all these systems in synchronization, the organization built two additional interfaces for the inventory and distribution systems. Given these four additional interfaces, the organization is faced with a decision to consolidate these purchasing systems into a single purchasing system and the six interfaces into two interfaces. The cost and technical advantages to the organization may prove worthwhile.

Figure 20.4
The As-is model may highlight to the organization any redundant systems within its architecture.

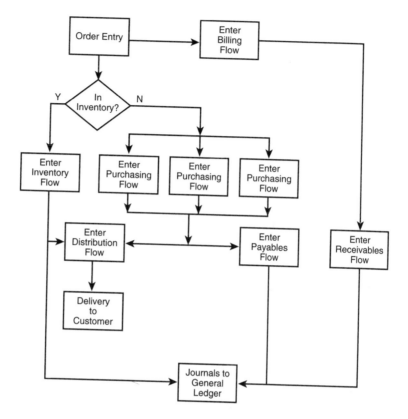

Taking a strategic look at a corporate computing architecture is enlightening. For those organizations that maintain current models of their processes, the existing models can be used. For organizations without existing models, the number of different systems, operating systems, database engines, interfaces, reporting tools, and maintenance personnel comes as a surprise. As highlighted in Figure 20.4, a well-documented process can highlight new areas that are ripe for enhancement.

FUNCTIONAL AND TECHNICAL MANAGERS SHOULD DOCUMENT THIS MODEL

Functional and technical managers should work together to accomplish the baseline model. These managers should come from both the project team and the end-user community. As stated earlier, project team synergy is critical to a successful project, but so is synergy between the project team and the end-user community. This joint activity is a tremendous opportunity for team building between the project team and end users. Also, the information technology professionals, referred to as technical managers, and the business professionals, referred to as functional managers, must also learn to work together.

Figure 20.5
Management defining a solid As-is model is the best start for any project.

I succeeded, now my project team can also succeed!

Use of management staff for this activity is important to gain that strategic look at the organization's processes. Managers are outside the details of the process and can more easily reflect on the integration between functional areas and are chartered to change business processes when the need arises. Use of this layer of the workforce speeds the model documentation and helps build the executive sponsorship discussed in other chapters.

FUNCTIONAL AND TECHNICAL PROJECT TEAM MEMBERS SHOULD FULLY UNDERSTAND THE AS-IS MODEL

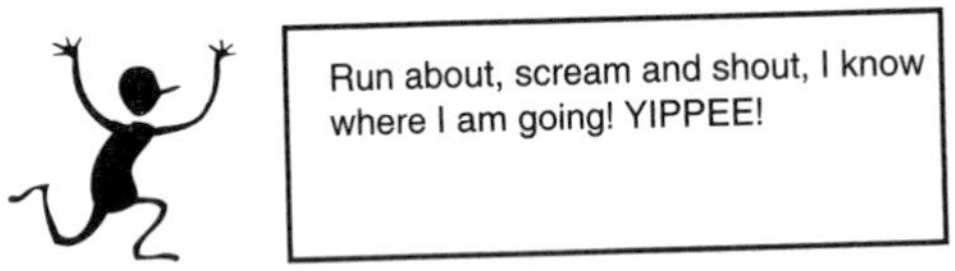

Figure 20.6
Understanding the As-is model is the best starting position for project team staff.

Run about, scream and shout, I know where I am going! YIPPEE!

At the point in the project when the project team staffing is occurring, the project management staff must fully convey all aspects and details of the As-is model to all project team members. From this model and the To Be model discussed in Chapter 21, "Establishing the 'To Be' State," the project will define its implementation strategy.

Without knowing the organization's beginning business processes, the organization will have difficulty discretely defining the implementation strategy to achieve the To Be model defined later.

Let's look at an example of a portion of a baseline model.

The example in Figure 20.7 shows a purchasing process and, for consistency, uses the PeopleSoft Purchasing terminology. It includes the Requestor (Customer) who is the initiator of the process. In this example, a customer desires an item and enters an online requisition. This entry is the event that spawns the purchasing process.

It also defines the users and executioners of the process. Two other user roles of requisition—approver and buyer—are identified. The requestor is a user of the process; they have a need to be fulfilled by the process. The approver and buyer are enablers of the process. This identification process enables an organization to analyze the number of human interface points in their process and the number of different organizations required during the process.

Figure 20.7
The As-is model is high level and shows the major activities and their inter-relationships.

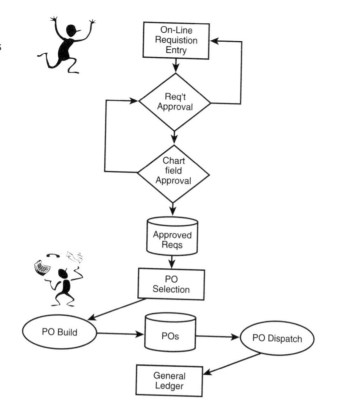

The model identifies decision points, internal management control points, and batch processes. When designing business processes, organizations must balance the need for multiple decision points and management oversight with the efficiency/cost of the process. The same applies to internal management controls (IMCs). The greater the number of IMCs, generally, the greater the cost. The key to IMCs is to collect the data for control without tasking the system end user with an additional workload.

These decisions on the extent of internal management controls, cost tradeoffs between management control points, and so forth are the reasons for managers to develop and approve the As-is model. During this strategic look at the organization and its processes, managers have a unique opportunity to analyze their current practices and can use the project as a change agent to streamline their organizations, and improve the integration between their organization and the organizations with whom they conduct business.

All processes have a discrete beginning and end point.

> **Note**
>
> One point that I did not address is the level of detail required or desired. This level is specific to each and every organization. Each organization must decide for itself the level of detail required for accomplishing the goals and objectives stated for the As-is model.

MEASURING THOSE PROCESSES: GETTING INTERNAL MEASUREMENTS

This topic is sometimes termed a *benchmarking study* or an internal benchmarking study. This effort is focused on determining how the existing business performs. This performance can be measured in terms of transaction volume, time to process a transaction, number of errors, and so on. Any measure that focuses on the cost or speed of doing business is appropriate. Remember that cost is measured in dollars, human resources expended, and computing resources expended. Each of these drivers should be analyzed, if possible.

Benchmarking aids an organization in two ways. First, it provides discrete requirements that are easily measurable. A project team can make preparations to meet these benchmarks and use either testing or additional benchmarking studies after implementation to confirm compliance with the stated requirements. Secondly, an organization can use the benchmarks as performance goals to measure functional process improvement against the best organizations. By measuring current performance against stated goals, objective performance measurement is accomplished.

Some organizations may routinely collect this type of information. The manufacturing industry is generally a good example. This industry may collect the number of cars produced on a line, the number of defects identified by their inspections, the number of defects identified after the vehicle passed inspection, and the amount of paint used on each vehicle. Each measure gets to the heart of how much it costs to do business.

The technology industry may collect the resource utilization of each main computing device and forecast the time for a hardware replacement or upgrade. It may collect the number of developers required to correct errors or payable technicians to run a pay cycle on a legacy finance system.

Each organization should investigate the monetary (cost driver), human, and computing resources (resource drivers) needed for each activity in their business processes. After collection of actual data, the organization then compares itself against the best performers within its industry. This comparison may yield areas of improvement that are translated into requirements for the To Be model. For those organizations that do not collect this type of information, the organizations may want to conduct a study of their existing processes and look for more unconventional ways to calculate many of these figures. For example, in the purchasing flow, most organizations have paper records on requisition submission and fill dates. These organizations can then compute the transaction time for a requisition. Those same organizations can determine the number of people in each department involved in the process. From these figures, one can compute the transaction volume per person. By using either developer staffing levels or contract costs, that same organization can compute maintenance costs.

Some organizations may require additional effort to collect good baseline performance, but each organization will benefit greatly from having collected the data.

After the cost and resource drivers are identified, management can determine the areas to target for improvement. But what should the numbers be? The section "Getting External Measurements" discusses this in more detail later in this chapter.

Let's go back to the example. Our organization measured the system performance of the online requisition entry in terms of transaction time (15 minutes per transaction), number of errors (30% error rate), and support (25 help desk calls per day). Also, the organization has measured the transaction volume for requisition approvals at five transactions per day. This organization considered these values to be high as compared to their benchmarking study, so change is required. Part of this organization's benchmarking study was to collect from industry the most efficient organizations with respect to these indicators as well as the key processes that enabled this stellar performance. The organization included their performance on the As-is model and defined requirements to reach the performance of industry best practitioners. Keep in mind that it may take years to reach the performance goals. So functional managers and project managers should phase their performance improvements to attainable levels within a given timeframe.

IDENTIFYING KEY PERFORMANCE INDICATORS

Key performance indicators are those process activities or decision points that have the most impact on the process. In looking at the prior example, let's assume the organization defined a key performance indicator as the requisition approval time. Thus, any improvement in this area would reap the most benefit in terms of process improvement.

Organizations should identify the key performance indicators for their business process or industry and target them for improvement. To enhance the team's ability to improve the performance measure, the organization can also investigate the reasons for its current level of performance. The analysis of performance indicators may reveal multiple causes for the metric calculations. Going back to the prior example, there could be three reasons for the current performance:

1. The current computing capacity slows the requirement approvers' capability to process transactions.

2. It is difficult to locate background information to properly review the transactions for approval.

3 The requirement approvers have higher priority tasking and cannot spend the time to process transactions.

As you can see, there are now three distinct areas to probe for improvement opportunities rather than believing that the measure as defined is the best the organization can do.

Figure 20.8
Organizations can include performance measurements or requirements in the model.

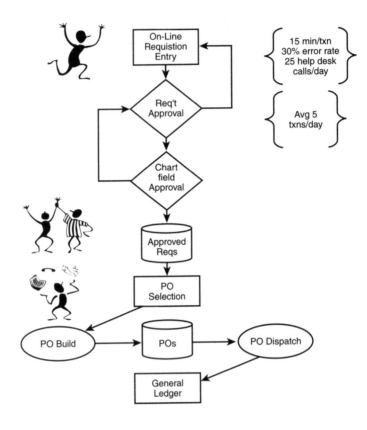

IDENTIFYING CRITICAL SUCCESS FACTORS

Critical success factors are similar to key performance indicators, but are not necessarily the same. The main difference is that key performance indicators are focused on the process and only the process, whereas critical success factors may focus on elements outside the process.

Let's take the manufacturing example again and highlight how forces outside the organization can affect the organization's performance. In a production line, the performance of the line is dependent on the "just in time" delivery of raw materials and work in progress. These elements are then assembled into the organization's finished goods. A critical success factor for this organization is the on-time delivery of these raw materials and work in progress. Should this supply chain get disrupted, the capability of the line workers to produce their finished goods is disrupted. Let's say that each line should produce 100 goods per week, but each Thursday after producing 90 goods, the materials for Friday production don't arrive. Through no fault of its own, this line cannot meet its stated goals. The ontime delivery of the materials for this line is a factor critical to its success.

Now why are the shipments late? After investigation, you find that the guards at the gates are in a shift change during the time when the shipments arrive. So another critical success factor could be either to alter the guard shift change patterns or to change the arrival times for the shipments. Although this may seem an outlandish example, it states a point about critical success factors. They are traditionally outside the purview of either the functional or project teams.

There are many ways to define critical success factors. However, the most common methods are

- Interviews with key executives—You will hear common themes about how they believe objectives will be achieved.

- Observation of coworkers—They will react to what is believed to be important to the higher level of management.

- Analysis of current state data—After all the processes are modeled, you will be able to identify which processes work well and which ones do not. By identifying what is common about those that work well, you will be able to identify a success factor.

GETTING EXTERNAL MEASUREMENTS

Figure 20.9
Organizations can investigate how their business colleagues conduct business.

So how does the guy down the street accomplish this task?

DEFINING INITIAL REQUIREMENTS

Figure 20.10
Benchmarking can aid the performance requirements definition process.

So how good do I want my organization to be?

PART

III

CH

20

The measurement of internal and external processes enables a project manager to compare the differences. After this comparison and identifying what areas are the primary focus for improvement, an organization can define the project objectives and initial and phased performance goals.

It is critical for project managers to work with management to define the project goals if business leader support is to be gained. After this support is obtained, the business leaders must communicate these goals to the rest of the organization. Organizational commitment is critical to implementing change supported by the project. In addition, these goals will become a way for the project to measure its own success. (For example, was the team able to achieve all the objectives? What was the value provided by the project?) To many in the business world, these goals become the business case for the project.

The second decision a project manager and functional user community should make is the speed at which the organizations will pursue these new goals. At this point, the project manager can synchronize the functional performance goals with the technical performance goals and the introduction of new automation into the organization. The other consideration is the sensitivity of the organization to change and the speed at which the organization is willing to change.

These new goals provide a transition to the To Be model.

DEFINING INDUSTRY BEST PRACTICES

Figure 20.11
A process is a best practice when multiple organizations successfully use the same practice.

I will take the best that everyone else has to offer and combine them to make my organization even better!

The identification and decision to implement industry best practices provide the last transition into the To Be model. Project managers have three paths for identification of industry best practices:

- Best practices are identified during the benchmarking activity in concert with the measurement of other organizations' efficient processes. During this research phase, organizations will identify processes they want to measure. In general, these processes represent a best practice. Therefore, in addition to measuring the process, organizations should document the business process model, observe the personnel executing the process, and identify the internal management controls and external management control points. A full understanding of the process enables functional managers to implement similar processes with their organizations.

- The consulting staffs of PeopleSoft and its implementation partners are well schooled in the best practices of each industry. This knowledge comes from both past experience and consulting experience. The advantage consultants have is the large number of different organizations they are able to see. Also, most of these organizations are undergoing best practice analyses, thus giving the consultant visibility into the efforts of a large number of organizations. This breadth and depth of experience provides a valuable resource for organizations implementing PeopleSoft.

- The PeopleSoft modules are designed with the best practices of industry in mind, so the PeopleSoft customers can use these practices in making their organization as efficient as possible and aid the organization in meeting their performance goals. PeopleSoft dedicates personnel called *product strategists* to determine the direction of each product line. These product strategy personnel consult industry professionals, implementation partners, and existing clients to determine the industry best practices and incorporate any changes into future releases of the product line.

After identification of the practices, the project manager, in concert with the functional user community, can determine the timing of the practices implementation. These practices are incorporated into the To Be model.

PART

III

CH

20

CHAPTER 21

ESTABLISHING THE "TO BE" STATE

In this chapter

by Mark Gibson

TRANSITIONING FROM THE PAST TO THE FUTURE

In Chapter 20, "Establishing the Baseline or the 'As-Is' State," you learned how the organization establishes the current state of its business processes. The implementing organization documents these processes divorced from the PeopleSoft application software. The process of developing the "As Is" model enables the organization to take a fresh look at how business is accomplished. Diagramming the processes forces the implementing organization to review the activities required in any business process. The inter-relationships between these activities become evident as well as any areas ripe for enhancement. Implementing organizations use industry best practices gathered either during a benchmarking phase or through the practices integrated into the PeopleSoft application software. This divorced focus enabled the implementing organization to begin the project from a position of knowledge and experience, thus building confidence and momentum before going forward with the implementation.

PREPARING FOR THE FUTURE

Now that the implementing organization has established its current business processes (the past), it can focus on where it wants to take those business processes (the future). Organizational and project managers can create this vision of the future. This future vision and the path to accomplish it are the focus of the "To Be" model. The *To Be* model is a pictorial depiction of the implementing organization, its locations, its software modules, and their inter-relationships. It includes detailed decision points, the data sources used during the decisions, and the user roles who make the decisions.

CHALLENGES ASSOCIATED WITH THE FUTURE

The challenge for project managers is to balance the future vision with the project realities such as cost, schedule, human resources, and risk. Ideally, the development of an "As Is" model and the evolution of the "To Be" model will fuel excitement within the team as old barriers and thorns are removed with the anticipated new system. Channeling this enthusiasm into an achievable project plan is a critical early goal for the project manager. Prototyping becomes a good asset to manage both user excitement and expectations. Prototyping the system is an evolution of gathering requirements, training the project team in system operation options, and determining desired system configuration settings. The project manager wants to achieve a psychological state of excitement about functionality that the implementing organization can use and the project manager can implement. Also, the project manager wants to temper enthusiasm for technology or functionality that might put the project at unreasonable risk as well as setting the end users' expectations for when the functionality will be implemented. New functions that will increase efficiency or remove barriers and thorns may be scheduled for some time after the initial rollout. This phasing can reduce the implementing organization's enthusiasm and must be managed.

CHAPTER STRUCTURE

This chapter discusses techniques for developing the "To Be" model and determining the scope of the vision—how an organization can document the vision, and how these models are used throughout the project lifecycle. The model is best divided into two separate parts, each developed during successive implementation phases.

The *high-level model* is developed first during the initial project startup phase. It gives project managers and corporate executives an initial look at the project cost, schedule, staffing, business case, and functional rollout plan. The second model, also called the *low-level model*, is developed by the project team and end users during the prototyping phase and evolves as the user community focuses on the desired business processes and supporting software, hardware, and telecommunications suite. The technical project team members evolve the technical design as the detailed requirements unfold.

By developing the "As Is" and "To Be" model, the organization and project team can determine the best path between the two. As the detailed requirements unfold during the prototyping phase, project managers will continually evaluate the evolving requirements in the context of the strategy documents such as technical, training, implementation, and testing, and the project constraints of cost, schedule, staffing, risk, and technology contained in the project plan. The project plan contains the best path from the past to the future.

THE HIGH-LEVEL PROCESS MODEL

The high-level process model is developed as part of the initial project scope efforts. This model is represented by process flow diagrams and definitions of how the PeopleSoft modules will interface to any legacy systems. It provides initial requirements, defines data conversion needs, and documents the functional phasing plans. Project managers should consider the impact on these high-level process flows when making system change decisions. Project managers and their counterparts within the end-user community should spend the time to map out the system software architecture. This architecture decision is best made by managers who can integrate the software implementation options with the strategic business objectives of the organization. Workers at a more detailed level may not have the visibility into the organization's strategic direction. Sometimes this model is referred to as "System Architecture." In the coming sections, we will document the characteristics of this model, its uses and benefits, and illustrate an example.

SYNCHRONIZING THE PROCESS DIAGRAMMING TOOLS WITH THE MODEL DEVELOPMENT

When beginning the "To Be" model, organizations have three tool options for developing this model. Each of these routes will lead to success; however, the most efficient routes depend on each organization. Organizations can also use any number of process diagramming tools to develop the "To Be" model. Microsoft PowerPoint, Visio, and the PeopleSoft Business Process Designer are three examples of engines that support this type of modeling. If the organization is considering either workflow or navigation using the PeopleSoft Navigator, the PeopleSoft Business Process Designer is the best choice.

MODIFYING THE "AS IS" MODEL

For the organizations who developed an "As Is" model, as discussed in Chapter 20, "Establishing the Baseline or the 'As-Is' State," modifying this model may make the most sense. During the modeling, benchmarking, and best practices analysis that occurred during the development of the "As Is" model, the implementing organization identified desired improvements to its existing business processes. The "To Be" model is the appropriate place to document these changes. Because the "As Is" model already exists, use of the same tools to develop it is appropriate for developing the "To Be" model.

STARTING WITH A CLEAN SHEET

The organizations who have not documented their current business processes and who did not develop the "As Is" model have two options: (1) develop the model from a clean sheet of paper, or (2) use the PeopleSoft vanilla business processes documented in the Advantage Toolkit (ATK). Those organizations who want to start fresh should next consult with either their Professional Services Manager (PSM) or hired consulting staff to determine whether workflow or the Navigator will be used. If neither will be used, development of the "To Be" model should occur within any of the industry diagramming tools the organization is comfortable using. The user base of this tool will include management and the eventual end users, so the implementing organization should consider the full array of users before making this decision.

If the organization implements either workflow or the PeopleSoft Navigator, the PeopleSoft Business Process Designer is the best tool for the job. Here's why: Both workflow and the Navigator require documentation of business processes within the Business Process Designer. By documenting the business processes in the Business Process Designer, the implementing organization can eliminate duplicating these processes in multiple tools. If the organization has other uses for the business process diagrams such as in-house marketing, user training, and so on, the investment may be cost-effective.

ADVANTAGE TOOLKIT (ATK) VANILLA PROCESSES

The Advantage Toolkit (ATK) documents business processes both at the high level and low level. These process flows are documented in PowerPoint, Visio, and the Business Process Designer. Organizations that decide to use these process flows will be "jumpstarted" in the development of the "To Be" model and potentially eliminate the time required to determine the structure and formatting of the flows as well as the intimidation factor of beginning such a large task.

The flows documented in both PowerPoint and Visio are synchronized with the vanilla flows documented in Business Process Designer. This is a good option for any organization struggling with how to begin.

It consists of process flow diagrams such as the example in Figure 21.1.

Figure 21.1
The "To Be" model should depict the flow within each functional module, as well as between the functional modules.

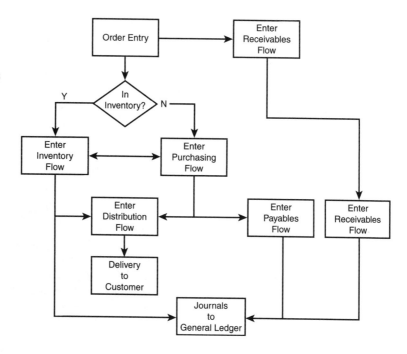

MANAGING THE PROCESS

How is this process managed? First, process modeling is best accomplished by gathering the key users of the business process into a single room and using a white board for illustration. As in any meeting, a facilitator can initiate discussion among the group and a scribe can record the evolving business process. This individual must also question the evolving design and gain the input of all group members. Sometimes the roles of facilitator and scribe can be filled by the same person if the implementing organization's sole product is a business process diagram. If textual requirements, comments, or data are collected, a separate scribe should focus on collecting this data.

Now let's look at the process itself. There are many proven methods to conduct a process modeling session, starting with either the "As Is" model or the ATK vanilla processes. From either of these models, the organization can look at improvements to its software architecture and business processes. For example, the organization may have multiple legacy systems for the entry of customer orders, all of which were written in different programming languages. This architecture required users to identify which order entry system to key in their orders. An inordinate number of orders were entered into the wrong system, causing rework cycles and accounting problems. The organization could consolidate those entry systems into a single system, thus eliminating the rework cycles and improving organizational efficiency.

BUSINESS OBJECTIVES AND HIGH-LEVEL REQUIREMENTS

After considering all manner of architectural improvements, the business objectives and high-level requirements of the system are considered. Let's go back to our previous example. This organization determined that multiple order entry systems were inefficient and defined a business objective of reducing order entry errors and limiting the technical staff to a single programming language and operating system. The business case documented cost savings associated with these objectives that would help pay for the software implementation. This organization realized cost savings by reducing the number of programming languages and operating systems to one. The single language and operating system reduced costs by reducing the number of support staff and license fees. For example, previously the organization staffed three individuals for each of three programming languages. Each individual work-load was one-third of a staff year. Because each individual was paid a full year's salary, the organization had triple the payroll. When the organization went to a single programming language, only one programmer was required, thus reducing the language support costs by 150%. The same scenario is true for operating systems, database engines, and so forth. During the course of developing its "To Be" model, the organization determined that a single order entry system would satisfy both of its business objectives.

Finally, after the software architecture becomes more concrete, the project manager can use the evolving decision to add detail to the project plan. By defining requirements, interfaces, data conversion needs, and required PeopleSoft modules at each phase, the project manager can draft an initial project plan. This project plan will include the project schedule and budget constraints. The project team and end users may need to adjust their architecture or project plan to meet cost, schedule, human resource, and risk constraints.

This is an example of a flow containing all PeopleSoft modules. The level of detail depicted here is at the module level. Early in the prototyping phase, the project team is learning about their purchased modules, how they fit together, and how these modules will fit into the overall enterprise. Until the team can gain sufficient detailed knowledge of the modules, process modeling at levels deeper than the module level is fruitless. Therefore, the high-level module should include activities such as Entering Time, Place Order, Send Journal Entries to GL, Configure Products, Bill Customers, and Enter Benefits.

Each activity box denotes an independent PeopleSoft application module and shows the interconnectivity between the modules. For example, the Order Management module operated by the Sales Organization will pass sales orders to either the Warehouse Managers or Purchasing Managers depending on whether the order is sourced from inventory or a purchase order. From an architecture perspective, it denotes the replacement of any existing legacy applications and the integration points between different functional end user communities. These points are critical to the project manager's assessment of project scope and are used in developing those portions of the project plan pertaining to interface development, data conversion, legacy system shutdown, training of functional and technical personnel in the new systems, and retraining of personnel with expertise in systems destined for shutdown.

To continue the example, both the warehouse and purchasing managers will pass the completed Material Stock Request from Inventory or the received goods to the distribution manager for delivery to the end customer. The Financial Managers are involved at the point of sale in preparing the invoices from Billing and posting a receivable to the General Ledger. The Accounts Payable Manager receives purchase orders from the Purchasing Manager to both create payments and post an Accounts Payable transaction to the General Ledger.

A second example (Figure 21.2) illustrates a flow containing both PeopleSoft modules and legacy system applications. The two examples also illustrate differences in style, in that the second example includes clip art and some high-level requirements of the system.

Figure 21.2
The "To Be" model depicts the interfaces between Legacy systems and PeopleSoft.

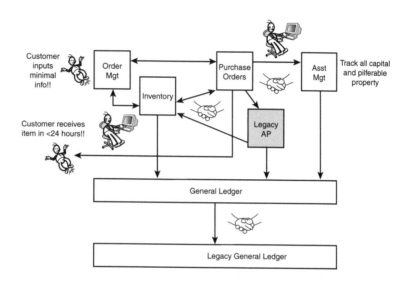

Here the organization chose to use the Screen Bean characters to document the points of customer interaction, the hands shaking to document interface points, and the man at the terminal to depict points of manual intervention with the system. You can see an interface to a legacy General Ledger system and derive training needs for General Ledger. Also, from this diagram, the organization can derive the shutdown of existing purchasing, order entry, and inventory systems. The shutdown of these systems defines a data conversion requirement and retraining of existing personnel. Again, notice the arrows illustrating the data flow from one functional module to the next.

High-level performance requirements or expectations were also documented. The Asset Management module must track both capital equipment and the smaller pilferable items such as software, laptop computers, and so forth. This organization has a more complex structure and documented its points in a slightly different manner.

HIGH-LEVEL MODULE PROJECTS PHASING STRATEGY

The last characteristic of a high-level module is its capability to illustrate the project's phasing strategy. Project managers and organizations have two approaches to the project; one is the "big bang," in which all functionality is deployed to all sites simultaneously. The second approach is to break up the deployment. The chapter on implementation methodology will speak to this topic in more depth, but this model is where organizations can document a phasing strategy. Multiple diagrams are drawn each representing the system at different points in time.

For example, the phasing strategy may have the financial applications rolling out in the spring, integrated with legacy distribution modules. During this time, interfaces to those legacy systems are required. In the winter, the PeopleSoft distribution modules roll out replacing the legacy systems. In this example, the organization has decided to build temporary interfaces to its legacy distribution applications. This illustrates the final advantage of the "To Be" model. The project manager can study the phasing strategy to look for implementation efficiencies. The project manager may determine that building interfaces for six months is not cost-effective, and the project can be implemented more efficiently by rolling out all the modules in the spring.

The ultimate goal of the high-level process flow/architecture is to define streamlined and efficient processes based on best practice and state-of-the-art technology. To successfully realize these goals, it is important that these are agreeable to both the project team and the end-user community. To obtain such agreement and to achieve corporate buy-in, it is important to involve the client in the analysis and decision making process.

USES OF THE HIGH-LEVEL MODEL

Now that the implementing organization has developed and successfully managed the high-level model, how does the implementing organization use this model? Another good question is: Why should an implementing organization spend the time and money to develop this model?

There are several uses of the high-level model, each of which is a good reason for developing it, but the aggregate sum of all these uses constitutes an overwhelming argument for spending the time and money to develop the high-level model. Figure 21.3 shows the uses of the high-level model.

DEFINING HOW PEOPLESOFT WILL INTERFACE INTO YOUR EXISTING ARCHITECTURE

As depicted in the preceding examples, the model can identify to the corporation all the interfaces required to complete the architecture. In the second example, the model identified interfaces between the Purchase Orders modules and the Inventory and Legacy Accounts Payable modules, and the General Ledger and a legacy General Ledger system. Depending on the hardware architecture, new servers, new client workstations, and possibly new telecommunication paths and devices could be required.

Figure 21.3
Uses of the high-level model.

I really hate documents! so why do I need this model?

The model identified which PeopleSoft modules were to be purchased and which functional user community personnel would require training on a new automation package. Project managers and end-user managers from every walk of life can derive a great deal of information about the future computing environment from this high-level model.

PROVIDING THE PROJECT STRUCTURE AND SCOPE

One of the greatest challenges facing every project manager is the management of requirements and balancing the evolving requirements against the project schedule and budget. This model puts bounds around the functionality to be developed by the project and to be reused from existing legacy systems.

Additionally, the evolving requirements need organization. They tend to exist on paper in a list and may or may not be complete. The model structures both the thought process of designing a system and the approach the project team will undertake during the project execution. By documenting all aspects of the project, project team members and end users can systematically think through those aspects. Without this model, project team members tend to become focused in discrete areas and may not think through or, more importantly, address required functions. Project managers cringe at the last-minute scope changes. Both the high- and low-level models discussed later mitigate this risk.

Lastly, it provides the integration points to the individual functional groups. Individual groups will form who works on the Purchasing or Inventory modules. These modules have points where they integrate, data that they share, and will have implementation decisions to make together. The model identifies these points to project team members so that communication will take place.

PROVIDING A BASIS FOR PROTOTYPING

The current trend in development methodologies is the use of prototyping as a means of speeding implementation times while providing a solution that more closely matches the end-user community needs. This process of prototyping needs structure and a systematic method of accomplishment. The high-level model provides discrete paths through the system architecture for end users to explore. By providing the universe of paths, the end users can ensure that all possible paths are explored and the more detailed processes documented in the low-level model are satisfactorily accomplished within the system.

It focuses the project team on discrete tasks during prototyping. The project team will develop the low-level model, identify detailed requirements, identify discrete panel and low-level security roles, identify job-level processes, and evolve the training needs. Just as with

PART

III

CH

21

the Project managers, it helps the project team think through the implementation tasks and focus those efforts.

The model provides the project manager a quantifiable means of tracking progress through prototyping. As the low-level model and system evolves, the project manager can lose the forest for the trees. The day-to-day activities evolve into detailed implementation decisions or reviews of customization designs. The high-level model is the big picture. By tracking progress against the big picture, the project manager can assess project positioning at any given time and brief that positioning to the organization's senior executives to maintain that critical sponsorship during the project.

PROVIDING A BASIS FOR BOTH INTEGRATION AND SYSTEM TESTING

Like the prototyping processes before them, the formal integration and system tests can leverage the same model. Because the model documents the full scope of functionality, it provides a good basis for any formal reviews of the functionality. The formal reviews will attempt to examine all aspects of the functionality within a context recognizable by the functional user community and systematically explore the system for errors. With a good model of the full functionality, a test that covers the full model has a reasonable chance of exploring the entire system. The model also provides a medium for testing based on risk reduction, if project funding constraints do not allow for full examination of the system. Project managers can use the model to choose those aspects of the system deemed most risky and focus the testing there.

PROVIDING A BASIS TO TIE THE INFORMATION TECHNOLOGY SOLUTION TO THE IMPLEMENTING ORGANIZATION'S BUSINESS OBJECTIVES

The second example also illustrated how an organization can incorporate its high-level requirements or business objectives into the model. These objectives are included in a cost-benefit analysis commonly used to justify the project. Given the importance of these goals, project managers can plan these requirements into their technical designs and have a far greater chance of achieving the objectives.

SETTING EXPECTATIONS AT A REASONABLE AND SUSTAINABLE LEVEL

User and project team expectations can run the full spectrum of expectations. Many end users and teams have unbounded enthusiasm for the project, but others may be satisfied with the current systems and resist the change. Staff at either of these extremes or somewhere in the middle of the spectrum requires management of their expectations throughout the implementation.

The easier group to deal with have unlimited enthusiasm for the new project. The whole environment is fresh and clean, and the optimism is unbounded. With this optimism come expectations of the project. What will it accomplish? When will certain functionality be available to their office? How much better will the environment be? All project team members bring their own view of the project.

The more difficult group is those staff who are satisfied with current systems and must be won over. These individuals tend to compare the new system with the old or tend to recreate the old business processes in the new system. This approach has merit if the implementing organization is satisfied with the current processes. These staff members can be especially challenging.

The risk Project managers face is keeping the team focused on the strategic goals and phasing strategy, if applicable. This model provides the project team's first look at the real project. It answers some of the questions about functionality and timing. And as the project progresses, it provides the project manager and team an anchor to keep them focused on the project goals and objectives.

During prototyping, project team members can lose focus and get caught up in the euphoric frenzy that accompanies the rapid evolution of a system. The risk becomes the desire to include additional features or functionality planned for a later phase. Project managers can use this anchor to mitigate this risk.

IDENTIFYING REQUIRED SKILLS OF THE PROJECT TEAM AND END-USER COMMUNITY

One of the challenges facing all project managers early in the project is the number of skill sets required for their project team. The project manager must split the team among functional and technical people, decide whether outside consulting support is required, and whether people conversant in the legacy systems are required. This model will aid the project manager in these decisions. Let's go back to the first example, which contained only PeopleSoft modules.

This model does not contain any interfaces to legacy systems, so legacy expertise is not required. This organization does have extensive new functionality to learn and master, so outside consulting is an option. Given that the model includes Order Management, Inventory, Purchasing, General Ledger, and so on, these functional areas are required on the team. This project manager should consult those managers for good personnel to implement those modules. Also, the project manager must consider technical staff. Will the project include customizations? In this case, the manager will require programmers and their management to support the project. Will new hardware or software operating systems be procured? In this case, the manager needs expertise in these areas. How about trainers? Telecommunication specialists?

The model will aid the project manager in thinking through the staffing needs.

PROVIDING A COMMUNICATION AND MARKETING VEHICLE FOR STRONG EXECUTIVE SPONSORSHIP

The high-level model provides a concise pictorial view of the project goals and objectives. Combined with an "As Is" model and a cost-benefit analysis, project managers are armed with ammunition to sell their project to senior organization executives and build organization commitment and excitement about the project. Because the models are concise and consist of a few pages, they can be used for briefing slides to brief senior management on the merits of the project and, if need be, justify the expenditure of funds for the effort.

PROVIDING A BASIS FOR BUSINESS PROCESS RE-ENGINEERING

One of the most important advantages of this model is that it provides the managers in an organization the time together and the opportunity to think about the automation environment and make good business decisions about the future environment. It also allows the managers to visualize the future state of the system and may provide a new perspective. Given the early timing of the model, the project manager has the opportunity to make significant enhancements to the organization's computing environment. By taking the time to think about how your organization conducts its business, managers can greatly improve their current situation.

Combined with the "As Is" model, the high-level model highlights the changes the organization's computing environment will undergo. By highlighting those changes, personnel can more easily see the benefits defined in the cost-benefit analysis. Organizations can also use the highlighted changes in training the end-user community.

THE LOW-LEVEL MODEL

The low-level model, as the name implies, delves much more deeply into the business processes of the organization as well as addressing the PeopleSoft specific implementation issues that arise during any implementation. Whereas the high-level model was generic and used as a basis for thought and architecture design, the low-level model does the following:

- Integrates the desired business processes with the purchased PeopleSoft modules
- Documents the specific processes associated with each user role
- Documents the base tables used by the software
- Identifies any misfits that spawn customizations of the software

As important as the high-level model is in designing and documenting the strategic approach to the project, the low-level module documents the tactical approach to the project. It represents the link between the strategic model and the future system and provides the project manager with a review and control point for project scope and detailed design issues. The tendency of project teams is to forget the low-level model in favor of the "more fun" activities of operating the new system, coding customizations, and configuring the system. Project managers should resist this temptation and maintain their management control points for scope and tactical direction of their project teamwork.

TECHNIQUES FOR DEVELOPING THE LOW-LEVEL MODEL

The low-level model is developed during the prototyping project phase in conjunction with the other scoping activities of detailed requirements, definition, fits and gaps, functional designs of customizations, required reports, and support tools. All these activities occur simultaneously, creating a period of time in which the end users discuss proposed processes, configure the system to implement the theoretical process, try out the theoretical process on the system, and determine whether the implementing organization wants to implement the process. This prototyping approach enables the end users to "test drive" a theoretical process prior to going to production with it. The end users can modify the processes and reconfigure the system on-the-fly to gain the best business process achievable for that organization.

The challenge for project managers is to manage the user expectations and constrain the timing of this process. Project teams and especially end users have a lot of fun during prototyping and may have difficulty settling down on the best business processes. This schedule risk, as well as how to get started, is a significant challenge for project managers during prototyping.

Figure 21.4
The low-level model may change the high-level model.

Now I remember why I must change my high-level model!

During the development of this low-level model, information may come to light that changes the high-level model (Figure 21.4). As the old cliché goes, "the devil is in the details." The high-level model may require updating and modification to reflect enlightenment. Project managers should be keenly aware when changes of this nature prove necessary. Given that the high-level model is briefed to senior executives and approved, any changes may affect the previous decisions.

Project managers have two options on how to get prototyping and low-level model development started. Both of these techniques begin with the theoretical discussion of the future business process.

MODIFYING THE HIGH-LEVEL MODEL

Earlier in this chapter, project teams learned how to build a high-level model. This high-level model is an excellent starting point for the low-level model. Basically, the project team will increase the level of detail documented in the high-level model.

Let's look at an example. Figure 21.5 is a portion of a high-level "To Be" model dealing with sales orders.

In the upper left corner of the model is the sales order entry functionality activity box. From this high-level box, Figure 21.5 will drill down one level of detail focused on the functionality within this single activity box.

Figure 21.5
One level of detail drill-down from high-level model to low level model.

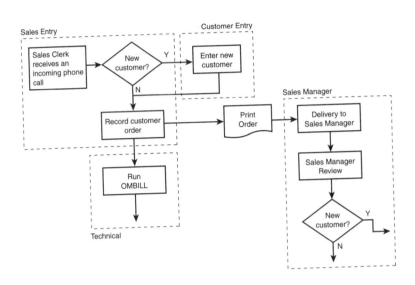

In this example, the Sales Order activity box was expanded to include the more detailed activities that encompass it. We will discuss the different aspects of this model in the section "Uses of the Low-Level Model."

USING THE VANILLA BUSINESS PROCESSES DEFINED IN THE ATK

The second option available to project managers is to use the vanilla business processes documented in the Advantage Toolkit (ATK). These lower-level business processes provide project teams with further detail than provided in the high-level ATK business processes and also document industry best practices.

The documentation of industry best practices with the ATK can also serve the project teams who want assistance with those best practices and are unable to conduct independent research.

USES OF THE LOW-LEVEL MODEL

The low-level model includes a lot of detail about the organization, its business processes, its internal management controls, and reporting needs. What are the uses of this model, and what benefit does the project team derive from this effort? This section examines how the model is used, why it is beneficial to an implementing organization, and how a project manager can use this model to successfully implement PeopleSoft and transition the implementing organization from the past to the future.

IDENTIFYING DETAILED REQUIREMENTS

As with the high-level model, the low-level model will uncover unknown requirements (Figure 21.6). An analogy near and dear to my heart is when I went jogging for the first time in a long time. Naturally, I ran farther than I should have and discovered muscles that I never thought I had. The same applies here. As the project team and end users work through the details of the organization's business processes, details of what the low-level security implementation should be will fall out, including new reports resulting from a new process, a new panel security class, how the software executes these processes, and how the detailed functional requirements are uncovered. By using a process model to define the requirements, the project team is engaged to systematically think through and document all aspects of the evolving business process. Project managers can use the following checklist to ensure that the project team is capturing all the different types of functional requirements.

- Functional Requirements
- Technical Infrastructure Requirements
- Data Management Requirements
- Security and Access Requirements
- Interface Requirements
- Performance Requirements
- Reporting Requirements
- Audit and Control Requirements

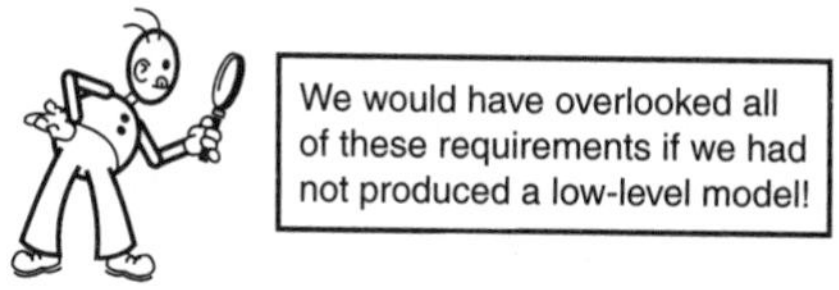

Figure 21.6
Assisting the project team to think through the detailed requirements.

We would have overlooked all of these requirements if we had not produced a low-level model!

Let's look again at our Order Entry example depicted in Figure 21.5.

From this example, we can derive the need for many requirements:

FUNCTIONAL REQUIREMENTS   Functional requirements include

> Entry of customer orders online
> Entry of customer orders while Sales Entry clerks and customers are on the phone
> On-line entry of customer data

TECHNICAL AND INFRASTRUCTURE REQUIREMENTS   Technical and infrastructure requirements include

> Print capability for Sales and customer entry clerks
> Data Management requirements
> Sales Manager approval of sales order after order is taken

SECURITY AND ACCESS REQUIREMENTS   Security and access requirements include defined security roles for Sales Entry, Customer Entry, Technical, and Sales Manager.

Notice in the figure that the Print Order deliverable box does not have an associated security role. This is an example of the advantage of using the process model. We defined a physical report, but up until now have overlooked granting access to this report to the Sales Entry role. By diagramming the whole detailed process, we easily identified an error and corrected it before any production impact occurred.

INTERFACE REQUIREMENTS   Internal interface: OMBILL batch process.

Project managers should include both internal PeopleSoft processes that integrate the different modules and, more importantly, the interfaces to systems outside of PeopleSoft. The definition of these interfaces will help define the development tasks of writing the interfaces. If the project manager includes the base application tables on the model, it can facilitate the data mapping inherent to any data conversion or interface development.

PERFORMANCE REQUIREMENTS   Performance requirements include:

Sales Order entry during initial customer phone call

Sales Order entry panel load in five seconds

The performance requirements can be defined inside and outside the model. In this example, a functional requirement was defined as the entry of order while the sales entry clerk was on the phone with the customer. This functional requirement spawns a more detailed technical performance requirement. The time it takes for the sales entry clerk to enter an order must be less than the time the customer is willing to stay on the phone. This definition is soft as stated here, but technical staff should define this time in terms of minutes to enter the order or panel response time, and so on. The exact definition of performance requirements is known only to the implementing organization.

REPORTING REQUIREMENTS   Review of the model indicates a desire to print the customer order for delivery to the Sales Manager. This paper printout defines a reporting requirement. As the model unfolds, many other reports will come to light.

Use of the model for definition of reporting requirements also provides the project manager and business leaders to validate the needs for existing reports and provides a mechanism to streamline those reporting requirements.

AUDIT AND CONTROL REQUIREMENTS   Audit and control requirements include automated reviews of sales orders after they are entered.

The capability and desire of the implementing organization to keep electronic records of data changes and the needs of business leaders for internal management control are also defined within this model. For business leaders to manage their organization, they require internal management controls. Documentation of these controls in the model provides a good mechanism for these leaders to define the points in the new process where auditing or control is needed. In this example, the review of sales orders is considered an internal management control requirement.

PROVIDING A BASIS FOR DETAILED FIT ANALYSIS

As the organization defines the detailed processes, the prototyping activities can begin. When sufficient detail begins to unfold in the processes, the PeopleSoft system can be configured to meet the unfolding process. After the system is configured, the project team and end-user community can walk through their proposed new business process within PeopleSoft and "test drive" it.

This activity of configuring the system to proposed business processes and the analysis of how well the system can execute those proposed business processes is the detailed fit analysis. By modeling the processes, the project team has a complete guide to all the business processes to examine. The project team can systematically analyze all the defined processes until satisfaction is achieved.

The system can be configured in many ways to satisfy the business requirements of the implementing organization. But on occasion, the business requirements cannot be implemented in the desired fashion. At this time, we have a gap between PeopleSoft and the proposed business process. The project manager can handle this gap by either changing the business process or customizing the software.

Let's look at a couple of examples.

THE ORDER ENTRY PHASE   During the Order Entry, our high-level requirement was "Customer inputs minimal info" as shown in Figure 21.2.

Upon review of the system, we find that the Order Management module has multiple methods of entering sales orders. Depending on the organization's needs, Sales Entry staff can enter comprehensive orders or use a streamlined entry panel where much of the required information is defaulted. Furthermore, organizations could use two different order entry panels within the Order Management module to enter customer orders. Let's look at one of the initial Order Entry panels found in Figure 21.7.

Figure 21.7
The PeopleSoft Order Entry screen can meet a requirement of a streamlined entry of orders.

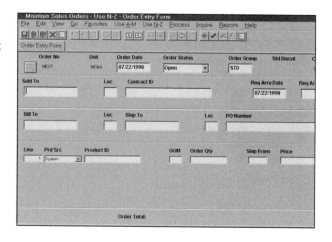

Here is the streamlined Order Entry panel in Order Management. It allows the entry of only the organization sold to, product desired, and order quantity—a nice, quick way of entering your customer product desires. By populating these three fields, the user can default information such as bill to and ship to destinations, and ship from locations. This capability may satisfy your needs.

During the development of the low-level model and prototyping, the project team can investigate each option and determine the best fit.

Now, let's look at the options in Purchasing.

THE REQUISITION PANEL   On the Requisition panel (Figure 21.8), you see a similar setup. Here the entry staff enters the desired items on each line and the rest is defaulted. Each of these panels has different capabilities and is designed for different personnel within your organization. The decision for the project team is which panel to use for each detailed purpose.

Figure 21.8
The Requisition panels can also fulfill this requirement.

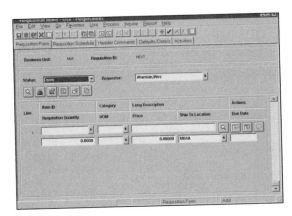

So when deciding how to implement the requirement for "Customer inputs minimal info," the project team will examine multiple options during the prototyping phase, and document their decisions in the low-level model.

Figure 21.9
The project team at work.

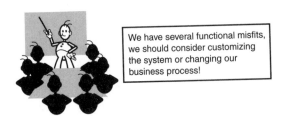

We have several functional misfits, we should consider customizing the system or changing our business process!

IDENTIFYING AREAS FOR CHANGE

As the examination of discrete functional areas continues, organizations will identify areas where the desired business process does not fit with the manner in which vanilla PeopleSoft is written (Figure 21.9). This can be a functional area unique to your organizations or just a practice that works very well in the organizations, but PeopleSoft does not operate in that fashion. These instances are called "misfits." When misfits are identified, the organizations can decide to customize the system or to change their business process.

This decision is far-reaching and should be made only after thoroughly thinking through the implications. Things to consider when making this decision are customizations are supported by the individual organizations, upgrade paths can be more difficult if modifications to delivered objects are made, and the delivered methodology is a better way of doing business. Organizations must consider these aspects when deciding to customize or change their business process. PeopleSoft delivers a full development environment with all software sales, so customizations are part of most implementations. Organizations should take great care when making these decisions.

PROVIDING A BASIS FOR DETAILED JOB/ROLE DESCRIPTIONS

One of the first questions asked by end users is, "How do I fit into the new organization?" This is an excellent question and can be answered with the low-level model (Figure 21.10). During the model development, we determined which activity boxes, decision points, and so on users would need access to. Compiling these individual access needs into discrete roles is well suited to process modeling. In the process of modeling, related tasks are naturally grouped closely together, creating synergy for the definition of a role. Also, the handoffs between different roles is easily identified and managed using a process model.

Figure 21.10
How do the employees fit into the model?

So where do I fit into the new processes and PeopleSoft?

As the low-level model evolves, the day-to-day activities of individuals within the organizations may change, or at least they may not know how they fit into the "New World Order." So during the prototyping phases, the parts of the processes that apply to individuals/roles within the organizations will become clear. At what point does the customer enter an order or requisitions? When does the purchasing department pick up the PO build process? Do employees now enter their benefits info via the Web or continue to submit the annual benefits review paperwork? All these questions are answered by breaking up the low-level model into "job-level processes."

These "job-level" processes will then drive the panel security role, low-level security roles, and client hardware needs for individuals whether they be power users on a high-powered desktop workstation or an occasional user who only requires Web access.

PROVIDING A BASIS FOR DEVELOPING A TRAINING PLAN

A low-level model assists the training or project manager in two activities of training plan development: (1) the identification of training needs, and (2) the development of the training curriculum. By using the detailed role descriptions and business processes, the development of a training plan is eased.

First, let's examine the identification of training needs. As the low-level model unfolds, the identification of the activities, decision points, and reporting needs of each role are documented. This information assists the training manager in determining what capabilities each security role must have to successfully operate PeopleSoft. Let's return to our Order Entry example shown in Figure 21.1.

Our Sales Entry role will require the capability to enter sales orders online while the customer is on the phone. Our Customer Entry role will require the capability to enter customer data. Now that the project team has the required capability, the business leaders can begin to identify the individuals within the implementing organizations who will fill those roles. When the training manager knows the needed capabilities of the individuals, the manager can poll the individuals to identify where to focus training.

Additionally, the training manager will need to develop a training curriculum to train these individuals in PeopleSoft. The business processes to be implemented and the manner they are to be implemented in PeopleSoft defines the training curriculum for the training manager. The training curriculum can become the execution of the low-level model business processes within the PeopleSoft panels. The low-level model defines this information for the training manager.

IDENTIFYING A BASIS FOR DEVELOPING CUSTOMIZATIONS

When the fit analysis is complete, the output is a list of misfits or gaps in the vanilla system. Previously, we discussed the decision point of either changing the business process or changing the system. Given the decision to modify or customize the system, the low-level model will assist project managers and technicians by providing the business process for the functional design and defining the points of interaction with the software.

Software designs have a endless number of design document formats, but one of the items that is consistent is the use of a business process model to define "how the software should work." From this functional design, the technicians will produce technical designs perhaps including pseudocode, and so forth. During the development of the functional design, the project team can leverage the desired business processes defined in the low-level model.

With the inclusion of the PeopleSoft base tables and the mapping of the business model to PeopleSoft, the low-level model assists the technician in determining where in the code to insert the customization. In object-oriented development, the technician must determine whether new tables are needed or existing tables can be used, what code is to be written, and on what table, field, or control to put the code. This customization design decision has two options:

- Modify an existing table—The technician can begin the design decisions using the base tables associated with the business process to be modified. Because the business process to be modified uses a certain base table, that table is the logical place to begin investigating the proper table, field, and control for the new code. The model will only provide a starting point because PeopleSoft uses many functions stored on FUNCLIB tables and temporary tables.

- Add a new table—The new tables added by the technician may require a relationship to existing PeopleSoft tables. Given the need for these relationships, the low-level model documents the base tables in use by the business process. These base tables again provide a starting point for the technician to determine the proper relationship between existing PeopleSoft tables and any new tables.

IDENTIFYING A BASIS FOR DEVELOPING INTERFACES

Interface development is a critical and time-consuming task in any implementation. The low-level model and the inclusion of the base tables provide technicians starting points for developing interfaces to non-PeopleSoft systems. The model provides the points within business processes where the interfacing systems interact, the base tables needed for the interface, and the points where humans interact with the system.

BUSINESS PROCESS INTERACTION   In the low-level model, project teams define the processes at a detailed level including the processes associated with non-PeopleSoft systems. With modeling at this level of detail, the activity boxes or decision points where the interface will occur are known. By showing the business process, the model will assist the technician in technical design decisions such as data transmission rates or methods. For example, let's assume the implementing organization manufactures shoes. The organization is using PeopleSoft inventory and interfacing it with another shipping system.

In this example, the organization wants to pick finished shoes from inventory and load them onto a transportation medium such as a truck. The organization has a need for real-time transmission of data from inventory on what shoes fit the order to the shipping software. Additionally, the loaded shoes are scanned and update inventory on the shipment. In this example, the frequency of data transmission over the interface must be nearly instantaneous, so the technician must decide between potential database triggers or running a script every few minutes. By understanding the business process and the performance requirements, the technician can make an informed design decision.

DATA MAPPING ASSISTANCE   When building this interface, the technician will want to map data elements from the PeopleSoft base tables to the interfacing system tables. By including the base tables in the model, the technician has a ready reference of these tables.

IDENTIFICATION OF HUMAN INTERFACE POINTS   The last aspect of the low-level model we will discuss is the human interface points. We have already discussed how some of the organization's personnel will operate PeopleSoft, but we did not discuss the support staff and their interaction. The support staff can drive many of the cost savings organizations, so the importance of examining their role is great. Let's look at another purchasing example.

In this example (shown in Figure 21.11), the organization's purchasing department has received a requisition from an end user and wants to process that requisition into a purchase order. After sourcing the requisitions, the purchasing department has many options on how to build their POs and dispatch them. Buyers can choose consolidation methods, build POs as approved or pending an approval cycle, or they can override the suggested vendor.

Figure 21.11
Building purchase orders.

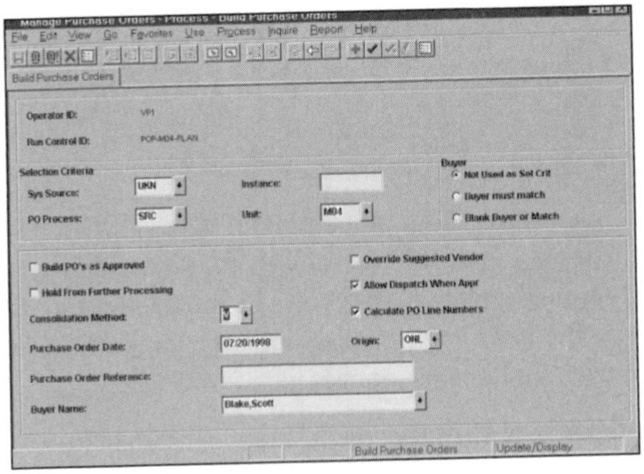

The details of these processes and the timing of using each of these switch settings evolve during the prototyping sessions as the end users from the Purchasing department examine their options and decide on the best approaches.

With all the options and functionality that PeopleSoft delivers, project teams and end users will spend many weeks working through all the possible scenarios. As I have tried to point out, the vastness of the options and volume of decisions is enormous. An organization has no chance of keeping track of this information without a robust low-level model.

IDENTIFYING BASIS FOR DATA CONVERSIONS

The conversion of system data into PeopleSoft is also a time-consuming and critical task in the process of implementing PeopleSoft. The accuracy of data provides the link between the real world and the world as perceived by the system. If these two worlds get out of synchronization, the system does not assist the implementing organization in its business but becomes a burden. The low-level model assists in the determination of what data requires conversion and what tables the data should populate.

When examining the business processes of the implementing organization, the project team will highlight the system capabilities this implementing organization will use. These desired capabilities then define how the system is configured and which tables must be populated to achieve the desired business processes.

For example, the implementing organization's business process defines that Sales and Use taxes will be manually entered onto a voucher. The PeopleSoft system has the capability to calculate this information, but the implementing organization wants to perform this function manually. Given this manual entry requirement, the tables associated with calculation of Sales and Use tax do not require population.

For those tables that do require population, technicians will want to map the fields from the PeopleSoft system to the fields of the current system. The base table definitions associated with the business process provide the technician with a starting point for that data mapping.

IDENTIFYING REQUIRED REPORTS

The low-level model provides a good mechanism to identify the reports the implementing organization will require while using the new business processes. During the process of thinking through the details of the business, management control points or points for reporting will surface, thus spawning a need for a written report.

Continuing with the Sales Order example, the defined business process defines a management control point as the documentation of completed sales for traveling salespersons or entry of sales orders by data entry staff. For example, these staff members are given bonuses based on the volume of orders that they generate. This compensation scheme spawns a need for a printed report that indicates the volume of business generated per employee during a given timeframe. Now that the reporting requirement is identified, the project team will identify a delivered report or relay the need to the report development staff for development of a custom report.

Project managers and business leaders can also use the model to streamline the number of printed reports produced by the implementing organization. This streamlining can occur in two ways, by consolidating similar reports, or eliminating reports that do not have a role in the new business process. For organizations that could benefit from consolidating reports, development of the low-level model will facilitate communication between business leaders who otherwise may not speak. When these leaders and project team members are communicating in the context of the new business process model, they will have the opportunity to identify the similarities in their reporting needs and consolidate reports. When the reports are consolidated, the implementing organization has reduced its maintenance requirement and the cost of that requirement.

The second option for project managers is the elimination of unused reports. Over time, some organizations define requirements for reports, but do not update the reporting needs when the business needs change. For example, many years ago, the implementing organization was organized on a geographic basis such as the Northeast, South, Midwest, and West. General managers were responsible for all business within those geographic regions. As a result of this responsibility, these general managers required a monthly income statement as well as multiple production reports to run these regional business centers. Two years ago, the implementing organization reorganized along product lines. This reorganization changed the responsibility of the general managers to specific product lines worldwide. The new reporting requirement of product line–based reports was spawned and implemented, but the requirements for regional reports were never eliminated. For two years, this organization has continued to produce regional reports that went unused. This fact was not immediately evident to the technical staff who produced the report, but printing the report was an unnecessary expense.

This project manager could use the low-level model to identify the product line reporting requirement as well as many others, but eliminate all reports that are not specifically required by the new business. Implementing organizations have a tendency to start with the existing reports and reproduce them. Project managers should resist this tendency as it is prone to creating unneeded reports.

When reports are identified in the context of the model and even decision points within the model, the format and content of the report become evident. To continue with the general manager income statement example, the formatting of the report by product line becomes immediately evident as well as the need to define either an accounting period or a period of time to use in the income development. Let's assume that the low-level model defines this report as an external reporting requirement, the general manager will want to have amplifying detail behind the numbers. This desire to have amplifying detail yet the ability to print summary level detail makes a strong argument for writing the report in Nvision.

PROVIDING A MORE DETAILED BASIS FOR BOTH INTEGRATION AND SYSTEM TESTING

By definition, the low-level model is a depiction of the future system and how it should be operated. For organizations that build business process–based tests, the low-level model defines the functional testing required, including what security roles should execute each business process. Additionally, the low-level model organizes the detailed requirements documented during the prototyping activities aiding the reporting of requirements satisfaction.

During the development of test plans for both Integration and System testing, the testing organization defines the breadth and depth of the tests required to satisfy the implementing organization that the system will function and all its requirements are met. The challenge for a testing organization is how to organize the test and the requirements into an efficient and robust plan. During the development of the low-level model, the project team defined the requirements and synchronized them with the business flows. The logical conclusion is to satisfy all the business processes, and the implementing organization can be satisfied that all the requirements are satisfied. The business processes are complete, thus completing a large portion of the test plan. The testing organization should include additional tests outside of functional tests such as performance and capacity tests to complete a robust test plan.

SUMMARY

The high-level and low-level business process models are critical to any PeopleSoft implementation. These models provide the critical structure upon which to build a successful implementation and business.

The high-level "To Be" model can be built using the "As Is" model, from a clean sheet of paper, or using the vanilla business processes defined in the PeopleSoft Advantage Toolkit

(ATK). Building this model is cost-effective and makes good sense because it offers the following benefits:

- Provides the project structure and scope
- Provides a basis for prototyping
- Provides a basis for both integration and system testing
- Provides a basis to tie the Information Technology solution to the implementing organization's business objectives
- Sets project team and end-user expectations at a reasonable and sustainable level
- Identifies required skills of the project team and end-user community
- Provides a communication and marketing vehicle for strong executive sponsorship
- Provides a basis for business process re-engineering

The low-level "To Be" model is equally critical to a successful implementation. It is built using either the high-level "To Be" model or using the vanilla business processes defined in the PeopleSoft Advantage Toolkit (ATK). Development of this model aids the project manager in many ways including

- Identifying detailed requirements
- Providing a basis for detailed fit analysis
- Providing a basis for detailed job/role descriptions
- Providing a basis for developing a training plan
- Identifying basis for developing customizations
- Identifying basis for developing interfaces
- Identifying basis for data conversions
- Identifying required reports
- Providing a more detailed basis for both integration and system testing

CHAPTER 22

REVOLUTION VERSUS EVOLUTION

In this chapter

by Carl Upthegrove

Implementations of computerized business systems such as PeopleSoft will alter the way your company does business. These types of systems, often called Enterprise Resource Planning (ERP) systems, affect many, if not all, aspects of the business: finance, human resources, manufacturing, distribution, and planning. Does this enterprisewide venture mean you have to re-engineer your processes? Can you leave things the way they are and just start using PeopleSoft with your existing processes? Or can the result be something between these two? In this chapter, you will take a look at what *can* be done, what *may* be done, and why you should choose one course or another.

Some Important History

Computerizing business processes has been going on now for over 40 years. Soon after computers were invented, people began to see their usefulness in business.

A bit of background here will help to put things in perspective. If you have good knowledge of the history of the computer in business and what is known as "packaged software applications," you might want to skip to the next section. Otherwise, take a few moments to read this section on how the use of the computer in business has changed over the past 30 or 40 years.

When computer systems first began to be used in business, the primary purpose was to automate tasks that were done manually. Tasks such as creating an accounts receivable aging report or multiplying hours times rate to calculate pay were very structured and repetitive, and thus the most likely to be automated. When a process was designed, the tasks themselves required very little thinking from the person who performed them. As IBM was fond of saying, "People should think; machines should work." This simply meant that a process was designed and then a computer program was written to simulate it. The computer did the work and people were free to think. Because the process existed first and the program was written to perform that work exactly as it was done manually, there was seldom, if ever, an issue of changing the business process to take advantage of the power of the computer. Much has changed since those early days.

Often today when the decision is made to purchase and implement a computer system, the thought of changing the business process is at the heart of the decision. And if the business process change is not the driver for the project, the questions will soon arise about whether the business processes should be reviewed and considered for change.

Packaged Software

One of the most significant changes in the use of computers for business came with the introduction of package software. *Package software* is a product or set of programs that are purchased to perform a specific business process or group of processes. This differs from developing these products in-house. As mentioned previously, in the early days the computer program was written for the specific business process and was done for a specific company, or even a specific department within a company. This meant that the program could be designed to perform the process almost exactly as it was done manually. Most of the early uses of computers in business were financial applications, such as payroll and accounting. These were, for the most part, applications that required performing repetitive calculations.

It wasn't too long before people began to realize that many of these applications were very similar from one business to another. Because of the standard way in which accounting is done, each business must perform these business processes in a similar way. Was there not then some economy of scale if a computer program could be written once and used many times? After all, it took a long time and cost quite a lot of money to develop a computer program to perform that business process.

In fact, packaged software was a revolutionary idea at the time, and many people felt it was not feasible to write a computer program so that it could be used in many different businesses. Even though each business was similar, there were differences. Accounting applications were required to come up with results in a common format, but the way those results were obtained might be different from business to business. Each business was unique, or at least the people who ran the business wanted to think so. So the challenge was to develop applications that could be used by several businesses, even several types of businesses, and yet still not require changes in the business process.

Looking back, it is easy to see why accounting-type applications were the first to be done in this manner. Adding, subtracting, and other arithmetic calculations were the same whether a manufacturing company, a grocery chain, or even a bank did them—the actual calculation was the same. It soon became apparent, however, that the business process was not quite the same. That is, the "*how* things were done" was different, even if the "*what* was done" was the same. *How* versus *what* is the heart of the business process. That will be dealt with in greater detail later in this chapter.

During this era, when packaged software was first coming onto the market, companies that were considering computerizing a business process were faced early in the decision-making process with the question, "Do we buy a package or write it ourselves?" In many cases, the drive behind this decision was how much change might be required in the business to accommodate the software. Because of the inflexibility of the software products in those days (and even today in some cases), and because of the expense involved with the purchase and implementation of these packages, changing the package was not usually a valid consideration. Even today, these decisions are important.

So, if modifying the package was not a realistic option, it left only one course of action: Change the business process. However, changing the business process was not the best action for that part of the business—rather, accommodating the software package would have been a better approach. This resulted in changes to how business was done, which were, in many cases, not in the best interest of that business process but were required only because of the software package. In many cases, there were, and still are today, valid reasons for changes to a business process to accommodate a software package for the "greater good" of the business in its entirety. However, as will be discussed later in this chapter, the climate today is much different than the climate a few years ago for these types of decisions.

So, packaged software was where the issue of changing the business process really began to become an issue. As already mentioned, changing the business process today is still a large part of the decision to buy a software package; however, the situation is quite different.

QUESTIONS TO ASK REGARDING A PEOPLESOFT IMPLEMENTATION

DECIDING FACTORS TOWARD IMPLEMENTING PEOPLESOFT

The decision to implement PeopleSoft may have resulted from a failure in the existing system because of growth, an outdated existing system, or other reasons. At any rate, the decision to review the business process has already been made and is part of the decision on what new system to purchase. This is discussed in more detail later as part of the topic of Business Process Re-engineering (BPR). But some other force may have driven the decision to implement PeopleSoft. Or PeopleSoft may have been purchased to address some other business need but it affects other processes indirectly.

It is important for everyone—the key decision-makers, the project team, and the users—to understand what the business drivers were that led to the decision to implement PeopleSoft. Decisions need to be made about what processes to review, how much change the organization can absorb, how critical change is to the success of the project, and other issues. Knowing what drove the decision to implement PeopleSoft will help with these other decisions that will impact the business. If the decision-making criteria are not known to the project managers, a process of interviews with those who make the decision should be undertaken to add this information to the project knowledge base.

THE OPPORTUNITY TO MAKE CHANGES

The decision to move to PeopleSoft provides an opportunity to look closely at business processes, especially because it impacts the entire business or at least affects many aspects of the business. Often, when a process is designed and is in use, it is seldom if ever reviewed. Usually, only a significant event will cause a company to review one or more of its business processes. After all, as the old saying goes, "If it isn't broke, why fix it?"

Probably the three most significant events that lead to reevaluating a business process are

- The decision to implement a new computerized system for that process
- The failure of the existing process
- An ownership change in the business

Change in ownership is certainly not a topic for discussion here, but the other two events are covered in the following sections.

Business Process Re-engineering and Continuous Improvement

In recent years, the concept of Business Process Re-engineering (BPR) has been a hot topic. Another hot topic that preceded that by a few years was Continuous Improvement (CI). Both these concepts deal with the idea that changes to business processes can improve the results of the business. BPR tends toward the revolutionary approach, at least in its pure form. Continuous Improvement represents the evolutionary style of change. It is certainly not the purpose here to delve into either of these concepts in any detail, but there is an important link between business process change and the implementation of a computerized application dealing with that business process.

Business Process Re-engineering

In the case of BPR, it is likely that a BPR project has preceded the implementation (although a BPR project may be undertaken concurrently with the implementation of a new system). BPR projects are usually initiated by senior management and are a result of either a known failure in the business processes or a potential failure of one or more of those processes. In some cases, the BPR resulted in the realization that a new computer system was required to accomplish the desired business goals which were sought in the BPR. In that case, there is an opportunity to take advantage of that work. The BPR effort will have identified what the new business processes are and it will be possible to map the new software product with that business process. During the mapping process, it is still possible that a change in the business process may be considered. This is due to new information becoming available with an understanding of the new computer system. Data will also have been identified, and that also can be mapped to the PeopleSoft system. This mapping may result in some new data or a new process being required, which will result in decisions about modifications to the system. This topic is dealt with elsewhere in this book.

Continuous Improvement

In the case of CI, the approach is likely to be somewhat different. By its definition, CI is an ongoing process and therefore does not have the project-type style seen in a BPR. For that reason, in a CI environment the implementation of a new software product may be the trigger for a CI review of certain business processes. In this case, the review of the process can be done with the new software product in mind. This calls for a dual approach: the assessment of the business process concurrent with the beginning of an implementation project. The following sections can be helpful in understanding this process.

Business Processes: Change a Little, Change a Lot—What Drives the Decision?

If you are completely re-engineering your business, you have already made the choice to rethink all the ways you perform every business process. But, let's be honest, that is a very dramatic choice that costs a lot of money, involves a lot of people, and most likely happens only in a handful of cases. The more likely scenario is that the choice to implement PeopleSoft has raised the issue of what processes should be changed and how dramatically?

These choices should be made during the planning stages and be driven to a very large degree by the needs of the business. It is advisable to avoid noticing the need for a process change in the middle of the implementation and letting the software drive the change. Doing that is quite similar to the example in the early days of package software, where the real reason for the change was to make the business adapt to the software.

Early in the project, time should be budgeted to review all the major business processes that will be affected by the implementation. The implementation consultants can be helpful at this stage, because they can assist in pointing out what parts of the business are affected based upon experience and knowledge.

METHODOLOGIES FOR ANALYZING BUSINESS PROCESSES

There are several methodologies of analyzing your business processes. Most use some sort of a decomposition method, where the business is broken down from the highest form to each process step-by-step. For example, at the highest level, you may have a retail store. That store must purchase items to sell, receive those items, stock the items, pay the invoices associated with the items, sell the items, receive payment, and so on. Afterward, each of those processes can be broken down the same way. This continues down to the lowest process.

During this work, it is important to note the relationships between the processes: What processes pass data to other processes? *Why* is that data passed? *What* does the other process do with the data? Asking these questions helps focus the team on *what* is being done and *why*. This is essential in making decisions on what business processes need to be reviewed for possible change.

ADDRESSING THE ISSUE OF WHAT VERSUS HOW

The next step addresses the issue of *what* versus *how*. It is often very difficult for users of a process, either manual or computerized, to separate *how* they do something from *what* it is they are doing. It takes special attention, time, and some creative thinking to separate the *what* from the *how*. But this is critical to establish the real need for change. If *what* is being done needs change, that is a much bigger issue than *how* it is being done.

If you ask a person *what* he or she does, for example, the person might tell you, "I look at a spreadsheet for past sales numbers, and call marketing to ask how much they think they are going to sell, and look at a screen from an existing system to get information about production rates, and then tell another person to make so many units for next week." What the respondent *does* is plan production; what the person told you was *how* he or she plans production.

What is being done is really the business process—for example, receiving goods, issuing a purchase order, or processing a new hire. These are all processes. Whether the new hire fills out a form or enters data onto a computer screen is *how* that process is accomplished. Whether there is a copy of the purchase order on the receiving dock to validate the receipt is *how* the process takes place. These are fairly simple examples; in most cases, it is much more difficult to assess what part of the transaction is *what* is being done and what part is *how* it is being done. However, this becomes very important in determining complexity and risk associated with making decisions about what processes to change and how to change them. In some, or even many, of the cases, *how* the process is executed can be a byproduct of the software.

In the example of the new hire filling out a form versus entering data on a computer, the exact format of how the data gets into the system is not the important issue. The important issue is whether the data being entered is consistent with the needs of the business. If the business needs to know that the new hire has certain technical skills, the process must account for that. In other words, *what* is being asked is important, not *how* the data gets into the system.

Now that you know *what* is being done, decide *which* of the processes need to be changed. When this is complete, the next step is to identify which of the processes are most important within the business. There is a law or principle known as Paerado's Law or the 80/20 principle. This law is applied in business to help focus effort on the 20 percent of the business that generates 80 percent of the result. For example, 20 percent of the customers generate 80 percent of the sales or 20 percent of the equipment requires 80 percent of the maintenance attention. The goal is to work on the 20 percent of the business that yields the 80 percent of the benefit, and that is what needs to be examined here. All projects live with time and money constraints; that is just a fact of business life. Therefore, care must be taken to focus the efforts of the team on those processes that will produce the most benefit—the most "bang for the buck." It is critical to have access to senior-level managers at this point. If they are not part of the team either as active members or part of the steering team, they must be consulted. It is difficult in organizations both large and small to have people see what really matters to the organization as a whole unless they are at a senior level. Every group naturally feels its area is critical to the business—and it may be—but some areas have a greater impact than others. To decide which business processes will yield the most result, one or more members of senior management must either participate in the choice or review the choices and approve them. This also effects ownership by a senior-level sponsor of the choices.

CRITICAL FACTORS IN DECIDING REVOLUTION OR EVOLUTION

Recall that re-engineering projects usually take the revolutionary approach, and doing business in the continuous improvement manner usually is associated with evolutionary change. However, either of these approaches might take on the characteristics of either revolution or evolution. What factors need to be taken into consideration when a team makes a decision about taking a more revolutionary or evolutionary approach?

THE REVIEW PROCESS

As mentioned previously, time and money always limit what we would like to do. Even in BPR projects, stopping the entire business long enough to review and analyze each business process is unlikely. So what does get done and how is the decision made?

The first step can be to eliminate those processes that will not need to be reviewed. Maybe this is because they are outside the project scope. An accounting-based project does not need to take time to review the human resources business processes. If the project is focusing on pension and benefits, addressing the purchasing process is not relevant. Possibly, some of these processes have recently been assessed, and there is no need to replow that field.

After it is decided what not to do, the focus should be on those processes that impact the business the most. A distribution business is likely to be impacted greatly by order-taking and inventory processes. On the other hand, a company that manufactures commercial aircraft may not care nearly as much about order management, because it takes only a few orders a year. It is really important for the team members to have very good knowledge of the business to help in making these choices. It is also important to avoid the trap of dealing with the processes that are the most easily understood and easiest to document. Later, during the actual implementation, those processes will not be the ones that cause the problems.

ANOTHER REVIEW PROCESS

Another criterion is what business processes are generally known to be due for change. Every business has processes that the users know don't work correctly. Maybe the process is just outdated, or maybe it is done because some other process requires it. Don't overlook the obvious.

As a business process is reviewed and assessed for potential change, it is important to keep track of the links from that process to others. A change in a purchasing process has the possibility of affecting inventory processes and accounts payable processes as well as others. An expected small change can quickly grow into a much larger change when the links are identified and analyzed. For example, it may seem to be a small change for a warehouse to consolidate all its data entry to one time each day. However, if purchasing, manufacturing, and accounting are using that data, the change will affect them. Those groups might find that the frequency of the receipt of the data changes their processes.

CHANGE IN THE ORGANIZATION AND HOW MUCH IT CAN ABSORB

When a business process is reviewed, it must be considered for change. Review alone does not mean change is required, but in deciding which processes to review, improvement should be a criterion. It serves no purpose to attempt to change more than the organization can absorb. Change is not easy; in fact it can be painful, even though the end result is desirable. Some organizations accept more change than others because they are more used to it. A high-tech company is likely to be more accustomed to change than a government agency. An organization that has recently gone through a significant change may be less tolerant than one where change has not taken place for some time.

CHANGE AND THE PEOPLESOFT IMPLEMENTATION

Many projects involving the implementation of PeopleSoft products are driven by the need for change in the business processes. PeopleSoft and similar systems are often the catalyst for change. Change is not easy, and one way to facilitate change is by combining the business process change with the move a PeopleSoft product. The managers of the business know that change is required and difficult, but the implementation of PeopleSoft will make that change easier, so the two go hand in hand.

Often, it is easier for users to visualize the change in the business process when it is represented in a software product. For example, the process of entering a sales order might need to be moved from a paper system, where the order is faxed into an office and entered into a system, to a remote system, where the order is entered via the Internet by the customer. If the user has never seen the process done any other way than the way it is done now, he or she may have difficulty imagining the new process without knowing the new system.

CHANGE BROUGHT ON BY BUSINESS PROBLEMS

Change in the midst of other critical pressures on the business might be overwhelming. There are times when PeopleSoft is implemented in an environment where the business is in jeopardy and a quick implementation is seen as critical to saving the business. For example, if the business is losing customers and having financial problems because orders are not shipping, there may be several causes. Some may be in the warehouse, some in manufacturing, and some in order management. And these problems may be the source of others in accounting and planning. There are no absolutes, but it is advisable to avoid a lot of change during a crisis. In a case such as this, it would be even more important than usual to identify for change only those processes that are very critical to the business. When things are back on track, other business processes can be reviewed.

PROPER INFRASTRUCTURE HELPS FACILITATE CHANGE

Some organizations have a better infrastructure for accepting change. Many organizations have team members and managers trained in change management. Change management recognizes that change does not happen easily or painlessly. One of the most overlooked aspects of implementing an ERP system, such as PeopleSoft, is the change that the organization must undergo. There are several ways to gain knowledge in change management, and although the topic is too broad for coverage here, it is very important to know that change must be managed for it to occur beneficially. In some cases, team members can be recruited from other departments or divisions that are trained to facilitate change.

Change requires time. A very fast-paced project is less likely to be able to tolerate change than one that has a longer timeline.

Another aspect of infrastructure that can help with the PeopleSoft implementation is having sufficient staff to backfill positions that become open as the implementation team is formed. Some companies have a corporate culture that enables the depth in personnel, and others do not. The lack of sufficient staff will cause the implementation team members to try to do their regular job in addition to the project. This makes change nearly impossible.

MULTIPLE PHASES TO THE IMPLEMENTATION PROJECT MAY BE HELPFUL

When a lot of business processes need to be addressed in a PeopleSoft implementation project, it is worthwhile considering a multiphased project. A multiphased project divides the entire scope of the project into smaller pieces. This can be done in different ways. One way is to divide the project by department or division of the organization. This is often not easy because it becomes necessary to determine who goes first, and some departments, divisions, or parts of the business must wait for their improvement while others begin to reap the benefits. But it is easier to make those kinds of decisions in the early stages of the project, during planning, rather than realize during the implementation that it will not be possible to get everything done.

Another way to separate project phases is by product. For example, it may be best to complete all financial projects before beginning any manufacturing or distribution projects. This also creates decisions such as how to interface the new systems with existing legacy systems for a limited period of time. PeopleSoft is very flexible in this regard, because it was designed to be broken into components when needed. This makes the creation of interfaces much easier because the data and table structure is easy to access.

Implementation projects have been known to run in length from a few weeks on the extreme low end to several years on the high end. Unfortunately, there is no magic number for how long a project should last. Some organizations can support massive projects that run for two or three years and still be successful, although these are rare. Some organizations begin to feel stressed when implementations run longer than a few months. One year is usually a good time to use as a benchmark. If during the planning it appears that the project will go beyond a year, it might be a good time to take a serious look at splitting the project into phases. Phased implementations have certain risks as well, and they are not always advisable; but they can be worth taking a hard look at in many cases.

Another issue of phased implementations is scope creep. What can be done with legitimate issues that arise during an implementation, issues that need to be included but that will push the project beyond the planned date? In a phased project, there is the opportunity to assign things to a later phase. If what has arisen must be done in the current phase, it might be possible to rearrange priorities and move something in the current phase to a later phase. Of course, the following phases must be completed, and it is always good to keep a larger project plan, which keeps all phases in the eye of management.

RE-EVALUATION OF THE SCOPE OF THE CHANGE AND WHAT DROVE IT

The process of deciding how much change should be undertaken can be an interactive process. After all the processes that are to be reviewed are compiled, it may be necessary to reevaluate some. What looked like an evolution may have grown to a revolution.

Projects nearly always grow over time, so it is useful to keep going back to the original basic business drivers. Perhaps the organization has statements that define its reason for being; if so, everything that is being undertaken should be clearly linked back to that purpose. Focus on the key items that make the organization successful.

KEEPING THE BUSINESS DRIVERS IN FOCUS

Late in a project, this question will often come up: "Why did we start this whole business in the first place?" Change is never easy, and when several changes are happening at once it is easy to forget why things were begun and how the current situation came to be. Here are some ways to avoid getting totally lost.

A simple clear project charter should be developed based on the original business drivers that led to the project. That project charter should be available to everyone throughout the project and referred to often. If the project charter is well written, it should serve as a reminder of what is to be accomplished and why. When decisions need to be made and when questions arise about how something fits into the project, the charter should easily provide the answer.

Another document that is very useful is the project scope document. The scope document outlines what is going to be done and should contain some language about why the limits are set where they are. Like the charter, this document should be accessible and used frequently.

Also, during regular project meetings it is useful to review the project progress in view of the original objectives. This reminds everyone, in a very nonthreatening way, what the purpose of the project really is. It might seem trivial, but even people with years of experience in projects such as these can get so caught up in the day-to-day work that they lose sight of the project objectives.

CHANGING METHODS FOR DOING BUSINESS

Is change for change's sake or is change for the right reason? What are the right reasons for change? Change improves profitability, reduces cost, improves customer service, takes advantage of technology, improves market share, becomes more responsive to the marketplace, improves flexibility, and improves responsiveness.

Every organization has its own reasons for change. And every organization has its own way of implementing change. But change should be undertaken only with a purpose, and that purpose should be clear to everyone in the project team. This takes a lot of work up front, not only to fully understand why the change is needed but also to communicate the need for the change and the result of the change to people in the organization. Change is easier for people to deal with when they understand it. Change that is not supported by management is unlikely to succeed, but just as important is support from the users. Change that is not understood and accepted by those in the organization who must live with it on a day-to-day basis is also not likely to be successful. Time and effort spent early in a project helping everyone in the organization understand the changes that will be taking place will pay handsome dividends in the long term. Working in groups to discuss the process changes and getting feedback from all the concerned parties is a useful technique. Not everyone will understand or accept the change immediately, and it can be frustrating to those who do understand what needs to be done and why. But when people gain an understanding and appreciation, everything is much easier.

Summary

How much to change, how to execute the change within the organization, and how to manage that change are significant to any PeopleSoft implementation. The history section in this chapter highlighted how the times have changed and how the implementation of a PeopleSoft system can be used as a catalyst of changes. Important questions were described to help identify opportunities associated with change and help you decide which effort is the right course: a full Business Process Re-engineering or a Continuous Improvement change. Finally, you explored a very important topic: how to manage the change resulting from the PeopleSoft implementation.

GETTING THE IMPLEMENTATION READY

CHAPTER 23

NO PAIN, NO GAIN: GIVING UP THE BEST AND BRIGHTEST

In this chapter   *by Perry Keating*

STARTING AN IMPLEMENTATION: HOW TO AVOID PAIN

What causes an implementation to fail? Rarely is it failures of the software or problems with hardware. The basic truth is that implementation failure is a people problem. Ill-conceived strategies, oversold products, weak specifications—all have the people box in the implementation checked yes. The root of such failure is something far more than just a generic version of people—it's the commitment of the organization to the implementation, the focus of the leadership, and the strength of the implementation team. Strong leaders and teams can quickly overcome almost any of the other issues. This is where the famous saying heard in every gym in America, "No pain, no gain," applies.

How? In the gym, if you don't push yourself, you aren't doing enough to achieve your goals. The physical exertion making you exceed your current fitness levels is what makes achieving the next level possible. Now, let's apply "No pain, no gain" to implementation.

BRINGING IN THE "BEST AND BRIGHTEST"

Company X has decided to implement PeopleSoft. The implementation project will touch areas all across the company, from your planners to your shop floor teams, from your supply chain to your receivables department. A successful implementation will help Company X transform key performance indicators such as time-to-market, rework, and scrap, but a poor implementation can cost a company millions of dollars in write-offs and—in some cases—put the company itself at risk. Good examples are the $100+ million dollar write-off at Applied Materials, and the near bankruptcy of Fox Meyer, all due to poor implementations.

So how does a company protect itself from the extraordinary pain of financial losses or bankruptcy? If bankruptcy represents full-fledged cardiac arrest, the best thing to help avoid it is to commit some of your time every day to working out and staying in shape. Corporately speaking, it's by committing those resources that are considered your best and brightest people to these implementation teams for the duration.

Most of you who are in the corporate world are muttering, "I can't do that! I need those people on their current assignments. Without them, things will stall and I won't make money." In other words, "I can't waste my time in the gym—I'll lose time in the office." Yes, the downside is that the best and brightest are away from their daily tasks, personal schedules are temporarily stressed with higher workloads, and junior people are forced to step up to help cover assignments. But stop and review the upside: Because these outstanding employees grow with the company, they need a detailed understanding of the new system and the location and type of information hidden in the company. This is a real impetus for their continued personal career growth. As these people take on their assignments in the implementation, enhancing the company's future, others in the original departments will step up to fill in. This will help this new leadership tier of employees grow, enhance their careers, and build a stronger team for the company.

To apply an analogy from the sports world, it's in the playoffs that the best players rise to the occasion. In the case of an implementation, the best players will rise to the top both on the implementation teams and in the departments operating semi-shorthanded. Yes, the daily operations of the existing business administration will be stressed, but isn't that the basis for any change, the way a company grows, the way a human body gets healthier?

Now let's not fool ourselves; this process is difficult and somewhat risky to the organization. You must be prepared to deal with the possibility of workforce problems and issues that grow out of this higher stress situation. Some companies build additional incentives in to keep employees committed, both on the project and the remaining workforce. These incentives can be quite positive if tied to project milestones or knowledge of the new system. If this seems excessive, remember that personnel with implementation experience are a hot commodity in today's market. If you are not careful, you will train your project personnel only to lose them to a higher bidder. This may also prove true for remaining personnel in the current tight labor environment. Despite your best efforts, you may still lose some employees during this more stressful period, but you can minimize the effects by dealing with the issues up front.

THE BEST AND THE BRIGHTEST: HOW LONG IS THE COMMITMENT?

It's now established that Company X will loan its best and brightest to the implementation. This being the case, the next question is for how long. Simply put, for the duration. This isn't a rotational position for staff members to "get some experience" for a few months and return to their departments. Each team member must go up a learning curve before they're fully effective; teams must "hit their stride." An implementation represents an ongoing learning process, so it's a difficult environment for people to step in and out. This long-term project commitment is essential for all members of a team, be they company employees or independent consultants. Rotations are demoralizing and inefficient and insert unnecessary risk into the environment. Team spirit, good working relationships, and commitment are three essential elements that must be fostered. Applying the best and the brightest to the long term demonstrates company commitment to the project and frequently lends to the strong team spirit and necessary communications.

IN FOR THE DURATION: NOW WHAT DO THEY DO?

Now it's established that the best and brightest from across the company will take on roles in the implementation. The next question: What are those roles and what are the responsibilities represented by these roles?

So where does this leave us? The concept of using the best and the brightest is not new, nor is it difficult to grasp in theory. In practice it is somewhat more challenging. The organization will feel pain, either for the short term during the implementation, or for the long term, as it struggles to use a poorly implemented system. Process re-engineering, system prototyping, business process definition, and so on, all require deep understanding of both the software and the customer business. Outside consultants can provide system understanding and even process "best practices," but they do not understand your business, your requirements, and your culture. You must have a strong implementation team and that team must include resources that understand your business. There is an added benefit to incorporating input from your best, which is the credibility they lend your implementation project. These team members are your company's informal leaders, and where they go the rest of your teams will follow. There is no quantifiable price to this added value!

THE IMPLEMENTATION TEAM

Figure 23.1
Sample implementation organization.

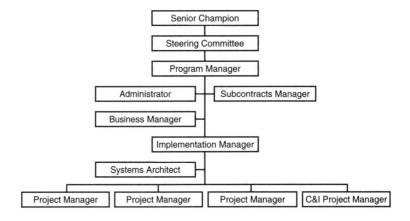

Noteworthy, too, are the four positions that have reporting lines not directly in line with the entire organization (that is, business manager, subcontracts manager, systems architect, and administrator). These positions aren't to be taken lightly because they sit off the direct line of authority. Quite the contrary, these positions are important elements supporting the proper operation of a large, complex implementation or, as in the case of the systems architect, in developing and executing the against the systems specifications.

The last oddity on this organization chart is the position of the conversions and interface (C&I) project manager. This position is explained in more detail later, but for now realize that this is one of the most critical positions in any PeopleSoft implementation. It requires the team's best individual because it's extraordinarily demanding. It will touch every part of the implementation, every legacy system, every process that uses any sort of information technology. It can play the single largest role in funding requirements and change traffic.

As you read on, keep in mind that this team is meant to be integrated and should operate in that spirit. Each team should be included in the decisions of the surrounding teams, because each segment of the implementation will later be integrated as part of the greater whole. So just as a baseball team has a team captain, the implementation team (and the implementation) will have a senior champion.

THE SENIOR CHAMPION

As noted in Chapter 22, "Revolution Versus Evolution," the leading critical success factor is having a committed senior implementation/change champion with the leadership and drive exemplified by RRAG's Colin Green. According to *Information Week* magazine (June 20, 1994,

"Missteps, Miscues"), one leading reason an implementation will fail is the lack of a committed senior executive. Whether focused on BPR or systems (which usually go hand in hand), the senior executive is the linchpin that holds the implementation together. If that person is a strong leader who establishes direction and drives his/her people from above, the project's chances for success grow immeasurably. If he/she is disinterested, unconnected, separated from the project by layers of management, or generally out of touch with the project, scope creep is bound to set in and the implementation course destined to wander. This will inevitably lead to the implementation stalling and finally failing.

PART

IV

CH

23

A leading Fortune 500 company is the perfect example of this type of failure. This manufacturer selected and performed partial implementations on *two* of the three major ERP packages. The first package was partially installed, training was in progress, and implementation teams were forming when the process was brought to a halt, the software shelved, and the second package initiated. Almost a year and a half later, the second package was stopped, the first company re-engaged in negotiations, and the competition reopened. The course of the 18-month implementation of the second package was like passage through Dante's *Inferno*:

- The scope of the projects wandered.

- Teams organized and dissolved.

- Support package/implementations analysis stopped and started by different subteams over the same package.

- Discussions and strategies developed on whether particular systems were required when the user community had already implemented them on the shop floor.

- The user community was never engaged.

- Leadership above the manager level never committed to decisions and frequently deferred to other team members (who in turn deferred back to management).

- Throughout, contractual issues plagued the project.

Why did all this happen? No single point of accountability on the company side was ever chosen—there was no senior champion. Questions were answered with questions; directions were left unclear. Specifications were never analyzed, nor were they clarified. The specifications were never frozen so that there was room to vary and, thus, there was room for enormous scope creep as the specifications altered from time to time. Directions to the third-party implementation teams varied from department to department because no two departments had a common understanding or worked together.

The effect was mass chaos as the implementation began to fail. This onrushing failure rapidly led to arguments about scope creep, work and rework, and subcontracts approved by one group and not by another. Critical implementation elements and systems also were poorly defined. Project segments moved forward with little or no concurrence. Large amounts of effort were being spent on doing the wrong things, which led to deteriorating team morale. A depressed team meant a near rebellion, which meant a disregard for the advice being given by the third-party consulting organization despite their long successful history in ERP implementations. Finally, the implementation went south—exactly what you would expect without senior management direction. The management team who didn't manage then reopened competition.

Now compare this with the RRAG effort (which started at roughly the same time). The commitment of the CEO, Colin Green, had placed a singular focus on the endgame completion of the implementation. The third-party consultants and the implementation teams were working in concert. Scope creep occurred, but it was minimal and controlled by change orders. During the same year and a half period that the Fortune 500 project descended into madness, RRAG brought one of its divisions up on an ERP. Though it wasn't nearly as large as the Fortune 500 company, the division was up and running, working out the bugs, and driving toward recognizing the projected benefits stream.

Looking back at this example, what's the role of a senior champion such as Colin Green? What must he bring to the team? What must his involvement be? All good questions.

The senior champion must be the general that leads at the front and by example. He must demonstrate the commitment that he and the board have to the project. One of his most important responsibilities is to communicate without reservation that the implementation and the changes in corporate business processes are the direction the business is heading, supported by senior management. This individual *must* be able to

- Reallocate resources without question
- Release employees that hamper progress
- Hire needed talent (be it third-party assistance or new personnel)
- Control the user community, the IT community, and any third-party subcontractor
- Have significant influence over funding allocation
- Continually correlate the implementation endgame and the corporate strategy

It's highly advisable that this individual maintain extremely current knowledge of the project, attending—if not indeed running—regular program management meetings, holding random meetings with the project teams, and running regular quality checks. Evidence from past implementations demonstrates that another "bullet" in the senior champion's control should be *tiger teams*, small teams of highly qualified troubleshooters who can descend on an issue and resolve it quickly. This overall type of involvement shows the employees the direction they must go if they want to have a future at Company X. It helps them realize that change is a reality and that holding on to the past is a waste of time and career-limiting. More positively, it helps to foster the creative energy needed to resolve issues and creates a winning team spirit, which is critical to any team.

THE STEERING COMMITTEE

The senior champion has one more significant role: He (and if a third-party implementer is present, his consulting mirror) will chair the steering committee. This committee, frequently filled by senior company (and consulting) officials, must act to implement the following:

- Keep the implementation strategy current
- Ensure that the implementation has the necessary resources to succeed

- Oversee program management reviews as part of quality assurance
- Administer and change control board decisions

This steering committee will act to resolve issues that become bogged down in the politics between departments or between company and consulting personnel. They must always act with the implementation and company strategy in mind, and be able to react quickly to prevent already lingering issues from continuing. These issues linger because they have been debated at lower levels and reach the steering committee only because of lack of resolution.

THE PROGRAM MANAGER

Next down the ladder of critical players in a PeopleSoft implementation is the program manager. This is a *program* manager, not a project manager. This individual is responsible for tracking the cost, schedule, performance, and risk of the entire implementation, which is composed of multiple projects and subcontractors. It's the program manager's job to

- Maintain accurate work breakdown structures
- Calibrate individual performance to tasks
- Task against the WBS
- Understand the risk/risk mitigation
- Understand the monetary and time issues surrounding the contract

Experience has shown that weekly assessment of the cost position against budget, estimates to complete, and projected burn rates are all effective cost-related views that will help a program manager keep surprises out of the implementation.

Unlike the implementation manager or project manager, the program manager has a certain amount of politicking to do. It's the program manager's job to work with the other managers to ensure that the required resources are onsite or properly allocated, and to act as the last line of quality assurance after the implementation manager and project manager but before the steering committee.

Note

Many implementations, when performed, will find the company leadership avoiding the program manager and even the program mentality. They will look on an implementation as the installation of software and try to cut costs by eliminating program management budgets. When asked why, the common retort is that program management is redundant or has no requirement. If the program manager is doing his job right, it should almost seem as if it's a boring task, but certainly not redundant or not required. Experience would advise, though, that program management be placed where it belongs—in each and every project. Each project will require a portion of the program manager's time or his "top cover" skills to protect it from resource loss or political strife, while continually monitoring progress and working to mitigate risk across the projects (and the program). Therefore, each project should build into its individual budgets the money to cover this time (frequently 10% to 20% depending on program and project size, deadlines, and projected risk).

WORKING PAPERS FOR THE IMPLEMENTATION

One lesson that can be drawn from the operations methodology of the "Big Five" accounting firms is the development and constant maintenance of working papers. *Working papers* is a collection of documentation across the lifecycle of the implementation. A complete set of working papers will include hard or soft copies of all contracts, contractual changes, communications, proposals, work plans, SOW, WBS, project reports, and program reports—that is to say, any documentation created during an implementation down to meeting notes. All this material is archived in reverse date order in the program manager's office, and it's his responsibility to maintain them (whether or not it's handled on a daily level by an administrator is up to the PM, but the PM has the final accountability due to tremendous legal bearing downstream). If working paper files are required by a team member for reference, it's checked out in a formal methodology.

Why is this essential? Because this is a best practice that will keep the program honest and create an audit trail that may be necessary for technical or legal reasons later on or even after the implementation. This is even more essential when contracting with a third-party implementation firm or one or more software/hardware subcontractors. The old saying is that good fences make good neighbors, and if that's the case, this is a nice solid, five-foot, cement-sunk storm fence.

Why treat an implementation as a program and not a project?
A program is composed of several projects, all designed to finally integrate into a greater whole. It's budgeted for at the program and project level. A program is a high-visibility effort requiring senior commitment and attention and usually requires a separate management team/office to be established, focused on running the effort. In no way should a program that's a multilevel, highly complex effort be confused with a simpler project. The projects are complex and demanding, and it's the management requirement of multiple tiers that's an initial differentiator.

Operationally, the program varies from the project, as it will affect the overall way in which the company performs its business. Also, when on the scale of an ERP, it's likely to be part of the company's operating infrastructure for the next 20–30 years. The information technology infrastructure and the method a company uses to access and apply its information will be a major sub-element of company strategy. Simply put, this is an effort that bears with it short- and long-term operational, monetary, and strategic consequences. Program-level efforts denote the type of organization, focus, and commitment necessary to establish success. The authority to direct change must come from the company's highest levels, as it will require a senior champion as an acting change agent. A project frequently stops at the division, department, or even the cell level.

THE IMPLEMENTATION MANAGER

On the next stop down the implementation totem is the implementation manager. Whereas the program manager focuses on running the implementation from a risk, schedule, performance, and cost level; the implementation manager focuses on team interaction/ coordination, enacting the implementation strategy (that is, implementation sequencing— what module goes in when to maximize benefit and minimize redundancy), working with the specifications and the systems architect, and focusing on technical issues. Although the implementation manager reports to the program manager, the two should function as a "dynamic duo." These two team members must have complementary skill sets: It's really the implementation manager's job to act as a foreman in the day-to-day running of the project, whereas it's the job of the program manager to keep resource issues off the implementation manager's worry list and keep company politics from getting into the critical path.

The implementation manager will work with the project managers on a regular basis to ensure coordination between project efforts. Frequently, more complex problems, like an ERP, will benefit from an implementation manager treating the project teams on an integrated basis. The implementation manager will ensure that team members from the various projects attend all meetings of the other projects and work with the other projects to ensure that efforts are concerted and coordinated, and touch points are designed for ease of interaction/operability. When it comes to a highly complex implementation, the benefits gained from the use of integrated project teams (IPTs) are substantial as integration is the key concept that will deliver the major benefits multiplier to the company. It's these teams that will work together over the program lifecycle to design and implement smooth touch points between departments or processes. This will create the smooth, uninterrupted flow of information that, in an extreme example, could run from advanced planning and scheduling efforts all the way to the manufacturing execution system, and from the engineer-to-order systems all the way to the after-market support systems.

When it comes to change orders and project-level disputes, the implementation manager should act as a clearinghouse. Depending on the complexity, the implementation manager can act as the systems configuration manager, but on larger projects he's well advised to delegate this responsibility to another teammate. Whether the implementation manager needs to make this a full-time position is directly proportional to the accuracy of the initial systems specification, the amount of user interaction on the development of the specification, and the overall complexity of the effort. Loose specs, or those developed with user input, will frequently demand repeated change to the systems spec. This will involve the repeated development of new statements of work and the associated support material, as it must frequently entail contractual and budgetary changes. It's this type of complex operation that will require a full-time configuration manager working for the implementation manager. Again, it's the responsibility of the IM to keep the new work associated with changed configurations in concert and executable without significant task alterations of resource realignment, while leveling the details of developing the SOWs and supporting change package documentation efforts (and librarying) to the configuration manager.

THE PROJECT MANAGER

With the jobs of program manager and implementation manager established, it's logical to look next at the project manager. By this point, most of the strategic concern, company politics, and contractual issues are above you. The project manager focuses her team on a particular tactical element, be it a process, software module, or department. Examples would be implementing a financials suite into the Finance department, a supply chain suite into the Procurement department, or an execution package on the shop floor.

Project managers should have a single statement of work with a very clearly defined single focus. Yes, part of this focus is the integration to surrounding packages and elements, but most of the focus is to get a single string of concurrent modules implemented in a specific time frame to support a single corporate entity or process, all as part of the great program. The program manager and the implementation manager must work to keep all extraneous activities such as resource problems and political infighting off the project manager's plate. This is the tactical battle of the implementation, and a strong, concise focus is what will permit a project manager to deliver a low-risk, on-time, on-budget project implementation.

So what are the day-to-day responsibilities of a project manager? As the tactical leader of a small team of technical or functional implementors, it's her job to maintain performance to the project plan; work with users and IT personnel that influence the particular project; and work to set up, configure, design, and build a solution that meets the needs of the user community. Through the project she will also act as quality assurance with an increasing role as the solution moves into testing, and as the daily proponent of the integrated process team concept, working with the other project leads and other potential subcontractors. The role will vary from true operational requirements such as requesting additional resources to mitigate forecast risk, to a true management role of helping teammates meet career goals or balancing work and personnel demands.

> **Tip**
>
> Frequently, some of the greatest bonds on an implementation team will form between a client project manager and her consulting mirror because together they will fight common management battles for the good of their project. If indeed this type of unity displays itself, it's to be fostered. It's an important element in getting and keeping the teams focused on the end game of a successful implementation.

CONVERSIONS AND INTERFACE PROJECT MANAGER

Welcome to the world of black magic and voodoo. No matter what else you learn from this text, learn that conversions and interfaces represent the long lead item that can easily make or break an implementation. During the initial phases of an implementation, if the team doesn't aggressively pursue accurate detail concerning the required number of conversions and interfaces, something is very wrong. All the data in the legacy systems must find its way across into the new world. Hopefully (and most cost-effectively), this is done through a one-time conversion. If not, the interfaces must be designed, built, tested, and maintained for the life of the legacy system or until a replacement system becomes the impetus to rewrite it or convert the data permanently and eliminate the interface maintenance money pit. It's for these reasons that the best of the nest from the implementation team lead this project.

What's required is a person with strong attention to detail and the creative mind to build ways around interfaces and into either vendor-predeveloped and -supported interfaces of conversions. This person will have a very strong team reporting to him and will live and die by the implementation team's ability to act in an integrated method. The more integrated the implementation, the sooner the conversions and interfaces can be designed, built, and so forth. Otherwise, an implementation runs a major risk of stalling because parallel tasking runs its course and everyone is left waiting for the data to come across an incomplete conversion or interface channel. The demand to maintain schedule and mitigate risk is a very real and a constant challenge for this project manager and team. Errors by this squad can cost hundreds of thousands—nay millions—of dollars in rework, idle time, and slippage. For this reason, the C&I project manager should have constant fear of the implementation manager, the program manager, and even the senior champion. Getting resources to this project and keeping it on track is one big key to a successful implementation.

SYSTEMS ARCHITECT

If everyone else on the team represents the construction crew, the systems architect is the person who designed the house. A good systems architect is one who can make the difference between a logical, capable, integrated system or a major mess of boxes and imperceptible lines on a wall chart. Having a full-time architect on the program—particularly in the early phases of the program—is the only practice, let alone a best practice. It's recommended that as the systems architecture reaches a stable state, other unbiased systems architects review it for logic and coherence. In other words, make sure that the blueprints are right before laying the foundation. A little extra precaution here can keep risk down later.

As the implementation moves through design, building, transition, and production, the systems architect role will diminish to an advisor. He will constantly play a role in optimizing the implementation strategy or the conversions and interface strategy.

Tip

Avoid the trap of rolling the architect off the program. If something does come apart, the architect would be one of the key fix-it persons you have.

It's also important to document the systems architecture and to always have at least one member of the IT and user staff that apprentices under the prior architect before that person leaves the position. As long as the system is in use, the company should always have readily available the blueprints and someone who can read them.

CONFIGURATION MANAGER

At this point, we've reviewed the primary roles in an implementation, but just as a good army has strong logistics behind it, a good implementation has good support function underpinning the daily operations. It's these support functions that will endure a smooth function of the business side of the implementation and keep the proper contracts and records in place to protect the implementation from legal hazards and scope creep. Although the position of the configuration manager was touched on earlier, a brief recap is in order.

The systems configuration as established by a locked and mutual systems specification is only a starting point. The belief that any such specification is set in stone is up there with the belief that the IRS is here to help you. This spec will change repeatedly during the course of the implementation as the teams learn more about the new system, the legacy system, the business processes, what the company wants to run its operations, and the prioritization of the implementation potential driven by needs or cost. It's the configuration manager's responsibility to ride herd on the change process and to work with the project teams and systems architect to develop coherent changes to the prior configuration. She must also work with the project managers to develop risk analysis, cost-benefit analysis, budgets, SOWs, and WBSs to support the implementation change. When these analyses are complete, the configuration manager will work with the program manager during presentations to the steering committee, and finally will act as librarian archiving the past configurations and tracking the alterations.

> **Tip**
>
> Frequently, the configuration manager job is an excellent position in which to develop new team members. It permits working with members of the entire program, technical exposure as well as functional exposure, and over time it will give this individual a strong feeling for the architecture, the system, and time capabilities. In some cases, this position can be designed as a rotational position as new team members join the implementation team, but this is usually driven by the luxury of time, which is rare in this environment.

SUBCONTRACTS MANAGER

You may have consultants helping you implement. You may have third-party software that feeds the systems (for example, tooling maintenance systems, time and attendance systems, or program management systems, to name a few). You may have hired a third party to develop your conversions and interfaces. No matter what, it's highly unlikely that any implementation won't go off without the participation of a subcontractor in some shape or form. For this reason—and just like any good program, be it a system, a fighter plane, a ship, or a car—a good subcontracts manager is worth his weight in gold.

The subcontract manager's role on an implementation will vary with the size of an implementation. Major multimillion-dollar implementations may require a full-time sub-contracts manager, whereas smaller efforts might see the program manager wearing two hats and picking up the subcontracting tasks himself.

BUSINESS MANAGER

Like the subcontracts manager, the business manager's role will vary with the complexity and size of the implementation. The basic description of the position is an implementation team member who focuses her efforts on maintaining the proper accounting and billing structure. The definition itself indicates that this position is actually more of a position for an implementation being staffed in part by third-party implementors who need to track and bill time and expenses. If the implementation is being performed by 100 percent internal resources, this job may simply entail the tracking of hours against the tasks as a function of measuring opportunity costs or maintaining projected program budgets.

The business manager's role is that of the team's accountant. Like the systems architect, the job is more intensive up front as the policies and procedures are established. When a proper tracking and billing method is set, the role can be turned over to the implementation administrator or performed on a partial full-time equivalent basis.

ADMINISTRATOR

The administrator is the person who acts as the keeper of all documentation, the work paper librarian, and the repository for all timesheets, internal and external communications, and so on. When an implementation reaches a size in which 20 or more people are reporting up through the organization, it's logical to engage a full-time administrator who can assist in maintaining SOWs, WBS, timesheet policies, and the like. Depending on the administrator's experience and the complexity of the engagement, she may be able to take over the business manager or subcontracts manager roles over time. It's important that these extra positions initially be established by experienced personnel, but a good administrator will be more than capable of keeping the positions functioning.

THE OVERALL TEAM STRUCTURE

Over the past dozen pages, the organization of a mid- to large-size implementation has been laid out. Although you might be saying to yourself that your implementation is too small to require such depth or that you can make do with what you have, I would encourage you to start off with something too large and pare back, rather than start off with too small an implementation staff and end up scrambling for resources as you fall further behind schedule.

Regarding the best and the brightest, separating with these people for the course of the implementation will help to mitigate implementation risk, protect company dollars, and build stronger company players for the future. Again, if you find that you've unnecessarily overstaffed, cut back and reallocate, but heed a very simple warning that you must start with what you think is too much and tailor the team as the requirements develop and dictate. If not, it's a simple rule that you'll fall behind. An implementation can be a difficult train to catch after it has left the station.

So to close, just remember that you should overstaff initially and get the best and the brightest committed. They are on the implementation for the duration, and they must all work together in an integrated fashion under strong, committed leadership.

CHAPTER 24

ADAPTATION VERSUS CUSTOMIZATION

In this chapter   *by Carl Upthegrove*

THE RISK OF DOING CUSTOMIZATIONS, OR NOT DOING THEM

The reasons for not making customizations to any package software products are well known. Customization takes time and will lengthen the implementation plan. It costs money, and how much it will cost is often difficult to estimate. It makes upgrading more difficult because all the customizations must be reviewed when an upgrade from one release to another is done to ensure that the customizations are not impacted by code changes that are part of the upgrade. It creates risk that the customizations will not work properly either within themselves or with the PeopleSoft products they touch.

There are also risks associated with not doing customization. After all, it is important that the key business processes that drove the decision to implement the new system be properly addressed. A significant business process may not work properly without a customization. Users may reject the system if it does not work properly for them, or if it creates so much additional work that they cannot be effective or efficient, and they perceive that because of the new system they "look bad" in the eyes of management.

Even though nearly every implementation project begins with the idea that the products will be used "plain vanilla," or as is, some customizations are almost always done. PeopleSoft applications are much easier to customize than most other products, due to the technology in PeopleTools. However, it is still good policy to consider each customization request very carefully.

WHAT CUSTOMIZATION IS ALL ABOUT

Customization, modification, making changes—just what are we talking about here? If we change the location of a field on a panel, is that a customization? What if we combine fields from two panels onto one; is that a customization? Is a modification the same as a customization? Is any change to the system a customization?

There is no rule for just what constitutes a modification or customization. Something that is perceived as minor in one project might be major in another. However, in general, changes to the system fall into groups.

If the change deals with the presentation of data and information on a panel, it will most likely not be considered a significant customization. That also goes for combining data from two or more panels onto one. These types of changes are fairly easy to do; they don't impact the table structure and make no changes to any process logic. They of course need to be documented and must be considered during a release upgrade, but there are PeopleSoft products to assist in dealing with these types of customizations or modifications during the upgrade.

CUSTOMIZATIONS TO THE TABLE STRUCTURE

Changes that affect the table structure are more significant. Changes to the table structure most often occur when it is necessary to add data elements, for example, a field that is required by the organization but is not in the standard PeopleSoft product. In some cases, additional tables are created and fields from those tables are added to existing panels. In some cases, completely new panels are created that contain fields from new tables and/or existing standard PeopleSoft tables. These types of changes are still relatively easy to do with PeopleTools but will present some added challenges during a release upgrade.

CUSTOMIZATIONS TO THE PROCESSING LOGIC

Changes that affect existing processing logic are the most significant. An example of processing logic might be when an update occurs to a table. In the case of receipt of goods, the update might take place immediately when the goods are received, or there might need to be a quality inspection task that takes place first. This quality inspection task might affect the process by which the inventory quantity is updated.

PeopleSoft works with tables and creating these tables. Adding, changing, and deleting data in one of those tables is managed with PeopleTools. When a process needs to be done that uses data from those tables to perform a task or create some output, PeopleSoft uses one or more products to do that processing. These products may include COBOL, SQR, Accuate, or another product. These processes contain processing logic that runs from fairly simple to quite complex. Changing that logic or adding to it can also run from simple to very complex. These changes are the most significant, risky, and difficult to manage. They also are the most difficult to deal with during an upgrade. For these reasons, changes of this type should be considered more closely and carefully.

In the case of some customizations, they can be created as "subsystems" and then integrated with the standard PeopleSoft products. For example, a separate process can be defined that gets input from or provides output to a PeopleSoft product rather than modifying PeopleSoft directly. A separate process specific to the situation is developed independently of the basic PeopleSoft product. This has several advantages in that it is less risky, easier to define and test, and simpler to deal with at upgrade time. The use of PeopleSoft's tools makes this type of customization reasonably easy to do and easy to deal with at the time of an upgrade. It can also require less knowledge of the standard system and can therefore be done by staff members who do not have a deep knowledge of the PeopleSoft products. Especially for a first-time PeopleSoft implementation, this is often a good choice.

So a customization can consist of something minor such as changing how data is presented, or it can be more complicated such as adding a new data element or changing a process. It can also be creating a separate system that is supported by or supports the standard PeopleSoft products and does not directly affect the PeopleSoft code.

THE BUSINESS ISSUES THAT IMPACT THE CUSTOMIZATION DECISION

As noted earlier, whatever business objectives that drove the decision to undertake the implementation of the PeopleSoft products in the first place should also be the driver behind the choice of what to customize and what not to change. No product will work exactly the way everyone would like. Even totally customized systems seldom meet everyone's needs. Therefore, compromises must be made.

PROJECT MANAGEMENT HELPS PROVIDE SOME CONTROL

A good project management methodology should contain some policies to address requests for customization. This policy should identify who will make the decisions about customizations and what the criteria will be. This helps both management and the users to better understand what is being done and why. It also helps prevent "on the spot" decisions from being made that may conflict with the logic used on a similar decision elsewhere in the project.

CUSTOMIZATION CRITERIA

The criteria for doing a customization should be clear. Is the customization required to run the business? It may be helpful to create a severity index. This severity index can become part of the lexicon of the project, allowing people to have an agreed-upon system to ranking requests and helping to eliminate personal and emotional views on how important a customization might be. For example, a severity code of 4 would indicate that this process is critical to the business and must work exactly as defined. A code of 3 might indicate a process that needs customization, but there is some flexibility in how the process can be executed. A code of 2 would indicate that a customization is desirable but not really needed for the business, and a code of 1 would indicate that a customization is preferred but has no real impact on doing business. Obviously other rating scales can be developed as suits the project. The advantage of some rating criteria such as this is that they can be created in an unemotional manner before any specific customization is asked for, and they can be applied with less subjectivity than simply one person or a group of people making a choice.

CORPORATE INTEREST TOWARD CUSTOMIZATION

Corporate interests often play a part in whether or not a customization is done. Consistency across the company can be an important issue, especially with large projects that span multiple divisions or geographical locations. In this case, the choice of whether or not to do a customization may be linked to whether all the affected organizations are impacted in the same way. Will a customization in one area create a problem in another area? Are all the parts of the organization using one version of the product, or will individual parts of the organization have their own versions? For example, will remote sites be required to provide accounting data to a central site for consolidation? If so, is it important that all sites be on the same release? If data and information regularly flow from site to site and unit to unit, it is advisable to have all units on the same version. When this is the case, all upgrades need to be done within the same time frame, and customization has an effect on that.

FLEXIBILITY

Flexibility on the part of users also plays a part in deciding whether a customization needs to be done or not. Some organizations can cope more easily than others with changes to how something is done. If the users are flexible and tend to adapt easily to changes of this type, customization may not be as important. However, if the organization tends to resist change and a small customization to how a panel looks or how data is accessed can overcome a major obstacle in retraining, perhaps the customization is the easier choice.

WILLINGNESS TO FOREGO UPGRADES

Willingness to forego upgrades or wait a while can enter into the decision. PeopleSoft historically has offered new releases approximately every 18 to 24 months. These new releases usually have significant technological and/or functional enhancements. For example, release 7.0 offered an enhanced PeopleTools product, which made PeopleTools easier to use. Release 7.5 had significant new functionality in areas such as Manufacturing and Production Planning. If a lot of customizations have been made to the products, or if those customizations are large and complex, that may impact the decision of how soon the organization can take advantage of the upgrade. It will also impact the cost of the upgrade. Each customization must be examined to determine the impact it will have given the new functionality in the system, and that takes time and costs money.

PART

IV

CH

24

THE TIMING OF A NEW RELEASE

The timing of a new release will also enter into the decision of whether or not to do a customization. If the implementation project is begun early in the release cycle, little may be known of what functionality is in the next release. If the project is begun later in the release cycle, PeopleSoft staff should be consulted early in the decision process to get their input on what might be available in the next release and how that will affect the decision on whether to do a customization. New functionality that closely approximates what is being called for in the customization request may be contained in the next release. If so, it may be a better choice to forego the customization and implement the next release as soon as possible to gain that functionality.

Cooperative development is a possibility in some cases. With any significant customization request, PeopleSoft should be consulted to determine whether the company is considering any cooperative development initiatives in that area. PeopleSoft and its customers will sometimes share development of major modifications or customizations that will have value for other PeopleSoft customers.

THE TECHNICAL ENVIRONMENT

The technical environment in which the project is taking place is also a consideration when deciding how much customization to undertake. What might seem quite simple to one organization would be a much more serious challenge to another organization. The technical environment involves factors such as

- Hardware—How much is available and what type?
- People—Are there enough staff and do they possess the needed skills and organizational maturity?
- Experience—Have things like this been done before?

The size of the IT staff can obviously have a bearing on the impact of customization. Customizations can be small IT projects and need to be managed as such. The same methodology used for creating a system will be of use in creating customization for a PeopleSoft product. Tasks such as functional design, technical design, unit testing, and system testing need to be part of the customization plan. Coding standards that are used for other projects should also apply here. For that reason, an organization with a limited IT staff may not have the people available to do a large number of customizations or to do customization of a complex nature. If a customization is absolutely required for the business, this lack of staff may be overcome with the use of temporary additions to the staff or contractors. PeopleSoft can provide help either from the PeopleSoft Professional Services Group or through reference to a business partner. In some cases, PeopleSoft will agree to do a customization through the Strategic Customization Services organization within PeopleSoft Professional Services. This group will provide a quote for doing the customization if it meets their requirements of reusability and availability in a future release, among other criteria. Consult with PeopleSoft through your PeopleSoft representative or via www.peoplesoft.com on how to take advantage of this service.

THE APPROPRIATE TECHNICAL SKILLS

PeopleSoft utilizes some proprietary technology such as PeopleTools and PeopleCode. An organization that possesses experience with this technology will find it easier to execute customizations than will an organization in which this knowledge is missing. Whether or not people on the staff have this knowledge and experience should be a very serious consideration when making decisions about customizations. Not only is this training and background essential to doing the customization, but it is also important when reviewing the effects of the customization at upgrade time. PeopleSoft provides training and education in all the technology used by the products. Taking advantage of this education can be very useful, but of course nothing really beats the experience of having been through it. If the organization is new to PeopleSoft or the team assembled for the project is new to this technology, small customizations are very realistic to consider. Things mentioned earlier such as changing panels and making some minor modifications to tables might fall in this category. Very large or complex customizations require assistance from PeopleSoft Professional Services or a provision for a ramping up of the skills needed to ensure that the customization is done properly. If the team is new to PeopleSoft and does not have experienced leadership from outside, extra time for testing should be included in the project plan.

SUMMARY

The final choice of whether to do a customization or not will be dependent on many things. Is it really required for the business or just nice to have? Does the organization have the proper skill set and sufficient staff to ensure that the work is done properly and in a timely manner? What will be available from PeopleSoft in the near future that might address the business need? Can it be supported in the environment going forward?

The answers to these questions and the decisions on what customizations to do and not do can have a significant impact on the success of the PeopleSoft implementation. Keep in mind that Pareto's Law usually applies. If the project appears to require more than 20% modifications or customizations, it is probably at high risk. Review each of the requests for business need and feasibility.

CHAPTER 25

IMPLEMENTATION SERVICES

In this chapter

by Perry Keating

SELECTING CRITICAL RESOURCES

A process for assembling a project team for PeopleSoft implementation consists of three steps: identify skill requirements, assess the in-house information technology (IT) group, and finally evaluate outside consultants.

During the development of the work breakdown structure (WBS), you identify the skill requirements to complete the implementation of a PeopleSoft application. Suppose that you've identified the requirements for three programmers, two analysts, one technical writer, one trainer, one quality assurance specialist, three users, and yourself (of course) as the project leader.

The first place to look for these people is in-house within the IT group. Bear in mind that people with the necessary expertise may not be available when you need them or may be too busy to assist you in your project. You may even find out that your project doesn't have a high enough priority to warrant dedication of resources from the IT group. The advantages of using the in-house IT group is that its members are familiar with the processes, the standards, and the procedures the company is following, as well as the organization's culture and mores. The disadvantage could be a lack of knowledge of PeopleSoft applications—hence, you would have to look outside for consultants.

Consultants should be technically proficient with PeopleSoft applications and should bring other business "best practices" experience to the project. As long as goals and objectives are clearly defined and plans include detailed tasks, subtasks, schedules, and deliverables, the higher-priced consultants bring value to the project. There is a danger that the consultant team will leave when training has been attended and assimilated by all hands. Then the technological expertise leaves with it. One way to ensure that this does not happen is to have a composite team of the best and the brightest from in-house as well as a small team of PeopleSoft-savvy consultants to handle the project.

The hybrid team mitigates the disadvantages of the in-house IT group and avoids the pitfalls of the outside consultant team. The critical elements in the hybrid team's success are communication, communication, and more communication.

FACILITATING SYSTEM ADMINISTRATION

What is the first step when you have the hybrid team in place? Database controls must be established very early in the implementation life cycle. These controls must be maintained throughout the life of the implementation. Not establishing controls is often the early critical error that sinks the implementation.

SELECTING THE DATABASE ADMINISTRATOR

Designate a database administrator (DBA) early in requirements definition to develop and enforce controls over the database. Assign the following responsibilities to the DBA:

- Control the database structure
- Control the software interfaces to the database
- Establish database security, backup, and recovery procedures
- Evaluate database performance

The DBA should control the database design and documentation, and develop and enforce policies and procedures needed to control access to the database and safeguard its integrity.

Select a DBA who understands input/output processing, data structures, and the intricacies of the operating system and the selected database management system (DBMS).

Note

PeopleSoft RDBMS choices include a wide variety of platforms, including Microsoft SQL Server, DB2, Oracle, Sybase, and Informix. In 1998, PeopleSoft's focus had been toward Windows NT and SQL Server as the platforms of choice.

CONTROLLING THE DATABASE STRUCTURE

Establish the DBA as the focal point of configuration control over the database structure. Require the DBA to assess the impact of changes to the database structure before authorizing such changes. During the requirements definition phase, identify the logical structure and content of the database from the user's perspective. During the design process, define the physical structure and content in terms of its schema and subschemas.

PART

IV

CH

25

Establish standards for naming and declaring data items and files.

Document all database entities and their attributes in a data dictionary. Define the data item content, format, location, usage, ownership, and access/modification rights for each database file. Ensure that redundant data items are either updated concurrently or reconciled periodically.

ENSURING DATABASE SECURITY, BACKUP, AND RECOVERY

Develop procedures to troubleshoot, monitor, reorganize, back up, and recover the database. Safeguard the database from natural and human hazards and from accidental and malicious damage. An example of malicious damage might be a disgruntled employee coming back to do harm before he or she leaves your organization. Two common safeguard methods are

- Multiple password level (for example, database, file, data item, access, and update)
- Audit trails that detail the date, time, and user ID for each access and/or update

Plan for multiple database copies. Provide a separate copy for implementation, build, and acceptance testing, each with its own set of access controls. This allows each effort to proceed independent of database changes made during the other two efforts.

Anticipate database failures and develop standard responses to them. For each type of failure (hardware, software, or accidental change), create detection and recovery procedures. Include capabilities in the software product to detect data inconsistencies. If possible, maintain a transaction log containing before and after images of changed records to facilitate recovery. Periodically, back up the database. In case of a failure, restore the backup copy and reapply the logged transactions.

UNDERSTANDING THE RESOURCE-OBJECTIVE MATCH (A.K.A. STRATEGY)

In reality, the Resource-Objective Match is similar to a "make or buy" decision or a trade-off study to determine whether alternative A is better than alternative B.

In this case, the objective is to implement the PeopleSoft Manufacturing module in the fourth quarter of your current fiscal year. The alternatives available are to use the existing IT group of 100 or to use the 80 consultants that are available for additional IT work. The selection criteria are schedule, quality of deliverable, success on budget, and the highest return on investment (ROI) of the committed resources. Criteria are weighted as follows: ROI is significantly more important than schedule, quality deliverables, and budget combined. The evaluation indicates that the short-term costs of the consultants exceed the budget and that the IT group can spare only 10 people for the effort. The project requires 20 people, so you can either hire 10 more people or use 10 or 20 consultants.

There are long-range cost implications for adding to your work force, so it appears that adding to the workforce in the long run yields a poor ROI. You can select a hybrid solution by mixing 10 of your IT group with 10 consultants because this gives you the most return for your resource investment.

ESTABLISHING PRIORITIES

The best way to establish priorities is to develop a completed network plan. This is not a telecommunications "network" plan, but a project network plan developed by following these steps:

- Decide what you want to accomplish (that is, go from the as is to the to be model).
- What activities will be needed to achieve success?
- In what sequence will these activities be needed?
- What tasks lead directly to achievement?
- How much time will each task/activity take?
- Milestone calculations: earliest and latest dates it can occur, and how long it can be delayed
- Critical path calculation: the total time required to achieve overall success

The network plan becomes a road map for managers, task leaders, and project members. For example, a simple color scheme can be used to track progress: green for normal progress, yellow for observed delay, and red for serious delay. So how do you prioritize? Because green indicates safe, you note those activities and tasks that show green and are on schedule. However, the cautionary yellow indicates an observed delay in which schedule recovery is possible; these tasks require management attention. Red indicates a serious delay and schedule recovery is unlikely; these tasks/activities require immediate attention and urgent management action.

So there you have it—a technique that can help you prioritize your project, a completed network plan. A plan in which a Pert/CPM network analysis has been completed. All milestones are laid out in a logical sequence and time estimates are made for each activity; when earliest/latest dates, slack, and the critical path are completed, your job is to plan the work and then work the plan. When this is done properly, progress will occur.

SUMMARY

There are many differing opinions as to whether an organization should seek the help of consultants or an IT shop. Such topics as selecting critical resources and facilitating system administration are key tasks, regardless of which route the organization chooses to take. When you are deciding on options, database security, backup and recovery, understanding the resource-objective match, and establishing priorities all come into play.

STARTING THE IMPLEMENTATION

CHAPTER 26

PROJECT PLANNING

In this chapter

by Mike Fauscette

As any good sailor will tell you, it is essential for a successful trip to carefully lay out your course in advance. This is not to say that the plans are static—not at all. Thousands of small course corrections will inevitably be required to reach your destination. Implementation projects are complex and can be costly in both money and resources, so managing and increasing the potential for success is imperative. Laying out a route to a destination inherently implies a clear understanding of the destination. Or, in other words, how do you know you're there if you didn't know where you were heading in the first place? That's really what project planning is all about—determining your destination and the route to take to get there. Without it, you're lost at sea.

By reading this chapter, you can

- Gain a basic understanding of an implementation methodology and the process of selecting one
- Learn how to take your basic requirements and turn them into a project scope, defining the project boundaries
- Learn how to examine project risk and determine the true danger zone
- Gain an understanding of the process of ensuring project quality and establish a process for building quality into your project from the start
- Examine methods for managing your system configuration

PROJECT SUCCESS FACTORS

Experience shows that there are several common threads to a successful project. The following list describes some of these factors. Although the list is not exhaustive, it can provide some insight into what a successful project should include.

- The project uses a proven implementation methodology.
- You have a clear understanding of your destination goals (business objectives) that are tied to your organization's overall goals.
- You tie your solution to your business objectives.
- You clearly define your project scope and manage it throughout the implementation.
- Project controls are defined up front and used by the project management team.
- The project has the highest level of executive sponsorship and that sponsorship is visible to the entire organization.
- The project team has the appropriate number of resources, and those resources have the correct skill set.
- A method for ensuring project quality is built in from the start.
- Communications, both internal to the project team and external to the organization, are planned and happen according to the plan.
- The project solution meets the organization's objectives.

IMPLEMENTATION METHODOLOGIES

What is an implementation methodology? Certainly you will be bombarded with a multitude of methodology options from internal IT departments and implementation partners. Although each methodology will offer some different options and features, they all share some common elements.

First of all, let's figure out just what we mean when we talk about an implementation methodology. A *methodology* is really a structure or framework around which your implementation planning is conducted. In other words, it's the map on which your course (project plan) is laid out. The methodology (or map) provides you with the lay of the land and helps you avoid the pitfalls of the implementation. By providing discipline to the implementation project, it frees the project management team up to focus on the details of planning and controlling the project, while also providing flexible options for meeting your business objectives. By using the methodology as a checklist for guiding your implementation planning, you can avoid the omission of key elements of the project.

You might be asking, do I really need a methodology? The simple answer is that by using one, you lower your implementation risk considerably. We will examine risk management in greater detail later in this chapter, but understand at this point that everything you can do to lower project risk significantly is crucial to a successful implementation. Selecting and using a methodology, one that is a good fit with your organization, is a key factor in risk reduction.

SELECTING AN IMPLEMENTATION METHODOLOGY

If the selection of a methodology is a key success factor, how do you sift through all the available approaches and find the one that is right for you? First, let's look at what implementation approaches are out there.

Your internal IT department is a good place to start. If your organization has a seasoned IT department, with expertise in implementing large-scale enterprise projects, they may have an established methodology that has proven itself in your organization. There are several advantages to its use. It's probably a close match with your organizational culture. There will be in-house experts to work with your project team and assist with project planning. Problems arise with internal methodologies when any of the following situations occur:

1. The methodology is not a previously documented approach to implementation (no folk tales allowed here; this must be a formal approach to implementations to reap its true benefit).

2. The internal staff is not experienced in projects of this scope and magnitude.

3. You have selected a prime implementation partner with their own methodology, and they do not have a good understanding of the internal approach to the implementation, or their methods are tried and true with PeopleSoft implementations.

4. You don't have an internal IT department or use a third-party outsourced vendor.

Implementation partners bring a wealth of implementation experience to the table. They will undoubtedly have an established method for the PeopleSoft implementation that will offer many options to the project team. When you are selecting a partner, a close examination of their methodology will give you a good understanding of their overall approach to the implementation. One of the criteria for selecting a partner is an understanding of their corporate culture and its compatibility with your own. After all, you plan to establish a fairly long-term relationship with the partner; you need to ensure that your people can work effectively together. The methodology is a piece of this culture. Examine it carefully in your partner selection and train the entire team in the methodology when the project is underway.

PEOPLESOFT'S IMPLEMENTATION APPROACH AND TOOLS

PeopleSoft offers a well-documented implementation approach and some tools to enhance the implementation. If you are using PeopleSoft Professional Services, their methodology will be available for use on the project. Express, the PeopleSoft rapid results implementation approach, has three basic routes to cover most customer implementation needs. In addition to Express, PeopleSoft has developed an Implementation Toolkit to assist in managing your implementation project. You can use this Advantage Toolkit with any methodology to speed up the implementation of PeopleSoft applications.

COMMON IMPLEMENTATION ACTIVITIES

Although every methodology contains unique activities and terminology, several activities are common to most. In general, the project can be divided into the following categories:

- Prepurchase planning—This includes developing the initial requirements for a system, establishing project sponsorship, examining business objectives and goals, assessing architecture, contacting and reviewing vendors, vendor selection, and so on. Some of the material developed here will be invaluable in the next segment, project planning, and carry over into that segment to gain more detail.

- Project planning—Activities that are associated with project planning include developing/refining of requirements; conceptualizing a solution; defining project scope and controls; developing a quality management plan; communication plan and configuration management plan; recruiting and training a project team; establishing your project infrastructure (hardware, software, network, and facilities); selecting a partner, and so on.

- Prototyping (sometimes called conference room pilots or joint application development sessions)—Includes software installation, definition of initial business rules (setup), development of prototype scenarios or scripts, prototyping sessions, development of detailed requirements, fit analysis, and validation of the conceptual solution.

- Development and setup—Any gaps or misfits requiring customizations are addressed, interfaces are programmed, data conversion programs are developed, custom reports are developed, all programs are unit tested, and software business rule decisions are finalized and set up. User procedures are documented, including training material.

- Testing—Testing is conducted based on the testing strategy of the selected implementation methodology. At a minimum, unit or process testing, integration testing, and system testing should be planned and executed. In addition, a parallel testing plan may be required.

- Training—User training material is developed, instructors are trained, material is piloted, and the user community is trained in the software and new operational procedures.

- Rollout—The rollout of the solution is executed based on the implementation strategy.

THE ONE AND ONLY PROJECT MANAGER

The development of an effective project team might be compared to the management structure of a winning professional sports team. There is an owner and front office, and a head coach. There are also other coaches responsible for various specialties, and the management team may include player coaches as well. The steering team and the executive sponsor are much like the owner and front office. They provide strategic direction and oversight to the project team. The head coach and the coaching staff handle the daily management of the team. This model is readily transferred to the implementation team. The coaching staff or the project management team provides the tactical direction for the project.

Just as the team has a head coach, so the project team needs a single leader. It is essential for the success of the project that one resource has the responsibility, accountability, and authority to lead the entire team. There are several key success factors related to the project manager, including:

- Organizational credibility
- Authority over project resources
- Responsibility and accountability for project progress
- Proper skill set:
  - Management
  - Leadership
  - Planning
  - Facilitation
- Competencies:
  - Project management tools
  - Risk management
  - Personnel management

PART

V

CH

26

It is difficult, or should I say, almost impossible for the project management role to be a shared responsibility. Critical decisions will be required, and strong leadership is a necessity. This is a full-time role on the project team, and anything less increases the risk of failure! It is very difficult for an outsider to manage the implementation as well. A partner-provided project advisor could be of benefit, especially if the project manager is not experienced in software implementations, but cannot take the place of an organizationally savvy member of your staff who spans both the technical and functional areas of the project.

The rest of the management team will vary based on the scope of the implementation. The implementation will run more smoothly with detailed focused team leads for the various teams that make up the overall project team. Referred to as a tiered leadership model, it is very effective at providing consistent and efficient team leadership. Partner-provided leads to manage their staff are also a bonus source of leadership and project management expertise.

ESTABLISHING AND MANAGING PROJECT SCOPE

Establishing and managing project scope is a challenging and important task in the implementation planning phase. A solid, well-defined project scope is high on the list of project success factors. If this is true, what do we really mean when we discuss project scope?

Project scope might be defined as the boundaries around the project (see Figure 26.1). Just as a country must have clearly defined boundaries, so must a successful project. A complete project scope really contains three key elements:

1. Those things that will be done during the implementation project (in scope)

2. Those things that will not be done during the implementation project (out of scope)

3. A documented process for moving things from one to the other (scope management and change process)

Figure 26.1
Assessing project scope.

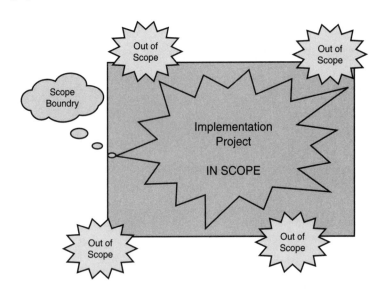

Why is the project scope so important? The scope document will be used and referenced throughout the project. It sets the proper expectations for management and the user community. The scope assists in providing focus for the project team on what is important in the implementation project, and with limited resources and time, it is essential that your team work on what is important. You cannot afford wasted efforts on out-of-scope activities.

DEVELOPING THE PROJECT SCOPE

There are many methods for establishing and documenting the project scope. The document itself may be very detailed or somewhat high level. You must choose the format and level of detail that will be successful in your organization. This is often driven by the needs of the project team to manage the expectations of the steering committee/executive sponsors, the user community, and the implementation partners. What it must do is clearly provide a picture of the implementation project. Often the implementation partner will request a detailed scope for their work, often called a *statement of work*. This will assist both the partner and your management team on managing the responsibilities of the partner team. We will look at this in more detail later in the chapter.

The project scope generally contains the following information:

- Assumptions and constraints
- Software functionality
- Software packages, specific applications, and versions
- Technology initiatives
- Interfaces
- Data conversions
- Other project-related initiatives

For the preceding information, the document should cover both the in- and out-of-scope details for each project phase.

How do you develop the project scope? The diagram in Figure 26.2 shows the basic steps.

Developing the project scope is an evolution that involves many different areas of the project team. Because it contains elements from all areas of the project, both technical and functional input will be required. The scope is built from an understanding of the organization's goals and strategic business objectives, as well as the tactical assumptions and constraints on the project team. The business objectives are the measure of success for the project. Even so, don't be misled into thinking that the project must meet all the objectives to be successful. That is, in fact, one of the functions of the scope, to identify the objectives that fall within the boundaries of the project at hand. Objectives outside the current project boundaries need to be addressed either by other projects or future phases of the current project.

PART

V

CH

26

Figure 26.2
Developing project
scope.

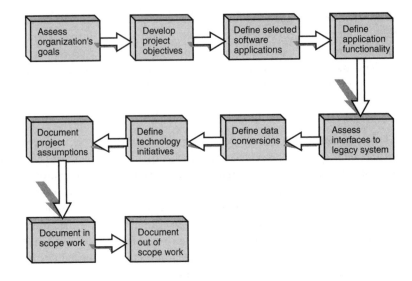

DEFINING CONSTRAINTS AND ASSUMPTIONS

Constraints and assumptions must be clearly defined in the scope document. Project
constraints are internal and external factors that impact the location of project boundaries.
An example of a project constraint might be the need to meet a calendar deadline imposed
by management on the project. The replacement of existing non-Y2K-compliant systems
is a project constraint. *Constraints* are factors that impact the locations of the project boundaries, and *assumptions* are factors that impact the way you move to those boundaries. In
other words, assumptions are factors whose presence is key to the success of the project.
Assumptions might include factors like the availability of certain key resources for the
project team, or the purchase of certain equipment by a specific date.

FOCUSING ON SOFTWARE FUNCTIONALITY

After constraints and assumptions are identified, the focus of the scope turns to the software
itself. The functionality of the individual PeopleSoft applications is assessed against the
business objectives. Decisions are made to implement certain functionality based on the
business objectives. Other software might also be included, for areas that fall outside of
the PeopleSoft products. This section can be as detailed as necessary, and might include
a list of functionality by application, with an assessment of in or out of scope for each
associated function.

LOOKING AT EXISTING SYSTEMS

After the new software is defined, a look at existing systems is necessary. Systems are examined to determine whether they will be replaced by the new software, or will be a candidate
for an interface. Interfaces should be identified at a high level, with more detail coming
later in the project. Data conversions should also be assessed. Again, this is more of a high-
level view of the conversions and in most cases comes from the superseded systems. Data
conversions are addressed in more detail later.

POTENTIAL TECHNOLOGY INITIATIVES

Next the focus shifts to potential technology initiatives. There may be many possibilities for the inclusion of new technology in the implementation project. For instance, you may decide to implement some of PeopleSoft's Web-based self-serve applications or eCommerce solutions. You should conduct a practical assessment to determine the impact to the project of each new initiative. In this assessment, compare the benefit of the new technology to the overall impact on the project, including time line and budget. There is a tendency to embrace technology for technology's sake; instead, the technology must be linked to a business objective! In other words, use technology when it can be demonstrated to support or meet a business need, but not simply because the technology is available.

The project scope is developed for the entire implementation project. It should then be subdivided based on the implementation strategy. The scope should address each phase of the project if the project contains multiple phases, in effect establishing the scope for each phase. The same logic applies to individual phases as to the project as a whole.

After the project boundaries are documented, clearly showing what's a part of the project scope and what's out of bounds, the scope should be communicated to and approved by the project sponsors. A key to the successful management of the scope is to have this formal approval and communication of the scope to the project team, implementation partners, senior management, and the end users. There can be no confusion over the scope of the project; communication will help prevent this.

HAVING AN IMPLEMENTATION PARTNER

An additional section may be required in the scope if an implementation partner will be used for the project. This involves the partner responsibilities and accountabilities. To prevent confusion and misunderstandings, it is very helpful to include a section that defines the partner's roles and responsibilities. Often the partner will require some type of scope statement, sometimes in the form of a statement of work. This statement of work, or scope, outlines all you require of the partner. Of course, this area may change, just as in the scope as a whole. The process for scope change must include a method for modifying the scope of work for the partner. Generally the partner will have a predefined method for communicating these changes; ensure that this method conforms to your own. Miscommunication in this area can be particularly costly, and more importantly can threaten your close relationship with the partner organization.

SCOPE MANAGEMENT

After the scope is established, a method for continuing maintenance of the scope should be put in place. This involves building a scope change process to govern the inevitable request for a change in scope. Very few projects successfully avoid some form of scope change. In fact, many times the change is necessary to successfully meet the implementation objectives. This happens for many reasons; the original scope may have omitted an important factor of the implementation, new requirements may have arisen, changes in the business environment may drive a need to change the scope of the implementation, or emerging technology may allow for the accomplishment of a business objective that couldn't have been met at the time the scope was developed. The alternative to creating a scope management process is scope creep. *Scope creep*, or the incremental change of the project scope over time, can seem very innocuous, occurring in small steps over the duration of the project, but those small steps can add up to a large change in scope. Uncontrolled, scope changes can be very costly to the project resources, in both time and budget.

The simplest method to manage the project scope and more specifically, changes in scope, is to develop a simple review and approval process for scope changes. This process involves the submission of a scope change form (either a paper form or some type of electronic form, email form, intranet-based form, and so on) through a formal approval and feedback cycle. Although simpler is definitely better in this instance, the form should record some basic information. This information should include the following:

1. Requestor
2. Date of submission
3. Reference to original scope
4. Description of proposed change
5. Business justification
6. Project impact (additional time, cost, and so on)
7. Alternatives to making the change, if any
8. Approval routing

The entire process can be incorporated into an issue tracking system. This approach is explained in detail in Chapter 27, "Project Tracking."

Figure 26.3 shows a simple scope change process.

Figure 26.3
The scope change process.

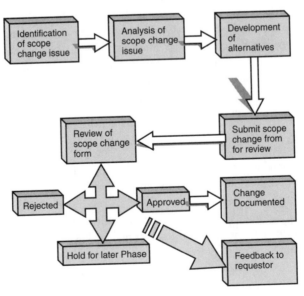

RISK MANAGEMENT

As stated previously, implementation projects are complex and can be costly in both money and resources, so managing and increasing the potential for success is imperative. The implementation necessitates change in your business, and as a change driver, presents a degree of risks to the organization. Change can take the form of new functionality, new processes, changes in infrastructure, and the replacement of existing systems. Because of this change and the natural resistance to change, strategies to reduce the project risks are critical to the implementation's and the organization's success. One of the best ways to increase your potential for success is to define, understand, and manage the project risks. Although this is a simple and straightforward statement, the process of risk management can seem quite challenging. It is not always a simple task, but assessing the high-risk areas of the project and defining a strategy to mitigate them can control risk. By identifying the high-risk activities, you meet them head-on and fully aware. This strategy keeps the project team prepared and the management team informed.

Where does the greatest risk lie? The perception of risk and the actual risk are often not the same. Often the perception of risk is much greater around later key project activities like system test or go live, affectionately referred to as crunch time. Historically though, there is much more project risk around poor or improper planning, poor scope management, or improper system design. Properly planned and designed, the risks associated with crunch time are manageable. Don't be misled; certainly, there is much anxiety around the system test and the cut over to the production system, but risk management and planning can significantly reduce the potential for problems. Figures 26.4 and 26.5 illustrate this idea.

Figure 26.4
Perception of risk.

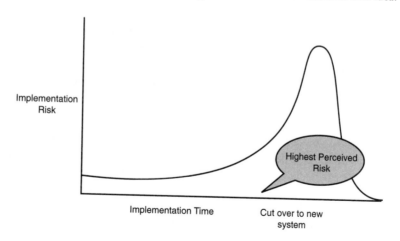

Figure 26.5
Actual risk.

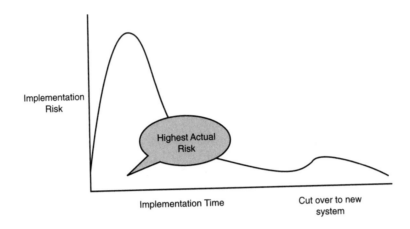

Project risks can be broken down into several key areas including the following:

- Application/technological risks—Risks in this area are related to the software and its fit with the organization, as well as the fit with your architecture and the new technologies you employ.
- Project risks—These risks relate to project planning and execution issues. Organizational experience or history is a factor. Project risks also include budgetary constraints and planning factors, such as the ability of the organization to develop precise goals and objectives.
- Change risks—The implementation of the new software solution drives change in the organization. This type of risk is related to both the natural resistance to change in the user community and the business risk associated with the shift to a new way of attaining organizational goals.
- People risks—People risks surround both the project team resources and the user community. The project resource risks are related to skills, experience, and availability. User risks range from skills and knowledge to receptivity to change.
- Business process risks—Risks related to business processes and their changes are the most visible project risks. The system drives many changes in both the interaction with the system and the support structure around these processes.

There are several key areas that have historically proven to be high risk factors to project success. Some common high risk areas are

- Project planning—Failure to define a detailed, realistic project plan.
- Staffing—Too few resources or not the correct resources assigned. Project team is not properly trained.
- Project sponsorship—No project sponsor, or project sponsor does not have the organizational clout to provide project support.
- Funding—Project is under-funded.

- Leadership—No full-time project manager assigned (part-time project manager) or more than one project manager defined (co-leadership).

- User training—Training strategy not defined during planning phase of project, instead too little/too late.

- Change management—No plan to deal with the change the implementation will bring to the organization, including plans to develop items like system user processes, procedures, and training, or a poorly executed change management plan.

- User procedures—No plan to develop user procedures or train users on new procedures.

- Schedule—Project schedule is not realistic based on resources and scope.

PHASING AS A RISK REDUCTION STRATEGY

A *project phasing strategy* is a method for reducing project risk by dividing the implementation project into manageable segments or pieces. The alternative to phasing a project is implementing the entire project in one single rollout, or "big bang." The big bang approach is generally the highest risk approach to an implementation, straining scarce resources and infrastructure as well as increasing the risk on business operations. The big bang is usually an appropriate choice in a project with limited scope, which is organizationally or functionally contained.

Phasing the project lowers the implementation risk by maximizing project resources and minimizing organizational complexity, while building team confidence by gaining an early project success. Phasing can be accomplished by structuring the project timeline in several different ways. There are four basic methods of phasing: organizational, geographical, functional, and by volume. Let's look at each method:

1. Organizational—Phasing by the organizational method involves rolling out the PeopleSoft applications to a limited part of the organization first. This strategy is useful if there are resource constraints on the project team. It can also be used when there are process risks, referred to as a pilot program, where a limited part of the organization proves out the process solution.

2. Geographical—Geographical phasing rolls out the solution by sequencing the implementation of the software in various geographic sites. This method is common in organizations that are geographically dispersed and allows the most effective use of project resources.

3. Functional—The functional phasing approach implements limited functionality/applications in the initial phase. In subsequent phases, increasing functionality or complexity is added. Functional phasing can lower technological risk and maximize project resources.

4. Volume—Phasing by the volume method limits the rollout to a select volume of data or users first. This method is used to lower the risks when there are data integrity or performance issues.

Developing a phasing strategy involves careful analysis of the implementation risks, the organization, and the project scope, constraints, and assumptions. Any one method may be used, or the methods can be used in combination to meet the project objectives and mitigate risks.

> **Note**
>
> Assume ownership for your implementation project and the software around which it is built. This is a simple statement, yet ownership is as difficult as it is crucial to success. A transfer of knowledge is certainly required to reach a high level of competence, but from the outset of the project, the team must assume the responsibility for the system. This responsibility is then transferred to the end users. They must be involved in the project and this involvement must be visible to the organization. Early organizational buy-in is one of the keys to implementation success.

BUILDING QUALITY IN FROM THE BEGINNING

How do you ensure that the implementation meets established standards and conforms to your expectations? In other words, is there a way to build quality into the project processes? Quality is a popular topic, yet as much as it is discussed, it is often misunderstood and misused. Many projects miss the mark, and a key contributor to this failure is an informal or casual approach to quality. It is easy to overlook the benefits of a formalized approach to quality, but as you have already seen, effort invested in proper planning early pays great dividends throughout the project. The key is formalizing the quality process for the project, and that's the function of the quality plan.

The goal of project quality processes is to ensure conformance to the established project standards. A quality system, integrated into the daily project activities, will provide predictable and measurable outcomes or deliverables. Deliverables are really the outcomes of the planned project activities. Project deliverables drive the design of the system, and as such are the keystone of an implementation that meets established business objectives. In the common, informal approach to quality, the deliverables are not developed in a predictable manner, but are really based on corporate mythology. This lack of formality is often attributable to the absence of a formal quality process, established for the project in a quality plan.

ESTABLISHING METHODS AND STANDARDS FOR QUALITY

A quality plan establishes methods designed to identify problems before they happen. To accomplish this goal, the plan establishes standards for project deliverables and a method for ensuring conformance to those standards. A proactive approach to project deliverables and project processes is essential for good quality management.

The first element of this process is to establish standards for project deliverables. Standards are established for deliverables by the use of templates. These standards and templates are often provided as a part of the selected implementation methodology. Templates provide the recipe for the development of the deliverable and a sample of the finished product. The templates are composed of instructions, a checklist, and the sample or model. The development of a deliverable is a process of transition from template to standard. Completeness of the deliverable is measured as progress from template to standard. This process is represented in Figure 26.6.

Figure 26.6
Development of standard deliverables.

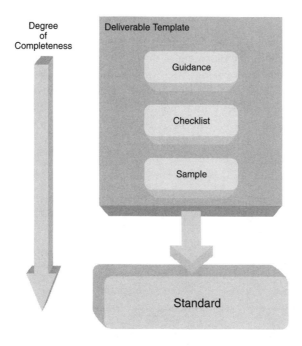

The quality plan establishes a process of measuring the deliverables' progress from template to standard. Project deliverables can take many forms. Just as the project plan is a deliverable, so also is the user readiness. Although it is simpler to measure the development of a plan or strategy document against its template, the method still is effective for less tangible deliverables. User training readiness, for example, is measurable in user competence on the system after training, or level of training. The standard is accurate job performance or competence. This might be referred to as user certification, which is in reality the measure of the user's progress from template (training course attendance) to standard (competent system user).

USING TEMPLATES AND STANDARDS

The use of templates and standards takes the quality process from subjective appraisal to objective assessment. The objective assessment of the deliverable is the insurance of quality, based on the process established in the quality plan. This is the formality required to build in quality to the implementation project.

In an implementation project, processes are developed to accomplish the development of deliverables. Project planning develops these processes. In addition to ensuring the quality of deliverables, the quality plan must also monitor these implementation processes. Examples of project processes include status reporting, issue resolution, and business process decomposition. Processes fall in two categories, one-time events and continuous. Each of these can be measured for completeness against a standard. The template for a process can be a flowchart with the standard execution against the process flow.

CHECKING DEVELOPMENT OF DELIVERABLES

The second element in the development of the quality plan is the creation of a method or procedure to check the development of deliverables and the progress of project processes. This is accomplished by creating a cycle of reviews and audits. *Reviews* measure the development of the project deliverables from template to standard. They can be informal, during deliverable development, as simple in- progress checks and more formal at deliverable completion. *Audits* are oriented towards the measurement of project processes against standards. Project standards are the established plans and policies developed in the project planning segment of the project. Often these processes can most easily be represented as a flowchart.

The outputs from review and audits are some form of issue or corrective action form. The quality process outlined in the plan should address the method for dealing with these issues. Figure 26.7 demonstrates a simple audit and review process.

Figure 26.7
The audit and review process.

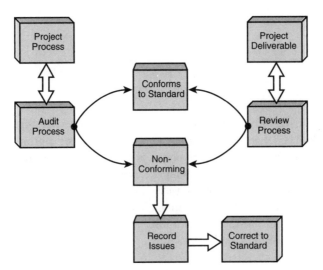

PUTTING QUALITY IN A PLAN

Using the principles outlined, a plan is developed to drive the management of quality in the implementation project. The plan puts the process in practical terms—simpler is definitely better here. Manage the process, don't overmanage! It is easy to go overboard in the level and intensity of quality management. Here is a simple outline of a quality plan:

1. Establish project templates and standards
2. Manage project processes
3. Project review processes
4. Project audit processes
5. Take corrective action

CONFIGURATION MANAGEMENT

You've purchased a major software product, or suite of products, and now you must keep track of its configuration! In addition to the complexity of the software you are implementing, you are also managing a project to implement the system, a project that creates and updates deliverables in a multiple team setting. High on the list of risk reduction strategies, a documented process for configuration management is critical for implementation success. The configuration management plan addresses both the configuration of the system and also the control of project deliverables. A system is required that defines policies and procedures for the management of files, objects, data, and security. Managing the configuration includes understanding the current configuration of the software and the project deliverables, tracking the changes that occur, and providing a structure for overseeing the incorporation of the changes. This structure ensures version control for both software and project deliverables.

ESTABLISHING A BASELINE

For the software itself, this should be an easy question. The PeopleSoft product is delivered and installed as a specific version of the product. This is a known quantity at installation. If you change nothing, the software would remain the installed version. This, however, will not be the case! We will look at what changes in the next section of this chapter.

For project deliverables, establishing the current state may not be as easy. Version control, or accurately tracking changes to deliverables, is crucial, especially in the team environment, where deliverables are developed by several individuals and are under constant revision. Establishing a structure around deliverable development and maintenance is the only way to keep them under control. The earlier the formality and discipline in version control are developed and enforced, the easier it will be to know where you are now with your deliverables.

SOFTWARE CHANGES

The implementation project is in reality a controlled process of changing the out-of-the-box PeopleSoft software into your custom solution. These changes include

- Establishing business rules (setup)
- Operator security/operator profiles
- Workflow configuration (user roles and role users, routings, and rules)
- Interfaces

- Modifications
- Fixes (see the section "Software Fixes" in this chapter)
- Reports

MANAGING CHANGE IN SOFTWARE AND PROJECT DELIVERABLES

The main purpose of the configuration plan is to provide the formalized method for managing change of your software and the project deliverables. A process should be defined for each, as well as a method for approving changes before they are implemented. The following questions should be addressed:

1. Who will manage the change control process?
2. What method will be used to communicate the change request?
3. How will changes be reviewed and approved?
4. How will the changes be recorded?
5. How will the change be migrated from test to production?
6. How does the change plan integrate with the test plan?
7. What naming conventions will be used to capture and identify changed objects and deliverables?
8. What tools will be used to control change?
9. How will the process change in a post-production environment? (Configuration management will continue into the post-production world; put this in place in the plan!)

Figure 26.8
The change control process.

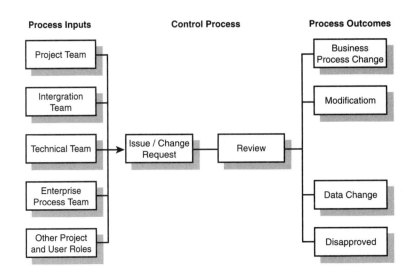

The following list provides some helpful hints and tips on change management.

- The use of a central data repository for all configuration changes will greatly enhance your change management efforts.

- An automated method for requesting change streamlines the process. Integration with an issue tracking tool adds greatly to this functionality.

- Combine change control standards with the project controls plan to ensure the use of these standards for all deliverables and changed/new objects.

- Capturing changes, including setup or business rules definition, will make future upgrades much easier.

- Design a configuration management plan that will continue to serve the organization into production.

- Use of change control functionality, included in PeopleTools, will enhance your change control efforts.

Software Fixes

PeopleSoft posts software fixes on the Customer Connection Internet site. You have access to that site through your customer number and a specific assigned logon. Your PeopleSoft account manager can assist in your initial access to the site. Fixes and supporting documentation are posted regularly as they are developed both as individuals and sometimes as bundled fixes. It is imperative that you establish a procedure in the early stages of the project to evaluate the fixes and determine which should be applied to your installed software. The process generally includes

1. Evaluation of fixes by functional team members for applicability.
2. Determination of the method for communicating to the technical team which fixes are to be applied.
3. Technical approval by an authorized technical team member.
4. Configuration manager approval, oversight, and tracking.
5. Application of the fix to the initial test environment, dependent on your test plan.
6. Testing the fix according to the test plan.
7. Migrating the fix according to the CM plan.
8. Recording the configuration change!

Issue Tracking Tools

You can use many methods to track changes in the system. One of the simplest and most effective methods is to design an automated change control tool. You can integrate this tool with an overall project issue tracking system. The tool itself can be constructed using many different database software packages. There are several commercially available packages that you can purchase as well.

One method that bears consideration is the construction of a tool in the PeopleSoft application using PeopleTools. There are several benefits to this approach. These benefits include the following:

1. The tool is available to all team members.
2. Use of the tool reinforces learning the standard navigation in PeopleSoft.
3. The construction of the application in PeopleTools reinforces learning the tool set.
4. The tool can be designed to meet your exact needs.
5. Through use of workflow, you can automate many aspects of approvals in the system.

Figure 26.9 shows a simple layout of a change and issue tracking tool.

Figure 26.9
Change and issue tracking tool layout.

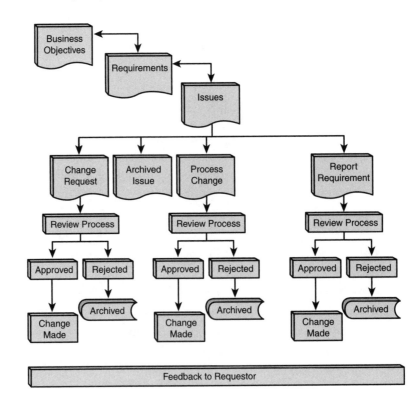

MANAGING DELIVERABLES

In managing deliverables, versioning and standardization are essential. Versioning can be accomplished through the diligent use of revisions and revision dating of documentation. Standardization is a little more involved. The project standards can be established in the configuration management plan or in the project controls documentation; the most important thing is to have written standards that are enforced from the beginning of the project.

Standardization involves several elements, including the use of predetermined software for each type of deliverable (for example, the use of a single word processing package, a drawing package, a spreadsheet, and so on), the use of standard naming conventions for the deliverables, and the use of a standard directory structure for saving the documents in a shared location for the project team. Often organizations have standard software already available for the different types of deliverables, so sticking to the company standards is the most advisable course. Naming conventions can take many forms. One simple way to name files is to use the corresponding work breakdown structure (WBS) number and name from the project plan. The only difficulty here is that the WBS number must then remain constant, something that may be a challenge, depending on the project management software used. Here is an example of this naming structure:

- 1.2.1 Project Scope
- 1.3.4 Requirements
- 1.5.3 Project Organization
- and so on

A file directory structure can also take on a similar approach. Figure 26.10 shows this in practice.

Figure 26.10
Sample directory structure.

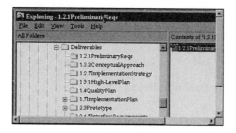

MIGRATIONS AND ENVIRONMENTS

Establishing a formal migration strategy can prevent many problems in configuration management. The first step in this process is identifying the different environments that the project will utilize and mapping them out. The environments usually will include, as a minimum, the following:

- System (SYS)—The initial "vanilla" installed PeopleSoft database.
- Prototype (PROTO)—The environment for use during prototype sessions, usually treated as a throwaway environment or "sandbox."
- Development (DEV)—The environment used for all development work.
- Testing (TEST)—The environment(s) used for testing. There may be several depending on the project test strategy (unit test, integration test, system test, and so on).
- Quality Assurance (QA)—The final environment prior to production, used for final certification of objects before they are moved into production.

- Training (TRN)—A copy of the production database, with predictable exercises/data set up to use for system user training.
- Production (PROD)—The actual production environment.

Figure 26.11 illustrates a simple migration/environment map.

Figure 26.11
Sample environment/migration map.

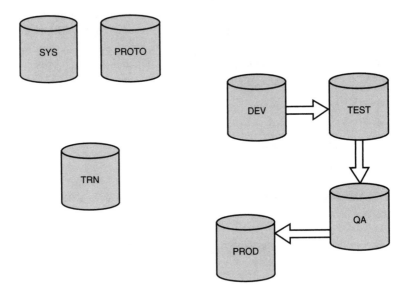

Other considerations in migrations are as follows:

- Manual migration process.
- Automated process for moving objects en masse.
- Possible use of PeopleSoft application upgrader for moving objects.
- Regression of a moved object back to development for corrections to problems discovered during testing.
- Clearly established lines of authority and responsibility—Who performs what types of moves? Is the DBA responsible for all moves?

THE PROJECT KICKOFF

You've reached your first major project milestone! The kickoff provides a transition from project planning and organization to project execution. It can provide an opportunity to get signoff on planning deliverables from the steering committee/project sponsor as well as an opportunity to educate the entire team on the direction of the project going forward. It is useful to involve the entire project team, the steering team/sponsor, the partner organization, and PeopleSoft. The meeting can also provide an excellent vehicle to establish some of the formal project communications. The kickoff meeting should accomplish the following:

1. Establish the implementation team, including the communication of roles and responsibilities

2. Review the project schedule/timeline

3. Establish project communications

4. Provide a transition from project planning to project execution

5. Establish a relationship with PeopleSoft account management and support

6. Communicate standard PeopleSoft support procedures for issue resolution

7. Set a positive, upbeat tone for the team

SUMMARY

Let's take a few minutes and see where we are in this process. We have talked about implementation methodologies and how you might go about selecting one to support your project. You looked at basic project success and risk factors and have seen how they might affect the implementation. By gaining an understanding of project scope, you now know how to accurately draw boundaries around your project. You have examined the process for "building quality" into your daily project activities and looked at methods for managing your changing system configuration. In effect, you now are armed with the tools and processes to accurately plot your course and a process to define your destination.

PART
V

CH
26

CHAPTER 27

PROJECT TRACKING

In this chapter

by Mike Fauscette

You know your destination, but how do you stay on the course and reach your intended goal on time? Not a simple question by any means, but an essential question for project success. If you executed your planning phase correctly, as seen in the previous chapter, you have selected a map, identified your destination, and plotted a good and true course. With that course in hand, you must now discern a method for monitoring your progress and provide the vehicle for executing necessary course changes. This is the process for managing your success, and that success is measured by reaching your intended goal (implementing a PeopleSoft system that meets or exceeds your business objectives), in control for project cost (on or under budget), and in control for time (on or ahead of schedule).

This chapter offers effective ways to monitor and track your progress to your project plan. Specifically, you will

> Learn how to develop an effective project plan
>
> Examine various project tracking tools and their use
>
> Gain an understanding of the use of project tracking tools to track project progress
>
> Learn to provide clear project status to the project team and project management
>
> Examine methods for making course corrections if you have wandered from your plan
>
> Understand and use issue-tracking methods to facilitate and speed your implementation
>
> Learn how to re-evaluate risk and apply risk management to the execution of the project

Tracking a project effectively and efficiently requires the combination of a good tracking process, a standard tracking tool, and no small measure of discipline. To establish this process, you first must develop a workable, manageable project plan. As you will see, that first step, the development of an effective project plan, will facilitate the tracking process.

DEVELOPING THE PROJECT PLAN

Although there is no strict recipe for the creation of a project plan, there are basic guidelines that will take you painlessly through the process (well, almost painlessly). We will discuss tracking tools later in the chapter, so for the moment we will assume that you are using a standard project management software package, something similar to Microsoft Project.

GATHERING PLANNING DELIVERABLES

So where do you start? First, gather the planning deliverables developed in the last chapter, as these will form the basis of the project plan. Remember that a deliverable is simple: a discrete and complete unit of work from a task on the project plan. These input deliverables include the project requirements, scope, organization, quality plan, risk management plan, project milestones or timeline, and so on. With your planning documentation gathered, you can begin the development of the plan. Planning assumptions should be detailed and examined as well. Planning assumptions include factors such as a fixed project end date (a management mandate to complete the project by a specific time), personnel constraints, overtime limits for personnel, and so forth. These assumptions have a direct bearing on the plan, including sequencing of tasks, task assignments, and durations.

LISTING STANDARD TASKS AND TASK DURATIONS

The most probable next stop is your chosen methodology. It is here that you should find a list of standard tasks and standard durations for those tasks. This is, of course, one of the advantages to the use of a standard methodology. In many cases, you might even be given a standard project plan template to aid in the plan development!

Determine or incorporate milestone dates. Your project will often have some externally driven milestones. These external dates might relate to project assumptions. Project completion might be fixed by management to meet other business objectives. Milestone dates like this are treated as project constraints. You will also need to establish your own project milestone dates to support your project objectives. If you developed a high-level project plan early in the project planning phase, this plan will be the source of those milestone dates for use in detail plan development. The milestone dates form the framework for task durations.

List the tasks to be accomplished in the implementation, or draw on the list from the methodology. The level of detail for these tasks is generally a hotly debated topic. There are several positions in the debate: the "no such thing as too much detail" faction, the "just point me in the right direction and we'll handle the details" faction, and the "tell me which road to take and we'll handle the driving" faction. Although there is no simple answer to this dilemma, there are some good rules of thumb. It is generally most effective to manage to the deliverable level. That is, develop a plan that correlates the task steps on the plan to a single project deliverable. An example of this level of detail would be a task on the plan for Develop Project Scope, or one for Develop Interface to Legacy General Ledger System.

Other factors have a direct impact on this, as well. The size, complexity, and duration of an implementation are directly related to the level of detail in the plan. The task-level detail is directly related to the complexity and duration; in other words, in a simple, less complex implementation, less detail is required in the plan, but for a large, complex implementation, more detail is necessary to stay on course. For example, a simple, single business unit implementation of the PeopleSoft General Ledger application—a project that might only last three to four months and have a small project team—may require only a high-level task plan. On the other hand, a full enterprise-level implementation of the complete PeopleSoft Financial, Distribution, Human Resources, and Manufacturing applications would require a much more detailed plan, simply to prevent the omission of critical tasks. The experience level of the project team is also a factor in the level of detail necessary to keep the team on track. A more experienced team will generally require much less detail task management.

TRACKING TASK DETAIL

Too much detail...why is this a problem? As you examine the process for tracking a project, consider the purpose of the project plan. It is a tool that acts as a checklist, and aids in keeping the project on track. It will be someone's responsibility to update this plan on a regular basis, most often weekly. A plan with too much detail creates several problems in the execution of your project tracking activity. First, it simply is too difficult to feed. What I mean is that if it is more than a full-time job to keep the plan in sync with reality, updated with weekly status, it is not an effective management tool. What I'm talking about is taking the plan to a task list level, often referred to as a punch list in the construction trade. You might equate this to your personal To Do List: a level of detail that guides your daily activity, but in much more detail than can be effectively tracked in a project plan. The inclination to include too much detail will provide comfort to many managers at the outset of the project, but will be a curse as you try to execute the plan. This is the second issue with too much detail; it draws focus away from the management of the project, and places that focus on the difficult task of updating the plan. The plan is a checklist, and project management uses the plan to monitor progress; if it is too high maintenance, it will not accomplish this. Don't misinterpret this: These details are important, but they just don't belong on the project plan. A method for disseminating this kind of detailed information is useful, but on a different operational level. We will discuss task lists again later in this chapter.

EXAMINING THE SEQUENCING OF THE TASKS

Now you have an appropriate list of tasks to be performed during the implementation. What's next? The next step is to examine the sequencing of the task. Certain project tasks are dependent on deliverables developed in previous tasks; in fact, the development of the detailed project plan is a good example. As noted, you need several key project planning deliverables to effectively develop the project plan. Project tasks could be diagrammed to show their dependencies, often a helpful exercise. There are competing objectives in this exercise; you want to accomplish tasks in the most expeditious manner, while sequencing them in a manner that provides all prerequisites for each task. A failure in either area will cost you time in the implementation. Figure 27.1 shows a simple dependency diagram.

Figure 27.1
A simple task dependency diagram.

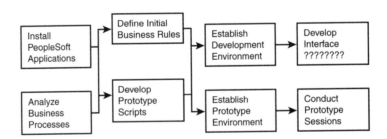

This diagram is an oversimplification of what would usually be a very complex flow, but it does show the basic concept. It is essential to determine which tasks are dependent and which tasks can be accomplished with parallel efforts. Project constraints, especially resource constraints, will also have a dramatic effect on the sequencing of tasks. The availability of key project resources will impact which tasks can be accomplished in parallel, and which work can be accomplished sooner to gain more time in the implementation. Other constraints may also affect task sequencing. You might need to accomplish tasks sooner in the sequence that are critical to the project's success. This must be balanced with true dependencies in the deliverables, but can be very effective in shortening the implementation timeline. For example, if you have a large number of interfaces, you might want to start development of the interface specifications and the interfaces themselves, earlier in the project. Data conversion might be another example. For instance, if you have a Year 2000 issue, or a large number of legacy systems with data to convert, you might decide to start the development of data conversion programs in parallel to the prototype effort. The caution with this approach is to ensure that you have enough information to begin the activity early, and that any dependencies are satisfied adequately to support valid work.

The second task in developing the dependencies and sequencing is to establish the project critical path. What exactly is a critical path? The critical path is the tasks and their sequencing or dependencies that control the project timeline. Said another way, the critical path is a representation of the most important tasks, which have two common traits shown as follows:

- They are critical for project success.
- Their interdependencies and duration control the project end date (or end dates to key segments of work).

Changes in the critical path dates will impact the project end date. Obviously then, it is essential that tasks on the critical path remain on schedule, or the overall schedule will be impacted. It is an excellent management tool, and should be used to ensure that the resources involved in these critical tasks understand the "big picture" importance of their assigned work and the impact of not keeping these tasks on schedule.

PLANNING TASK DURATIONS

With the sequencing of the project tasks and the critical dependencies determined, the next activity is to examine each task and assign a planned duration. This activity is both science and a little art in execution; and of course, the planned duration is just that, a reasonable estimate of what it will take to accomplish the task. Don't give it any more weight than that; the estimate is your best educated guess at the duration of the task. Your chosen methodology can provide some assistance in determining estimates, as will your own experience, and that of your project team. Table 27.1 provides some standard "rules of thumb" for some key task durations.

TABLE 27.1   GENERAL IMPLEMENTATION TASK DURATION GUIDELINES

Task	Criteria
Installing PeopleSoft System	Generally scheduled for one week.
Train Project Team	Based on actual project team training schedule, most PeopleSoft Training courses are four peopledays in length.
Building A Baseline Process Model	Estimate five peopledays per enterprise process for complete analysis.

continues

TABLE 27.1 CONTINUED

Task	Criteria
Developing Prototype Scenarios or Scripts (including analysis of new processes, defining initial system business rules, collecting and loading sample data and developing the actual script)	Plan two peopleweeks per application; activity is very dependent on availability of knowledgeable resources and the complexity of the processes. If detailed process analysis is not conducted in the development of a baseline model, more time might be required to analyze the business processes.
Perform Prototyping (includes the Fit Analysis)	Two to three peopledays per script or scenario, adjust for complexity of process.
Establish Development and Test Environments (includes security, collecting, and and business rules)	Development data collection and two to three peopledays per application, one to two peopledays for security, and moving/setup of business rules.
Finalize Business Rules	Five peopledays per application.
Develop Modification Functional Design	Three peopledays per modification (complexity of modification will have an impact on duration).
Develop Modification Technical Design	Two peopledays per modification (complexity of modification will have an impact on duration).
Develop Modification	Eight peopledays per modification (complexity of modification will have an impact on duration).
Unit Test Modification	Four peopledays per modification (complexity of modification will have an impact on duration).
Develop Interface Functional Design	Three peopledays per Interface (complexity of Interface will have an impact on duration).
Develop Interface Data Map	Two peopledays per Interface (complexity of Interface will have an impact on duration).
Develop Interface Technical Design	Two peopledays per Interface (complexity of Interface will have an impact on duration).
Develop Interface	Two peopledays per Interface (complexity of Interface will have an impact on duration).
Unit Test Interface	Four peopledays per Interface (complexity of Interface will have an impact on duration).
Develop Report Functional Design	Two peopledays per Report (complexity of Report will have an impact on duration).

Task	Criteria
Develop Report Technical Design	One peopleday per Report (complexity of Report will have an impact on duration).
Develop Report	Two peopledays per Report (complexity of Report will have an impact on duration).
Unit Test Report	One peopleday per Report (complexity of Report will have an impact on duration).
Develop Integration Test Scripts	Two to three peopledays per script, adjust duration based on complexity of script/process.
Integration Testing	Two to three peopledays per test script, adjust duration based on complexity of script/process.
Develop System Test Scripts	Two to three peopledays per script, adjust duration based on the complexity of the business process to be tested.
Perform System Testing	Two to three peopledays per script, adjust duration based on the complexity of the test script.

Based on the durations and the sequencing/dependencies of the tasks, preliminary beginning and end dates can now be established. At this stage, the scheduling tool selected most probably will establish these dates for you. If not, it's basically a math problem to determine the controlling dates for each task and enter them in your schedule (start date plus planned duration equals end date).

ASSIGNING RESOURCES TO TASKS

The next step in the development of the project plan is very critical, that is, the assignment of resources to tasks and the subsequent leveling of the resources. In the typical minimally staffed implementation, this activity can be a great challenge. In a strict project management sense, the resources should be assigned to the tasks and then the project leveled to accommodate the resource loading. Of course, you might find your timeline doubling, or at least extending well beyond your project deadline constraints. What do you do now? Well, the obvious answer would be to add resources to the project plan. Or, another possibility is to extend the workweek beyond "normal" hours.

The first suggestion, bring on more resources, although the most straightforward answer, might simply be a luxury that is not available to your project. Additional consulting resources might provide an alternative, but only in certain types of tasks. Outside consultants cannot replace the business knowledge necessary to implement the system. They can, however, provide software and technical expertise, as well as training support to your project. This, too, might be a luxury your budget cannot afford. Knowledgeable PeopleSoft consulting resources are in high demand, and availability of these resources can be challenging as well.

The second suggestion, planning for more than "normal" work in the project plan, is a risky proposition. There are times in the project that work outside the "normal" schedule will be required to keep the project on track. If you plan up front using large amounts of overtime, the team simply will not have the reserve to make up deficits, not to mention the strong possibility of burning out key resources well before you have reached your goal.

What's the answer, you ask? Unfortunately there is no simple answer. Staffing is discussed elsewhere in this book, but we'll look at it briefly here as well. The approach that is most effective in minimizing project risk is to identify all the required resources by role at the beginning of the project. If you successfully fill the majority of these roles, both internally with full- and part-time personnel and externally with consulting resources, you shouldn't have major problems with resource loading. If the exercise of matching your task load to available resources proves that your staffing is inadequate, then face it head on. Either the time constraints or the staffing constraints must be adjusted; you can do it up front, and lower the risk of failure, or try to do it later, and suffer the consequences of project delays and loss of confidence in the plan (and planner). Take the high road and address these issues with your steering committee up front; their buy-in to the solution is the only safe course of action.

This strategy addresses major staffing shortfalls, but you might also discover minor issues in resource loading. This could be related to the availability of resources or having the correct resources to meet project task requirements. These minor staffing issues can usually be addressed by reassigning tasks to the correct resources or by addressing the availability of key resources with the steering committee. In general, a single full-time resource is considerably more valuable to the project than several part-time resources. It is very difficult for a key resource to effectively manage more than one critical job. (And of course, if you have chosen the "right" resources, their regular management will resist the loss of the resource and their time will be in high demand.) It will be a challenge to keep full-time resources focused on the tasks at hand, and almost impossible with personnel who report to more than one manager.

DEVELOPING TASK START/END DATES

The next step in developing the project plan is to adjust the task start/end dates for the impact of the resource loading. Often this function is accomplished through a process automated by your project planning tool. At the end of this step you have a complete project plan.

With a completed plan in hand, it is now time to gain approval from your steering team or executive sponsor. Executive buy-in to the plan is essential to ensure the right level of support during the implementation. It is also important for your organization to understand the high level of executive support needed for the project, thereby giving you the leverage you will need to staff the project. When approved, the plan should be distributed to the team members and communicated to the business owners involved in the project. The plan development process is illustrated in Figure 27.2.

Figure 27.2
Developing a project plan.

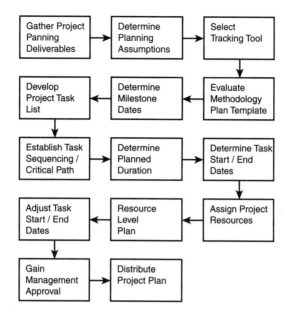

After all this effort, you should now have a complete and approved project plan. This tool can be used to track your progress and drive the success of the project.

STAYING THE COURSE: USING YOUR TRACKING TOOLS

With an approved project plan in hand, we can now examine methods for tracking progress against the plan. We will look at several areas of project tracking tools and their effective use in keeping the project on track. Tracking tools can be broken down into the following:

- Project plan
- Project reports
- Issue tracking

The following sections discuss these tracking tools in greater detail.

THE PROJECT PLAN

The project plan is the most basic project tracking tool. As previously stated, its use is the fundamental method for keeping the project on course. How do you accomplish this? First, let's look at keeping that nice shiny new project plan up-to-date. After all, it should represent something close to the project reality. In fact, this was one of the arguments for keeping the plan at a high enough level that updates can be accomplished on a routine basis.

PART

V

CH

27

UPDATING THE PROJECT PLAN

How often should the plan be updated? There is no standard timeframe. Once a week is probably the minimum, but the reporting structure of your executive sponsor might dictate more frequent reporting. The real answer is update as often as necessary to keep the plan current and yet balance the administrative burden on your project team.

> **Tip**
>
> A very useful, maybe necessary, role is that of a project administrator. This role would execute plan updates, collect information for status reports, draft those reports for the project manager's approval, and so on. This will relieve some of the burden on the project manager and allow more focus on the project issues.

The basic update to the project plan is usually in the form of percentage of completion on all started tasks. The method of tracking this is a simple mathematical calculation based on the completion of a task to its overall duration.

For example, a task that has a duration of 16 hours is 50 percent complete when eight hours of work have been accomplished. A reality check to this method is the percentage of completion as a representation of the work accomplished against the whole task, without regard to the planned duration. This presents a clearer picture of project status and the work remaining. The most effective approach combines both the completion of work and its relationship to the planned duration. This necessitates the tracking of the planned duration and schedule as a baseline and any subsequent revisions as changes to this baseline. This information is useful in tracking the accuracy of the original plan and for predicting the impact sliding tasks will have on the overall project timeline. Take into account a task's position on the critical path as well.

REPRESENTING THE TASK STATUS

Although the mathematical method just described is the most effective for tracking and reporting actual status, it is often too detailed to be used effectively in displaying problem areas in the project. An alternate method for displaying plan status that has proven an effective tool is adding a simple representation of the task status. This might, for example, take the form of a field on the plan for recording a "Red," "Yellow," or "Green" status for the task. In this example, Red represents a task that is slipping, Yellow a task that is in danger of slipping, and Green a task on track for scheduled completion. This more visual approach to reporting task status can be very effective in focusing the team and executive sponsors on problem areas. Table 27.2 shows an example of this approach.

TABLE 27.2 AN EXCERPT FROM A PROJECT PLAN

Task Name	Duration	Start	Finish	% Complete	Status	Dependency	Resource
3.14 Develop Reports	53	8/31/98	10/16/98	38%			
3.14.1 Create Report Functional Design	6	8/31/98	9/9/98	60%	Yellow	3.6.3	
3.14.11 GL Trial Balance	2	8/31/98	9/2/98	100%	Green		Mary Business_ analyst
3.14.12 Cost variance	2	9/4/98	9/9/98	25%	Red		Mary Business_ analyst

PROJECT REPORTS   556

Many other project reports might be necessary to track the progress of the project. Most project management tools come with standard reports that might meet many of your reporting needs. Often these standard reports can be modified and customized if they do not fit your exact requirements. For example, Microsoft Project contains the following report categories: overview reports, current activity reports, cost reports, assignment reports, workload reports, and custom reports.

- *Overview reports* show information over the entire project duration, including summary tasks, critical tasks, project milestones, cost and schedule information, and so on.
- *Current activity reports* show a variety of task information, such as unstarted, in progress, and completed tasks; tasks that are behind schedule; and tasks that will start or that should have started between the dates you specify.
- *Cost reports* show a full range of cost information, including budgets for all tasks over the entire project duration; tasks and resources that are overbudget; earned-value information for all tasks; and costs per task displayed for one-week periods.
- *Assignment reports* show resource assignment information, including task schedules for all resources over the entire project duration; tasks for only the resources you specify, displayed for one-week periods; and resources that are overallocated.
- *Workload reports* are crosstab reports showing task usage and resource usage information.

As you can see, these standard reports cover a myriad of project reporting needs.

You can also use the Custom Reports dialog box to create a new report or to customize or copy an existing report.

Using the complete project plan can be troublesome for individuals who are not used to the format or dealing with the large number of tasks. It is often more effective to produce reports for the project team that focus the resources on the tasks at hand. This can be accomplished through these reports. Some of the more useful reports in this area are "Tasks in Progress," "Tasks Starting Soon," "Tasks That Should Have Started," and "Completed Tasks."

"Tasks in Progress" will provide a reality check for the team on what has been reported in progress, and what work actually IS in progress (and of course one hopes these are the same, but...). In addition, this report is useful for reviewing dependencies on other tasks that need to start but are waiting for the completion of a dependent task.

"Tasks Starting Soon" is used to alert and prepare project resources. Resources can gather necessary tools, provide support, and verify that dependencies are complete.

"Tasks That Should Have Started" is a report that alerts management and the team to potential problems, possibly in status reporting or actual task slippage.

"Completed Tasks" is useful for validating status and for identifying dependencies on other tasks that should start soon. It can also show areas where work is progressing more quickly than planned, leading to a gain in the overall schedule.

STATUS REPORTS

Status reports are a special category of project reports that have many uses for the team. At a minimum, they keep senior management sponsors and team members aware of the project progress. They can also provide a great opportunity to keep the user community as a whole up-to-date on the project progress. The type and frequency of status reports should be determined during the project planning phase. At a minimum, the project manager should produce regular reports to the steering committee/executive sponsor. These reports can be an excellent vehicle for keeping the sponsors informed of project progress against the schedule as well as alerting them to open issues that require executive attention. Additional reports might also be required from the various teams/team leads on your project team. Weekly reports are useful at this level, but they should not put an onerous administrative burden on your team leads. After all, their focus should be on detailed task management/accomplishment, not on administrative reports!

PROJECT STATUS REPORT COMPONENTS

What makes up a good project status report? This is often driven by your organization and sponsor's needs. The following are some of the topics that should be discussed in a status report:

■ Accomplishments and task completions—List all tasks that have been completed during the current reporting period.

■ Resource issues and problems—List any problems associated with project staffing.

■ High-level project issues—Focus should be on issues that need executive attention; project issue tracking is discussed later in this chapter.

■ Budget summary—Summarize the project expenditures to date, budget to actual.

■ Overall project status—This should focus on key milestones, milestone accomplishment, and potential for problems meeting scheduled milestone dates. A simple Red, Yellow, and Green system works well here as well.

■ Team lead status reports—These should focus on a more detailed level. The focus is more on the specific team, its issues and accomplishments. Categories in a team lead status report include:

  • Accomplishments and status of assigned tasks. This can be the vehicle for updating the individual task percentage completion.

  • Detailed team issues that need project management attention.

ISSUE TRACKING

Issue tracking is a critical task for project success. There are many methods for tracking project issues. We will look at a few simple ones. It is surprising how many projects do not have a clearly defined method for tracking project issues and resolutions. Something that sounds very simple is often very challenging for project teams. Here are some of the success factors for effective issue tracking:

■ Define a simple process for recording and tracking all project issues.

■ Train all team members in the use of the issue-tracking process.

■ Give all team members access to the issue-tracking tool.

■ Enforce the use of the tool!

■ Routinely review the issue log for complete use and timely resolution of issues.

■ Keep all issues in one tool. Categorize the issues to break them out to their proper area of responsibility.

The issue-tracking process can be thought of as an outgrowth of the planning process. Issues should be easily tracked back to project requirements to be valid. This concept and the relationship of issues to requirements and objectives are represented in Figure 27.3.

PART
V

CH
27

Figure 27.3
Relationship of issues to project require- ments and objectives.

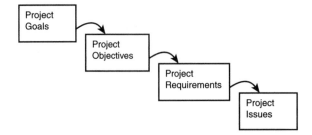

All issues, then, should have a clear link to a project requirement. If an issue does not have a clear link, is it really a valid issue?

A basic process for tracking and resolving issues is essential. Establish this process and clear- ly communicate it to the entire team. Figure 27.4 shows a sample of an issue process.

Figure 27.4
The issue process.

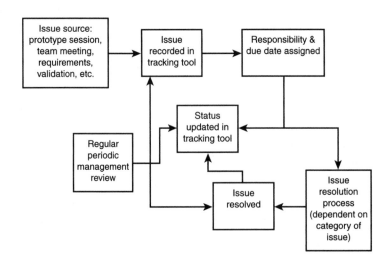

Issues can be divided into several categories, including software fit, business process fit, reporting, software deficiencies (which might be subdivided into issues with the base prod- uct and issues with customizations), data, interface, personnel, and budget. These issues touch all areas of the project.

Issue tracking can be accomplished using a variety of tools. Several commercial products are available that can simply be purchased and used by the team. In addition, the tool could be as simple as a spreadsheet or a custom developed database product. Figure 27.5 illustrates a spreadsheet format.

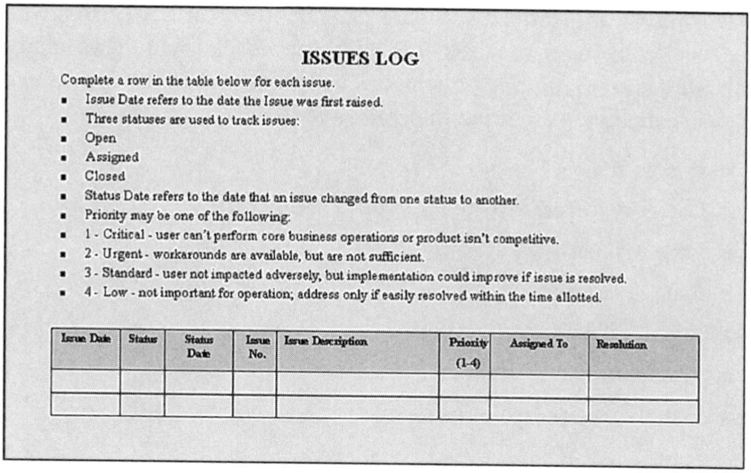

Figure 27.5
A simple issue log.

ISSUES LOG

Complete a row in the table below for each issue.

- Issue Date refers to the date the Issue was first raised.
- Three statuses are used to track issues:
- Open
- Assigned
- Closed
- Status Date refers to the date that an issue changed from one status to another.
- Priority may be one of the following:
- 1 - Critical - user can't perform core business operations or product isn't competitive.
- 2 - Urgent - workarounds are available, but are not sufficient.
- 3 - Standard - user not impacted adversely, but implementation could improve if issue is resolved.
- 4 - Low - not important for operation; address only if easily resolved within the time allotted.

Issue Date	Status	Status Date	Issue No.	Issue Description	Priority (1-4)	Assigned To	Resolution

MAINTAINING AN ISSUES LOG

The following process describes how to use the issue log shown in Figure 27.5:

Complete a row in the table for each issue.

Issue Date refers to the date the issue was first raised.

Three types of status are used to track issues. They are as follows:

- Open
- Assigned
- Closed

Status Date refers to the date that an issue changed from one status to another.

Priority can be one of the following:

1. Critical—User can't perform core business operations or product isn't competitive.
2. Urgent—Workarounds are available, but are not sufficient.
3. Standard—User not impacted adversely, but implementation could improve if issue is resolved.
4. Low—Not important for operation; address only if easily resolved within the time allotted.

CUSTOM DEVELOPED ISSUE TRACKING TOOLS

A custom tool can be developed using a variety of programming tools like Microsoft Access. Another possibility would be to use the PeopleTools program delivered with the PeopleSoft applications. This approach has the added benefit of giving your developers experience with the tool set and, when in use, giving your project team experience navigating in the PeopleSoft application. The developed tool could also include the other key pieces of the

PART

V

CH

27

issue process, as identified in Figure 27.5. In other words, a section could be created for project goals, objectives, requirements, and issues. Each could then be linked with its parent. The subsequent reporting possibilities would greatly aid the project team. Each issue record should contain the following information or fields:

- Reported date
- Category (software, process, report, and so on)
- Issue number
- Issue description
- Reported by
- Priority
- Assigned to for resolution
- Status
- Status date
- Solution/resolution
- Solution/resolution date

We will examine the use of the issue tracking tool in more detail in Chapter 30, "Prototyping."

As you have seen, the three tools—project plan, project reports, and issue tracking—are interrelated and are key to effective tracking. It is imperative to define both the tools and the process for using these tools on a daily basis. It also is incumbent on the project manager to ensure that these tools are used…they are useless if not kept up-to-date. Now that you know how to track the project, let's look at what happens when you catch yourself going off course.

KEEPING THE PROJECT ON TRACK

Armed with all of the tools we have discussed, and with your project planning safely behind you, your project will sail along smartly, right? With a clear destination (your project objectives), the correct map (your planning deliverables), and the right course laid out to your destination (your project plan), you will stay on course. At least that is what "should" happen, but just in case, what do you do if your project strays off course?

RECOGNIZING PROBLEMS

As with any problem, the first step is actually recognizing that the problem exists. There are several potential problems that might arise and lead the project astray. The greatest potential for problems is slippage of deliverable due dates. Slippage, if improperly managed, can have dramatic effects on the project timeline. This type of problem can occur for a variety of reasons, including unrealistic planned dates, resource problems (too few, incorrect skill set, and so on), scope creep, and external problems out of the direct control of the project team (for example, information on legacy systems involved in an interface, data conversion, and so on).

Controlling Recognized Problems

How do you recognize and control slippage? The simplest method is properly executing project plan updates and status reporting. Any potential for slippage should be readily evident in both the plan updates and the status reports and can be dealt with aggressively. It is key to note the potential for slippage at the first sign of trouble and head it off! The use of the "red, yellow, green" status on the project plan can be a great assist in catching the problem early. Just the focus on each task required to make the determination for the status should yield the attention required to head off the problems.

Strategic Direction

It is very easy to focus on the details during the implementation and, in effect, be overwhelmed with the volume of the task at hand. The project team carries the tactical role throughout the implementation, but strategy is also critical to project success. Someone must also step back and look at the big picture from time to time. The goals and objectives of the project provide the measure of the strategic progress of the project. The project manager and the steering team are responsible for strategic direction. This is often difficult for the project manager, who is often trapped in the day-to-day details of managing the project.

One method of ensuring that the strategic direction remains intact is through the overt link between goals, objectives, requirements, and issues. We have discussed this process before in the issue tracking section. Remember that if you cannot trace an issue back to a requirement, to an objective, and ultimately to a goal, the validity of the issue is in question. This is also true of requirements. As long as the goals and objectives are a true representation of the strategic direction of the project, this method will keep that element of the project on track. A simple exercise of questioning the lineage of issues and requirements will go a long way in guaranteeing the correct strategic direction. In addition, choosing an executive-level steering team and focusing them on the "big picture" will provide the proper direction and serve to pull the project manager back out of the details from time to time, focusing on the strategic direction.

Getting Off Track from the Task

What happens when you identify that you have strayed from your intended course? Having the courage to admit the error and fostering an environment where team members can admit mistakes will go a long way toward solving these problems. Again, if you don't know that there is a problem, how can you determine the solution? Depending on your corporate culture, this can be very difficult. Honest and complete status reports and plan updates are the key to finding problems early and determining the correct solution. It is significantly easier to make small course corrections than major course changes. By tracking progress closely, you can avoid major surprises in your project and greatly reduce your burden for change. This process also increases executive confidence and credibility for the project team.

SMART PEOPLE ARE NOT ENOUGH

Or if it was that easy, anyone could do it! The real secret to successfully managing your project is following sound fundamentals; those fundamentals are outlined in this book. Many companies go into their implementation project with serious misconceptions about the level of effort, discipline, and skill required to be successful. Leaving out any one of the key elements of success is a step down the road to failure. You've seen that you must have the correct number of team members with the correct skill set, solid basic project planning, and disciplined execution to the plan. Having the right project team, without solid leadership and planning will not pull you through. Even hiring the "best" partner is not the key. Good, basic project management is the answer!

SUMMARY

Project tracking is an important element in a successful project. Establishing the tools to be used, having a clear process, and educating your project team will go a long way towards keeping the project on track. The project plan, project reports, and issue tracking form the basics of your project management tool set. Diligently execute the process for each tool, and you will be able to identify problems early and get them resolved. Do not be afraid to accurately report project status; it is much easier to correct issues as they are happening rather than after the fact. Issues that are ignored have a way of growing and can have disastrous effects later in the project.

CHAPTER 28

PROJECT INFRASTRUCTURE

by Mark Gibson

In this chapter

ESTABLISHING THE FOUNDATION FOR A SUCCESSFUL PROJECT

Successful projects are built from the ground up. Similar to a house or other building, the successful project begins with a sound foundation or infrastructure. From this infrastructure, the project manager and the project team will build the remaining portions of the project. In the Information Technology (IT) profession, the term *infrastructure* commonly refers to the network of clients, servers, routers, and other network devices through which end users communicate. Although this telecommunications infrastructure is extremely important to the successful project, a project infrastructure is focused on many other aspects of the project.

A project infrastructure consists of four main attributes:

- Structure of the Implementation/Development Team
- Structure of the Software Implementation/Development Environment
- Project Strategies
- Fundamental Project Plans and Processes, the Quality Plan

Throughout this chapter, we will discuss how to build a successful project team including the number of staff required and the mix of functional, technical, and management staff. We will discuss when to hire staff and how to effectively organize them to meet the needs of your PeopleSoft implementation.

The software implementation environments and their structures can be critical to the efficiency with which the PeopleSoft implementation proceeds. We will discuss what file server, Web server, and database environments are required to effectively implement and manage the PeopleSoft system. When multiple implementation phases are required or desired, we will examine additional optional environments the prudent project manager might choose to construct.

Multiple high-level strategies, such as training and testing strategies, become important to provide guidance to the project team as they work through the details of the implementation. These strategies are used by the project team in developing more detailed plans, such as training plans for end-user training and test plans to be used during execution of integration, system, or parallel testing.

Finally, we will discuss the Quality Plan and its various components. Most would desire a PeopleSoft implementation that not only resulted in a launch, but that also was deemed a quality implementation. We will examine different ways to ensure quality and discuss options to include in the project team's approach to achieving quality for the implementing organization.

STRUCTURE OF THE IMPLEMENTATION/DEVELOPMENT TEAM

A project manager must balance many factors in determining the staff required to successfully implement a project. The project manager must strike a balance among technical staff, functional staff with expertise in each software module, consulting staff, and the in-house project team. But first, an examination of the implementation life cycle is prudent. Each project begins with the establishment of the project infrastructure and a high-level "To Be" model. This documents the new PeopleSoft modules, any legacy system interfaces, hardware, operating systems, project organization, and basic implementation strategies, such as testing, training, configuration management, quality management, and database instance migration and management.

After the project manager has a firm understanding of the project scope, duration, and strategies, the manager can look at the staffing requirements from two perspectives: First, what specific skill sets does the project manager need? Second, how many personnel does the project manager need in each skill set? The prudent project manager can leverage the project infrastructure and the To Be model to aid in these decisions. Remember, the high-level To Be model defines the PeopleSoft modules scheduled for implementation and the legacy systems involved. The strategies mentioned in the previous paragraph speak to the technical staff required to manage the project. After this scope is defined, the project manager can assess the range of required skill sets.

After determining the specific skill sets, the project manager should look at the number of staff members required to complete each of the tasks. The project manager can build this staff using either in-house workers or consulting organizations. In the next few pages, we will examine both the number of staff required and the options from which project managers can obtain this staff. First, let's examine the number of staff required and whether or not a project needs consulting staff. This decision is based on cost, technical risk, the needs of the organization for best practices, and the aggressiveness of the schedule.

NUMBER OF STAFF REQUIRED

The number of staff required is a function of project size. Which leads us to the question of "How does a project manager know the size of the project?" The answer lies in two parts. First, the high-level To Be model defines the number of PeopleSoft modules needed as well as the number of interfaces, conversions, and possible customizations. The project strategies will define staffing needs in the areas of testing, training, configuration management, change management, and so on. The project manager must examine these strategies before determining any additional staffing needs. Project staffing can be divided into four categories: functional, technical, management, and other, such as testing, training, or configuration managers.

Secondly, PeopleSoft surveys its customers annually to determine, among other things, the number of staff used during an implementation. The Implementation Surveys also provide an indication of project size by company size. These survey results provide the project manager with the staffing profiles chosen by other PeopleSoft customers. The surveys are broken down by company size for a more discrete look at the needs of the implementing organization.

USE OF THE HIGH-LEVEL TO BE MODEL AND PROJECT STRATEGIES

In Chapter 21, "Establishing the To Be State," the high-level system was defined. This system included the PeopleSoft modules being implemented and the interface points to existing systems. Later in this chapter, the technical and various other strategy documents are defined. All these sources can assist the project manager in defining the project team.

The modules identified in the high-level To Be model define the different skill sets required on the project team. Let's assume a purely financial implementation. The implemented PeopleSoft modules include General Ledger, Accounts Payable, Accounts Receivable, Billing, Asset Management, Treasury, and Project Costing. The project team will require individuals skilled in each of these functional areas. The number of individuals on the project team skilled in each area is driven by three considerations: the structure of the organization, the physical location of the individuals within each organization, and the training strategy. Let's look at each of these options individually.

STRUCTURE OF THE ORGANIZATION   Many organizations are divided into multiple divisions, each acting as a separate business entity. An example might be a General Ledger Business Unit. Given these divisions' degree of autonomy from each other, they might desire to have their own in-house experts to guide their division's staff. Under these circumstances, the project manager might want to include a member of each division on the project team to ensure harmony during the first few months after implementation. In the preceding example and assuming two divisions in this example company, the project manager would staff two individuals in the role of implementing each module.

PHYSICAL LOCATION OF THE INDIVIDUALS   The physical location of the end users is also a key consideration when determining the size and composition of the project team. Consider the location of end users during the first few weeks after the Go-Live. End users will have a decreased level of support from the help desk as those individuals begin to accept and resolve cases. The level of support from the help desk will be lowest during the time when end user need for the support is greatest. The physical dislocation of end users from the project team exacerbates this anomaly. Under the circumstances, in which a small group of end users is physically located away from each other, the project manager might consider augmenting the staff with individuals from each physical location. This augmentation can be for the duration of the testing cycles, can also include the prototyping project activities, or can be for the entire project.

TRAINING STRATEGY   The training strategy is the final project attribute to consider when staffing based on the To Be model and strategies. Later in this chapter, we will discuss the use of project team members for training the end users. Under this scenario, the project manager should consider the numbers of trainers required and augment the project team with these individuals. Again, the project manager can augment the project team during the entire implementation phase, prototyping phases, and/or testing phases.

USE OF THE PEOPLESOFT IMPLEMENTATION SURVEYS

Project Managers can also use the PeopleSoft Implementation Surveys to determine the size of their project staff. PeopleSoft conducts these surveys annually to determine the implementation options chosen by its customers. The surveys also break down the staffing relative to the size of the implementing organization. For the Human Resources (HR) suite, the number of employees determines the company size. For the Financials, Distribution, and Manufacturing (FDM) suite, the gross annual revenue determines the company size.

Table 28.1, Total Team Size, is a compilation of the PeopleSoft Implementation Surveys from 1996–1998 for the FDM and HR suites.

TABLE 28.1   TOTAL TEAM SIZE (FTES)

Human Resources (HR)

Year	In-House	Consultants	Total
1996	10.80	6.70	17.50
1997	9.32	8.18	17.50
1998	11.02	10.33	21.35

Financials, Distribution, & Manufacturing (FDM)

Year	In-House	Consultants	Total
1996	10.10	6.60	16.70
1997	9.23	10.58	19.81
1998	11.92	9.72	21.64

From 1996 to present, project teams have consistently increased in the size of both the in-house and consulting staff. In 1998, the average HR project team consisted of 11 in-house members and 10 consultants. The FDM teams consisted of 12 in-house members and 10 consultants. Table 28.1 provides an indication of the average size of an average HR or FDM implementation. Tables 28.2 and 28.3 highlight the average project team size broken out by company size.

Tables 28.2 and 28.3 clearly show increased staffing levels as the company size increases. These tables also show increasing staff levels from 1996 to 1998 with the exception of FDM implementations for companies with revenues exceeding 5 billion. These implementations demonstrated a decreasing level of consulting staff and fluctuating in-house staff. These statistical anomalies are, most likely, because of the smaller number of large implementations during 1998.

TABLE 28.2   TOTAL HR PROJECT TEAM SIZE BY COMPANY SIZE

	Average In-House (FTEs)			Average Consulting (FTEs)		
	1998	**1997**	**1996**	**1998**	**1997**	**1996**
<5K	6.70	6.85	8.40	7.82	4.92	4.70
5–10K	9.99	7.72	10.00	9.07	4.88	12.90
10–50K	11.35	12.81	13.20	10.36	9.19	8.60
>50K	15.55	13.22	26.30	20.23	10.87	8.90

TABLE 28.3   TOTAL FDM PROJECT TEAM SIZE BY COMPANY SIZE

	Average In-House (FTEs)			Average Consulting (FTEs)		
	1998	**1997**	**1996**	**1998**	**1997**	**1996**
<1B	9.59	9.51	12.70	7.84	7.12	5.30
1–5B	12.80	8.44	7.60	8.51	7.62	5.60
>5B	14.86	17.10	9.50	5.83	8.42	8.60

Project team sizes in 1998 range from 17.43 to 20.69 for FDM and from 14.52 to 35.78 for HR implementations. These tables do not provide any indication as to the number of modules implemented; therefore, project managers should be cautious when determining their staffing profiles. Another data point available for use by project managers is the relative mix of managers, functional, and technical staff.

RELATIVE MIX OF STAFF

In the previous section, the number of staff members was examined. Another consideration is the relative mix of the staff. How many project managers do I need? How many functional and technical staff does the project require? Again, the tables are based on the PeopleSoft Implementations Reports from 1996, 1997, and 1998.

DEFINITIONS

Functional staffs are the business experts within each professional discipline. For financials, they consist of accountants working with general ledgers, payroll clerks working on company payroll, receiving clerks working with receiving purchased goods, or shop floor managers working with the workcenters. Each of these individual functional disciplines should have representation on the project team during the implementation of their respective modules.

Technical staff members are those project team members who are proficient in the writing of code, in batch processing, or in any information technology area that supports the functional staff. These individuals are traditionally titled Database Administrators, System Administrators, Help Desk technicians, or programmers. Management staff consists of the project managers or process leads, defined later in this chapter.

MIX OF MANAGEMENT STAFF

Table 28.4 from the PeopleSoft Implementation Surveys documents the average number of project team members in each category and breaks the number down into both internal and consulting staff. The mix of management staff is stable across both HR and FDM implementations at a single internal and single consultant project manager for the entire project. This number is stable until the projects become large. With a project of this size, the team organizations tend to be process model oriented and thus have process leads. For example, a company with >5 billion in revenue would organize the project team into process teams, such as Procure to Pay, Order to Cash, Time to Payroll, or Schedule to Produce. Leading each of these teams is a process team leader and these individuals are categorized as management staff. Under these conditions, the number of management staff will grow to nearly five internal and five consultants filling these roles.

PART

V

CH

28

MIX OF FUNCTIONAL AND TECHNICAL STAFF

The relative number of functional and technical staff is nearly the same. For example, for an FDM implementation the ratios of internal functional to technical staff are 2.5/2.3, 2.25/2.65, and 3.58/3.1 for the years of 1996, 1997, and 1998, respectively. The consulting staff shows a similar relationship. The ratios of consulting staff possibly highlight a tendency to keep more technical staff than functional staff. This trend is probably because of the number of specialists that can be needed. These individuals would implement self-service Web applications, workflow, Electronic Data Interchange (EDI), or Online Analytical Processing (OLAP) reports, or serve as testing, configuration, or change managers.

These nearly equal ratios lend credence to the two-person development team concept. This concept of using two developers on a single task has gained favor since the advent of the rapid prototyping/development approach. The consultants appear also to support this model but at a slightly lower two-thirds of a consultant for each functional/technical project team member.

MIX OF OTHER TECHNICAL STAFF

Table 28.4 also documents the various other technical specialties, such as Database Administrators (DBA), System Administrators (SNA), or network specialists. The project need for these specialties is relatively constant at 2 DBAs, 1.5 SNAs, and 1.5 network and personal computer specialists. The number of consultants tends to be slightly higher than in-house staff.

SYNOPSIS

The data gathered over the last three years tends to suggest most PeopleSoft customers staff an equal number of functional and technical staff. The number of functional staff is driven by the number of PeopleSoft modules being implemented, and augmented by any additional staff needed to support the training strategy. Project managers are staffed at a single consultant and single internal manager per company except in large companies. In these large companies that tend to organize around business processes, the number of process leads will increase the number of management staff. Other technical specialties, such as DBAs, SNAs, or testing and configuration managers, are staffed at rates of one member in each category from internal sources and one from a consulting firm.

There is no significant difference between the FDM and HR product lines. The total staff size averages approximately 10 staff members from both the consultancy and in-house staff. If consultants are not used, the number of in-house staff should be at least doubled.

TABLE 28.4 PROJECT TEAM COMPOSITIONS
PEOPLESOFT FINANCIALS, DISTRIBUTION, AND MANUFACTURING PROJECT TEAM COMPOSITION

Implementation Effort

Team Member	Internal FTE Average Actual			Internal FTE High/Low			Consulting FTE Average Actual			Consulting FTE High/Low		
	1998	1997	1996	1998	1997	1996	1998	1997	1996	1998	1997	1996
Project Manager	1.27	1.11	1.2	9/.25	4/.25	4/.25	1.03	1.05	.8	5/.10	4/.20	1/.25
Functional Analyst	3.58	2.25	2.5	25/.20	13/.25	8/.25	2.49	2.26	1.8	15/.10	12/.25	4/.25
Technical Analyst	3.1	2.65	2.3	15/.05	10/.25	7/.25	2.64	3.11	2.5	20/.10	20/.25	5/.25
Database Administrator	.79	.62	.5	5/.05	2/.10	1.5/.1	.91	.91	.4	5/.10	3/.10	1/.1
Network Specialist	.54	.41	.4	5/.05	1/.10	1.5/.1	.75	1	0	2/.10	1/1	0/0
PC Specialist	.59	.47	.4	3/.01	2/.10	1.5/.2	.92	1.25	1	2/.10	2/1	1/1
Other*	2.05	1.72	2.7	8/.20	8/.25	10/.25	.98	1	0	2/.20	2/.50	0/0
Totals	11.92	9.23	10.1				9.72	10.58	6.6			

PEOPLESOFT HUMAN RESOURCES PROJECT TEAM COMPOSITION

Implementation Effort

Team Member	Internal FTE Average Actual			Internal FTE High/Low			Consulting FTE Average Actual			Consulting FTE High/Low		
	1998	1997	1996	1998	1997	1996	1998	1997	1996	1998	1997	1996
Project Manager	1.12	1.09	1	7/.10	7/.25	10/.1	.95	.90	.7	6/.05	3/.10	2/0
Functional Analyst	2.95	2.38	2.4	20/.10	8.5/.30	20/0	2.13	1.72	1.2	21/.01	12/1	4/0
Technical Analyst	3.12	2.59	2.4	23/.05	12/.25	18/0	2.73	2.24	1.9	25/.05	15/.20	10/0
Database Administrator	.74	.63	.6	4/.03	2/.10	4.5/0	.8	.69	.5	4/.10	2/.25	2/0
Network Specialist	.51	.43	.4	4/.01	1/.05	1/0	.66	.57	.2	2/.05	1/.25	1/0
PC Specialist	.57	.54	.5	4/.01	2/.10	5/0	.79	.60	.3	4/.05	1/.20	2/0
Other*	2.01	1.66	3.4	7/.10	7/.10	24/0	2.27	1.46	2	6/.25	6/.25	8/0
Totals	11.02	9.32	10.8				10.33	8.18	6.7			

CONSIDERATIONS BETWEEN IN-HOUSE STAFF AND CONSULTANTS

Project managers also have to decide whether to use in-house staff, consultants, or both. This decision is based on the availability and expertise of in-house staff and their prior experience in implementing PeopleSoft applications. The availability of PeopleSoft consultants has historically been a concern, but PeopleSoft has taken steps to ensure the availability of consulting staff when needed. Staffing shortages in some specialties do still exist and are supplemented by implementation partners.

Annually, PeopleSoft publishes many statistics pertaining to the balance points its customers have chosen. Table 28.5 is compiled from the 1996, 1997, and 1998 Implementations Report. It portrays the percentages of customers who currently use consultants, have not used consultants, and plan to use consultants. The three-year trend shows that the percentage of customers using consultants is rising. In 1998, the percentage of customers either using or planning to use consultants exceeded 94 percent for FDM and 95 percent for HR. Data on Manufacturing, Distribution, and Student Administration was not available for the entire three-year period; therefore, it was not included.

The trend over the past several years indicates an increasing use of consultants on PeopleSoft implementations. Because the percentage of customers that either are using or plan to use consultants approaches and even exceeds 90 percent, the data indicates that a prudent project manager would hire consultants to assist with the implementation.

TABLE 28.5 CUSTOMERS USING CONSULTANTS ON THEIR IMPLEMENTATIONS

	% That Have Used Consultants			% That Have Not Used Consultants			% That Plan To Use Consultants		
	1998	1997	1996	1998	1997	1996	1998	1997	1996
PeopleSoft Financials	86.5	81.5	78	5.7	11.3	14	7.8	7.2	8
PeopleSoft HRMS	87.6	86.6	84	7.9	9.2	11	4.5	4.2	5

CONSIDERATIONS BETWEEN FULL- AND PART-TIME STAFF

Many project managers assume that any staff member is better than no staff member. Although the short-term gains acquired using this strategy might prove valuable, the long-term consequences of this strategy usually outweigh the benefits. Project Managers tend to believe that by using this strategy the project cost is lower and that the project will gain wider exposure throughout the organization. In most instances, these assumptions prove false.

Full-time staff members are critical to the project success. This includes both consulting staff and in-house staff. Full-time staff are critical because they have the greatest sense of loyalty to the project, will provide a majority of the project work, can maintain a current vision of the project direction, and provide the main source of external marketing.

Let's assume an ideal case of a part-time consultant who makes periodic visits to an implementing organization. Part-time consultants require time to re-acquire knowledge of the project and where it has progressed since their last visit. Many things, such as business processes, setup settings, and corporate direction, could change between visits. At the beginning of each visit, the consultant must understand these changes. Even if no changes occur, the consultant must understand the progress made and the future direction. Toward the end of the visit, the consultant's productivity decreases as the time before leaving decreases past the point that any new tasks are started. This leads to dead time at the end of the visit. This ramp-up and ramp-down time is unavoidable and unproductive. A full-time consultant only goes through this process once, thus increasing the percentage of productive time at the implementing organization.

The same applies to in-house staff with one exception. The in-house staff will have difficulty focusing on the tasks even when they are working on the project because they have full-time jobs. These folks tend to maintain a level of interest in their non-project job resulting in less focus on project work. Additionally, they will have difficulty maintaining the current vision for the implementation. This vision includes current requirements and the need to resolve issues. Part-time members are not as fluent in project details and can have out-of-date information. Because they are associated with the project and are more easily accessible than full-time project team members, end users who have questions about the project will go to these folks. The project's main avenue for marketing then becomes the part-time member. This can prove problematic when inaccurate visions of the project status, resolutions to issues, and requirements reach the end users. This equates to negative external marketing and is an undesired effect of part-time in-house staff.

Part-time staff has a role in a PeopleSoft implementation project and can provide great value. During any implementation, short discrete tasks will arise that are ideal for a part-time staff member. These tasks will be of short duration and independent of the project as a whole. For example, reporting on vanilla tables can be a good use of part-time staff. This staff member either can be hired for a short duration or could work half days. Another example might be a performance tuner, who would only be staffed for one to four weeks while a finite number of processes or panels are tuned.

TIMING OF THE PROJECT STAFF BUILDUP

The optimum time for beginning a staffing buildup is one of the most important decisions a project manager will make. This decision can have dramatic impact on the ultimate project cost, the morale of the staff, and the degree to which the staff comes together to form an integrated, focused team. Under the assumption that project cost includes both consultants and in-house staff, staffing too early will increase the hours/salaries that the project budget incurs. Without sufficient project work to sustain them, project team members will become disillusioned, lose the enthusiasm they brought to the project, and can become impediments to project success. Disillusioned project team members might thwart team-building efforts and slow the assimilation of the team into a cohesive unit. Multiple factors affect this decision, including availability of in-house staff, availability of consultant staff (if desired), and status of implementation planning.

Before any staff is brought onboard, a project manager must know what staff is available within the implementing or consulting organizations. The prudent project manager will poll the implementing organization to attain the best and the brightest project team members. With respect to consulting services, PeopleSoft has in-house consulting staff as well as a variety of implementation partners. The project manager can balance the availability and experience of these resources against the project budget and schedule. One important point to remember is that the lowest unit-cost resources do not always make the best choice. In any instance, the initial planning phases should be complete. These planning phases were discussed in Chapters 20, "Establishing the Baseline or the As-Is State," and 21, "Establishing the 'To Be' State." Given that these models are high-level and serve as a springboard for process re-engineering, these tasks are better accomplished by the management staff.

Bringing on detailed staff members too early will result in an anxious staff that does not yet have sufficient tasking to support the enthusiasm they usually bring to a new project. Without sufficient tasks, they quickly become disillusioned and lose the enthusiastic attitude that is so valuable. Project managers are better served by bringing on staff later on the project than too early. Under this scenario, the staff has sufficient tasks to complete, and the downside is a schedule that begins slightly behind schedule. Project managers can for a short duration make up this time by increasing working hours or extending the work week. Making up for a disillusioned staff is a far greater task to overcome.

Management staff

The best time to bring on staff is different for the project management, functional, and technical staff. The early stages of the project entail determining high-level To Be models; establishing strategies for testing, training, and so on; and establishing project schedules and budgets. This is the most important time in the project and should be supplemented by external project management guidance. If external project management support is to be used, this support should be onboard before any decisions about project scope, phasing, schedule, budget, or strategy are made. Guidance from resources with experience on large-scale implementations can be of immense help. Good decisions at this point in the project can save hundreds of thousands and sometime millions of dollars.

Functional and Database Administrators

The functional and database administration staff is the next staff to come onboard. After the completion of the mentioned project startup activities, the project will proceed into intense learning phases in which the software operation is discussed in detail. This phase is sometimes called pilot, prototyping, rapid prototyping, discovery, and so on. This detailed functional knowledge is best suited for the functional team members who can learn about the options of how to configure the software. Later, the actual software build will occur. DBA support is required at this stage to build the initial instances and maintain them as product updates are delivered.

Under some circumstances, an organization might have a firm understanding of the software capabilities and might be able to skip this discovery phase and proceed immediately into building the production system. These circumstances are rare and should be discussed extensively with project management support before deciding to take this path.

Technical Staff

Technical staff is the last to assimilate into the team. These members are best assimilated late in the discovery phase after most of the software options have been examined. These staff members will support the actual system build, interfaces, customizations to the delivered software, writing custom reports, and performing multiple other technical tasks. Building up this staff at this time enables them to gain functional and technical knowledge about the To Be system operation. For instance, the entering of user data will populate certain tables, this data is edited upon entry, and the delivered batch processes further manipulate the data and populate other tables. PeopleSoft also delivers interface points in the software and scripts that are usable for interface work. Gaining this knowledge in preparation for the development phase is critical for the technical staff. Up until this time, these decisions were not necessary.

Technical staff members are less likely to be patient during the discovery phase when the functional community examines all the software options. This decision process is frustrating to technical minds and results in the disillusionment mentioned previously. The functional community can feel pressured by technical staff that "just want a decision." Functional staff must be given time to work through the improvement of their business and they are best served by working through this task without technical support.

Team Organization

Project team organization can play a significant role in the success of the project. Project managers should organize the project team in a similar fashion to how the project work is organized. Keeping this synchronization intact will minimize the volume of communication required to make the project successful and thus reduce the risk that insufficient communication will jeopardize the project.

Project managers can organize their project teams in three different configurations, including functional process teams, software modules, and a matrixed technical staff. Additionally, project managers should address other staffing needs, such as testing, training, and configuration management staff.

Functional Process Teams

Functional process teams are characterized by their orientation to the fundamental business processes of "schedule to ship," "order to cash," "procure to pay," and so on. This project team organization is well suited to large and small implementations. The structure orients the project team with the functions requiring the most volume of communication, orients the business and steering committee to easily understandable functions, and is easily translatable into test teams.

Because PeopleSoft is structured into software modules, any module can be implemented on its own. This structure is flexible and requires the project team to synchronize the setup of modules. This synchronization requirement is most pronounced between modules in the traditional fundamental business processes. For example, the setup synchronization between purchasing, accounts payable, and general ledger is more pronounced than the setup between production management and purchasing. In this example, the vendors, vendor locations, items, and tax must use the same set IDs for each Business Unit combination. The experts/consultants implementing each of these modules will spend a great deal of time coordinating their setup. Having these individuals working on the same sub-team tends to enhance their interaction and facilitate a more coordinated solution.

The fundamental business processes are well understood by high-level company executives including the steering committee members. Because the project manager will maintain a communications channel with these executives, a common ground of terminology that is linked to the organization of the project work is advantageous. By maintaining this linkage between the project work and terminology understood by executive management, the project manager can minimize the time spent developing briefings and re-organizing data to suit the reporting and oversight needs of the steering committee.

Assuming a testing strategy that is business-process oriented, the process teams naturally dovetail with a test plan based on these fundamental business processes. Project managers have many options in determining the best suited testing strategy for the implementing organization. Given a strategy revolving around the "procure to pay" or "order to cash" processes, the test can be derived from the To Be model, which is a derivative of the fundamental business processes. Project managers can assign testing assets to tests based on the synergy throughout the project team organization, test plan, and business processes.

SOFTWARE MODULE

Project managers can also organize their teams around the software modules. This approach is particularly effective for smaller companies or companies who are implementing a small number of modules at a time. Many PeopleSoft customers implement just the General Ledger or Accounts Payable modules. Under these circumstances, the implementation is limited in scope and consists of more technical work; therefore, a business process orientation is less helpful.

Large implementations can also use this organizational structure, but its use can be problematic. One of the advantages of the business process model was organizing the project team into units which have the greatest need to communicate. Because this communication is critical to project success, this orientation minimized any communication risks. The software module structure does not facilitate the communication channels as easily. Project team members are expected to understand the coordination needs and get together when required. The consulting staff will have a greater understanding of these needs than the internal project team until the internal project team has a thorough understanding of the system setup.

The project manager desiring to use this model should closely manage the communication risks, especially during the initial system setup. Close management of these early project activities will provide the project manager with the severity and probability of the risk. Over time, the probability of this risk occurring will decrease as the project team becomes self-sufficient in system setup activities.

MATRIXED TECHNICAL STAFF

With either the business process or software module organizational structures, the project manager might set up a matrix of the technical staff. Under this organizational scenario, the technical staff is not assigned to any particular business process or software module. Under this scenario, the project manager should staff a technician with supervisory responsibility over the team.

This structure provides the project manager with great flexibility in assignment of the technical staff to tasks. By matrixing the staff, each staff member is exposed to more of the full application suite. After the technical staff gains familiarity with the whole suite, the project manager has maximized the implementing organization's flexibility in assigning staff to tasks for ongoing support. This structure is especially valuable when resolving critical production problems. Given that the project manager will not know beforehand where critical production problems will occur, a well trained, matrixed organization is best suited to engage numerous critical production problems anywhere in the system.

The disadvantage of this structure is near-term risk. Technical staff should have an in-depth understanding of the entire system before the implementing organization goes live on the system. Training each technical staff member in the entire system is difficult in the time frame of most PeopleSoft implementations. The risk of not having a fully trained technical staff is manageable by hiring additional consulting support until technical training is complete. Although this option exists, it is expensive and should be carefully considered before undertaking it.

UTILITY INFIELDER

This concept stems from the now common practice on baseball teams of keeping an individual who can play multiple positions on the field. Usually the player is not as skilled at each position as the starter, but can fill in during unforeseen circumstances when the starter is not available. These circumstances are rarely known with sufficient advance notice to facilitate an orderly transfer of responsibilities.

The same concept is applicable to a PeopleSoft implementation. During the course of the implementation, primary project team members become ill, get injured, or fall behind in their tasks, and as a result the project is at risk of falling behind schedule because of these unforeseen circumstances.

Having a utility infielder would provide the project manager with added flexibility to adjust to the ever-changing implementation challenges. For example, the project is one week away from a critical test and has two reports that remain in development. Each report development is lead by a technician. One technician becomes ill and will not return for two weeks. The project manager is faced with a hard decision, either postpone the test or start the test without the report. If the project manager has a utility infielder staffed, this individual can pick up the work and complete it.

There are two prominent issues with this philosophy. First, the project manager must staff an additional member and the cost of this can be prohibitive. Under these circumstances, the project manager can consider staffing a more senior member who is not completely task-loaded. This individual would be capable of picking up additional workload during peak periods. The project manager could staff an extra individual to serve the same purpose.

Second, this individual will require time to become familiar with the work before they can be productive. Project managers can minimize this familiarization period by staffing this position with a technical lead. The technical lead position was discussed previously in this chapter. The technical lead will, because of the position, remain familiar with all ongoing work, thus minimizing the familiarization period.

STRUCTURE OF THE SOFTWARE IMPLEMENTATION/DEVELOPMENT ENVIRONMENT

The structure of the software implementation/development environment can have a great impact on the success of the project. The structure of this environment also impacts the efficiency of the implementation. The project should consider multiple basic tenets on structuring a project team environment that supports the successful implementation. This structure will consist of the multiple database instances each serving unique implementation functions, several optional instances for special implementation strategies, file server and Web server environments, and various peripherals, such as PeopleSoft client.

BASIC CONCEPTS

Dr. Randall Jensen documented multiple basic tenets that he felt were critical to a successful software development environment. Although he spoke about a custom coding environment, the same tenets prove true in a PeopleSoft implementation environment. His tenets include

- Dedicate the project area
- Minimize communications barriers
- Provide utensils for creative work
- Avoid sharing resources
- Maintain the project's space

DEDICATE THE PROJECT AREA

A dedicated area for the project team is a concept commonly referred to as a war room. This concept has gained favor along with the rapid prototyping/implementation approach. Project managers should provide the project team with office space physically separated from but close to the end-user community. Having a dedicated area enables the project team to coordinate activities without disturbing the rest of the office. Especially early in the prototyping phase, the project teams will engage in many discussions every day. This high volume of conversation might not be appropriate for a more traditional office environment.

MINIMIZE COMMUNICATIONS BARRIERS

The use of offices for project team members is a traditional manner of establishing the hierarchy of the project team. It aids new managers in establishing a power base. Project managers should minimize any barriers to communication because they will hinder the project team and endanger the project success. Other examples of barriers include quiet periods, physical separation of project team members in different rooms or floor of the building, permanently assigned non-project team members to the office space, or assigning all project team members to cubicles.

PROVIDE UTENSILS FOR CREATIVE WORK

Creativity is a key ingredient in any successful implementation. As project team members conduct prototyping or design a customization or report, their ability to envision new and elegant solutions to problems or implementation challenges greatly enhances the end user's satisfaction with the system and its effectiveness. Many tools can be employed by project managers to assist their teams in being more creative. White boards enable members to freelance new or modified business processes, and corkboards enable the posting of documents, announcements, or slogans. Conference tables with plenty of chairs enable project team members to call meetings to discuss any number of implementation options, business process changes, or design documents. Project managers should also consider providing technical staff with quiet areas, like an office with a closed door, to focus on detailed technical tasks. Although these areas will limit communication, quiet focus time is a necessity for technicians engaged in detailed work. These technicians should not be allowed to permanently reside in a quiet area, but they should use these areas during intense development periods.

AVOID SHARING RESOURCES

Dedication of project team resources is a critical facet of successful implementation. The PeopleSoft implementation surveys contain many testimonials of current PeopleSoft customers that speak to the need for dedicated project team members. The other resource to consider is computing resources. An implementation environment is taxing on both server and client resources. The prudent project manager will attempt to acquire and maintain dedicated server resources. During the prototyping, data conversion, and interface development tasks, the response of the system to queries, running scripts, and loading data can have a tremendous impact on the productivity of the project team. Sharing these resources with another project or a production system can lead to reduced productivity and schedule delays.

MAINTAIN THE PROJECT'S SPACE

Over the course of an implementation, the size of the project team will vary. The staffing profile will build to a peak during the prototyping and testing phases, and then decrease as the rollout occurs. Project managers can feel pressure to replace transferred project team members with other individuals. These individuals might be from another project or the result of new employee hiring. The prudent project manager will resist having the project space invaded. This invasion will tend to decrease communication and team unity just when the rollout is occurring. For the same reasons, early in the project, the project manager obtained dedicated project space. This space should be maintained for the duration of the project. If the invasion of space is inevitable, the project manager should keep the project team in close proximity to each other. This will mean moving individuals into a new workspace.

PEOPLESOFT ENVIRONMENTS

The second element in structuring the development/implementation environment is the construction of multiple PeopleSoft databases/environments to support the many implementation and production tasks. Throughout the implementation, the project team will engage in project tasks, such as prototyping, interface development, conversion of existing system data to PeopleSoft, customization development, and testing. Sometimes during the implementation, but certainly after the Go-Live, the project or production team will upgrade PeopleTools versions, product updates, apply patches, and upgrade to a new Generally Available (GA) release. The implementing organization will need a database in which to perform these tasks.

Most implementing organizations will chose a phasing strategy to reduce implementation risk. Other organizations can distribute their PeopleSoft database across multiple servers in different physical locations. Both of these scenarios require additional database instances to support the management of multiple configurations simultaneously.

The PeopleSoft system consists of database instances, but also file server, Web server, and client environments. These environments must also be managed to effectively implement or maintain the PeopleSoft system. The configuration of these environments and the management and deployment of that configuration can play a significant role in the success or failure of a PeopleSoft implementation.

In the following pages, we will discuss each of the environments and the options available to the project manager. Project managers might chose to create additional environments or instances, but caution should be exercised in creating large numbers of instances. The risk of losing control of the proper system configuration increases with the number of instances/environments created. The additional hardware cost and decreased server performance realized by multiple file server environments could slow performance at the client workstation and thus reduce project team productivity.

REQUIRED DATABASE INSTANCES

PeopleSoft implementations require multiple database instances to support different project and maintenance activities. These activities range from product demonstrations and upgrades to testing and production. The prudent project manager will host these instances on several different hardware boxes to effect the best use of available computing power, protect the production system, and maximize server performance, thus facilitating increased project team productivity. The six required PeopleSoft database instances are

- Demonstration
- Application Upgrader
- System Instance
- Prototyping
- Development
- Test/Quality Assurance (QA)
- Production

Each of these instances, its uses during both the implementation and production, and its preferred hardware positioning are discussed in the following pages. When initially installed, PeopleSoft creates three instances. The demonstration and application upgrader instances are discussed in the following sections. The system instance is an instance containing no setup or demonstration data. From this instance, the project team will create all remaining instances. Project managers should always keep this instance free of any setup or demonstration data.

DEMONSTRATION   The demonstration (DMO) database is built during the initial installation of PeopleSoft. It is unique in that it contains setup and transaction data provided by PeopleSoft. Each PeopleSoft customer DMO database contains the same data. This uniqueness makes it an invaluable tool for troubleshooting errors.

During the implementation from prototyping through production, the system might not operate as intended. If this occurs, three possibilities exist for this occurrence:

- An individual erred in their operation of the system.
- The system was not setup to operate in the desired fashion.
- A software error occurred.

The DMO database is a great tool for resolving this issue. If, after using PeopleBooks or consulting staff, an individual is convinced that they are properly operating the system, they can try to reproduce the same error in the DMO database. Because this instance contains the proper setup, the individual can reproduce the error with assurance that the error is not the result of a setup problem. The opposite is also true. If the problem is not reproducible within the DMO database, the individual should look at the setup for the resolution of the problem. However, if customizations are involved, the DMO database will not assist in troubleshooting the problem.

Using DMO for this purpose requires maintaining and controlling the configuration of this instance identically to the production instance. All tools releases, product updates, and patches that are applied to the other instances must be applied to the DMO database.

A second use of the DMO is for demonstrations. During the early project activities as the functional and technical staff are beginning to learn the system, the DMO database can be used to highlight functionality and systems architecture. Although implementing organizations will have demonstrations during the sales cycle, great value is gained by working through the panels, manipulating data hands-on, and examining the object structures. Until the project team develops the concept for their first prototype, the DMO instance can provide a fertile ground for training and familiarization with the system.

APPLICATION UPGRADER   The application upgrader (AUD) instance is another unique instance and has a specialized purpose. This instance contains no setup or transaction data, either. It consists purely of the object definitions that make up the record definitions, panel definitions, fields, and so on. Given this unique characteristic, this instance has a single purpose. Its purpose is to support system maintenance.

The PeopleSoft application designer provides the capability to push new and revised object definitions to the instances that need the updates. After new or revised object definitions are received in a patch, product update, or GA release, the upgrade project is first applied to the AU instance and then pushed to the other required instances.

PROTOTYPING   Early in the implementation, the project team will iteratively configure, evaluate, and re-configure the system during the prototyping phase. Successive loading and reloading of setup and a sample of converted data characterize this phase. Given the dynamic nature of these activities, a separate instance for these activities is suggested.

DEVELOPMENT   During the course of a PeopleSoft implementation, project teams will convert existing system data into PeopleSoft tables, build custom reports, build interfaces to the existing systems, and potentially customize the PeopleSoft applications to fit specific organizational needs. During each of these activities, technical staff will require an instance in which to code the changes; a development instance serves this need.

Early in the implementation, project teams will use the prototyping instance to define the system requirements. Project teams will also define the To Be models that will highlight the data to be converted, interfaces to be built, custom reports, and customizations to the applications. The results of these activities are a fit analysis. This fit analysis generates the list of development work to be accomplished in the development instance.

Early in the project, the prototyping instance can be used to create the development instance. The prototyping instance has much of the projected setup data and enables unit testing to be conducted on the projected setup data. Later in the project, the testing/QA instance and eventually the production instances are best used to create the development instances because they are more representative of the eventual environment in which the development work must operate.

PART

V

CH

28

In projects where a lot of customization is occurring, project managers might consider having multiple development environments or refreshing these environments frequently. Under these circumstances, the transaction data will become corrupted, hindering the capability of technicians to effectively code and unit test the customizations. Project managers can either create multiple development environments to segregate development projects or refresh the environments frequently. Each of these approaches maintains a more realistic environment for development for a longer time.

TEST/QUALITY ASSURANCE (QA)   The testing phases are critical to the success of any implementation. Planning a robust series of tests requires the use of an instance dedicated to this endeavor. Later in the chapter, we will discuss the use of integration and system testing cycles. Project managers have the option of using one or two instances to achieve these two tests. In either case, the DBAs should build the test instance(s) from the production instance. After completion of a successful test, project managers should restrict access to this instance. If problems do occur in production after the implementation date, these instances can assist technicians in troubleshooting those problems.

PRODUCTION   The culmination of any implementation lives on the production database. Project teams will work for many weeks to reach this milestone. How to build the production database instance is one of the most hotly debated topics during PeopleSoft implementations. There are two schools of thought: 1) Build the instance early in the implementation cycle, or 2) Build the instance just before going live. Each of these methods has been successfully used by a multitude of live PeopleSoft customers and each uses the SYS instance as a source for the production instance. But everyone agrees that organizations should host this instance separately from any of the other instances. This hosting scheme minimizes any potential impact from other implementation environments.

Project managers can build the production instance early in the implementation in conjunction with the integration test build. This timing assumes a robust prototyping phase where requirements and system setup are discretely defined and believed to be final. At this point, the production database is built using the system setup documents defined and refined during the prototyping sessions. The production instance is built from the system setup documents. The integration test instance is then created from production.

This approach has three advantages: 1) It validates the system setup documents and the proper configuration of the system using those documents, 2) It places the burden of validating the production database setup on the testing cycle, and 3) It front loads much of the data conversion activities. By testing a virtual image of the production database, the implementing organization is able to virtually test the production instance. Any errors discovered during testing are corrected in the test instance and production. This approach requires correcting errors discovered during testing in two database instances.

Project managers can also build the production instance just before going live. This approach reduces the burden of maintaining two database instances during the test cycles, but relies heavily on the implementing organization's documentation skills. During the test cycle, errors are corrected in the test instance and setup documentation. Data conversion files and scripts are staged for loading just before the go-live date. Just before the go-live date, the production database is created and configured using the system setup documents and staged data conversion files and scripts.

This approach has three large disadvantages in that it back loads the production instance build risk too late in the implementation cycle when little time is available to mitigate this risk. It relies heavily on the configuration manager to accurately document all system settings, and it removes the test cycle as a means to correct any setup errors from sources as simple as missed keystrokes.

OPTIONAL DATABASE INSTANCES

Many implementing organizations will choose to phase in the PeopleSoft functionality. In 1998, the PeopleSoft Implementation Surveys reported 71.2 percent of HR and 78.9 percent of FDM customers used a phased approach. This phasing could be functional phasing, in which the software modules were implemented a few at a time; geographic phasing, in which different locations were implemented over time; or organization phasing, in which the divisions within an implementing organization were implemented over time.

Other organizations might choose to distribute the PeopleSoft system across multiple servers. These servers are traditionally in different physical locations. Many manufacturing customers have chosen this approach to protect their production capabilities during network difficulties. Other multi-national corporations choose this approach to maintain a common set of applications while maintaining centralized financial capabilities. Any of these scenarios require the use of additional database instances to support these unique implementation needs.

PRE-PRODUCTION   For implementing organizations that are distributing their architecture across multiple servers and do not desire to replicate the production database on each server, a pre-production instance will be required. In this situation, the implementing organization has multiple sites that will go-live in time-dispersed phases. This scenario requires a production-like database that is free of all transaction data but has a complete system setup. This pre-production instance can serve that purpose. The implementing organization will create production databases from this instance as each phase goes live.

PRODUCTION PATCH   This instance is required for all organizations implementing with a phased approach. The type of phasing is not significant as long as there is time between the first and last rollout. The requirement for this instance stems from the potential need to apply patches and updates to the production instance(s) between the time when the first and last rollout occurs. During this time an instance to test new patches is required before the patch is rolled out to production sites.

For example, an implementing organization will rollout in two phases, one in April and one in August. In May, PeopleSoft delivers a tools and product update that the implementing organization decides to deploy to the August site. The implementing organization desires to test the update before deployment, so an instance is required for this purpose. The test/QA instances are in use for testing the August rollout, so another instance is required, the production patch instance. This instance is another test instance for this special purpose.

INTEGRATION AND SYSTEM TESTING   For implementing organizations that are phasing the rollouts and planning multiple integration and/or system tests, the timing of those tests might overlap. Under these circumstances, the overlapping tests will require multiple test instances to support the concurrent tests. Project managers should consider the resource load of conducting multiple concurrent tests, but if this scenario is required, then project managers will need to create a test instance for each concurrent test.

PEOPLESOFT ENVIRONMENTS

The PeopleSoft system consists of not only database instances but also the executables, scripts, layouts, and reports hosted on the file server. The PeopleTools executable, Structured Query Reports (SQRs), nVision layouts, and Crystal Report files are also hosted on the file server. This environment must be managed during the implementation and production time periods.

Implementing organizations will usually only require one file server environment. Some organizations that either are customizing the applications or desire to distribute their architecture might desire to create more than one of the file server environments.

In most situations, organizations that are customizing SQRs, nVision reports, and/or Crystal Reports can use a single file server or Web server environment upon which to develop. During development, technicians should use a development directory/folder for the in-progress work. When execution of the files is required, the technician can use the Configuration Manager to change the pointer to the development directory/folder. This approach will enable technicians to change between development and production files at will.

Organizations that are heavily customizing SQRs or Crystal Reports might desire to create a development environment. Creating a separate environment for development under these circumstances eases the burden on the organization's configuration management staff. While developing, a risk exists that technicians will mistakenly save development work into the production directories/folders. Using a separate environment removes this risk.

Organizations that are distributing their architecture might desire to keep a separate file server environment. This environment is copied for each distributed server. This approach will eliminate the need to remove the various logs before replicating to a new distributed server.

PERIPHERALS

The final component of the PeopleSoft system is the end-user workstations or clients. PeopleSoft provides the capability for either a fat or thin client depending on the preference of the implementing organization. With either of these configurations, the contents of the client workstation should be considered. Additional peripheral devices are common with the PeopleSoft system including bar code scanner, full-page scanners, and check printers. We will discuss both the clients and peripherals and their part in defining the project infrastructure.

PEOPLESOFT CLIENTS   The client workstations provide the portal for all users except DBAs and SNAs to access the system. Project managers have several concepts to consider when evaluating how the clients fit into the project infrastructure. These concepts include the number of clients required, configuring a fat or a thin client, needs for additional clients to support training, or other project activities, and the access each client has to the various implementation/development environments.

The first concept to consider is the number of clients required to support the project. Project managers should consider the number of individuals who need access and the timing of this access. Generally, all full-time project team members should have a dedicated client workstation. These individuals will have a consistent level of work throughout the implementation. Early in the implementation, they will setup the system by entering Business Units, vendors, customers, employees, bills, routings, and initial security roles. These activities will require full-time use of a workstation.

The second concept to consider is whether to configure fat or thin clients. PeopleSoft has the flexibility to run the applications from either a server-based (thin client) or client-based (fat client) executable. The configuration manager contains the executable locations and is the location for defining fat or thin clients. Project and technical managers can evaluate the best solution for their implementing organization. This configuration option is easily changed during the implementation if the original decision proves problematic.

The decision is centered around the load on the servers, which might change during the implementation. By running many processes, reports, and so forth on the client, the server load is reduced. Especially during peak server load periods, such as interface development and data conversion, the fat client configuration can improve server performance. During other periods, such as prototyping or training, thin clients might be more appropriate. Project managers might also consider configuring technical staff with fat clients, because these staff members are assigned most of the tasks that load the servers. Functional staff could be configured with thin clients, because these staff members generally operate within the PeopleSoft panels. The project manager must balance server performance/team productivity with server size and software licenses fees, because additional client licenses for software, such as COBOL or SQR, might be required to configure fat clients.

The third concept is the use of clients for special tasks. Throughout the implementation, the project team will undertake activities that involve groups larger than 2–3 staff members. These activities include training, prototyping, testing, and so on. During these activities, having clients grouped together might prove advantageous. For example, a set of end users planned to train on the system with project team members. The team planned a concentrated training schedule during the week and planned to use a single instructor. Under these conditions, a group of clients, possibly in a separate room, would be an advantage. This approach enables the training group to conduct training conversations without conflicting with any conversations undertaken by the other project team members. Project managers can consider having a group of clients for use when these circumstances arise.

The final concept is the access to individual environments. In an earlier section, we discussed the various database instances required or desired as well as potentially using different file and Web server environments for specific project tasks. Because of the need for project team activities to be conducted on different instances and environments, full-time project team members should have access from their dedicated workstation to each of these instances and environments.

The various instances are easily configured for three-tier operation within the configuration manager. Project team members can select the instance to log in to on the PeopleSoft login screen. Two-tier operation requires the client to be configured with the proper open database connectivity (ODBC) Data Source within the Windows Control Panel. The PeopleSoft login screen is again used, but the instance name must be known and hand typed. File server environments are not as easily configured. The pointers to these environments are contained within the Registry and are also modified within the configuration manager. These changes are generally more than what a project manager would want the functional staff to contend with, and so a batch file provides a reasonable alternative for the functional staff to change file server environments.

MISCELLANEOUS PERIPHERALS   The PeopleSoft applications provide a great deal of functionality to assist the implementing organization in its business, but many other peripheral devices and their accompanying software might be required to fulfill all the business needs of the organization. For example, many manufacturing and/or distribution firms use bar code scanners to increase data entry efficiency during the manufacturing, warehousing, and shipping functions. The project manager should account for these bar code scanners and the accompanying servers and software necessary to realize these business efficiencies. Other examples include full-page scanners for storing faxed invoices or purchase orders and printer cartridges with embedded signatures for payroll or vendor checks. All of these examples illustrate a need for project and technical managers to think through these miscellaneous peripherals.

The As Is and To Be models can assist managers in identifying the wide variety of peripherals their project might require. Documentation of these needs enable the project manager to plan for any additional funding required or evaluate the utility of existing equipment for these purposes.

PROJECT STRATEGIES

The building of a project infrastructure also entails developing, documenting, and disseminating multiple basic project strategies. These strategies will form the basis for the more detailed plans developed later by the project team. Project managers and technical managers will dedicate time early in the implementation to set this foundation for their respective staffs to plan the details of

- The technical architecture to include hardware and telecommunications designs, decisions on operating systems, and other technologies required for project success.

- The data conversion and reporting designs that include how project team members will convert existing system data and how the reporting infrastructure will function.

- The testing strategy and the various tests the project team will execute before going live during any project phase.

- The training strategy for both end users and project team members, including the types of training and how it will be delivered to the required individuals.

These strategies provide implementing organization management with a mechanism to set strategic goals and directions for the organization. They also provide the steering committee and project manager with a management control to steer the work of the project team ensuring that the detailed work remains aligned with the implementing organization's strategic direction.

Many organizations have these strategies in place and can leverage those existing strategies for use during their PeopleSoft implementation. Under these circumstances, the strategies should be passed on to any hired consulting staff to ensure the consultant's alignment with the strategic direction of the implementation organization.

TECHNICAL STRATEGY

The technical strategy provides the mechanism for management to guide the strategic direction of the technical architecture. This strategy will include attributes, such as the network architecture including the server hardware platforms used, the physical location of these servers, the network management system used, and server and client operating systems.

Establishing this base technical architecture sets the stage for all future work. Project managers can use the early implementation phases especially prototyping to evaluate this technical architecture if any questions or concerns exist. Project managers should also include any peripheral devices, such as bar code scanners, full-page scanners, or special check printers, in this strategy. This early identification of these hardware requirements enables the project manager to begin negotiations with these vendors and establish a more accurate budget.

SERVER/CLIENT HARDWARE AND SOFTWARE PLANNING

The basic configuration of the servers and clients is critical to establish early in the project. Because most project activities should be accomplished on production-like hardware and software, establishing these platforms is a prerequisite to the prototyping activities. In many organizations, these decisions were made long ago when the network infrastructure was built. Nevertheless, some organizations desire to make an infrastructure change, and these organizations should make this decision early so as to take advantage of executing project activities, beginning with prototyping on the server and client production operating system and, if possible, the server hardware platform.

NETWORK PLANNING

The underlying network of an implementing organization should be examined early in the project. PeopleSoft will send a great deal of traffic across a network, so organizations should become familiar with the bandwidth needs and ensure that their network has sufficient capacity. PeopleSoft will provide estimated network load requirements or will evaluate an implementing organization's network and provide recommendations.

For those larger organizations that have a Wide Area Network (WAN), a network management system might be an option worth investigating. There are many different systems available to monitor network components, such as server, routers, hubs, and even individual clients. These systems are designed to provide network operators with instantaneous information about outages within the network. Having this information before the end users do enables network operators to correct outages with minimum impact to production operations.

Organizations, especially multinational organizations, should examine the means by which end users will connect to the PeopleSoft system. In today's diverse workforce, some organizations might have sales people who are constantly on the road and therefore might choose either a Web-based or dial-up connection into their PeopleSoft system. Other employees might have direct connections through either a Local Area Network (LAN) if they are close to the server(s) or a WAN connection if they are not so close to the server. An implementing organization should examine their workforce and determine the best connection for each end user. Based on this decision, the organization might desire to examine different means to ensure good connections for these end users.

TECHNOLOGY ENABLERS

Many vendors have products that assist implementing organizations in both managing their networks and ensuring their PeopleSoft system maintains consistent performance and reliability. In the previous section, network management systems were mentioned as a consideration in network planning. These systems are also a means by which technology from other vendors can ensure the consistent network, and therefore PeopleSoft system, performance that end users insist on and deserve.

There are many different vendors that have products that can achieve these goals. In this section, mention will be made of two. Cisco has a product/service called Cisco Assure. This service uses the priority functionality within the TCP/IP (Transmission Control Protocol/Internet Protocol) stack to increase the reliability of PeopleSoft transactions across the implementing organization's network. By increasing the priority of PeopleSoft transactions, those transactions maintain a more consistent performance even during times of peak network load.

Throughout this chapter, consistent references to centralized and distributed network architectures have been made. This concept refers to the hosting of the PeopleSoft database on one or several geographically dispersed servers. The implementing organization should decide the architecture early in their decision to implement PeopleSoft. Two PeopleSoft partners, TIBCO and STC, capably handle this technology. These technologies are relatively new and implementing organizations should consider some level of proficiency with this technology before beginning a PeopleSoft implementation.

DATA AND REPORTING STRATEGY

The data and reporting strategy provides management with a mechanism to determine how the implementing organization desires to handle the acquisition of data for the implementation, the transfer of data either on a one-time basis during data conversion or continuously when interfacing systems, and the long term storage of historical data. This strategy also documents how the implementing organization wants to manage the extraction of data for reporting purposes. Establishing these high-level strategies provides the directions from which to develop the detailed plans.

DATA CONVERSION

During the implementation, the project team will convert existing system data into the PeopleSoft format. The project team must consider the sources of this data and the tools to be used for its extraction and loading into PeopleSoft.

The sources of data can be critical to both the successes of the early days of the implementation and the difficulties of the activity. Data to be converted can exist in multiple locations for an implementing organization. The accuracy of this data might not be equal in each source. Implementing organizations should have a good feel for the accuracy of the data before it is loaded into PeopleSoft. This is especially true in modules that have a great deal of automation, such as Inventory, Production Management, Production Planning, and Payables.

After the sources are determined, PeopleSoft provides multiple tools to assist technicians, and other vendors can provide tools as well. PeopleSoft provides three tools to assist in the conversion of data. DataMover is a tool for executing SQL scripts from formatted data files. It provides a central repository for the storage of scripts and a common user interface for their execution. Import Manager is unique in that it uses the data validation within PeopleSoft to ensure the referential integrity of the loaded data. This tool provides a common user interface for mapping flat files into PeopleSoft tables. This tool is best used for loading medium-sized files consisting of 1000–3000 rows. SQR is the high-end tool for loading large data files. Technicians write data conversion files in SQR and load large volumes of data quickly. PeopleSoft also delivers a testing tool, SQA Robot, which is routinely used for loading small volumes of data. This tool has the capability to retrieve data from a comma-delimited ASCII file and to simulate a user typing data into the PeopleSoft panels. This tool is not designed for data conversion, but it can be effectively used for small data loading tasks. Because the data is loaded through the PeopleSoft panels, the data validation checks are all satisfied using this method.

PART

V

CH

28

ARCHIVING

Over time, the PeopleSoft database will get to a size at which the implementing organization will determine that the archiving of the data is a necessity. The decision on the means to archive should be made during the initial project startup. Implementing organizations have two options when assessing their archiving solution. PeopleSoft has an archiving solution, or organizations can consider custom development work. The initial offering from PeopleSoft is written in PeopleTools, is executed from the PeopleSoft database, and uses PeopleSoft security to limit user access. The tool uses SQL scripts to move data from the PeopleSoft database into an archive database. If development work is required to implement the archiving approach, this work should be included in with the customization work.

SYSTEM MANAGEMENT

Application and system management is another consideration for the implementing organization. PeopleSoft contains multiple tables that will need periodic maintenance. The supply chain end users will add or update customers and vendors; the manufacturing users will update work-centers, bills, and routings; the accountants will add accounts and maintain the various trees that affect consolidations and financial reports. Technicians will periodically purge the Process Scheduler request table or audit files. The various tables that the organization will update, who will update them, and the process for getting these updates made should be decided early in the project. These early decisions will facilitate the detailed decisions on security; that is, what user roles have access to updating these previously mentioned tables and whether workflow will be used during any needed approvals.

INTERFACES

For those organizations that will build interfaces between the existing system and PeopleSoft, the interface architecture must be determined and the mode of transferring data from one system into another. These decisions will also drive the detailed plans and development work that will occur later in the project. Because all the methods entail differing amounts of work and differing staff skill sets, making these decisions early will enable the project manager to include this information in staffing decisions and in establishing a budget.

Implementing organizations have three basic options when determining their interface architecture and mode of information transfer: 1) batch file transfer, 2) real-time transfer, or 3) near real-time transfer. Batch file transfers are used by many organizations having separate systems and effect their data transfer mostly at night. Near real-time tools, such as SQR or COBOL, can effect transfers and run at user-defined time intervals. Real-time transfers are effected instantaneously when transactions are saved to either the PeopleSoft database or an existing system database.

REPORTING

Implementing organizations should also choose how they will report the information that they collect. Decisions, such as use of the production hardware for reporting or using an offline-reporting server, should be made. The organizations should also choose which reporting tools they intend to use. They can choose nVision, an Excel-based reporting tool that provides real-time access to data, such as financial reports or production IDs. Alternatively, end users can use Crystal Reports with query access to write their own reports and free the technicians of much of this workload. SQRs, on the other hand, are used for reporting needs that join large numbers of tables and require advanced SQL to achieve the desired results. Online Analytical Processing (OLAP) can also be used for real-time analysis of data by end users and can provide the end users with greater flexibility in generating the reports that are needed.

Although this decision cannot be made with absolute certainty, the initial training requirements and any knowledge transfer requirements are made based on this initial reporting estimate. Project managers and implementing organizations can determine some of their technical staffing needs by determining the amount of reporting that end users will need to accomplish.

TESTING STRATEGY

The strategy for ensuring the quality of the implementation includes a strategy for testing the system before going live. Testing is a critical risk mitigation measure used by implementing organizations to ensure proper system operation, validate documentation, validate end-user training, and validate knowledge transfer from consulting staff to the implementing organization. Project managers have multiple levels of testing available to ensure a quality implementation. This strategy sets the stage for the test-plan development in which the detailed tests are described, management mechanisms defined, and success factors defined.

Organizations should choose which levels of testing are required after the completion of a system-related task. These tasks would include the configuration of Business Units, vendors, employees, and so on; the development of interfaces, data conversion scripts, or custom reports; or prelaunch preparations. The level of testing required by each organization depends on the number of customizations and the amount of risk of having improper system operation upon going live that the implementing organization is willing to assume.

Project managers will also define the testing infrastructure. This infrastructure includes the use of testing tools either for functional tests or for performance and capacity testing. The management of the test will be defined in the testing strategy. These management interests include how test results are recorded and reported, how incidents will be recorded and tracked to closure, and how test planners will organize requirements into tests.

DEFINITION OF THE TESTING PHASES

Project managers have many types of testing available to ensure that they have a successful project and a quality implementation. In this section, the discussion will be limited to five types of testing: 1) unit testing, 2) integration testing, 3) system acceptance or user acceptance testing, 4) parallel testing, and 5) performance and capacity testing. Project managers should define the requirements for testing early so that planners can incorporate this guidance into their detailed schedules, cost estimates, and staffing requirements.

Unit testing is the most basic level of testing. This form of testing is commonly executed by developers and is commonly called *code and unit testing*. This term was coined because developers commonly will write a few lines of code then execute it to ensure it operates as they envisioned. Thus they code and unit test throughout the development process. This type of testing is commonly required for customized code, data conversion scripts, and interfaces.

Integration testing is the first stage in a testing program where all aspects of the system are brought together. Hence the name integration which refers to that process of combining all the different aspects of the project into a cohesive system that operates in an "integrated" fashion. Integration of a system is routinely a process that begins with the system basics, and then systematically adds complexity until the entire requirements set is satisfied. This process for combining all aspects of the system will be carefully documented in the Integration test plan. The testing strategy will include the need for the phase, its goals and objectives, and the universe of system components that will be integrated.

System acceptance testing is the culmination of the project development activities. The goal of this test phase is a decision to Go-Live. This phase is a validation of user training, project team readiness to support a production system, the production server, network, and clients. Because the system requirements were met in the integration test, this test is a validation of that system in the production environment, and it satisfies the project manager and steering committee that the company business will not be shut down upon going live. The test can also be used as a practice session for the upcoming Go-Live.

Parallel testing is a unique phase for those organizations that desire a path of the least risk. During this phase, the existing systems and PeopleSoft are run simultaneously to ensure consistent results before shutting down the legacy system. This testing phase can be valuable for those organizations that have configured PeopleSoft to run like their existing system. If either configuration or business process changes have been made during the PeopleSoft implementation, the validation of one system against the other might prove problematic.

Performance and capacity testing is a phase in which the speed of the system is measured as well as the throughput of transactions. For organizations with large transaction volumes, this testing phase can identify potential bottlenecks that could hinder system performance and therefore the end user's capability to run the business. For robust testing of this nature to occur, the implementing organization will require a suite of tools to effectively control system variables, such as concurrent users, server central processing unit (CPU) load, memory usage, or LAN segment loads.

TESTING INFRASTRUCTURE

To effectively execute and manage tests, project managers will require resources of multiple varieties. Based on the testing phase decisions, the project and test managers might require tools, and they will require testers, test planners, and a hardware platform for the database instances. Each of these resources should be included in the test strategy to ensure its effectiveness.

Testing tools can serve multiple purposes. SQA Robot and its supporting suite of applications, for example, can serve as a repository and management tool for requirements and software defects; assist with data conversion; execute functional tests; and with a load testing tool, provide system variable control for performance and capacity testing. Project managers should consider

- How the requirements will be collected, managed, and their satisfaction reported.

- How identified defects will be recorded and managed, including those defects that PeopleSoft will assist in correcting.

- How the test scripts will be collected, executed, and the results recorded.

- How to build a test program that is repeatable and that considers the inevitable tools update, product update, and upgrade processes.

Test and project managers should decide how the tests will be executed and by whom. The decision to use human testers should occur early so the test manager and business managers can prepare for those project needs. In the previous paragraph, functional test tools were introduced, and they can assist the test and project managers by pre-recording test scripts and providing a simulated user if a sufficient number of human testers is not available.

The project team must also prepare a hardware platform and database instances for the testing phases. Depending on the phase of testing, the project and test managers might determine that a separate hardware platform and database instance will satisfy the needs. For example, in a system test, this would provide the project with the opportunity to dry run the Go-Live. Under these circumstances, the project team can execute the data conversion scripts on live data, thus confirming the validity of the scripts and proper system operation after the conversion. The team can practice maintaining customer and vendors and the management processes surrounding those tasks.

MANAGEMENT INTERESTS

Project managers should also consider various other management processes, including results recording and reporting and software incident and defect tracking. Each of these high-level business decisions will guide the test manager in documenting the detailed processes required to properly execute a test.

During the process, tests are run and the results of each test should be documented. Will the project team use a paper test script and record the results on paper? Will the scripts be all electronic and results recorded online? Will the test team use an automated test tool and have the results recorded automatically? These decisions should be included in the testing strategy so project and test managers can staff the test and estimate both the cost and schedule for the activity.

During the test, incidents will occur in which the testers do not immediately know if the system operated properly. Under these circumstances, a test incident should be logged and investigated. The process for identifying, logging, and resolving incidents should be documented. Some incidents result in a defect within the PeopleSoft plain vanilla software.

Project managers should document how the interaction with the PeopleSoft Global Support Center (GSC) will occur.

Finally, the project manager should define how the results of the test are to be reported. Definition of results, such as the passing or failing of each requirement or the percentage of requirements satisfied should be defined. Also the project manager should define the timing of the report. This early identification of reporting requirements allows the test manager to prepare report formats or data analysis tools and is critical when short reporting time frames are required.

TRAINING STRATEGY

Training of both the end users and the project team is of paramount importance to those implementing organizations that desire self-sufficiency at the end of the project. An implementation cannot be successful if the implementing organization does not have users who can operate the system. A focus area for the prudent project manager is the training of both the project team and the end-user community.

The project manager has multiple options available when determining the best strategy for the implementing organization. The manager should focus on both the project team and the end-user community. One of the key decisions is whether to establish a core competency within the implementing organization or to outsource this training. Either strategy can serve the company well. In this section, we will examine four strategies for training, two for establishing a core competency within the implementing organization and two outsourcing options.

TRAIN THE TRAINER

The first option for the project manager to build an in-house core competency is the Train the Trainer (TTT) approach. With this philosophy, the implementing organization builds a critical mass of individuals who are proficient across the full range of PeopleSoft applications and technology. This critical mass of individuals is then available to train the rest of the end-user community.

To begin building this core set of individuals, the project manager can chose the consulting staff to train the critical end users who will act as the trainers. The key end users chosen are critical to successful implementations at key sites.

One of the best ways to motivate a staff to learn a new application is to establish that staff as the trainers. The knowledge that an individual will train his or her peers is a motivator in two respects. The first motivator is a positive feeling that they are deemed the champion of the application and will train their peers. The second motivator is a negative feeling of embarrassment if the individual cannot adequately answer the questions of their peers. Both of these motivators will produce a better-trained resource.

PROJECT TEAM TRAINS

The project manager might also choose to have the project team train the end users. This approach is similar to the Train the Trainer approach in that the implementing organization develops a critical mass of individuals who are proficient in the full range of applications and technology. The benefits and motivators are the same. The distinguishing factor lies in whether the project team members will be assimilated back into the organization.

The project manager should consider the level of proficiency desired during the first 6–12 months after implementation. During this period, the end-user community will gain an in-depth level of proficiency with the PeopleSoft system. After 12 months, the proficiency of the end-user community will rival that of a well-trained project team.

Given a need for assistance during this 12-month period, the training strategy should determine whether the implementing organization desires to have the expertise at the field sites or centralized into a help desk. Training end users to train their staff distributes PeopleSoft expertise into the field where the need is greatest. This approach could require a greater number of individuals to be proficient depending on the size and dispersion of the implementing organization. Training the project team generally implies a more centralized proficiency center that can be used for a help desk. The implementing organization should consider the size and dispersion of the organization, the size of the project staff, and how close to the end users the organization will desire to keep the proficient staff when making the decision on training strategies.

CONSULTANTS TRAIN

Project managers can also have the hired consulting staff train the end-user community. These training sessions can be held during multiple phases of the project, but should not be completed until approximately two weeks before the implementation date. Because individuals tend to forget training they do not use, the two-week date will increase the recall of the training once the system is available for use. End users can use the prototyping sessions, testing phases, and formal training sessions to learn the system.

PEOPLESOFT TRAINS

The final option available to train end users is a program that PeopleSoft offers. Using the demonstration database, PeopleSoft will conduct end-user training for an implementing organization. Implementing organizations can choose to travel to a PeopleSoft office or have an instructor come on-site and conduct the training.

FUNDAMENTAL PROJECT PLANS AND PROCESSES, THE QUALITY PLAN

The final attribute of a project infrastructure is the fundamental plans and processes that will define the approach to the work. The project strategies define the context for the work, whereas the plans define how the project team will approach the work. These processes and plans provide a consistent methodology for all project team members to follow.

Following a consistent methodology provides the project manager with consistent data upon which to analyze and report on the effectiveness of the project team. Without consistent methods of performing project tasks, the project team can become confused and errors will occur. The results of these errors are databases that do not contain the same patches or that contain conflicting development work. These errors create confusion within the project team, result in lost production time, and lead to lower morale because project work is lost or performed against the wrong baseline. Following a consistent methodology provides the project manager with a forum to minimize these errors and maximize team productivity.

During the staffing buildup, new project team members will desire to understand fundamental processes, such as how to have a change approved, who will migrate changes through the different database instances, and how to log system issues. Each of these fundamental processes is documented in various plans, the sum of which is deemed the quality plan.

The combination of all these documents provides the project manager with a mechanism to not only successfully implement the system, but also to provide a quality implementation. This quality implementation is defined as an implementation at the lowest cost providing the implementing organization with the capability to maximize their business goals and value of ownership. The quality plan consists of five main sections:

- Project Management Controls
- Configuration Control Process
- Review and Audit Process
- Change Management Process
- Communication Plan

In the following pages, we will deal with each of these sections individually.

PROJECT MANAGEMENT CONTROLS

During the implementation, project managers will provide guidance to the project team and manage the completion of activities and the quality of the deliverables associated with each activity. The project management controls will fulfill this purpose. Many mechanisms exist for project managers to manage their implementations. In this chapter, the discussion is limited to those controls that are specific to a PeopleSoft implementation.

USE OF AN ISSUES LOG

Throughout the implementation, the project team, management, and end users will identify software or business processes that are not functioning as expected, security access to a panel or report that is needed, or a new service or tool required by the project team or end-user community. Each of these examples represents an issue requiring the attention of the project team, management, or the steering committee.

The project team should maintain a list of these issues and provide a mechanism for tracking and communicating resolutions. The issues log will serve this purpose. The mechanism for maintaining the issue log can be a simple as a spreadsheet or word processing table containing information, such as the issue description, date identified, issue solution, person with the action, and issue status (Open or Closed). These issues are then tracked to closure.

PRODUCT UPDATES, TOOLS RELEASES, AND PATCHES

Periodically, PeopleSoft will deliver code enhancements in the form of application product updates, tools updates, and patches. Implementing organizations are expected to maintain their production environment with these enhancements. Organizations will also make their own improvements periodically over time. At times, the frequency of these updates appears problematic, but prudent project managers will control and manage the flow and these code enhancements into production and the amount of testing required before the migration to production. These program management controls will ease the maintenance of the system while reducing the risk of PeopleSoft code enhancements adversely affecting the production system.

Project managers should create a process for migrating new code into the production environment under both routine and emergency circumstances. This process should include the testing program and approvals required before migrations to production are executed. Under routine circumstances, product updates, tools releases, and new custom code and reports are easily planned, tested, and migrated based on user priorities and business objectives. Project managers are free to schedule these migrations. Emergency patches involve a much shorter time frame between problem identification and migration to production. Given this shorter time frame and the user stress that normally accompanies a production problem, the project manager must develop a process executable in a much shorter time period while maintaining control of the configuration in the production environment. In all cases, this process should contain testing.

RECURRING FUNCTIONAL MAINTENANCE

Many organizations will implement modules, such as Payroll, Purchasing, or Accounts Payable that require routine maintenance. Previously, the concepts of updating the employee, vendor, and customer list were mentioned. In this section, the discussion is limited to two potential maintenance items: tax updates and exchange rates.

Many governments regularly change payroll tax rates and rules. PeopleSoft will deliver these changes to customers on an annual basis for migration to the production instances. Project managers should include these updates into the regular system maintenance plan.

Another more frequent maintenance item is the update of exchange rates. For those implementing organizations that have implemented the multi-currency functionality, the maintenance of exchange rates is critical to their business. Given the relative criticality to the business, project managers should consult their business leaders to determine the proper interval for maintaining these rates.

PART

V

CH

28

CONFIGURATION CONTROL PROCESS

The management and control of the system configuration is a vital component of any project. PeopleSoft implementations are no different. Project managers can eliminate a serious risk to project success and ease the transition during the first few days after Go-Live by maintaining good configuration control. PeopleSoft has four main areas that should be controlled with a good configuration management (CM) process. The details of how PeopleTools and more specifically Application Designer can assist in this function as discussed in Chapter 3, "PeopleTools."

Project managers should control four types of code during their PeopleSoft implementations:

- PeopleSoft objects
- File server procedures
- Non-PeopleSoft code
- Setup and converted data

Application Designer provides the functionality to adequately control and migrate PeopleSoft objects between databases. Application Designer uses a concept of a project to store the components of the customization together. Developers can develop new code; record definitions, fields, panels, and menus; store them within a project; and when ready, migrate them to a test or production instance. Project managers can create a project for each production release, store multiple projects within this "super-project," and migrate all the functionality together.

PeopleSoft does not provide specific tools to manage the other three types of code. Implementing organizations can use either a vendor CM tool or a manual CM program. With either solution, the project team should control all new SQR processes, Crystal Reports, SQR Reports, and nVision layouts stored on the file server. Implementing organizations might develop interfaces or conversion routines that are executed against existing systems. These routines should also be controlled. Finally, project managers should manage the setup of the system including Business Units, employees, and so on and any of the data converted from existing systems. The goal of a good CM program is to maintain the capability to rebuild the system if a disaster would occur. Although not discussed in this chapter, routine backups are also critical to this goal.

REVIEW AND AUDIT PROCESS

Periodically throughout this chapter, the discussion has centered on the concept of a quality implementation. The definition of this quality implementation included the concepts of minimizing life cycle cost of the PeopleSoft implementation and maximizing the value of owning PeopleSoft. One of the ways the implementing organization can affect the implementation quality is by conducting reviews and audits of project deliverables.

Project managers and steering committees should include periodic reviews and audits throughout the implementation cycle and even during production. The timing and nature of these reviews is part of the management style of the project manager and steering committee. The use of multiple reviews can assist the implementing organization in achieving a quality implementation. Several options are available to implementing organization.

At major milestones, the steering committee should review the current state of the project. These major milestones should include the Go-Live decision, completion of integration testing, completion of the final prototype, and completion of the project infrastructure. These reviews should include topics such as the high-level and detailed business processes for the areas for which the committee members have responsibility, the satisfaction of all requirements in an integration test, and the readiness of the system and end users for going live. Many times the steering committee reviews are at a level too high for members to provide guidance and actually steer the implementation. Committee members should resist a review that consists merely of budget and schedule status.

Project management reviews can be conducted at two different levels: process and design. All project managers should focus on the fundamental project processes identified earlier in this chapter. Although the project managers might have configuration or test managers to assist with these processes, the prudent project manager focuses on the processes the project team is executing. This level of review enables the project manager to maintain control of the project while allowing the project team the autonomy to exploit their talents. Some project managers might desire to assist project team members in the review of strategic designs, especially the designs of major customizations or critical interfaces and conversions.

Project teams should also review their own work and the work of hired consultants. Errors do occur during the implementation and a peer review of customized code, setup information, interface designs, test scripts, and so on will eliminate many errors before the errors impact cost or schedule. These reviews are best accomplished with small groups and have an informal mood. A single reviewer is not uncommon or unwise. Project managers should vary the reviewers so that each project team member both reviews and is reviewed by individual peers.

End-user reviews are also critical during the prototyping phases, development of customizations, and final satisfaction of system requirements just before a before a go-live decision. Because the end users will eventually make or break the system, their opinion should be heard early and often during the implementation. Project managers should plan these reviews to solicit their input, but also to begin training and obtain their buy-in on the system to be implemented. Project managers can use the end-user reviews as a tool to achieve all these goals.

CHANGE MANAGEMENT PROCESS

The implementation of a new computing system might represent quite a cultural change for many implementing organizations. End users and business leaders might resist this change for any number of reasons. Project managers and steering committees have the challenge of developing a strategy for overcoming any resistance and ultimately gaining the backing of all the employees of the implementing organization. Winning over all employees might be too high a goal to achieve but winning over critical business leaders is a must if the initial project success is to last over time.

PART

V

CH

28

COMMUNICATION PLAN

Communication is always a key to coordinating the activities of any staff. The larger and more spread out the project, the more an effective communication plan will impact the success of the project. Project managers should consider the communication within the project team and steering committee. The approaches to communicating the various aspects of the project plan should be included in the communications plan.

Project managers should focus attention on communicating within the project team. The communication channels should be from the project manager/steering committee to project team members and the reverse, up from the project team to the project manager. Project teams routinely wonder how steering committee meetings went, or what the business leaders thought of the new business processes designed during prototyping. These casual curiosities are a great stressor for many team members. A few minutes addressing these types of questions will assist in maintaining good morale among the team members. Project managers can also assist with communication channels up the management hierarchy by soliciting questions and answering them in real-time. Allowing project team members to express concerns and even to openly vent frustration tends to build a level of trust after management addresses some of the concerns.

Coordination of project tasks should also be addressed by the communication plan. The setup of many PeopleSoft modules requires a tight integration of setup data to operate properly. For example, the purchasing and payables modules will use the same vendors. The setup of location data for example must be coordinated and agreed upon by all parties to ensure proper defaulting of location data from the Purchase Order to the Voucher. Another example centers on interface design. Both the receiving and supplying parties must synchronize the mapping of data elements between the two systems. Close coordination and effective communication will greatly enhance the chances for success. The project manager should establish guidelines for establishing and maintaining these communication channels.

Many project teams are distributed across multiple physical locations. In these teams, the communication is both more difficult and even more critical. The physical separation of individuals tends to make communication more difficult. Previously in the chapter, the informal nature of reviews and communication was stressed. When groups are distributed, more formal communication channels and reviews are necessary to ensure the accurate delivery of data between parties. Project managers should consider having distributed groups document their intentions and designs in written form. This documentation might be in the form of email or even design documents. Project managers must consider the risk of miscommunication against the additional overhead generated by documentation.

SUMMARY

Successful projects are built. Just like buildings or other structures, they begin with a solid foundation and the finishing work is applied later. Project managers who spend time laying a solid foundation can rely on that foundation throughout the implementation and use it as a basis for the implementing organization's long-term system management strategies. Project infrastructures consist of four major attributes:

- Structure of the implementation/development team
- Structure of the software implementation/development environment
- Project strategies
- Fundamental project plans and processes, the quality plan

When structuring the implementation/development team, the project managers must consider many aspects and juggle many variables to lay a solid foundation. These aspects include

- Number of staff required
- Relative mix of staff
- Considerations between in-house staff and consultants
- Considerations between full- and part-time staff
- Timing of the project staff build-up
- The organization of the team into functional process teams, module based teams, or matrixed technical teams

When looking at ways to maximize the productivity of the project team, the prudent project manager will consider the software implementation and development environment as well as the structure of the team. Project managers again have multiple concepts to consider. The discussion touched on multiple topics including

- Some basic concepts for building an effective environment, including dedicating a project area, minimizing communication barriers, providing utensils for creative work, avoiding sharing resources, and maintaining a project team's space.
- Defining the required database instances that include demonstration, application upgrader, prototyping, development, test/QA, and production.
- Defining optional database instances required under unique circumstances that include pre-production for distributed architectures, production patch when phased implementation strategies are used, and separate integration and system acceptance testing instances when multiple tests are run simultaneously.
- Defining the requirements for the file server environments.
- Defining the peripherals needed for the implementation, such as client workstations.

To establish a solid foundation for project success, the project manager should document multiple strategies that guide the project team in their detailed project activities. These strategies include

- The technical strategy that includes the determination of the hardware and software architecture. This section would document the server and client operating systems, the database engine, the hardware vendors, the network configuration and its bandwidth requirements, and different enablers of the technology, such as network management systems or PeopleSoft specific vendor products such as Cisco Assure or bar code scanners.

PART

V

CH

28

- The data and reporting strategies that provide guidance on conversions, interface, and archiving.

- The testing strategy documents the phases of testing, the tools available to support the testing requirements, and several management considerations.

- The training strategy that introduces multiple options for end-user training that is available to the implementing organizations. These options included training trainers; using the project team to train, consultants to train, or utilizing the PeopleSoft supplied end-user training.

The final brick in the project foundation are the fundamental project processes and controls. The discussion included

- Project management controls that assisted the project manager and steering committee in maintaining a position of guidance throughout the implementation. Examples of the PeopleSoft specific controls included the use of an issue's log; the handling of product updates, tools release, and patches; and the handling of recurring maintenance.

- Configuration control processes for maintaining documentation of the PeopleSoft objects, file server procedures, non-PeopleSoft code, and setup and conversion data.

- Review and audit processes designed to assist all the levels of the implementing organization (steering committee, project manager, project team, and end users) in ensuring a quality implementation. A quality implementation is an implementation in which the total cost of ownership is minimized and the value of ownership is maximized.

- The change management processes for managing the cultural changes that might occur as a result of a PeopleSoft implementation.

- The communication plan for facilitating effective communication up and down the project team hierarchy and out to the rest of the implementing organization.

Project managers have many different variables to juggle during the course of an implementation. Documenting the foundation for the work of the project team will greatly enhance the chances of project success and provide the project manager with the mechanism for setting high-level goals for the project team. This foundation is critical to the success of the project and the implementing organization's business with PeopleSoft.

CHAPTER 29

PROJECT PUBLIC RELATIONS

In this chapter   *by Perry Keating*

UNDERSTANDING THE IMPORTANCE OF PUBLIC RELATIONS

Project Public Relations is necessary to ensure that you have a successful implementation of PeopleSoft modules.

Successful Project Public Relations involves three key elements: quality communication, a communications blueprint, and an external communication interface control document. Each element will be discussed in this chapter.

Quality communication is so important because it is a two-way street. If you are transmitting and the other person is not receiving, there is a communications gap in the process. You must always remember to keep people informed. As Thomas Jefferson observed, "When you don't keep people informed, you can get one of three things: rumor, apathy, or revolution." These results could be catastrophic to your implementation project because you can't afford to have management operating on rumors from the cafeteria or the coffee shop. If your project team begins to show apathy, your schedule and quality deliverables are in jeopardy. A revolt by end users to reject the To Be model would be difficult to overcome and would almost guarantee project failure.

To combat all these problems and ensure that your project gets completed, you devise sure-fire ways to increase quality and teamwork by becoming a key communicator, a catalyst for change, a team player, and a coach. PeopleSoft has two items that can help you accomplish better communications: integration tools and electronic commerce technologies.

INTEGRATION TOOLS

The integration tools that can help you are the Message Agent, the Workflow Administrator, the Forms API, and the EDI Manager.

- Message Agent processes messages sent to PeopleSoft by external systems, such as email systems, interactive voice response systems, kiosks, other workflow systems, and the Internet. The Message Agent also enables external applications to reuse the business logic built into PeopleSoft panel groups.

- Workflow Administrator provides tools needed to keep your workflow running smoothly by enabling you to define and assign roles, set workflow defaults, schedule agents, and monitor the workflow through the system.

- Forms API enables PeopleSoft applications to route forms to an electronic forms package as part of an integrated workflow solution.

- EDI Manager provides the tools you need to manage electronic commerce transactions with your trading partners. It defines the data mappings that EDI Agents use to transfer data between the transaction files and the tables in your PeopleSoft database.

PEOPLESOFT AND ELECTRONIC COMMERCE

PeopleSoft takes an integrated approach to electronic commerce, just as it does with enterprise applications.

The scope of technologies under the umbrella term of *electronic commerce* for PeopleSoft includes Web/Internet, electronic data interchange, electronic funds transfer, interactive voice response, kiosks, fax server technology, workflow, email, and groupware. An integrated approach to the many types of technologies is essential. These technologies are categorized into three major groups: system-to-system, system-to-people, and people-to-people.

PLANNING INTERNAL COMMUNICATIONS

You need an internal communications plan as soon as you take on the implementation of the PeopleSoft Manufacturing Module project.

The integrated internal communications plan is one of the basic tools for effective communication of project work and status. It allows you to provide timely information on the project to all interested personnel.

Key factors for developing effective internal communications are identified communications interfaces; schedule status; resource allocation utilization; cost status; issue promulgation; and information media selection.

- Identified Communications Interfaces—A number of people need to know about the project. An appropriate sponsor, typically identified as the Executive Sponsor, is the single most important determinant of success.

    The project team and the project support team as well as other corporate organizations such as sales, engineering, purchasing, manufacturing and finance. Each user group as well as trainers should also be included.

- Schedule Status—A variety of graphic presentations can effectively compare planned versus actual performance. The most common of these is the Gantt chart that portrays activity over time.

- Resource Allocation Utilization—This resource-loading chart plots number of people by month during the activity. It shows the rate at which resources are being used and can easily show when a slippage is imminent.

- Cost Status—This graph shows what actual monies are being spent over time against plan.

- Issues Promulgation—The questions that you should ask to ensure that you are communicating are

    - Will there be any future problems?
    - Is personnel supply in jeopardy?
    - Is the staff dissatisfied?
    - Are you dealing with recurring problems?

- What are you lacking?
- Are there long lead deliveries?
- Are you accepting change outside of scope?

■ Information Media Selection—Several media are available for you to influence communication flow: Project Manager interviews, project baseline updates, status review meetings, and personnel time reports. Regardless of the medium you select—email, voice mail, status reports, or review meetings—you need to develop media for collecting data. When you design your own data forms, make sure that the forms are simple and easy to complete. You also need to ensure that all people are aware of its end use.

Tip

Following the integrated internal communications process will provide you with a project team and management that is well informed and working to obtain the planned status of the enterprise.

FACILITATING EXTERNAL INTERFACES

To influence the external perception of your project, you need to follow the external interface process. The process has four steps: design information packet, develop information packet, implement information packet, and assess impact.

1. Design the information packet. Determine who the audience is and what information you are trying to send. Is the audience an analyst, a supplier, a partner, a subcontractor, or a competitor? The outcome is the capture of all requirements for the information packet.

2. Develop the information packet. You need to select a medium for transmission of the information packet. It can be an article in a magazine, a report, or a press release. It can be verbal, written, or both. The outcome is complete when a rehearsal of the developed information packet has been sent to a "practice audience" for feedback.

3. Implement the information packet. This step is the actual transmission of the information packet to the target audience. There should be some means of monitoring the audience to ensure that the information packet is received.

4. Assess the impact. See if the target audience takes the action that you want them to take. You may have to return to Step 1 and repeat the process to get the desired results.

SUMMARY

In summary, the external interface control process enables you to make sure that rumor, gossip, and competitive interference doesn't get out of control. This value-added process allows you to influence analysts, bankers, and competitors.

CHAPTER **30**

PROTOTYPING

In this chapter

by Mike Fauscette

The process of prototyping—what is it and what will it do for you? Prototyping is a word used by PeopleSoft to refer to a process that is commonly referred to as a conference room pilot or a joint application development (JAD) session. Although these terms can be misleading, they represent a process crucial in the implementation of PeopleSoft products. In fact, according to PeopleSoft, this process is what puts the "rapid" in Rapid Implementation. All well and good, but what is it? You might think of it as an opportunity for your trained project team members to have some scripted hands-on experience with the applications; or as an opportunity to validate business requirements; or even an opportunity to examine the "fit" of the new software for your business. Prototyping is all these things and more. For the sake of this book (and to standardize the term), let's define *prototyping* as the project team's process of using the application software to analyze the key business requirements, thereby blending the software and the customer business processes into a viable business solution or model. And now you're thinking, that's easy for you to say, but what does that mean to my project team?

In the simplest terms, prototyping is a process that takes several inputs (business processes, setup or business rule decision documentation, initial system business requirements) and, by having team members perform scripted demonstrations of the key business processes in the PeopleSoft system (using vanilla or unmodified software), accomplishes a detailed fit analysis/requirements validation. Through the execution of the scripts, the documentation of issues, and the subsequent resolution of issues, the system is designed to meet your needs. This is an extremely effective approach for several reasons including the following:

- Requirements can be visually matched with the software process, either validating the requirement or generating a new requirement for a software or process modification.

- Knowledge transfer starts early in the implementation by having the team execute the major software processes through the prototype scripts. Because this usually occurs directly following attendance of the various PeopleSoft training courses, it also reinforces the learning process.

- The majority of the fit/gap issues are identified and resolved as a team early in the implementation.

- Early user involvement ensures that the system designed will actually meet user needs and requirements.

- Additional outputs of the process may include user role descriptions, reporting requirements, and data conversion requirements.

That's prototyping in a nutshell. Let's look at the process graphically in Figure 30.1.

You will refer back to this figure often during the discussion of prototyping. Which processes do you prototype? Everything you do in your business? The answer is not a simple one, but, in general, the idea is to prototype the most important or critical processes to your business. This is probably around 60%–80% of your business processes. In other words, don't prototype every process and every exception. Some areas of the software will be an obvious fit to your business and will not require the same depth of modeling as others. Use your own judgment to determine what is right for your business.

Figure 30.1
A typical PeopleSoft prototyping example.

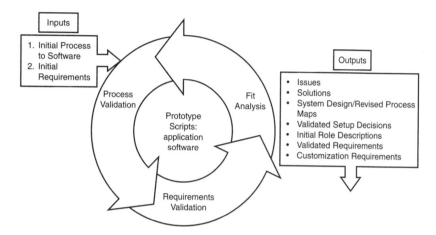

With this overview, let's look at what you can expect to accomplish in this chapter:

1. Define the prototype process.
2. Demonstrate the basic procedures for business process analysis.
3. Determine the prerequisites for starting the prototype process.
4. Determine a method for defining initial business rules to support the prototype.
5. Examine various methods for scripting prototype sessions.
6. Learn how to manage fit issues and the resolution process.
7. Examine the prototype process in detail, learning a successful model for executing your prototype sessions.

PROTOTYPE PREREQUISITES

Prior to starting the actual prototype sessions, several things must be in place to facilitate the process. These include

- Clear business objectives (as discussed in Chapter 26, "Project Planning," it is crucial to the design of a system to understand the objectives for the end result). Business objectives might be as simple as automating specific manual processes or could be complex and measurable, for example decreasing on-hand inventory.

- A high-level picture of what the end system will look like, including enterprise process maps that are tied to the new system. (We'll discuss this key input in the section "Business Processes Analysis" later in this chapter).

- Initial requirements list. (Again developed in the planning phase of the project, and tied to business objectives.)

- Detailed business process maps. (See the section "Business Processes Analysis" later in the chapter.)

- Prototype scenarios or scripts. (See the section "Scripting Scenarios" later in this chapter.)

- Installed PeopleSoft system with workstations for the prototyping team members. (We will discuss the logistics in the section "Prototype Logistics" later in this chapter.)

- A prototype environment configured to the desired prototype configuration. (See discussion in the section "Prototype Data Decisions" later in this chapter.)

- A trained prototyping team (often several subteams made up from your implementation team are used, a cross-functional and technical mix, based on the process to be prototyped). At a minimum, each of the team members involved should have attended basic PeopleSoft training for the applications that are involved in the prototype process, so that there is at least one "expert" per application involved. For example, if you are prototyping a complete Order-to-Cash process (utilizing all PeopleSoft applications possible), you would need someone trained in Order Management, Inventory, Accounts Receivable, Billing, and General Ledger. In addition, depending on how the process is designed, you might need representation for other applications. In a manufacture-to-order business, for example, you would need representation from the manufacturing applications and Order Configurator. You would need also representation for any legacy systems that may be tied to the process through interface.

Let's look at some of these critical items in more detail.

BUSINESS PROCESSES ANALYSIS

In a process-oriented implementation of the PeopleSoft applications (certainly the recommended approach to enterprise software implementation!), it is essential to have a solid understanding of the processes that drive your business. There are several ways to develop this understanding, and several partner organizations can be instrumental in this process. Although we have examined the development of the To Be model in Chapter 21, "Establishing the 'To Be' State," because of the critical nature of the process, we will outline one approach to the implementation using business process analysis as the foundation for modeling the system design.

Early in the planning process, the framework for the detailed analysis of your business processes is initiated. The first stages are at "40,000 feet" and involve an analysis of your business at the enterprise level. This analysis ties the high-level flow of your business together with several enterprise-wide processes. Examples of these types of processes might be the procure-to-pay process, the order-to-cash process, or the plan-to-produce process. These enterprise processes are broad-reaching process flows that link the entire organization. A generic order-to-cash enterprise process might look like the following simple process shown in Figure 30.2.

As you can see, this is a very high-level view of the organization and the process. Although this may represent the current activities of the organization, it should capture the direction of the organization in the future state or system. There may be some inaccuracies at this level, due to the lack of experience with the new system, but the important point is to represent your business as accurately as possible, looking to the future with your new system. By taking this approach, you can map this concept of your new process to the software that you have, or will purchase. (Yes, this process could support the selection process as well.)

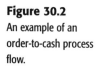

Figure 30.2
An example of an order-to-cash process flow.

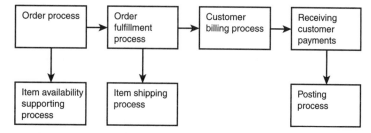

CONDUCTING A FIT ANALYSIS

With the initial enterprise processes mapped, you can conduct a first attempt at a fit analysis based on the available software applications. A *fit analysis*, or *gap analysis*, is a comparison of the functionality required to accomplish the documented business process, with the process in the software. The analysis validates the "fit" or identifies a gap that must be resolved. One method for this analysis is to take the enterprise process and overlay the applications that you have purchased. Interfaces might also be included in this analysis. The representation of the new system, or your solution for your enterprise needs, could be built by overlaying the applications to the identified process. That might look like Figure 30.3.

Figure 30.3
An example of a PeopleSoft fit analysis.

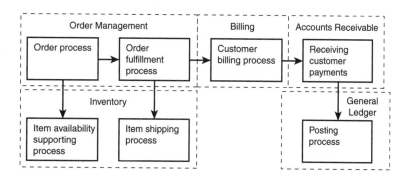

This preliminary fit analysis is very high level, but can head off any initial issues. For example, in the model in Figure 30.3, if you had not purchased the inventory application, it would be obvious that you have a gap in the basic functionality necessary to accomplish the process. To address the issue, you could either build an interface to an existing inventory system or purchase the inventory application. The end result of this evolution is a conceptual model of the end system design at a high level. This conceptual solution is the starting point for the subsequent business process analysis.

PROCESS DECOMPOSITION

With this conceptual model and the enterprise processes that it represents, the team then starts to drill down into the details of your business. This drill-down process is called *process decomposition*. Each enterprise process is broken down into multiple business processes. The business processes are then broken down into their activities and steps. Figure 30.4 illustrates this concept.

Figure 30.4
Process decomposition drills down to the activity level.

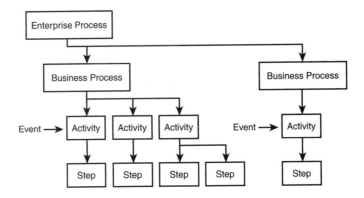

Here are some commonly used business process analysis terms:

- Business process—Actions necessary to fulfill some business request.
- Activity—A set of standard steps, triggered by some event(s), that should be completed in that work session.
- Event—A trigger for some business activity.
- Step—A work action (manual or system) that creates some business output.

In the model in Figure 30.4, you see that the enterprise process can have one or many related business processes. Each business process is then broken down into activities and steps. The relationship between activities and business processes is also one to many; one business process may have several related activities. Steps are also directly related to activities in the same manner. The activities represent groups of steps, usually accomplished in one continuous business period (for instance one shift) and triggered by one or more business event. For example, an activity might be receiving goods into inventory. The event that triggers the activity is the receipt of an inventory item. The steps represent the individual tasks required to accomplish the activity and relate directly to a panel in PeopleSoft, or an individual manual task.

With these business processes defined, we can move into the other prerequisite tasks.

PROTOTYPE DATA DECISIONS

To facilitate the prototyping process, the team must decide on the sample or demo data that will be used during the sessions. This is a rather difficult decision for most project teams. The options include

- Use the delivered PeopleSoft demo database with no changes.
- Use the delivered PeopleSoft demo database, but customize some of the setup and data to represent your business.
- Use a blank database and build a sample of your business.

Let's examine the benefits and costs of each approach.

Using the delivered demo database has several advantages. It is already set up and contains sample data. Its use can significantly speed up the time it takes to get the prototype sessions started. In addition, because it is already set up from PeopleSoft, the chance of introducing a setup problem is virtually eliminated. The downside of this approach, however, is significant. Unless you happen to be in the same business as represented in the demo database, the data will be totally unfamiliar to your team. The setup, although standard, also probably will not be a good match for your implementation. In many ways this is a risky approach to the prototype, and is the least desirable.

The second approach is a hybrid approach, using the demo database but adding some data, and modifying setup enough to reasonably model your business. The advantage to this approach is readily obvious; you gain the requisite similarity to your business and yet save some setup time. The downside, though, may not be so obvious. One issue is the modification of setup options in a fully configured system. Unless you are extremely careful and thorough, your setup changes may have unpredictable results. You will also find that some confusion cannot be avoided between the existing demo data and the new company data. Although a more desirable approach than the first option discussed, it does still carry some substantial project risks.

By far the most desirable approach is to fully configure a blank database with sample data and initial business rule configuration decisions. The advantages of working with a true representative sample of your data and validating your setup decisions make the investment of time and effort it takes worthwhile. The downside is the investment of time and the resources necessary to work through the initial business decisions, as well as the time to build the database. However, this will be offset by the gain later in validated business rule decisions and a more accurate system design.

With critical data decisions made, we can now examine the process for making that data useful for prototyping.

SETUP, CONFIGURATION, AND DEFINITION OF INITIAL BUSINESS RULES

Defining your initial setup or business rules and database configuration is a key element in the success of your prototype. This is especially true if you are working with a pristine or unconfigured database instead of the delivered demo. Several issues need to be addressed depending on the applications involved in your business solution. One of the first major debates will involve the setup of business rules and setIDs. The concept is discussed in detail in the application chapters of the book, but suffice it to say that these decisions have far-reaching ramifications in the performance of the PeopleSoft applications.

Other business rules that need to be defined include the following:

- General setup
- System configuration
- Navigator
- Define install options

- Define currency codes
- Define executable locations
- Define locations
- Define forecast sets
- Define personal data
- Define planner codes
- Define states
- Create SetID
- Define accounting calendars
- Define account types
- Define chart fields (Account, Department, Product, Project)
- Define trees and tree structures
- Define units of measure
- Define statistics codes
- Define business calendars
- Module-specific setup (varies by PS application)
- Assign operator preferences
- Run controls
- Operator security

With setup complete, you can now focus on the development of the prototype scripts.

SCRIPTING SCENARIOS

With clearly defined business processes in hand, now it's time to build some prototype scripts or scenarios. The scripts are your road map to the validation of your processes and requirements. They also enable a relatively inexperienced project team to navigate successfully through the business processes in the PeopleSoft system.

SCRIPTING SCENARIO APPROACHES

There are several different approaches to developing and organizing your prototype scenarios. One of the simplest methods is to use the enterprise processes to organize the scenarios into manageable groups of supporting business processes. The business processes then become the headers for each script. This approach allows for easier scheduling of blocks of scripts by enterprise process, with detailed daily scheduling by business process.

The scripts themselves can take many forms. If your organization has a familiar test script format, it is possible to adopt that for use during the prototype, with some basic modification. If not, there are several simple formats that have worked successfully. Often your implementation partner will have a suggested format as well. No matter which format you utilize, there are a few items that should be included on your scripts. The following categories are essential information for effective prototype scripting:

- Business process flow.

- Navigation for the process in the PeopleSoft applications to the panel level—The level of detail for the script is debatable, but the minimum for successful prototype seems to be the panel level. Field-level detail is not required during the prototype, as it would be during testing, because there is no validation of expected results.

- Assumptions—This may include setup assumptions as well as process assumptions.

- Requirements to be validated by the prototype session.

- Roles—Define which roles will perform each step of the process. If you don't know at this point, leave blanks for update during the prototype session.

- Opportunities for process improvements.

- Questions or open issues that were identified during the initial high-level fit analysis.

PART

V

CH

30

Scripts developed with this information will form a sound basis for the prototype sessions. There is an added benefit to the script development process. With the addition of field-level detail, they will serve as a good portion of your system test scripts and can be the basis for development of user procedures and training material.

PROTOTYPING SESSIONS

With a properly configured prototype database and scripts developed, you're almost ready to begin your prototype sessions. First, however, there are a few other concerns that must be addressed. We'll call these concerns prototype logistics and scheduling.

PROTOTYPE LOGISTICS

Before the prototype sessions can begin, facilities must be established that are conducive to the accomplishment of your goals. We already mentioned that the installation of the PeopleSoft system is a prerequisite. In addition, client workstations must be procured and configured for use on the prototype system. How many workstations? That depends on several factors. The obvious issue here is team size and access to the system. One approach that seems to be very effective is a combination of a conference room, complete with a workstation and projection system, for conducting the main sessions, and smaller team rooms with several workstations, useful for detailed research on the process/system. It is useful if most or all of the project team has the prototype system available to do individual research and to reinforce training.

PROTOTYPE SCHEDULING

Detailed scheduling is also very important. The sessions will usually involve team members from several areas and also extended team members, serving as subject matter experts in the affected business area. To tie the sessions all together and ensure that the correct people are available for each session, it is necessary to put out a detailed prototype schedule. The schedule should include the enterprise process, the business process, the location of the session, the date and time, the lead resource responsible for the session, and all the attendees. The format is unimportant, and might be as simple as a spreadsheet or could be handled by a groupware scheduling program.

SESSION FORMAT

The format for the sessions follows a simple pattern. As a rule of thumb, it generally takes two to three days to work through a business process. The duration changes based on the complexity of the process and the fit. Daily the most efficient use of the schedule seems to be a four- to six-hour prototype session focused on the process, followed by a two- to four-hour issue session dealing with any issues raised in the prototype session. Separating the time tends to keep you on track, preventing the team from getting bogged down on a single issue. Issues are recorded during the session and then reviewed during the issue portion of the day. Keeping the process moving is the responsibility of the identified lead for the session.

VALIDATING THE PROCESS

Let's look at the process portion of the sessions in detail. Scripts should be prepared and handed out to each member of the team present. Identify a person to record issues and someone to "drive" the software. (You probably want to rotate this duty, as it builds familiarity with system navigation.) It's helpful to review the requirements that should be validated during the session with all present. (They should be on your script, right?) At this point you are ready to start working through the script. The team member who is "driving" for this session starts at the beginning of the script and executes the process as scripted. Other team members observe, comment, and validate the requirements. As a requirement is validated, it is checked off. As issues arise, they are recorded. If need be, walk though sections of the script as many times as necessary to understand the process, and then move on. Your goals are to validate the requirements, resolve small issues, record issues that are not easily resolved, gain understanding of the process, and move on. Don't forget to address related areas of each process; for instance, this is the perfect opportunity to examine and review reporting requirements related to the process. Role assignments should be validated and defined as each step of the process is performed. Remember that roles in the system do not equate to organizational "jobs" at this stage. Later in the process you will map these roles to your own job titles. Also remember that a part of the validation in the session is that the initial setup and configuration of the software meets your needs. If changes in setup are required, make those changes and rerun the process. Prototyping is an iterative process; don't be afraid to repeat sessions as necessary to understand the process and support solutions.

At the end of the allotted time, the session stops and the team breaks off to address the day's issues. This can be a single group session, or you may choose to break up into smaller teams to address specific areas of concern.

ISSUE SESSIONS

The issue sessions are an open forum to address the issues that arise during the process sessions. Issues could be anything from "gaps" in the software functionality to processes that are identified as ineffective. Unresolved issues from previous days may also be put on the agenda for more discussion. The goal should be to resolve all open issues from the day's session. (Okay, realistically some issues will be more involved and will require either more research or involvement from team members not present, and thus will need to be tabled until a later session.) As you might guess, the use of an issue tracking tool is critical in this process. The layout of an effective tool is discussed elsewhere in this book. At the end of the day, you will have validated several requirements, generated reporting requirements, generated issues, found solutions for some issues, validated the portion of the process and modified your process flows to reflect any changes, determined which processes need to be modified and possibly rescheduled a portion of the session, generated basic role definitions, generated some modification requirements, and validated setup decisions. Update your prototype schedule and continue the process as scheduled.

The prototype sessions continue until all the scheduled processes have been validated. As stated previously, rarely will you prototype all your business processes. The goal is to prototype the ones most critical to your business. The processes that fall out of the range for the prototype sessions must also be examined, but this can be accomplished by your team in a more traditional fit analysis format. Certainly the system can and must be used in this process, but it is not usually productive to continue the formal prototyping sessions for those less critical processes and exceptions. The outputs will continue to be refined for some time after the end of prototyping, but a solid foundation will exist for the design of your system. The solutions you developed can be pushed rapidly into the proper forum for implementing the solution (development for modifications, business owners for process changes, reporting team for reports, and so on).

With a clear understanding of the prototype process, it is now time to look at the outputs from your sessions.

PROTOTYPING OUTPUTS

Let's take a closer look at the outputs from your prototyping sessions. As outlined in the beginning of the chapter (refer to Figure 30.1), the basic deliverables are

- Validated requirements
- Issues
- Solutions
- Validated business processes (system model, process flows, and so on)
- Validated setup decisions
- Initial role descriptions
- Customization requirements

Requirements, as you have seen, are initially developed in the project planning activities and are linked directly to business objectives. As the prototype sessions play out, the requirements are validated and detailed requirements are developed. These detailed requirements fit into several subcategories:

- Functional or business process requirements.
- Technical and technology requirements. (These include database, architecture or network, middleware, process scheduling, workstations, two- and three-tier, backup, performance monitoring, and so on.)

- Data management requirements including data conversion, archiving, and database sizing.

- Security and access requirements. This has a direct relationship to role descriptions.

- Interface requirements.

- Performance requirements.

- Audit and control requirements.

- Reporting requirements.

Requirements gathering and definition will continue outside of the sessions, but a solid foundation can be established during the prototype.

Issues and Solutions

Issues and solutions also flow out of the sessions, as you have seen. The goal of resolving all open issues is a good one, but of course some issues will remain open for some time. Issues must be prioritized and assigned to a responsible team member. Open issues should have a due date for resolution as well. The issue management process is explained elsewhere in this book, and will continue throughout the implementation. The basic outcomes for an open issue are a solution or a decision to carry the open issue forward due to a need for more information, and so on. Solutions can take the form of a process change, a software change (see customization requirements below), or a closed issue (a decision to not address an issue, or that an issue is not valid IS a solution).

Updated Business Process Maps

Updated business process maps or flows form the basis of your designed system or system model. The model you develop is a significant portion of your system. There are some decisions open at this time in the project, but the bulk of the system processes are defined. If you updated your business and enterprise process flows continually during the prototype, this deliverable is probably 80% complete at the end of prototype. The other 20% or so can be filled in as the requirement definition is completed.

Note

> PeopleSoft's Business Process Designer can be used to capture your business processes in the system if desired.

Setup documentation should be updated to reflect your end configuration of the prototype system. The prototype process should produce enough knowledge to work though most setup/business rules issues and reach final decisions. This business rule documentation forms the foundation for establishing several environments for use during the rest of the implementation process. Figure 30.5 shows one approach for using this setup information in configuring the project database structure.

Figure 30.5
Sample database environments.

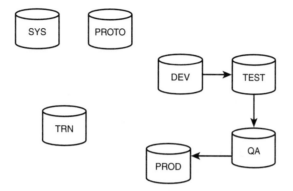

The prototype database environment is used extensively during the prototype, but is not copied or carried forward into subsequent versions of your environment. There will be way too much transactional data in the environment to use it as a model for future environments. It is much safer to configure a new database instance using what was learned and documented during the prototype!

ROLE DESCRIPTIONS

Initial role descriptions are a key deliverable that will be used in several areas of the project. Role definitions are matched against security and access requirements to develop security profiles for each role, matching the role to the required operator class(es). Roles should be standardized across all areas of the business. If your System Design includes the use of workflow, these user roles form the heart of your workflow setup. Your analysis should include the definition of the role and its function in and out of the system (tied to processes), the way information is routed to and from the role, and any event or process drivers that trigger role responses and actions. Also document any other role tool and support requirements that may arise in the process. Role definitions may also be used as a driver in the user training program. Often user training is developed on a role level. Role definitions are often refined further and finalized after the prototype.

Customizations that are documented during the prototype should be handled as outlined in your configuration management plan, change management plan, or other procedure for dealing with proposed software changes. Generally a specification for the proposed change is created and reviewed/approved through the established process. The specification should contain both a functional and technical analysis of the modification, with a clear link to the business driver for the change. The formal review/approval process usually includes sign-off from the business process owner and the technical team before reaching the overall authority for software change approval. Include any other options for addressing the issue and address any performance concerns.

And that's all there is to it! You should now have a prototype of your future system, fully documented and ready for development.

PROTOTYPING TIPS

The following tips on prototyping should be useful to your project team:

- Establish an approval process for your solutions.

- Establish a communication approach for your solutions and system design or model. This should include the project team and business owners.

- Ensure that the user community is represented in each session with the appropriate process owners; their buy-in at this stage is critical for the long term success and will minimize change management issues later.

- The sessions will progress much more smoothly if all involved have been through some PeopleSoft training. A familiarity with the basic navigation of the system is a must.

- During the sessions, don't fall into the trap of detailed analysis and debate on an obvious misfit in the software. Document the issue and move on with the session; deal with the issue during the issue session.

- Include workflow issues in your session. Visualizing the use of workflow can be instrumental in laying out appropriate uses.

- Get sign-off from the team immediately when a process is approved.

- Update the process flows daily; don't allow your model to become outdated.

- Involve members of your technical team as needed to resolve technical issues. Technical buy-in on all modification is essential.

- Keep project scope close at hand to ensure that the team stays on track.

- The use of time management techniques like time boxing is critical to keep the sessions moving in a positive direction.

- Do not fall into the trap of irrelevant "what if" scenarios. These are costly in both time and commitment. There is always an exception to every normal process. Remember the goal is to make the process fit the majority of your business; exceptions can be dealt with in the future.

- Feel free to break up into smaller groups or assign work outside the session to deal with difficult issues.

- Remember that this is a visual process. The more you can use the system or process flows to demonstrate the outcome, the more effective your sessions will be.

- Prioritize your issues and deal with the highest priority first.

- Focus on the business objectives and requirements; you are building and shaping the direction of the new system, not analyzing your old system.

- Involve the right team members and extended team members in each session, and use the schedule to ensure that they are present for the correct sessions.

SUMMARY

As you can see, the prototype activity is the heart of a successful rapid approach implementation. It often is difficult to dedicate the time and resources to prototyping, but you can now understand the necessity. A thorough and complete prototype will yield many benefits to the project and help prevent serious issues late in the project from derailing the implementation.

PART

V

CH

30

CHAPTER 31

INTEGRATING PEOPLESOFT WITH EXISTING APPLICATIONS

In this chapter

by Rob Townsend

THE REASON FOR THE MESSAGE AGENT SERVER

PeopleSoft understands the importance and complexity of integrating existing applications with the PeopleSoft software. There are many different ways customers do business, and sometimes the functionality provided with PeopleSoft does not correlate with all the customer's business requirements. Sometimes a new application can be developed using PeopleTools, but other times an existing solution is already available in another software application. In the latter case, an integration is required if the data needs to be shared between the PeopleSoft applications and the third-party application in order to provide a full system solution.

With the introduction of third-party applications into an existing software product, PeopleSoft or otherwise, a new level of complexity is reached in the overall system architecture. Many factors come into play regarding the interface between the two applications that need to be considered. Does the interface need to be real-time or batch-driven? What are the expected volumes? Are the volumes regarded in terms of transactions per minute or transactions per day? What are the error handling requirements?

Because of the complexity of software integration and the requirement variations between customers, it is difficult to provide a single tool or utility that can meet the demands of every customer. PeopleSoft offers a flexible solution with the Message Agent Server, which provides a simple and direct interface to the PeopleSoft data. The Message Agent Server is a utility that allows third-party applications to insert or retrieve data directly through the existing PeopleSoft applications. The Message Agent Server uses the existing PeopleSoft applications as an entry point for inserting and retrieving data.

When you initially think of an application that is driven by a database, such as PeopleSoft, the first thought for interfacing with other applications is to insert, update, and delete data directly from database tables. Well, the business logic in PeopleSoft exists on a layer above the database known as PeopleTools and PeopleCode. If inserts, updates, and deletes to tables are performed directly to a PeopleSoft database, the business logic is bypassed and the result could be compromised data integrity.

For example, the paycheck direct deposit information for an employee can be broken down into percentages that are split across several bank accounts. Suppose that 20% goes to a savings account and the remaining percentage goes into a checking account. It is PeopleCode that prohibits a user from entering percentages totaling greater than 100%. PeopleCode checks for the total percentages and issues an error message if the amount does not equal 100%.

If the interface from a third-party application is designed to perform direct inserts into the direct deposit table, it is possible to enter any combination of %ages. The database itself doesn't have the business logic to prevent a total greater than 100%.

When you use the Message Agent Server, an incoming transaction to the Direct Deposit panel will follow the same business logic as if the data were being entered manually. PeopleCode verifies that the percentages total 100% and issues an error message otherwise.

This is the reason it is important for an interface to use the Message Agent Server—so that the business logic and data integrity follow the same constraints as the online data.

THE MESSAGE AGENT SERVER AND THE MESSAGE AGENT API

Two components make up the Message Agent: the Message Agent Server and the Message Agent API. Often the terminology between the two gets misused, so let's clarify the difference between them, and then we will dive into greater detail about each piece.

There is a process that runs on the Application Server that receives incoming data and passes it to PeopleSoft panels. This process is typically called the Message Agent Server and is like a robotic online user. More commonly, this is what people are talking about when they say "The Message Agent."

There is also the Message Agent API. The Message Agent API is a set of functions that allow users to develop their own Application Programming Interfaces (APIs) between a third-party application and PeopleSoft. Basically, the Message Agent API functions are used to create programs that can feed data to the Message Agent Server process running on the Application Server. Typically, the Message Agent API is used in C/C++, Visual Basic, and more recently Java applications that are developed specifically for integrating a third-party application with PeopleSoft.

THE MESSAGE AGENT SERVER

With PeopleSoft version 7.5 come some really terrific changes to the Message Agent Server. In earlier versions of PeopleSoft, the Message Agent (previously referred to as the Message Agent Monitor) was an executable that ran on a Windows 95 or Windows NT desktop. It was written to replicate the same actions a user performs when navigating to a PeopleSoft panel, inserting data into the panel, and saving. And, this is exactly what it did. In fact, when the Message Agent Monitor navigated to the panel, you could actually see the screen flashing as it cycled through the panels and inserted data into them.

One of the major problems with the Message Agent Monitor was its slow performance and lack of robustness. The Message Agent Monitor was not much faster than a regular user because it had to physically navigate to the panels and wait for all the PeopleCode to execute. It was also a Windows-based executable that was prone to all risks that are inherent to any Windows applications. Although the Message Agent Monitor worked, it was due for a complete overhaul.

For PeopleSoft 7.5, the Message Agent was completely rewritten with many improvements. In PeopleSoft 7.5, the Message Agent Server is an additional process that runs as part of the Application Server processes. It starts along with the other processes when the Application Server is booted, and it is certified to run on Windows NT or any of the supported UNIX platforms. The Message Agent Server process name is PSAPISRV, and it is shown among the list of Application Server processes in Figure 31.1.

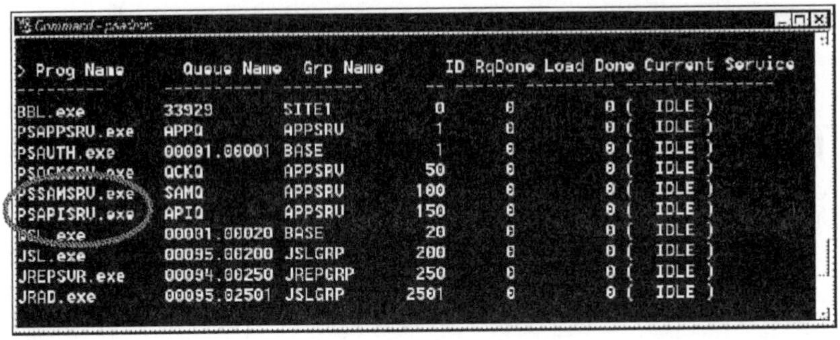

Figure 31.1
Application Server
processes.

```
Command - psadmin                                                    _ □ ×
> Prog Name       Queue Name  Grp Name      ID RqDone Load Done Current Service

  BBL.exe         33929       SITE1          0     0      0 (  IDLE )
  PSAPPSRU.exe    APPQ        APPSRU         1     0      0 (  IDLE )
  PSAUTH.exe      00001.00001 BASE           1     0      0 (  IDLE )
  PSQCKSRU.exe    QCKQ        APPSRU        50     0      0 (  IDLE )
  PSSAMSRU.exe    SAMQ        APPSRU       100     0      0 (  IDLE )
  PSAPISRU.exe    APIQ        APPSRU       150     0      0 (  IDLE )
  PSQLSRU.exe     00001.00020 BASE          20     0      0 (  IDLE )
  JSL.exe         00095.00200 JSLGRP       200     0      0 (  IDLE )
  JREPSUR.exe     00094.00250 JREPGRP      250     0      0 (  IDLE )
  JRAD.exe        00095.02501 JSLGRP      2501     0      0 (  IDLE )
```

MESSAGE AGENT PERFORMANCE GAINS

With this new design come very impressive performance gains. The performance benchmarks show the 7.5 Message Agent Server to be between 6 to 20 times faster than the previous Message Agent Monitor. The new design does not require the Message Agent Server to physically navigate to the PeopleSoft panel to service a message request. Also, the Message Agent Server runs as part of the Application Server rather than on the Windows client desktop. The Application Server is the middleware product, and processing power, behind the PeopleSoft three-tier environment. It uses BEA Technology's Tuxedo as an intermediary to transmit messages from a client to a database. A three-tier configuration is beneficial in improving performance across a Wide Area Network as well as reducing network traffic. The network traffic reduction comes from smaller Tuxedo packets that are sent to service the requests traditionally handled by large SQL transactions.

The Message Agent Server process is named PSAPISRV and is another process that is started when the Application Server is booted. The new design of the Message Agent Server provides better performance, improved robustness, and greater scalability.

In the configuration file of the Application Server, there is a variable for each process that specifies the number of instances that get started when the Application Server is booted. This gives the Message Agent greater scalability because if a single instance of the Message Agent process is not enough to handle the transaction volumes, the Application Server configuration file can be updated so that multiple instances of PSAPISRV are started.

The following snippet is a section from the PSAPPSRV.CFG file that shows the Message Agent Server configuration. The Min Instances and Max Instances variables can be set so that multiple instances of the PSAPISRV process are started.

```
[PSAPISRV]
;================================================
; Settings for PSAPISRV
;================================================
Min Instances=2
Max Instances=5
Spawn=1
Service Timeout=300
Recycle Count=100000
Allowed Consec Service Failures=0
```

The 7.5 Message Agent Server is *stateless*, which means it can service several incoming requests but process them one at a time. This improves the reliability of the Message Agent Server because the failure of one incoming request will not affect the servicing of subsequent requests. Figure 31.2 gives a graphical layout of how the Message Agent Server is configured in the three-tier environment.

Figure 31.2
The Message Agent Architecture.

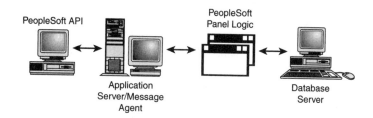

Because the Message Agent Server is now a process that runs on the Application Server, there is no GUI interface to deal with. Instead of physically going to each panel and inserting data, the Message Agent Server logically goes to each panel. Without the need of the GUI, the Message Agent Server is able to process transactions much more quickly than the previous version, but it still utilizes the business logic in the PeopleSoft applications.

Now that you have a basic understanding of the Message Agent Architecture, it is time to begin developing an Application Programming Interface (API) for the third-party application to communicate with PeopleSoft.

CODING THE MESSAGE AGENT API

Let's talk a little bit about the Message Agent API. The Message Agent Server receives and services requests from third-party applications. But how do the requests actually get from the third-party application to the Message Agent Server? This is where the Message Agent API comes into play. The Message Agent API is delivered in the form of a C or OLE/COM interface, which provides a set of functions that can be used to give specific orders to the Message Agent Server.

First, you create a Message Definition using the Application Designer that identifies which Menu, Panel Group, Mode, and Search Record the Message Agent Server should access. This is also where you map the fields from your API to the fields on the PeopleSoft panel. For more information on creating a Message Definition, take a look at the PeopleTools PeopleBook. It gives a pretty good walkthrough on creating Message Definitions.

The next step is coding the API and including the Message Agent API functions that enable you to interact with the Message Agent Server. The first few steps in coding the API are making a connection to the Message Agent Server and passing the name of the Message Definition indicating which menu, panel group, and so on, the application will be accessing. After this initial call to the Message Agent Server to pass the Message Definition, the rest is up to you!

A fairly wide variety of functionality is provided with the Message Agent API. You can set the value of fields in the panel, retrieve the result set from a search dialog box to display to a user, or return the text of an error message. A complete description of all the Message Agent functions is available in the Integration Tools section of the PeopleTools 7.5 PeopleBook. Also, there are many examples of Message Agent API programs in the PeopleBooks that can help you write that killer application.

For coding the API, you have a choice of an OLE Automation language, C/C++, or the Java programming language. To code an API using an OLE Automation language, you must reference the PSMAS.TBL file, which should be located in the \bin\CLIENT\WINX86 directory of the file server. To code your API in C/C++, you need to include the PSMSGAPI.H file in your programs. For Java coding, you need to use the delivered JMAC, which is basically a wrapper around the Message Agent API so that it can be used in a scripting language.

In addition to writing a custom API from scratch, there are several Message Agent APIs that come delivered with a standard PeopleSoft install. You might actually be using them already! Before starting to develop a new API, you should see if the delivered ones meet your business requirements. Why reinvent the wheel?

Available Message Agent API Programs

There are some Message Agent API programs that come with the standard PeopleSoft install. These programs were developed by PeopleSoft and come in the form of a compiled executable. Unfortunately, the source code is not available because it is considered proprietary information. Nevertheless, these programs provide a good example of the functionality that can be reached using the Message Agent API and the Message Agent Server.

The Database Agent is an API that detects certain conditions in the database by running a user-defined query and then triggers workflow to invoke a business process. If you aren't using the Database Agent in your implementation yet, chances are you will or could benefit by it. The Database Agent uses the Message Agent API to send the data retrieved from the query to the target panel defined in the Message Definition. Remember the Message Definition is the object that tells the Message Agent Server which panel to navigate to as well as the mappings from the API to the actual panel. When the Message Agent Server inserts data into the target panel, there is workflow PeopleCode that executes when the panel is saved. This workflow PeopleCode can be written to route messages to users that notify them that the condition defined in the query has been met.

Also, the Database Agent can be used as an integration API from one database to another. For example, suppose you have a third-party application that is used to enter purchase orders. The purchase orders need to be inserted into the PeopleSoft Procurement module for tracking purposes. The Database Agent could be used in this scenario by querying a staging table that contains the purchase order data from the third-party system and then inserting the data into the PeopleSoft Purchase Order panel via the Message Agent Server.

This is an efficient and stable integration that does not require any additional API code. Everything is already available in the PeopleSoft install.

In addition to the Database Agent, PeopleSoft also delivers an API that is used for retrieving data from a Lotus Notes database. PeopleSoft delivers a PSNOTES.EXE program that can be used to pass data from Lotus Notes to PeopleSoft. This application queries the Lotus Notes Database and checks for any forms that need to be sent to PeopleSoft. If any are found, it sends the form data to the Message Agent Server, which inserts it into PeopleSoft. This whole process is a Message Agent API that collects the data and the Message Agent Server that processes the data and inserts it into PeopleSoft.

SOME TIPS FOR A SUCCESSFUL INTEGRATION

The first priority that should be taken into consideration when integrating applications, whether PeopleSoft or any other software in general, is making sure the data is correct. This should be the number one priority before anything else is considered. You must be sure that the data being manipulated, both during the input and output transactions, is accurate and in the correct form that the database is expecting.

The one proven method of ensuring that this data is correct is to get down to the database level and query the tables before and after the transactions occur. First, insert or update data through the PeopleSoft online system and query the applicable tables for the results. Next, use your custom API to insert or update data via the Message Agent Server and then query the applicable tables. The result set should be the same between PeopleSoft and your custom application. This process should be performed for as many different scenarios as possible to ensure that the API and the online result set are the same.

SUMMARY

Integrating third-party applications with PeopleSoft can be a tricky task. There are many different ways to approach a software integration, but PeopleSoft delivers a viable solution in the Message Agent Server. The Message Agent provides the security of inserting data directly through the PeopleSoft panels to utilize the existing business logic. It also provides stability and quick performance by running as part of the Application Server.

CHAPTER 32

IMPLEMENTATION PITFALLS

In this chapter

by Carl Upthegrove

IMPLEMENTATION PROJECTS

PeopleSoft implementation projects, like any software implementation projects, have certain characteristics, good and bad, that can be learned over time and then shared. Consequently, there are many potential problems that might come up during a PeopleSoft implementation. Some of these pitfalls are generic to ERP projects; others are more specific to PeopleSoft implementations. The information presented in this chapter is a guide that has been created from the experience of others. It identifies the types of pitfalls that typically plague a PeopleSoft implementation, and gives some ideas on how to avoid the pitfalls or deal with them after they have occurred.

LACK OF FOCUS (BUSINESS GOALS)

Implementing one or more PeopleSoft product suites is a significant business decision. It requires a commitment of the organization's resources, money, people, and time. Many projects end up as failures—or at least less successful than they might otherwise be—as a result of a lack of focus on the business drivers that spawned the project. It is easy to get "lost in the trees" during an implementation. When a PeopleSoft implementation project is under-way, a lot of people are performing a lot of functions in a fast-paced environment. Meetings are being held, decisions are being made, resources are being allocated, and in general everything is moving along. How does the project team ensure that everything doesn't go off course?

UNDERSTANDING PROJECT OBJECTIVES

From the very beginning, everyone should be aware of what the project objectives are. In the project charter, there will be a very eloquently worded set of business objectives. Usually, these are general and quite high-level. However, it helps to break those business goals down to more specific goals for each phase and subsection of the project. If the project is dealing with the implementation of a new distribution system, how does that affect the warehouse? What about the team working on interfaces to a legacy accounts payable system? Does it have a specific goal? Breaking these types of questions down and discussing them on a regular basis helps to maintain focus. That focus helps ensure that the decisions made by each subunit of the project will be directed toward the larger goal.

AVOIDING COMMUNICATION PROBLEMS

Communication may well be the most written about, talked about, difficult, and important aspect of our lives as humans. That goes as well for the business world and the world of systems implementation. Communication certainly fits in any discussion of potential pitfalls in implementing PeopleSoft products.

Before the Kickoff

There probably is no time more critical for communicating well than at the beginning of a project. The sooner the communication plans are developed and executed, the better the chance for success. Before the kickoff is the time to get "buy-in" by involving everyone in the project. The users, the project team, and management all need to be receiving information and providing input.

During the early stages of any project, only a few people ordinarily are involved. That makes sense. At that early stage there is a lot of uncertainty; so the fewer people involved, the quicker decisions can be made and the easier it is to change direction if needed. Also, in the early stages there is less work to be done, so the number of people involved can be kept small. However, as everything moves forward, the natural tendency is to keep communication to the original small group. That is one of the more common mistakes made in projects, but it is not that hard to avoid. Early on, identify people who will be affected by the project as it grows. Keep that list of affected people with the project files and don't hesitate to add names. It is dynamic. Except in some very particular situations communicating with more people than necessary is less risky that communicating with fewer people than needed.

Even before the project kicks off, develop communication vehicles, such as email groups, newsletter updates, project logos, and slogans. Several projects being done in PeopleSoft Student Administration have continuously updated Web sites. Some of this may seem trivial and even a bit hokey, but it works and can prevent problems later in the project. While the group is still small, be prepared to accept input from others not in it.

Communication is input and output. It serves two important purposes. First, people feel involved when they are allowed to contribute. Receiving information is a passive activity. Providing input requires understanding, thought, and the sharing of that thought and knowledge. Second, small groups can become so stubborn in their thinking that important ideas are missed or certain considerations are excluded. Allowing input from other concerned people in the organization can prevent going down a course that does not take into consideration the true impact of the project on the organization.

Communication is never easy, and deciding how much information to send out and how much input to allow is never exact. Beginning early in the project helps develop communication skills that are critical to success.

During the Project

In an ongoing project, everything is moving very quickly. There just is not enough time to get it all done. During these times, good managers prioritize and work on the most important items first. This is often where communication within the project can fail. Communication takes time; good communication takes a lot of time. Mark Twain once said, "I'm sorry this letter is so long but I didn't have enough time to send a short one." Good communication is clear, concise, thorough, and accurate. To create this type of memo, email, or even voice mail requires thought and organization—and that requires time. During the heat of battle, good communication is often sacrificed and that is just when it is needed most. One way to avoid this problem is to make sure that everyone knows what information he or she is responsible for maintaining and disseminating. Communication is not solely the responsibility of the project manager or managers. Everyone can be involved. Something as simple as a status report can seem overwhelming if only one person does it. If sections are divided among members of the team, it takes less time, is easier to accomplish, and will probably even be more thorough and accurate.

Regular meetings are essential. Ideas exchanged and even decisions made at the water fountain, in the break room, and in the hallways may be valuable but often exclude important aspects of the project. The frequency of the project meetings can be agreed upon by the team, but whether the meetings are daily, weekly, or biweekly, they should be scheduled and held regularly and on time. By having regular meetings and enforcing timeliness, you will ensure that they will be useful and efficient. Poorly organized and poorly run meetings are a sore subject in nearly every organization. It is advisable to get some good material on how to have useful meetings and incorporate that into the planning of the project, because successful meetings are essential to project success.

Another potential pitfall in communication during the project is failure to let everyone know of decisions that result in course changes. No matter how well planned the project is, no plan can anticipate every eventuality. The larger the project, the more critical the planning, but projects of any size will be adversely affected when part of the team is going forward with old information. The best way to avoid these types of problems may be to maintain a log of decisions and review these at each project meeting.

After Everything is Up and Running

Now that the project is a success, don't forget to tell everyone. It seems odd but there are plenty of examples of projects that are completed but only the project team knows. A "go-live" party is one useful way to send out the message that a lot has been accomplished. Another way is to publish something telling the organization what has been done and what benefit it will receive. No matter how the project is done, it is not over until everyone has been notified.

With Management

Management support is *key* to the success of a PeopleSoft project. PeopleSoft implementation projects typically have an executive sponsor and usually have another key member of management who participates in regularly scheduled meetings. However, others in management need to be in the communication loop. Early in the project, seek out the members of management impacted by the project. Try to arrange face-to-face meetings to explain what is being done, how it will be accomplished, and most importantly *why*. If possible, enlist the executive sponsor to gain access to these members of the management team and to show the overall importance of the project. During these meetings, attempt to identify which members of management are the most likely allies of the project and who, if anyone, will be opposed. Remember, management is not of one mind. The project's success can be influenced greatly by finding key supporters and identifying potential opponents.

IDENTIFYING USERS AND THEIR ROLES

Just exactly who are the users of the system? In most cases, they are not the people in the organization who are involved with the selection of the system or the initial planning. In some companies, the people who will actually use the system are brought into the process early and participate throughout; however, that is an exception and for very good reason. The people in an organization who will actually use the system cannot be freed up to work on a project of this type. They are busy doing what they do to add value to the company. For that reason, teams are developed, usually from the Information Technology (IT) community, who act as liaisons between the actual users and the project.

So, if the real users are not directly involved on a day-to-day basis, how does the project keep them involved? Meetings with the users should be regularized so that the users are kept informed and can provide input. Also, during key times in the project, these users can be scheduled to participate in some way, even if in a limited manner. For example, during the prototype or conference room pilot segment is an ideal time for the users to participate. Testing is another point where user involvement is ideal. One thing to keep in mind: The users have the most impact on the success or failure of the implemented system. Understanding and acceptance is the key to that success.

Communication is critical to the success of the project as it begins, during the project, and after the project is complete. A good understanding of how important communication is and a good plan on how that communication will take place between team members, with management, and with users, is critical.

PART

V

CH

32

INSUFFICIENT BUDGET

"There is never enough time or money." "If we just had a little more time." "If we had a large enough budget, we could have done a much better job." The two most precious resources that any organization manages are time and money. Let's start with the subject of budget.

There are several troublesome issues with budget planning. The following is a listing of some of these issues and some ideas on how to handle them:

The organization has never done anything quite like this before.

It is a good idea to use the experience of others. Some good sources of information are PeopleSoft consultants. PeopleSoft consultants and project managers have experience with other PeopleSoft implementations and should be very helpful during the budget planning. Another good source of information is other PeopleSoft customers. PeopleSoft or its partners can help put customers in touch with other customers who have implemented PeopleSoft in a similar environment.

The budget must be developed and approved before enough is known about how much will be undertaken and how it will be done. The best way to prevent this from being a problem is to plan thoroughly and early. The sooner the planning begins, the more that will be known by budget time. No plan is ever perfect—after all it is a plan—but a detailed plan is much easier to use to create a budget than one that is very high-level and general. It is also possible to budget some contingency money. Add a line in the budget to deal with unforeseen costs.

UNREALISTIC TIME FRAME

The other precious resource is time. Projects are budgeted for both time and money, and in some cases, time becomes more precious than money. During the software selection process, critical events are usually identified. A critical event is something that prompts action. A common example is the famous Y2K issue (see Chapter 2, "PeopleSoft: Where It Came From and How It Fits," for more on PeopleSoft's solution to this). Many organizations found themselves in a situation where their systems would not support transactions after a certain date, usually from 24 to 6 months prior to January 1, 2000. The critical event became that date; the implementation must be complete by that date or serious problems would occur for the business. Other examples are the opening of a new facility or the merger of two businesses; or maybe the system presently in use will be inoperative at a certain date. When conditions such as these exist, time cannot be extended. The project must be complete by that critical event.

In other cases, management imposes a deadline, and even though no serious impact may come to the business, a serious impact may befall some careers if the project is not done on time.

ISSUES AND IDEAS WITH TIME FRAMES

You have been given a deadline that you know you cannot meet.

Phases for the project may help. Often it is desirable to structure the project so that some very noticeable results are obtained quickly. In almost any project, there are activities that can be postponed into a second phase without a serious impact on the business. Look at those processes that are not critical, and consider reports and inquiries that are "nice to have" but are not required to run the business. These are not easy choices to make, and plans must be developed to ensure that the later phases do happen—but it is better than delaying the entire project.

Here are some time issues you might encounter:

We can't get it done with only the team we have.

Often, projects are started with an insufficient number of people on the team. It may be possible to use temporary staff to do the day-to-day jobs of the team members to free them up for work on the project. It might be that job rotation can be done. Does the same person need to be on the implementation team full time for the life of the project or could two or more people rotate through that position? Another idea is breaking the work down into small activities that can be spread out among people who may not have the skills or knowledge to do the entire job. It might be desirable to have a team member do much of the setup data entry for knowledge gathering, but it could be done by less skilled people and done in less elapsed time. In the case of one PeopleSoft Select midmarket implementation of version 7.5 by Atlantic Duncans International (ADI) with a trade council, recently trained and experienced staff were brought in as needed to take care of some of the simpler tasks or the unexpected tasks that often show up during ERP projects. This utilization of temporary staff kept the project on time (and within budget!), because the core project team was able to concentrate on what it was assigned to do.

LACK OF SENIOR MANAGEMENT COMMITMENT

A very real potential pitfall for a PeopleSoft project is lack of management commitment. It is not enough to simply approve the expenditure and stop by occasionally and ask how the team is doing. Key management people must be an active part of the project. They must attend all regularly scheduled meetings. They must gain and maintain a good understanding of what is being done and how it is being done. They don't need to know all the details, but they must have a real interest and participate in the project directly. The team must have regular access to these key management people to help ensure that decisions that are being made will not conflict with other parts of the business and will not need to be readdressed or even overturned at a later time.

As discussed in other parts of this book, PeopleSoft projects impact the business; that is their purpose. Benefits cannot be realized without some change, and change is difficult and painful. When an organization undertakes a PeopleSoft project, it must experience some change to realize the business benefits that were the reason for the project in the first place. And change cannot be effective in an organization without key management support. Changes need to be reviewed and approved by the members of the organization who will be most affected by the change. It does no good for the IT department just to propose a change in an accounting policy or procedure; the accounting staff must support that change.

Without key management commitment, conflicts cannot be effectively resolved. All organizations have conflict; it is natural and a useful part of doing business. However, during system implementation, when those conflicts result in a stalemate because a decision cannot be made due to conflicting goals, the issue needs to be raised to a senior level quickly.

PART

V

CH

32

PITFALLS ASSOCIATED WITH PLANNING

"Now I see why everything is not going according to plan—we have no plan." One aspect of implementation projects that is almost always underappreciated is planning. Time taken early to develop a well–thought-out plan that involves as many parts of the organization as practical is time well spent. Successful PeopleSoft projects *must* be well planned before they begin. Imagine constructing a building by just getting a lot of carpenters, masons, electricians, and other skilled people together and telling them to go ahead. The chances of having a building where people could safely work or live are slim at best. But that is exactly what many organizations try to do with software projects. It is important to know that poor planning is one of the most common reasons why projects fail or provide only part of the desired benefit. *Plan to succeed!*

The topics covered so far in this chapter, while very important to a PeopleSoft implementation, also apply to other systems projects or projects in general. The following section addresses a potential pitfall that is slightly more technical in nature, and one that is more specific to PeopleSoft.

MAINFRAME VERSUS CLIENT/SERVER

PeopleSoft is part of a breed of business application software commonly called client/server applications. One characteristic of these applications is that they are based on client/server technology. The client/server technical architecture or environment will not be addressed here. However, it should be noted that business applications designed for a client/server environment differ from those designed for mainframe and so-called minicomputers. When managers begin work on a client/server project with only the knowledge they have gained working on mainframe projects, they could find themselves on the brink of a serious problem.

NEW SKILL SETS

Along with client/server technology came the need for a whole new set of skills: new programming languages, new hardware, networks, and even knowledge of the Internet. Client/server architecture makes use of servers, networks, one or more operating systems, and client workstations. That is only the core hardware and software. Many organizations find these skills either missing or underrepresented in their staff. If the organization has never done any client/server projects prior to implementing PeopleSoft, it is likely at least some or many of these skills will be missing.

First, PeopleSoft has its own proprietary languages, such as PeopleTools and PeopleCode. There are also some processes within PeopleSoft that might require knowledge of COBOL and SQR. Much of the training for this can be obtained through PeopleSoft's Education Services classes or the classes of several authorized training and consulting companies where other items, such as Crystal Reports, nVision, Process Scheduler, Workflow, are taught.

Then, network administrators or network operations managers are needed to set up and manage the network. Network staff often are responsible for the client workstations also, depending on the size of the organization.

Database administrators (DBAs) are required. DBAs possess knowledge that is unique to the operating system; so, for example, an Oracle DBA will not be the right fit if the operating system is Informix, DB2, or one of several others.

NEW TECHNOLOGY

Technology knowledge is also an important part of implementing a client/server application. In addition to having staff members who are trained in the specific skills, it is important for the Information Technology staff, the project team, and—in many cases—users, to understand how this new technology is deployed in a specific organization. To take full advantage of all this new client/server technology, the organization must understand its power and how best to apply that power to the business goals of the organization.

MORE CHOICES WITH CLIENT/SERVER

Just when the information technology world looked like it might settle down, along came client/server technology. One of the goals of client/server technology is *open systems*. Open systems mean the organization is able to mix and match hardware, software, databases, networks, and client workstations in the client/server environment. In the days of mainframes, and to some extent, the minicomputer, application software products ran on only one or an extremely limited number of hardware platforms. For example, a pension and benefits system written to run on an IBM 3090 was not transferable to a UNISYS machine or an NCR system. Products designed for a DEC PDP/11 didn't operate on an IBM System 38 or AS/400. The problem was that you may find the application software you want, but if you had other applications running on different hardware, you had a problem. Did you find the money to spend on the hardware-specific version of the other application, add a different brand of hardware, or what?

The IT community provided some answers. PeopleSoft's applications run on multiple platforms, databases, networks, and workstations. The organization must make decisions about how to deploy PeopleSoft. How about Hewlett-Packard servers running HPUX with Ethernet and NT4.0 workstations? or Compaq servers running NT4.0 with token ring and Windows95 workstations? All the options have decision points associated with them. Will the network be fast enough? Can more servers be added easily? Will Windows95 become obsolete too soon?

The world of client/server presents many more flexible choices, which mean more effective implementations and savings, but also mean more decisions. This brings the possibility of more problems and pitfalls, especially early in the project.

MORE VENDORS INVOLVED

There was a time when organizations purchased nearly all hardware and sometimes even the system software from one vendor and application software from another vendor. With a PeopleSoft implementation, in a client/server environment, that is not the case. Hardware can come from several different vendors. The servers are purchased from one vendor, the network hardware from one or more vendors, clients possibly from yet another vendor, and so on. Of course, on the software side, the database comes from one vendor, there may be middleware from another vendor, and finally the application from PeopleSoft.

PART

V

CH

32

This means it is time for a system integrator or integrators. The system integrator is likely to be yet another vendor. One or more implementation partner is almost always involved in PeopleSoft implementations, which means another vendor.

Having all these vendors can add significant complexity. The server might be one brand from one vendor, and the client is another. The networking software comes from a separate vendor and the networking hardware from yet another. In addition to the PeopleSoft applications, there may also be application software from other vendors. If the organization is not experienced in dealing with this, serious problems can result. Unfortunately, there is no easy way to simplify this situation, nor would that really be desirable, because it would eliminate flexibility; however, being aware of this complexity can help the organization prepare for the impact.

More Flexible Software

Part of this difference between traditional mainframe systems and client/server systems such as PeopleSoft is due to the flexibility of the client/server architecture.

When organizations first began to use computers for processing data, all the applications were custom-designed and written for a specific purpose for a specific organization. In time, packaged software was developed. (For a somewhat more detailed discussion, see Chapter 24, "Adaptation Versus Customization"). Although custom programs most frequently fit the specific organization's needs exactly, they take a long time to design and develop, or program. When packaged software applications came on the market, they dramatically reduced the time an organization had to commit to designing and programming the system. However, these products lacked flexibility and did not fit each organization's need as precisely as the custom systems. PeopleSoft is a sort of hybrid between custom-designed programs and packaged applications. PeopleSoft products are packaged applications in the sense that the design and programming is done; however, through use of PeopleTools and even third-party applications, PeopleSoft can be tailored to the specific needs of a company or a sub-unit of a company if necessary. This has a significant impact on how the implementation project must be planned and managed.

PeopleSoft is a very flexible system, and flexible systems require configuration, which leads to the need for some decision making on how that configuration will be done. In many—if not most—organizations, making decisions is one of the most time consuming and difficult processes that can be undertaken. Project planning for client/server products such as PeopleSoft is often done by people who have been through only mainframe projects in the past. The situation is quite different with a mainframe system (and this includes most mini-computer systems as well, such as AS/400, DEC, and so on). In most cases, the users were given little choice about how the processes would be implemented. These systems were too rigid to change easily, and therefore change was very costly in both time and money. The seemingly positive impact? Less time was required to implement the system. When the users were trained, there were only limited decisions to be made about how to set up the system. This differs dramatically from how a PeopleSoft implementation is managed.

The PeopleSoft products are designed with a great deal of flexibility. This leads to decisions on configuration, or how to set up the system, and also decisions about how the system will be used. The positive side of this is quite obvious; PeopleSoft can be set up to closely mirror many different business environments, and therefore works well in many types of organizations. However, sufficient time must be allotted in the project plan to handle these decisions.

Consultants in PeopleSoft's Professional Services Group (PSG) and partner implementation organizations are trained to assist the customers during this setup and prototyping work. However, often not enough time has been planned to actually carry out this work.

A More Dynamic Atmosphere

Change in business today is much faster than ever because of the globalization of the marketplace. The rapidity of change impacts a much larger part of an organization. Technology is a major cause of this, but it also suffers from the dynamic environment, which changes frequently. System projects of the past could count on a business environment that was likely to remain constant at least for the life of the project. Today, that is not always the case. Projects must take into account potential change to the organizational structure, the personnel involved, and even the ownership of the organization. Although it is not possible to plan for changes that are completely unknown, by structuring the project in certain ways, change is less disruptive. As mentioned earlier, the project can be planned in phases, with no phase longer than 12 months. Special emphasis can be put on how the project spans organizational boundaries, such as divisions, departments, and separate companies. Changes might take place in one part of the business but not another, or the project itself might precipitate change where none was anticipated. PeopleSoft products are developed with consideration for how they can work, not only with other PeopleSoft products but also with legacy systems and even competitor's products. This is a major advantage in today's dynamic world and may be exploited during an implementation project.

Another consideration is the frequency of new releases of PeopleSoft products. Along with new releases, of course, comes new functionality. The timing of those new releases and what new functionality they contain must be considered during the planning of the project. If a new release is only a few months away and the project is expected to last longer than that, some consideration should be made for how the new release might be included in the project. On the other hand, if a project is beginning just as a release is made available, it would be doubtful that delaying the project, even for new functionality, would be advisable.

Lack of User Involvement in the Planning and Deployment of the PeopleSoft Products

After more than three decades of using computer systems, user involvement would not seem to be a problem. But it is. It also does not seem that getting users involved would be all that difficult because most are aware of how critical computers are to at least their jobs, if not their lives. But it is. Generally if an organization has any experience at all with software acquisition and implementation, that expertise is in the IT department. Most users' knowledge is the result of their involvement in a similar project elsewhere or just from exposure to another project. This isn't sufficient to generate interest or involvement. Involvement in this case means participation in the planning of the project and all the subsequent phases. In fact, ownership is not too strong a word to suggest how involved the users should be.

So the first hurdle is how to get the user involved. The next significant problem is availability of those users. Users seldom have time to add any more items to their already busy schedule. Because projects of this type usually begin with a business need, the users are probably aware of that need. The ideal time to begin user involvement is early, during the process of requirements-gathering or definition. The user's role at this time is generally one of participating in meetings that are facilitated by someone from IT or by an outside consultant. The user needs to have input into this process to ensure that the real requirements are detailed, and the user takes ownership of this part. The most difficult feature of this is finding a person or persons to facilitate the process so that people feel that this phase of the project is providing real value and that their ideas and opinions are being recognized.

The software selection process, during which time different software vendors are presenting their products, should also include users for many of the same reasons. When a decision is made, the users, like everyone else, will need to live with the decision. What better way to ensure cooperation than to have them be part of the process? It is important that this be seen not just as an exercise, but that the users' input is considered as seriously as the IT department's. This is easier said than done. Few people in IT have any training in how to involve users in these processes. To avoid problems later, help should be sought to assist in getting the proper level and type of involvement.

The project planning phase is also a very critical time to involve the users. Their time is probably not fully committed to the project. By involving them in developing the project plan, real conflicts can be avoided.

Caution

Without good knowledge of the implementation process for this type of system, the users are likely to underestimate the amount of time needed. It is very useful to provide some education and training in how projects of this type are run and how long they typically take (and why) prior to the project planning sessions. This can be done through project management classes offered by many sources.

Acknowledgment is not acceptance. The users may acknowledge that their participation is needed and may even agree to a certain time commitment, but when the pace of the project quickens and that time is actually required, there may be serious reluctance on their part to accept their roles. Two things help in this case. The first is management commitment. People in organizations usually understand that their priorities are set at least in part by their management. If management sends a clear signal that the project is important, acceptance by the users is much more likely. Second, you should have an infrastructure that enables participation. Users cannot be expected to simply add several hours per week to their already full schedule. Temporary workers, job rotation, or some other means must be employed to free the users if they are expected to fully participate.

When the Project Size Is Too Large

Nothing is ever quite as easy as it seems in the beginning. One potential pitfall in PeopleSoft projects is a project scope that is too large to start with. Almost all projects will have some sort of scope creep—that is, they will end up involving more than was anticipated. Managing scope creep is difficult enough, but when a project is extremely large to start, it is even more of a problem.

How big is too big? The answer to this question is unique to each project. The experience of the organization and of the project manager or managers has a lot to do with how big a project can be without risking loss of control.

Another important scope consideration is availability of resources. If there are only enough people and enough money available to fund the project as it is planned, it is probably too big. Some contingency resources are needed. No matter how well planned a project is, some reserve must be available to deal with unforeseen items that might crop up. No one has ever been criticized for being early and below budget.

One yardstick used in determining excessive project scope is the definition of the length of time before some business results are seen. Any project that exceeds one year before business benefits are realized is worth close scrutiny. There cannot be a definite time limit, but one year is often as long as an organization wants to wait for results from a commitment of resources. Another reason for a one-year time limit is that projects that exceed one year often benefit from being broken into phases. There is an old saying: "By the yard it is hard; by the inch it's a cinch." When a project is broken into phases, it is often easier to manage. It can be easier to staff, easier to assess potential problems, and easier to identify results. In addition, people tire of projects that go on and on and never seem to close. It seems that when a really large project (and its staff) becomes institutionalized, it loses its effectiveness. Over time, people on the team become too far removed from the business, and the original goals of the project diminish or get lost entirely.

When sizing the project, let the business dictate what needs to be done. What critical business issues are being dealt with in the project? What is the timetable on those critical issues? After the critical business issues are dealt with, look for things to cut back in the scope.

Excessive Modifications

It would be unfair to expect any application software product to meet the business needs exactly. PeopleSoft products are designed to be as flexible as possible, but there may still be situations where modifications are required to get the product to meet the business need. The issue of change in business process versus modification is very important. Excessive modifications can be a very serious problem to both the implementation and the ongoing support of the system.

Although there are very few "plain vanilla" implementations, the risk of doing too many modifications is also a real one. Modifications require not only time and money to develop, but also present potential problems when they are integrated into the system with interfaces. Each potential modification should be looked at to determine whether it really needs to be done. Can the process be changed? Is there a workaround that will avoid the need for a modification? Will a future release of the product have the functionality that is needed?

LACK OF SKILLED RESOURCES

It seems that it is a new world when it comes to the resources needed for a PeopleSoft project. An endemic lack of skilled resources can create some real problems in a PeopleSoft implementation. The skills needed to manage a project of this type as well as serve as a team member are in short supply. This situation will likely change over time, but for the foreseeable future the demand for PeopleSoft skills will outstrip supply. This applies in many cases for other skill sets needed for a PeopleSoft implementation.

TECHNICAL SKILLS

Technical skills really fall into two broad categories. The first are skills that are PeopleSoft-specific, such as PeopleTools, PeopleCode, Application Engine, and other technical products that are part of the PeopleSoft product line. The second are skills that are not specific to PeopleSoft. These include database skills, network skills, SQR, and others.

In the case of PeopleSoft-specific skills, PeopleSoft and its implementation partners can be a good resource for those people. As mentioned before, PSG of PeopleSoft is an organization that can provide consultants who have both training and experience with these PeopleSoft tools. In some cases, PSG can also provide technical assistance in some of the more generic areas, such as database administration and network support. Another source of PeopleSoft-specific skills is PeoplePartners. These are firms that have a formal relationship with PeopleSoft and whose consultants have been trained by PeopleSoft consultants. They may have participated in release testing and other programs that give them exposure to the latest PeopleSoft products. PeopleSoft also identifies PeopleFriends. These are individuals who are working independently but have a relationship with PeopleSoft. A PeopleSoft Account Manager or PSG Practice Manager can provide contacts with PeoplePartners and PeopleFriends. There is also a complete listing of the PeopleSoft partners in Appendix C, "PeopleSoft Partner Program," of this book. Consultants with non–PeopleSoft-specific skills are often available through these same channels or through the partners as well.

PROJECT MANAGEMENT

Project management is an interesting mix of PeopleSoft-specific knowledge, general project management skills, and just good management talent. Many organizations feel that they can manage their PeopleSoft implementation with existing in-house managers. This is not always a wise choice. Many projects have encountered problems late in the process that could have been avoided if some outside assistance had been used early. Unless an organization has someone who has led a PeopleSoft implementation in the past, it would be wise to consider engaging a project manager with PeopleSoft implementation experience.

PeopleSoft, through the PSG or the PeopleSoft partners, also can provide project managers. In the case of PeopleSoft, this is most commonly done when PSG is engaged as an *implementation partner* with the organization that is implementing the PeopleSoft products. In the case of the PeoplePartner, this is usually done when it is the prime vendor for the implementation services contracted by the organization. In either case, the project manager will begin working with the customer very early in the project, possibly even before the final license agreements are signed. This provides the customer with information and experience early in the process and saves time and money.

FUNCTIONAL EXPERTISE AND PRODUCT KNOWLEDGE

The third type of consulting skills is product knowledge and functional expertise. This means consultants who have actually worked in a business similar to that of the customer. They may come with an accounting background, or possibly have been a human resource manager. They may have specific business experience in a financial services organization, a manufacturing plant, or the public sector. In addition, these consultants have a thorough knowledge of the PeopleSoft products they represent.

As with technical consultants and project managers, these consultants may be engaged as part of an agreement with either PeopleSoft PSG or a partner firm that runs for the length of the implementation. Alternatively, they may be engaged on an individual basis for a specific task. It is not unusual for both situations to occur during the implementation cycle.

PART

V

CH

32

SUMMARY

Throughout this chapter, the focus has been on pitfalls and how to avoid them. Many are generic and revolve around subjects such as communication, budgets, and planning. Some are more specific and appear in client/server systems implementations such as PeopleSoft. Usually, not all of these pitfalls appear in every project, but some most certainly will. Knowing about them and some possible ways to deal with them can help improve the project's chances for success.

As the System Rolls Out

CHAPTER 33

TRAINING, EDUCATION, AND SUPPORT

In this chapter

by Paul Greenberg

TRANSFERRING KNOWLEDGE ABOUT THE PEOPLESOFT APPLICATIONS

PeopleSoft is not simple. When implemented, it can be overwhelming. End users look at it and say, "How do I do this?" IS managers look at it and say, "What if it breaks down? Who do I talk to?" Consultants or employees on implementation teams say, "Where do I learn this stuff?" Luckily, the options for support and training from PeopleSoft and its partners are myriad. These include online help, telephone hotline, hard-copy documentation, tip lines, and Internet sites, to mention the main ones. In fact, PeopleSoft has become so well focused in this area, especially given its people-friendly corporate profile, that the company has grouped the training and support offerings under a single program called PeopleSoft Advantage. This chapter examines the numerous options available.

PEOPLESOFT ADVANTAGE

PeopleSoft Advantage was developed in 1998 to take care of the tasks of the full implementation lifecycle, which is often defined as the life of the application from the first thought of a new system through evaluation, selection, conversion, training, going live, and startup support. Though by no means the only offering for training and support in the PeopleSoft market, it is the most comprehensive on the market today. Its value derives from both its comprehensive nature and its accessibility. It is a combination of planning, toolkits, knowledgebases, methodologies, and training. It is available from the beginning of an implementation to ongoing support for the implementation through upgrades and training. In other words, you're covered from head to toe.

PRE-IMPLEMENTATION SUPPORT SERVICES

When the implementation is in its planning stages, it can be a confusing process to you, the customer. You have never been through this before. What if you indicate that you need something in the Statement of Work (the SOW is the contract between the customer and the system integrator) and then you don't need it? That could be a wasted several thousand (or tens of thousands of) dollars. "What if" becomes the operant for the earliest stages that come with built-in anxieties. To that end, PeopleSoft Advantage provides the customer with services ranging from strategic planning, comparative examinations, and Return on Investment (ROI) analysis. Needless to say, the services put PeopleSoft in a great light, but they are quite valuable in helping to determine whether you will get a good return on your PeopleSoft expenditures, and, if you will, how to plan for that in the early stages of the implementation. PeopleSoft will provide you with the Strategic Investment Model toolkit, which evaluates products purchased, implementation direction, and the costs to maintain this complex system. The results will show what the return is likely to be. You can maximize this return through strategic planning.

IMPLEMENTATION SUPPORT SERVICES

There is one certainty during the implementation—change in scope is inevitable. It is a virtual impossibility that every facet of an implementation or every user need can be anticipated at the start. Customization will probably be warranted in some areas that were not identified clearly in the Statement of Work simply because of previously unknown pitfalls or a customer's newly determined need or interest. PeopleSoft and its partners have had longstanding experience with this through collective thousands of implementations. Both PeopleSoft and its partners have professional service organizations that are available to help determine how to handle these changes best.

Tip

Change in scope can also be expensive. The Statement of Work binds PeopleSoft and its partners, but any significant changes necessitate a change order, which is often costly. Each implementation partner has its own way of dealing with change and its interpretation of the magnitude of change. Some are lenient; some are very strict. If you are planning an implementation, set out the parameters prior to the implementation for how change orders will be handled. This can save you a lot of money and heartache later.

PeopleSoft Advantage offers several implementation services that are typically included with the cost of the application license or the ongoing maintenance contract:

- Implementation-specific services such as PeopleSoft Express, the rapid implementation methodology designed to speed up the efficiency of the implementation, and the Express Implementation Toolkit, which provides models and tools that represent best practices from 1987 to date.

- Offsite lab facilities including the PeopleSoft Global Support Center, which tracks technical and functional difficulties with PeopleSoft and provides both personalized support during the implementation and a substantial knowledgebase of problems and solutions gleaned from the hundreds of version 7.5 and prior version implementations over the past years.

- The PeopleSoft Application Upgrader is a toolkit that is part planner, part ROI analyst, and part marketing. In part, it provides change management tools, allowing you to see how the changes that you are making now will impact an upgrade in the future.

- PeopleSoft Plugged In is an email newsletter with the latest information on PeopleSoft for you, the customer.

- The Customer Connection is a Web-based extranet for PeopleSoft customers only. All customer-related services including online technical support, white papers for those interested in deeper knowledge of the products or of specific business processes, education services and class schedules, and a myriad of other offerings are available 24 hours a day, 7 days a week. This carries well beyond the completion of the implementation through post-implementation care and maintenance.

POST-IMPLEMENTATION SUPPORT SERVICES

Post-implementation is usually the knottiest phase of support. There are an unbelievable number of tasks that have to be accomplished for knowledge transfer from the implementation team to those MIS folks that are going to maintain the system. Additionally, this is the point where the end users have to learn how to use the system and be comfortable with it day to day. This is where consideration has to be given to the future of the system—are there going to be future customizations and/or point upgrades or full upgrades? There is also an "angst factor." Nerves get frayed when it is time to take over and fly yourself. What if there are problems?

Never fear, PeopleSoft is here! In addition to the availability of the Customer Connection, PeopleSoft has developed a significant post-implementation support capacity that can be contracted for at extra cost. Contact your PeopleSoft representative for specific scope and costs.

- Customer Care Business Center—This is designed for solving ongoing business problems such as contract maintenance.

- PeopleSoft Advisor Program—PeopleSoft provides subject matter experts related to the modules you've installed. For example, if you have Payroll installed, PeopleSoft will provide content on year-end close and changes in the tax laws that you might need.

- Professional Services Organization—These are the PeopleSoft consultants who are there to not only provide implementation support through complete teams, but also incremental support for upgrades, technical problems, and any other services that need rapid onsite attention.

Additionally, there are the aforementioned Global Support Center and the Customer Connection.

The PeopleSoft Global Alliance Partners can provide similar services. When you buy the PeopleSoft software licenses, you buy the right to utilize these services whether a partner does the implementation for you or PeopleSoft itself does.

TRAINING AND EDUCATION

Despite the friendliness of the company and the easygoing modularity of the software, the learning curve is steep—and it isn't cheap. For example, the typical commitment to train a single General Ledger user could exceed 8 to 10 days and $5,000 plus travel expenses. Training is a necessary part of the success of any PeopleSoft implementation and its aftermath, otherwise known as "use of the product." Whether you are a partner or a customer, training is as essential as the implementation itself. Luckily, as we move to the millennium, and—as Internets, extranets, and intranets become *de rigueur*—the variety of options available increase. The increase in both offerings and delivery methods makes the cost of training more efficient, and the knowledge transfer more effective.

PEOPLESOFT UNIVERSITY (PSU)

PeopleSoft has consolidated its training and education offerings under PeopleSoft University. Both its partners and its customers can attend multiple course offerings covering all recent releases of all PeopleSoft modules in a variety of environments. Course delivery is done at the PSU, onsite, online, and soon, via satellite-based distance learning straight to your desktop. This is what you can look forward to when you need a PeopleSoft education.

CUSTOMER/NON-PARTNER TRAINING

There are abundant programs that are offered to you as a PeopleSoft customer or you as a non-partner PeopleSoft consultant or company. The partners are welcome to take these courses too, but they have several programs that are made available to them beyond the ones outlined here.

INSTRUCTOR-LED COURSES FOR LICENSED CUSTOMERS

The most popular and most old-fashioned PeopleSoft course offerings are instructor-led courses. Held at more than 100 PeopleSoft facilities around the world or, if given by an end user partner at an authorized partner facility, these courses cover the gamut of PeopleSoft modules and technical tools. Classroom instruction is hands-on and the class size is limited to no more than 14 people. These courses are ordinarily where customer implementation teams and PeopleSoft consultants are given functional and technical training.

For example, new course offerings from PeopleSoft include

- Enhanced PeopleTools I and II courses, which add business process models, reporting options, debugging, and other technical advances
- Advanced Technical Curriculum including

    PeopleSoft Globalization, which takes advantage of the version 7.5 globalization features

    Executive Overview of PeopleTools

    Advanced SQR for PeopleSoft

    EDI Manager

    Overview of Enterprise Performance Management

This is offered in addition to the more than 100 classes on existing modules.

PART

VI

CH

33

Tip

Be smart and register early for these classes. PeopleSoft is often booked months in advance for any given module. Even though the burden has eased a bit with the certified Partner Service Providers, the backlog is still heavy.

A typical course sequence would involve functional training in a number of areas. For example, Payroll r.6.0, Payroll Foundation 7.5, Payroll I 7.5, Payroll I/II 7.5, Payroll II 7.5, and Payroll Interface 7.5 would be available for Payroll module trainees. The course sequence would depend on factors such as how quickly they have to be ready to implement Payroll. If the need is urgent, they could take the Payroll I/II five-day course rather than the "more leisurely" Payroll I and Payroll II six days of courses.

If travel is a problem, PeopleSoft and partners will ordinarily make arrangements for onsite training under various circumstances.

Tip	Even though it might be stating the obvious, make sure that training both internal implementation/maintenance teams and end users is built into the initial contract and statement of work. An oversight like this might be very costly later.

COURSES FOR NON-LICENSED CUSTOMERS

A limited series of 26 courses is available to non-licensed customers in the PeopleSoft Pro course (see the section "PeopleSoft Pro Certification"). The courses are primarily fundamentals and overviews for application and business process design, PeopleTools, various modules, and third-party products such as Crystal Reports and Essbase.

END-USER TRAINING (EUT)

PeopleSoft and its partners offer a wide variety of end-user training options. The glue for almost all the offerings is the PeopleSoft End-User Training (EUT) courseware. The creation of these materials came from the dramatically increased demand from customers and partners for end-user training over the past two years. PeopleSoft staff realized that to maintain the quality and integrity of their instructional materials and to standardize the training and still meet the demand sufficiently, they had to develop resources that would be amenable to a necessarily fast-paced learning environment. The result was the EUT materials.

The EUT courseware is flexible and customizable. It consists of an Online Library, Student Exercises, and Training Services.

THE ONLINE LIBRARY

The Online Library is the core of End-User Training. This is an easily navigable knowledgebase that logically follows the modules you have implemented. Each module has an overview/introduction that has hyperlinks to specific information that is highlighted in the introduction. Following the introduction is a more detailed discussion of the fundamentals of the module and then a step-by-step instructional manual on how to follow critical-path PeopleSoft procedures. Instructions can be as high level as how to use the menus in the Online Library for specific business processes identified in your implementation.

STUDENT EXERCISES

What are classroom materials without tests? The EUT materials provide three levels of exercises:

Level 1—A single procedure with inclusive steps that are defined by the Online Library.

Level 2—Multiple procedures with inclusive steps.

Level 3—Scenarios that have no formally defined steps with the Online Library as a reference.

END-USER TRAINING SERVICE OFFERINGS

The ability to customize the End-User Training materials is one of its biggest advantages. Both PeopleSoft and the implementation partners in the PeopleSoft Services Provider (PSP) program can customize the Online Library and the student exercises to client specifications. If you want to bring it in-house, there are workshops in customizing and delivering End-User Training for your employees. Further courses are available to partners in managing projects in End-User Training implementations.

The instructor-led part of this offering can be done either by PeopleSoft or its partners at your site or, in a more limited way, at either PeopleSoft or a partner training facility.

The current EUT instructional materials offerings are General Ledger, Payables, Human Resources, Payroll, HR for Canada, Receivables, Purchasing, Benefits Administration, and, finally, Time and Labor. Several other offerings are in the offing.

PEOPLESOFT CERTIFIED SERVICE PROVIDERS (PSP)

PeopleSoft has elected to work with a number of business partners to educate them and maintain a high level of competency in their knowledge of PeopleSoft applications. These partners must complete a specified series of courses and demonstrate proficiency to be considered as qualified by PeopleSoft. Most of these business partners are qualified in various degrees to assist customers with system integration and implementation services. In addition, some are qualified to assist with user training, system upgrades, and customization services. These business partners should be contacted directly to determine their current offerings and capabilities.

As of mid-1999, the following companies were certified PSPs:

> Andersen Consulting
>
> Answerthink (formerly Delphi Partners)
>
> Bianco Hopkins
>
> Cambridge Technology Partners
>
> CSC Pinnacle
>
> Deloitte and Touche

PART

VI

CH

33

Ernst & Young LLP

The Hunter Group (A Renaissance Worldwide Company)

Noblestar Systems

PriceWaterhouseCoopers

RWD Technologies

ROMAC International

Sierra Systems

Technology Solutions Company

Usertech

PEOPLESOFT PRO CERTIFICATION

PeopleSoft Pro certifications are 32 role-based courses that fall into four basic tracks. This is something like the "be all that you can be" program for PeopleSoft. The concept is simple. You are an HR professional or a financial professional or a manufacturing and distribution professional or a technical guru. Within these four tracks, there are roughly eight job roles that have specific courses identified for them. When you've gone through the recommended course series, you are a "pro" and can receive a PeopleSoft certificate stating that you have completed this path. See Table 33.1 for an example of how this process works.

> **Caution**
>
> This path does not mean formal certification. It simply recognizes that you have completed a course of study successfully.

TABLE 33.1 AN EXAMPLE OF A JOB-ROLE-BASED COURSE SEQUENCE

PeopleSoft Pro for HR Professionals: Payroll Interface Pro

Course
PeopleTools I or PeopleTools Foundation
SQL/SQR for PeopleSoft
Introduction to Human Resources
Introduction to Benefits
Payroll Interface

ONLINE SERVICES

PeopleSoft is moving into the next millennium with a strong Web-based focus in its applications. This extends to the training programs too. From the standard EdWeb offering, which allows you to register courses online, to the advanced PeopleSoft

Knowledge Broadcasts, a satellite-based distance learning initiative, PeopleSoft is covering all online bases for the year 2000. Read on for more detail.

PeopleSoft Knowledge Broadcasts

One of the most exciting 1999 education initiatives has been the PeopleSoft Knowledge Broadcasts. This is a fine-tuned form of distance learning.

Distance learning is traditionally done via satellite. The PeopleSoft Knowledge Broadcast system involves both satellites and PCs, and through a point-and-click interface allows fully interactive learning in real-time with instructors. The courses can be small or large, at the workplace or at a central facility. There is no need to even use the corporate network. The Broadcast capacity includes real-time interaction with the instructor and classmates with live questions. Additionally, multimedia-based instruction is supported including animated materials. The current offerings include overviews of all the major modules and several offerings such as Service Industries Industry Overview, and Public Sector Industry Overview. It also includes more sophisticated courses—Managing Your Human Capital-Knowledge Management, Preparing to Go Live, and Projecting Your ROI with the PeopleSoft Strategic Investment Model—a cornucopia, indeed.

PeopleSoft Knowledge Center

The PeopleSoft Knowledge Center is a Web-based online learning center that provides self-paced learning in basic PeopleSoft and PC skills. There are three flavors being offered through 1999.

The Content Edition is the core offering. Its purpose is to offer you or your employees a Web-based training program in the fundamental skills such as Navigating PeopleSoft Menus or Introduction to PeopleSoft RDBMS. It is delivered straight to the desktop through a corporate intranet.

The Competency Edition includes the Content Edition and job roles. The job roles training is an organized path toward more specific responsibilities. This edition allows customization and development of courses, exercises, and assessment tools. This is a PeopleSoft-focused course development tool.

The Enterprise Edition includes all the skills in the Content and Competency editions but is integrated into the PeopleSoft HRMS module so that you can manage individual skills development efficiently. This edition is expected before 1999 ends.

PeopleSoft Performance Solutions

This is one of the lesser services that PeopleSoft offers, but one could have some importance to a few strategic customers. This is an online service that identifies "knowledge gaps." In other words, it identifies what knowledge and performance management practices need to be implemented to effectively improve corporate competence in those areas and then measures that same performance improvement.

PART

VI

CH

33

EdWeb

The EdWeb service is offered through the Customer Connection and allows you to check the current group of course offerings and availability and then register for those courses—online.

PARTNER TRAINING

The demand for training has exceeded the supply of instructors and has stretched the PeopleSoft bandwidth. Consequently, PeopleSoft has wisely created programs for business partners to be certified in teaching their instructors to train customers. These programs put the partner through a rigorous certification process including observation of the partner courses by PeopleSoft-employed instructors prior to the partner's certification as a Training Partner. The result? The PSU Masters Training Program.

PSU MASTERS TRAINING PROGRAM

The PSU Masters Training Program is the crown jewel for partners who want to train clients. PeopleSoft's three-week Train the Trainer (TTT) program both trains the partner instructors and provides partner training delivery tools that include case studies, business process maps, troubleshooting data, and reference data. During the first two weeks, the partner trainer trainee is in an intensive classroom environment with nightly homework and exams—all those things that make adults remember and shudder. Following that, a qualification week is arranged within 90 days of completing the TTT course. During this week, a PeopleSoft instructor who determines whether or not the instructor is qualified to teach observes the partner instructors. Currently, Intro to HR, Intro to Benefits Administration, Purchasing, Payables, and Benefits Administration are available under this program.

SUMMARY

When it comes to education, PeopleSoft is an innovative company. From its traditional instructor-led courses to its distance-learning hybrids, the Knowledge Broadcasts, the more than 100 courses provide you and the partners doing your implementations with extraordinary opportunity to not only know what you are doing, but to measure its return—a fine result, indeed.

THE ENTERPRISE WAREHOUSE

In this chapter

by Ari Katanick

The operational data that resides in your PeopleSoft ERP and HR applications is your company's lifeblood. Your PeopleSoft system manages the vital information about your financial operations, products, business processes, and personnel, and a multitude of other information. However, trying to access this information for decision support purposes can be difficult for several reasons:

- PeopleSoft's systems are transaction-intensive, and its database table structures are highly normalized. PeopleSoft comes delivered with thousands of tables with complex interrelationships. These tables have been optimized for transaction processing, and reporting from these tables doesn't produce optimal performance.

- To support decision making, you may need to consolidate data from several source systems. Your operational data may be located in several places, on several different systems and platforms. This creates a challenge for consolidating this data.

- Decision support reporting may require aggregating information or joining several database tables. Reports of this type can be server-intensive in nature, and this can create a performance impact on your mission-critical PeopleSoft applications.

For these reasons, implementing your PeopleSoft applications is only the first step in creating an enterprisewide decision support system. You cannot manage your operations with your ERP and HR applications alone. You need to consolidate information from all your various production systems, aggregate and enrich that information, and then create high-value reports from this information. Today's business climate demands that enterprises leverage their operational data by turning it into information that enables more effective business decisions and helps companies gain a competitive advantage. To aid you in this cause, PeopleSoft delivers its Enterprise Performance Management (EPM) line of products.

PeopleSoft's EPM line is composed of three types of products (see Figure 34.1):

- PeopleSoft's Enterprise Warehouse is the backbone of the EPM line. It is the main repository of enterprise information. The Enterprise Warehouse extracts information from PeopleSoft applications and other sources to stage, store, and make information available for analysis purposes.

- PeopleSoft's Analytic Applications are rule-based applications that transform data into management information. These applications perform complex calculations to build decision support data, such as cost management, product and customer profitability, and capital return on investment. PeopleSoft's current Analytic Application offerings are Activity Based Management (ABM), Funds Transfer Pricing (FTP), and Risk Weighted Capital (RWC).

- PeopleSoft's Workbenches are a set of role-based, predefined report templates. These templates report from the enriched data resident in the Enterprise Warehouse. The Workbenches are built using PeopleSoft's DecisionMaster reporting tool, which will be discussed in more detail later in this chapter.

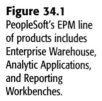

Figure 34.1
PeopleSoft's EPM line of products includes Enterprise Warehouse, Analytic Applications, and Reporting Workbenches.

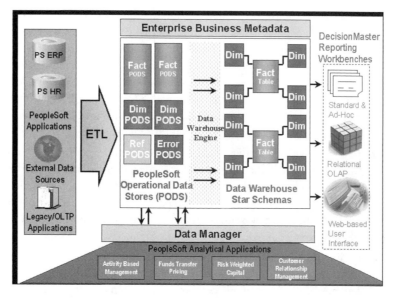

THE ARGUMENT FOR BUILDING A DATA WAREHOUSE

A data warehouse is used to consolidate, standardize, integrate, and then serve data consumers. The data in the warehouse is stored in table structures that are optimized for reporting and not transactional in nature. The purpose of the data warehouse is to facilitate the downstream decision making process. This is in contrast to the application efficiency and throughput purpose of your transactional PeopleSoft systems.

Why should you build a data warehouse? There are several reasons why you would want to take on this type of project:

- To offload reporting from your PeopleSoft transactional systems—In order to ensure that your PeopleSoft transactional processes complete in an acceptable amount of time, you want to limit the number of nontransactional activities that occur on your system. By offloading reporting, you free server processing time for those mission-critical transactional needs.

- To create table structures that are optimized for reporting—Your PeopleSoft application table structures are optimized for transactional processing. Reporting from the delivered structures may be difficult and take lots of processing time. By creating table structures that support reporting, it will be easier to build reports and will improve report processing time.

- To provide an environment with tools that ease report creation—PeopleSoft's Enterprise Warehouse is set up so that simpler queries and reports can be written by less technically knowledgeable personnel. This will free some of your IS department from its user support activities. This will also eliminate your end users' wait time for the IS department to produce the reports they need.

- To provide a repository of information that encompasses your PeopleSoft systems, other production systems, and even external data—A data warehouse combines information from many of your production systems and external data to create a single source for reporting. Information from external sources and legacy systems that were previously unavailable in reports can now be included for use in decision support. By having a single source for reporting, it also frees the end user from having to identify the system that houses the data. Having a single source also enables you to consolidate your various production systems' reporting personnel.

- To provide an avenue that enables you to store information for a longer span of time— Your transactional system may require only a year's worth of data for transactional processing. Your reporting needs may require you to store information for a longer duration. To report year-to-year comparisons, you need to store several years' worth of information. A data warehouse enables you to store more information without affecting the performance of your transactional system.

- To provide a mechanism that improves the measurement and visibility of corporate performance—Traditionally, management teams don't have the business information they need to make strategic decisions. By building a data warehouse and decision support system, you provide management with data that reflects the performance of the company. These performance measurements can also be subdivided by business unit, department, or customer. This creates a full view of corporate performance and also a method of finding areas of improvement.

- To prevent people who only need to query and report transactional information from having any access to your PeopleSoft or other production system databases—The users of your data warehouse will have a different security schema than your PeopleSoft transactional users. Security for reporting reflects an "allowed to know" access, and security for your transactional PeopleSoft systems reflects an "allowed to affect" access. By building a data warehouse, you prevent "allowed to know" users from having any "allowed to affect" access to your PeopleSoft or other production systems.

- To have the ability to align your information with your corporate strategy—Developing a data warehouse provides a consistency of data content and structure across your various applications. This consistency helps ensure that the information focus is the same as your corporate focus. A data warehouse can ensure that your users have the information they need to implement your corporate strategy.

- To have access to informational knowledge that can give you a competitive advantage— Your organization may have already spent billions of dollars on IT projects that have focused on automating manual processes to improve efficiency. As more companies improve their processes, your efficiency advantage becomes less apparent. You can now focus on arming your managers with better information to enhance decision making and to improve the effectiveness of management decisions. This effectiveness advantage is what a data warehouse will provide for you.

Building a data warehouse isn't an easy task. To help you with this, PeopleSoft delivers the Enterprise Warehouse. The Enterprise Warehouse comes delivered with several tools, templates, and technologies to help you build your corporate warehouse.

INTRODUCING PEOPLESOFT'S ENTERPRISE WAREHOUSE

PeopleSoft's Enterprise Warehouse is the complete set of tools and technologies that make up the framework behind PeopleSoft's EPM line of products. These tools and technologies include integration with ETL tools, a data warehouse engine, data enrichment tools, integration with third-party reporting tools, and an analytical reporting tool (DecisionMaster). This chapter explores these tools and technologies in further detail.

EXTRACT, TRANSFORM, AND LOAD (ETL) TOOLS

The first steps in building your data warehouse is to extract the data from your source systems; transform that data into a consistent, meaningful, and usable state; and load that data into PeopleSoft's Enterprise Warehouse. An ETL tool manages the process of extracting, transforming, and loading the data. To do this, PeopleSoft partners with four ETL vendors. These vendors are Acta, Ardent, Informatica, and Prism. All four vendors needed to pass a certification process that included demonstrating the following:

- The ability to extract from PeopleSoft application tables (support PeopleSoft version 6.0 and up)—The ETL vendors were asked to create prebuilt physical data models for PeopleSoft's applications. These models are delivered as templates with the Enterprise Warehouse and are updated and maintained by the ETL vendors. The flexibility of the ETL tools enables customers to easily modify the data within the Enterprise Warehouse by adding or deleting data elements or by integrating data from your other production systems.

- The ability to extract from non-PeopleSoft sources—This includes, but is not limited to, DB2, VSAM, and flat-files. The ETL vendors were required to be able to maintain several simultaneous connections, not only with PeopleSoft application databases, but also with non-PeopleSoft applications, data, and platforms.

- The ability to capture and handle changed data—The ETL vendors needed to show the ability to identify changed data from the source systems and to process it correctly. The ETL vendors also needed to be able to identify duplication of data and determine whether a set of data had already been processed. This feature prevents the same record from being inserted more than once.

- The ability to apply complex transformations and aggregations—PeopleSoft's ETL partners have graphical tools to create cleansing and transformation rules by selecting from included arithmetic operators and functions. These transformations are then performed in memory by the ETL processing engine. These in-memory transformations result in higher performance and enable greater flexibility than performing them in native SQL. The ETL partners needed to show the ability to aggregate detail records to summarized levels.

- The ability to insert, update, and refresh data in the Enterprise Warehouse—The vendors also needed to be able to perform bulk loads with high throughput performance.

- The ability to filter source data according to user-defined rules.

- The ability to validate data according to predefined rules—This includes, but is not limited to, referential integrity and invalid data types. The ETL partners had to adhere to PeopleSoft's Error Processing design when building its templates (see Figure 34.2). This design included the need to capture error data and write these errors, with appropriate messages, to PeopleSoft's Error PODS. The ETL partners were also required to support the reprocessing of a batch of data if the errors were manually corrected using PeopleSoft's Error Modification panels, or if a decision was made to back out a batch load and reprocess it.

Figure 34.2
PeopleSoft's ETL partners had to adhere to PeopleSoft's Error Processing design.

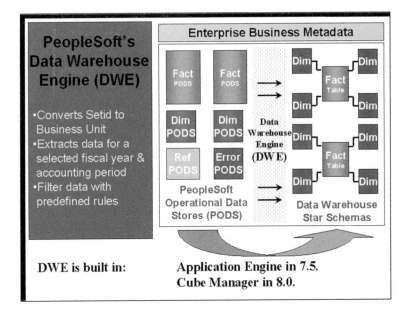

There are many advantages to using an ETL tool over building custom interface programs. ETL tools feature point-and-click graphical tools for modeling your extractions, transformations, and loads. These tools save development and maintenance costs by housing all your warehouse's interface efforts in one location. The ETL tools support many platforms and environments, and this enables you to concentrate your efforts on data cleansing rather than on data movement. The ETL tools are easy to use and implement. The graphical design tools are process-oriented, and your existing IT resources can learn to use these quickly and easily without having to write custom code. The ETL tools provide scheduling software that incorporates event- or time-based scheduling. This enables easy automation of the warehouse building process and easier system administration and maintenance.

The PeopleSoft ETL templates offer you many time-saving features. PeopleSoft's ERP and HR systems house thousands of tables, and finding the data that is needed in them is not always easy. In addition, PeopleSoft uses data structures such as trees and effective date tables that are difficult to write queries from. The ETL templates identify the tables required for PeopleSoft's Analytic Applications and Workbenches and also contain prepackaged transformations that simplify and facilitate the extraction of Trees and effective date records. Each of the ETL partners provide ready-to-use ETL templates to extract and transform PeopleSoft source application data and load PeopleSoft's Enterprise Warehouse.

PeopleSoft will bundle Informatica's ETL tool and the appropriate templates for the Enterprise Warehouse in future version's of EPM. This doesn't mean that they will terminate its relationships with its other ETL partners. It only means that PeopleSoft will deliver and support Informatica's tools and templates and that the other ETL vendors (Ardent, Acta, and Prism) will deliver and support their own tools and templates.

PeopleSoft Operational Data Stores (PODS)

The ETL tools load their data into the PeopleSoft Operational Data Stores (PODS), which is housed within the Enterprise Warehouse. The PODS store information that is transactional in nature. This information is retained for a short period of time (generally not longer than three months). The PODS are used to integrate information from the source systems and to provide this data as input for PeopleSoft's Analytical Applications. The Analytical Applications enrich the data in the PODS, and then the data becomes a source for the data warehouse's Star Schemas.

PeopleSoft delivers four types of PODS:

- Fact PODS store data containing measures (numeric data, such as posted total amount, inventory count, and so on). These PODS contain the meat of your raw decision support data and will be the basis of the Analytic Application's calculations.

- Dimension PODS contain textual descriptions and attributes about business entities (code translations, such as department or product codes and descriptions). Dimension PODS are used to further define the keys of the fact tables and are used for multidimensional reporting.

- Reference PODS contain normalized common attributes about a fact or dimension (code translations that are shared, such as employee and manager IDs). This simplifies maintenance of data and reduces the amount of table space required. Reference PODS may serve more than one Dimension or Fact PODS.

- Error PODS contain errors identified in the data migration process. All Fact PODS have corresponding Error PODS. Errors are typically missing or invalid attributes of facts or dimensions. The Error PODS include an Error Message table that identifies and documents the type of error that occurred.

THE DATA WAREHOUSE ENGINE

The purpose of the Data Warehouse Engine (DWE) is to move, aggregate, and filter data from the PODS to the data warehouse star schema structures. The DWE also converts the dimension table's SetIDs to business units in order to make access to the data easier for the end user to understand for constructing queries.

Star schemas are built for simplicity and speed. Their design is intuitive for an end user, and they are optimized for multi-dimensional reporting. They are also easy to maintain, and their design reduces the number of necessary joins to do reporting. PeopleSoft builds its star schemas with a single fact table that may hold detail and summary data. Positioned around that fact table are several dimension tables that are highly denormalized. The fact table's primary key contains only one key column per dimension. Each dimension is maintained in a single dimension table. Star schemas do not follow classic relational database design because their tables are considered static (that is, updates are not done online). So, it is acceptable to break database normalization rules when designing star schemas in order to optimize access for reporting.

PeopleSoft's Application Engine, a set processing tool, supplies the power behind the DWE in its current release (version 7.5 of EPM). In future releases, PeopleSoft's Cube Manager will supply the power behind the DWE (version 8.0 and beyond). In release 8.0, Cube Manager will begin support of building star schemas from a combination of a detail source and PeopleSoft tree. For more information about the capabilities of PeopleSoft's Cube Manager, please see Chapter 4, "PeopleTools Reporting."

The differences between the PODS and star schema tables are summarized in Table 34.1.

TABLE 34.1 PODS AND STAR SCHEMA DIFFERENCES AT A GLANCE

PODS	Star Schemas
Keyed by SetID, Dimension ID, and Effective Date	Keyed by Business Unit and Dimension ID
Normalized Tables	Denormalized tables
Stores current rolling month	Aggregated into accounting periods
Supports PeopleSoft's Analytical Applications	Supports PeopleSoft's Reporting and Workbenches
Used for data enrichment and storage	Used for data presentation
Table prefixes: Fact table (_F00) Dimension tables (_D00) Error tables (_E00) Reference tables (_R00)	Table prefixes: Fact tables (_FCT) Dimension tables (_DIM) History tables (_HST)

Figure 34.3
PeopleSoft's Data
Warehouse Engine
(DWE).

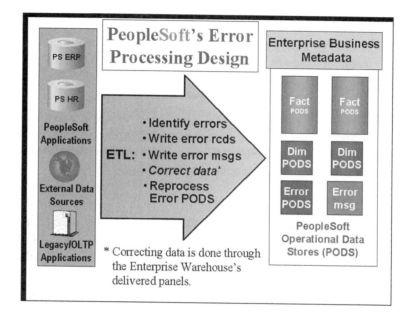

DATA MANAGER

PeopleSoft's EPM line comes delivered with several data enrichment tools. These tools are used by the Analytical Applications to enrich the warehoused data for decision support. Data Manager is one example of these enrichment tools.

Data Manager is a very powerful allocation engine. It can apportion a source measure (such as costs, revenues, or account balances) to a target table with one to many dimensions (such as allocating cost over customer and product). Data Manager offers several methods of allocations:

- Copy—This type of allocation copies the raw PODS data from the source to the target without changing the numeric values of the data.

- Spread Even—This allocation type apportions the measure of the source evenly to the target.

- Prorata—This type of allocation proportions the source measure to the target through a predefined calculation.

- GL Mapper—This allocation type apportions PeopleSoft's General Ledger account balances to EPM's Ledger accounts.

- Tree Aggregation—This type of allocation aggregates measures based on the hierarchy defined in a PeopleSoft Tree.

PART

VI

CH

34

REPORTING AND WORKBENCHES

PeopleSoft delivers all its standard reporting tools with its EPM product line (see Chapter 4 for more information on PeopleSoft's standard reporting tools). PeopleSoft also includes two additional reporting tools with EPM: Actuate and DecisionMaster. PeopleSoft's Workbenches are built using these other tools.

EPM reports can be used to view key performance indicators, view summaries and exceptions, review rules, validate engine output, and assess organizational performance relative to business initiatives. PeopleSoft delivers a number of reporting templates with EPM that enable you to produce valuable analysis with little customization.

ACTUATE

Actuate is an object-oriented Web-reporting tool. Actuate reports are created with drag-and-drop screen painting similar to Crystal Reports and have the same complex programming logic available with Sqribe's SQR. Actuate reports can be scheduled, executed, secured, and distributed with their delivered Report Server.

Actuate reports are "live" documents. Report objects can contain "links" to other reports or sections of the same report. Actuate stores data with its reports, and this enables much more sophisticated searching than with just pure text searching. Actuate reports can be distributed via its client software or through its Web agent. Actuate reports may also be generated as HTML and distributed via a URL address.

Actuate's Reporting tools are integrated with PeopleSoft's PS/Query product through the Open Query API. Release 7.5 of EPM is delivered with approximately 35 Actuate reports that display application engine output, validate models, and report on profitability.

DECISIONMASTER

DecisionMaster is a browser-based, analytic reporting tool that is developed by PeopleSoft and leverages Information Advantage's ROLAP engine. DecisionMaster can perform ad hoc, analytical, and rule-based exception reporting. The ad hoc reporting tool is easy to learn and use. This allows end users the freedom to write their own queries against the star schema tables in the warehouse. By allowing your end users to service their own reporting needs, your IT organization can be freed to perform more productive warehouse development activities. End users' self service also eliminates their need to wait for IT to code their reports.

DecisionMaster reports are "live" reports. After a report, is run, an end user has full analytic abilities for data exploration. The end user can drill up and down on the hierarchies, rotate the axis, and/or do calculations and subtotaling. DecisionMaster's rule-based exception reports reduce your end users' report examination time by presenting information to them only when it hits alert status. DecisionMaster provides multicolored exception highlighting to enable you to specify different types and levels of exceptions. DecisionMaster's ad hoc, analytical, and rule-based exception reporting give your end users the tools they need to service their reporting needs.

DecisionMaster is flexible to meet the needs of all user types in your organization. It offers several different user interfaces to accommodate the diverse types of end-user skill levels. There is a separate interface for power, casual, and auto-fed users. These interfaces also can be customized to meet your organization's individual needs.

DecisionMaster provides automated, publish, and subscribe report distribution. An end user can subscribe to a set of reports and when they are run, they will be delivered (published) for the end user to view. DecisionMaster's browser-based interface makes it easy to deploy its reports and ad hoc tools. The Web-based user interface enables you to initiate, retrieve, and view any reports. It also enables you to manage your inbox, subscriptions, the master report library, report scheduler, report security, and personal folders. This gives you the added convenience of going to only one place for all your reporting needs.

DecisionMaster supports both NT and UNIX platforms. This enables it to be scalable to support any size organization while keeping the tool's performance at acceptable levels. DecisionMaster's tools are all HTML-based, which also means there are no plug-ins for you to administer.

In summary, DecisionMaster is a decision support analytic tool that provides rule-based exception reporting, ad hoc reporting, and online analysis in a graphical, browser-based environment. Using DecisionMaster's reporting capabilities will improve your strategic decision making ability by providing accurate and timely exception-based reports and by allowing your users to interactively analyze this data further through slicing and dicing.

WORKBENCHES

PeopleSoft's Workbenches are a set of industry-specific, role-based predefined DecisionMaster reports and queries based on the information stored in the Enterprise Warehouse. Workbenches provide "out of the box" reporting that also includes built-in calculations for company metrics and key performance indicators. These predefined reports save developer time and enable a faster return on your PeopleSoft EPM investment. The workbenches also enable you to change the delivered reports and to add new custom-built reports. This enables you to fully customize the Workbenches to support your organization's unique informational needs.

DATA WAREHOUSING WORDS OF CAUTION

PART

VI

CH

34

Although PeopleSoft delivers the basic structure, enrichment, and reporting for your data warehouse project, you might still run into the following problems:

- You might find problems with the data in the source systems that feed the Enterprise Warehouse. Some of these problems might have gone undetected in your source systems. At this point, you need to decide where to fix the problem. It may take a long time to get these problems fixed in your source systems, so you may have to "temporarily" fix them through the ETL transformation.

■ You will discover a need for data that isn't currently captured in any of your existing systems. In this case, you will be pressed with the decision to either build a custom system, buy a software vendor's system, or modify an existing source system to capture this data.

■ You might need to spend a lot of research time during the transformation step of the ETL portion of the Enterprise Warehouse implementation. The departments defined in your PeopleSoft HR system might not match those in your PeopleSoft ERP system. Your PeopleSoft ERP data may be stored at different levels than the detail from your other source systems. These issues tend to creep up while building a data warehouse because you are forced to standardize facts and dimensions based on source systems that may have been developed and implemented by different IT people in your organization and at different times. These issues may create the need to build transformations that can identify and match customer names stored in two different systems that have two different formats. During the transformation step, you might also uncover different deviations of the same customer name within the same source system. These source system and integration problems create the need to validate data through the ETL tool, and you will need to spend much time configuring the ETL tools to handle your complex data transformations.

■ The full cycle of loading, enriching, and presenting the warehouse data will take a lot of CPU time. In order to benefit from the Workbenches and reports, you must first extract, transform, and load the data into the PODS. After loading into the PODS, you will enrich the data by using the tools and rules within the Analytic Applications. After enriching the data, you need to aggregate and present it in a format optimized for reporting. DecisionMaster and your other reporting tools then need to build and distribute their reports. All these processes need to run before the end user can see the information they use to make their business decisions. All these processes take time to run, and you need to plan your data warehouse building window appropriately. Luckily, the data in your warehouse is used for decision support, and this enables a more lenient batch processing window.

■ You will be challenged to avoid scope creep. When the end users start to understand the power of their new reports and Workbenches, they'll ask for more information. The best way to avoid scope creep is to release the warehouse in several phases. Building and maintaining your data warehouse will be an ongoing development initiative. After each phased release of the warehouse, your end users will want you to add more data, dimensions, and reports. This enables you to add benefits with each release of the warehouse while providing a useful system for your end users.

■ The system that you are building will be a high-maintenance system. Although PeopleSoft is providing you with the basis on which you will build, changes to your existing source systems may require changes to your data warehouse. These changes, in combination with new requirements from your end users, require your organization to build and maintain a long-term, competent warehouse IT staff.

SUMMARY

The information that makes up the PeopleSoft ERP and HR applications is some of the most vital of a company's information structure. The PeopleSoft Enterprise Warehouse system manages the vital information about your financial operations, products, business processes, personnel, and a multitude of other information.

PART VII

Taking PeopleSoft to the Next Millennium

CHAPTER 35

PEOPLESOFT 2000 AND BEYOND

In this chapter   *by Paul Greenberg*

A Look at the Future

As we get closer to the new millennium, most companies are installing software that will solve or patch their Y2K problems. Since November 1997, PeopleSoft has been repositioning itself to not be just a Y2K software in the eyes of clients or a dramatic fix for the customers' Y2K problems. In a sense, there was a customer perception of PeopleSoft as Y2K software with a whole lot more. Now, PeopleSoft has, more or less, altered that perception to be more like: "We are what your entire corporation needs for its engine and the foundation upon which all else may rest." PeopleSoft's applications as they are now deal with Y2K, or the January 1, 2000 problem, and much of the appeal of ERP software and a good deal of the reason for its sales has been the rush to Y2K compliance. But what happens after 2000 is here? What does PeopleSoft plan to do so that you still want it?

PeopleSoft Defines Its Strategy for 2000 and Beyond

PeopleSoft's solution-concept is actually consistent with its philosophy and the content of its applications: understand the market demand, listen to what the potential clients want, and respond to those demands/needs by building the appropriate enterprise-level applications. What does that entail? First, recognize that Year 2000 issues end in the year 2000. Second, recognize that corporations are looking for the easiest and most cost-effective ways to work. They don't want to be bothered with having to choose 50 different companies to define their IT needs. They would prefer one. Third, recognize that globalization doesn't mean spreading the enterprise across the world in multiple locations. It means integrating all business processes with a single product across those multiple multilingual locales. How? PeopleSoft Advantage and PeopleSoft Enterprise Solution Assembly Architecture— industry-focused solutions and business process models. Behind these rather lofty names are fundamental business applications that look at the millennium as an opportunity to make PeopleSoft more than just a big fix to the Y2K problem. In principle, should PeopleSoft succeed, they will be ubiquitous across the enterprise by 2000, having penetrated the pores of the financial and human resources processes of any given company that does business with them.

There is one other significant recognizable change that is applications-related. In 1998, for the first time, PeopleSoft service revenues outstripped software license revenues. Although not a critical factor to your company, it will have dramatic impact on how PeopleSoft does business with your company in the ensuing years. It means that value-added services and products will be how PeopleSoft expands its offerings to make them "complete."

PeopleSoft Enterprise Solution Architecture

In PeopleSoft's millennial vision, when it becomes the application suite of choice to a company, it will mean all things to all people. Its applications and services will be as important as the operating system or relational database or hardware layers that it is built on. You will depend on PeopleSoft for all your mission-critical applications except perhaps your word processor. To that end, it created the PeopleSoft Enterprise Solution Architecture, a domain of products and services that provide specific corporations in specific industries with the means to run their entire enterprise and account for all their business processes, including all internal and external sources such as suppliers and vendors.

PeopleSoft E-Business Strategy

Studies in early 1999 from various analysts came up with a curious fact. ERP implementations have a net Return on Investment (ROI) of negative dollars. The number varied, but more than one study reflected a dollar loss when using classic measurements for ROI determination. However, these same studies indicated that the direct benefit measured with these benchmarks was not truly sufficient to value ERP. With additional investments in several areas such as analytic applications, front-office applications (for example, Siebel or Vantive sales and marketing applications) or e-commerce, the ROI skyrockets beyond what each of those extended areas would return by themselves. As of 1999, as the traditional ERP markets slow, PeopleSoft announced an aggressive e-business strategy to define the push to the millennium.

PeopleSoft E-Commerce Strategy at 40,000 Feet

The twenty-first century is the era of e-business. Across the globe, e-business has been awkwardly defined as e-commerce, that is, buying services and products over the Web or doing banking over the Web or any number of Web "transactions." There has been a redefinition of the nature of the future model corporation, also awkwardly, as the "virtual corporation," a combination of Internet, intranet, and extranet features that combine the core business entity with its suppliers, vendors, and customers. Although there is truth to this, the reality is more the current buzzword for this network ecosystem. Current corporate reality is a highly integrated chain of suppliers, vendors, and customers that are symbiotically functional.

PeopleSoft's e-business inspiration is to layer this process utilizing its own applications by integrating them with other applications (e-business backbone), providing a gateway (e-business portal) to Web services such as Employee Self Service (ESS), grouping the applications according to domain such as procurement or human resources (e-business communities), and providing global service opportunities both internally or externally within these communities (e-business merchants).

PeopleSoft Business Network

PeopleSoft has taken this inspiration and molded it into a single applied vision, The PeopleSoft Business Network (PSBN). The PSBN is an extension of PeopleSoft applications and a reflection of its corporate culture. From the first day that David Duffield founded the company (see Foreword and Chapter 1), customer service was a priority. The PSBN both reflects the contemporary market reality and is founded on strong customer service commitments. Conceptually, PSBN is a network that combines Internet, intranet, and extranet enterprise value chains through electronic Web-based portals to provide total product/services/transaction capacity in a visually interesting fashion.

PART

VII

CH

35

Each enterprise will be able to effectively utilize an entire set of customer, vendor, and employee transactions within a company (an e-business community) or from external sources (e-merchants program). All this is combined under the PSBN (not to be confused with the sports channel).

Electronic Communities

Electronic communities are the Web-enabled core content delivery units of the PeopleSoft Business Network. They are components organized around discrete business processes, that is, Benefits Administration or Human Resources and the personnel involved with that process. The community brings together the necessary resources to allow a person with a role in a particular domain, such as a Benefits Coordinator or Personnel Manager, to utilize all the products and resources to make his/her job easier, more effective, and hopefully, transparent.

For example, there are Workforce Communities that include employees and managers that might involve recruiting, training, or procurement. Because this is an extremely large community in numbers of staff, it might involve the groupware "community," which includes email, calendaring and scheduling, and other groupware functions. There are also Executive and Expert Communities supported by the e-business backbone, which can use the Balanced Scorecard and the Enterprise Performance Management tools (see next section) to analyze and monitor the benchmarks that characterize organizations. Finally, there are communities of Suppliers, Customers, and Producers, also known as the supply chain.

E-Merchants

An e-merchant is a certified business partner who provides services or products to the communities. These are the suppliers in the supply chain. They are PeopleSoft users who might be involved in supplying specific services in benefits administration to the users of the PeopleSoft Benefits Administration module. These e-merchants will be screened and approved by PeopleSoft before they enter the "community." PeopleSoft will function as the "Homeowners Association" to assure the potential customers of quality and good service.

E-Backbone

The e-backbone consists of enterprise-specific applications and content. The form varies—analytical, transactional, static, collaborative, singular, and so on—but the backbone provides the convergence of the information so that it can be managed and published effectively to those who need it or, in some cases, want it. This is the information technology nucleus of the PSBN. It consists of management resource applications such as financials and human resources; it consists of transactions hubs, event and workflow engines, integrated application links, and a universal security platform. All told, this is the centerpiece of the entire PSBN network.

E-PORTAL

The portal is the gateway and interface to the communities for role-based personnel. It will provide highly compelling content via attractive interfaces that will be personally customized to the individual type of user and eventually the specific user. The user accesses a particular community through a portal. The portal gateway, which in concept is no different than Yahoo, defines the view to the user. It also can link to other portals and other communities. In its ideal form, it would be the gateway to an extended enterprise that would consist of role-based communities.

PEOPLESOFT ENTERPRISE PERFORMANCE MANAGEMENT

PeopleSoft Enterprise Performance Management consists of measuring-stick applications jointly developed with KPMG that are loosely called "analytic" applications. The concept is in part a consistent derivative of Enterprise Resource Optimization (see Chapter 2, "PeopleSoft: Where It Came From and How It Fits"), which simply identifies the need to rapidly respond to changes in the marketplace by changing the business processes and procedures and technologies across the enterprise. Analytic applications are designed to enable better decision-making and identify measurement benchmarks to reduce risk and improve cost- and action-effectiveness at all levels of an organization.

In 1997, PeopleSoft introduced its Performance Measurement system, the forerunner of Enterprise Performance Management. The measurements for this software product were based on the work of Dr. Robert Kaplan and Dr. Robin Cooper of the Harvard Business School, who called the new breed accounting "Stage IV" and defined it in the following way:

> "Year 2000 Management Reporting and Control Systems will be fully integrated, with a common set of information, entered once and accessible to all, supporting both internal and external reporting. The management systems will provide performance information for operational and strategic control, and accurate measurement of product and customer profitability."
>
> *Introduction to PeopleSoft Performance Measurement: An Integrated Financial System to Enhance Decision Making and Organizational Performance*—White Paper, by Tom Mescall and David Ogden, October 1997

The foundation for Performance Measurement was the Activity-Based Costing (ABC) proposals of Doctors Kaplan and Cooper. Critical to this concept was the idea that there were essential performance measurements that were not numerical, yet as critical to the bottom line as the dollars and cents that were normally used to value success. These measurements were often things such as customer service, product design, business process re-engineering, innovation, and learning, among others. All these intangible and tangible measurements needed to be integrated into a system that could identify, through analysis, the value of a person, process, company, network, or any other identifiable unit. This is the foundation of the now-classic book by Dr. Kaplan, *The Balanced Scorecard*.

PART

VII

CH

35

ENTERPRISE PERFORMANCE MANAGEMENT—1999 AND BEYOND

Performance measurements and business process analyses are now a mainstream part of contemporary enterprise performance. With the rapid growth of information technology and the implementations of complex information systems, CIO and CTO careers rise and fall on the success or failure of the choices they make. Entire companies can be forced into collapse by bad decisions. How do you integrate the information provided by a multiple number of databases that are often on different platforms or tied into legacy systems? With all this disparity, how do you then identify the measurements? Are they geography, finance, innovation, education, service, or all of these? What are the impacts of the day-to-day realities and results on the strategic planning by the company? Analyzing this increasingly complex series of processes, transactions, and static identifiers is the basis for Enterprise Resource Management.

ENTERPRISE WAREHOUSE

The enterprise warehouse is the repository of all data, regardless of source of the information. It draws all the data for analysis from PeopleSoft, legacy systems, and other databases. It uses the Extract, Transform & Load (ETL) technology to extract data from any third-party source and transfer it to the Enterprise Warehouse. From here, the tools for analysis can go into action.

PEOPLESOFT BALANCED SCORECARD

The Balanced Scorecard is the command and control center of the analytic tools. It consists of benchmark performance indicators as outlined in Dr. Kaplan's *The Balanced Scorecard*. It is a tool that allows executive management to determine and communicate the strategic direction of the enterprise through the measurement of such indicators as financial performance, customer knowledge, and business process effectiveness down to the level of the individual.

PEOPLESOFT WORKBENCH

The Workbench consists of either functional or role-based user interfaces designed for specific content subscription. What this means is that it allows a user with a particular responsibility such as manager, coordinator, or employee to receive specifically defined information in an area such as Human Resources or Accounting and Control and then analyze and share the information with the appropriate colleagues.

THE ANALYTIC APPLICATIONS

The analytic applications investigate the information in the Enterprise Warehouse to allow management to make strategic and tactical decisions based on how the information is analyzed and presented.

ACTIVITY BASED MANAGEMENT (ABM)   Activity-Based Management (ABM) is an application that measures strategic cost assessment and multidimensional profitability. It is both an application and a methodology developed by Dr. Robert Kaplan, Dr. Robin Cooper, and KPMG Peat Marwick.

Funds Transfer Pricing (FTP)   Not to be confused with File Transfer Protocol, Funds Transfer Pricing (FTP) assesses costs and credits across a balance sheet to provide new means of looking at financial product profitability for Financial Services institutions. It is aimed at the association of interest expense with particular products in any given enterprise. This was developed in conjunction with Andersen Consulting.

Risk Weighted Capital (RWC)   Risk Weighted Capital (RWC) is an application that examines real Return on Investment by looking at inherent risk through multiple levels of capital allocation. It prices risk associated with a transaction. It is integrated with FTP. It was developed in conjunction with Andersen Consulting.

Total Compensation Management (TCM)   Total Compensation Management (TCM) analyzes the effectiveness of changes in policy and its impact on organizational performance.

Asset Liability Management (ALM)   Also developed in conjunction with Andersen Consulting, Asset Liability Management (ALM) incorporates global best practices for assessment of risk based on external practices including market impact on holdings and investments.

All the preceding are far from the only value-added solutions that PeopleSoft is adding to its arsenal in the new millennial era. E-commerce and slicing and dicing the data for strategic analyses are the most attractive parts of the new PeopleSoft dimensions. They are broad and wide-ranging, suitable to any data in any enterprise or for linking any "community of enterprises." That deals with the horizontal developments, but what are the vertical, more narrowly focused new domains?

Industry Solutions: Templates & Maps

Vertical markets are fast becoming part of the PeopleSoft millennial strategy. The corporation restructured in 1998 by creating three divisions, each of which had a general industry focus, and subunits with specific industries, such as health care, retail, public utilities, and so on. To facilitate rapid implementations and prepackaged modules, PeopleSoft has developed industry maps that identify the modules that are needed to provide specific industries with what they need. They are also releasing templates that are accelerated versions of the methodologies necessary to implement the modules for a specific industry.

Globalization in a Single Package

One dilemma that PeopleSoft had to solve was how to handle the multinational growth of the corporate world. One prior approach ERP companies had used was the provision of localized versions in the appropriate languages, but this did not utilize the power of the applications to centralize information in a commonly accessible wrapper. However, PeopleSoft recognized that multiple cultures; different sets of ethics and work practices; national, local and international legislative differences; and vastly different currency systems would make the problems insurmountable unless some common ground was identified.

Common business practices and thus best practices are identified and presented in coherent packages such as global HRMS. PeopleSoft not only is developing these global enterprise packages but also has designed a Global Strategic Investment Model to try to identify the benefits and potential return on global enterprise investments in PeopleSoft.

Now we have e-commerce, analytic applications, vertical specificity, and globalization. These are all new and not the original meat-and-potatoes of PeopleSoft. But how is PeopleSoft reshaping that meat-and-potatoes? The company built its foundation on its fuzzy relationship with its customers and staff. Yet with the year 2000, a new approach to the old standard is also necessary.

PEOPLESOFT ADVANTAGE: TO THE ADVANTAGE OF THE CUSTOMER

PeopleSoft's reputation was established with its emphasis on customer-friendly service. However, with PeopleSoft Advantage, it takes on a new dimension. PeopleSoft customer service now includes pricing models, time-efficient implementations, and implementation tools for the internal customer project teams that make life and business processes much friendlier. The following sections discuss these components.

PEOPLESOFT EXPRESS: THE FASTEST ROUTE ON THE IMPLEMENTATION PATH

The fixed price implementation model became popular in the mid-1990s, pioneered by Cambridge Technology Partners. This model originally was intended to provide a definitive cost for an implementation rather than the standard time and materials hourly rate that had prevailed. Lowering the stress levels of CIOs and CTOs was its original purpose. If you know for sure that there is a certain cost, the risk is shared between the customer and the contractor. If it goes over the projected project date, the customer loses nothing because he is paying the same price regardless of time or scope increase. However, as the '90s ended, it became apparent that fixed didn't mean cheaper necessarily. Implementations either were planned for time and materials, or were fixed so they would last a year or more. This could be deadly in any very competitive sector because the time to do the implementation could eat into the time to improve the business that the implementation was for. Thus rapid implementations were born.

Rapid implementations, regardless of ERP package, have a certain generic feel. They are a combination of toolkits and templates, well-established methodologies, built-in business processes, and best practices. The idea was to make the implementations cheaper and faster. By late 1997, PeopleSoft had developed the Select program, using a rapid implementation methodology called SelectPath for midmarket companies defined as being under $250 million in revenue. Aside from the standard features mentioned earlier, SelectPath's unique defining characteristic was the use of best-of-breed software such as Seagate Software's Crystal Reports for report writing, Convoy for data migration, Rational's SQA for testing and Sqribe's SQR for authoring (used universally in much of PeopleSoft's customization). PeopleSoft developed a considerably larger scale rapid implementation methodology called

DirectPath. Due to the success of the program and the increasing client clamor, in late 1998, PeopleSoft announced a much-refined rapid implementation program called Express. The core of Express was the PeopleSoft Implementation Toolkit, with standardized templates and tools. The implementation time is reduced to months for multiple modules. In mid-1999, Express was just beginning to penetrate the PeopleSoft community.

PEOPLESOFT LIFECYCLE TOOLS

These tools are part of the Advantage Program announced at the 1998 PeopleSoft Users Conference. They are Web-based knowledge management tools and templates based on more than ten years of PeopleSoft business process experience. For example, one of the templates is the "Application Features Checklist," which enables a project team to understand specific features so that the assessment time during a gap fit analysis is shortened. The other templates are "Table Setup Sequencing" and "Data Conversion Mapping." The Application Features Checklist is augmented with four implementation models that have been used successfully on PeopleSoft projects. The combination is designed to help you determine what steps, processes, and activities will work for your project.

Note

Knowledge Management, a term made popular by Jeff Papows, President of Lotus Development Corporation, is a recently ubiquitous and little understood term. It has been defined from a level as simple as document management–the storage of documents from different sources–to the far more complex issue of how to effectively analyze and utilize vast stores of information from multiple sources.

PEOPLESOFT IMPLEMENTATION TOOLKIT

The PeopleSoft Implementation Toolkit manages the project activities, documentation of implementation decisions, and project facilitation. There are two primary types of models used in the toolkit: process models and data models. The process models depict the routes and business process flow of your organization. The data models are entity-relationship diagrams that provide detailed pictures of the PeopleSoft application data structures and their relationships to each other. Additionally, implementation process models and setup process models are also provided by the toolkit.

The other major piece of the Implementation Toolkit is the Implementation Workbench. This is an automation tool for work management, documentation, and object migration for a given implementation.

Work management features track project personnel, tasks, time estimates, and progress.

Documentation features document the above and store it in a knowledgebase to prepare for future upgrades.

Object migration features are used to easily transfer completed work from one environment to the next as it goes through the phases of setup, prototype, testing, and training.

PART

VII

CH

35

PEOPLESOFT REPOSITIONS ITSELF TOWARD THE FUTURE

PeopleSoft's steps into the next millennium are actually both a dramatic repositioning of their products and a straightforward extension of their present position. They recognize that being implemented for their Year 2000 compliance goes away on January 1, 2000 and the euro became the real deal on January 1, 1999, so the foundation for the red hot ERP market is going to be altered in the near future. PeopleSoft's repositioning is simple. Extend customer service directly into the enterprise solutions and prepare for the virtual corporation by building new tools, making the applications far more customer-friendly and useful, and providing the services to integrate it all, despite disparate sources. This way PeopleSoft becomes not just an ERP application set, but instead an enterprisewide set of applications that provide a nearly complete set of business processes and tools and database repositories to run your entire business—a good future for a great application and company.

> **Note**
>
> PeopleSoft and ERM: One of the hottest current markets is Enterprise Relationship Management (ERM), a k a Customer Relationship Management (CRM). These are true so-called front office applications, applications designed to handle such day-to-day operations such as sales and marketing. While applied to a company with the benefits of PeopleSoft and all the data behind it, the ERM applications return enormous value. To that end, even though they did not develop their own products, PeopleSoft allied themselves with Siebel Systems and Vantive Corporation, two of the largest companies in the ERM/CRM world, both of whom have serious Web-based customer management tools that encompass inventory management, call centers, customer information, analytic marketing and sales tools, demand planning, and several other critical features that can use the full benefit of PeopleSoft.

SUMMARY

All over the world, people are planning parties to celebrate the next century. IT departments are fearful of the next century because they have no clue what will happen with the triggering of the so-called Millennium Bug. As we head toward the final months of the century, the ERP market is slowing down because the IT departments have been implementing last-minute Y2K fixes, rather than supporting very large implementations. Yet, although a slowdown is forecast, there is growth for PeopleSoft in the air. Why? Because the company chose to change the way ERP is perceived. No longer the big, best back engine, but instead a sleek application set that not only integrates all your business functions and information systems, but can now slice and dice and analyze your data, provide a community for your e-commerce needs, and knock down implementation time. As PeopleSoft implementations go from the back end to the front end and from large time-consuming projects to sleek short-term ventures, you can save enough time to go join those celebrants at the hotels on January 1, 2000.

APPENDIXES

Working with Systems Integrators

In this appendix

by Jennifer Caria and Paul Greenberg

All things start as a concept but rapidly become real if agreed upon. One of the "realest" things that all enterprise decision makers in the IT kingdom must decide is who they are going to use to do their PeopleSoft implementation. There are a myriad of choices, but, fundamentally, it boils down to three types of service providers: the vendor itself, a large integrator, or a small integrator. All have their advantages and disadvantages. Which one is used is a complex corporate decision beyond the purview of this appendix.

WORKING WITH A SMALL INTEGRATOR

The most enigmatic of the three choices is the small integrator. Why should you use the most resource-poor of the lot? As enigmatic as the question is, the answer is easy. Flexibility and pricing are the advantages.

A small PeopleSoft provider is characterized by annual revenue in the range of $3–$50 million. The PeopleSoft practice usually has between 30 and 200 consultants, and the market that they ordinarily work in is the midmarket, which is defined by PeopleSoft as an enterprise with revenues under $250 million. The best small integrators are usually Service partners of PeopleSoft through its Global Alliance Partner (GAP) program, a highly selective partnership program developed by PeopleSoft in the late 1980s to weed out those companies that didn't meet rigorous standards defined by the vendor. Currently, there are roughly 60 of these partners, large and small, in the services sector.

The true value of the smaller partner is flexibility and pricing. If you are interested in using a partner of PeopleSoft, big or small, you know that it has met a rigorous standard, so the quality of its work is at least going to be good. The smaller integrator uses its size to stay close to the customer need. Often, it uses the classic PeopleSoft methodologies to do its implementations because it hasn't had the size or the need to develop its own regular or rapid implementation methodology. Smaller integrators are able to work more closely with the client because their size forces them to integrate with the client tightly. The client need becomes the partner need.

Pricing is more than competitive, because the smaller integrator has more to prove than the larger well-established company. The senior staff at the smaller integrators will often have multimodule experience because they need to cover more territory due to the smaller size of the company. The advantage is that the same consultant can work continuously on a project, and the client knows the caliber of that consultant throughout. There is less cycling of consultants, which often goes on during larger lengthy projects, because it is in the interest of the smaller firm to keep its billable staff on long-term assignments.

A good case in point is Atlantic Duncans International (ADI), a Chantilly, Virginia–based ERP consultancy specializing in staff augmentation and midmarket implementations. This double-edged business strategy has given ADI's 300-plus consultants a wealth of experience they otherwise would not have had. ADI implementation team staff members often cut their teeth on the larger integrator/partner projects that were beyond ADI's then-current scope. In turn, these consultants became the leads of ADI teams as they gained experience in multiple PeopleSoft modules and in technical and project leadership.

That piggybacking gave ADI strengths that weren't the norm in PeopleSoft consultancies of ADI's size, because their best consultants became part of their implementation teams.

Pricing is also a small consultancy advantage, especially in this era of small client budgets. Because of the competition among the hundreds of small firms, the standout smaller firms are those that not only differentiate themselves with expertise but also distinguish themselves with price.

FINDING A NICHE

It is often hard to distinguish between the myriad of small consultancies out in the marketplace—another reason that many potential clients steer clear of them. However, the smartest of the smaller firms finds a niche they might dominate; for example, a vertical market specialty, such as PeopleSoft implementations in the utilities domain; or a horizontal specialty, such as the Employee Self Service market; or even a modular specialty, such as the PeopleSoft supply chain offering or one called Time & Labor. The results often lead to a practice that has more experienced project teams in its niche than the largest integrators or even the vendor may have. That can allow a small company to dominate the market. It also provides serious comfort to the client because of the small integrator's experience.

That type of strategy is increasingly important to small integrators. For example, Live Wire, Inc., a Boston-based PeopleSoft and e-commerce consultancy, has focused its expertise in the PeopleSoft Student Administration modules. Although Live Wire has been involved in many non–Student Administration modules, such as Time & Labor or the suite of PeopleSoft Financials, it is gaining an increasingly good reputation as a specialist in both Student Administration and the e-commerce–focused aspects of higher education. That makes Live Wire a prime candidate for work at the campuses that need the newly announced PeopleSoft eCampus Community product, the e-commerce–enabled version of PeopleSoft's Campus Community.

"Even though our expertise has extended beyond just the Higher Education market into areas like the financial services, retail, and high tech services industries, we made a decision to become expert in PeopleSoft Student Administration to distinguish ourselves from other equally-sized and even larger integrators," said Nachi Junankar, president of Live Wire. "This gave us not only a differentiator, but a value to our clients and partners that couldn't be found too many other places. It also allowed us to focus on creating an excellence that we could not have done if we were just generalists."

Small integrator? Large integrator? Whether your company chooses either one is subject to multiple internal decisions. However, it is good to know that there are small companies out there you can trust.

WORKING WITH A LARGE SYSTEMS INTEGRATOR

When searching for your organization's PeopleSoft integrator, it may appear that the quickest selection approach is to match integrator size to organization size. Many large integrators identify themselves as linked to organizations with revenues over $250 million, such as in the Fortune 1000. Some integrators, as is the case of KPMG LLP, find they have the flexibility of scope and knowledge to reach the midmarket client, as well. This adaptability makes them extremely appealing to a multitude of market prospects.

In the PeopleSoft space, most of the large system integrators are recognized PeopleSoft service partners who have met the high-level standards needed to be a Global Consulting Alliance (GCA) partner or a participant in the less strenuous Global Alliance Partner (GAP) program. Held to a rigorous selection process, GCA partners, like all Service partners in the PeopleSoft GAP program, have met and exceeded critical standards for service, support, and size. Only a handful of the 60 or so GAP program members are termed GCA partners as well; the bulk of GCAs are defined as the Big Five consulting organizations.

This level and scope of alliance as a GCA partner or large integrator provides the PeopleSoft customer with a significant array of benefits in system integration. Among them are depth of knowledge and capabilities; comprehensive services, which stretch beyond the ERP implementations; global coverage; and PeopleSoft investment.

KNOWLEDGE AND CAPABILITIES

Without a doubt, the large integrator brings to the customer a wealth of knowledge and capabilities. If it first appears that the large integrator is too broad and impersonal, it should be levied with the information that the sheer scope of the integrator's size means that consultants are available at all client locations and throughout multiple geographies—regionally, nationally, or globally. This ability to respond to the client's geographic needs allows the large implementer to deploy practitioners to the locations where the client does business, often in multiple teams and across multiple geographic lines.

It is not just the physical capability that is impressive, but also the ability to deploy knowledge. The PeopleSoft market defines the client into seven industry groups. The implementer must understand those client industries, too. In the case of KPMG LLP, a global staff of nearly 1,100 PeopleSoft practitioners carries the message that PeopleSoft implementations can be successfully staffed and managed for clients virtually around the globe. No closeness to, or understanding of, the client is compromised as a result of size; rather, the increased number of practitioners allows the large integrator to staff the client engagement with the right capabilities, both technically and functionally. The client connection is extremely tight and intact, perhaps bolstered even further with the knowledge that such a dedicated and significant investment is made to the client.

"The amazing depth of our practitioner knowledge is demonstrated not only in terms of their understanding of the PeopleSoft product, but in relation to that of the client's businesses and their industries. The over 13.5 year average of KPMG practitioner's consulting experience is a momentous force which we are able to offer to our client's PeopleSoft investments," stated Michael J. Donahue, KPMG managing partner and PeopleSoft Global Partner-in-charge. "The scope of our practitioners' consulting intelligence and industry understanding interconnects us to the client; the interplay of the provider/customer integration team is what leads to our numerous substantial successes." KPMG LLP deploys its

PeopleSoft practitioners through six mirroring industry-based lines of business, with dedicated PeopleSoft implementers receiving upward of 160 hours of product training annually.

COMPREHENSIVE SERVICES

Another massive differentiator of the large integrator may be its array of service beyond the PeopleSoft ERP implementation. Many of the GCA partners have capacities to integrate diverse packages and systems. As is the case with KPMG, PeopleSoft implementations can be enhanced by KPMG comprehensive knowledge in areas such as architecture, Web development, infrastructure, data security, and systems integration. Brought to the implementation are well-rounded consulting strategy and process skills, including services such as change management, program management, and business transformation. KPMG's versatility may encompass the offering of outsourcing services.

The GCA and large integrator may also be able to enhance the PeopleSoft implementation with specialized products that increase the customer's total value of the PeopleSoft product. For example, in providing what GCA partner KPMG calls an end-end end solution, impacting supply chain or customer value management, the PeopleSoft implementation becomes even more integrated and meaningful to the client's technical and strategic structure.

"KPMG sees our PeopleSoft implementations as a huge opportunity to assist clients not only from an ERP standpoint, but as the total organization. We are poised to assess client needs, develop integration plans, and work with them to help ensure that large-scale organizational rewards are reaped. These benefits springboard from the smart initial decision to implement PeopleSoft," said Donahue.

GLOBAL CAPABILITIES

The global stretch of the large integrator is not limited merely to the practitioner's physical ability to be staffed at the client site, wherever it may be. It is the partner's ability to encourage the initial implementation on a global scale when strategic demand suggests this is necessary. This means that the partner's geographic offices, worldwide knowledge and solution centers, and comprehensive services are fixed firmly on the client's global map.

What does all this mean in real terms? It means understanding the geographies, regulations, and standards of the governments, cultures, and business norms where PeopleSoft clients operate. It means creating an organized structure to use this global reach and knowledge. KPMG LLP has found solid rewards for its PeopleSoft clients and for itself by organizing globally focused Swat teams. Its purpose is not only to carry well-shaped marketing, sales, and client relationship approaches to the global scenes, but to assist in further development of KPMG PeopleSoft practice work through the establishment of KPMG offices and centers worldwide. As an example, KPMG's three National Solution Centers, which study and develop information on PeopleSoft implementations and provide technical assistance on topics such as upgrades and infrastructure, serve as the model for the ongoing organization of global centers. Such a capability gives KPMG a tremendous ability to be proactive and responsive to global customer needs.

PEOPLESOFT INVESTMENT

The large integrator, whether GCA or not, invests heavily in PeopleSoft by the nature of the sheer size of its retained consultant force.

Temporal and monetary investments, too, may play a large role in the large integrator's PeopleSoft relationship. It may range from prerelease testing of PeopleSoft, to sponsorship of PeopleSoft marketing and sales programs, to large-scale involvement at PeopleSoft's annual Global Conferences. Additionally, to both provide a market edge and strengthen the alliance between the GCA and PeopleSoft, often the large integrator will invest directly in the creation of a PeopleSoft product with PeopleSoft.

For example, KPMG was selected to co-develop Enterprise Performance Management with PeopleSoft. From its role in prerelease testing to its continued enhancement of EPM's Enterprise Warehouse and Balanced Scorecard, KPMG provided a foundation of knowledge and support that created value-added products and offerings for PeopleSoft clients across the spectrum. The ability of KPMG and the other GCAs to work in alliance with PeopleSoft is one of the greatest strengths of the large integrator.

MAKING YOUR CHOICE

Surely, no matter what size or scope a PeopleSoft implementation may be, there will be an integrator appropriately targeted for the implementation. When needs are of the scale where a "large" integrator is deemed critical, it is important for customers and prospects to sift through the various elements of that integrator's capacities. When the needs call for a smaller integrator, look for the specialties of that integrator. Cheap doesn't mean good. By examining the large integrator's depth of knowledge and capabilities, its comprehensive services that stretch beyond the ERP implementations, its global coverage, and the impact of its PeopleSoft investment, a decision on the PeopleSoft large integrator can best be made. Looking at specialty, pricing, and flexibility of the small integrator when they are called for provides you with the best decision on the lesser scale.

THE CAST

LIVE WIRE, INC.

Live Wire, Inc., is a Boston-based PeopleSoft and e-commerce consultancy. Founded in 1997, Live Wire has developed a successful PeopleSoft practice, which provides PeopleSoft implementation services, and an e-commerce practice, which provides eCRM, online procurement, e-commerce architecture, online registration on the campuses, and other e-commerce capabilities to the higher education, financial, retail, telecommunications, and services markets. The Live Wire Web site is

`www.live-wire.net`

KPMG LLP

KPMG LLP is the U.S. member firm of KPMG International. In the U.S., KPMG partners and professionals provide a wide range of accounting, tax, and consulting services. As a provider of information-based services, KPMG delivers understandable business advice—helping clients analyze their businesses with true clarity, raise their level of performance, achieve growth, and enhance shareholder value. KPMG International's member firms have more than 6,700 partners and 92,000 professionals in 157 countries. KPMG's Web site is

`http://www.us.kpmg.com`

ATLANTIC DUNCANS INTERNATIONAL

Atlantic Duncans International (ADI) is a Chantilly, VA–based ERP consultancy. As a successful GAP of PeopleSoft, ADI has specialized in both midmarket implementations and staff augmentation. More recently, ADI has been establishing itself in the world of e-commerce and CRM, with partnerships with companies such as Siebel and Ariba. The ADI Web site is

`www.atlgr.com`

PeopleSoft Web Sites

In this appendix

by Paul Greenberg

PeopleSoft has spawned several rather creative independent Web sites for the purpose of furthering the PeopleSoft creed. They are viewed as a place where users, consultants, and customers can get together and hash out problems; find out the latest news; learn about the technical and nontechnical aspects of PeopleSoft; look for work in the field; and, in general, increase their knowledge of the products. This appendix briefly gives you the tour of the existing Web sites that are exclusively devoted to PeopleSoft. Not included are Web sites for retained search firms and headhunters who may have a PeopleSoft bias but are primarily in existence to gather résumés.

INDEPENDENT WEB SITES

PEOPLEBUD ON THE BEACH

www.geocities.com/siliconvalley/9295

This is, by far, the most comprehensive and eclectic of all the devoted PeopleSoft Web sites. Run by someone who clearly loves PeopleSoft, the site offers the most comprehensive coverage of existing PeopleSoft projects, news, and resources, and even offers such diversions as the Barbie site (Mattel is a user of PeopleSoft). It carries links to dozens of ongoing PeopleSoft projects, particularly in the realm of higher education. It even carries a slightly dated but very useful bibliography of articles on PeopleSoft. It styles itself "The Way Cool PeopleSoft Resource Site"—and it is.

THE PEOPLESOFT FAN CLUB AND USER FORUM

www.peoplesoftfans.com

This site is part of a group of erpfans.com sites that span the Internet. A central point for information exchange, it carries a unique feature called Fan Book, which is effectively a forum for PeopleSoft personals where, as a PeopleSoft user or consultant, you can post an ad, a warning to others, a request for knowledge exchange, or simply a comment on how great PeopleSoft is. The links provided on this site are direct PeopleSoft Web site links or PeopleSoft competitors.

THE PEOPLESOFT USERS GROUP

www.ps-users.com

Thissite is actually a subscription for a listserv that is probably the most active PeopleSoft technical site. Modeled something like the old Compuserve technical forums, there is an ongoing technical discussion and problem-sharing that is emailed in near–real time to the subscribers of the list. This is very valuable for clients and consultants.

SLERP

www.slerp.com

This is a well-constructed "technofunctional" site with solid technical message boards. The fact that the PeopleTools message board is the road most traveled is indicative of the type of participant at this site. There are not only message boards but technical presentations and a section called Nuggets that are short technical solutions to common PeopleSoft problems discussed and fixed on the Web site. This is the only site that gives away gifts such as a Palm Pilot III to its users.

PEOPLESOFT ASSIST

www.peoplesoftassist.com

This site is geared toward the PeopleSoft consultant, rather than the software. There are four basic areas on the site that are focused on furthering the interaction and lives of PeopleSoft consultants. Knowledgebank is a message board for support, similar to how the ps-users listserv mentioned earlier works. Also included is coverage of the latest news, PeopleSoft books, and product-oriented PeopleSoft-related links. A section called Careers focuses on a job bank and an Internet job search. Finally, and most interestingly, there is a Networking segment that has a still-motion chat-like general discussion and, uniquely, free email to PeopleSoft consultants!

PeopleSoft Partner Program

In this appendix

by Paul Greenberg

In 1999, PeopleSoft began to make dramatic changes in the way it views its partners. No longer would it be good enough for partners to profess their support for PeopleSoft, the proof had to be in the pudding. This meant that partners had to produce within certain guidelines or they would not become or remain partners. This caused a dramatic reduction in the numbers.

When push came to shove, however, the principles that guided the different partner programs were not really altered; they merely were enforced much more directly. This appendix gives you the principles, in brief, for each partner category: Services, Software, and Platform Alliance.

GENERAL PRINCIPLES

PeopleSoft views its partners as complementary and complete. This means that the partners' skills complement what PeopleSoft offers—either through a more finely honed group of already existing skills, such as expert student administration implementations (for example, Kaludis Consulting) or through a new set of skills or new product, such as Convoy's PeopleSoft data migration and mapping tool. In addition, PeopleSoft looks to partners who have industrial expertise in a particular vertical market, such as SPL, public utilities specialists. The review process is strict and extensive, ranging from the submission of a business plan from the prospective partner to a serious due diligence process by PeopleSoft. When a company is accepted first as a prospective partner, it is given the rights to buying software at partner prices but not much else. However, that is the first step in the process toward completion. Finally, after all is completed, if accepted, full partnership is granted and the company is certified by PeopleSoft as a legitimate contender in PeopleSoft's world.

SERVICE PARTNERS

Service partners can be small or large, but they are governed by the same criteria. PeopleSoft reviews their applications by the following criteria:

- Extensive knowledge of implementation methodologies, including Express
- Industry-specific expertise
- Extensive implementation history
- High customer satisfaction ratings
- Investment in PeopleSoft skills maintenance

Strategic partners must also show the ability to deploy PeopleSoft on a multinational and global level.

In return for acceptance in the partnership program—a one-year renewable contract—PeopleSoft offers the partners participation in the beta testing programs of new products, favorable prices for demonstration and internal usage software, and resources to make the partnership work effectively (including joint delivery services). These valuable resources allow the partners to work closely with PeopleSoft, ensuring the success of both.

SOFTWARE ALLIANCE PARTNERS

PeopleSoft's strategy toward Software Alliance partners is somewhat different than toward Services partners. Software Alliance partners act as third-party developers for complementary products that integrate with PeopleSoft. They vary in what they do. For example, Brio has SQR, the development language of PeopleSoft, and Convoy (recently acquired by Neon) has ConvoyDM, the data mapping and migration tool for PeopleSoft. There are dozens of other products that handle such disparate categories as extraction transformation and load, forms, decision support, demand planning, expatriate management, and OLAP reporting. A wide variety indeed!

To become a PeopleSoft Software Alliance partner, a company must have an application or product that works, that PeopleSoft sees value in, and that becomes certified. Throughout the partnership, PeopleSoft will work closely with the product development team through the PeopleSoft Integration Team (PIT) Crew to help streamline the integration of the partner product with PeopleSoft. This includes training, design, development, support, documentation, and certification.

PART

VIII

APP

C

PLATFORM ALLIANCE PARTNERS

Platform Alliance partners are perhaps the most important to PeopleSoft because they represent the databases and the hardware that PeopleSoft rests on. For example, in the database arena, it is partnered with

- Oracle
- Sybase
- Informix
- IBM (DB2)
- Microsoft (SQL Server)

In the hardware world, some of its partners are

- Compaq
- Intel
- Hewlett-Packard
- Sun Microsystems
- IBM (AS/400 and System 3090)
- Unisys

Each of these partners has had its platform certified by PeopleSoft teams that are expert in the particular platforms. The certifications are done at the Pleasanton, California–based PeopleSoft Solutions Center.

INDEX

Fresh lemonade
from California.
Darjeeling tea
from the Himalayas.
Biscotti from Tuscany.
Yup, business sure
wouldn't be what
it is today without
the Internet.

KPMG

Assurance
Tax
Consulting

Customer Management
Supply Chain
World-Class Finance
Knowledge Management
World-Class Human Resources
e-Strategy and e-Processes
e-Integration
e-Outsourcing

We're helping businesses use the Internet
to connect with suppliers, manufacturers,
vendors and customers in ways they never
have before. In short, we're showing them
how to gain a competitive edge.

**For further information on our
e-engineering and PeopleSoft
capabilities, contact:
www.kpmgconsulting.com**

It's time for clarity.™

Special Edition Using

The One Source for Comprehensive Solutions™

The one stop shop for serious users, *Special Edition Using* offers readers a thorough understanding of software and technologies. Intermediate to advanced users get detailed coverage that is clearly presented and to the point.

Special Edition Using Linux, 5th Ed.
Jack Tackett, Jr. and Steven Burnett
0789721805
$49.99 US

Special Edition Using TCP/IP
John Ray
0789718979
$29.99 US

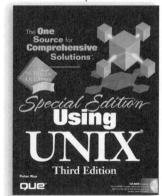

Special Edition Using UNIX, 3rd Ed.
Peter Kuo
0789717476
$39.99 US

www.quecorp.com

All prices are subject to change.

Other Related Titles

UNIX Hints and Hacks
Kirk Waingrow
0789719274
$19.99 US

Working with Unicenter TNG, 2nd Ed.
Rick Sturm
0789720825
$39.99 US

Windows NT Hints and Hacks
John Savill
0789719185
$19.99 US

C++ from Scratch
Jesse Liberty
0789720795
$29.99 US

Caldera OpenLinux Installation and Configuration Handbook
Gary Wilson
0789721058
$39.99 US

Complete Idiot's Guide to Networking Your Home
Mark Thompson and Mark Speaker
0789719630
$16.99 US

Windows 98 Installation and Configuration Handbook
Rob Tidrow
0789715104
$39.99 US

Complete Idiot's Guide to Networking, 2nd Ed.
Bill Wagner and Chris Negus
0789718022
$16.99 US

Platinum Edition Using HTML 4, XML, and Java 1.2
Eric Ladd
078971759X
$59.99 US

Using Linux
Bill Ball
0789716232
$29.99 US

Easy Lotus Notes R5
Cate McCoy
0789721066
$24.99 US

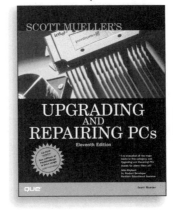

Upgrading and Repairing PCs, 11th Ed.
Scott Mueller
0789719037
$59.99 US

How Networks Work, 4th Ed.
Frank Derfler and Les Freed
0789715953
$29.99 US

www.quecorp.com

All prices are subject to change.